Programming in Visual Basic

Version 6.0

Update Edition

D1398421

Programming in Visual Basic

Version 6.0

Update Edition

Julia Case Bradley
Mt. San Antonio College

Anita C. Millspaugh
Mt. San Antonio College

McGraw-Hill
Irwin

Boston   Burr Ridge, IL   Dubuque, IA   Madison, WI   New York   San Francisco   St. Louis
Bangkok   Bogotá   Caracas   Kuala Lumpur   Lisbon   London   Madrid   Mexico City
Milan   Montreal   New Delhi   Santiago   Seoul   Singapore   Sydney   Taipei   Toronto

McGraw-Hill Higher Education

*A Division of The **McGraw-Hill** Companies*

PROGRAMMING IN VISUAL BASIC 6.0 UPDATE EDITION

Published by McGraw-Hill/Irwin, an imprint of The McGraw-Hill Companies, Inc. 1221 Avenue of the Americas, New York, NY, 10020. Copyright © 2002 by The McGraw-Hill Companies, Inc. All rights reserved. No part of this publication may be reproduced or distributed in any form or by any means, or stored in a database or retrieval system, without the prior written consent of The McGraw-Hill Companies, Inc., including, but not limited to, in any network or other electronic storage or transmission, or broadcast for distance learning.

Some ancillaries, including electronic and print components, may not be available to customers outside the United States.

This book is printed on acid-free paper.
Printed in China

6 7 8 9 0 CTP/CTP 0 9 8 7

ISBN-13: 978-0-07-251381-3
ISBN-10: 0-07-251381-0

Publisher: *George Werthman*
Sponsoring editor: *Steve Schuetz*
Developmental editor: *Craig S. Leonard*
Senior marketing manager: *Jeff Parr*
Associate project manager: *Destiny Rynne*
Production supervisor: *Debra R. Sylvester*
Senior designer: *Jenny El-Shamy*
Lead supplement producer: *Marc Mattson*
Senior producer, Media technology: *David Barrick*
Cover design: *Peter Siu*
Typeface: *11/13 Bodoni*
Compositor: *GAC Indianapolis*
Printer: *CTPS*

Library of Congress Cataloging-in-Publication Data

Bradley, Julia Case.
    Programming in Visual Basic version 6.0 update edition / Julia Case Bradley, Anita C. Millspaugh.
      p. cm.
    ISBN 0-07-251381-0 (alk. paper)
    1. BASIC (Computer program language) 2. Microsoft Visual BASIC. I. Millspaugh, A. C. (Anita C.) II. Title.
QA76.73.B3 B698 2002
005.26'8—dc21   2001044260

www.mhhe.com

Preface

As the world turns to graphical user interfaces, computer programming languages are changing to accommodate the shift. Visual Basic 6 is designed to allow the programmer to develop applications that run under Windows without the complexity generally associated with Windows programming. With very little effort, the programmer can design a screen that holds standard Windows elements such as command buttons, check boxes, option buttons, text boxes, and list boxes. Each of these Windows objects operates as expected, producing a "standard" Windows user interface.

Visual Basic is easy to learn, which makes it an excellent tool for understanding elementary programming concepts. In addition, it has evolved into such a powerful and popular product that skilled Visual Basic programmers are in demand in the job market.

About This Text

This textbook is intended for use in an introductory programming course, which assumes no prior knowledge of computer programming. However, many of the later chapters are appropriate for an advanced-level course. The later chapters are also appropriate for professional programmers who are learning a new language to upgrade their skills.

This text assumes that the student is familiar with the Windows operating environment.

Approach

This text incorporates the basic concepts of programming, problem solving, and programming logic, as well as the design techniques of an event-driven language.

Chapter topics are presented in a sequence that allows the programmer to learn how to deal with a visual interface while acquiring important programming skills such as creating projects with loops, decisions, and data management.

The later chapters may be used in various sequences to accommodate the needs of beginning and advanced-level courses, as well as a shorter quarter system or a semester-long course. For a shorter course, the professor may choose to skip the chapter on data files and cover only the first of the two database chapters.

New in This Edition of the Text

This updated edition of the text provides some new material and some reorganization. The biggest changes are:

- A new appendix introducing VB.NET, the next version of Visual Basic.

- The inclusion of ActiveX Data Objects (ADO) in the two database chapters: Chapters 11 and 12. The older-technology DAO controls were replaced with ADO.

- The addition of selecting and sorting Recordsets using the Find method and Filter and Sort properties in Chapter 12.

- The modificaton of the random file project in Chapter 10 to allow coverage without first covering Chapter 9.

- The addition of the Data Environment to Chapter 12, along with displaying related tables in a grid. SQL selection was removed from the chapter—postponed to the advanced text.

- The addition to Chapter 9 of a discussion of multitier applications.

- The addition of two case studies to each chapter.

Introduced in the Previous Edition

The features introduced in the Visual Basic 6.0 Edition have been retained. The text places an emphasis on the planning steps of project design to encourage students to develop good programming habits from the start.

The programs conform to Microsoft's newly published coding conventions, which define a three-character prefix for variable names to indicate data type.

The new formatting functions (`FormatNumeric`, `FormatCurrency`, `FormatPercent`, and `FormatDateTime`) simplify the formatting of output. And the new Validate event and CausesValidation properties simplify the validation of input data.

The advanced techniques chapter (Chapter 15) includes sections on creating an MDI project with parent and child forms, as well as creating shortcut menus.

Students and instructors will appreciate the appendix, "Tips and Shortcuts for Mastering the VB Environment." This reference brings together many helpful tips that can save a programmer significant amounts of time.

The instructor materials include suggested coding standards and masters of forms for project planning that can be reproduced and distributed to students. The solutions to all exercises are available to instructors for downloading on the Web.

Introduced in Visual Basic 6

The upgrade from Visual Basic version 5 to version 6 is significant, but not as great a change as the upgrade from version 4 to version 5. The major changes allow developers to use VB for Web page development and perform more robust data management.

VB version 6 introduces new formatting functions to simplify formatting output for display or print. Many new string and numeric functions are also introduced, as well as the new Validate event for input controls and the CausesValidation property for most controls.

Introduced in Visual Basic 5

Visual Basic 5:

- Runs much faster than previous versions and incorporates more features required for professional application development. VB5 is now competitive with C++ for object-oriented program development.

- Incorporates many helpful new features in the editor, making it easier for beginners as well as advanced programmers to enter and edit code. For example:
  - Drag-and-drop editing for moving and copying lines.
  - Pop-up lists of available data types when declaring variables.
  - Pop-up lists of allowable properties and methods for controls.
  - Tips showing formats and arguments for functions and statements that appear automatically as you enter program code.

- Is easier to debug than previous versions. For example:
  - Data tips, similar to tooltips, display the current contents of variables, properties, and expressions, and pop up when you point to the expression during break time.
  - You can easily set breakpoints in code by clicking in the margin of a statement.
  - During break time, you can drag the highlighted line to set the next statement to execute.

- Includes many new controls. For example:
  - Many ActiveX controls for programming on the Web.
  - A new Web Browser control that allows you to retrieve and display Web pages in an application.

Chapter Organization

Each chapter begins with identifiable objectives and a brief overview. Numerous coding examples as well as hands-on projects with guidance for the coding appear throughout. Thought-provoking feedback questions give students time to reflect on the current topic and to evaluate their understanding of the details. The end-of-chapter items include a chapter review, questions, programming exercises, and four case studies. The case studies provide a continuing-theme exercise that may be used throughout the course.

Chapter 1 walks the student through the creation of a first Visual Basic project, incorporating command buttons and labels. The programming environment is introduced along with the concepts of objects and their related properties, methods, and events. Students are taught to create a new folder and store their project inside the folder.

Chapter 2 continues coverage of controls, including text boxes, option buttons, check boxes, frames, images, lines, and shapes. It also covers some of the finer points of using the environment and working with keyboard access keys, multiple controls, and alignment. The color constants are used at this point to lead the novice programmer into Chapter 3, which introduces variables and constants. The text includes naming conventions to make the scope and data type of a variable or constant easier to determine from the coding syntax. Standards also provide for the use of `Option Explicit` to force the declaration of all variables and constants.

Chapter 4 introduces the relational and logical operators and their use with the `If` statement. Input validation and message boxes are also covered. In Chapter 5 students learn to set up custom menus and to write their own sub functions and sub procedures. Multiple forms, global variables, and standard code modules are presented in Chapter 6.

Chapter 7 incorporates list boxes and combo boxes into the projects, providing the opportunity to discuss looping procedures and printing lists of information. The list concept leads logically into the use of variable arrays and control arrays in Chapter 8.

Chapter 9 introduces the terminology of object-oriented programming and provides a step-by-step tutorial for creating a new class, instantiating objects of the new class, creating a collection class to hold references to the objects, and displaying and modifying objects from the collection. It also introduces the concepts of multitier applications.

Chapter 10 covers both sequential and random files, but the material may be covered in sections.

Chapters 11 and 12 deal with the use of Visual Basic as a front end for database programming. The projects display and update tables created by a database application such as Microsoft Access. Chapter 12 includes using a data-bound grid, error trapping, and the Data Environment.

The drag-and-drop feature of Windows programming is introduced in Chapter 13. This chapter normally brings great enthusiasm from students as they learn to deal with the source and target objects. The examples and assignments provide a blend of practical and just-for-fun applications. This approach is also true of Chapter 14, which introduces the graphics methods and graphics controls.

Chapter 15, the final chapter, covers various topics that build a bridge from Visual Basic to other applications. These include using and creating ActiveX controls, the Windows API, DLLs, OLE, Visual Basic for Applications, and MDI and SDI applications, and creating shortcut menus.

Acknowledgments

We would like to express our appreciation to the many people who have contributed to the successful completion of this text. Most especially, we thank our students at Mt. San Antonio College who helped class-test the material and who greatly influenced the manuscript.

Many people have worked very hard to design and produce this text, including George Werthman, Steve Schuetz, Craig Leonard, Destiny Rynne, Jenny El-Shamy, Betsy Blumenthal, and Bette Ittersagen.

We greatly appreciate Diane Murphey, Theresa Berry, and Dennis Fraser for their thorough technical reviews, constructive criticism, and many valuable suggestions. Thanks also to Theresa for writing the Instructors Manual and the exercise solutions. And most important, we are grateful to our families for their support and understanding through the long days and busy phone lines.

We want to thank our reviewers, who have made many helpful suggestions:

Gary R. Armstrong
Shippensburg University

Dennis Clarke
Hillsborough Community College

Charles Massey
University of North Carolina—Asheville

Ronald L. Burgher
Metropolitan Community College

Diane Murphey
Oklahoma Panhandle State University

Sheila J. Pearson
Southern Arkansas University

Thomas S. Pennington
Maple Woods Community College

Anita Philipp
Oklahoma City Community College

Hwang Santai
Purdue University–Fort Wayne

Debbie Tesch
Xavier University

Judy Yaeger
Western Michigan University

The Authors

We have had fun teaching and writing about Visual Basic. We hope that this feeling is evident as you read this book and that you will enjoy learning or teaching this outstanding programming language.

Julia Case Bradley
Anita C. Millspaugh

To the Student

The best way to learn to program in Visual Basic is to do it. If you enter and run the sample projects, you will be on your way to writing Windows applications. Reading the examples without trying to run them is like trying to learn a foreign language or mathematics just by reading about it. Enter the projects, look up your questions in Visual Basic's excellent Help files, and make those projects *run*.

Format Used for Visual Basic Statements

Visual Basic statements and functions are shown in `this font`. Any values you must supply are in *italics*. Optional items are in [square brackets]. Braces and a vertical bar indicate that you must choose one or the other value {one | other}.

Example:

```
[Let] {Variable|Object.Property} = Expression
```

As you work your way through this textbook, note that you may see a subset of the available options for a Visual Basic statement. Generally, the options that are included will reflect those covered in the chapter. If you want to see the complete format for any statement, refer to online Help in the MSDN library or on the Web.

J.C.B.
A.C.M.

Contents

1

Introduction to Visual Basic   1

Writing Windows Applications with Visual Basic   2
   The Windows Graphical User Interface   2

Programming Languages— Procedural, Object Oriented, and Event Driven   3
   The Object Model   3
   Versions of Visual Basic   4

Writing Visual Basic Projects   4
   The Three-Step Process   4
   Visual Basic Projects   5

The Visual Basic Environment   6
   The Form Window   6
   The Project Explorer Window   6
   The Properties Window   7
   The Form Layout Window   7
   The Toolbox   7
   The Main Visual Basic Window   7
   The Toolbar   7
   The Form Location and Size Information   8
   Help   8
   Design Time, Run Time, and Break Time   8

Writing Your First Visual Basic Project   8
   Set Up Your Visual Basic Workspace   9
   Plan the Project   13
   Define the User Interface   13
   Set Properties   17
   Write Code   22
   Visual Basic Code Statements   22
   Code the Event Procedures for Hello World   24
   Run the Project   26
   Save the Project   28
   Open the Project   30

   Modify the Project   30
   Print the Project Documentation   35

Sample Printout   36
   The Form Image   36
   The Code   37
   The Form as Text   38

Finding and Fixing Errors   39
   Compile Errors   39
   Run-Time Errors   40
   Logic Errors   40
   Project Debugging   41
   Naming Rules and Conventions for Objects   41

Visual Basic Help   42
   The MSDN Viewer   43
   Context-Sensitive Help   44

2

More Controls   51

Introducing More Controls   52
   Text Boxes   53
   Frames   53
   Check Boxes   53
   Option Buttons   54
   Images   54
   Setting a Border and Style   56
   The Shape Control   56
   The Line Control   57

Working with Multiple Controls   57
   Selecting Multiple Controls   57
   Deselecting a Group of Controls   58
   Moving Controls as a Group   58
   Setting Properties for Multiple Controls   59
   Aligning Controls   59

Designing Your Applications for User Convenience   61
   Designing the User Interface   61
   Defining Keyboard Access Keys   62

Setting the Default and Cancel Properties of Command Buttons   63
Setting the Tab Order for Controls   63
Setting the Form's Location on the Screen   64
Creating ToolTips   65

Coding for the Controls   66

Clearing Text Boxes and Labels   66
Resetting the Focus   66
Setting the Value Property of Option Buttons and Check Boxes   66
Changing the Font Properties of Controls   67
Changing the Color of Text   68
Changing Multiple Properties of a Control   68
Concatenating Text   69
Continuing Long Program Lines   69
Using the Default Property of a Control   70

Programming Hints   77

3

Variables, Constants, and Calculations   87

Data—Variables and Constants   88

Data Types   89
Naming Rules   90
Naming Conventions   90
Constants—Named and Intrinsic   92
Declaring Variables   94
Scope of Variables   96

Calculations   99

Val Function   99

Arithmetic Operations   100

Order of Operations   101
Using Calculations in Code   102

Formatting Data   102

A Calculation Programming Example   106

Planning the Project   106

The Project Coding Solution   110

Counting and Accumulating Sums   111

Summing Numbers   111

Counting   111
Calculating an Average   112

Programming Hints   118

4

Decisions and Conditions   127

If Statements   128

Flowcharting If Statements   130

Conditions   130

Comparing Numeric Variables and Constants   131
Comparing Strings   132
Testing for True or False   135
Comparing the Text Property of Text Boxes   135
Comparing Uppercase and Lowercase Characters   136
Compound Conditions   136

Nested If Statements   137

Using If Statements with Option Buttons and Check Boxes   140

A "Simple Sample"   141
Checking the Value of an Option Button Group   142
Checking the Values of Multiple Check Boxes   142

Displaying Messages in Message Boxes   143

Selecting the MsgBox Icon   144
Displaying a Message String   144

Input Validation   145

Checking for Numeric Values   145
Checking for a Range of Values   146
Checking for a Required Field   146
Performing Multiple Validations   147

Calling Event Procedures   147

Debugging Visual Basic Projects   156

Pausing Execution with the Break Button   156
Forcing a Break   156
Using the Immediate Window   157
Checking the Current Values of Expressions   158
Stepping through Code   158

Debugging Step-by-Step Tutorial   159

Test the Project   159

Break and Step Program
Execution   160
View the Contents of Properties,
Variables, and Conditions   161
Continue Project Execution   162
Test the White Total   163
Correct the Red Total Error   163
Correct the White Total Error   164
Force a Run-Time Error   165

5

Menus, Sub Procedures, and Sub Functions   173

Menus   **174**
Defining Menus   174
Creating a Menu—Step-by-Step   176
Coding for Menu Commands   179
Modifying a Menu   179
Toggling Check Marks
On and Off   181
Standards for Windows Menus   181

Common Dialog Boxes   **181**
Using a Common Dialog Box   183
Using the Information from
the Dialog Box   184
Setting Current Values   186

Writing General Procedures   **187**
Creating a New Sub Procedure   187
Passing Variables to Procedures   188
Passing Arguments ByVal
or ByRef   189
Function Procedures versus
Sub Procedures   190
Writing Function Procedures   190
Writing a Function with
Multiple Arguments   192
Calling a Function with
Multiple Arguments   192
Reusing Procedures   192
Breaking Calculations into
Smaller Units   194

Programming Hints   **205**
Creating Executable Files   205

6

Multiple Forms   213

Multiple Forms   **214**
Creating New Forms   214

Adding and Removing Forms   215
The Hide and Show Methods   216
The Load and Unload
Statements   218
The Me Keyword   218
Referring to Objects on a
Different Form   219

Standard Code Modules   **219**

Variables and Constants in
Multiple-Form Projects   **220**
Global Variables and Constants   221
Static Variables   221
Guidelines for Declaring
Variables and Constants   222

An About Box   **223**

A Splash Screen   **225**

Using Sub Main for Startup   **226**
Coding the Standard
Code Module   226
Coding the Splash Screen
Event Procedure   227
Setting the Startup Form or
Procedure   227

Programming Hints   **244**
Working with Maximized
Forms   244

7

Lists, Loops, and Printing   251

List Boxes and Combo
Boxes   **252**
Filling the List   253
Clearing the List   255
The ListIndex Property   255
The ListCount Property   256
The List Property   256
Removing an Item from a List   257
List Box and Combo Box Events   257

Do/Loops   **258**
The Boolean Data Type
Revisited   261
Using a Do/Loop with
a List Box   261

For/Next Loops   **262**
Negative Increment or Counting
Backward   264
Conditions Satisfied
before Entry   265

Altering the Values of the
Loop Control Variables   265
Endless Loops   265
Exiting For/Next Loops   266

Using the MsgBox Function   **267**
Function Return Values   268
Specifying the Buttons and/or
Icons to Display   268
MsgBox Example   269

Using String Functions   **269**
Examples Using Left, Right,
and Mid Functions   270
The Len Function   270
Selecting Entries in a List Box   271

Sending Information
to the Printer   **271**
Printing to the Printer   272
Formatting Lines   272
Selecting the Font   276
Terminating the Page or the Job   276
Printing the Contents
of a List Box   276
Printing the Selected Item
from a List   277
Aligning Decimal Columns   277

8

Arrays   **293**
Control Arrays   **294**
The Case Structure   **295**
Testing Option Buttons
with the Case Structure   297
Single-Dimension Arrays   **299**
Subscripts   300
More on Subscripts   301
For Each/Next Statements   **301**
Initializing an Array Using
For Each   302
User-Defined Data Types   **303**
Accessing Information with
User-Defined Data Types   304
Using Array Elements
for Accumulators   **305**
Table Lookup   **306**
Coding a Table Lookup   309
Using List Boxes with Arrays   **309**
The ItemData Property   310
Using Nonsequential ItemData
Values   311

Adding Items with ItemData
to a List   312
Multidimensional Arrays   **313**
Initializing Two-Dimensional
Arrays   314
Nested For/Next Example   314
Printing a Two-Dimensional
Table   314
Summing a Two-Dimensional
Table   315
Lookup Operation for
Two-Dimensional Tables   316
Programming Hints   **324**
The Array Function   324

9

OOP—Creating
Object-Oriented
Programs   **333**
Visual Basic and Object-
Oriented Programming   **334**
Objects   334
Object-Oriented Terminology   335
Reusable Objects   336
Classes   **337**
Assigning Property Values   337
Creating a New Class—
Step-by-Step   **339**
Define a New Class Module   339
Define the Class Properties   340
Add Property Procedures   340
Code a Method   343
Add General Remarks   343
Save the Class Module   343
Creating a New Object
Using a Class   **344**
Define and Use a New Object   344
Save the Form and the Project   346
Run the Project   347
Choosing When to Create
New Objects   **347**
Using the Set Statement   348
Early Binding versus
Late Binding   349
The Initialize and Terminate
Events   **349**
Terminating Projects   **350**
Collections   **351**
Creating a Collection   351

Creating a Unique Key in the
CProduct Class 352
Creating the CProducts Class 352
Adding Objects to a Collection 353
Removing a Member
from a Collection 354
Accessing a Member
of a Collection 355
Returning the Count Property 355
Setting a Default Property 355
Using For Each/Next 356

Using a Collection in a Form—
Step-by-Step 358
Modifying the User Interface 358
Declaring the Collection Object 359
Coding the Add Procedure 359
Coding the Display Procedure 359
Coding the Clear Procedure 360
Running the Project 360

Using the Object Browser 360
Examining VB Objects 361
Examining Your Own Classes 362

Using a List Box to
Store the Keys 362
Using the List Box to Display an
Object 364
Using the List Box to Remove an
Object 364

Avoiding Global Variables 364
Adding Properties to Forms 365

Programming Hints 380
Multitier Applications 380

10

Data Files 387

Data Files 388
Data Files and Project Files 388
Data File Terminology 388
File Organizations 389
Opening and Closing Data Files 389
The FreeFile Function 391
Viewing the Data in a File 391

Sequential File Organization 391
Writing Data to a Sequential
Disk File 392
Creating a Sequential Data File 392
Reading the Data in
a Sequential File 393
Finding the End of a Data File 394
Locating a File 394

Trapping Program Errors 395
The On Error Statement 395

The Err Object 397
The Err.Number Property 397
Raising Error Conditions 398
Coding Error-Handling
Routines 398
The Resume Statement 399
Handling Errors 400
The Exit Function and Exit Sub
Statements 401
Saving Changes to a File 403
Sequential File Programming
Example 404

Random Data Files 408
Fixed-Length Strings 409
Defining a Record for a
Random File 409
Opening a Random File 409
Reading and Writing a
Random File 410
Accessing Fields in a
Random Record 411
Finding the End of a
Random File 412
The Seek Function 412

Using a List Box to Store
a Key Field 413
Trimming Extra Blanks
from Strings 414
Retrieving a Record from the File 414
Displaying the Selected Record 415

Updating a Random File 415
Locking the Contents
of Controls 417
Adding Records 417
Deleting a Record 418
Editing Records 419
The Read and Write
Procedures 420

Programming Hints 434
The InputBox Function 434
Using the InputBox to Randomly
Retrieve a Record 435

11

Accessing Database
Files 441

Visual Basic and Database
Files 442
Database Formats Supported
by Visual Basic 442
Database Terminology 442
Creating Database Files
for Use by Visual Basic 443

Using the ADO Data Control   **444**

*The Data Control and
Data-Bound Controls*   446

**Viewing a Database File—
Step-by-Step**   **453**

Design and Create the Form   453
*Set the Properties for the
Data Control*   455
*Set the Properties for the
Data-Bound Controls*   457
Write the Code   458
Run the Project   459

**Navigating the Database
in Code**   **460**

The Recordset Object   460
*Using the MoveNext,
MovePrevious, MoveFirst,
and MoveLast Methods*   460
Checking for BOF and EOF   460

**Using List Boxes and
Combo Boxes as Data-Bound
Controls**   **461**

*Setting up a Lookup Table
for a Field*   461

**Adding a Lookup Table and
Navigation—Step-by-Step**   **462**

Modify the User Interface   462
Change the Properties   463
Write the Code   464
*Testing the Navigation and
Lookup Tables*   466

Updating a Database File   **466**

Adding Records   466
Deleting Records   467

Preventing Errors   **468**

Protecting an Add Operation   468

Programming Hints   **478**

Putting It Together   492

**Validation and Error
Trapping**   **493**

Locking Text Boxes   493
*Validating Data in the
Validate Event*   494
Trap Errors with On Error   495
*Programming Example Showing
Validation Techniques*   498

Searching for Records   **503**

The Find Method   503
No Record Found   504
Bookmarks   505
The Filter Property   505

Sorting a Recordset   **506**

**Working with Database
Fields**   **507**

Referring to Database Fields   508
*Loading Datebase Fields into a
List Box*   508
*An Example with Find, Filter,
and Sort*   508

**The Data Environment
Designer**   **512**

*Connection and Command
Objects*   513
*Adding a Data Environment
Designer*   513
Creating Connections   514
Adding Commands   514
*Creating a Data Environment—
Step-by-Step*   515
*Navigating Recordsets for Data
Environment Objects*   517
One-to-Many Relationships   518
Relation Hierarchies   519
*Creating a Relation Hierarchy—
Step-by-Step*   519
Build the Relation Hierarchy   520

12

Data Handling—
Grids, Validation,
Selection,
and Sorting   485

Displaying Data in Grids   **486**

A Grid Control—Step-by-Step   486
*Displaying the Record
Number and Record Count*   491
The MoveComplete Event   492

13

Drag-and-Drop   531

Drag-and-Drop Terminology   **532**

The Source and the Target   532
Source Object Properties   532
*DragOver and DragDrop
Events*   532

A Step-by-Step Example   **533**

Create the User Interface   533
Set the Properties   534
Write the Code   534

Run the Project 536
Add Command Buttons 537
Run the Completed Project 538

Dragging and Dropping Multiple Objects 539
Passing the Source Argument 539
Changing the Icon of the Target Image 540
Setting the DragIcon Property of Source Controls 540
Blanking Out an Image 541

The Toybox Program 542
The Procedures 542
The Project Coding Solution 543

Programming Hints 551
Manual Drag-and-Drop 551

14

Graphics 555

The Graphics Environment 556
The Coordinate System 556
Picturebox Controls 557

Colors 557
The RGB Function 557
The Visual Basic Intrinsic Color Constants 558
The QBColor Function 558

The Graphics Methods 559
The Cls Method 560
The PSet Method 560
The Line Method 562
The Circle Method 563
The Step Keyword 566

Layering 567

More Properties for Your Graphics Controls 568
Controlling Pictures at Design Time 568
Controlling Pictures at Run Time 569
Moving a Picture 569

Simple Animation 570

The Timer Control 571

More Graphics Techniques 574
Custom Coordinate Systems 574
PaintPicture Method 574

The Scroll Bar Controls 575
Scroll Bar Events 577

A Fun Programming Example 577
The Project Coding Solution 579

15

Advanced Topics in Visual Basic 583

ActiveX 584
Using ActiveX Controls 584
The Tabbed Dialog Control 585
Browsing the Web from a Visual Basic Project 589
Creating Your Own ActiveX Controls 590

Dynamic Link Libraries 593
The Declare Statement 594
Passing Arguments ByVal and ByRef 595
Calling a DLL Procedure 596
Finding the Reference Information for DLLs 596
Accessing System Information with a DLL 597
Placing Tabs for Columns in a List Box 598

Object Linking and Embedding 600
Object Linking 600
Object Embedding 600
Creating OLE Objects at Run Time 602

Visual Basic for Applications 603
Recording an Excel Macro 604
A Sample Excel Visual Basic Application 605
Help with Visual Basic in Excel 608

Multiple Document Interface (MDI) 608
Creating an MDI Project 609
Adding Menus to an MDI Project 609
Creating a Window Menu 609

Defining Shortcut Menus 612
Defining the Menu 612
Coding for the Menu 613

The Report Designer 613
Begin the Project 614
Set Up the Data Source 614
Design the Report 617
Print the Report from a Form 621

Appendix A
Answers to Feedback Questions   627

Appendix B
Functions for Working with Dates, Financial Calculations, Mathematics, and String Operations   639

Appendix C
Tips and Shortcuts for Mastering the VB Environment   649

Appendix D
A Preview of Microsoft's VB.NET   659

Glossary   **673**

Index   **679**

1

Introduction to Visual Basic

At the completion of this chapter, you will be able to . . .

1. Describe the process of visual program design and development.

2. Explain the term *event-driven programming*.

3. Explain the concepts of objects, properties, and methods.

4. List and describe the three steps for writing a Visual Basic project.

5. Describe the various files that make up a Visual Basic project.

6. Identify the elements in the Visual Basic environment.

7. Define design time, run time, and break time.

8. Write, run, save, print, and modify your first Visual Basic project.

9. Identify compile errors, run-time errors, and logic errors.

10. Look up Visual Basic topics in Help.

Writing Windows Applications with Visual Basic

Using this text, you will learn to write computer programs that run in the Microsoft Windows environment. Your projects will look and act like standard Windows programs. Visual Basic (VB) provides the tools you need to create windows with familiar elements like menus, text boxes, command buttons, option buttons, check boxes, list boxes, and scroll bars. Figure 1.1 shows some sample Windows user interfaces.

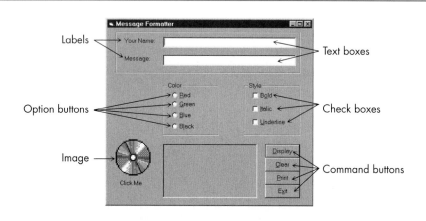

Graphical user interfaces for application programs designed with Visual Basic.

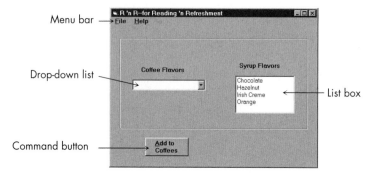

The Windows Graphical User Interface

Microsoft Windows uses a **graphical user interface**, or **GUI** (pronounced "gooey"). The Windows GUI defines how the various elements look and function. As a Visual Basic programmer, you have available a toolbox of these elements. You will create new windows, called ***forms***. Then you will use the toolbox to add the various elements, called ***controls***. The projects that you will write follow a relatively new type of programming called ***event-driven programming***.

Programming Languages—Procedural, Object Oriented, and Event Driven

There are literally hundreds of programming languages. Each was developed to solve a particular type of problem. Most traditional languages, such as BASIC, C, COBOL, FORTRAN, PL/I, and Pascal, are considered *procedural* languages. That is, the program specifies the exact sequence of all operations. Program logic determines the next instruction to execute in response to conditions and user requests.

The newer programming languages, such as C++ and Visual Basic, use a different approach: **object-oriented programming** (OOP) and event-driven programming. Microsoft refers to Visual Basic as an event-driven programming language, which has many (but not all) elements of an object-oriented language such as Java. Each release of Visual Basic moves it a little closer to a true object-oriented language.

In the event-driven model, programs are no longer procedural; they do not follow a sequential logic. You, as the programmer, do not take control and determine the sequence of execution. Instead, the user can press keys and click on various buttons and boxes in a window. Each user action can cause an *event* to occur, which triggers a Basic procedure that you have written. For example, the user clicks on a command button labeled Calculate. The clicking causes the button's Click event to occur, and the program automatically jumps to a procedure you have written to do the calculation.

The Object Model

In Visual Basic you will work with **objects**, which have **properties** and **methods**.

Objects

Think of an object as a thing, or a noun. Examples of objects are forms and controls. *Forms* are the windows and dialog boxes you place on the screen; *controls* are the elements you place inside a form, such as text boxes, command buttons, and list boxes.

Properties

Properties tell something about an object, such as its name, color, size, location, or how it will behave. You can think of properties as adjectives that describe objects.

When you refer to a property, you first name the object, add a period, and then name the property. For example, refer to the Caption property of a form called Form1 as Form1.Caption (say "form1 dot caption").

Methods

Actions associated with objects are called *methods*. Methods are the verbs of object-oriented programming. Some typical methods are Move, Print, Resize, and Clear.

You refer to methods as Object.Method ("object dot method"). For example, a `Print` method can apply to different objects. `Printer.Print` sends the output to the printer object; `Form1.Print` sends output to the form called Form1.

Versions of Visual Basic

Microsoft Visual Basic for Windows comes in a **Working Model**, a **Learning Edition**, a **Professional Edition**, and an **Enterprise Edition**. Anyone planning to do professional application development that includes the advanced features of database management should use the Professional Edition or Enterprise Edition.

In addition to the various editions of Visual Basic, you must also be aware of the release number. This text is based on release 6.0, the current release. Although most of the projects in this text can be written with an earlier release, the menus and screens may not look the same as the text screen shots. Also, several new elements and statements were added in release 6.0. In short, you should use release 6.0 with this text.

Next to each new or changed feature you will see an icon.

Writing Visual Basic Projects

When you write a Visual Basic project, you follow a three-step process for planning the project and then repeat the process for creating the project. The three steps involve setting up the user interface, defining the properties, and then creating the code.

The Three-Step Process

Planning

1. *Design the user interface*. When you plan the **user interface**, you draw a sketch of the screens the user will see when running your project. On your sketch, show the forms and all the controls that you plan to use. Indicate the names that you plan to give the form and each of the objects on the form. Refer to Figure 1.1 for examples of user interfaces.

    Before you proceed with any more steps, consult with your user and make sure that you both agree on the look and feel of the project.

2. *Plan the properties*. For each object, write down the properties that you plan to set or change during the design of the form.

3. *Plan the Basic code*. This step is where you plan the procedures that will execute when your project runs. You will determine which events require action to be taken and then make a step-by-step plan for those actions.

    Later, when you actually write the Visual Basic **code**, you must follow the language syntax rules. But during the planning stage, you will write out the actions using **pseudocode**, which is an English expression or comment that describes the action. For example, you must plan for the event that occurs when the user clicks on the Exit command button. The pseudocode for the event could be *Terminate the project*.

Programming

After you have completed the planning steps and have agreement from your user, you are ready to begin the actual construction of the project. You will use the same three-step process that you used for planning.

1. *Define the user interface.* When you define the user interface, you create the forms and controls that you designed in the planning stage.

   Think of this step as *defining* the objects you will use in your project.

2. *Set the properties.* When you set the properties of the objects, you give each object a name and define such attributes as the contents of a label, the size of the text, and the words that appear on top of a command button and in the form's title bar.

   You might think of this step as *describing* each object.

3. *Write the Basic code.* You will use Basic programming statements (called Basic code) to carry out the actions needed by your program. You will be surprised and pleased by how few statements you need to create a powerful Windows program.

   You can think of this third step as defining the *actions* of your program.

Visual Basic Projects

Each Visual Basic project consists of at least two, and usually more, files.

1. The .vbp file, called the **project file**, is a small text file that holds the names of the other files in the project, as well as some information about the VB environment. *Note:* If you are using release 2.0 or 3.0 of Visual Basic, project files have a .mak extension.

2. Each form in your project is saved in a file with a .frm extension. To begin, your projects will have only one form (and therefore one **form file**). Later, you can expect your projects to have several forms, with one .frm file for each form.

   A form file holds a description of all objects and their properties for the form, as well as the Basic code you have written to respond to the events.

   In Visual Basic each of these form files is referred to as a ***form module***.

3. Optionally, your project can have .bas extension files. These files hold Basic statements that can be accessed from any form. As soon as you begin writing multiform projects, you will need .bas files.

   .bas files are called ***standard code modules***.

4. Additional controls, called *custom controls*, are stored in files with a .ocx extension. If you include controls in your project that are not part of the standard control set, the .ocx file names will be included in the project.

5. After you save a project, Visual Basic automatically adds one more file to your project with an extension of .vbw. This file holds information about each of your project's forms.

Store each Project in its own folder

Tip

Before creating any files for your project, first create a new folder on disk. Save your .vbp file, .frm files, and .bas files into the new folder. Then if you want to copy or move the project to another disk, you will get all the pieces. It is easy to miss parts of a project unless all files are together in one folder.

The Visual Basic Environment

The **Visual Basic environment** is where you create and test your projects. Figure 1.2 shows the various windows in the Visual Basic environment. Note that each window can be moved, resized, opened, and closed. Your screen may not look exactly like Figure 1.2; in all likelihood you will want to customize the placement of the various windows.

F i g u r e   1 . 2

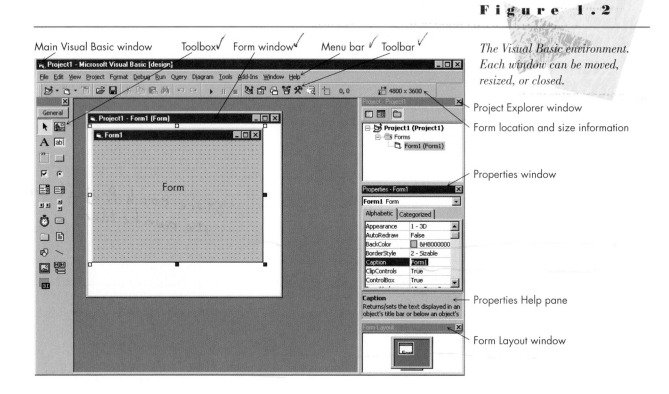

Main Visual Basic window   Toolbox   Form window   Menu bar   Toolbar

The Visual Basic environment. Each window can be moved, resized, or closed.

Project Explorer window

Form location and size information

Properties window

Properties Help pane

Form Layout window

The Form Window

The **Form window** is where you design the forms that make up your user interface. You can use standard Windows techniques to change the size and location of the form.

When you begin a new project, Visual Basic gives your new form the default name *Form1*. As soon as you save the file, you will give it a new (more meaningful) name.

The Project Explorer Window

The **Project Explorer window** holds the filenames for the files included in your project. The window's title bar holds the name of your project (.vbp) file, which is *Project1* by default until you save it with a new name.

The Properties Window

You use the **Properties window** to set the properties for the objects in your project. See "Set Properties" later in this chapter for instructions on changing properties.

The Form Layout Window

The position of the form in the form layout window determines the position of the form on the desktop when execution of the project begins.

The Toolbox

The **toolbox** holds the tools you use to place controls on a form. You may have more or different tools in your toolbox, depending on the edition and release of Visual Basic you are using. See Figure 1.3 for a labeled version of the toolbox.

Figure 1 . 3

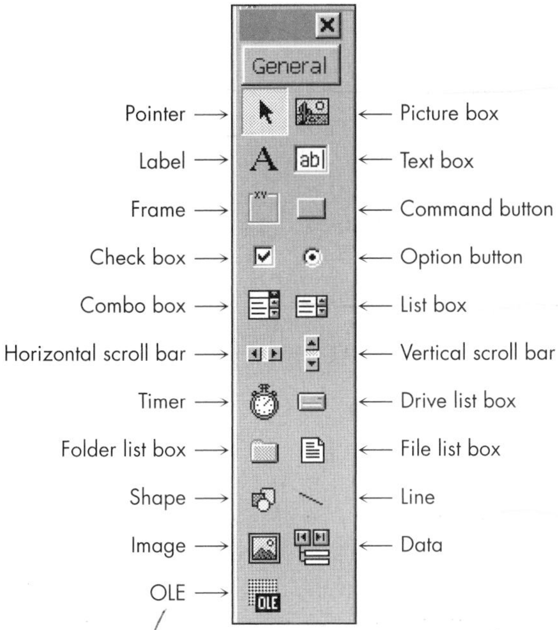

The toolbox for Visual Basic. Your toolbox may have more or fewer tools, depending on the edition and release you are using.

General

Pointer → ← Picture box
Label → ← Text box
Frame → ← Command button
Check box → ← Option button
Combo box → ← List box
Horizontal scroll bar → ← Vertical scroll bar
Timer → ← Drive list box
Folder list box → ← File list box
Shape → ← Line
Image → ← Data
OLE →

object linking & embedding

The Main Visual Basic Window

The Main Visual Basic window holds the VB menu bar, the toolbar, and the form location and size information.

The Toolbar

You can use the buttons on the **toolbar** as shortcuts for frequently used operations. Each button represents a command that can also be selected from a menu. Figure 1.4 shows the toolbar buttons.

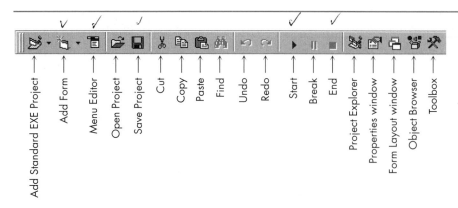

The Visual Basic toolbar. Each button represents a command that you can execute by clicking the button or by choosing a command from a menu.

The Form Location and Size Information

The two small diagrams at the right end of the Visual Basic toolbar (refer to Figure 1.2) show the position of the form on the screen along with the size of the form.

Help

Visual Basic has an extensive Help feature that is greatly changed and expanded in Version 6.0. Help now includes the Microsoft Developer Network library (MSDN), which contains several books, technical articles, and the Microsoft Knowledge Base, a database of frequently asked questions and their answers.

Help includes the entire reference manual, as well as many coding examples. In addition, you will find Microsoft on the Web with a submenu containing various resources. Take some time to investigate the options on the Help menu.

Note: The Working Model edition of VB 6.0 does not include the Help files.

Design Time, Run Time, and Break Time

Visual Basic has three distinct modes. While you are designing the user interface and writing code, you are in **design time**. When you are testing and running your project, you are in **run time**. If you get a run-time error or pause project execution, you are in **break time**. The title bar notation in Figure 1.2 indicates that the project is currently in design time.

Writing Your First Visual Basic Project

For your first event-driven project, you will create a form with three controls (see Figure 1.5). This simple project will display the message "Hello World" when the user clicks the Push Me command button and will terminate when the user clicks the Exit button.

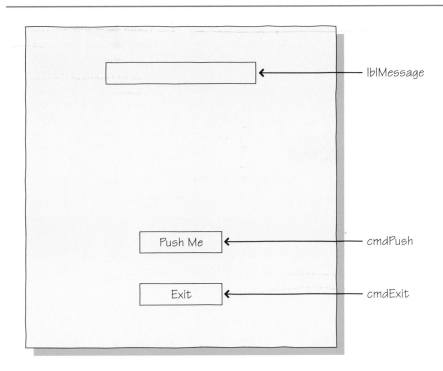

The Hello World form. The "Hello World" message will appear in the label when the user clicks on the Push Me command button.

Set Up Your Visual Basic Workspace

Before you can begin a project, you must run Visual Basic and set up your workspace the way you want it.

Run Visual Basic

STEP 1: Click on the Start button and move the mouse pointer to *Programs*.

STEP 2: Locate *Microsoft Visual Studio 6.0*. (If it doesn't appear, go on to the next step.)

STEP 3: Locate *Microsoft Visual Basic 6.0*.

STEP 4: Click on *Microsoft Visual Basic 6.0* (Figure 1.6) in the submenu.

Note: If you see the dialog box pictured in Figure 1.7, check the box that says *Don't show this dialog in the future.* If you are using a shared computer lab, check with your instructor before checking this box.

The Visual Basic project will begin and display the VB environment on the screen (refer to Figure 1.2).

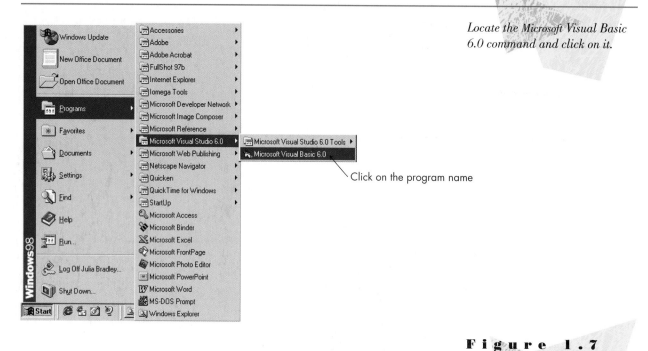

Locate the Microsoft Visual Basic 6.0 command and click on it.

Click on the program name

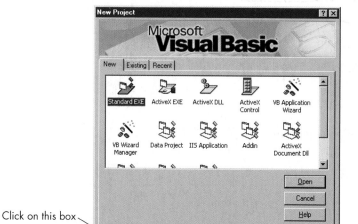

Click on this box

The New Project dialog box may appear when you start Visual Basic. Click on the check box to prevent the box from appearing for each project.

Set Up Your Workspace

STEP 1: Open the Visual Basic *Tools* menu and choose *Options.* Select the *Editor* tab if necessary. Then check each of these options, changing any that do not match (Figure 1.8).

Code Settings:	
Auto Syntax Check	Selected
Require Variable Declaration	Selected
Window Settings:	
Drag-and-Drop Text Editing	Selected
Default to Full Module View	Selected
Procedure Separator	Selected

Figure 1.8

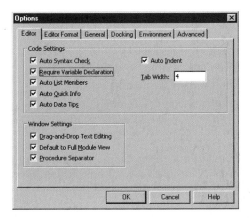

Choose **Options** *from the* **Tools** *menu and select the* **Editor** *tab; make sure the options are set properly.*

STEP 2: Click on the *General* tab of the Options window and make sure the following options are selected (Figure 1.9). When you are finished, click OK.

Form Grid Settings:	
Show Grid	Selected
Align Controls to Grid	Selected
Show ToolTips	Selected

STEP 3: If the Project Explorer window is not displaying, open the *View* menu and select *Project Explorer*.

STEP 4: If the Properties window is not displaying, open the *View* menu and select *Properties Window*. (You may move or resize the Form window by dragging its title bar.)

STEP 5: If the toolbox is not displaying, open the *View* menu and select *Toolbox*. You may have to scroll down the *View* menu if the command is not visible.

STEP 6: Maximize the Form window by clicking on its Maximize button.

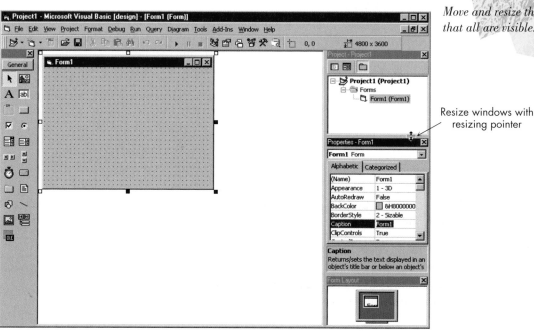

Set these options on the General tab of the Options window.

STEP 7: Adjust the size and location of the various windows if necessary. You can point to the divider between the Project Explorer window and the Properties window and drag to resize. Each window may be floating or docked, so your screen may not look like the examples. Try to make your screen layout similar to Figure 1.10.

Move and resize the windows so that all are visible.

Resize windows with resizing pointer

Plan the Project

The first step in planning is to design the user interface. Figure 1.11 shows a sketch of the form that includes a label and two command buttons. You will refer to the sketch as you create the project.

Figure 1.11

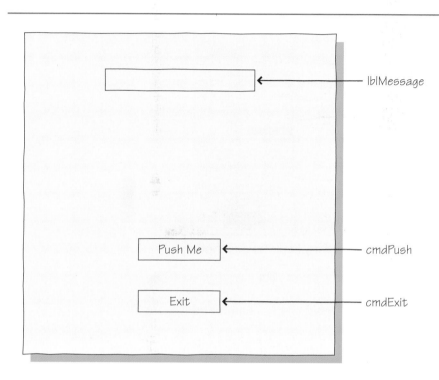

A sketch of the Hello World form for planning.

The next two steps, planning the properties and the code, have already been done for this first sample project. You will be given the values in the steps that follow.

Define the User Interface

Set Up the Form

Notice that the new form in the Form window has all the standard Windows features, such as a title bar, maximize and minimize buttons, and a close button.

STEP 1: Resize the form in the Form window: Drag the handle in the lower-right corner down and to the right (see Figure 1.12).

STEP 2: Look at the Form Layout window in the lower-right corner of the screen (refer to Figure 1.12). The small picture of a form on the monitor shows the location where your form will appear when the project runs. You may drag the picture to a different location. (*Note:* Monitors have differing resolutions, and the location you choose when designing your project may not appear the same on a different monitor.)

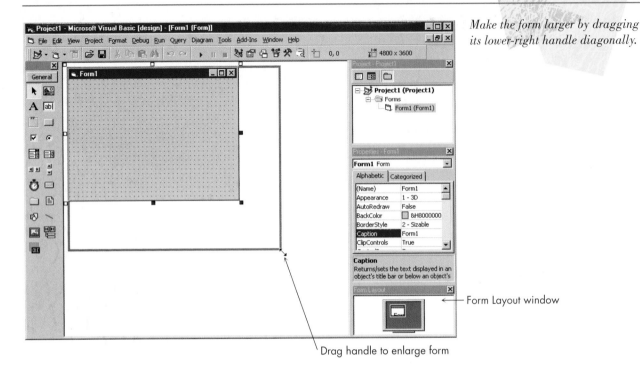

Make the form larger by dragging its lower-right handle diagonally.

Form Layout window

Drag handle to enlarge form

Place Controls on the Form

You are going to place three controls on the form: a **label** and two **command buttons**.

STEP 1: Point to the label tool in the toolbox and click. Then move the pointer over the form. Notice that the pointer becomes a crosshair, and the label tool looks like it has been pressed, indicating it is the active tool (Figure 1.13).

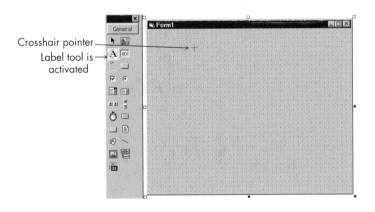

Crosshair pointer
Label tool is activated

When you click on the label tool in the toolbox, the tool's button is activated and the mouse pointer becomes a crosshair.

STEP 2: Point to the upper-left corner where you want the label to begin, press the mouse button, and drag the pointer to the opposite corner (Figure 1.14). When you release the mouse button, the label and its default contents (Label1) will appear (Figure 1.15).

Figure 1.14

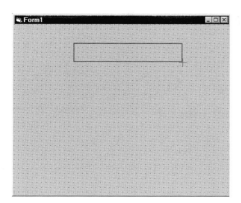

Drag the mouse pointer diagonally to draw the label on the form.

Figure 1.15

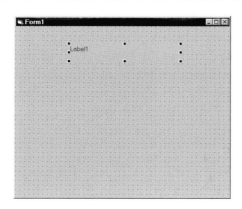

The newly created label has eight small handles, indicating that it is selected. Notice that the contents of the label are set to Label1 by default.

When you pause, Visual Basic's ToolTip pops up, indicating the size of the control in *twips,* which is a printer's measurement system. One twip is 1/1440 inch.

The label has eight small square **handles**, indicating that the control is currently selected. While a control is selected, you can delete it, resize it, or move it. Refer to Table 1.1 for instructions for selecting, deleting, resizing, and moving controls. Click outside of a control to deselect it.

Table 1.1

Select a control	Click on the control.
Delete a control	Select the control and then press the Delete key on the keyboard.
Move a control	Select the control, point inside the control (not on a handle), press the mouse button, and drag it to a new location.
Resize a control	Make sure the control is selected; then point to one of the handles, press the mouse button, and drag the handle. Drag a side handle to change the width, a bottom or top handle to change the height, or a corner handle to resize in two directions.

Selecting, deleting, resizing, and moving controls on a form.

STEP 3: Draw a command button on the form: Click on the Command button tool in the toolbox, position the crosshair pointer for one corner of the button, and drag to the diagonally opposite corner (Figure 1.16). The new command button should have selection handles.

Figure 1.16

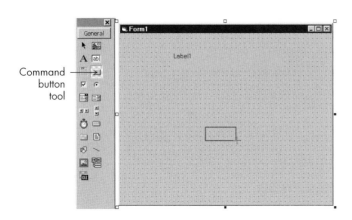

Command button tool

Select the Command button tool and drag diagonally to create a new command button control.

STEP 4: Create another command button using this alternative method: Point to the Command button tool in the toolbox and double-click. A new command button of the default size will appear in the center of the form (Figure 1.17).

Figure 1.17

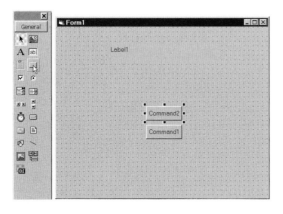

Place a new command button on the form by double-clicking the Command button tool in the toolbox. The new button appears in the center of the form.

STEP 5: Keep the new command button selected, point anywhere inside the button (not on a handle), and drag the button below your first button (Figure 1.18). As you drag the control, you see only its outline; when you release the mouse button, the control is actually moved to its new location.

Figure 1.18

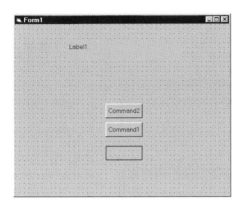

Drag the new command button (Command2) below Command1. An outline of the control shows the new location for the control.

STEP 6: Select each control and move and resize the controls as necessary. Make the two buttons the same size and line them up.

STEP 7: Point anywhere on the form except on a control and click the right mouse button. On the *Shortcut* menu, select *Lock Controls* (Figure 1.19). Locking prevents you from accidentally moving the controls. When your controls are locked, white handles, rather than the dark handles, surround a selected control.

> *Note:* You can unlock the controls at any time if you wish to redesign the form. Just click on *Lock Controls* on the *Shortcut* menu again to deselect it.

Figure 1.19

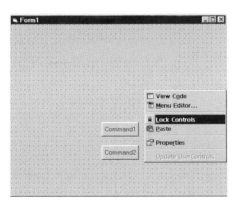

After the controls are placed into the desired location, lock them in place by selecting Lock Controls from the Shortcut menu.

At this point you have designed the user interface and are ready to set the properties.

Set Properties

Set the Name and Caption Properties for the Label

STEP 1: Click on the label you placed on the form; selection handles will appear. Next click on the title bar of the Properties window to make it the active window (Figure 1.20).

If the Properties window is not visible, you can press the F4 key to show it.

Notice that the Object box at the top of the Properties window is showing *Label1* (the name of the object) and *Label* (called the ***class*** of the object).

Figure 1.20

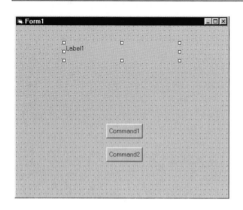
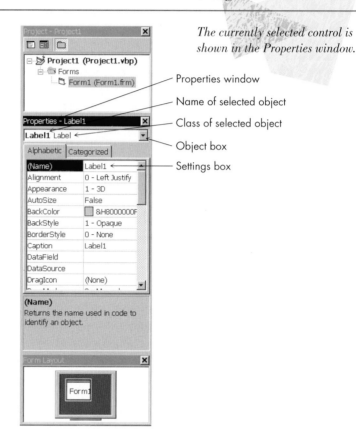

The currently selected control is shown in the Properties window.

Properties window

Name of selected object

Class of selected object

Object box

Settings box

STEP 2: Select the Name property. Click on *(Name)* and notice that the Settings box shows *Label1*, the default name of the label (Figure 1.21).

Figure 1.21

The Properties window. Click on the Name property to change the value in the Settings box.

Settings box

STEP 3: Type "lblMessage" (without the quotation marks). See Figure 1.22.

Figure   1 . 2 2

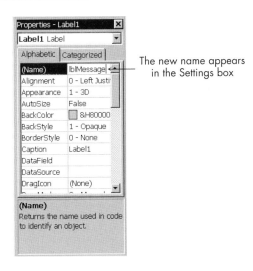

The new name appears
in the Settings box

Type "lblMessage" into the
Settings box for the Name
property.

STEP 4: Click on the Caption property to select it. Scroll the list if necessary.
The **Caption** property of a label determines what will be displayed
on the form. Because nothing should display when the project begins,
you must delete the value of the Caption property (as described in the
next two steps).

STEP 5: Double-click on *Label1* in the Settings box; the entry should appear
selected (highlighted). See Figure 1.23.

Figure   1 . 2 3

Double-click in the Settings box to
select the entry.

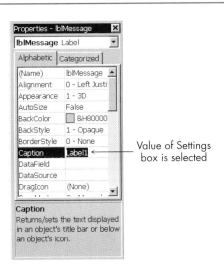

Value of Settings
box is selected

STEP 6: Press the Delete key to delete the value of the Caption property. Notice
that the label on the form now appears empty (Figure 1.24).

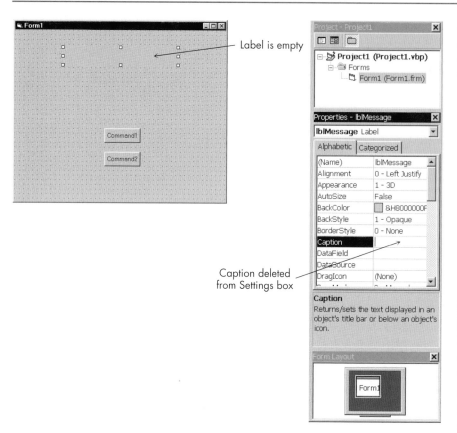

Label is empty

Caption deleted
from Settings box

Delete the value for the Caption property from the Settings box; the label on the form also appears empty.

Tip

Don't confuse the Name property with the Caption property. You will use the Name property to refer to the control in your Basic code. The Caption property tells what the user will see on the form. Visual Basic sets both of these properties to the same value by default, and it is easy to confuse them.

Set the Name and Caption Properties for the First Command Button

STEP 1: Click on the first command button (Command1) to select it and then look at the Properties window. The Object box should show the name *(Command1)* and class *(CommandButton)* of the command button. See Figure 1.25.

Problem? If you should double-click and another window appears, simply close the window by clicking on the new window's close button.

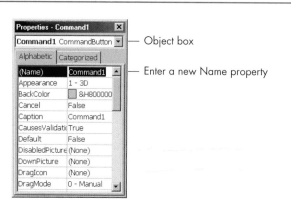

— Object box

— Enter a new Name property

Change the Name property for the first command button.

STEP 2: Change the Name property of the command button to "cmdPush" (without the quotation marks).

Although the project would work fine without this step, we prefer to give this button a meaningful name, rather than use Command1, its default name.

STEP 3: Change the Caption property to "Push Me" (without the quotation marks). This step changes the words that appear on top of the button.

Set the Name and Caption Properties for the Second Command Button

STEP 1: Select Command2 and change its Name property to "cmdExit".

STEP 2: Change the Caption property to "Exit".

Change the Caption Property for the Form

STEP 1: Click anywhere on the form, except on a control. The Properties window Object box should now show the form as the selected object (*Form1* as the object's name and *Form* as its class).

STEP 2: Change the Caption property to "Hello World by *Your Name*" (again, no quotation marks).

The Caption property of a form determines the text to appear in the title bar. Your screen should now look like Figure 1.26.

Tip ✓

Always set the Name property of controls before writing code. If you change the name of an object after the code is typed, the code becomes separated from its object and the program does not run properly.

F i g u r e   1 . 2 6

Change the form's Caption property to set the text that appears in the form's title bar.

The form's Caption appears in the title bar

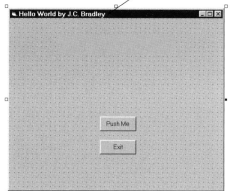

Change the form's Caption property in the Settings box

Write Code

Visual Basic Events

While your project is running, the user can do many things, such as move the mouse around; click on either button; move, resize, or close your form's window; or jump to another application. Each action by the user causes an **event** to occur in your Visual Basic project. Some events (like clicking on a command button) you care about, and some events (like moving the mouse and resizing the window) you do not care about. If you write Basic code for a particular event, then Visual Basic will respond to the event and automatically execute your procedure. *VB ignores events for which no procedures are written.*

Visual Basic Event Procedures

You write code in Visual Basic in **procedures**. For now, each of your procedures will be a **sub procedure**, which begins with the words *Private Sub* and ends with *End Sub*. (Later you will also learn about function procedures.) *Note:* Many programmers refer to sub procedures as *subprograms* or *subroutines*. *Subprogram* is acceptable; *subroutine* is not, because Basic actually has a different statement for a subroutine, which is not the same as a sub procedure.

Visual Basic automatically names your **event procedures**. The name consists of the object name, an underscore (_), and the name of the event. For example, the Click event for your command button called cmdPush will be *cmdPush_Click*. For the sample project you are writing, you will need a cmdPush_Click procedure and a cmdExit_Click procedure.

Visual Basic Code Statements

This first project requires three Visual Basic statements: the **remark**, the **assignment statement**, and the **End statement**.

The Remark Statement

Remark statements, sometimes called *comments*, are used for project documentation only. They are not considered "executable" and have no effect when the project runs. The purpose of remarks is to make the project more readable and understandable by the people who read it.

Good programming practices dictate that programmers include remarks to clarify their projects. Every sub procedure should begin with a remark that describes the purpose of the sub. Every project module should have remarks that explain the purpose of the module and provide identifying information such as the name of the programmer and the date the module was written and/or modified. In addition, it is a good idea to place remarks within the logic of a project, especially if the purpose of any statements might be unclear.

When you try to read someone else's project, or your own after a period of time, you will appreciate the generous use of remarks.

Visual Basic remarks begin with an apostrophe. Most of the time your remarks will be on a separate line that starts with an apostrophe. You can also add an apostrophe and a remark to the right end of a line of code.

The Remark Statement—Examples

```
'This project was written by Jonathon Edwards
'Exit the project
lblMessage.Caption = "Hello World" 'Assign the message to the Caption property
```

The Assignment Statement

The assignment statement assigns a value to a property or variable (you learn about variables in Chapter 3). Assignment statements operate from right to left; that is, the value appearing on the right side of the equal sign is assigned to the property named on the left of the equal sign. It is often helpful to read the equal sign as "is replaced by." For example, the assignment statement in the example would read "lblMessage.Caption is replaced by Hello World."

The Assignment Statement—General Form

```
[Let] Object.Property = value
```

The value named on the right side of the equal sign is assigned to (or placed into) the property named on the left. The Let is optional and may be included if you wish. You may find that using Let improves the readability of your projects.

The Assignment Statement—Examples

```
lblTitle.Caption = "A Snazzy Program"
lblAddress.Caption = "1234 South North Street"
lblTitle.FontSize = 12
Let lblTitle.FontBold = True
```

DIM A VAR A S INTEGER
AVAR= 7
String
AVAR= "ABC"

Notice that when the value to assign is some actual text (called a *literal*), it is enclosed in quotation marks. This convention allows you to type any combination of alpha and numeric characters. If the value is numeric, do not enclose it in quotation marks. And do not place quotation marks around the terms *True* and *False*, which Visual Basic recognizes as special key terms.

The End Statement

The End statement stops execution of a project. In most cases, you will include an End statement in the sub procedure for an Exit button or an *Exit* menu choice.

The End Statement—Example

Terminates Program execution
"Quit" button

```
End
```

Code the Event Procedures for Hello World

Code the Click Event for the Push Me Button

STEP 1: Double-click on the Push Me command button. The Visual Basic **Code window** will open with the first and last lines of your sub procedure already in place (Figure 1.27).

F i g u r e   1 . 2 7

Name of object   The event

```
cmdPush              Click

Option Explicit

Private Sub cmdPush_Click()

End Sub
```

The Code window, showing the first and last lines of the sub procedure.

STEP 2: Press the Tab key once to indent and then type this remark statement:

```
'Display the Hello World message
```

STEP 3: Press Enter and notice that Visual Basic automatically changes remarks to green (unless you or someone else has changed the color with the Environment option).

Follow good coding conventions and indent all lines between `Private Sub` and `End Sub`. Also, always leave a blank line after the remarks at the top of a sub procedure.

STEP 4: Press Enter again and then type this assignment statement:

```
lblMessage.Caption = "Hello World"
```

Note: When you type the period after lblMessage, a list box appears showing the properties and methods available for a label control. Although you can type the entire word *Caption*, you can allow the Visual Basic editor to help you. As soon as you type the *C*, the list automatically scrolls to the word *Caption*. You can press the spacebar to select the word and continue typing the rest of the statement.

This assignment statement assigns the literal "Hello World" to the Caption property of the control called lblMessage. Compare your screen to Figure 1.28.

Figure 1.28

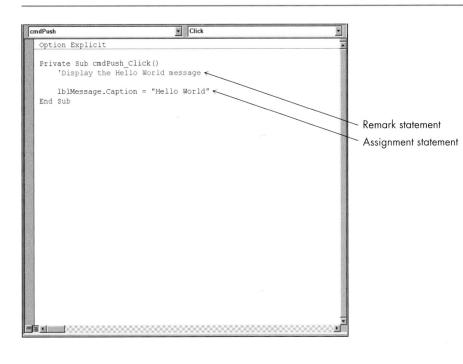

Type the remark and assignment statement for the cmdPush_Click event.

STEP 5: Return to the form by clicking on the View Object button on the Project Explorer window (Figure 1.29).

Figure 1.29

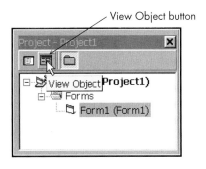

View Object button

Click on the View Object button to return to the form.

Code the Click Event for the Exit Button

STEP 1: Double-click on the Exit command button to open the Code window for the cmdExit_Click event.

STEP 2: Press Tab once and type this remark:

```
'Exit the project
```

STEP 3: Press Enter twice and type this Basic statement:

```
End
```

STEP 4: Make sure your code looks like Figure 1.30 and then click on the Code window's Close button.

Figure 1.30

Code window Close button

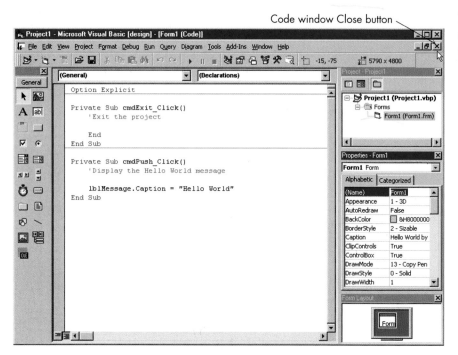

Type the remark and End *statement for the cmdExit_Click event and close the Code window.*

Run the Project

After you have finished writing the code, you are ready to run the project. Use one of these three methods:

1. Open the *Run* menu and choose *Start*.
2. Press the Start button on the toolbar.
3. Press F5, the shortcut key for the *Start* command.

Start the Project Running

STEP 1: Choose one of the three methods shown above to start your project running.

Notice that the Visual Basic title bar now indicates that you are in run time and that the grid dots have disappeared from your form (Figure 1.31). (The grid dots help you align the controls; you may turn them off if you prefer.)

Figure 1.31

Now in run time

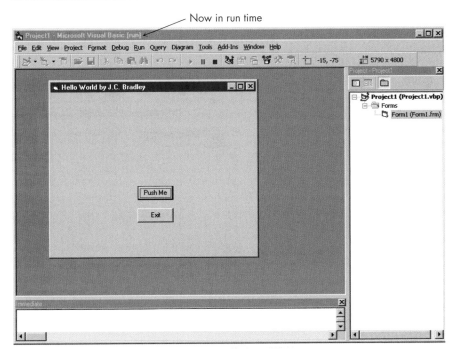

When you run the project, the Visual Basic title bar indicates run time and the form's grid dots disappear.

Tip

If your form disappears during run time, click its button on the task bar.

Click the Push Me Button

STEP 1: Click the Push Me button. Your "Hello World" message appears in the label (Figure 1.32).

Figure 1.32

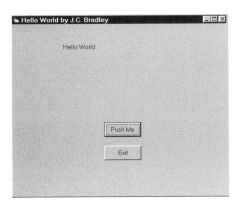

Click on the Push Me button and "Hello World" appears in the label.

Click the Exit Button

STEP 1: Click the Exit button. Your project terminates, and you return to Visual Basic design time.

(Problems? See "Finding and Fixing Errors" later in this chapter.)

Save the Project

Of course, you must always save your work often. Except for a very small project like this one, you will usually save your work as you go along.

Create a Folder

It is very easy to lose parts of a Visual Basic project and neglect to include all of the files when you copy a project from one disk to another. Therefore, you should always create a new folder on disk before saving your first file.

Note: Because of the way Visual Basic stores its project files, it is sometimes difficult to make it recognize that you have changed the location of a file. Always create your folder *first* and save into the folder—do not save somewhere else first and plan to organize later.

Save the Form File

STEP 1: Open the Visual Basic *File* menu and choose *Save Form1 As*. This option allows you to save the current form.

STEP 2: Check the *Save in* box and change to the correct drive.

STEP 3: Click on the *Create New Folder* button (Figure 1.33).

F i g u r e   1 . 3 3

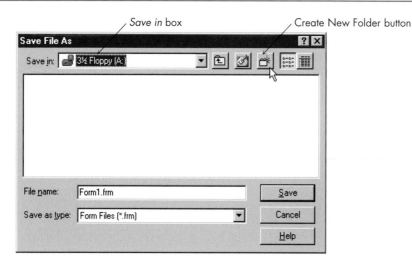

Save in box   Create New Folder button

The Save Form As dialog box. Click on the Create New Folder button and name the new folder.

STEP 4: Type the name of your new folder as "Hello" (without the quotation marks) and press Enter.

STEP 5: Open the new folder by double-clicking on it.

STEP 6: In the *File name* box, type "Hello" (without the quotation marks; see Figure 1.34). Visual Basic will add the correct .frm extension to the filename.

Your new folder should appear in the *Save in* box

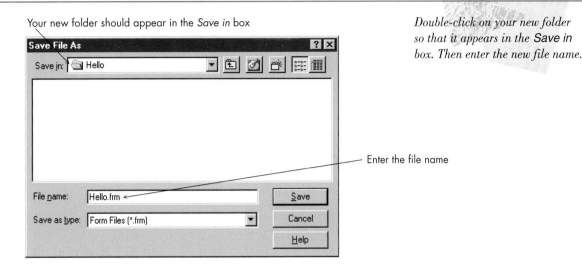

Double-click on your new folder so that it appears in the Save in box. Then enter the new file name.

Enter the file name

STEP 7: Check the *Save in* list again to make sure the file will be saved in your new folder. Then press Enter or click *Save* to save the form file.

Save the Project File

STEP 1: Open the *File* menu and select *Save Project As* to save the project (.vbp) file.

STEP 2: Check the *Save in* box; your new folder should still be showing.

STEP 3: In the *File name* box, type "Hello" (without the quotation marks; see Figure 1.35). This file will be saved as *Hello.vbp*, since Visual Basic adds the correct file extension.

The Save Project As dialog box. Make sure the correct folder is selected and type the name of the project file in the File name box.

STEP 4: Press Enter or click *Save* to save the project file.

Open the Project

Now is the time to test your save operation by opening the project from disk.

Open the Project File

STEP 1: Either click on the Open Project button on the toolbar or choose *Open Project* from the *File* menu.

STEP 2: In the *Open Project* dialog box, check the *Look in* box. Your Hello folder should still be set correctly.

When you begin a new session, you will need to change to your drive and directory before you can open a project.

STEP 3: You should see your project name, Hello.vbp, in the file list box (Figure 1.36). Click on the filename and then click on the Open button (or double-click on the filename).

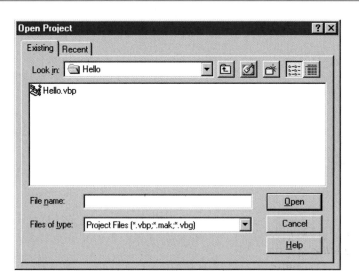

The Open Project *dialog box. Select the correct folder and find your project name in the file list.*

STEP 4: If you do not see your form on the screen, check the Project Explorer window—it should say *Hello.vbp* for the project. Click on the View Object button, and your form will appear.

Modify the Project

Now it's time to make some changes to the project. We'll change the size of the "Hello World" message, display the message in two different languages, and display the programmer name (that's you) on the form. We'll also provide a button that will print the form.

Change the Size and Alignment of the Message

STEP 1: Right-click somewhere on the form to display the *Shortcut* menu and select *Lock Controls* to unlock the controls so that you can make changes.

STEP 2: Click on the label on your form, which will make dark selection handles appear. (If your selection handles are white, you must unlock the controls, as described in Step 1.)

STEP 3: Widen the label on both ends by dragging the handles wider. (Drag the right end farther right and the left end farther left.)

STEP 4: With the label still selected, scroll to the Font property and click to select it. The Settings box shows the currently selected font.

Notice the new button with an ellipsis on top, which appears in the Settings box (Figure 1.37). The button is called the *Properties* button; the ellipsis indicates that clicking on the button will display a dialog box with choices.

Figure 1 . 3 7

Click on the Properties button to see the choices for the Font property.

Properties button

STEP 5: Click on the Properties button to display the *Font* dialog box (Figure 1.38). Select 12 point if it is available. (If it isn't available, choose another number larger than the current setting.) Close the *Font* dialog box.

Figure 1 . 3 8

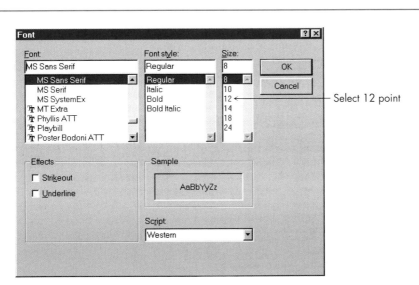

Choose 12 point from the Font dialog box.

Select 12 point

STEP 6: Select the Alignment property. The Properties button that appears with the down-pointing arrow indicates a drop-down list of choices. Drop down the list and choose *2—Center*.

Add a New Label for Your Name

STEP 1: Click on the Label tool in the toolbox and create a new label along the bottom edge of your form (Figure 1.39). (You can resize the form if necessary.)

F i g u r e 1 . 3 9

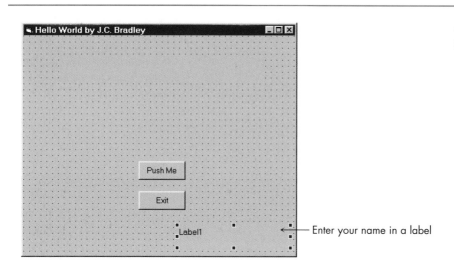

Add a new label for your name at the bottom of the form.

Hello World by J.C. Bradley

Push Me

Exit

Label1 ← Enter your name in a label

STEP 2: Change the label's Caption property to "by Your Name". (Use your name and omit the quotation marks.)

Change the Location and Caption of the Push Me Button

Label1   cmdPush

Because we plan to display the message in one of two languages, we'll change the caption on the Push Me button to English and move the button to allow for a second command button.

STEP 1: Select the Push Me button and change its Caption property to English.
STEP 2: Move the English button to the left to make room for a Spanish button (see Figure 1.40).

Add a Spanish Button

cmdSpanish

STEP 1: Add a new command button. Move and resize it as necessary, referring to Figure 1.40.
STEP 2: Change the Name property of the new button to cmdSpanish.
STEP 3: Change the Caption property of the new button to Spanish.

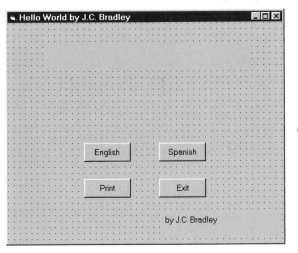

Label 2

Move the English button to the left and add a Spanish button and a Print button.

Add an Event Procedure for the Spanish Button

STEP 1: Double-click on the Spanish button to open the Code window for cmdSpanish_Click.

STEP 2: Press the Tab key once and add a remark:

```
'Display the Hello World message in Spanish
```

STEP 3: Press Enter twice and type the following Basic code line:

```
lblMessage.Caption = "Hola Mundo"
```

STEP 4: Close the Code window.

Add a Print Button

cmdPrint

STEP 1: Move the Exit button to the right to make room for the Print button.

STEP 2: Add a new command button; move and resize it to match Figure 1.40.

STEP 3: Change the Name property of the new button to cmdPrint.

STEP 4: Change the Caption property of the new button to Print.

Lock the Controls

STEP 1: When you are satisfied with the placement of the controls on the form, display the Shortcut menu and select *Lock Controls* again.

Add an Event Procedure for the Print Button

To print the form, we will use the `PrintForm` method, which prints the current form without its title bar or borders.

STEP 1: Double-click on the Print button to open the Code window for the cmdPrint_Click event.

STEP 2: Indent and add a remark that tells what you plan to do in the subprogram.

STEP 3: Leave a blank line and indent the following code statement:

```
PrintForm
```

That's all there is to it. The actual format for a method is Object.Method (object dot method). However, we can omit the object in this case, since it defaults to the current form.

Save and Run the Project

STEP 1: Save your project again. You can use the *Save File* and *Save Project* menu options or click on the Save button on the toolbar, which saves both.

STEP 2: Close the Code window and run your project again. Try clicking on the English button and the Spanish button. You can click on the Print button any time you wish. (Problems? See "Finding and Fixing Errors" later in this chapter.)

Add General Remarks

Good documentation guidelines require some more remarks in the project. Always begin each procedure with remarks that tell the purpose of the procedure. In addition, each project file needs identifying remarks at the top.

The **General Declarations section** is a good location for these remarks.

STEP 1: Click on the View Code button in the Project Explorer window; the Code window appears.

Your Code window may appear with or without an `Option Explicit` statement at the top. If you *do* see the `Option Explicit` statement, click at the left end of the line and press Enter; then skip to Step 3. (You will learn about the `Option Explicit` statement in Chapter 3. If the statement doesn't appear for this project, that's OK.)

STEP 2: Use the Code window's scroll bar to scroll to the top of the Code window. Then click in front of the first line and press Enter, creating a blank line.

STEP 3: Move the insertion point up to the blank line and type the following remarks, one per line (Figure 1.41):

```
'Hello World project
' by Your Name  (use your own name here)
' Today's date  (fill in today's date)
' This project will display a "Hello World" message in two
' different languages, and print the form on the printer.
```

F i g u r e   1 . 4 1

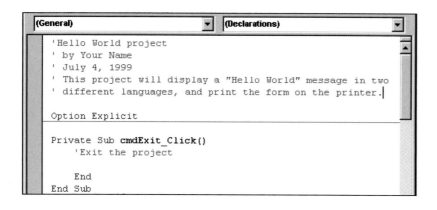

Enter remarks in the General Declarations section of the form module.

Explore the Code Window

STEP 1: Notice the two drop-down list boxes at the top of the Code window.

You can use these lists to move to any procedure in the Code window.

STEP 2: Click on the left down-pointing arrow to view the list of objects. Notice that every object in your form is listed there (Figure 1.42). At the top of the list, you see *(General)*.

F i g u r e   1 . 4 2

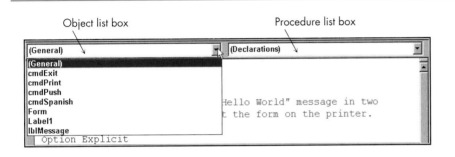

View the list of objects in this form module by dropping down the object list. Select an object from the list to display the sub procedures for that object.

STEP 3: Click on *(General)* to select it. Then notice the Procedure list, on the right, which says *(Declarations)*. This method is the quick way to jump to the General Declarations section of a module.

STEP 4: Drop down the Object list (the left list) and select *cmdSpanish*. The insertion point jumps to the event procedure for cmdSpanish.

STEP 5: Look at the Procedure list box (the right list box); it says *Click*. You are currently viewing the cmdSpanish_Click event procedure.

To write code for more than one event for an object, use the Procedure drop-down list.

STEP 6: Drop down the Procedure list and view the list of events available for the selected object. You can jump to another procedure by selecting its name from the list.

Finish Up

STEP 1: Close the Code window.

STEP 2: Save the project again.

Print the Project Documentation

Select the Printing Options

STEP 1: Open the *File* menu and choose *Print*. The *Print* dialog box appears (Figure 1.43).

STEP 2: Click on the check boxes to select the printing options you want.

Range	
Selection	This option is available only when you have selected (high-lighted) text in the Code window.
Current Module	This option will print all of the current module (form file).
Current Project	This option will print all modules in the project. Since this project has only one module, the two options give the same result.
Print What	
Form Image	Print a picture of the form as it appears at design time.
Code	Print all procedures and the General Declarations section.
Form as Text	Print a description of every object and its properties.

STEP 3: Select all three check boxes for *Print What* and click OK.

F i g u r e   1 . 4 3

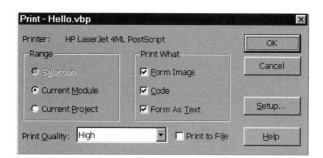

Select the options you want in the Print dialog box.

Sample Printout

This output is produced when you choose to print the form image, the code, and the form as text.

The Form Image

When you select *Form Image,* the form prints without its title bar or borders. See Figure 1.44.

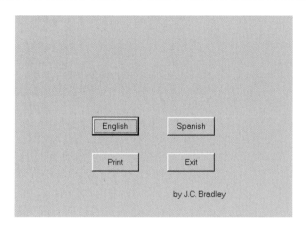

The Code

The *Code* selection prints all module procedures, as well as the General Declarations section.

```
'Hello World project
' by Your Name
' July 4, 1999
' This project will display a "Hello World" message in two
' different languages, and print the form on the printer.
Option Explicit

Private Sub cmdExit_Click()
    'Exit the project

    End
End Sub

Private Sub cmdPrint_Click()
    'Print the form

    PrintForm
End Sub

Private Sub cmdPush_Click()
    'Display the Hello World message

    lblMessage.Caption = "Hello World"
End Sub

Private Sub cmdSpanish_Click()
    'Display the Hello World message in Spanish

    lblMessage.Caption = "Hola Mundo"
End Sub
```

The Form as Text

The output produced when you select *Form as Text* lists the objects and properties in the module.

```
VERSION 5.00
Begin VB.Form Form1
   Caption             =  "Hello World by J.C. Bradley"
   ClientHeight        =  4392
   ClientLeft          =  48
   ClientTop           =  276
   ClientWidth         =  5664
   LinkTopic           =  "Form1"
   LockControls        =  -1 'True
   ScaleHeight         =  4392
   ScaleWidth          =  5664
   StartUpPosition     =  3 'Windows Default
   Begin VB.CommandButton cmdPrint
      Caption          =  "Print"
      Height           =  372
      Left             =  1560
      TabIndex         =  5
      Top              =  3120
      Width            =  972
   End

   Begin VB.CommandButton cmdSpanish
      Caption          =  "Spanish"
      Height           =  372
      Left             =  3120
      TabIndex         =  4
      Top              =  2400
      Width            =  972
   End

   Begin VB.CommandButton cmdExit
      Caption          =  "Exit"
      Height           =  372
      Left             =  3120
      TabIndex         =  2
      Top              =  3120
      Width            =  972
   End

   Begin VB.CommandButton cmdPush
      Caption          =  "English"
      Height           =  372
      Left             =  1560
```

```
   TabIndex           = 1
   Top                = 2400
   Width              = 972
End
Begin VB.Label Label1
   Caption            = "by J.C. Bradley"
   Height             = 372
   Left               = 3240
   TabIndex           = 3
   Top                = 3840
   Width              = 2292
End
Begin VB.Label lblMessage
   BeginProperty Font
      Name            = "MS Sans Serif"
      Size            = 12
      Charset         = 0
      Weight          = 400
      Underline       = 0 'False
      Italic          = 0 'False
      Strikethrough   = 0 'False
   EndProperty
   Height             = 372
   Left               = 840
   TabIndex           = 0
   Top                = 480
   Width              = 4092
   End
End
Attribute VB_Name = "Form1"
Attribute VB_GlobalNameSpace = False
Attribute VB_Creatable = False
Attribute VB_PredeclaredId = True
Attribute VB_Exposed = False
```

Finding and Fixing Errors

You may have already seen some errors as you entered the first sample project. Programming errors come in three varieties: **compile errors**, **run-time errors**, and **logic errors**.

Compile Errors

As Visual Basic attempts to convert your project code to machine language (called *compiling the code*), it finds any compile errors. You get compile errors when you break the syntax rules of Basic and sometimes when you use an illegal object or property.

For example, try spelling *End* as *ennd* or using the word *Quit* instead of *End*. The compiler can only translate the exact spelling of a word and cannot recognize either of these words; they would both cause a Compile Error message box.

You also receive a compile error if you accidentally use the wrong punctuation or place the punctuation in the wrong place. The compiler cannot understand `lblMessage,Caption` or `lblMessage.Caption;`.

The editor may find compile errors as you move off the offending line. Or the compile error may not be found until you try to run the project. Before Visual Basic can actually run your code, it attempts to compile the code into machine language. If VB finds compile errors, it displays the Code window, highlights the offending line, and enters break time.

After you have corrected your compile errors, you can click the Run button to continue the compile and run, or click the Stop button to end.

One type of compile error that is all too common for beginning programmers is the inconsistent spelling of object names. For example, if you set a label control's Name property to `lblMessage`, you must always refer to it with that exact spelling. The following line of code will generate a compile error. Can you spot the problem?

```
lblMessages.Caption = "Hello World"
```

Run-Time Errors

If your project halts during execution, that's a run-time error. Visual Basic displays a dialog box, goes into break time, and highlights the statement causing the problem. Statements that cannot execute correctly cause run-time errors. The statements are correctly formed Basic statements that pass the syntax checking of the compiler; however, the statements fail to execute. Run-time errors can be caused by attempting to do impossible arithmetic operations such as calculate with nonnumeric data, divide by zero, or find the square root of a negative number.

Logic Errors

With logic errors, your project runs but produces incorrect results. Perhaps the results of a calculation are incorrect or the wrong text appears or the text is OK but appears in the wrong location.

Beginning programmers often overlook their logic errors. If the project runs, it must be right—right? All too often, that statement is not correct. You may need to use a calculator to check the output. Check all aspects of the project output: computations, text, and spacing.

For example, the Hello World project in this chapter has event procedures for printing "Hello World" in English and in Spanish. If the contents of the two procedures were switched, the program would work but the results would be incorrect.

The following code does not give the proper instructions to display the message in Spanish:

```
Private Sub cmdSpanish_Click
    'Display the Hello World Message in Spanish

    lblMessage.Caption = "Hello World"
End Sub
```

Project Debugging

If you talk to any computer programmer, you will learn that programs don't have errors, but that programs get "bugs" in them. Finding and fixing these bugs is called **debugging**.

For compile errors and run-time errors, your job is easier. Visual Basic displays the Code window with the offending line highlighted. However, you must identify and locate logic errors yourself.

If you are able to see the problem and fix it, you can continue project execution from that location by clicking on the Run button, pressing F5, or choosing *Start* from the *Run* menu. You can restart execution from the beginning by selecting *Restart* from the *Run* menu or by pressing Shift +F5.

Visual Basic has some very helpful tools to aid in debugging your projects. The debugging tools are covered in Chapter 4.

Naming Rules and Conventions for Objects

Using good consistent names for objects can make a project easier to read and understand, as well as easier to debug. You *must* follow the Visual Basic rules for naming objects, procedures, and variables. In addition, conscientious programmers will also follow certain naming conventions.

The Naming Rules

When you select a name for an object, Visual Basic requires the name to begin with a letter. The name can be up to 40 characters in length and can contain letters, digits, and underscores. An object name cannot include a space or punctuation mark.

The Naming Conventions

This text follows the industrywide naming conventions, which help make projects more understandable: Always begin a name with a lowercase three-letter prefix, which identifies the object type (such as label, command button, or form) and capitalize the first character after the prefix (the "real" name of the object). For names with multiple words, capitalize each word in the name. All names must be meaningful and indicate the purpose of the object.

Examples

lblMessage
cmdExit
frmDataEntry
lblDiscountRate

Do not keep the default names assigned by Visual Basic, such as Command1 and Label3. Also, do not name your objects with numbers. The exception to this rule is for labels that never change during project execution. These labels usually hold items such as titles, instructions, and labels for other controls. Leaving these labels with their default names is perfectly acceptable and is practiced in this text.

Refer to Table 1.2 for the list of object prefixes.

Table 1.2

Object Class	Prefix	Example
Form	frm	frmDataEntry
Command button	cmd	cmdExit
Text box	txt	txtPaymentAmount
Label	lbl	lblTotal
Option button	opt	optBold
Check box	chk	chkPrintSummary
Frame	fra	fraSelection
Horizontal scroll bar	hsb	hsbRate
Vertical scroll bar	vsb	vsbTemperature
Image	img	imgLogo
Picture box	pic	picLandscape
Combo box	cbo	cboBookList
List box	lst	lstIngredients
Shape	shp	shpBox

Recommended naming conventions for Visual Basic objects.

Visual Basic Help

The Visual Basic **Help** facility is great! With Help, you really don't need a printed manual. You can look up any Basic statement, object, property, method, or programming concept. Many coding examples are available, and you can copy and paste the examples into your own project, modifying them if you wish.

The VB Help facility is greatly changed and expanded in Version 6.0. Help now includes all of the Microsoft Developer Network library (MSDN), which contains several books, technical articles, and the Microsoft Knowledge Base, a database of frequently asked questions and their answers. You can either install all of the MSDN library on your hard drive or network or keep the CD in the drive to reference its topics. *Note:* If you are using the Visual Basic Working Model, you don't have MSDN unless you purchase it separately. You can access MSDN on the web at http://msdn.microsoft.com. Or, if you want to go directly to the VB Help, add this link to your favorites:

http://msdn.microsoft.com/library/default.asp?URL=/library/devprods/vs6/vbasic/vbcon98/vbstartpage.htm

The expanded Help is a two-edged sword: You have available a wealth of materials, but it may take some time to find the topic you want.

The MSDN Viewer

The MSDN files are actually HTML pages that can be viewed in a browser such as Internet Explorer. In fact, the MSDN viewer is a customized version of Internet Explorer.

The Viewer window (Figure 1.45) is divided vertically into two panes: the navigation pane on the left, which can be hidden if you wish, and the topics pane on the right. In the navigation pane you can select a subset of the complete documentation, which can help you narrow down your search. The MSDN library holds documentation for all of Visual Studio, which includes Visual C++, Visual J++, Visual FoxPro, Visual InterDev, Visual SourceSafe, and several software development kits (SDKs).

F i g u r e   1 . 4 5

Use the MSDN library Viewer window to select and view Help topics.

In the navigation pane you can choose to view the library contents by the table of contents, by the index, or by searching for a phrase. You can also add pages to the Favorites list for future reference. You select a topic in the navigation pane and view the topic's text in the topic pane (on the right).

A good way to start using the MSDN library is to view the topics that demonstrate how to look up topics in the viewer. Open the *Contents* tab and select *MSDN Library Visual Studio 6.0/Welcome to the MSDN Library/MSDN Library Help/Locating Information in the MSDN Library*. Then select from *Navigating Using the Table of Contents, Finding Information with the Index, Finding Information with Full-Text Search*, and *Creating a List of Favorite Topics*.

event *22*

event-driven programming *2*

event procedure *22*

form *2*

form file *5*

form module *5*

Form window *6*

General Declarations section *34*

graphical user interface (GUI) *2*

handle *15*

Help *42*

label *14*

Learning Edition *4*

logic error *39*

method *3*

object *3*

object-oriented programming *3*

procedure *22*

Professional Edition *4*

Project Explorer window *6*

project file *5*

Properties window *7*

property *3*

pseudocode *4*

remark *22*

run time *8*

run-time error *39*

standard code module *5*

sub procedure *22*

toolbar *7*

toolbox *7*

user interface *4*

Visual Basic environment *6*

Working Model *4*

R e v i e w   Q u e s t i o n s

1. What are objects and properties? How are they related to each other?

2. What are the three steps for planning and creating Visual Basic projects? Describe what happens in each step.

3. What is the purpose of these Visual Basic file types: .vbp, .frm, .bas, and .ocx?

4. When is Visual Basic in design time? run time? break time?

5. What is the purpose of the Name property of a control?

6. Which property determines what appears on the form for a label control?

7. What is the purpose of the Caption property of a command button? the Caption property of a form?

8. What does *cmdPush_Click* mean? To what does cmdPush refer? To what does Click refer?

9. What is a Visual Basic event? Give some examples of events.

10. What property must be set to center text in a label? What should be the value of the property?

11. What is the General Declarations section of a form module? What belongs there?

12. What is a compile error, when does it occur, and what might cause it?

13. What is a run-time error, when does it occur, and what might cause it?

14. What is a logic error, when does it occur, and what might cause it?

15. Tell the class of control and the likely purpose of each of these object names:

    lblAddress

    cmdExit

    txtName

    optTextBlue

16. What does *context-sensitive Help* mean? How can you use it to see the Help page for a command button?

Programming   Exercises

1.1 For your first Visual Basic exercise, you must first complete the Hello World project. Then add command buttons and event procedures to display the "Hello World" message in two more languages. You may substitute any other languages for those shown. Use Figure 1.44 as a guideline but feel free to modify the user interface to suit yourself (or your instructor).

Make sure to use meaningful names for your new command buttons, following the naming conventions in Table 1.2. (Begin the name with lowercase "cmd".) Include remarks at the top of every procedure and in the General Declarations section of the module.

"Hello World" in French: *Bonjour tout le monde*
"Hello World" in Italian: *Ciao Mondo*

1.2 Write a new Visual Basic project that displays a different greeting, or make it display the name of your school or your company. Include at least three command buttons to display the greeting, print the form, and exit the project.

Include a label that holds your name at the bottom of the form and change the Caption property of the form to something meaningful.

Follow good naming conventions for object names; include remarks at the top of every procedure and in the General Declarations section of the module.

Select a different font name and font size for the greeting label. If you wish, you can also select a different color for the font. Select each font attribute from the *Font* dialog box from the Properties window.

1.3 Write a project that displays four sayings, such as "The early bird gets the worm" or "A penny saved is a penny earned." (You will want to keep the sayings short, as each must be entered on one code statement. However, when the saying displays on your form, long lines will wrap within the label if the label is large enough.)

Make a command button for each saying with a descriptive Caption for each, as well as command buttons to print the form and to exit the project.

Include a label that holds your name at the bottom of the form. Also, make sure to change the Caption property of the form to something meaningful.

You may change the Font properties of the large label to the font and size of your choice.

Make sure the label is large enough to display your longest saying and that the command buttons are large enough to hold their entire Captions.

Follow good naming conventions for object names; include remarks at the top of every procedure and in the General Declarations section of the module.

1.4 Write a project to display company contact information. Include command buttons and labels for the contact person, department, and phone. When the user clicks on one of the command buttons, display the contact information in the corresponding label. Include command buttons to print the form and to exit.

Include a label that holds your name at the bottom of the form and change the Caption property of the form to something meaningful.

You may change the Font properties of the labels to the font and size of your choice.

Follow good naming conventions for object names; include remarks at the top of every procedure and in the General Declarations section of the module.

CASE STUDIES

Very Busy (VB) Mail Order

If you don't have the time to look for all those hard-to-find items, tell us what you're looking for. We'll send you a catalog from the appropriate company or order for you.

We can place an order and ship it to you. We also help with shopping for gifts; your order can be gift wrapped and sent anywhere you wish.

The company title will be shortened to VB Mail Order. This name should appear as the Caption on the first form of every project that you create throughout the text for this case study.

Your first job is to create a project that will display the names and telephone numbers for the contact persons for the customer relations, marketing, order processing, and shipping departments.

Include a command button for each department. When the user clicks on the button for a department, display the name and telephone number for the contact person in two labels. Also include identifying labels with Captions "Department Contact" and "Telephone Number".

Be sure to include a command button for Exit and another for Print Form.

Include a label at the bottom of the form that holds your name and give the form a meaningful Caption.

Test Data

Department	Department Contact	Telephone Number
Customer Relations	Tricia Mills	500-1111
Marketing	Michelle Rigner	500-2222
Order Processing	Kenna DeVoss	500-3333
Shipping	Eric Andrews	500-4444

Valley Boulevard (VB) Auto Center

Valley Boulevard Auto Center will meet all of your automobile needs. The center has facilities with everything for your vehicles including sales and leasing for new and used cars and RVs, auto service and repair, detail shop, car wash, and auto parts.

The company title will be shortened to VB Auto Center. This name should appear as the Caption on the first form of every project that you create throughout the text for this case study.

Your first job is to create a project that will display current notices.

Include four command buttons with the Captions: "Auto Sales", "Service Center", "Detail Shop", and "Employment Opportunities". One label will be used to display the information when the command buttons are clicked. Be sure to include command buttons for Exit and Print Form.

Include your name in a label at the bottom of the form.

Test Data

Command Button	Label Caption
Auto Sales	Family wagon, immaculate condition $12,995
Service Center	Lube, oil, filter $25.99
Detail Shop	Complete detail $79.95 for most cars
Employment Opportunities	Sales position contact Mr. Mann 551-2134 x475

Video Bonanza

This neighborhod store is an independently owned video rental business. The owners would like to allow their customers to use their computers to look up the aisle numbers for movies by category.

Create a form with a command button for each category. When the user clicks on a command button, display the corresponding aisle number in a label. Include command buttons to print the form and to exit.

Include a label that holds your name at the bottom of the form and change the caption property of the form to Video Bonanza.

You may change the font properties of the labels to the font and size of your choice. Include additional categories if you wish.

Follow good programming conventions for object names; include remarks at the top of every procedure and in the General Declarations section of the module.

Test Data

Command Button	Location
Comedy	Aisle 1
Drama	Aisle 2
Action	Aisle 3
Sci-Fi	Aisle 4
Horror	Aisle 5
New Releases	Back Wall

This chain of stores features a full **Very Very Boards** line of clothing and equipment for snowboard and skateboard enthusiasts. Management wants a computer application to allow their employees to display the address and hours for each of their branches.

Create a form with a command button for each store branch. When the user clicks on a command button, display the correct address and hours.

Include a label that holds your name at the bottom of the form and change the caption property of the form to Very Very Boards.

You may change the font properties of the labels to the font and size of your choice.

Follow good programming conventions for object names; include remarks at the top of every procedure and in the General Declaratons section of the module.

Store Branches: The three branches are Downtown, Mall, and Suburbs. Create hours and locations for each.

2

More Controls

At the completion of this chapter, you will be able to . . .

1. Use text boxes, frames, check boxes, option buttons, images, shapes, and lines effectively.

2. Set the Appearance property to make controls appear flat or three-dimensional.

3. Select multiple controls and move them, align them, and set common properties.

4. Make your projects easy for the user to understand and operate by defining access keys, setting a default and a cancel button, controlling the tab sequence, resetting the focus during program execution, and causing ToolTips to appear.

5. Clear the contents of text boxes and labels.

6. Change font attributes, such as bold, italic, underline, size, and color, during program execution.

7. Code multiple statements for one control using the `With` and `End With` statements.

8. Concatenate (join) strings of text.

9. Make a control visible or invisible by setting its Visible property.

Introducing More Controls

In Chapter 1 you learned to use labels and command buttons. In this chapter you will learn to use several more control types: text boxes, frames, check boxes, option buttons, image controls, shapes, and lines. Figure 2.1 shows the toolbox with the tools for these controls labeled. Figure 2.2 shows some of these controls on a form.

F i g u r e   2 . 1

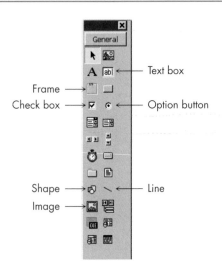

The toolbox showing the controls that are covered in this chapter.

F i g u r e   2 . 2

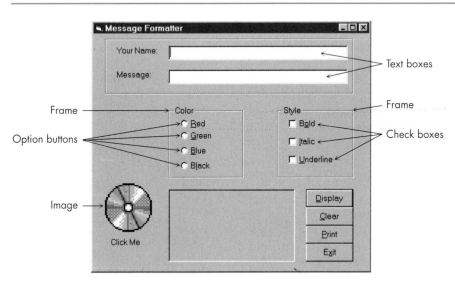

This form uses text boxes, frames, check boxes, option buttons, and an image.

Each class of control has its own set of properties. To see a complete list of the properties for any class of control, you can (1) place a control on a form and examine the properties list or (2) click on a tool or a control and press F1 for context-sensitive Help. VB will display the Help page for that control, and you can view a list of the properties and an explanation of their use.

Text Boxes

No Caption

Use a **text box** control when you want the user to type some input. The form in Figure 2.2 has two text boxes. The user can move from one box to the next, make corrections, cut and paste if desired, and click the Display button when finished. In your program code you can use the **Text property** of each text box.

Example

```
lblName.Caption = txtName.Text
```

In this example whatever the user enters into the text box is assigned to the Caption property of lblName. If you want to display some text in a text box during program execution, assign a literal to the Text property:

```
txtMessage.Text = "Watson, come here."
```

You can set the **Alignment property** of text boxes to change the alignment of text within the box. However, you must also set the **Multiline property** to True, or VB ignores the Alignment.

The values for the Alignment property, which can be set only at design time (not at run time), are

0 – Left Justify
1 – Right Justify
2 – Center

The three-letter prefix for naming a text box is "txt".

Examples

txtTitle
txtCompany

Frames

Frames are used as containers for other controls. Usually, groups of option buttons or check boxes are placed in frames. Using frames to group controls makes your forms easier to understand.

Set a frame's Caption property to the words you want to appear on the top edge of the frame. The three-letter prefix for naming a frame is "fra".

Examples

fraColor
fraStyle

Check Boxes

Check boxes allow the user to select (or deselect) an option. In any group of check boxes, any number may be selected. The **Value property** of a check box is set to 0 if unchecked, 1 if checked, or 2 if grayed (disabled). You can write an event procedure to execute when the user clicks in the box. In

Chapter 4, when you learn about If statements, you can take one action when the box is checked and another action when it is unchecked.

Use the Caption property of a check box for the text you want to appear next to the box. The three-letter prefix for naming a check box is "chk".

Examples

    chkBold
    chkItalic

Option Buttons

Use **option buttons** when only one button of a group may be selected. Any option buttons placed directly on the form (not in a frame) function as a group. A group of option buttons inside a frame function together. The best method is to first create a frame and then create each option button inside the frame. You must be careful to create the button inside the frame; don't create it on the form and drag it inside the frame—it still belongs to the form's group, not the frame's group. Therefore, you should not create an option button by double-clicking on its toolbox tool; instead, click to select the tool and use the crosshair pointer to draw the option button control.

The Value property of an option button is set to True if selected or to False if unselected.

You can write an event procedure to execute when the user selects an option button. In Chapter 4 you will learn to determine in your code whether or not a button is selected.

Set an option button's Caption property to the text you want to appear next to the button. The three-letter prefix for naming an option button is "opt".

Examples

    optRed
    optBlue

Images

An **image** control holds a picture. You can set an image's **Picture property** to a file with an extension of .bmp, .wmf, .ico, .dib, .gif, .jpg, .emf, or .cur. First place the image control on a form and then select its Picture property in the Properties window. Click on the Properties button (Figure 2.3) to display the *Load Picture* dialog box where you can select a filename (Figure 2.4).

You can use any picture file (with the proper format) that you have available. You will find many icon files included with Visual Basic. Look in the Icons folder, under the Graphics folder, beneath the VB folder (Figure 2.5).

Note: For the graphics files to install with Visual Basic, you must do a custom install and specifically request that the graphics files be included.

Default path for icon files:

```
Program Files
    Microsoft Visual Studio
        Common
            Graphics
                Icons
```

Figure 2.3

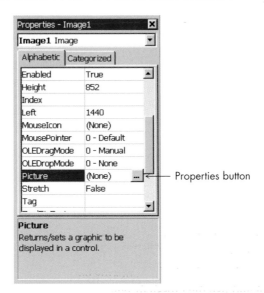

Click on the Picture property for an image control, and a Properties button appears. Click on the Properties button to view the Load Picture dialog box.

Figure 2.4

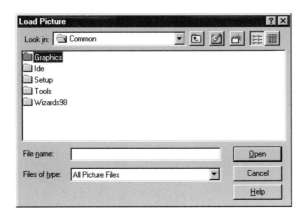

The Load Picture dialog box. Make your selection here for the picture file you want to appear in the image control.

Figure 2.5

Find the Visual Basic icon files in several folders beneath the Microsoft Visual Studio\Common\Graphics\Icons folder.

Image controls have several useful properties that you can set at design time or run time. For example, set the **Stretch property** to True to make the picture enlarge to fill the control. You can set the **Visible property** to False to make the image disappear.

For example, to make an image invisible at run time, use this code statement:

```
imgLogo.Visible = False
```

The three-letter prefix for naming an image is "img".

Tip

To remove a picture from a form or image, select the Picture property value in the Properties window and press the Delete key.

Setting a Border and Style

Most controls can appear to be three-dimensional (refer to Figure 2.2) or flat. Labels, text boxes, check boxes, option buttons, and images all have an **Appearance property**, with choices of 0 − Flat, or 1 − 3D. To make a label or an image appear three-dimensional, you must first give it a border. Set the BorderStyle to 1 − Fixed Single. The Appearance property defaults to 1 − 3D.

Feedback 2.1

Create an image control that displays an enlarged icon and appears in a "sunken" box. (Make up a name that conforms to this textbook's naming convention.)

Property	Setting
Name	*imgBig*
Stretch	*True*
Appearance	*1 − 3D*
BorderStyle	*1 − Fixed Single*
Visible	*True*

The Shape Control

You can use the **shape control** to place rectangles, squares, ovals, and circles on a form (Figure 2.6). Shapes can enhance the readability of a screen or add some fun. You may wish to use shapes to create a company logo or to separate a form into sections.

Use the shape tool in the toolbox (refer to Figure 2.1) to draw a shape on the form. Then you can determine its shape by setting its Shape property. The property values are

0 – Rectangle
1 – Square
2 – Oval
3 – Circle
4 – Rounded Rectangle
5 – Rounded Square

Figure 2.6

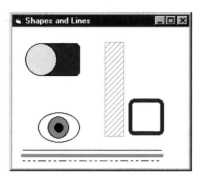

You can draw, move, and resize shape controls in the same manner as the other controls. By changing properties, you can select the style and color of the shape's outline, the color of its fill, and whether it is transparent or solid.

The naming prefix for shape controls is "shp", such as *shpRectangle*.

The Line Control

You can draw a line on a form by using the **line control**. You may want to include lines when creating a logo, or you may simply want to divide the screen by drawing a line. Click on the line tool (refer to Figure 2.1) and use the crosshair pointer to drag a line; you may rotate the line in any direction and stretch it until releasing the mouse button.

Change properties of line controls to set the color and style of the line. You can determine the thickness of a line by changing its Borderwidth property.

The naming prefix for a line control is "lin", for example, *linLogo*.

Working with Multiple Controls

You can select more than one control at a time, which means that you can move the controls as a group, set similar properties for the group, and align the controls.

Selecting Multiple Controls

There are two methods of selecting multiple controls. If the controls are near each other, the easiest method is to use the mouse to drag a selection box around the controls. Point to one corner of a box surrounding the controls, press the mouse button, and drag to the opposite corner (Figure 2.7). When you release the mouse button, each control will have light gray selection handles (Figure 2.8).

Figure 2 . 7

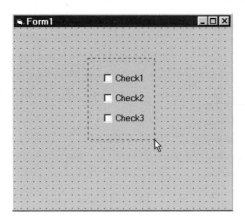

Use the pointer to drag a selection box around the controls you wish to select.

Figure 2 . 8

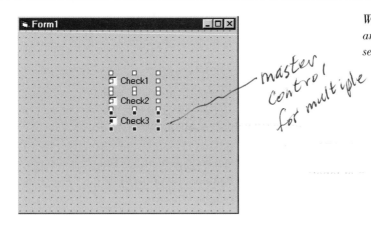

When multiple controls are selected, each has selection handles.

master control for multiple

You can also select multiple controls, one at a time. Click on one control to select it, hold down the Ctrl key or the Shift key, and click on the next control. You can keep the Ctrl or Shift key down and continue clicking on controls you wish to select. Ctrl–click (or Shift–click) on a control a second time to deselect it without changing the rest of the group.

When you want to select most of the controls on the form, use a combination of the two methods. Drag a selection box around all of the controls to select them all and then Ctrl–click on the ones you want to deselect.

Deselecting a Group of Controls

When you are finished working with a group of controls, it's easy to deselect them. Just click anywhere on the form (not on a control) or select another (single) control.

Moving Controls as a Group

After selecting multiple controls, you can move them as a group. Point inside one of the selected controls, press the mouse button, and drag the entire group to a new location (Figure 2.9). As you drag the mouse pointer, an outline of the controls moves. When you release the mouse button, the controls move to their new location.

Figure 2.9

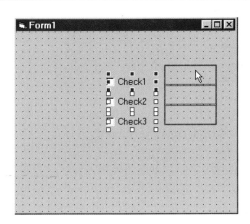

Drag a group of selected controls. An outline of the controls moves as you drag, and then the group moves when you release the mouse button.

Setting Properties for Multiple Controls

You can set some common properties for groups of controls. After selecting the group, check the Properties window. Any properties shown in the window are shared by all of the controls and can be changed all at once. For example, you may want to set the appearance for all your controls to three-dimensional or change the font used for a group of labels.

Aligning Controls

After you select a group of controls, it is easy to resize and align them using the options on the *Format* menu. Figure 2.10 shows the *Align* submenu, and Figure 2.11 shows the *Make Same Size* submenu. Select your group of controls, choose *Make Same Size*, and then use the *Align* option. You may also move the entire group to a new location.

Figure 2.10

Choose the alignment for multiple selected controls from the Align submenu.

Figure 2.11

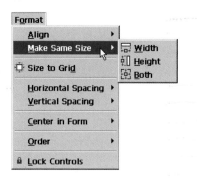

Use the Make Same Size submenu to resize multiple selected controls to make them all the same size.

To set the spacing between controls, use the *Horizontal Spacing* (Figure 2.12) and/or Vertical Spacing (Figure 2.13) options on the *Format* menu. These options enable you to create equal spacing between controls or to increase or decrease the space between controls.

Figure 2.12

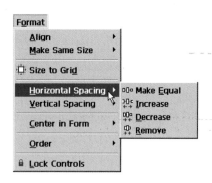

Use the Horizontal Spacing submenu to change the horizontal alignment of multiple selected controls.

Figure 2.13

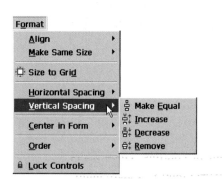

Use the Vertical Spacing submenu to change the vertical alignment of multiple selected controls.

Another way to align controls on a form is to select them and set their location using properties. For example, if you have a group of controls to align vertically, select them all and set their Left property to the same value. You can also set the Width property so the controls are all the same size. To set the controls to align horizontally, set them to the same Top property. See Figure 2.14.

Figure 2.14

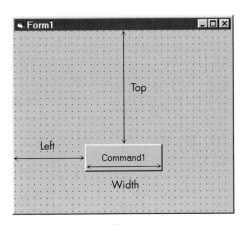

A control's Top property is its distance in twips from the top of the form; the Left property is its distance from the left edge of the form; and the Width property is the width of the control.

INPUTBOX(—, —, 4000, 1000)

The numbers you see in the Settings box for Left, Top, and Width may look strange. The measurements are shown in twips, which is a measuring system from the printing industry. One **twip** is $\frac{1}{20}$ of a printer's point or $\frac{1}{1,440}$ of an inch. If you define a control to be 1,440 twips wide, theoretically it is 1 inch wide. Actually, when it prints on the printer, it is 1 inch. However, on the screen it may be smaller or larger, depending on the resolution of monitors.

Designing Your Applications for User Convenience

One of the goals of good programming is to create programs that are easy to use. Your user interface should be clear and consistent. One school of thought says that if users misuse a program, it's the fault of the programmer, not the users. Because most of your users will already know how to operate Windows programs, you should strive to make your programs look and behave like other Windows programs. Some of the ways to accomplish this goal are to use controls in the standard way, define keyboard access keys, set a default command button, and make the Tab key work correctly. You can also define ToolTips, those small labels that pop up when the user pauses the mouse pointer over a control.

Designing the User Interface

The design of the screen should be easy to understand and "comfortable" for the user. The best way that we can accomplish these goals is to follow industry standards in relation to color, size, and placement of controls. Once users become accustomed to a screen design, they will expect (and feel more familiar with) applications that follow the same design criteria. Design your applications to match other Windows applications. Take some time to examine the screens and dialog boxes in Microsoft Office as well as those in Visual Basic.

Microsoft has done extensive program testing with users of different ages, genders, nationalities, and disabilities. We should take advantage of this research and follow the guidelines.

One recommendation about interface design concerns color. You have probably noticed that Windows applications are predominantly gray. A reason is that many people are color blind. Also, gray is easiest and best for the majority of users. Although you may personally prefer brighter colors, if you want your applications to look professional, you will stick with gray.

Colors can indicate to the user what is expected. Use a white background for text boxes to indicate that the user is to input information. Use a gray background for labels, which the user cannot change. Labels that will display a message or result of a calculation should have a border around them; labels that provide a caption on the screen should have no border (the default).

Group your controls on the form to aid the user. A good practice is to create frames to hold related items, especially those controls that require user input.

This visual aid helps the user understand the information that is being presented or requested.

Use a sans serif font on your forms, such as the default MS Sans Serif, and do not make them boldface. Limit large font sizes to a few items, such as the company name.

Defining Keyboard Access Keys

Many people prefer to use the keyboard, rather than a mouse, for most operations. Windows is set up so that most everything can be done with either the keyboard or a mouse. You can make your projects respond to the keyboard by defining **access keys**. For example, in Figure 2.15 you can select the OK button with Alt + o and the Exit button with Alt + x.

The underlined character in a Caption defines an access key. The user can select the OK button by pressing Alt + o and the Exit button with Alt + x.

You can set access keys for command buttons, option buttons, and check boxes when you define their Caption properties. Type an ampersand (&) in front of the character you want for the access key; Visual Basic underlines the character.

For example, type the following Captions:

```
&OK      for OK
E&xit    for Exit
```

When you define access keys, you need to watch for several pitfalls. First, try to use the Windows-standard keys whenever possible. For example, use the x of Exit and the S of Save. Second, make sure you don't give two controls the same access key—it confuses the user. The first time someone presses the access key, it selects the first button; the next time he or she presses the same key, it selects a different button.

Setting the Default and Cancel Properties of Command Buttons

Are you a keyboard user? If so, do you mind having to pick up the mouse and click a button after typing text into a text box? Once a person's fingers are on the keyboard, most people prefer to press the Enter key, rather than to click the mouse. If one of the command buttons on the form is the *default button*, pressing Enter is the same as clicking the button. You can always identify the default button on a form by its darker outline. Referring to Figure 2.15, the OK button is the default.

You can make one of your command buttons the default button by setting its **Default property** to True. When the user presses Enter, that button is automatically selected.

You can also select a *cancel button*. The cancel button is the button that is selected when the user presses the Esc key. You can make a command button the cancel button by setting its **Cancel property** to True. An example of a good time to set the Cancel property is on a form with OK and Cancel buttons. You may want to set the Default property to True for the OK button and the Cancel property to True for the Cancel button.

Setting the Tab Order for Controls

In Windows programs one control on the form always has the **focus**. You can see the focus change as you Tab from control to control. For controls such as command buttons and option buttons, the focus appears as a light dotted line. For text boxes, the insertion point (also called the cursor) appears inside the box.

Some controls can receive the focus; others cannot. For example, text boxes and command buttons can receive the focus, but labels and images cannot.

The Tab Order

Two properties determine whether the focus stops on a control and the order in which the focus moves. Controls that are capable of receiving focus have a **TabStop property**, which you can set to True or False. If you do not want the focus to stop on a control when the user presses the Tab key, set the TabStop property to False.

The **TabIndex property** determines the order the focus moves as the Tab key is pressed. As you create controls on your form, Visual Basic assigns the TabIndex property in sequence. Most of the time that order is correct, but if you want to Tab in some other sequence or if you add controls later, you will need to modify the TabIndex properties of your controls.

When your program begins running, the focus is on the control with the lowest TabIndex (usually 0). Since you want the insertion point to appear in the first text box on the form, its TabIndex should be set to 0. The next text box should be set to 1; the next to 2; and so forth.

You may be puzzled by the properties of labels, which have a TabIndex property, but not a TabStop. A label cannot receive focus, but it has a location in the tab sequence. This fact allows you to create keyboard access keys for text boxes. When the user types an access key, such as Alt + N, the focus jumps to the first TabIndex following the label. See Figure 2.16.

F i g u r e   2 . 1 6

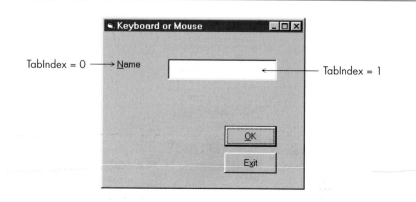

To use keyboard access keys for a text box, the TabIndex of the label must precede the TabIndex of the text box.

Setting the Form's Location on the Screen

When your project runs, the form will appear in the upper-left corner of the screen by default. The easiest way to choose a location for your form is to use the Form Layout window (Figure 2.17). Drag the image of the form to the screen location where you want the form to appear. Figure 2.18 shows the setting to make your form appear centered on the screen.

F i g u r e   2 . 1 7

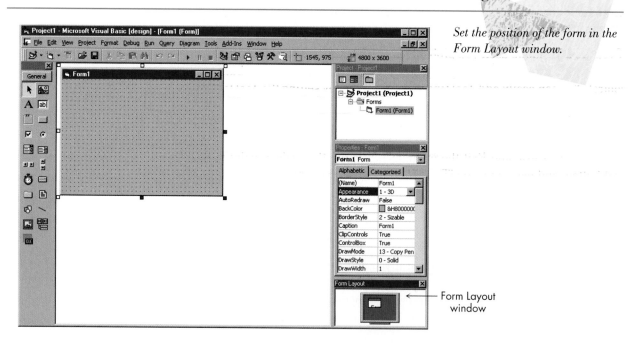

Set the position of the form in the Form Layout window.

Drag the form to the center of the screen.

Note: If the Form Layout window does not appear on your screen, choose *View/Form Layout Window.*

You can also set the form's screen position by setting the StartupPosition property of the form. Figure 2.19 shows your choices for the property setting. To center your form on the user's screen, set the StartupPosition property to *2 – Center Screen.*

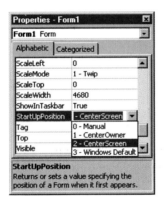

Set the StartupPosition property of the form to 2 – Center Screen to make the form appear in the center of the screen.

Creating ToolTips

If you are a Windows user, you probably appreciate and rely on ToolTips, those small labels that pop up when you pause your pointer over a toolbar button or control. You can easily add ToolTips to your projects by setting the ToolTipText property of any control that you want to display a ToolTip.

To define a ToolTip for a command button, add a new command button to a form. Change the button's Caption property to Exit and set its **ToolTipText property** to "Close and Exit the program". Now run the project, point to the Exit button, and pause; the ToolTip will appear (Figure 2.20).

Figure 2.20

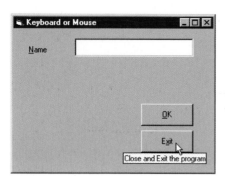

Coding for the Controls

You already know how to set initial properties for controls at design time. You may also want to set some properties in code, as your project executes. You can clear out the contents of text boxes and labels; reset the focus; and change font attributes, such as bold, underline, italic, and the color of text.

Clearing Text Boxes and Labels

You can clear out the contents of a text box or label by setting the property to an **empty string**. Use "" (no space between the two quotation marks). This empty string is also called a *null string*.

Examples

```
txtName.Text = ""          'Clear the contents
lblMessage.Caption = ""    'Clear the contents
```

Resetting the Focus

As your program runs, you want the insertion point to appear in the text box where the user is expected to type. The focus should begin in the first text box. But what about later? If you clear the form's text boxes, you should reset the focus to the first text box. The **SetFocus method** handles this situation. Remember, the convention is Object.Method, so the statement to set the insertion point in the text box called txtName is

```
txtName.SetFocus 'Make the insertion point appear here
```

Setting the Value Property of Option Buttons and Check Boxes

Of course, the purpose of option buttons and check boxes is to allow the user to make selections. However, often you need to select or deselect an option in code. You can select or deselect option buttons and check boxes at design time (to set initial status) or at run time (to respond to an event).

To make an option button appear selected initially, set its Value property to True in the Properties window. In code, assign True to its Value property:

```
optRed.Value = True 'Make button selected
```

For check boxes, the procedure is slightly different, since the Value property has three settings: 0 – unchecked, 1 – checked, and 2 – grayed. You can set the initial state by making a selection in the Properties window. At run time, use these code statements:

```
chkBold.Value = 1            'Make box checked
chkItalic.Value = 0          'Make box unchecked
```

You can also use the Basic constants Checked and Unchecked to set the Value property in code:

```
chkBold.Value = Checked      'Make box checked
chkItalic.Value = Unchecked  'Make box unchecked
```

Although a check box's Value property is set to 0, 1, or 2, sometimes you can treat its Value as True or False. For example, you can assign the Value of a check box to another property that must be True or False:

```
optDisplay.Value = chkScreen.Value 'Set option button Value _
                                    to check box Value
```

In the previous example, the Value of the option button is set to True if the check box is checked and to False if the check box is unchecked.

Feedback 2.2

1. Write the Basic statements to clear the text box called txtCompany and reset the insertion point into the box. *txtCompany.Text = " " txtCompany.SetFocus*
2. Write the Basic statements to clear the label called lblCustomer and place the insertion point into a text box called txtOrder. *lblCustomer.Caption = " " txtOrder.SetFocus*
3. What will be the effect of each of these Basic statements?
   (a) chkPrint.Value = 1 *Chk box is checked*
   (b) optColor.Value = False *option button not selected*
   (c) imgDrawing.Visible = False *image not visible*
   (d) lblLocation.BorderStyle = 1 *appearance set to 3-D, Border style is fixed*
       lblLocation.Appearance = 1
   (e) lblCity.Caption = txtCity.Text *assigns value to lblCity.Caption by value in txtCity.Text*

Changing the Font Properties of Controls

It is easy to define initial properties of a text box or a label. You just select *Font* in the Properties window and display the *Font* dialog box. There you can change the name of the font, the size, the style (bold, italic, underline), and the color. But what if you want to change Font properties while the program is running? For that, you need to set Font properties in code.

Visual Basic has a special object called a **Font object**. A Font object has several properties, including Name, Size, Bold, Italic, Underline, and StrikeThrough. You can set each of the properties for the Font object and access it through the Font property of a control.

Font = "Courier New"
so decimals align

Examples

```
txtName.Font.Bold = True      'Set the font to bold
lblMessage.Font.Size = 12     'Change to 12-point font
lblTitle.Font.Italic = True   'Set the font to italic
```

Changing the Color of Text

You can change the color of text by changing the **ForeColor property** of a control. Actually, most controls have a ForeColor and a BackColor property. The ForeColor property changes the color of the text; the BackColor property controls the color around the text.

The Color Constants

Visual Basic provides an easy way to specify some of the most-used colors. These eight names are called **color constants**.

```
vbBlack
vbRed
vbGreen
vbYellow
vbBlue
vbMagenta
vbCyan
vbWhite
```

Examples

```
txtName.ForeColor = vbRed
lblMessage.ForeColor = vbWhite
```

Changing Multiple Properties of a Control

By now you can see that there are times when you want to change several properties of a single control. In versions of Visual Basic previous to version 4, you had to write out the entire name (Object.Property) for each statement.

Examples

```
txtTitle.Visible = True
txtTitle.ForeColor = vbWhite
txtTitle.Font.Bold = True
txtTitle.Font.Italic = True
txtTitle.SetFocus
```

Of course, you can still specify the statements this way, but now Visual Basic provides a statement to make this task easier—the **With** and **End With statements**.

The With and End With Statements—General Form

```
With ObjectName
    Statement(s)
End With
```

You specify an object name in the With statement. All subsequent statements until the End With relate to that object.

The With and End With Statements—Examples

```
With txtTitle
    .Visible = True
    .ForeColor = vbWhite
    .Font.Bold = True
    .Font.Italic = True
    .SetFocus
End With
```

The statements beginning with With and ending with End With are called a *With block*. The statements inside the block are indented for readability. Although indentation is not required by VB, it is required by good programming practices.

The real advantage of using the With statement, rather than spelling out the object for each statement, is that With is more efficient. Your Visual Basic projects will run a little faster if you use With. On a large, complicated project, the savings can be significant.

Concatenating Text

At times you need to join strings of text. For example, you may want to join a literal and a property. You can "tack" one string of characters to the end of another in the process called **concatenation**. Use an ampersand (&), preceded and followed by a space, between the two strings.

Examples

```
lblMessage.Caption = "Your name is: " & txtName.Text
txtNameAndAddress.Text = txtName.Text & txtAddress.Text
lblFontSize.Caption = "The current fontsize is " & txtMessage.Font.Size & " points."
```

Continuing Long Program Lines

Basic interprets the code on one line as one statement. You can type *very* long lines in the Basic Code window; the window scrolls sideways and allows you to keep typing. However, this method is inconvenient. It isn't easy to see your program code, and printers can't handle the extra width. (Some printers wrap long lines to the next line; others just drop the extra characters.)

When a Basic statement becomes too long for one line, use a **line-continuation character**. You can type a space and an underscore, press Enter, and continue the statement on the next line. It is OK to indent the continued lines. The only restriction is that the line-continuation character must appear between elements; you cannot place a continuation in the middle of a literal or split the name of an object or property.

Example

```
lblGreetings.Caption = "Greetings " & txtName.Text & ": " & _
    "You have been selected to win a free prize. " & _
    "Just send us $100 for postage and handling."
```

Using the Default Property of a Control

Each class of control has one property that is the default property. When you use the default property of a control, you do not have to name the property. For example, the Text property is the default property for a text box. Therefore, these two statements are equivalent:

```
txtCompany.Text = "R 'n R - for Reading 'n Refreshment"
txtCompany = "R 'n R - for Reading 'n Refreshment"
```

This text uses the complete form for consistency, readability, and understandability. You may choose to refer to the default property of controls in your projects, however. Table 2.1 shows controls and their default properties.

Tip

Although Basic allows concatenation with the + operator, the practice is not advised. Depending on the contents of the text box, the compiler may interpret the + operator as an addition operator rather than a concatenation operator, giving unpredictable results.

T a b l e   2 . 1

Controls and their default properties.

Control	Default Property
Check box	Value
Combo box	Text
Command button	Value
Frame	Caption
Horizontal scroll bar	Value
Image	Picture
Label	Caption
Line	Visible
List box	Text
Menu	Enabled

(continued)

(continued)

Control	Default Property
Option button	Value
Picture box	Picture
Shape	Shape
Text box	Text
Timer	Enabled
Vertical scroll bar	Value

Your Hands-On Programming Example

For this example you will write a program that uses many of the new controls and topics introduced in this chapter. The program will input the user's name and a message, display the two items concatenated in a label, and change the format of the label. Using option buttons and check boxes for selection, the user can make the label bold, underlined, or italic and change its color.

You will include command buttons to display the message in the label, clear the text boxes and label, print the form, and exit. Include keyboard access keys for the command buttons; make the Display button the default button and make the Clear button the cancel button.

Place a logo on the form. Actually, you will place two images with different sizes for the logo on the form. Each time the user clicks on the logo, it will toggle the large and small versions of the logo.

Add a ToolTip to the logo that says "Click here".

Planning the Project

Sketch a form (Figure 2.21), which your users sign off as meeting their needs. *Note:* Although this may seem unnecessary, it is standard programming practice and documents that your users have been involved and approve the design.

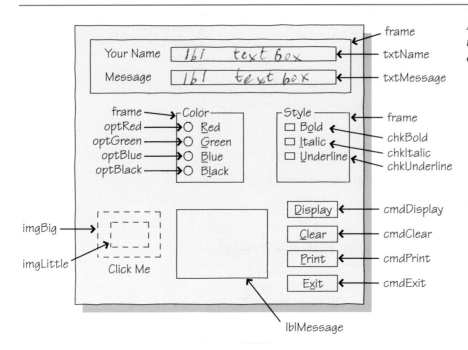

A planning sketch of the form for the hands-on programming example.

Plan the Objects and Properties

Plan the property settings for the form and for each control.

Object	Property	Setting	
Label1	Caption	Your Name:	*Hint:* Do not change the name of this label.
txtName	Name	txtName	
	Text	(blank)	
Label2	Caption	Message:	
txtMessage	Name	txtMessage	
	Text	(blank)	
fraColor	Name	fraColor	
	Caption	Color	
optRed	Name	optRed	*Hint:* Don't forget to draw the option buttons *inside* the frame.
	Caption	&Red	

(continued)

Object	Property	Setting
optGreen	Name	optGreen
	Caption	&Green
optBlue	Name	optBlue
	Caption	&Blue
optBlack	Name	optBlack
	Caption	B&lack
fraStyle	Name	fraStyle
	Caption	Style
chkBold	Name	chkBold
	Caption	B&old
chkItalic	Name	chkItalic
	Caption	&Italic
chkUnderline	Name	chkUnderline *Hint:* If you can't see option button or check box captions, make your objects wider.
	Caption	&Underline
imgBig	Name	imgBig
	Stretch	True
	Picture	Microsoft Visual Studio\Common\Graphics\Icons\Computer\Cdrom01.ico
	Visible	True
	ToolTipText	Click here
imgLittle	Name	imgLittle (Note that the two images are in the same location, one on top of the other.)
	Stretch	True
	Picture	Microsoft Visual Studio\Common\Graphics\Icons\Computer\Cdrom02.ico
	Visible	False
	ToolTipText	Click here
Label3 (or some other number)	Caption	Click Me

(continued)

Tip

To use the VB icon files, you must install them when you install VB. If you don't have the files, reinstall VB, select Custom Install, and choose to install the graphics files.

Object	Property	Setting
lblMessage	Name	lblMessage
	Caption	(blank)
	Alignment	2 - Center
	Appearance	1 - 3D
lblMessage	Name	lblMessage
	BorderStyle	1 - Fixed Single
cmdDisplay	Name	cmdDisplay
	Caption	&Display
	Default	True
cmdClear	Name	cmdClear
	Caption	&Clear
	Cancel	True
cmdPrint	Name	cmdPrint
	Caption	&Print
cmdExit	Name	cmdExit
	Caption	E&xit

Plan the Event Procedures

You will need event procedures for each command button, option button, check box, and image.

Procedure	Actions—Pseudocode
cmdDisplay_Click	Set lblMessage to both the name and message from the text boxes (concatenate them).
cmdClear_Click	Clear the two text boxes and label. Reset the focus in the first text box.
cmdPrint_Click	Print the form.
cmdExit_Click	End the project.
optRed_Click	Make the ForeColor of lblMessage red.
optGreen_Click	Make the ForeColor of lblMessage green.
optBlue_Click	Make the ForeColor of lblMessage blue.
optBlack_Click	Make the ForeColor of lblMessage black.
chkBold_Click	Set lblMessage's Font.Bold property to match the check box (selected or deselected).

(continued)

Procedure	Actions—Pseudocode
chkItalic_Click	Set lblMessage's Font.Italic property to match the check box (selected or deselected).
chkUnderline_Click	Set lblMessage's Font.Underline property to match the check box (selected or deselected).
imgBig_Click	Make imgBig invisible (Visible = False). Make imgLittle visible (Visible = True).
imgLittle_Click	Make imgLittle invisible. Make imgBig visible.

Write the Project

Follow the sketch in Figure 2.21 to create the form. Figure 2.22 shows the completed form.

● Set the properties of each object, as you have planned.

● Working from the pseudocode, write each event procedure.

● When you complete the code, thoroughly test the project.

F i g u r e   2 . 2 2

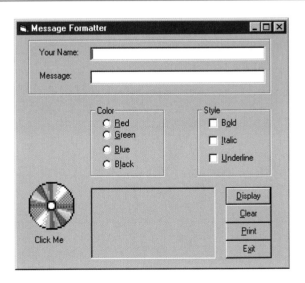

The form for the hands-on programming example.

The Project Coding Solution

```
'Project:         Chapter Example 2.1
'Date:            July 1999
'Programmer:      J.C. Bradley
'Description:     This project uses labels, text boxes, option buttons,
'                 check boxes, images, and command buttons to change
'                 the properties of text.
```

```
'Folder:          Ch0201
Option Explicit
```

```
Private Sub chkBold_Click()
    'Change the message text to/from bold

    lblMessage.Font.Bold = chkBold.Value
End Sub
```

```
Private Sub chkItalic_Click()
    'Change the message text to/from italic

    lblMessage.Font.Italic = chkItalic.Value
End Sub
```

```
Private Sub chkUnderline_Click()
    'Change the message text to/from underline

    lblMessage.Font.Underline = chkUnderline.Value
End Sub
```

```
Private Sub cmdClear_Click()
    'Clear the text controls

    With txtName
        .Text = ""                  'Clear the text box
        .SetFocus                   'Reset the insertion point
    End With
    lblMessage.Caption = ""
    txtMessage.Text = ""
End Sub
```

```
Private Sub cmdDisplay_Click()
    'Display the text in the message area

    lblMessage.Caption = txtName.Text & ": " & txtMessage.Text
End Sub
```

```
Private Sub cmdExit_Click()
    'Exit the project

    End
End Sub
```

```
Private Sub cmdPrint_Click()
    'Print the form

    PrintForm
End Sub
```

```
Private Sub imgBig_Click()
    'Switch the icon

    imgBig.Visible = False
    imgLittle.Visible = True
End Sub
```

```
Private Sub imgLittle_Click()
    'Switch the icon

    imgLittle.Visible = False
    imgBig.Visible = True
End Sub
```

```
Private Sub optBlack_Click()
    'Make label black

    lblMessage.ForeColor = vbBlack
End Sub
```

```
Private Sub optBlue_Click()
    'Make label blue

    lblMessage.ForeColor = vbBlue
End Sub
```

```
Private Sub optGreen_Click()
    'Make label green

    lblMessage.ForeColor = vbGreen
End Sub
```

```
Private Sub optRed_Click()
    'Make label red

    lblMessage.ForeColor = vbRed
End Sub
```

Programming Hints

1. To make the text in a text box right justified or centered, you must set the Multiline property to True, in addition to setting the Alignment property.
2. You can use the Value property of a check box to set other properties that must be True or False. For example:

```
txtMessage.Font.Bold = chkBold.Value 'Sets Bold property to True or _
                                      False to match check box
```

3. Always test the tab order on your forms. Fix it if necessary by changing the TabIndex properties.

4. You can create multiple controls of the same type without clicking on the tool in the toolbox every time. To create the first of a series, Ctrl–click on the tool; the tool will remain active and allow you to keep drawing more controls. Click on the pointer tool (the arrow) when you are finished.

5. Always remember to create an option button inside its frame. If you double-click to create an option button, it does not belong to the frame. You can make an option button belong to a frame by cutting and pasting it inside the frame.

6. Use text boxes when you want the user to enter or change the text. Use label controls when you do not want the user to change the data. You can set the BorderStyle and BackColor properties of a label so that it looks just like a text box, but cannot be changed.

Summary

1. Text boxes are used primarily for user input. The Text property holds the value input by the user. You can also assign a literal to the text property during run time.

2. Frames are used as containers for other controls and to group like items on a form.

3. Check boxes and option buttons allow the user to make choices. In a group of option buttons, only one can be selected; but in a group of check boxes, any number of the boxes may be selected.

4. Image controls hold a graphic, which is assigned to the Picture property.

5. The Appearance property of many controls can be set to 0 – Flat or 1 – 3D, which determines whether the control appears flat or three-dimensional.

6. You can select multiple controls and treat them as a group, including setting common properties at once, moving them, or aligning them.

7. Make your programs easier to use by following Windows standard guidelines for colors, control size and placement, access keys, default and cancel buttons, and tab order.

8. Define keyboard access keys by including an ampersand in the caption of command buttons, option buttons, and check boxes.

9. Set the Default property of one command button to True so that the user can press Enter to select the button. If you set the Cancel property to True, the button will be selected when the user presses the Esc key.

10. The focus moves from control to control as the user presses the Tab key. The sequence for tabbing is determined by the TabIndex properties of the controls.

11. Set the ToolTipText property of a control to make a ToolTip appear when the user pauses the mouse pointer over the control.

12. Clear the Text property of a text box or the Caption property of a label by setting it to an empty string.

13. To place the insertion point into a text box as the program is running, use the `SetFocus` method.

14. To change font attributes of a text box or a label, use the Font property of the control. The Font property refers to a Font object with properties for bold, italic, underline, size, etc.

15. Change the color of text in a control by changing the ForeColor property.

16. You can use the Visual Basic color constants to change colors during run time.

17. The `With` and `End With` statements provide an easy way to refer to an object multiple times without repeating the object's name.

18. Joining two strings of text is called *concatenation* and is accomplished by placing an ampersand between the two elements. (A space must precede and follow the ampersand.)

19. Use a space and an underscore to continue a long statement on another line.

20. Using the default property of a control allows you to refer to an object without naming the property.

Key Terms

access key   *62*
Alignment property   *53*
Appearance property   *56*
Cancel property   *63*
Check box   *53*
color constant   *68*
concatenation   *69*
Default property   *63*
empty string   *66*
focus   *63*
Font object   *68*
ForeColor property   *68*
Frame   *53*
image   *54*
line-continuation character   *70*
line control   *57*

Multiline property   *53*
option button   *54*
Picture property   *54*
`SetFocus` method   *66*
Shape control   *56*
Stretch property   *56*
TabIndex property   *63*
TabStop property   *63*
text box   *53*
Text property   *53*
ToolTipText property   *65*
twip   *61*
Value property   *53*
Visible property   *56*
`With` and `End With` statements   *69*

Review Questions

1. You can display program output in a text box or a label. When should you use a text box? When is a label appropriate?

2. How does the behavior of option buttons differ from the behavior of check boxes?

3. If you want two groups of option buttons on a form, how can you make the groups operate independently?

4. Explain how to make a graphic appear in an image control.

5. Describe how to select several labels and set them all to 12-point font size with one command.

6. What is the purpose of keyboard access keys? How can you define them in your project? How do they operate at run time?

7. Explain the purpose of the Default and Cancel properties of command buttons. Give an example of a good use for each.

8. What is a ToolTip? How can you make a ToolTip appear?

9. What is the focus? How can you control which object has the focus?

10. Assume you are testing your project and don't like the initial position of the insertion point. Explain how to make the insertion point appear in a different text box when the program begins.

11. During program execution you want to return the insertion point to a text box called txtAddress. What Basic statement will make that happen?

12. What Basic statements will clear the current contents of a text box and a label?

13. Explain how to change a label's Caption to italic at design time and at run time.

14. How are the `With` and `End With` statements used? Give an example.

15. What is concatenation and when would it be useful?

16. Explain how to continue a very long Basic statement onto another line.

17. What is the default property of a control? Give an example.

P r o g r a m m i n g   E x e r c i s e s

2.1 Create a project that will switch a light bulb on and off, using the user interface shown on page 81 as a guide.

Form: Include a text box for the user to enter his/her name. Create two images, one on top of the other. Only one will be visible at a time. Use option buttons to select the color of the text in the label beneath the light bulb image.

Include keyboard access keys for the option buttons and the command buttons. Make the Print button the default button and the Exit button the cancel button. Create ToolTips for both light bulb images; make the ToolTips say "Click here to turn the light on or off."

Project operation: The user will enter a name and click an option button for the color (not necessarily in that order). When the light bulb is clicked, display the other image and change the message below it. Concatenate the user name to the end of the message.

The two icon files are

Microsoft Visual Studio\Common\Graphics\Icons\Misc\Lightoff.ico
Microsoft Visual Studio\Common\Graphics\Icons\Misc\Lighton.ico

(You will need to find the location of the Graphics directory on your system to find the icons.)

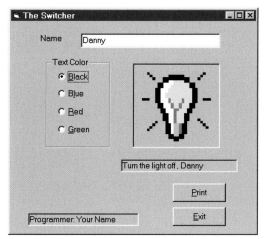 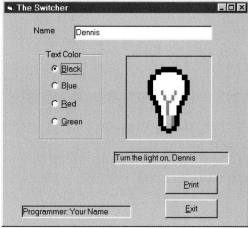

Coding: In the click event for each Color option button, change the color of the message below the light bulb. In the click event for the Print command button, print the form.

2.2   Write a project to display the flags of four different countries, depending on the setting of the option buttons. In addition, display the name of the country in the large label under the flag image. The user can also choose to display or hide the form's title, the country name, and the name of the programmer. Use check boxes for the display/hide choices.

Include keyboard access keys for all option buttons, check boxes, and command buttons. Make the Print button the default button and the Exit button the cancel button. Include ToolTips for the Print and Exit buttons.

You can choose the countries and flags. You will find more than 20 flag icons in Microsoft Visual Studio\Common\Graphics\Icons\Flags.

Hints: When a project begins running, the focus goes to the control with the lowest TabIndex. Because that control is likely an option button, one button will appear selected. You must either display the first flag to match the option button or make the focus begin in a different control. You might consider beginning the focus on one of the command buttons.

Set the Visible property of a control to the Value property of the corresponding check box. That way when the check box is selected, the control becomes visible.

Because all three selectable controls will be visible when the project begins, set the Value property of the three check boxes to *1 – Checked* at design time. Set the flag images to *Visible = False* so they won't appear at startup. (If you plan to display one image at startup, its Visible property must be set to True.)

Rather than stack the images as was done in the chapter example, you might consider another method of setting up the four flag images. Try placing four small invisible flag icons near the bottom of the form. When the user selects a different country's flag, set the Picture property of the large flag image to the Picture property of one of the small, invisible images.

Example:
```
imgFlag.Picture = imgMexico.Picture
```

Make sure to set the Stretch property of the large image control to True.

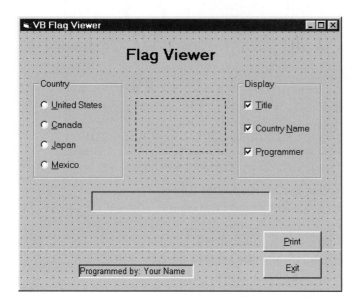

2.3   Write a project to display a weather report. The user can choose one of the
      option buttons and display an icon and a message. The message should
      give the weather report in words and include the person's name (taken
      from the text box at the top of the form). For example, if the user chooses
      the Sunny button, you might display "It looks like sunny weather today,
      John" (assuming that the user entered "John" in the text box).

      Include keyboard access keys for the option buttons and command
      buttons. Make the Exit button the cancel button. Include ToolTips for the
      Print and Exit buttons.

      You might consider the method of hiding and displaying images
      described in the hints for exercise 2. The four icons displayed are in the
      Microsoft Visual Studio\Common\Graphics\Icons\Elements folder and are
      called Cloud.ico, Rain.ico, Snow.ico, and Sun.ico.

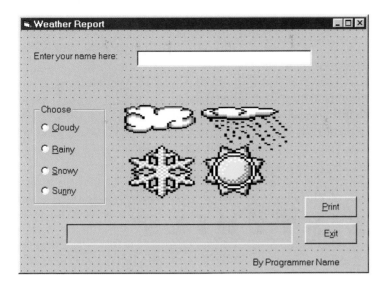

2.4 Write a project that will input the user name and display a message of the day in a label, along with the user's name. Include command buttons (with keyboard access keys) for Display, Clear, Print, and Exit. Make the Display button the default button and the Clear button the cancel button. Include ToolTips where appropriate.

   Include a group of option buttons for users to select the font size of the message. Give them a choice of three different sizes. *Hint:* Display the *Font* dialog box from the Properties window to determine the available sizes. Make sure your message label is large enough to display the longest message in the largest font size.

   Make your form display a changeable image. You can use the happy face icon files or any other images you have available (Microsoft Visual Studio\Common\Graphics\Icons\Misc\Face01.ico, Face02.ico, and Face03.ico).

   You may choose to have only one message of the day, or you can have several that the user can select from option buttons. You might want to choose messages that go with the different face icons.

   Optional extra: Include check boxes to change the font attributes of the message. Include Bold, Underline, Italic, and StrikeThru. Make sure to include keyboard access keys.

2.5 Create a project that allows the user to input information and then display the lines of output for a mailing label.

   Remember that fields to be input by the user require text boxes, whereas information to be displayed belongs in labels. Use text boxes for first name, last name, street address, city, state, and ZIP code; give meaningful names to the text boxes and set the initial Text properties to blank. Add appropriate labels to each text box to tell the user which data will be entered into each box and also provide ToolTips.

   Use command buttons for Display Label Info, Clear, Print Form, and Exit. Make the Display button the default button and the Clear button the cancel button.

   Use three labels for displaying the information for Line 1, Line 2, and Line 3.

A click event on the Display Label Info command button will display the following:

Line 1—The first name and last name concatenated together.
Line 2—The street address.
Line 3—The city, state, and ZIP code concatenated together. (Make sure to concatenate a comma and a space between the city and state, using ", ", and two spaces between the state and ZIP code.)

CASE STUDIES

VB Mail Order

Design and code a project that has shipping information.

Use an appropriate image in the upper-left corner of the form.

Use labeled text boxes for Catalog Code, Page Number, and Part Number.

Use two groups of option buttons on the form; enclose each group in a frame. The first frame should have a Caption of Shipping and contain buttons for Express and Ground. Use a Caption of Payment Type on the second frame and include buttons for Charge, COD, and Money Order.

Use a check box for New Customer.

Add command buttons for Print Form, Clear, and Exit. Make the Clear button the cancel button.

Add ToolTips as appropriate. *(Run Time)*

Form Load Event

cmd Quit, ToolTipText="End"

VB Auto Center

Modify the project from the Chapter 1 VB Auto Center case study, replacing the command buttons with images. Above each image place a label that indicates which department or command the image represents. A click on an image will produce the appropriate information in the special notices label.

Add an image that allows the form to be printed as well as an image that will clear the special notices label.

Include a ToolTip for each image to help the user understand the purpose of the image.

Add two option buttons that will allow the user to view the special notices label in a 10-point font or a 14-point font. Make sure that the label is large enough to hold the 14-point message.

Include a check box labeled Hours. When the check box is selected, a new label will display the message "Open 24 Hours--7 days a week".

Department/Command	Image
Auto Sales	Microsoft Visual Studio\Common\Graphics\Icons\Industry\Cars
Service Center	Microsoft Visual Studio\Common\Graphics\Icons\Industry\Wrench
Detail Shop	Microsoft Visual Studio\Common\Graphics\Icons\Elements\Water
Employment Opportunities	Microsoft Visual Studio\Common\Graphics\Icons\Mail\Mail12
Exit	Microsoft Visual Studio\Common\Graphics\Icons\Computer\Msgbox1
Print Form	Microsoft Visual Studio\Common\Graphics\Icons\Dragdrop\Drag1pg

Video Bonanza

Design and code a project that displays the location of videos using option button. Use an option button for each of the movie categories and a label to display the aisle number. A check box will allow the user to display or hide a message for members. When the check box is selected, a message stating "All Members Receive a 10% Discount" will appear.

Include command buttons (with keyboard access keys) for Clear, Print, and Edit. The Clear button should be set as the default button and the Exit as the cancel button.

Place a label on the form in a 24-point font that reads *Video Bonanza*. Use a line to separate the label from the rest of the interface. Include an image on the form.

Option Button	Location
Comedy	Aisle 1
Drama	Aisle 2
Action	Aisle 3
Sci-Fi	Aisle 4
Horror	Aisle 5

Create a project that will display an advertising screen for Very Very Boards. Include the company name, a slogan (use "The very best in boards" or make up your own slogan), and a graphic image for a logo. You may use the graphic included with the text materials (Skateboard.wmf) or one of your own.

Allow the user to select the color for the slogan text using option buttons. Additionally, the user may choose to display or hide the company name, the slogan, the logo, and the company name. Use check boxes for the display options so that the user may select each option independently.

Include keyboard access keys for the option button and the command buttons. Make the Print button the default button and the Exit button the cancel button. Create ToolTips for the company name ("Our company name"), the slogan ("Our slogan"), and the logo ("Our logo").

When the project begins execution, the slogan text should be red and the Red option button selected. When the user selects a new color, change the color of the slogan text to match.

Each of the check boxes must appear selected initially, since the company name, slogan, logo, and programmer name display when the form appears. Each time the user selects or deselects a check box, make the corresponding item display or hide.

Set the form's StartUpPosition property to 2—CenterScreen.

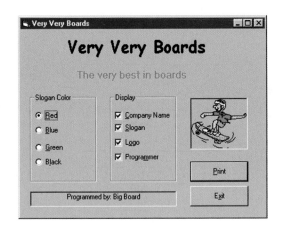

3

Variables, Constants, and Calculations

At the completion of this chapter, you will be able to . . .

1. Distinguish between variables, constants, and controls.

2. Explain and use the various data types.

3. Apply naming conventions that indicate scope and data type.

4. Declare variables using the `Dim` statement.

5. Select the appropriate scope for a variable.

6. Convert text input to numeric values using the `Val` function.

7. Perform calculations using variables and constants.

8. Format values for output using the formatting functions.

9. Accumulate sums and generate counts.

10. Format data for output.

11. Modify the environment to require `Option Explicit`.

In this chapter you will learn to do calculations in Visual Basic. You will start with text values input by the user, convert them to numeric values, and perform calculations on them. You will also learn to format the results of your calculations and display them for the user.

Although the calculations themselves are quite simple (adding, subtracting, multiplying, and dividing), there are some important issues to discuss first. You must learn about variables and constants, the various types of data used by Visual Basic, and how and where to declare variables and constants. Variables are declared differently, depending on where you want to use them and how long you need to retain their values.

The code below is a small preview that shows calculating the product of two text boxes. The first group of statements (the Dims) declares the variables and their data types. The second group of statements converts the text box contents to numeric and places the values into the variables. The last line performs the multiplication and places the result into a variable. The following sections of this chapter describe how to set up your code for calculations.

```
'Dimension the variables
Dim intQuantity          As Integer
Dim curPrice             As Currency
Dim curExtendedPrice     As Currency

'Convert input text to numeric and assign values to variables
intQuantity = Val(txtQuantity.Text)
curPrice = Val(txtPrice.Text)

'Calculate the product
curExtendedPrice = intQuantity * curPrice
```

Data—Variables and Constants

So far, all data you have used in your projects have been properties of objects. You have worked with the Text property of Text Boxes and the Caption property of Labels. Now it is time to consider working with values that are not properties. Basic allows you to set up locations in memory and give each location a name. You can visualize each memory location as a scratch pad; the contents of the scratch pad can change as the need arises. In this example, the memory location is called *intMaximum*.

```
intMaximum = 100
```

intMaximum
100

After executing this statement, the value of intMaximum is 100. You can change the value of intMaximum, use it in calculations, or display it in a control.

In the preceding example, the memory location called intMaximum is a **variable**. Memory locations that hold data that can be changed during project execution are called *variables;* locations that hold data that cannot change during execution are called ***constants***. For example, a customer's name will vary as the information for each individual is being processed. However, the name of the company and the sales tax rate will remain the same (at least for that day).

When you declare a variable or a named constant, Visual Basic reserves an area of memory and assigns it a name, called an *identifier*. You specify identifier names according to the rules of Basic as well as some recommended naming conventions.

The **declaration** statements establish your project's variables and constants, give them names, and specify the type of data they will hold. The statements are not considered executable; that is, they are not executed in the flow of instructions during program execution.

Here are some sample declaration statements:

```
Dim strName          As String              'Declare a string variable
Dim intCounter       As Integer             'Declare an integer variable
Const curDiscountRate As Currency = .15     'Declare a named constant
```

The next few paragraphs describe the data types, the rules for naming variables and constants, and the format of the declarations.

Data Types

The **data type** of a variable or constant indicates what type of information will be stored in the allocated memory space: perhaps a name, a dollar amount, a date, or a total. Note that the default data type is **variant**. If you do not specify a data type, your variables and constants will be variants. The advantage of using variant data type is that it's easy, and the variables and constants change their appearance as needed for each situation. The disadvantage is that variants are less efficient than the other data types; that is, variants require more memory and operate less quickly than other data types. The best practice is to always specify the data type.

Data Type	Use For
Boolean	True or False values.
Byte	A single ANSI character (code 0 to 255).
Currency	Decimal fractions, such as dollars and cents.
Date	An eight-character date.
Double	Double-precision floating-point numbers with 14 digits of accuracy.
Integer	Whole numbers in the range $-32,768$ to $32,767$.
Long	Larger whole numbers.
Single	Single-precision floating point numbers with six digits of accuracy.
String	Alphanumeric data: letters, digits, and other characters.
Variant	Converts from one type to another, as needed.

The most common types of variables and constants we will use are string, integer, and currency. When deciding which data type to use, follow this guideline: If the data will be used in a calculation, then it must be numeric (usually integer or currency); if it is not used in a calculation, it will be string. Use currency as the data type for any decimal fractions in business applications; single and double data types are generally used in scientific applications.

Consider the following examples:

Contents	Data Type	Reason
Social Security number	String	Not used in a calculation.
Pay rate	Currency	Used in a calculation, contains a decimal point.
Hours worked	Currency	Used in a calculation, may contain a decimal point. (Currency can be used for any decimal fraction, not just dollars.)
Phone number	String	Not used in a calculation.
Quantity	Integer	Used in calculations, contains a whole number.

Naming Rules

Each programmer has to name (identify) the variables and named constants that will be used in a project. Basic requires identifiers for variables and named constants to follow these rules: names must be 1 to 255 characters in length; they may consist of letters, digits, and underscores; they cannot contain any spaces or periods; and they may not be reserved words. (Reserved words, also called *keywords*, are words to which Basic has assigned some meaning, such as *print*, *name*, and *value*.)

Naming Conventions

When naming variables and constants, you *must* follow the rules of Basic. In addition, you *should* follow some naming conventions. Conventions are the guidelines that separate good names from bad (or not so good) names. The meaning and use of all identifiers should always be clear.

Just as we established conventions for naming objects in Chapter 1, in this chapter we adopt conventions for naming variables and constants. The following conventions are widely used in the programming industry:

1. Identifiers must be meaningful. Choose a name that clearly indicates its purpose. Do not abbreviate unless the meaning is obvious and do not use very short identifiers, such as *X* or *Y*.
2. Precede each identifier with a lowercase prefix that specifies the data type. This convention is similar to the convention we already adopted for naming objects and is widely used in the programming field.
3. Capitalize each word of the name (following the prefix). Always use mixed case, never all uppercase.

This text follows the coding conventions published by Microsoft in the MSDN Library Help that accompanies VB and is available online. To find the complete list of coding conventions, look up the following pages in the MSDN Library Help:

Visual Basic Documentation
 Using Visual Basic
  Programmer's Guide
   Visual Basic Coding Conventions
    Constant and Variable Naming Conventions
     Object Naming Conventions

Here is a list of the most common data types and their prefixes:

bln	Boolean
cur	Currency
dbl	Double-precision floating point
dtm	Date/time
int	Integer
lng	Long integer
sng	Single-precision floating point
str	string
vnt	Variant

Sample identifiers

Field of Data	Possible Identifier
Social Security number	strSocialSecurityNumber
Pay rate	curPayRate
Hours worked	curHoursWorked
Phone number	strPhoneNumber
Quantity	intQuantity
Tax rate	curTaxRate
Quota	intQuota
Population	lngPopulation

Feedback 3.1

Indicate whether each of the following identifiers conforms to the rules of Basic and to the naming conventions. If invalid, give the reason. Remember, the answers to all Feedback questions are found in Appendix A.

1. omitted *no data type, suffix*
2. int#Sold *no special characters*
3. i Number Sold *no blanks*
4. int.Number.Sold *no periods in I.D.*
5. sng$Amount *no special characters*
6. Sub *reserved word*
7. strSub *Valid meaningful?*
8. Caption *reserved word*
9. conMaximum *follows rules, but not conventions*
10. MinimumRate *needs prefix*
11. curMaximumCheck *Valid*
12. strCompanyName *Valid*

Constants—Named and Intrinsic

Constants provide a way to use words to describe a value that doesn't change. In Chapter 2 you used the Visual Basic constants vbBlue, vbRed, vbYellow, and so on. Those constants are built into Visual Basic—you don't need to define them anywhere. The constants that you define for yourself are called *named constants;* those that are built into VB are called *intrinsic constants.*

Named Constants

You declare named constants using the keyword Const. You give the constant a name, a data type, and a value. Once a value is declared as a constant, its value cannot be changed during the execution of the project. The data type that you declare and the data type of the value must match. For example, if you declare an integer constant, you must give it an integer value.

You will find two important advantages to using named constants rather than the actual values in code. The code is easier to read; for example, seeing the identifier curMaximumPay is more meaningful than seeing a number, such as 1,000. In addition, if you need to change the value at a later time, you need to change the constant declaration only once and not change every reference to it throughout the code.

Const Statement—General Form

```
Const Identifier [As Datatype] = Value
```

Naming conventions for constants require a prefix that identifies the data type as well as the "As" clause that actually declares the data type.

Although the data type is optional, the best practice is to always declare the data type. When you don't declare the data type, Visual Basic looks at the value given and chooses an appropriate data type.

This example sets the company name, address, and the sales tax rate as constants:

Const Statement—Examples

```
Const strCompanyName As String = "R 'n R--for Reading 'n Refreshment"
Const strCompanyAddress As String = "101 S. Main Street"
Const curSalesTaxRate As Currency = .08
```

Assigning Values to Constants

The values you assign to constants must follow certain rules. You have already seen that a text (string) value must be enclosed in quotation marks; numeric values are not so enclosed. However, you must be aware of some additional rules.

Numeric constants may contain only the digits (0–9), a decimal point, and a sign (+ or −) at the left side. You cannot include a comma, dollar sign, any other special characters, or a sign at the right side.

String literals (also called *string constants*) may contain letters, digits, and special characters, such as $#@%&*. The only problem comes when you want to include quotation marks inside a string literal, since quotation marks enclose the literal. The solution is to use two quotation marks together inside the literal; Visual Basic will interpret the pair as one symbol.

Example

`"He said, ""I like it."""` produces this string: `He said, "I like it."`

Although you can use numeric digits inside a string literal, remember that these numbers are text and cannot be used for calculations.

The string values are referred to as **string literal**s because they contain exactly (literally) whatever is inside the quotation marks.

Example constants

Data Type	Constant Value Example
Integer	5
	125
	2170
	2000
Single or currency	101.25
	-5.0
String literals	"Visual Basic"
	"ABC Incorporated"
	"1415 J Street"
	"102"
	"She said ""Hello."""

Intrinsic Constants

Intrinsic constants are system-defined constants. Several sets of intrinsic constants are stored in library files and available for use in your Visual Basic programs. For example, the color constants you used in Chapter 2 are intrinsic constants.

Intrinsic constants use a two-character prefix to indicate the source, such as *vb* for Visual Basic, *db* for Data Access Objects, and *xl* for Excel. In the next chapter we will use intrinsic constants for creating message boxes.

Declaring Variables

Although there are several ways to declare a variable, the most commonly used statement is the `Dim` statement.

Dim Statement—General Form

```
Dim Identifier [As Datatype]
```

If you omit the optional data type, the variable's type defaults to variant. It is best to always declare the type, even when you intend to use variants.

Dim Statement—Examples

```
Dim strCustomerName      As String
Dim intTotalSold         As Integer
Dim sngTemperature       As Single
Dim curPrice             As Currency
Dim vntChanging                         'Defaults to Variant type
```

The reserved word `Dim` is really short for *dimension*, which means "size." When you declare a variable, the amount of memory reserved depends on its data type. Table 3.1 shows the amount of memory allocated for each data type.

Note: Visual Basic does not require you to declare a variable before using it—see "Programming Hints" at the end of this chapter for details.

Table 3.1

The amount of memory allocated for each data type.

Data Type	Number of Bytes of Memory Allocated
Boolean	2
Byte	1
Currency	8
Date	8
Double	8
Integer	2
Long	4
Single	4
String (variable length)	10 bytes plus 1 byte for each character in the string.
Variant	Holding numbers—16 bytes. Holding characters—22 bytes plus 1 byte for each character in the string.

Entering Dim Statements

Visual Basic's Auto Fill In feature helps you enter `Dim` statements. After you type the space that follows `Dim VariableName As`, a shortcut menu pops up (Figure 3.1). This list shows the possible entries for data type to complete the statement. The easiest way to complete the statement is to begin typing the correct entry; the list automatically scrolls to the correct section (Figure 3.2). When the correct entry is highlighted, press Enter, Tab, or the space bar to select the entry, or double-click if you prefer using the mouse.

Figure 3.1

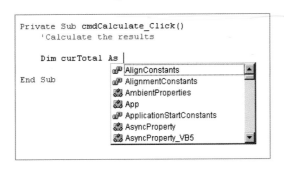

As soon as you type the space after As, the Auto Fill In menu pops up. You can make a selection from the list with your mouse or the keyboard.

Figure 3.2

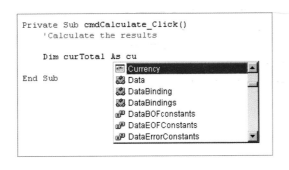

Type the first few characters of the data type and the Auto Fill In list will quickly scroll to the correct section. When the correct word is highlighted, press Enter, Tab, or the space bar to select the entry.

Note: Some people find the Auto Fill In feature annoying rather than help-ful. You can turn off the feature by selecting the *Tools/Options/Editor* tab and deselecting *Auto List Members*.

Feedback 3.2

Write a declaration for the following situations; make up an appropriate variable identifier.

1. You need variables for payroll processing to store the following:
    (a) Single-precision number of hours. *sngHoursWorked*
    (b) String employee's name. *strEmployeeName*
    (c) Department number (not used in calculations). *strDepartmentNumber*

2. You need variables for inventory control to store the following:
   (a) Integer quantity. *intQuantity*
   (b) Description of the item. *strDescription*
   (c) Part number. *strPartNumber*
   (d) Cost. *curCost*
   (e) Selling price. *curSellingPrice*

Scope of Variables

A variable may exist and be visible for an entire project, for only one form, or for only one procedure. The visibility of a variable is referred to as its **scope**. *Visibility* really means "this variable can be used or 'seen' in this location." The scope is said to be global, module level, or local. A **global** variable may be used in all procedures of a project and is discussed in Chapter 6. **Module-level** variables are accessible from all procedures of a form. A **local** variable may be used only within the procedure in which it is declared.

You declare the scope of a variable by choosing where to place the Dim statement.

Variable Lifetime

When you create a variable, you must be aware of its **lifetime**. The *lifetime* of a variable is the period of time that the variable exists. The lifetime of a local variable is normally one execution of a procedure. For example, each time you execute a sub procedure, the local Dim statements are executed. Each variable is created as a "fresh" new one, with an initial value of 0 for numeric variables and an empty string for string variables. When the procedure finishes, its variables disappear; that is, their memory locations are released.

The lifetime of a module-level variable is the entire time the form is loaded, generally the lifetime of the entire project. If you want to maintain the value of a variable for multiple executions of a procedure, for example, to calculate a running total, you must use a module-level variable (or a variable declared as Static, which is discussed in Chapter 6).

Local Declarations

Any variable that you declare inside a procedure is local in scope; it is known only to that procedure. A Dim statement may appear anywhere inside the procedure as long as it appears prior to the first use of the variable in a statement. However, good programming practices dictate that all Dims appear at the top of the procedure, prior to all other code statements (after the remarks).

```
Private Sub cmdCalculate_Click()
    'Calculate the price and discount

    Dim intQuantity          As Integer
    Dim curPrice             As Currency
    Dim curExtendedPrice     As Currency
    Dim curDiscount          As Currency
    Dim curDiscountedPrice   As Currency
    Const curDiscountRate    As Currency = 0.15
```

```
'Convert input values to numeric variables
intQuantity = Val(txtQuantity.Text)
curPrice = Val(txtPrice.Text)

'Calculate values
curExtendedPrice = intQuantity * curPrice
curDiscount = curExtendedPrice * curDiscountRate
curDiscountedPrice = curExtendedPrice - curDiscount
```

Notice the Const statement in the preceding example. You can declare named constants to be local, module level, or global in scope, just as you can variables.

Module-Level Declarations

At times you need to be able to use a variable or constant in more than one procedure of a form. When you declare a variable or constant as module level, it may be used anywhere in that form. Place the declarations (Dim or Const) for module-level variables and constants in the General Declarations section of the form. (Recall that you have been using the General Declarations section for remarks since Chapter 1.) If you wish to accumulate a sum or count items for multiple executions of a procedure, you should declare the variable at the module level.

Figure 3.3 illustrates the locations for coding local variables and module-level variables.

Figure 3.3

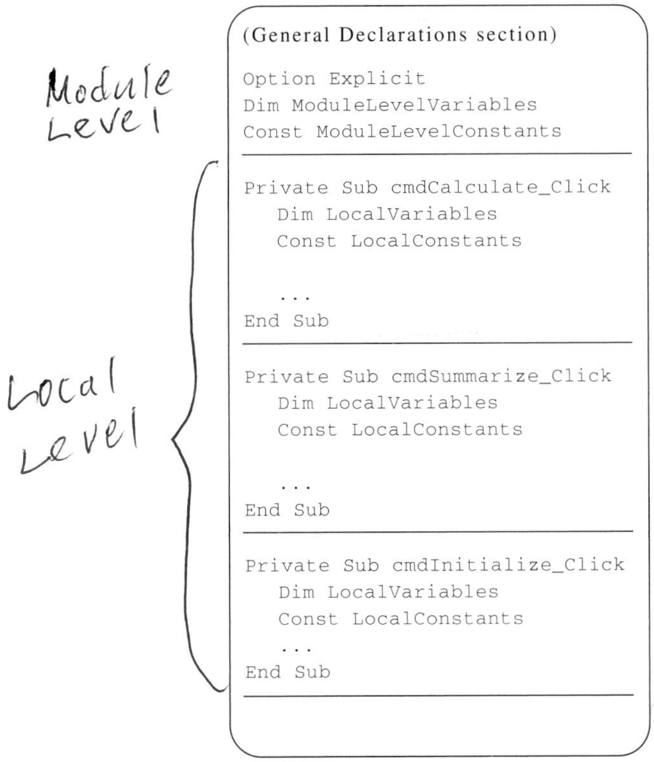

The variables you dimension inside a procedure are local. Variables that you dimension in the General Declarations section of a form are module level.

Module
Level

Local
Level

```
(General Declarations section)

Option Explicit
Dim ModuleLevelVariables
Const ModuleLevelConstants


Private Sub cmdCalculate_Click
    Dim LocalVariables
    Const LocalConstants

    . . .
End Sub


Private Sub cmdSummarize_Click
    Dim LocalVariables
    Const LocalConstants

    . . .
End Sub


Private Sub cmdInitialize_Click
    Dim LocalVariables
    Const LocalConstants
    . . .
End Sub
```

```
'General Declarations section of a form

Option Explicit

'Dimension module-level variables
Dim mintQuantitySum          As Integer
Dim mcurDiscountSum          As Currency
Dim mintSaleCount            As Integer
```

Including the Scope in Identifiers

When you use variables and constants, it is important to know their scope. For that reason you should include scope information in your naming conventions. To indicate a module-level variable or constant, place a prefix of m before the identifier. Local variables and constants do not have an additional prefix, so any variable without an initial m can be assumed to be local.

Examples

```
Dim mcurTotalPay As Currency
```

Note that the m stands for module level, and the cur stands for currency data type.

```
Const mintNumberQuestions As Integer = 50
```

The m stands for module level, and the int stands for integer data type.

Coding Module-Level Declarations

To enter module-level declarations, you must be in the Code window, in the General Declarations section (Figure 3.4). Recall how to display the General Declarations section:

1. Select *Code* from the *View* menu or click on the *View Code* button in the *Project Explorer* window.
2. In the Object list, select *(General)*.
3. In the Procedure list, select *(Declarations)*.
4. Place the Dim (or Const) statements in this section of code, after the Option Explicit statement.

F i g u r e   3 . 4

Code module-level declarations in the General Declarations section of a form module.

Feedback 3.3

Write the declarations (Dim or Const statements) for each of the following situations and indicate where each statement will appear.

1. The total of the payroll that will be needed in a Calculate event procedure and in a Summary event procedure. *DIM mCurTotal As Currency*
2. The sales tax rate that cannot be changed during execution of the program but will be used by multiple procedures. *Const mCurSalesTaxRate As Currency = .07*
3. The number of participants that are being counted in the Calculate event procedure, but not displayed until the Summary event procedure. *DIM mintParticipant Count As Integer*

all module levels

Calculations

In programming you can perform calculations with variables, with constants, and with the properties of certain objects.

The properties you will use, such as the Text property of a text box and the Caption property of a label, are actually strings of text characters. These character strings, such as "Howdy" or "12345", should not be used directly in calculations. Visual Basic tries to make assumptions about the property values you use in calculations. Those assumptions are correct most of the time, but are incorrect often enough that we must take steps to convert all property values to numeric before using them in calculations.

Use the Val function to convert the property of a control to its numeric form before you use the value in a calculation:

```
'Convert input values to numeric variables
intQuantity = Val(txtQuantity.Text)
curPrice = Val(txtPrice.Text)

'Calculate the extended price
curExtendedPrice = intQuantity * curPrice
```

Val Function

Visual Basic supplies many functions that you can use in your programs. A **function** performs an action and returns a value. The expression to operate upon, called the ***argument*** (or multiple arguments, in some cases), must be enclosed in parentheses.

The first Basic function we will use is Val. (Think of *val* as an abbreviation for *value*.) The Val function converts text data into a numeric value.

The Val Function—General Form

```
Val(ExpressionToConvert)
```

The expression you wish to convert can be the property of a control, a variable, or a constant.

A function cannot stand by itself. It returns (produces) a value that can be used as a part of a statement, such as the assignment statements in the following examples.

The Val Function—Examples

```
intQuantity = Val(txtQuantity.Text)
curPrice = Val(txtPrice.Text)
lngCustomerNumber = Val(mstrCustomerNumber)
```

When the Val function converts an argument to numeric, it begins at the argument's left most character. If that character is a numeric digit, decimal point, or sign, Val converts the character to numeric and moves to the next character. As soon as a nonnumeric character is found, the operation stops. Here are some examples of the values returned by the Val function:

Contents of Argument	Numeric Value Returned by the Val function
(blank)	0
123.45	123.45
$100	0
1,000	1
A123	0
123A	123
4B5	4
−123	−123
+123	123
12.34.8	12.34

Arithmetic Operations

The arithmetic operations you can perform in Visual Basic include addition, subtraction, multiplication, division, and exponentiation.

Operator	Operation
+	Addition
−	Subtraction
*	Multiplication
/	Division
^	Exponentiation

Order of Operations

The order in which operations are performed determines the result. Consider the expression 3 + 4 * 2. What is the result? If the addition is done first, the result is 14. However, if the multiplication is done first, the result is 11.

The hierarchy of operations, or **order of precedence,** in arithmetic expressions from highest to lowest is

1. Exponentiation
2. Multiplication and division
3. Addition and subtraction

In the previous example, the multiplication is done before addition, and the result is 11. To change the order of evaluation, use parentheses:

(3 + 4) * 2

will yield 14 as the result. One set of parentheses may be used inside another set. In that case, the parentheses are said to be *nested.*

Example

```
((intScore1 + intScore2 + intScore3)/3) * 1.2
```

Extra parentheses can always be used for clarity. The expressions

```
2 * curCost * curRate  and  (2 * curCost) * curRate
```

are equivalent, but the second is easier to understand.

Multiple operations at the same level (such as multiplication and division) are performed from left to right. The example 8 / 4 * 2 yields 4 as its result, not 1. The first operation is 8 / 4, and 2 * 2 is the second.

Evaluation of an expression occurs in this order:

1. All operations within parentheses. Multiple operations within the parentheses are performed according to the rules of precedence.
2. All exponentiation. Multiple exponentiation operations are performed from left to right.
3. All multiplication and division. Multiple operations are performed from left to right.
4. All addition and subtraction are performed from left to right.

Although the precedence of operations in Basic is the same as in algebra, take note of one important difference: There are no implied operations in Basic. The following expressions would be valid in mathematics, but they are not valid in Basic:

Mathematical Notation	Equivalent Basic Function
2A	2 * A
3(X + Y)	3 * (X + Y)
(X + Y)(X − Y)	(X + Y) * (X − Y)

Tip

Use extra parentheses to make the precedence clearer. The operation will be easier to understand and the parentheses have no negative effect on execution.

Feedback 3.4

What will be the result of the following calculations using the order of precedence?

Assume that: X = 2, Y = 4, Z = 3

1. X + Y ^ 2   *18*
2. 8 / Y / X   *1*
3. X * (X + 1)   *6*
4. X * X + 1   *5*
5. Y ^ X + Z * 2   *22*
6. Y ^ (X + Z) * 2   *2048*
7. (Y ^ X) + Z * 2   *22*
8. ((Y ^ X) + Z) * 2   *38*

Using Calculations in Code

Calculations are performed in assignment statements. Recall that whatever appears on the right side of an = (assignment operator) is assigned to the item on the left. The left side may be the property of a control or a variable. It cannot be a constant.

Examples

```
curAverage = curSum / intCount
lblAmountDue.Caption = curPrice - (curPrice * curDiscountRate)
txtCommission.Text = curSalesTotal * curCommissionRate
```

In the preceding examples, the results of the calculations were assigned to a variable, the Caption property of a label, and the Text property of a text box. In most cases you will assign calculation results to variables or to the Caption properties of labels. Text boxes are usually used for input from the user, not for program output.

Formatting Data

When you want to **format** data for display, either on the printer or on the screen, use the formatting functions. To *format* means to control the way the output will look. For example, 12 is just a number, but $12.00 conveys more meaning for dollar amounts.

VB 6 introduces four new formatting functions—FormatCurrency, FormatNumber, FormatPercent, and FormatDateTime. Refer to Appendix B for the Format function that was used in Visual Basic versions prior to 6.0.

When you use the formatting functions, you can choose to display a dollar sign, a percent sign, and commas. You can also specify the number of digits to appear to the right of the decimal point. Visual Basic rounds the value to return the correct number of decimal positions.

The FormatCurrency Function—Simple Form

```
FormatCurrency(NumericExpressionToFormat)
```

The `FormatCurrency` function returns a string of characters formatted as dollars and cents. By default, the currency value displays a dollar sign, commas, and two positions to the right of the decimal point. (Note: You can change the default format by changing your computer's regional settings.)

Usually, you will assign the formatted value to the property of a control for display.

The FormatCurrency Function—Simple Example

```
lblBalance.Caption = FormatCurrency(curBalance)
```

Examples

Variable	Value	Function	Output
curBalance	1275.675	FormatCurrency(curBalance)	$1,275.68
sngAmount	.9	FormatCurrency(sngAmount)	$0.90

Note that the formatted value returned by the `FormatCurrency` function is no longer purely numeric and cannot be used in further calculations. For example, consider the following lines of code:

```
curAmount = curAmount + curCharges
lblAmount.Caption = FormatCurrency(curAmount)
```

Assume that curAmount holds 1050 and lblAmount.Caption displays $1,050.00. If you want to do any further calculations with this amount, such as adding it to a total, you must use curAmount not lblAmount.Caption. The variable curAmount holds a numeric value; lblAmount.Caption holds a string of (nonnumeric) characters.

You can further customize the formatted value returned by the `FormatCurrency` function. You can specify the number of decimal positions to display, whether or not to display a leading zero for fractional values, whether to display negative numbers in parentheses, and whether to use the commas for grouping digits.

The FormatCurrency Function—General Form

```
FormatCurrency(ExpressionToFormat [, NumberOfDecimalPositions [, LeadingDigit _
    [, UseParenthesisForNegative [, GroupingForDigits]]]])
```

As you can see, the only required argument is the expression you want to format. You can choose to display a currency value in whole dollars by specifying zero for the number of decimal positions:

```
lblWholeDollars.Caption = FormatCurrency(curDollarAmount, 0)
```

For an explanation of the other options of the `FormatCurrency` function, see online Help.

The FormatNumber Function—Simple Form

```
FormatNumber(ExpressionToFormat)
```

The `FormatNumber` function is similar to the `FormatCurrency` function. The default format is determined by your computer's regional setting; it will generally display commas and two digits to the right of the decimal point.

The FormatNumber Function—Simple Examples

```
lblSum.Caption = FormatNumber(curSum)
lblCount.Caption = FormatNumber(intCount)
```

Both of these examples will display with commas and two digits to the right of the decimal point. You can specify the exact number of decimal digits, just as with the `FormatCurrency` function. This example will format the number with commas and no digits to the right of the decimal point.

```
lblWholeNumber.Caption = FormatNumber(intCount, 0)
```

The FormatNumber Function—General Form

```
FormatNumber(ExpressionToFormat [, NumberOfDecimalPositions [, LeadingDigit _
    [, UseParenthesisForNegative [, GroupingForDigits]]]])
```

See online Help for the explanation of the optional arguments of the `FormatNumber` function.

Examples

Variable	Value	Function	Output
mcurTotal	1125.67	FormatNumber(mcurTotal, 0)	1,126
curBalance	1234.567	FormatNumber(curBalance, 2)	1,234.57

The FormatPercent Function—Simple Form

```
FormatPercent(ExpressionToFormat)
```

To display numeric values as a percent, use the `FormatPercent` function. This function multiplies the argument by 100, adds a percent sign, and rounds to two decimal places. (As with the `FormatCurrency` and `FormatNumber` functions, the default number of decimal positions is determined by the computer's regional settings and can be changed.)

The FormatPercent Function—Simple Examples

```
lblPercentComplete.Caption = FormatPercent(sngComplete)
lblInterestRate.Caption = FormatPercent(curRate)
```

In the complete form of the `FormatPercent` function, you can select the number of digits to the right of the decimal point as well as customize other options, similar to the other formatting functions.

The FormatPercent Function—General Form

```
FormatPercent(ExpressionToFormat [, NumberOfDecimalPositions [, LeadingDigit _
    [, UseParenthesisForNegative [, GroupingForDigits]]]])
```

Variable	Value	Function	Output
curCorrect	.75	FormatPercent(curCorrect)	75%
curCorrect	.75	FormatPercent(curCorrect, 1)	75.0%
curRate	.734	FormatPercent(curRate)	73%
curRate	.734	FormatPercent(curRate, 1)	73.4%
curRate	.734	FormatPercent(curRate, 2)	73.40%

The FormatDateTime Function—General Form

```
FormatDateTime(ExpressionToFormat [, NamedFormat])
```

You can format an expression as a date and/or time. The expression may be a string that holds a date or time value, a date type variable, or a function that returns a date. The named formats use your computer's regional settings. If you omit the optional named format, the function returns the date using vbGeneralDate.

The FormatDateTime Function—Examples

```
lblStartDate.Caption = FormatDateTime(dtmStartDate, vbShortDate)
lblStartTime.Caption = FormatDateTime("1/1/00", vbLongDate)
lblDateAndTime.Caption = FormatDateTime(dtmSomeDate)
```

The actual values returned by the `FormatDateTime` function depend on the regional settings on your computer. These are the return formats based on the USA defaults.

Named Format	Returns	Example
vbGeneralDate	A date and/or time. If the expression holds a date, returns a short date. If it holds a time, returns a long time. If it holds both, returns both a short date and long time.	2/28/99 6:01:24 PM
vbLongDate	Day of week, Month Day, Year	Sunday, February 28, 1999
vbShortDate	MM/DD/YY	2/28/99
vbLongTime	HH:MM:SS AM/PM	6:01:24 PM
vbShortTime	HH:MM (24 hour clock)	18:01

Feedback 3.5

Give the line of code that assigns the formatted output and tell how the output will display for the specified value.

1. A calculated variable called mcurAveragePay has a value of 123.456 and should display in a label called lblAveragePay. *lblAveragePay.Caption = FormatCurrency (mcurAveragePay)* $123.46
2. The variable sngCorrect, which contains .76, must be displayed as a percentage in the label called lblPercentCorrect. *lblPercentCorrect.Caption = FormatPercent (sngCorrect)* 76.00%
3. The total amount collected in a fund drive is being accumulated in a variable called mcurTotalCollected. What statement will display the variable in a label called lblTotal with commas and two decimal positions but no dollar signs? *lblTotal.Caption = FormatNumber (mcurTotalCollected)*

A Calculation Programming Example

R 'n R—For Reading 'n Refreshment—needs to calculate prices and discounts for books sold. The company is currently having a big sale, offering a 15 percent discount on all books. In this project you will calculate the amount due for a quantity of books, determine the 15 percent discount, and deduct the discount, giving the new amount due—the discounted amount.

Planning the Project

Sketch a form (Figure 3.5) that meets the needs of your users.

Figure 3.5

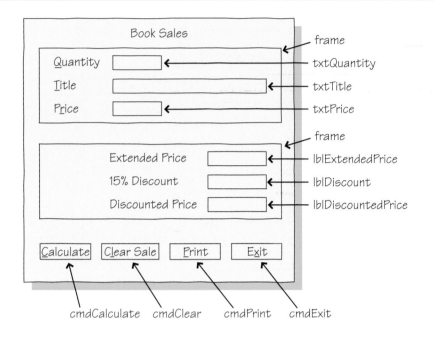

A planning sketch of the form for the calculation programming example.

Plan the Objects and Properties

Plan the property settings for the form and each of the controls.

Object	Property	Setting
Form	Name	frmBookSales
	Caption	R 'n R for Reading 'n Refreshment
Label1	Name	Label1
	Caption	Book Sales
	Font	Bold, 12 point
fraInput	Name	fraInput
	Caption	(blank)
Label2	Name	Label2
	Caption	&Quantity
txtQuantity	Name	txtQuantity
	Text	(blank)
Label3	Name	Label3
	Caption	&Title
txtTitle	Name	txtTitle
	Text	(blank)

(continued)

Object	Property	Setting
Label4	Name	Label4
	Caption	P&rice
txtPrice	Name	txtPrice
	Text	(blank)
fraOutput	Name	fraOutput
	Caption	(blank)
Label5	Name	Label5
	Caption	Extended Price
lblExtendedPrice	Name	lblExtendedPrice
	Caption	(blank)
	Alignment	Right Justify
	BorderStyle	Fixed Single
Label6	Name	Label6
	Caption	15% Discount
lblDiscount	Name	lblDiscount
	Caption	(blank)
	Alignment	Right Justify
	BorderStyle	Fixed Single
Label7	Name	Label7
	Caption	Discounted Price
lblDiscountedPrice	Name	lblDiscountedPrice
	Caption	(blank)
	Alignment	Right Justify
	BorderStyle	Fixed Single
cmdCalculate	Name	cmdCalculate
	Caption	&Calculate
cmdClear	Name	cmdClear
	Caption	C&lear Sale
cmdPrint	Name	cmdPrint
	Caption	&Print
cmdExit	Name	cmdExit
	Caption	E&xit

Plan the Event Procedures

Since you have four command buttons, you need to plan the actions for four event procedures.

Event Procedure	Actions—Pseudocode
cmdCalculate_Click	Dimension the variables and constants. Convert the input Quantity and Price to numeric. Calculate Extended Price = Quantity * Price. Calculate Discount = Extended Price * Discount Rate. Calculate Discounted Price = Extended Price − Discount. Format and display output in labels.
cmdClear_Click	Set each text box and label to blanks. SetFocus in the first text box.
cmdPrint_Click	Print the form.
cmdExit_Click	Exit the project.

Write the Project

Follow the sketch in Figure 3.5 to create the form. Figure 3.6 shows the completed form.

- Set the properties of each object, as you have planned.

- Write the code. Working from the pseudocode, write each event procedure.

- When you complete the code, use a variety of test data to thoroughly test the project.

Figure 3.6

The form for the calculation programming example.

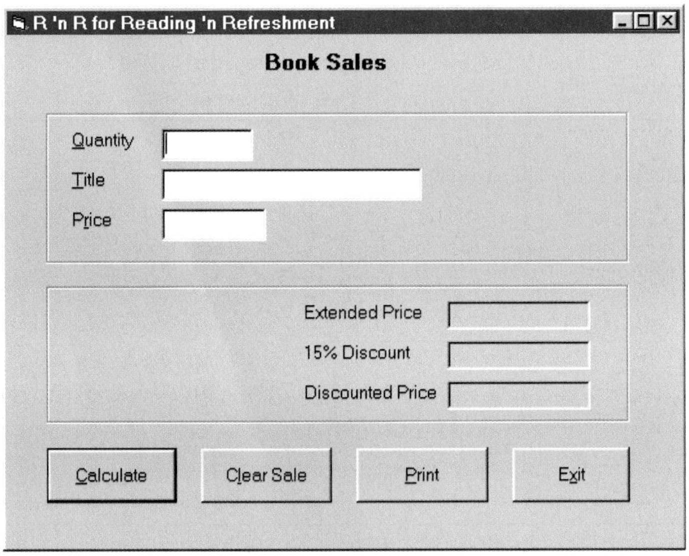

The Project Coding Solution

```vb
'Project:       Chapter Example 3.1
'Date:          February 1999
'Programmer:    J.C. Bradley
'Description:   This project demonstrates the use of variables,
'               constants, and calculations.
'Folder:        Ch0301

Option Explicit
Const mcurDiscountRate        As Currency = 0.15
```

```vb
Private Sub cmdCalculate_Click()
    'Calculate the price and discount

    Dim intQuantity           As Integer
    Dim curPrice              As Currency
    Dim curExtendedPrice      As Currency
    Dim curDiscount           As Currency
    Dim curDiscountedPrice    As Currency

    'Convert input values to numeric variables
    intQuantity = Val(txtQuantity.Text)
    curPrice = Val(txtPrice.Text)

    'Calculate values
    curExtendedPrice = intQuantity * curPrice
    curDiscount = curExtendedPrice * mcurDiscountRate
    curDiscountedPrice = curExtendedPrice - curDiscount

    'Format and display answers
    lblExtendedPrice.Caption = FormatCurrency(curExtendedPrice)
    lblDiscount.Caption = FormatNumber(curDiscount, 2)
    lblDiscountedPrice.Caption = FormatCurrency(curDiscountedPrice)
End Sub
```

```vb
Private Sub cmdClear_Click()
    'Clear previous amounts from the form

    txtQuantity.Text = ""
    txtTitle.Text = ""
    txtPrice.Text = ""
    lblExtendedPrice.Caption = ""
    lblDiscount.Caption = ""
    lblDiscountedPrice.Caption = ""
    txtQuantity.SetFocus
End Sub
```

```vb
Private Sub cmdExit_Click()
    'Exit the project

    End
End Sub
```

```
Private Sub cmdPrint_Click()
    'Print the form

    PrintForm
End Sub
```

Counting and Accumulating Sums

Programs often need to sum numbers. For example, in the previous programming exercise each sale is displayed individually. If you want to accumulate a total of the sales amounts, of the discounts, or of the number of books sold, you need some new variables and new techniques.

As you know, the variables you declare inside a procedure are local to that procedure. They are re-created each time the procedure is called; that is, their lifetime is one time through the procedure. Each time the procedure is entered, you have a new fresh variable with an initial value of 0. If you want a variable to retain its value for multiple calls, in order to accumulate totals, you must declare the variable as module level. (Another approach, using Static variables, is discussed in Chapter 6.)

Summing Numbers

The technique for summing the sales amounts for multiple sales is to dimension a module-level variable for the total. Then in the cmdCalculate_Click event for each sale, add the current amount to the total:

```
mcurDiscountedPriceSum = mcurDiscountedPriceSum + curDiscountedPrice
```

Reading this assignment statement from right to left, it says to add the curDiscountedPrice and the current contents of mcurDiscountedPriceSum and place the result into mcurDiscountedPriceSum. The effect of the statement is to add the current value for curDiscountedPrice into the sum held in mcurDiscountedPriceSum.

Counting

If you want to count something, such as the number of sales in the previous example, you need another module-level variable. Dimension a counter variable as integer:

```
Dim mintSaleCount as Integer
```

Then in the cmdCalculate_Click event procedure, add one to the counter variable:

```
mintSaleCount = mintSaleCount + 1
```

This statement, reading from right to left, adds one and the current contents of mintSaleCount, placing the result in mintSaleCount. The statement will execute one time for each time the cmdCalculate_Click event procedure executes. Therefore, mintSaleCount will always hold a running count of the number of sales.

Calculating an Average

To calculate an average, divide the sum of the items by the count of the items. In the R 'n R book example, we can calculate the average sale by dividing the sum of the discounted prices by the count of the sales.

```
mcurAverageDiscountedSale = mcurDiscountedPriceSum / mintSaleCount
```

Note: Error checking for division by zero is covered in Chapter 4.

Your Hands-On Programming Example

In this project, R 'n R—For Reading 'n Refreshment needs to expand its book sale project done previously in this chapter. In addition to calculating individual sales and discounts, management wants to know the total number of books sold, the total number of discounts given, the total discounted amount, and the average discount per sale.

Planning the Project

Sketch a form (Figure 3.7) that your users sign off as meeting their needs.

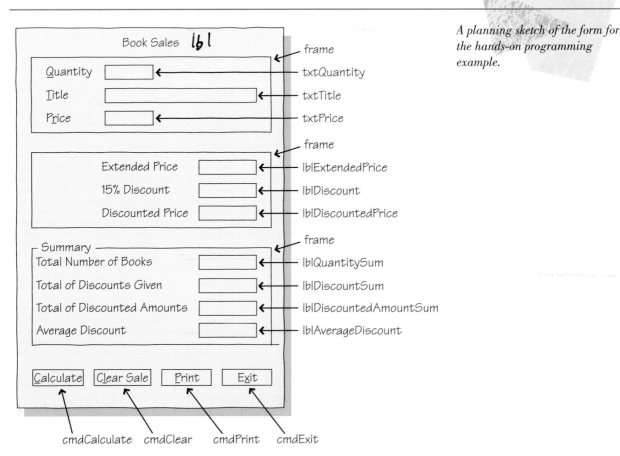

A planning sketch of the form for the hands-on programming example.

Plan the Objects and Properties

Plan the property settings for the form and each control. These objects and properties are the same as the previous example, with the addition of the summary information beginning with fraSummary.

Object	Property	Setting
Form	Name	frmBookSales
	Caption	R 'n R for Reading 'n Refreshment
Label1	Name	Label1
	Caption	Book Sales
	Font	Bold, 12 point
fraInput	Name	fraInput
	Caption	(blank)
Label2	Name	Label2
	Caption	&Quantity
txtQuantity	Name	txtQuantity
	Text	(blank)
Label3	Name	Label3
	Caption	&Title
txtTitle	Name	txtTitle
	Text	(blank)
Label4	Name	Label4
	Caption	P&rice
txtPrice	Name	txtPrice
	Text	(blank)
fraOutput	Name	fraOutput
	Caption	(blank)
Label5	Name	Label5
	Caption	Extended Price
lblExtendedPrice	Name	lblExtendedPrice
	Caption	(blank)
	Alignment	Right Justify
	BorderStyle	Fixed Single
Label6	Name	Label6
	Caption	15% Discount

(continued)

Object	Property	Setting
lblDiscount	Name	lblDiscount
	Caption	(blank)
	Alignment	Right Justify
	BorderStyle	Fixed Single
Label7	Name	Label7
	Caption	Discounted Price
lblDiscountedPrice	Name	lblDiscountedPrice
	Caption	(blank)
	Alignment	Right Justify
	BorderStyle	Fixed Single
cmdCalculate	Name	cmdCalculate
	Caption	&Calculate
cmdClear	Name	cmdClear
	Caption	C&lear Sale
cmdPrint	Name	cmdPrint
	Caption	&Print
cmdExit	Name	cmdExit
	Caption	E&xit
fraSummary	Name	fraSummary
	Caption	Summary
Label8	Name	Label8
	Caption	Total Number of Books
lblQuantitySum	Name	lblQuantitySum
	Caption	(blank)
	Alignment	Right Justify
	BorderStyle	Fixed Single
Label9	Name	Label9
	Caption	Total Discounts Given
lblDiscountSum	Name	lblDiscountSum
	Caption	(blank)
	Alignment	Right Justify
	BorderStyle	Fixed Single

(continued)

Object	Property	Setting
Label10	Name	Label10
	Caption	Total of Discounted Amounts
lblDiscountedAmountSum	Name	lblDiscountedAmountSum
	Caption	(blank)
	Alignment	Right Justify
	BorderStyle	Fixed Single
Label11	Name	Label11
	Caption	Average Discount
lblAverageDiscount	Name	lblAverageDiscount
	Caption	(blank)
	Alignment	Right Justify
	BorderStyle	Fixed Single

Plan the Event Procedures

The planning that you did for the previous example will save you time now. The only procedure that requires more steps is the cmdCalculate_Click event.

Event Procedure	Actions—Pseudocode
cmdCalculate_Click	Dimension the variables and constants.
	Convert the inputs Quantity and Price to numeric.
	Calculate Extended Price = Quantity * Price.
	Calculate Discount = Extended Price * Discount Rate.
	Calculate Discounted Price = Extended Price − Discount.
	Calculate the summary values:
	Add Quantity to Quantity Sum.
	Add Discount to Discount Sum.
	Add Discounted Price to Discounted Price Sum.
	Add 1 to Sale Count.
	Calculate Average Discount = Discount Sum / Sale Count.
	Format and display sale output in labels.
	Format and display summary values in labels.
cmdClear_Click	Set each text box and label to blanks.
	SetFocus in the first text box.
cmdPrint_Click	Print the form.
cmdExit_Click	Exit the project.

Write the Project

Following the sketch in Figure 3.7 create the form. Figure 3.8 shows the completed form.

● Set the properties of each of the objects, as you have planned.

● Write the code. Working from the pseudocode, write each event procedure.

● When you complete the code, use a variety of test data to thoroughly test the project.

Figure   3.8

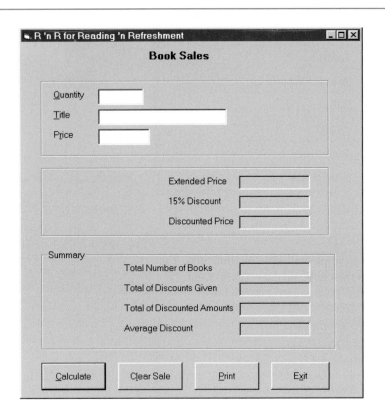

The form for the hands-on programming example.

The Project Coding Solution

```
'Project:        Chapter Example 3.2
'Date:           February 1999
'Programmer:     J.C. Bradley
'Description:     This project demonstrates the use of variables,
'                 constants, and calculations.
'Folder:          Ch0302

Option Explicit

'Dimension module-level variables
Dim mintQuantitySum            As Integer
Dim mcurDiscountSum            As Currency
Dim mcurDiscountedPriceSum     As Currency
Dim mintSaleCount              As Integer
Dim mcurAverageDiscount        As Currency
Const mcurDiscountRate         As Currency = 0.15
```

```vb
Private Sub cmdCalculate_Click()
    'Calculate the price and discount

    Dim intQuantity        As Integer
    Dim curPrice           As Currency
    Dim curExtendedPrice   As Currency
    Dim curDiscount        As Currency
    Dim curDiscountedPrice As Currency

    'Convert input values to numeric variables
    intQuantity = Val(txtQuantity.Text)
    curPrice = Val(txtPrice.Text)

    'Calculate values for sale
    curExtendedPrice = intQuantity * curPrice
    curDiscount = curExtendedPrice * mcurDiscountRate
    curDiscountedPrice = curExtendedPrice - curDiscount

    'Calculate summary values
    mintQuantitySum = mintQuantitySum + intQuantity
    mcurDiscountSum = mcurDiscountSum + curDiscount
    mcurDiscountedPriceSum = mcurDiscountedPriceSum + curDiscountedPrice
    mintSaleCount = mintSaleCount + 1
    mcurAverageDiscount = mcurDiscountSum / mintSaleCount

    'Format and display answers for sale
    lblExtendedPrice.Caption = FormatCurrency(curExtendedPrice)
    lblDiscount.Caption = FormatNumber(curDiscount)
    lblDiscountedPrice.Caption = FormatCurrency(curDiscountedPrice)

    'Format and display summary values
    lblQuantitySum.Caption = mintQuantitySum
    lblDiscountSum.Caption = FormatCurrency(mcurDiscountSum)
    lblDiscountedAmountSum.Caption = FormatCurrency(mcurDiscountedPriceSum)
    lblAverageDiscount = FormatCurrency(mcurAverageDiscount)
End Sub
```

```vb
Private Sub cmdClear_Click()
    'Clear previous amounts from the form

    txtQuantity.Text = ""
    txtTitle.Text = ""
    txtPrice.Text = ""
    lblExtendedPrice.Caption = ""
    lblDiscount.Caption = ""
    lblDiscountedPrice.Caption = ""
    txtQuantity.SetFocus
End Sub
```

```
Private Sub cmdExit_Click()
    'Exit the project

    End
End Sub
```

```
Private Sub cmdPrint_Click()
    'Print the form

    PrintForm
End Sub
```

Programming Hints

Use the `Option Explicit` statement to help avoid common coding errors.

Visual Basic does not require you to declare a variable before using it. When the variable is first used in the code, it will automatically become type Variant. However, good programming practice requires the declaration of all variables. The specification of a data type will save memory space. It is also to the programmer's advantage to declare all variables.

As an example of what might occur if the `Option Explicit` is not used, look at the following code:

```
Sub cmdCalcPay_Click()
    'Calculate Pay

    curHours = Val(txtHours.Text)
    curPayRate = Val(txtPayRate.Text)
    curPay = Hours * PayRate
    mcurTotalPay = mcurTotlPay + curPay
End Sub
```

Look carefully at this code, which does not generate any Visual Basic errors. What will be the values in curPay and mcurTotalPay? This type of error is difficult to spot visually and, unfortunately, very easy to make. *Hint:* The code has three errors.

Are you ready for the answers? curPay and mcurTotalPay will both be zero. Notice the different spellings of the variable names curHours/Hours, curPayRate/PayRate, and mcurTotalPay/mcurTotlPay.

You can avoid this type of error completely by setting the option that requires all variables to be declared prior to use. This technique will help in debugging projects because the compiler will detect misspelled variable names when the project is run.

The steps to setting `Option Explicit` are

1. From the *Tools* menu select *Options*.
2. On the *Editor* tab, make sure that *Require Variable Declaration* is selected.
3. Click the OK button.

When you turn on the *Require Variable Declaration* option, Visual Basic automatically adds the `Option Explicit` statements to all new forms you create after that point. VB does not add an `Option Explicit` statement to a form that has already been created. You can add an `Option Explicit` statement yourself to any existing form.

Summary

1. Variables and constants are temporary memory locations that have a name (called an *identifier*), a data type, and a scope. The value stored in a variable can be changed during the execution of the project; the values stored in constants cannot change.

2. The data type determines what type of values may be stored in a variable or constant. The most common data types are string, integer, currency, single precision, and Boolean. Any variable not explicitly given a data type defaults to variant.

3. Identifiers for variables and constants must follow the Visual Basic naming rules and should follow good naming standards, called *conventions*. An identifier should be meaningful and have a lowercase prefix that indicates the data type and the scope. Variable and constant names should be mixed upper- and lowercase.

4. Intrinsic constants, such as vbRed and vbBlue, are predefined and built into Visual Basic. Named constants are programmer-defined constants and are declared using the `Const` statement. The location of the `Const` statement determines the scope of the constant.

5. Variables are declared using the `Dim` statement; the location of the statement determines the scope of the variable.

6. The scope of a variable may be global, module level, or local. Local variables are available only within the procedure in which they are declared; module-level variables are accessible in all procedures within a form; global variables are available in all procedures of all modules in a project with multiple modules.

7. A Visual Basic function performs an action and returns a value. The expressions named in parentheses are called *arguments*.

8. Use the `Val` function to convert text values to numeric before performing any calculations.

9. Calculations may be performed using the values of numeric variables, constants, and the properties of controls. The result of a calculation may be assigned to a numeric variable or to the property of a control.

10. A calculation operation with more than one operator follows the order of precedence in determining the result of the calculation. Parentheses alter the order of operations.

11. The formatting functions `FormatCurrency`, `FormatNumber`, `FormatPercent`, and `FormatDateTime` can be used to specify the appearance of values for display.

12. You can calculate a sum by adding each transaction to a module-level variable. In a similar fashion, you can calculate a count by adding to a module-level variable.

13. A frequent cause of errors in Basic programming is the misspelling of variable names. You can avoid this error by including the `Option Explicit` statement in the General Declarations section of each module. VB will automatically add the `Option Explicit` statement to all new modules if you set the option to *Require Variable Declaration*.

Key Terms

argument *99*	lifetime *96*
constant *88*	local *96*
data type *89*	module level *96*
declaration *89*	order of precedence *101*
format *102*	scope *96*
function *99*	string literal *93*
global *96*	variable *88*
identifier *89*	variant *89*
intrinsic constant *93*	

Review Questions

1. Name and give the purpose of five types of data available in Visual Basic.
2. What does *declaring a variable* mean?
3. What effect does the location of a `Dim` statement have on the variable it declares?
4. Explain the difference between a constant and a variable.
5. What is the purpose of the `Val` function?
6. Explain the order of precedence of operators for calculations.
7. What statement(s) can be used to declare a variable?
8. Explain how to make an interest rate stored in sngRate display as a percentage with three decimal digits.
9. Should formatting functions be included for all captions and text display in a program? Justify your answer.

Programming Exercises

3.1   Create a project that calculates the total of fat, carbohydrate, and protein calories. Allow the user to enter (in text boxes) the grams of fat, the grams of carbohydrate, and the grams of protein. Each gram of fat is nine calories, whereas a gram of protein or carbohydrate is four calories.

Display the total calories for the current food item in a label. Use two other labels to display an accumulated sum of the calories and a count of the items entered.

Form: The form should have three text boxes for the user to enter the grams for each category. Include labels next to each text box indicating what the user is to enter.

Include command buttons to Calculate, to Clear the text boxes, to Print, and to Exit.

Make the form's caption "Calorie Counter".

Code: Write the code for each command button.

3.2 Lennie McPherson, proprietor of Lennie's Bail Bonds, needs to calculate the amount due for setting the bail. Lennie requires something of value as collateral, and his fee is 10 percent of the bail amount. He wants the screen to provide boxes to enter the bail amount and the item being used for collateral. The program must calculate the fee. He needs to print the screen form so that he can attach it to the legal documents.

Form: Include text boxes for entering in the amount of bail and the description of the collateral. Label each text box.

Include command buttons for Calculate, Clear, Print Form, and Exit.

The caption for the form should be "Lennie's Bail Bonds".

Code: Include event procedures for the click event of each command button. Calculate the amount due as 10 percent of the bail amount and display it in a label, formatted as Currency.

3.3 In retail sales, management needs to know the average inventory figure and the turnover of merchandise. Create a project that allows the user to enter the beginning inventory, the ending inventory, and the cost of goods sold.

Form: Include labeled text boxes for the beginning inventory, the ending inventory, and the cost of goods sold. After calculating the answers, display the average inventory and the turnover formatted in labels.

Include command buttons for Calculate, Clear, Print Form, and Exit. The formulas for the calculations are

$$\text{Average inventory} = \frac{Beginning\ inventory + Ending\ inventory}{2}$$

$$\text{Turnover} = \frac{Cost\ of\ goods\ sold}{Average\ inventory}$$

Note: The average inventory is expressed in dollars; the turnover is the number of times the inventory turns over.

Code: Include procedures for the click event of each command button. Display the results in labels. Format the average inventory as currency and the turnover as a number with one digit to the right of the decimal.

Test Data

Beginning	Ending	Cost of Goods Sold
58500	47000	400000
75300	13600	515400
3000	19600	48000

Check Figures

Average Inventory	Turnover
$52,750.00	7.6
44,450.00	11.6
11,300.00	4.2

3.4 A local recording studio rents its facilities for $200 per hour. Management charges only for the number of minutes used. Create a project in which the input is the name of the group and the number of minutes it used the studio. Your program calculates the appropriate charges, accumulates the total charges for all groups, and computes the average charge and the number of groups that used the studio.

Form: Use labeled text boxes for the name of the group and the number of minutes used. The charges for the current group should be displayed formatted in a label. Create a frame for the summary information. Inside the frame, display the total charges for all groups, the number of groups, and the average charge per group. Format all output appropriately. Include buttons for Calculate, Clear, and Exit.

Code: Use a constant for the rental rate per minute.

Test Data

Group	Minutes
Pooches	95
Hounds	5
Mutts	480

Check Figures

Total Charges for Group	Total Number of Groups	Average Charge	Total Charges for All Groups
$316.66	1	$316.66	$316.66
$16.67	2	$166.67	$333.33
$1,599.98	3	$644.44	$1,933.31

3.5 Create a project that determines the future value of an investment at a given interest rate for a given number of years. The formula for the calculation is

Future value = Investment amount * (1 + Interest rate) ^ Years

Form: Use labeled text boxes for the amount of investment, the interest rate (as a decimal fraction), and the number of years the investment will be held. Display the future value in a label formatted as currency.

Include command buttons for Calculate, Clear, Print Form, and Exit. Format all dollar amounts.

Test Data

Amount	Rate	Years
2000.00	.15	5
1234.56	.075	3

Check Figures

Future Value
$4,022.71
$1,533.69

3.6 Write a project that calculates the shipping charge for a package if the shipping rate is $0.12 per ounce.

Form: Use labeled text boxes for the package-identification code (a six-digit code) and the weight of the package—one box for pounds and another one for ounces. Use a label to display the shipping charge.

Include command buttons for Calculate, Clear, Print Form, and Exit.
Code: Include event procedures for each command button. Use a constant for the shipping rate, calculate the shipping charge, and display it formatted in a label.

Calculation hint: There are 16 ounces in a pound.

Test Data

ID	Weight
L5496P	0 lb. 5 oz.
J1955K	2 lb. 0 oz.
Z0000Z	1 lb. 1 oz.

Check Figures

Shipping Charge
$0.60
$3.84
$2.04

3.7 Create a project for the local car rental agency that calculates rental charges. The agency charges $15 per day plus $0.12 per mile.
Form: Use text boxes for the customer name, address, city, state, ZIP code, beginning odometer reading, ending odometer reading, and the number of days the car was used. Use labels to display the miles driven and the total charge. Format the output appropriately.

Include command buttons for Calculate, Clear, Print Form, and Exit.
Code: Include an event procedure for each command button. For the calculation, subtract the beginning odometer reading from the ending odometer reading to get the number of miles traveled. Use a constant for the $15 per day charge and the $0.12 mileage rate.

3.8 Create a project that will input an employee's sales and calculate the gross pay, deductions, and net pay. Each employee will receive a base pay of $900 plus a sales commission of 6 percent of sales.

After calculating the net pay, calculate the budget amount for each category based on the percentages given.

Pay

Base pay	$900; use a named constant
Commission	6% of sales
Gross pay	Sum of base pay and commission
Deductions	18% of gross pay
Net pay	Gross pay minus deductions

Budget

Housing	30% of net pay
Food and clothing	15% of net pay
Entertainment	50% of net pay
Miscellaneous	5% of net pay

Form: Use text boxes to input the employee's name and the dollar amount of the sales. Use labels to display the results of the calculations.

Provide command buttons for Calculate, Clear, Print Form, and Exit.

[handwritten notes:]
object .Enabled = True
else   = False (Gray Box)

$1000 × .02 = $20
80/160 = .5
.5 × 20 = $10

Figure Math 1st

C A S E   S T U D I E S

VB Mail Order

The company has instituted a bonus program to give its employees an incentive to sell more. For every dollar the store makes in a four-week period, the employees receive 2 percent of sales. The amount of bonus each employee receives is based upon the percentage of hours he or she worked during the bonus period (a total of 160 hours).

The screen will allow the user to enter the employee's name, the total hours worked, and the amount of the store's total sales. The amount of sales needs to be entered only for the first employee. (*Hint:* Don't clear it.)

The Calculate command button will determine the bonus earned by this employee, and the Clear button will clear only the name and hours-worked fields. A Print Form button will be available only after the calculation has been made—it will be disabled until the Calculate button is pressed the first time. When the Clear button is pressed, the Print Form button will become disabled (Enabled = False).

VB Auto Center

Salespeople for used cars are compensated using a commission system. The commission is based on the costs incurred for the vehicle.

Commission =
Commission rate × (Sales price − Cost value)

The screen will allow the user to enter the salesperson's name, the selling price of the vehicle, and the cost value of the vehicle. Use a constant of 20 percent for the commission rate.

The Calculate command button will determine the commission earned by the salesperson; the Clear button will clear the text boxes. A Print Form button will be available only after the calculation has been made—it will be disabled until the Calculate button is pressed the first time. When the Clear button is pressed, the Print Form button will become disabled (Enabled = False).

Video Bananza

Design and code a project to calculate the amount due and provide a summary of rentals. All movies rent for $1.80 and all customers receive a 10 percent discount.

The form should contain input for the Member number and the number of movies rented. Inside a frame, display the rental amount, the 10 percent discount, and the amount due. Inside a second frame, display the number of customers served and the total rental income (after discount).

Include command buttons for Calculate, Clear, Print (PrintForm), and Exit. The Print button should be disabled (Enabled = False) until a calculation has been made. The Clear button should reset the Print button's Enabled property to False.

The Clear command clears the information for the current rental but does not clear the summary information.

Very Very Boards rents snowboards during the snow season. A person can rent a snowboard without boots or with boots. Create a project that will calculate and print the information for each rental. In addition, calculate the summary information for each day's rentals.

For each rental, input the person's name, the driver's license or ID number, the number of snowboards, and the number of snowboards with boots. Snowboards without boots rent for $20; snowboards with boots rent for $30.

Calculate and display the charges for snowboards and snowboards with boots, and the rental total. In addition, maintain summary totals. Use constants for the snowboard rental rate and the snowboard with boots rental rate.

Create a summary frame with labels to indicate the day's totals for the number of snowboards and snowboards with boots rented, total charges, and average charge per customer.

Include command buttons for Calculate Order, Print, Clear, Clear All, and Exit. The Clear All command should clear the summary totals to begin a new day's summary. *Hint:* You must set each of the summary variables to zero as well as clear the summary labels.

Make your command buttons easy to use for keyboard entry. Make the Calculate button the default button and the Clear button the cancel button, and disable the Print button until a calculation is performed. *Hint:* Make the Print button disabled initially and enable it in the calculation procedure; disable the button in both the Clear and Clear All procedures.

4

Decisions and Conditions

At the completion of this chapter, you will be able to . . .

1. Use block Ifs to control the flow of logic.

2. Understand and use nested Ifs.

3. Read and create flowcharts indicating the logic in a selection process.

4. Evaluate conditions using the relational operators.

5. Combine conditions using And and Or.

6. Test the Value property of option buttons and check boxes.

7. Perform validation on numeric fields.

8. Call event procedures from other procedures.

9. Create message boxes to display error conditions.

10. Apply the message box constants.

11. Debug projects using breakpoints, stepping program execution, and displaying intermediate results.

In this section you will learn to write projects that can take one action or another, based on a condition. For example, you may need to keep track of sales separately for different classes of employees, different sections of the country, or different departments. You may want to check the value entered by the user to make sure it is valid and display an error message for inappropriate values.

If Statements

A powerful asset of the computer is its ability to make decisions and to take alternate courses of action based on the outcome.

A decision made by the computer is formed as a question: <u>Is a given condition true or false?</u> If it is true, do one thing; if it is false, do something else.

If *the sun is shining* Then	(condition)
go to the beach	(action to take if condition is true)
Else	
go to class	(action to take if condition is false)
End If	(See Figure 4.1.)

The logic of an `If...Then...Else` *statement in flowchart form.*

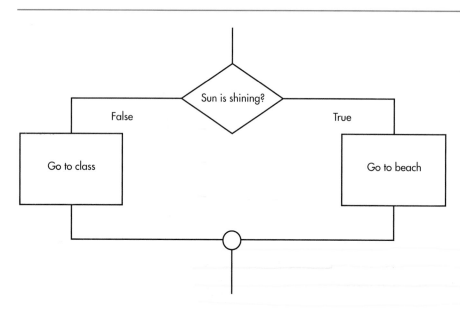

or

If *you don't succeed* Then	(condition)
try, try again	(action)
End If	(See Figure 4.2.)

The logic of an If *statement without an* Else *action in flowchart form.*

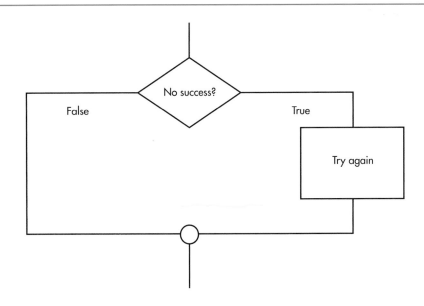

Notice in the second example that no action is specified if the condition is not true.

In an If statement, when the condition is true, only the Then clause is executed. When the condition is false, only the Else clause, if present, is executed.

If . . . Then . . . Else Statement—General Form

```
If (condition) Then
     statement(s)
[ElseIf (condition) Then
     statement(s)]
[Else
     statements(s)]
End If
```

A block **If...Then...Else** must always conclude with **End If**. The word Then must appear on the same line as the If with nothing following Then (except a remark). End If and Else (if used) must appear alone on a line. The statements under the Then and Else clauses are indented for readability and clarity.

Notice that the keyword ElseIf is all one word but that End If is two words.

If . . . Then . . . Else Statement—Examples

When the number of units in curUnits is less than 32, select the option button for *Freshman;* otherwise, make sure the button is unselected. (See Figure 4.3.) Remember that when an option button is selected, the Value property has a Boolean value of True.

```
curUnits = Val(txtUnits.Text)
If curUnits < 32 Then
    optFreshman.Value = True
Else
    optFreshman.Value = False
End If
```

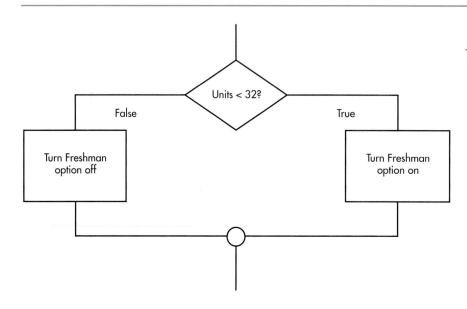

The If *statement logic in flowchart form. If the number of units is less than 32, the Freshman option button will be selected; otherwise, the Freshman option will be deselected.*

Flowcharting If Statements

A flowchart is a useful tool for showing the logic of an If statement. It has been said that one picture is worth a thousand words. Many programmers find that a flowchart helps them organize their thoughts and design projects more quickly.

The symbols used in this text are a subset of the available flowcharting symbols. The diamond-shape symbol (called a *decision symbol*) represents a condition. The two branches from the symbol indicate which path to take when the condition evaluates True or False. (See Figure 4.4.)

Conditions

The test in an If statement is based on a **condition**. To form conditions, six **relational operators** (Table 4.1) are used to compare values. The result of the comparison is either True or False.

Tip

Always take the time to indent properly as you enter an If statement. You will save yourself debugging time; the indentation helps to visualize the intended logic.

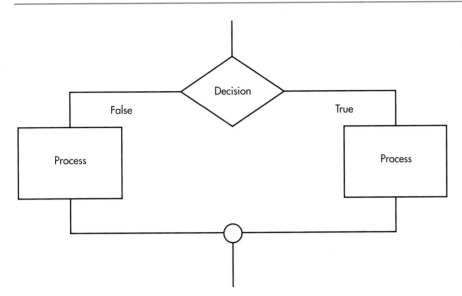

Table 4.1

The six relational operators.

Symbol	Relation Tested	Examples
>	greater than	`Val(txtAmount.Text) > mcurLimit` `frmMain.Height > mcurSize`
<	less than	`Val(txtSales.Text) < 10000` `txtName.Text < strName`
=	equal to	`txtPassword.Text = "101"` `optButton1.Value = True`
<>	not equal to	`optButton1.Value <> True` `txtPassword.Text <> "101"`
>=	greater than or equal to	`Val(lblCorrect.Caption) >= 1000` `frmMain.Height >= 500`
<=	less than or equal to	`txtName1.Text <= txtName2.Text`

The conditions to be tested can be formed with numeric variables and constants, string variables and constants, object properties, and arithmetic expressions. However, it is important to note that comparisons must be made on like types; that is, strings can be compared only to other strings, and numeric values can be compared only to other numeric values, whether a variable, constant, property, or arithmetic expression.

Comparing Numeric Variables and Constants

When numeric values are involved in a test, an algebraic comparison is made; that is, the sign of the number is taken into account. Therefore, negative 20 is less than 10, and negative 2 is less than negative 1.

Even though an equal sign (=) means replacement in an assignment statement, in a relation test the equal sign is used to test for equality. For example, the condition

```
If Val(txtPrice.Text) = curMaximum Then
```

means "Is the current numeric value stored in txtPrice.Text equal to the value stored in curMaximum?"

Sample Comparisons

intAlpha
5

intBravo
4

intCharlie
−5

Condition	Evaluates
intAlpha = intBravo	False
intCharlie < 0	True
intBravo > intAlpha	False
intCharlie <= intBravo	True
intAlpha >= 5	True
intAlpha <> intCharlie	True

Comparing Strings

String variables can be compared to other string variables or string literals enclosed in quotation marks. The comparison begins with the left most character and proceeds one character at a time from left to right. As soon as a character in one string is not equal to the corresponding character in the second string, the comparison is terminated, and the string with the lower-ranking character is judged less than the other.

The determination of which character is less than another is based on the code used to store characters internally in the computer. The code, called the **ANSI code,** has an established order (called the *collating sequence*) for all letters, numbers, and special characters. (ANSI stands for American National Standards Institute.) In Table 4.2, *A* is less than *B, L* is greater than *K,* and all numeric digits are less than all letters. Some special symbols are lower than the numbers, some are higher, and the blank space is lower than the rest of the characters shown.

Note: VB actually stores string characters in Unicode, a coding system that uses two bytes to store every character. Using Unicode, all characters and symbols in foreign languages can be represented. For systems that do not use the foreign symbols, only the first byte of each character is used. And the first byte of Unicode is the same as the ANSI code. For comparison, Unicode can store 65,536 unique characters, ANSI code can store 256 unique characters, and ASCII, the earlier coding method, can store 128 unique characters. The first 128 characters of ANSI and Unicode are the same as the ASCII characters.

Table 4.2

The ANSI collating sequence.

ANSI Code	Character	ANSI Code	Character	ANSI Code	Character
32	Space (blank)	64	@	96	`
33	!	65	A	97	a
34	"	66	B	98	b
35	#	67	C	99	c
36	$	68	D	100	d
37	%	69	E	101	e
38	&	70	F	102	f
39	' (apostrophe)	71	G	103	g
40	(	72	H	104	h
41	)	73	I	105	i
42	*	74	J	106	j
43	+	75	K	107	k
44	, (comma)	76	L	108	l
45	−	77	M	109	m
46	.	78	N	110	n
47	/	79	O	111	o
48	0	80	P	112	p
49	1	81	Q	113	q
50	2	82	R	114	r
51	3	83	S	115	s
52	4	84	T	116	t
53	5	85	U	117	u
54	6	86	V	118	v
55	7	87	W	119	w
56	8	88	X	120	x
57	9	89	Y	121	y
58	:	90	Z	122	z
59	;	91	[	123	{
60	<	92	\	124		
61	=	93	]	125	}
62	>	94	^	126	~
63	?	95	_	127	Del

txtPerson1.Text	txtPerson2.Text
JOHN	JOAN

The condition txtPerson1.Text < txtPerson2.Text evaluates False. The *A* in JOAN is lower ranking than the *H* in JOHN.

txtWord1.Text	txtWord2.Text
HOPE	HOPELESS

The condition txtWord1.Text < txtWord2.Text evaluates True. When one string is shorter than the other, it compares as if the shorter string is padded with blanks to the right of the string, and the blank space is compared to a character in the longer string.

lblCar1.Caption	lblCar2.Caption
300ZX	Porsche

The condition lblCar1.Caption < lblCar2.Caption evaluates True. When the number *3* is compared to the letter *P*, the *3* is lower, since all numbers are lower ranking than all letters.

Feedback 4.1

intCountOne	intCountTwo	intCountThree	txtFour.Text	txtFive.Text
5	5	−5	"Bit"	"Bite"

Determine which conditions will evaluate True and which ones will evaluate False.

1. intCountOne >= intCountTwo *True*
2. intCountThree < 0 *True*
3. intCountThree < intCountTwo *True*
4. intCountOne <> intCountTwo *False*
5. intCountOne + 2 > intCountTwo + 2 *False*
6. txtFour.Text < txtFive.Text *True*
7. txtFour.Text <> txtFive.Text *True*
8. txtFour.Text > "D" *False*
9. "2" <> "Two" *True*
10. "$" <= "?" *True*

Testing for True or False

You can use shortcuts when testing for True or False. Visual Basic evaluates the condition in an `If` statement. If the condition is a Boolean variable name, it holds the values True or False.

For example:

```
If blnSuccessfulOperation = True Then . . .
```

is equivalent to

```
If blnSuccessfulOperation Then . . .
```

Boolean variables hold the value 0 when False and negative 1 when True. You can actually test *any* variable for True or False. Visual Basic considers any numeric variable with a value of 0 to be False; any other value will evaluate True. The variable or expression is referred to as an **implied condition**.

Examples

```
intCounter = 10
If intCounter Then . . .        'Evaluates True

intTotal = 0
If intTotal Then . . .          'Evaluates False
```

Comparing the Text Property of Text Boxes

When you compare the Text property of a text box with another value, you must be careful. The Text property behaves like a variant. That is, if you use it like a string, it acts like a string; but if you use it like a number, it acts like a number. However, sometimes your intentions are not clear, and sometimes you are using the Text property as numeric, but the user enters nonnumeric data or no data at all.

Visual Basic compares one text box to another as strings and compares a text box to a numeric variable or constant with a numeric compare. You can force a numeric comparison on a Text property by using the `Val` function. You should always use the `Val` function on a numeric Text property when you need to compare or calculate. Remember, the `Val` function converts blank values to zero.

Examples

txtFirst.Text	txtSecond.Text	txtFirst.Text > txtSecond.Text	Val(txtFirst.Text) > Val(txtSecond.Text)
1	+1	True	False
2	100	True	False
+100	−100	False	True
0	(blank)	True	False

Comparing Uppercase and Lowercase Characters

When comparing strings, the case of the characters is important. An uppercase *Y* is not equal to a lowercase *y*. Because the user may type a name or word in uppercase, lowercase, or as a combination of cases, we must check all possibilities. The easiest way is to use the string function UCase or LCase, which returns the uppercase or lowercase equivalent of a string, respectively.

UCase and LCase—General Form

```
UCase(string)
LCase(string)
```

UCase and LCase—Examples

txtOne.Text Value	UCase(txtOne.Text)	LCase(txtOne.Text)
Basic	BASIC	basic
PROGRAMMING	PROGRAMMING	programming
Robert Jones	ROBERT JONES	robert jones
hello	HELLO	hello

An example of a condition using the UCase function follows.

```
If UCase(txtOne.Text) = "BASIC" Then
    'Do something
End If
```

Note that when you convert txtOne.Text to uppercase, you must compare it to an uppercase literal ("BASIC") if you want it to evaluate as True.

Compound Conditions

You can use **compound conditions** to test more than one condition. Create compound conditions by joining conditions with **logical operators**. The logical operators are Or, And, and Not.

Logical Operator	Meaning	Example
Or	If one condition or both conditions are true, the entire condition is true.	lblNumber.Caption = 1 Or lblNumber.Caption = 2
And	Both conditions must be true for the entire condition to be true.	txtNumber.Text > 0 And txtNumber.Text < 10
Not	Reverses the condition so that a true condition will evaluate false and vice versa.	Not lblNumber.Caption = 0

```
If optMale.Value = True And Val(txtAge.Text) < 21 Then
    mintMinorMaleCount = mintMinorMaleCount + 1
End If
If optJunior.Value = True Or optSenior.Value = True Then
    mintUpperClassmanCount = mintUpperClassmanCount + 1
End If
```

The first example requires that both the option button test and the age test be true for the count to be incremented. In the second example, only one of the conditions must be true.

One caution when using compound conditions: Each side of the logical operator must be a complete condition. For example,

```
optJunior.Value Or optSenior.Value = True
```

is incorrect.

Combining And and Or

You can create compound conditions that combine multiple And and Or conditions. When you have both an And and an Or, the And is evaluated before the Or. However, you can change the order of evaluation by using parentheses; any condition inside parentheses will be evaluated first.

For example, will the following condition evaluate True or False? Try it with various values for curSale, optDiscount, and txtState.Text.

```
If curSale > 1000 Or optDiscount.Value = True And UCase(txtState.Text) <> "CA" Then
 '(Calculate the discount)
End If
```

curSale	optDiscount.Value	UCase(txtState.Text)	Condition Evaluates
1500	False	CA	True
1000	True	OH	True
1000	True	CA	False
1500	True	NY	True
1000	False	CA	False

Nested If Statements

In many programs another If statement is one of the statements to be executed when a condition tests True or False. If statements that contain additional If statements are said to be **nested If** statements. The following example shows a nested If statement in which the second If occurs in the Then portion of the first If (Figure 4.5).

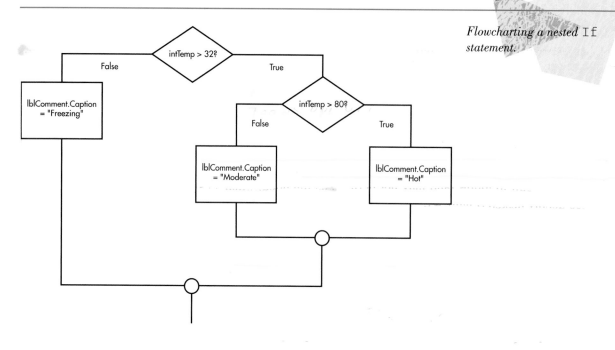

```
If intTemp > 32 Then
    If intTemp > 80 Then
        lblComment.Caption = "Hot"
    Else
        lblComment.Caption = "Moderate"
    End If
Else
    lblComment.Caption = "Freezing"
End If
```

To nest If statements in the Else portion, you may use either of the following approaches; however, your code is simpler if you use the second method (using ElseIf . . . Then).

```
If intTemp <= 32 Then
    lblComment.Caption = "Freezing"
Else
    If intTemp > 80 Then
        lblComment.Caption = "Hot"
    Else
        lblComment.Caption = "Moderate"
    End If
End If
```

```
If intTemp <= 32 Then
    lblComment.Caption = "Freezing"
ElseIf intTemp > 80 Then
    lblComment.Caption = "Hot"
Else
    lblComment.Caption = "Moderate"
End If
```

You may nest Ifs in both the Then and Else. In fact, you may continue to nest Ifs within Ifs as long as each If has an End If. However, projects become very difficult to follow (and may not perform as intended) when Ifs become too deeply nested (Figure 4.6).

Figure 4.6

A flowchart of a nested If statement with Ifs nested on both sides of the original If.

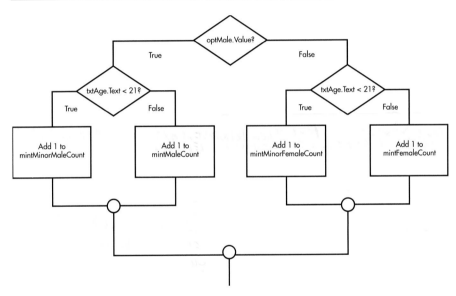

```
If optMale.Value = True Then
    If Val(txtAge.Text) < 21 Then
        mintMinorMaleCount = mintMinorMaleCount + 1
    Else
        mintMaleCount = mintMaleCount + 1
    End If
Else
    If Val(txtAge.Text) < 21 Then
        mintMinorFemaleCount = mintMinorFemaleCount + 1
    Else
        mintFemaleCount = mintFemaleCount + 1
    End If
End If
```

Tip

Indentation can help you catch errors. Visual Basic always matches an Else with the last unmatched If, regardless of the indentation.

Feedback 4.2

Assume that `intFrogs = 10`, `intToads = 5`, and `intPolliwogs = 6`.
What will be displayed for each of the following statements?

1. ```
If intFrogs > intPolliwogs Then
    optFrogs.Value = True   *Frogs opt on*
    optToads.Value = False   *Toads opt off*
Else
    optFrogs.Value = False
    optToads.Value = True
End If
```

2. ```
If intFrogs > intToads + intPolliwogs Then
    lblResult.Caption = "It's the frogs"      *It's the toads and the polliwogs*
Else
    lblResult.Caption = "It's the toads and the polliwogs"
End If
```

3. ```
If intPolliwogs > intToads And intFrogs <> 0 Or intToads = 0 Then
    lblResult.Caption = "It's true"
Else   *It's True*
    lblResult.Caption = "It's false"
End If
```

4. Write the statements necessary to compare txtApples.Text and txtOranges.Text. Display in lblMost.Caption which has more, the apples or the oranges. *If txtApples.Text > txtOranges.Text Then lblMost.Caption = "Apples" Else lblMost.Caption = "Oranges" End If*

5. Write the Basic statements that will test the current value of curBalance. When curBalance is greater than zero, the check box for Funds Available called chkFunds should be selected, the curBalance set back to zero, and intCounter incremented by one. When curBalance is zero or less, chkFunds should not be selected (do not change the value of curBalance or increment the counter).

*If curBalance > 0 Then*
*chkFunds.Value = Checked*
*curBalance = 0*
*intCounter = intCounter + 1*
*Else*
*chkFunds.Value = Unchecked*
*End If*

# Using If Statements with Option Buttons and Check Boxes

In Chapter 2 you used the Click event for option buttons and check boxes to carry out the desired action. Now that you can use `If` statements, you should not take action in the Click events for these controls. Instead, use `If` statements to determine which options are selected.

To conform to good programming practice and make your programs consistent with standard Windows applications, place your code in the Click event of command buttons. For example, refer to the Visual Basic *Print* dialog box (Figure 4.7); no action will occur when you click on an option button or check box. Instead, when you click on the OK button, VB checks to see which options are selected.
```

Figure 4.7

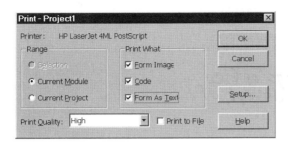

*The Visual Basic Print dialog box.
When the user clicks OK, the
program checks the state of all
option buttons and check boxes.*

In an application such as the message formatter project in Chapter 2 (refer to Figure 2.22), you could modify the code for the Display command button to include code similar to the following:

```
If optBlue.Value = True Then
    lblName.BackColor = vbBlue
Elseif optGreen.Value = True Then
    lblName.BackColor = vbGreen
Else
    lblName.BackColor = vbBlack
End If

If chkFastShip.Value = Checked Then
    curTotal = curTotal + curFastShipRate
End If
If chkGiftWrap.Value = Checked Then
    curTotal = curTotal + curWrap
End If
```

A "Simple Sample"

Test your understanding of the use of the If statement by coding some short examples.

Test the Value of a Check Box

Create a small project that contains a check box, a label, and a command button. Name the command button cmdTest, the check box chkTest, and the label lblMessage. In the Click event for cmdTest, check the value of the check box. If the check box is currently checked, display "Check box is checked" in lblMessage.

```
Private Sub cmdTest_Click()
    'Test the value of the check box

    If chkTest.Value = Checked Then
        lblMessage.Caption = "Check box is checked"
    End If
End Sub
```

Test your project. When it works, add an `Else` to the code that displays "Check box is not checked".

Test the Value of Option Buttons

Remove the check box from the previous project and replace it with two option buttons, named optFreshman and optSophomore and captioned "< 30 units" and ">= 30 units". Now change the `If` statement to display "Freshman" or "Sophomore" in the label.

```
If optFreshman.Value = True Then
    lblMessage.Caption = "Freshman"
Else
    lblMessage.Caption = "Sophomore"
End If
```

Can you modify the sample to work for Freshman, Sophomore, Junior, and Senior? In the sections that follow, you will see code for testing multiple option buttons and check boxes.

Checking the Value of an Option Button Group

Nested `If` statements work very well for determining which button of an option button group is selected. Recall that in any group of option buttons, only one button can be selected. Assume that your form has a group of buttons for Freshman, Sophomore, Junior, or Senior. In a calculation procedure, you want to add 1 to one of four counter variables, depending on which option button is selected:

```
If optFreshman.Value = True Then
    mintFreshmanCount = mintFreshmanCount + 1
ElseIf optSophomore.Value = True Then
    mintSophomoreCount = mintSophomoreCount + 1
ElseIf optJunior.Value = True Then
    mintJuniorCount = mintJuniorCount + 1
ElseIf optSenior.Value = True Then
    mintSeniorCount = mintSeniorCount + 1
End If
```

Checking the Values of Multiple Check Boxes

Although nested `If` statements work very well for groups of option buttons, the same is not true for a series of check boxes. Recall that if you have a series of check boxes, any number of the boxes may be selected. In this situation assume that you have check boxes for Discount, Taxable, and Delivery. You will need separate `If` statements for each condition.

```
If chkDiscount.Value = Checked Then
    'Calculate the discount
End If
```

```
If chkTaxable.Value = Checked Then
    'Calculate the tax
End If
If chkDelivery.Value = Checked Then
    'Deliver it
End If
```

Displaying Messages in Message Boxes

A **message box** is a special type of Visual Basic window in which you can display a message to the user. You can display a message, an optional icon, a title bar caption, and command button(s) in a message box (Figure 4.8).

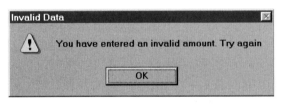
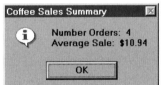

Two sample message boxes created with the MsgBox statement.

You may want to display a message when the user has entered invalid data or neglected to enter a required data value. Later in this chapter you will see several techniques for checking for valid input, called *validating* input data.

The MsgBox Statement—General Form

```
MsgBox "Message string" [, Buttons/icon][, "Caption of title bar"]
```

The *Message string* is the message you want to appear in the message box. The *Buttons* portion is optional; it determines the command buttons that will display and any icons that will appear. If you omit the *Caption of title bar*, the project name will appear in the message box title bar.

Note: It's considered very sloppy programming to display a message box with a title bar of "Project 1." Do not omit the caption unless you have given your project a meaningful name.

The MsgBox Statement—Example

```
If txtName.Text = "" Then
    MsgBox "Please Enter your name.", vbOKOnly, "Name Missing"
End If
```

Selecting the MsgBox Icon

For the button/icon entry, you can choose to use the numeric values in the following table or to use the Visual Basic constant. For example, you can display the Warning Query icon with either of these statements:

```
MsgBox "Let this be a warning", vbQuestion, "Error"
```

or

```
MsgBox "Let this be a warning", 32, "Error"
```

Button/Icon	Value	Constant
OK button	0	vbOKOnly
Critical Message icon	16	vbCritical
Warning Query icon	32	vbQuestion
Warning Message icon	48	vbExclamation
Information Message icon	64	vbInformation

Note: MsgBox can be used as a statement as explained here, which displays only an OK button. It can also be used as a function. When you use MsgBox as a function, you can choose the buttons to display (such as Yes, No, Cancel; or OK and Cancel). The function returns a value indicating which button was pressed. The MsgBox function is covered in Chapter 7.

Displaying a Message String

The message string you display may be a string literal enclosed in quotes or it may be a string variable. You may also want to concatenate several items, for example, combining a literal with a value from a variable. If the message you specify is too long for one line, Visual Basic will wrap it to the next line.

Combining Values into a Message String

You can concatenate a literal such as "Total Sales" with the value for the total sales:

```
Dim strMessage As String

strMessage = "Total Sales" & mcurTotalSales
MsgBox strMessage, vbOKOnly, "Sales Summary"
```

This example does not format the number. To remedy this condition, consider formatting the number before concatenating it to the string.

```
Dim strFormattedTotal          As String
Dim strMessage                 As String


strFormattedTotal = FormatCurrency(mcurTotalSales)
strMessage = "Total Sales" & strFormattedTotal
MsgBox strMessage, vbOKOnly, "Sales Summary"
```

Creating Multiple Lines of Output

To display multiple lines of output, you can insert a line feed/carriage return code into the line. Use the Visual Basic intrinsic constant vbCRLF to determine line endings. You can concatenate this constant into a message string to set up multiple lines. This step allows you to determine the position of the line break, rather than rely on word wrap.

In this example a second line is added to the MsgBox from the previous example.

```
Dim strFormattedTotal          As String
Dim strFormattedAvg            As String
Dim strMessage                 As String


strFormattedTotal = FormatCurrency(mcurTotalSales)
strFormattedAvg = FormatNumber(mcurAverageSale)
strMessage = "Total Sales" & strFormattedTotal & vbCRLF & _
     "Average Sale" & strFormattedAvg
MsgBox strMessage, vbOKOnly, "Sales Summary"
```

Tip

Create a "quicky" message box using the default button and an empty title bar:
```
MsgBox "My Message", , ""
```

Input Validation

Careful programmers check the values entered into text boxes before beginning the calculations. Validation is a form of self-protection; it is better to reject bad data than to spend hours (and sometimes days) trying to find an error only to discover that the problem was caused by a "user error." Finding and correcting the error early can often keep the program from producing erroneous results or halting with a run-time error.

Checking to verify that appropriate values have been entered for a text box is called *validation*. The validation may include making sure that data is numeric, checking for specific values, checking a range of values, or making sure that required items are entered.

Checking for Numeric Values

You can make sure that data entered is truly numeric with Visual Basic's IsNumeric function. The IsNumeric function returns True or False to indicate the result of the value checking.

The IsNumeric Function—General Form

```
IsNumeric(expression)
```

The `IsNumeric` function tests whether the value is numeric and therefore can be used in a calculation. If numeric, the result will be True; if not, the result is False. This function can help avoid problems in procedures that contain calculations. If the data cannot be converted to a number, the calculation cannot be performed and a run-time error will occur. The only way the programmer can prevent the user from making this type of error is to check the contents of the field after the data has been entered.

The IsNumeric Function—Example

```
If IsNumeric(txtQuantity.Text) Then
    intQuantity = Val(txtQuantity.Text)
    lblDue.Caption = curPrice * intQuantity
Else
    MsgBox "Nonnumeric data entered.", vbOKOnly, "Invalid Data"
End If
```

Checking for a Range of Values

Data validation may also include checking the reasonableness of a value. Assume you are using a text box to input the number of hours worked in a day. Even with overtime, the company does not allow more than 10 work hours in a single day. You could check the input for reasonableness with this code:

```
If Val(txtHours.Text) > 10 Then
    MsgBox "Too many hours entered", vbOKOnly, "Invalid Data"
End If
```

Checking for a Required Field

Sometimes you need to be certain that a value has been entered into a text box before proceeding. You can compare a text box value to an empty string literal.

```
If txtName.Text <> "" Then
    'Do Something
Else
    MsgBox "You must enter a value", vbOKOnly, "Required Field"
End If
```

Assume that you have a text box that must have an entry *and* must be numeric for calculations. If you use the `Val` function to convert the text to numeric and the text box is empty, what is the result? Right. Zero. If you want to check the text box for an empty string, you must do so *before* using the `Val` function.

Incorrect:

```
intQuantity = Val(txtQuantity.Text)
If intQuantity = "" Then 'Impossible test
```

Correct:

```
If txtQuantity.Text <> "" Then
    intQuantity = Val(txtQuantity.Text)
```

Performing Multiple Validations

When you need to validate several input fields, how many message boxes do you want to display for the user? Assume that the user has neglected to fill in five text boxes and clicked on Calculate. You can avoid displaying five message boxes in a row by using a nested If statement. This way you check the second value only if the first one passes, and you can exit the processing if a problem is found with a single field.

```
If txtName.Text <> "" Then
    If txtUnits.Text <> "" Then
        If optFreshman.Value = True Or optSophomore.Value = True _
            Or optJunior.Value = True Or optSenior.Value = True Then
                'Data valid — Do calculations or processing here
        Else
            MsgBox "Please select a Grade Level", vbOKOnly, "Error"
        End If
    Else
        MsgBox "Enter Number of Units", vbOKOnly, "Error"
        txtUnits.SetFocus
    End If
Else
    MsgBox "Please Enter Your Name", vbOKOnly, "Error"
    txtName.SetFocus
End If
```

Calling Event Procedures

If you wish to perform a set of instructions in more than one location, you don't have to duplicate the code. Write the instructions once, in an event procedure, and "call" the procedure from another procedure. When you **call** an event procedure, the entire procedure is executed and then execution returns to the statement following the call.

Cobol "perform"

The Call Statement (No Arguments)—General Form

```
[Call] ProcedureName
```

Notice that the keyword `Call` is optional and rarely used.

The Call Statement—Examples

```
Call cmdCalculate_Click
cmdCalculate_Click              'Equivalent to previous statement
```

In the programming example that follows, you will accumulate individual items for one customer. When that customer's order is complete, you need to clear the entire order and begin an order for the next customer. Refer to the interface in Figure 4.9; notice the two command buttons: *Clear for Next Item* and *New Order*. The command button for next item clears the text boxes on the screen. The command button for a new order must clear the screen text boxes *and* clear the subtotal fields. Rather than repeat the instructions to clear the individual screen text boxes, we can call the event procedure for cmdClear_Click from the cmdNewOrder procedure.

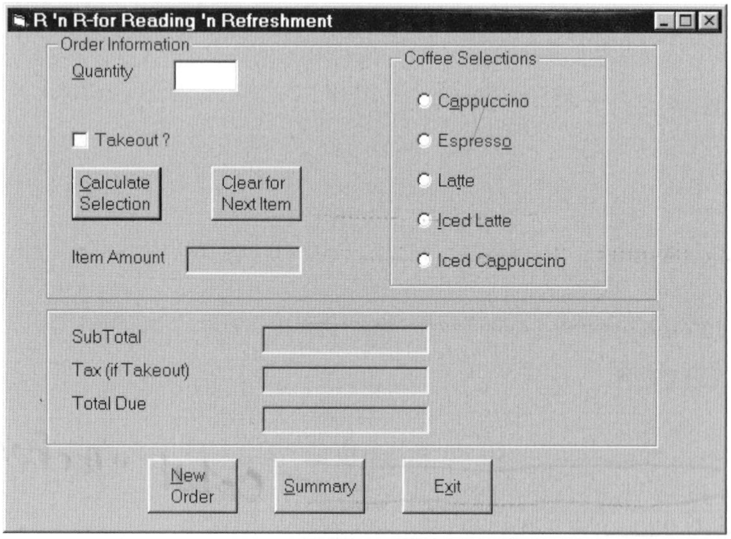

Figure 4.9

A form with command buttons that perform overlapping functions. The New Order button must do the same tasks as Clear for Next Item.

```
Private Sub cmdNewOrder_Click()
    'Clear the current item and the current order

    cmdClear_Click 'Call the procedure for the click event of cmdClear
    . . . 'Continue with statements to clear subtotals
```

In the cmdNewOrder_Click procedure, all the instructions in cmdClear_Click are executed. Then execution returns to the next statement following the call.

Your Hands-On Programming Example

Create a project for R 'n R—for Reading 'n Refreshment that calculates the amount due for individual orders and maintains accumulated totals for a summary. Have a check box for takeout items, which are taxable (8 percent); all other orders are nontaxable. Include option buttons for the five coffee selections—Cappuccino, Espresso, Latte, Iced Cappuccino, and Iced Latte. The prices for each will be assigned using these constants:

Cappuccino	2.00
Espresso	2.25
Latte	1.75
Iced (either)	2.50

Use a command button for Calculate Selection, which will calculate and display the amount due for each item. A button for Clear for Next Item will clear the selections and amount for the single item. Additional labels in a separate frame will maintain the summary information for the current order to include subtotal, tax, and total.

Buttons at the bottom of the form will be used for New Order, Summary, and Exit. The New Order button will clear the bill for the current customer and add to the totals for the summary. The button for Summary should display the average sale amount per customer and the number of customers in a message box.

Planning the Project

Sketch a form (Figure 4.10), which your users sign as meeting their needs.

The planning sketch of the form for the hands-on programming exercise.

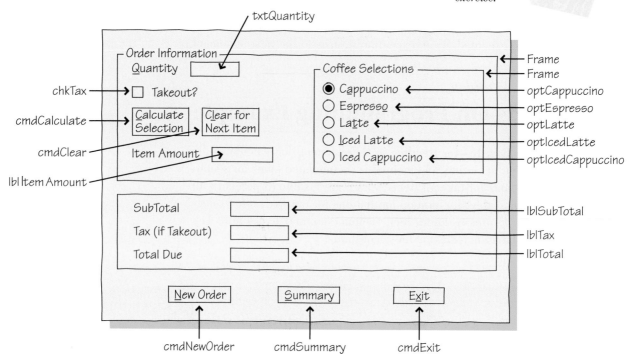

Plan the Objects and Properties

Plan the property settings for the form and each of the controls.

Object	Property	Setting
frmBilling	Name	frmBilling
	Caption	R 'n R for Reading 'n Refreshment
Frame1	Caption	Order Information
Frame2	Caption	Coffee Selections
Frame3	Caption	(blank)
optCappuccino	Name	optCappuccino
	Caption	C&appuccino
	Value	True
optEspresso	Name	optEspresso
	Caption	Espress&o
optLatte	Name	optLatte
	Caption	La&tte

(continued)

Object	Property	Setting
optIcedLatte	Name	optIcedLatte
	Caption	&Iced Latte
optIcedCappuccino	Name	optIcedCappuccino
	Caption	Iced Ca&ppuccino
Label1	Caption	&Quantity
txtQuantity	Name	txtQuantity
	Text	(blank)
chkTax	Name	chkTax
	Caption	Takeout ?
Label2	Caption	Item Amount
Label3	Caption	SubTotal
Label4	Caption	Tax (if Takeout)
Label5	Caption	Total Due
lblItemAmount	Name	lblItemAmount
	Caption	(blank)
	BorderStyle	1 - FixedSingle
lblSubTotal	Name	lblSubTotal
	Caption	(blank)
	BorderStyle	1 - Fixed Single
lblTax	Name	lblTax
	Caption	(blank)
	BorderStyle	1 - Fixed Single
lblTotal	Name	lblTotal
	Caption	(blank)
	BorderStyle	1 - Fixed Single
cmdCalculate	Name	cmdCalculate
	Caption	&Calculate Selection
	Default	True
cmdClear	Name	cmdClear
	Caption	C&lear for Next Item
	Cancel	True
cmdNewOrder	Name	cmdNewOrder
	Caption	&New Order

(continued)

Object	Property	Setting
cmdSummary	Name	cmdSummary
	Caption	&Summary
cmdExit	Name	cmdExit
	Caption	E&xit

Plan the Event Procedures

You need to plan the actions for five event procedures for the command.

Object	Procedure	Action
cmdCalculate	Click	Determine price per cup. Multiply price by quantity. Calculate tax if needed. Calculate total = subtotal + tax. Display the values.
cmdClear	Click	Clear the coffee selections. Clear the quantity and the item price. Disable the takeout check box. Set the focus to the quantity.
cmdSummary	Click	Display the average. Display the number of customers.
cmdNewOrder	Click	Clear the previous order. Accumulate total sales and count. Set subtotal and total due to 0. Enable takeout check box.
cmdExit	Click	Terminate the project.

Write the project

Follow the sketch in Figure 4.10 to create the form. Figure 4.11 shows the completed form.

- Set the properties of each object as you have planned.

- Write the code. Working from the pseudocode, write each event procedure.

- When you complete the code, use a variety of data to thoroughly test the project. Make sure the tab order is set correctly so that the insertion point begins in txtQuantity.

The Project Coding Solution

```
'Program Name:    Billing
'Programmer:      A. Millspaugh
'Date:            July 1999
'Description:     This project calculates the amount due
'                 based on the customer selection
'                 and accumulates summary data for the day.
'Folder:          Ch0401
```

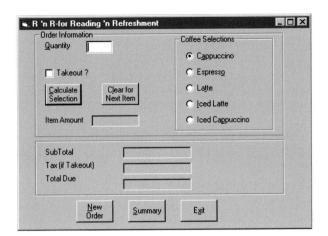

The form for the hands-on programming exercise.

```
Option Explicit
Dim mcurSubtotal                    As Currency
Dim mcurTotal                       As Currency
Dim mcurGrandTotal                  As Currency
Dim mintCustomerCount               As Integer
```

```
Private Sub cmdCalculate_Click()
    'Calculate and display the current amounts, add to totals

    Dim curPrice                    As Currency
    Dim intQuantity                 As Integer
    Dim curTax                      As Currency
    Dim curItemAmount               As Currency
    Const curTaxRate                As Currency = 0.08
    Const curCappuccinoPrice        As Currency = 2
    Const curEspressoPrice          As Currency = 2.25
    Const curLattePrice             As Currency = 1.75
    Const curIcedPrice              As Currency = 2.5

    'Find the price
    If optCappuccino.Value = True Then
        curPrice = curCappuccinoPrice
    ElseIf optEspresso.Value = True Then
        curPrice = curEspressoPrice
    ElseIf optLatte.Value = True Then
        curPrice = curLattePrice
    ElseIf optIcedCappuccino.Value = True Or _
            optIcedLatte.Value = True Then
        curPrice = curIcedPrice
    End If
```

```
        'Add the price times quantity to price so far
        If IsNumeric(txtQuantity.Text) Then
            intQuantity = Val(txtQuantity.Text)
            curItemAmount = curPrice * intQuantity
            mcurSubtotal = mcurSubtotal + curItemAmount
            If chkTax.Value = Checked Then
                curTax = mcurSubtotal * curTaxRate
            End If
            mcurTotal = mcurSubtotal + curTax
            lblItemAmount.Caption = FormatCurrency(curItemAmount)
            lblSubTotal.Caption = FormatNumber(mcurSubtotal)
            lblTax.Caption = FormatNumber(curTax)
            lblTotal.Caption = FormatCurrency(mcurTotal)
        Else
            MsgBox "Quantity must be numeric", vbExclamation, "Numeric Test"
            txtQuantity.SetFocus
        End If
End Sub
```

```
Private Sub cmdClear_Click()
    'Clear appropriate controls

    If mcurSubtotal <> 0 Then          'Clear only if calculation made
        optCappuccino.Value = True
        optEspresso.Value = False
        optLatte.Value = False
        optIcedLatte.Value = False
        optIcedCappuccino.Value = False
        lblItemAmount.Caption = ""
        chkTax.Enabled = False         'Allow change for new order only
        With txtQuantity
            .Text = ""
            .SetFocus
        End With
     Else
        MsgBox "No New Order to Clear", vbExclamation, "Customer Order"
    End If
End Sub
```

```
Private Sub cmdExit_Click()
    'Terminate the project

    End
End Sub
```

```vb
Private Sub cmdNewOrder_Click()
    'Clear the current order and add to totals

    cmdClear_Click
    lblSubTotal.Caption = ""
    lblTax.Caption = ""
    lblTotal.Caption = ""

    'Add to Totals
    If mcurSubtotal <> 0 Then        'Should not be able to add to counts if no
                                     'new order/customer. Prevents accidental
                                     'clicking
        mcurGrandTotal = mcurGrandTotal + mcurTotal
        mcurSubtotal = 0
        mcurTotal = 0                'Reset for next customer
        mintCustomerCount = mintCustomerCount + 1
    End If

    'Clear appropriate display items and enable check box
    With chkTax
        .Enabled = True
        .Value = Unchecked
    End With
End Sub
```

```vb
Private Sub cmdSummary_Click()
    'Calculate the average and display the totals

    Dim curAverage             As Currency
    Dim strMessageString       As String
    Dim strFormattedAvg        As String

    If mintCustomerCount > 0 Then
        If mcurTotal <> 0 Then
            cmdNewOrder_Click      'Make sure last order is counted
        End If
        curAverage = mcurGrandTotal / mintCustomerCount

        'Format the numbers
        strFormattedAvg = FormatCurrency(curAverage)
        'Concatenate the message string
        strMessageString = "Number Orders: " & mintCustomerCount & vbCrLf & _
            "Average Sale: " & strFormattedAvg
        MsgBox strMessageString, vbInformation, "Coffee Sales Summary"
    Else
        MsgBox "No data to summarize", vbExclamation, "Coffee Sales Summary"
    End If
End Sub
```

Debugging Visual Basic Projects

One of the advantages of programming in the Visual Basic environment is the availability of debugging tools. You can use these tools to help find and eliminate logic and run-time errors. The debugging tools can also help you to follow the logic of existing projects to better understand how they work.

You can use the buttons in the toolbar or the *Debug* menu to access Visual Basic's debugging tools. (See Figure 4.12.) The debugging tools include the Debug window, single-stepping through a project, and watching the contents of variables and expressions.

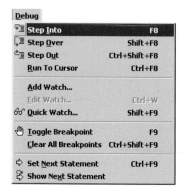

The debugging options on the Debug menu.

Pausing Execution with the Break Button

You can click on the Break toolbar button to pause execution. This step places the project into break time at the current line. The disadvantage of this method is that usually you prefer to break in the middle of a procedure. To choose the location of the break, you can force a break.

Forcing a Break

During the debugging process, often you want to stop at a particular location in code and watch what happens (which branch of an If...Then...Else; which procedures were executed; the value of a variable just before or just after a calculation). You can force the project to break by inserting a **breakpoint** in code.

```
If IsNumeric(txtQuantity.Text) Then
    lblDue.Caption = curPrice * txtQuantity.Text
Else
    MsgBox "Please Enter a Numeric Value", vbOKOnly, "Error"
End If
```

To set a breakpoint, place the cursor in the gray margin indicator area at the left edge of the Code window and click; the line will be highlighted in red, and a large red dot will display in the margin indicator (Figure 4.13). You can also set a breakpoint by placing the cursor on the line before which you want to break and clicking on the Set Breakpoint button, by choosing *Toggle Breakpoint* from the *Run* menu, or by pressing F9, the keyboard shortcut. The breakpoint line will change to red (unless colors have been altered on your system).

F i g u r e   4 . 1 3

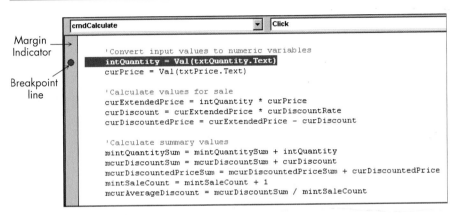

The highlighted line is set as a breakpoint. Note the dot in the gray margin indicator area.

After setting a breakpoint, start (or restart) program execution. When the project reaches the breakpoint, it will halt, display the line, and go into break time.

You can use *Toggle Breakpoint* again to turn off an individual breakpoint or clear all breakpoints from the *Run* menu.

Using the Immediate Window

The **Immediate window** is available at design time, run time, and break time. You can display the values of data or messages in the Immediate window while the project is executing. In break time you can use the Immediate window to view or change the current contents of variables or to execute lines of code. At design time you can view the window to see values from the previous run, but you cannot execute any code. You can display the window by selecting it from the *View* menu or use the shortcut Ctrl + G. You may want to move and resize the window to make it more visible. Figure 4.14 shows the Immediate window.

F i g u r e   4 . 1 4

You can execute program statements in the Immediate window.

Checking the Current Values of Expressions

You can quickly check the current value of an expression, such as a variable, a control, a condition, or an arithmetic expression. During break time, display the Code window and point to the name of the expression that you want to view; a small label will pop, similar to a ToolTip, which displays the current contents of the expression. If you want to view the contents of an expression of more than one word, such as a condition or arithmetic expression, highlight the entire expression and then point to the highlighted area; the current value will display.

Note: For True/False values, Visual Basic displays 0 for False and −1 for True.

The steps for viewing the contents of a variable during run time are

1. Break the execution (using the *Run* menu, the toolbar button, or a breakpoint).
2. Click on the View Code button in the Project Explorer window or select *Code* from the *View* menu.
3. Point to the variable or expression you wish to view.

The current contents of the expression will pop up in a label (Figure 4.15).

Point to a variable name, control name, condition, or arithmetic expression during break time to display the current value.

```
(General)                                    (Declarations)

        'Calculate summary values
        mintQuantitySum = mintQuantitySum + intQuantity
⇨       mcurDiscountSum = mcurDiscountSum + c intQuantity = 3
        mcurDiscountedPriceSum = mcurDiscountedPriceSum + curDiscountedPrice
        mintSaleCount = mintSaleCount + 1
        mcurAverageDiscount = mcurDiscountSum / mintSaleCount

        'Format and display answers for sale
        lblExtendedPrice.Caption = FormatCurrency(curExtendedPrice)
        lblDiscount.Caption = FormatNumber(curDiscount)
        lblDiscountedPrice.Caption = FormatCurrency(curDiscountedPrice)
```

Stepping through Code

The best way to debug a project is to thoroughly understand what the project is doing every step of the way. Previously, this task was performed by following each line of code manually to understand its effect. You can now use the Visual Basic stepping tools to trace program execution line by line and see the progression of the program as it executes through your code.

You step through code at break time. You can use one of the techniques already mentioned to break execution or choose one of the stepping commands at design time; the program will begin running and immediately transfer to break time.

Two stepping commands on the *Debug* menu are *Step Into* and *Step Over*. You can also use the toolbar buttons for Step Into and Step Over or the keyboard shortcuts shown on the menu (refer to Figure 4.12).

These commands force the project to execute a single line at a time and to display the Code window with the current statement highlighted. As you execute the project, by pressing a command button, for example, the Click event occurs. Execution transfers to the click procedure, the Code window for that procedure appears on the screen, and you can follow line-by-line execution.

Step Into

Most likely you will use the **Step Into** command more than you will use Step Over. When you choose Step Into (from the menu, the toolbar button, or F8), the next line of code is executed and the program pauses again in break time. If the line of code is a call to another procedure, the first line of code of the other procedure will be displayed.

To continue stepping through your program execution, continue choosing the Step Into command. When a procedure is completed, your form will display again, awaiting an event. You can click on one of your command buttons to continue stepping through code in an event procedure. If you want to continue execution without stepping, choose the Start command (from the menu, the toolbar button, or F5).

Step Over

The **Step Over** command also executes one line of code at a time. The difference between Step Over and Step Into occurs when your code has calls to other procedures. Step Over displays only the lines of code in the current procedure being analyzed; it does not display lines of code in the called procedures.

You can choose *Step Over* from the menu, from the toolbar button, or by pressing Shift + F8. Each time you choose the command, one more program statement executes.

Debugging Step-by-Step Tutorial

In this exercise you will learn to set a breakpoint; pause program execution; single step through program instructions; display the current values in properties, variables, and conditions; and debug a Visual Basic project.

Student Diskette?

Test the Project

STEP 1: Open the debugging project on your student diskette. The project is found in the Ch04Debug folder.

STEP 2: Run the project.

STEP 3: Enter color Blue, quantity 100, and press Enter or click on the Calculate button.

STEP 4: Enter another color Blue, quantity 50, and press Enter. Are the totals correct?

STEP 5: Enter color Red, quantity 30, and press Enter.

STEP 6: Enter color Red, quantity 10, and press Enter. Are the totals correct?

STEP 7: Enter color White, quantity 50, and press Enter.

STEP 8: Enter color White, quantity 100, and press Enter. Are the totals correct?

STEP 9: Exit the project. You are going to locate and correct the errors in the red and white totals.

Break and Step Program Execution

STEP 1: Display the program code and click in the gray margin indicator area for the first calculation line in the cmdCalculate_Click event procedure:

```
curQuantity = Val(txtQuantity.Text)
```

A breakpoint will be set on the selected line. Your screen should look like Figure 4.16.

F i g u r e   4 . 1 6

A program statement with a breakpoint set appears highlighted, and a dot appears in the gray margin indicator area.

STEP 2: Close the Code window.

STEP 3: Run the project, enter Red, quantity 30, and press Enter.

The project will transfer control to the cmdCalculate_Click procedure, stop when the breakpoint is reached, highlight the current line, and enter break time (Figure 4.17).

Note: The highlighted line has not yet executed.

STEP 4: Press the F8 key, which causes VB to execute the current program statement (the assignment statement). F8 is the keyboard shortcut for Debug/Step Into.

The statement is executed, and the highlight moves to the next statement (the If statement).

STEP 5: Press F8 again; the condition (optBlue) is tested and found to be False.

STEP 6: Continue pressing F8 and watch the order in which program statements execute.

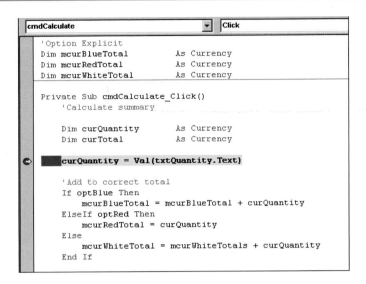

*When a breakpoint is reached
during project execution, Visual
Basic enters break time, displays
the Code window, and highlights
the breakpoint line.*

View the Contents of Properties, Variables, and Conditions

STEP 1: Scroll up if necessary and point to `txtQuantity.Text` in the breakpoint line. The current contents of the Text property pops up (Figure 4.18).

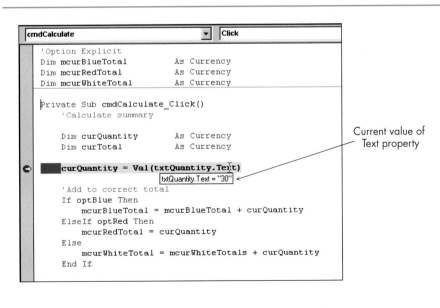

*Point to a property reference in
code, and the current content
pops up.*

STEP 2: Point to `curQuantity` and view the contents of that variable. Notice that the Text property is enclosed in quotes and the numeric variable is not.

STEP 3: Point to `optBlue` in the `If` statement; then point to `optRed`. The value that pops up is the current state of the Value property (the default property of an option button).

STEP 4: Point to `mcurRedTotal` to see the current value of that total variable. This value looks correct, since you just entered 30, which was added to the total.

Continue Project Execution

STEP 1: Press F5, the keyboard shortcut for the Start command. The Start command continues execution.

> If the current line is any line other than `Exit Sub`, execution continues and your form reappears. If the current line is `Exit Sub`, you must click on your project's Taskbar button (Figure 4.19) to make the form reappear.

Figure 4.19

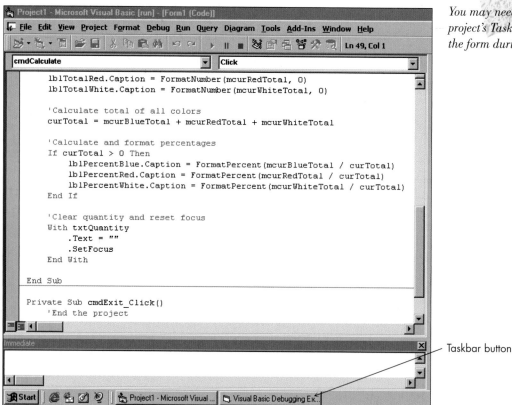

You may need to click on your project's Taskbar button to display the form during project execution.

Taskbar button

STEP 2: Enter color Red and quantity 10. When you press Enter, program execution will again break at the breakpoint.

> The 10 you just entered should be added to the 30 previously entered for Red, producing 40 in the Red total.

STEP 3: Use F8 to step through execution. Keep pressing F8 until the 10 is added to mcurRedTotal. Display the current contents of the total. Can you see what the problem is?

> *Hint:* mcurRedTotal has only the current amount, not the sum of the two amounts. The answer will appear a little later; try to find it yourself first.

> You will fix this error soon, after testing the White total.

Test the White Total

STEP 1: Press F5 to continue execution. If the form does not reappear, click the project's Taskbar button.

STEP 2: Enter color White, quantity 100, and press Enter.

STEP 3: When execution halts at the breakpoint, press F5 to continue.

STEP 4: Enter color White, quantity 50, and press Enter.

STEP 5: Press F8 several times when execution halts at the breakpoint until you execute the line that adds the 50 to the White total. Remember that the highlighted line has not yet executed; press F8 one more time, if necessary, to execute the addition statement.

STEP 6: Point to each variable name to see the current values (Figure 4.20). Can you see the problem?

Figure 4.20

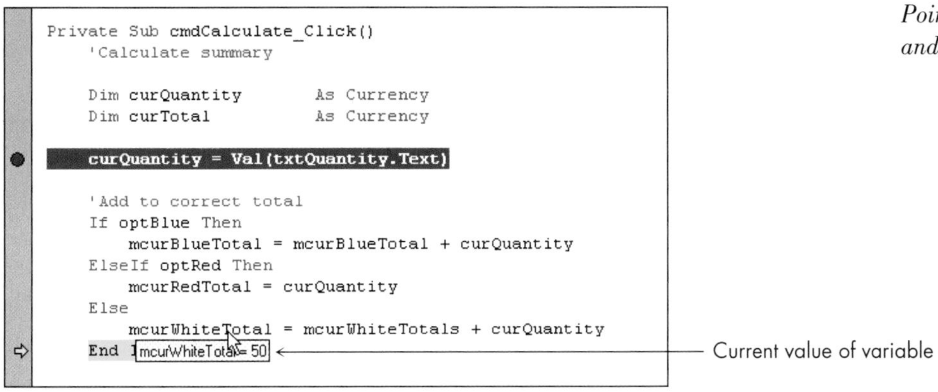

Point to a variable name in code, and its current value displays.

```
Private Sub cmdCalculate_Click()
    'Calculate summary

    Dim curQuantity       As Currency
    Dim curTotal          As Currency

    curQuantity = Val(txtQuantity.Text)

    'Add to correct total
    If optBlue Then
        mcurBlueTotal = mcurBlueTotal + curQuantity
    ElseIf optRed Then
        mcurRedTotal = curQuantity
    Else
        mcurWhiteTotal = mcurWhiteTotals + curQuantity
    End If  mcurWhiteTotal = 50
```

— Current value of variable

STEP 7: Identify all the errors. When you are ready to make the corrections, continue.

Correct the Red Total Error

STEP 1: Stop program execution by clicking on the End toolbar button (Figure 4.21).

End toolbar button

STEP 2: Locate this line:

```
mcurRedTotal = curQuantity
```

This statement *replaces* the value of mcurRedTotal with curQuantity rather than *adding* to the total.

STEP 3: Change the line to read

```
mcurRedTotal = mcurRedTotal + curQuantity
```

Correct the White Total Error

STEP 1: Locate this line:

```
mcurWhiteTotal = mcurWhiteTotals + curQuantity
```

Have you found the problem with this line? Look carefully at the spelling of the variable names. The compiler would find this error if the project included an `Option Explicit` statement.

STEP 2: First scroll up to the General Declarations section and remove the apostrophe from the `Option Explicit` statement.

STEP 3: Run the project again.

STEP 4: Enter color White and quantity 100; then press Enter.

The compiler displays a compile error message; click OK, and the Code window redisplays with the offending variable name highlighted (Figure 4.22).

F i g u r e   4 . 2 2

```
'Add to correct total
If optBlue Then
    mcurBlueTotal = mcurBlueTotal + curQuantity
ElseIf optRed Then
    mcurRedTotal = mcurRedTotal + curQuantity
Else
    mcurWhiteTotal = mcurWhiteTotals + curQuantity
End If

'Format totals in labels
lblTotalBlue.Caption = FormatNumber(mcurBlueTotal, 0)
lblTotalRed.Caption = FormatNumber(mcurRedTotal, 0)
lblTotalWhite.Caption = FormatNumber(mcurWhiteTotal, 0)
```

Problem area highlighted

After a compile error, the Code window displays with the problem area highlighted.

STEP 5: Remove the s from mcurWhiteTotals. The line should read:

```
mcurWhiteTotal = mcurWhiteTotal + curQuantity
```

STEP 6: Press F5 to continue project execution. Remember that you already entered White and 100.

STEP 7: Press F5 to continue when the project halts at the breakpoint.

STEP 8: Enter White, 50, and Enter.

STEP 9: At the breakpoint, click on the breakpoint line, and select *Toggle Breakpoint* from the *Debug* menu to clear the breakpoint.

STEP 10: Press F5 to continue and check the total on the form. It should be correct now.

STEP 11: Test the totals for all three colors carefully and then click Exit.

Force a Run-Time Error

STEP 1: Display the code window and locate this line:

```
If curTotal > 0 Then
```

STEP 2: Type an apostrophe at the beginning of the line; then place another apostrophe on the End If line (Figure 4.23). This practice, called *commenting out* a statement, is a useful way to test program code.

F i g u r e   4 . 2 3

```
          'Calculate total of all colors
          curTotal = mcurBlueTotal + mcurRedTotal + mcurWhiteTotal

          'Calculate and format percentages
        '   If curTotal > 0 Then
              lblPercentBlue.Caption = FormatPercent(mcurBlueTotal / curTotal)
              lblPercentRed.Caption = FormatPercent(mcurRedTotal / curTotal)
              lblPercentWhite.Caption = FormatPercent(mcurWhiteTotal / curTotal)
        '   End If

          'Clear quantity and reset focus
          With txtQuantity
              .Text = ""
              .SetFocus
          End With
End Sub
```

Add apostrophes

Convert statements to comments by typing an apostrophe at the beginning of the line. You can remove the apostrophes later to restore the lines.

STEP 3: Run the project. This time click the Calculate button without entering an Amount.

A run-time error will occur.

STEP 4: Click *Debug* on the error dialog box, and the Code window will display with the offending line highlighted.

STEP 5: Point to each variable name to see its value. Of course this error occurred because it is illegal to divide by zero.

STEP 6: Notice that the program is in break time. Click the End toolbar button to return to design time.

STEP 7: Remove the apostrophes from the If and End If lines.

STEP 8: Test the project carefully and thoroughly. If you have corrected all the errors, it should run correctly now.

Summary

1. Visual Basic uses the `If...Then...Else` statement to make decisions. An `Else` clause is optional and specifies the action to be taken if the condition is false. An `If...Then...Else` statement must conclude with an `End If`.

2. Flowcharts can help visualize the logic of an `If...Then...Else` statement.

3. The conditions for an `If` statement can be composed of the relational operators, which compare items for equality, greater than, or less than. The comparison of numeric values is based on the quantity of the number, while string comparisons are based on the ANSI code table.

4. The `UCase` and `LCase` functions can convert a text value to upper- or lowercase.

5. The `And` and `Or` logical operators may be used to combine multiple conditions. With the `And` operator, both conditions must be true for the entire condition to evaluate True. For the `Or` operator, if either or both conditions are true, the entire condition evaluates as True. When both `And` and `Or` are used in a condition, the `And` condition is evaluated before the `Or` condition.

6. A nested `If` statement contains an `If` statement within either the true or false actions of a previous `If` statement. Nesting an `If` statement inside of another requires the use of the `End If` clause. An `Else` clause always applies to the last unmatched `If` regardless of indentation.

7. The state of option buttons and check boxes should be tested with `If` statements in the event procedure for a command button, rather than coding event procedures for the option button or check box.

8. The `MsgBox` statement can be used to display a message to the person running the program. The programmer must supply the message and can optionally select an icon to display and enter a caption for the message box title bar.

9. Data validation checks the reasonableness or appropriateness of the value in a variable or property. Because an error will occur if the data placed in a text box are not numeric, a popular validation tool is the `IsNumeric` function.

10. One procedure can call another procedure.

11. A variety of debugging tools are available in Visual Basic. These include breaking program execution, displaying the current contents of variables, and stepping through code.

Key Terms

ANSI code   *132*

breakpoint   *156*

call   *147*

compound condition   *136*

condition   *130*

End If   *129*

If...Then...Else   *129*

Immediate window   *157*

implied condition   *135*

logical operator   *136*

message box   *143*

nested If   *137*

relational operator   *130*

Step Into   *159*

Step Over   *159*

validation   *145*

Review Questions

1. What is the general format of the statement used to code decisions in an application?
2. What is a condition?
3. Explain the purpose of relational operators and of logical operators.
4. Differentiate between a comparison performed on numeric data and a comparison performed on string data.
5. How does Visual Basic compare the Text property of a text box?
6. Why would it be useful to include the UCase function in a comparison?
7. Name the types of items that can be used in a comparison.
8. Explain a Boolean variable test for True and False. Give an example.
9. Give an example of a situation where nested Ifs would be appropriate.
10. When would you use a message box?
11. Give an example of three message box constants.
12. Define the term *validation*. When is it appropriate to do validation?
13. Define the term *checking a range*.
14. Explain the difference between Step Into and Step Over.
15. What steps are necessary to view the current contents of a variable during program execution?

Programming Exercises

4.1 Lynette Rifle owns an image consulting shop. Her clients can select from the following services at the specified regular prices: Makeover $125, Hair Styling $60, Manicure $35, and Permanent Makeup $200. She has distributed discount coupons that advertise discounts of 10 percent and 20 percent off the regular price. Create a project that will allow the receptionist to select a discount rate of 10 percent, 20 percent, or none, and then select a service. Display the price for the individual service in a label and have another label to display the total due after each visit is entered. Include command buttons for *Calculate*, *Clear*, *Print Form*, and *Exit*.

4.2 Modify project 4.1 to allow for sales to additional patrons. Include command buttons for *Next Patron* and *Summary*. When the receptionist clicks the *Summary* button, display the number of clients and the total dollar value for all services rendered in a summary message box.

4.3 Create a project to compute your checking account balance.

Form: Include option buttons to indicate the type of transaction—deposit, check, or service charge. A text box will allow the user to enter the amount of the transaction. Display the new balance in a label. Calculate the balance by adding deposits and subtracting service charges and checks. Include command buttons for *Calculate*, *Clear*, and *Exit*.

4.4 Add validation to project 4.3 by displaying a message box if the new balance would be a negative number. If there is not enough money to cover a check, do not deduct the check amount. Instead, display a message box with the message "Insufficient Funds" and deduct a service charge of $10.

4.5 Modify project 4.3 or 4.4 by adding a *Summary* command button that will display the total number of deposits, the total dollar amount of deposits, the number of checks, and the dollar amount of the checks. Do not include checks that were returned for insufficient funds, but do include the service charges. Use a message box to display the Summary information.

4.6 Piecework workers are paid by the piece. Workers who produce a greater quantity of output are often paid at a higher rate.

Form: Use text boxes to obtain the person's name and the number of pieces completed. Include a *Calculate* command button to display the dollar amount earned. You will need a *Summary* button to display the total number of pieces, the total pay, and the average pay per person. A *Clear* button should clear the name and the number of pieces for the current employee.

Include validation to check for missing data. If the user clicks on the *Calculate* button without first entering a name and number of pieces, display a message box. Also, you need to make sure to not display a summary before any data are entered; you cannot calculate an average when no items have been calculated. You can check the number of employees in the Summary event procedure or disable the *Summary* command button until the first order has been calculated.

Pieces Completed	Price Paid per Piece for All Pieces
1–199	.50
200–399	.55
400–599	.60
600 or more	.65

4.7 Modify project 2.3 (the weather report) to treat option buttons the proper way. Do not have an event procedure for each option button; instead use a *Display* command button to display the correct image and message.

4.8 Modify project 2.2 (the flag viewer) to treat option buttons and check boxes in the proper way. Include a *Display* command button and check the settings of the option buttons and check boxes in the button's event procedure, rather than code event procedures for each option button and check box.

....

CASE STUDIES

Calculate the amount due for an order. For an order, the user should enter the following information into text boxes: customer name, address, city, state (two-letter abbreviation), and ZIP code. An order may consist of multiple items. For each item, the user will enter the product description, quantity, weight, and price into text boxes.

You will need command buttons for *Next Item*, *Update Summary*, *Print*, and *Exit*.

For the *Next Item* button, validate the quantity, weight, and price. Each must be present and numeric. For any bad data, display a message box. Calculate the charge for the current item and add the charge and weight into the appropriate totals. Do not calculate shipping and handling on individual items; rather, calculate shipping and handling on the entire order.

When the *Update Summary* button is clicked, calculate the sales tax, shipping and handling, and the total amount due for the order. Sales tax is 8 percent of the total charge and is charged only for shipments to a California address. Do not charge sales tax on the shipping and handling charges.

The shipping and handling charges depend on the weight of the products. Calculate the shipping charge as $.25 per pound and add that amount to the handling charge (taken from the following table).

VB Mail Order

Display the entire amount of the bill in labels titled *Dollar amount due*, *Sales tax*, *Shipping and handling*, and *Total amount due*.

Test Data

Description	Quantity	Weight	Price
Planter	2	3	19.95
Mailbox	1	2	24.95
Planter	2	3	19.95

Test Data Output

	Nontaxable	Taxable
Dollar Amount Due	$104.75	$104.75
Sales Tax	0.00	8.38
Shipping and Handling	6.50	6.50
Total Amount Due	111.25	119.63

Handling

Weight	Handling
Less than 10 pounds	$1.00
10 to 100 pounds	$3.00
Over 100 pounds	$5.00

Create a project that will be used to determine the total amount due for the purchase of a vehicle. You will need text boxes for the base price and the trade-in allowance. Check boxes will indicate if the buyer wants additional accessories: stereo system, leather interior, and/or computer navigation. A frame for the exterior finish will contain option buttons for Standard, Pearlized, or Customized Detailing.

Have the trade-in allowance default to zero; that is, if the user does not enter a trade-in value, use zero in your calculation. Validate the values from the text

VB Auto Center

boxes, displaying a message box if necessary.

To calculate, add the price of selected accessories and finish to the base price and display the result in a label called *Subtotal*. Calculate the sales tax on the subtotal and display the result in a *Total* label. Then subtract any trade-in value from the total and display the result in an *Amount Due* label.

Include command buttons for *Calculate, Clear, Exit*, and *Print Form*. The *Calculate* button must display the total amount due after trade-in.

Item	Price
Stereo System	425.76
Leather Interior	987.41
Computer Navigation	1,741.23
Standard	No additional charge
Pearlized	345.72
Customized Detailing	599.99
Tax Rate	8%

Design and code a project to calculate the amount due for rentals. Movies may be in VCR (videotape) format or DVD format. Videotapes rent for $1.80 each and DVDs rent for $2.50. New releases are $3 for DVD and $2 for videotape.

On the form include a text box to input the movie title and option buttons to indicate whether the movie is in DVD or a videotape format. Use one check box to indicate whether the person is a member; members receive a 10 percent discount. Another check box indicates a new release.

Use command buttons for *Calculate, Clear for Next Item, Order Complete, Summary*, and *Exit*. The *Calculate* button should display the item amount and add to the

Video Bonanza

subtotal. The *Clear for Next Item* clears the check box for new releases, the movie title, and the option buttons; the member check box cannot be changed until the current order is complete. Include validation to check for missing data. If the user clicks on the *Calculate* button without first entering the movie title and selecting the movie format, display a message box.

The *Order Complete* button clears the controls on the form for a new customer.

The *Summary* button displays the number of customers and the sum of the rental amounts in a message box. Make sure to add to the customer count and rental sum for each customer order.

Very Very Boards does a big business in shirts, especially for groups and teams. They need a project that will calculate the price for individual orders, as well as a summary for all orders.

The store employee will enter the orders in an order form that has text boxes for customer name and order number. To specify the shirts, use a text box for the quantity, option buttons to select the size (small, medium, large, extra large, and XXL), and check boxes to specify a monogram and/or a pocket. Display the shirt price for the current order and the order total in labels.

Include command buttons to add a shirt to an order, clear the current item, complete the order, and display the summary of all orders. Do not allow the summary to display if the current order is not complete. Also, disable the text boxes for customer name and order number after an order is started; enable them again when the user clicks on the button to begin a new order.

When the user adds shirts to an order, validate the quantity, which must be numeric and greater than zero. If the data do not pass the validation, do not perform any calculations but display a message box and allow the user to correct the value. Determine the price of the shirts from the option buttons and check boxes for the monogram and pockets. Multiply the quantity by the price to determine the price, and add to the order total and summary total.

Use constants for the shirt prices.

Prices for the Shirts	Small, medium, and large	$10
	Extra large	11
	XXL	12
	Monogram	Add $2
	Pocket	Add $1

Display the order summary in a message box. Include the number of shirts, the number of orders, and the dollar total of the orders.

5

Menus, Sub Procedures, and Sub Functions

At the completion of this chapter, you will be able to . . .

1. Create menus and submenus for program control.

2. Display and use the Windows common dialog boxes.

3. Write reusable code in sub procedures and function procedures and call the procedures from other locations.

4. Create an executable file that can be run from the Windows environment.

Menus

You have undoubtedly used menus quite extensively while working with the computer. **Menus** consist of a menu bar with menu names, each of which drops down to display a list of menu commands. You can use menu commands in place of or in addition to command buttons to activate a procedure.

Menu commands are actually controls; they have properties and events. Each menu command has a Name property and a Click event, similar to a command button.

It is easy to create a menu for your form, using the Visual Basic menu editor. Your menu will appear across the top of the window and look like a standard Windows menu.

To use the menu editor, select *Menu Editor* from the *Tools* menu or click on the Menu Editor toolbar button (Figure 5.1).

F i g u r e   5 . 1

The Menu Editor toolbar button.

Defining Menus

You will use the Menu Editor window to set up your menus. Figure 5.2 shows the Menu Editor window with the various parts labeled.

F i g u r e   5 . 2

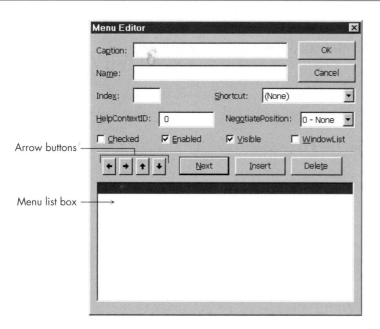

Define menus with the Menu Editor window.

Arrow buttons

Menu list box

The Caption

The Caption property holds the words you want to appear on the screen (just like the Caption property of a label or command button). Start creating a new menu by entering the Caption of the item you want for your first menu.

To conform to Windows standards, your first menu Caption should be File, with a keyboard access key. Use the ampersand (&) in the Caption to specify the key to use for keyboard access, as you learned in Chapter 2. For example, for File, the Caption should be &File.

The Name

The Name box indicates the name of the menu control, similar to other controls. The Name is required.

Naming Standards

The three-character prefix for a menu name is "mnu". Therefore, the name for the *File* menu should be mnuFile. For the commands on a menu use the prefix plus the name of the menu plus the name of the command. (You can abbreviate long names, if you do so consistently and clearly.) The name for the *Print* command on the *File* menu should be mnuFilePrint. The *Exit* command should be called mnuFileExit, which will trigger the mnuFileExit_Click event when the user selects it.

Submenus

The drop-down list of commands below a menu name is called a *menu*. When a command on the menu has another list of commands that pops up, the new list is called a **submenu**. A filled triangle to the right of the command indicates that a menu command has a submenu (Figure 5.3).

Figure 5 . 3

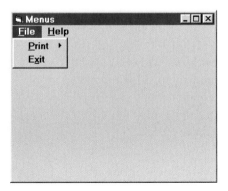

A filled triangle on a menu command indicates that a submenu will appear.

You specify menu names, menu commands, and submenu commands by their indentation levels. Menu names appear at the left of the list box; for a menu command, click on the Right arrow button to indent one level. For submenus, click on the Right arrow button again to indent two levels. The indentations show as dots (....) in the list box.

The Menu List Box

The menu list box contains a list of the menu items you have created and shows their indentation levels. You can move an item up or down, left or right by clicking on its name in the list box and clicking on one of the arrow buttons (refer to Figure 5.2).

```
&File
....E&xit
&Help
....&About
```

Separator Bars

When you have many commands in a menu, you should group the commands according to their purpose. You can create a **separator bar** in a menu, which draws a bar across the entire menu. To define a separator bar, type a single hyphen (-) for the Caption and give it a name. Even though you can never refer to the separator bar in code and it does not have a Click event, you must still give it a unique name. Call your first separator bar mnuSep1, your second separator bar mnuSep2, and so on.

Creating a Menu—Step-by-Step

You are going to create a project with one form and a menu bar that contains these menu items:

```
File            Help
  Exit            About
```

STEP 1: Display the Menu Editor window (refer to Figure 5.2) by selecting *Menu Editor* from the *Tools* menu or clicking on the Menu Editor toolbar button (refer to Figure 5.1).

STEP 2: Type the Caption (&File) and Name (mnuFile) for the first menu (Figure 5.4).

STEP 3: Click on the *Next* button or press Enter; the text boxes will clear, and the name of your first menu appears in the menu list box (Figure 5.5).

STEP 4: Click on the Right arrow button, which sets the indentation level for a menu command.

Figure   5.4

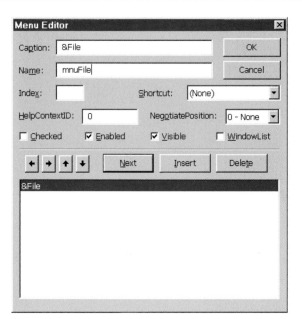

Type the Caption and Name for the first menu name.

Figure   5.5

After entering the first menu name, the text boxes clear and the Caption of the first menu appears in the menu list box.

STEP 5: Click in the Caption text box to set the focus and then type the Caption and the Name for the Exit menu command (Figure 5.6). Click on Next or press Enter.

*Type the Caption and Name for
the Exit menu command.*

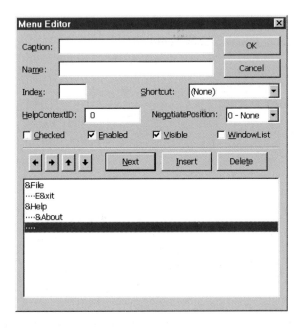

STEP 6: Click on the Left arrow (outdent) button to return to the previous level.

STEP 7: Repeat the steps to create the *Help* menu and the *About* command
indented below it (Figure 5.7).

*The completed menu appears in
the menu list box.*

Tip

You can rearrange the order of the
menus and menu commands.
Click on a name in the text box
and click on the up and down
arrows. Add or remove
items using the Insert and
Delete buttons.

STEP 8: Click OK when you are finished. The new menu will appear on your
form.

Coding for Menu Commands

After you create your form's menu bar, it will appear on the form in design time. Just select any menu command, and the control's Click event procedure will appear in the Code window where you can write the code. For example, in design time, open your form's *File* menu and choose *Exit*. The Code window will open with the mnuFileExit_Click procedure displayed (assuming you have followed the suggested naming conventions and named the Exit command mnuFileExit).

STEP 1: Code the procedure for the Exit by pulling down the menu and clicking on the word *Exit*. Type in the remark and the End statement.

STEP 2: Use a MsgBox statement in the procedure for the Click event of the *About* on the *Help* menu. The Message string should say "Programmed by" followed by your name (Figure 5.8).

F i g u r e 5 . 8

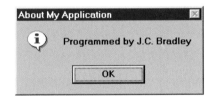

Display a message box for an About box.

Modifying a Menu

You can easily make changes to a menu bar you have created. With the form displaying in design time, display the Menu Editor window. Your complete menu will appear in the window.

You can click to select any menu item in the list box, and its information will appear in the top of the window where you can make modifications if desired. You can click on the Delete button to delete the selected item, or you can click Insert to insert a new blank line before the selection. To change the indentation level of any item, first select it and then click on the Left or Right arrow button. You can move an item up or down in the list by first selecting it and then clicking on the Up or Down arrow button.

Adding to Your Sample Menu

To add a new menu and commands to the previous sample project, display the menu editor. Click on &Help in the list box and click the *Insert* button, which inserts a blank line in the list box above &Help (Figure 5.9). Add the following items to your menu, one at a time. (You must insert a new line for each item, including the separator bar.) Make sure to click the right arrow to indent each menu item, including the separator bar. Separator bars must also be indented.

Tip

If you receive the message "Cannot use separator bar as menu name for this control," check your separator bar. It must be indented.

```
&Edit
....&Color
....-
....&Font
```

Click on the Insert button to insert a blank line above &Help.

Checked and Enabled

A menu command may contain a check mark beside it (**checked**), or it may be grayed (**disabled;** see Figure 5.10). An **enabled** menu item appears in black text and is available for selection, whereas the grayed out or disabled items are not available. A check mark placed next to a menu command usually indicates that the option is currently selected.

Menu commands can be disabled (grayed) or checked. A check mark usually indicates that the option is currently selected.

Check marks are often used on menu commands for options that can be toggled on and off. For example, for the option *Bold*, the check mark would indicate that Bold is currently selected. Choosing the *Bold* command a second time should remove the check mark and turn off the Bold option.

The check boxes in the menu editor for *Checked* and *Enabled* determine the beginning state for these options. By default, menu commands are unchecked and enabled. If you wish the menu item to be checked, then select the *Checked* check box. To make a menu item grayed (disabled), uncheck the *Enabled* check box.

Toggling Check Marks On and Off

If you create a menu option that can be turned on and off, you should include a check mark to indicate the current state. You can set the initial state of the check mark in the menu editor (refer to Figure 5.2). In code you can change its state by setting the menu item's Checked property.

```
Private Sub mnuFormatBold_Click()
    If mnuFormatBold.Checked = True Then
        mnuFormatBold.Checked = False
        txtChangeable.Font.Bold = False
    Else
        mnuFormatBold.Checked = True
        txtChangeable.Font.Bold = True
    End If
End Sub
```

Standards for Windows Menus

When you write applications that run under Windows, your programs should follow the Windows standards. You should always include keyboard access keys; if you include keyboard shortcuts (Ctrl + key), stick with the standard keys, such as Ctrl + P for printing. Also follow the Windows standards for placing the *File* menu on the left end of the menu bar and ending the menu with an *Exit* command; if you have a *Help* menu, it belongs at the right end of the menu bar.

Plan your menus so that they look like other Windows programs unless your goal is to confuse people.

Common Dialog Boxes

You can use a set of predefined standard dialog boxes in your projects for such tasks as specifying colors and fonts, printing, opening, and saving. The **common dialog** control, which is a custom control, allows your project to use the dialog boxes that are provided as part of the Windows environment.

To use the common dialog control, you first place a control on your form (Figure 5.11). You cannot change the size of the control, and its location doesn't matter, since it will be invisible when your program runs. In code, when you wish to display one of the standard dialog boxes, you will refer to properties and methods of the control. You don't need more than one common dialog control on your form even if you plan to use more than one type of dialog box; each time you refer to the control, you specify which dialog box you want.

Note: Windows determines the size of the dialog boxes; you cannot modify their size.

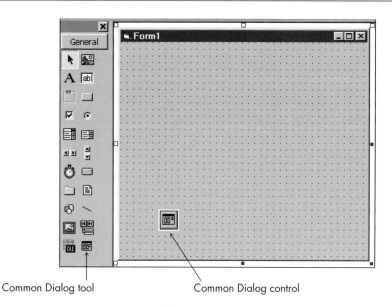

Use the common dialog tool in the toolbox to place a control on the form.

Common Dialog tool   Common Dialog control

The common dialog control may not appear in your toolbox. It is a custom control, and you must add it to Visual Basic before you can use it. Custom controls are stored in files with an extension of .ocx. To use the common dialog, you must have Comdlg32.ocx in your Windows\System folder. Open the *Project* menu and choose *Components*; you should see *Microsoft Common Dialog Control 6.0* in the list (Figure 5.12). Make sure that a check appears next to the item, and its tool should appear in your toolbox.

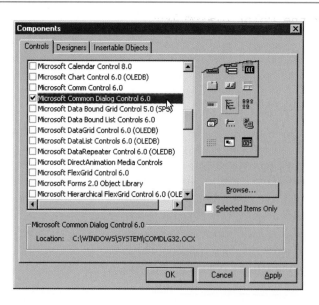

*Select the Common Dialog control in the **Components** dialog box to make the Common Dialog tool appear in the toolbox.*

When you name a Common Dialog control, use "dlg" as its three-character prefix.

Using a Common Dialog Box

After you place a Common Dialog control on your form, you can display any of its dialog boxes at run time. In code you specify which box you want with the Show method.

Show Method—General Form

```
Object.ShowMethod
```

The method can be one of the following:

Dialog Box	Method
Open	ShowOpen
Save As	ShowSave
Color	ShowColor
Font	ShowFont
Print	ShowPrint

For example, assume you have a common dialog control called dlgCommon and a menu item named mnuEditColor. You could display the *Color* dialog box in the Click event for the menu command:

```
Private Sub mnuEditColor_Click()
    'Display the Color Dialog Box

    dlgCommon.ShowColor 'Display the Color dialog box
End Sub
```

The Windows dialog box for choosing colors (Figure 5.13) will appear when the user clicks on the *Color* menu option.

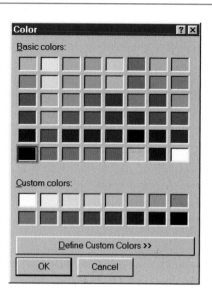

Using the Information from the Dialog Box

Displaying the *Color* dialog box doesn't make the color of anything change. You must take care of that in your program code. What *does* happen is that the user's choices are stored in properties that you can access. You can assign these values to the properties of controls in your project.

Color Dialog Box

The color selected by the user is stored in the Color property. You can assign this property to another object, such as a control or the form.

```
frmMain.BackColor = dlgCommon.Color
```

Because Basic executes the statements in sequence, you would first display the dialog box with the ShowColor method. (Execution then halts until the user responds to the dialog box.) Then you can use the Color property:

```
Private Sub mnuEditColor_Click()
    'Display the Color dialog box

    dlgCommon.ShowColor
    'Assign dialog box color to the form
    frmMain.BackColor = dlgCommon.Color
End Sub
```

When the *Color* dialog box displays, it shows black as the default color. If you want to initialize the box to show the form's currently selected color when it appears, you must set the control's Flags property to cdlCCRGBInit and set its Color property before showing the dialog box.

```
Private Sub mnuEditColor_Click()
    'Select the color and set initial color
```

```
With dlgCommon
     .Flags = cdlCCRGBInit          'Initialize the dialog box
     .Color = frmMain.BackColor     'Set initial color
     .ShowColor                     'Display dialog box
End With

'Assign dialog box color to the form
frmMain.BackColor = dlgCommon.Color     'Set color of form
End Sub
```

Font Dialog Box

Before you can use the `ShowFont` method, you must set the Flags property of the control. This coding step installs the fonts to appear in the list box. The value of the Flags property may be cdlCFScreenFonts, cdlCFPrinterFonts, or cdlCFBoth. If you forget to set the flags, an error will occur at run time that says "There are no fonts installed."

The Font properties for the common dialog control are different from those used for other controls. Instead of a group of properties for a Font object, each Font property is listed separately.

Font Object of Other Controls	Font Property of Common Dialog Control	Values
Font.Bold	FontBold	True or False (Boolean)
Font.Italic	FontItalic	True or False (Boolean)
Font.Name	FontName	System dependent
Font.Size	FontSize	Font dependent
Font.StrikeThrough	FontStrikeThru	True or False (Boolean)
Font.Underline	FontUnderline	True or False (Boolean)

Assign the FontName property before assigning the size and other attributes. The following code allows the user to change the font of a label.

```
Private Sub mnuEditFont_Click()
    'Display the Font dialog box

    With dlgCommon
        .Flags = cdlCFScreenFonts
        .ShowFont
    End With

    'Assign dialog box font to the label
    With lblEmployee.Font
        .Name = dlgCommon.FontName
        .Bold = dlgCommon.FontBold
    End With
End Sub
```

When the user clicks on the *Font* menu command, the *Font* dialog box appears on the screen (Figure 5.14).

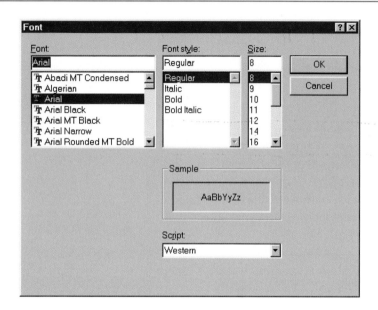

The Font *common dialog box.*

Setting Current Values

Before calling the common dialog box for colors or fonts, you should assign the existing values of the object properties that will be altered. This step will provide for the display of the current values in the dialog box. It also ensures that if the user selects the Cancel button, the property settings for the objects will remain unchanged.

```
Private Sub mnuEditFont_Click()
    'Display the Font common dialog box
    '  and make the changes in the label settings

    'Assign the current settings to the dialog box
    With dlgCommon
        .FontName = lblEmployee.Font.Name
        .FontBold = lblEmployee.Font.Bold
        .FontItalic = lblEmployee.Font.Italic
        .FontSize = lblEmployee.Font.Size
    End With
    'Set the method for Font dialog box
    With dlgCommon
        .Flags = cdlCFScreenFonts 'Specify screen fonts
        .ShowFont
    End With
```

```
        'Assign dialog box font to the label
        With lblEmployee.Font
                .Bold = dlgCommon.FontBold
                .Italic = dlgCommon.FontItalic
                .Name = dlgCommon.FontName
                .Size = dlgCommon.FontSize
        End With
End Sub
```

Writing General Procedures

Often you will encounter programming situations in which multiple procedures perform the same operation. This condition can occur when the user can select either a command button or a menu option to do the same thing. Rather than retyping the code, you can write reusable code in a **general procedure** and call it from both event procedures.

General procedures are also useful in breaking down large sections of code into smaller units that perform a specific task. By breaking down your calculations into smaller tasks, you simplify any maintenance that needs to be done in a program in the future. For example, bowling statistics for a league may require calculations for handicap and series total. If the method for calculating handicaps changes, wouldn't it be nice to have a procedure that calculates handicaps only instead of one that performs all the calculations?

Creating a New Sub Procedure

To add a new general procedure to a form:

STEP 1: Display the Code window for the form.
STEP 2: Select *Add Procedure* from the *Tools* menu.
STEP 3: Enter a name in the *Add Procedure* dialog box (Figure 5.15).

Figure 5.15

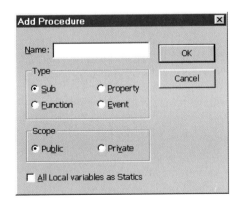

Use the **Add Procedure** dialog box to add a new general procedure to your form module.

STEP 4: Select *Private* for *Scope*. Choosing *Public* makes a procedure available from other project modules. *Note:* Leave the *Type* set to *Sub* for now.

STEP 5: Click OK.

In this example of a new general sub procedure, notice that the SelectColor sub procedure is not attached to any event.

```
Private Sub SelectColor()
    'Allow user to select a color

    dlgColor.ShowColor
End Sub
```

The coding of the new procedure is similar to the other procedures we have been coding, but is not yet attached to any event. Therefore, this code cannot be executed unless we specifically **call** the procedure from another procedure. To call a sub procedure, just give the procedure name, which in this case is SelectColor.

```
Private Sub cmdChangeMessage_Click()
    'Change the color of the message

    SelectColor
    lblMessage.ForeColor = dlgColor.Color
End Sub
```

```
Private Sub cmdChangeTitle_Click()
    'Change the color of the title

    SelectColor
    lblTitle.ForeColor = dlgColor.Color
End Sub
```

Passing Variables to Procedures

At times you may need to use the value of a variable in one procedure and also in a second procedure that is called from the first. In this situation you could declare the variable as module level, but that approach makes the variable visible to all other procedures. To keep the scope of a variable as narrow as possible, consider declaring the variable as local and passing it to any called procedures.

As an example, we will expand the capabilities of the previous SelectColor sub procedure to display the original color when the dialog box appears. Because the SelectColor procedure can be called from various locations, the original color must be passed to the procedure. Note that Visual Basic stores colors in Long Integer variables.

```
Private Sub SelectColor(lngIncomingColor As Long)
    'Allow user to select a color
```

```
    With dlgColor
        .Flags = cdlCCRGBInit              'Initialize the Color dialog box
        .Color = lngIncomingColor          'Set the initial color
        .ShowColor
    End With
End Sub
```

```
Private Sub cmdChangeMessage_Click()
    'Change the color of the message
    Dim lngOriginalColor As Long

    lngOriginalColor = lblMessage.ForeColor
    SelectColor lngOriginalColor
    lblMessage.ForeColor = dlgColor.Color
End Sub
```

```
Private Sub cmdChangeTitle_Click()
    'Change the color of the title
    Dim lngOriginalColor As Long

    lngOriginalColor = lblTitle.ForeColor
    SelectColor lngOriginalColor
    lblTitle.ForeColor = dlgColor.Color
End Sub
```

Notice that in this example the SelectColor procedure now has an argument inside the parentheses. This syntax specifies that when called, an argument must be supplied.

When a sub procedure definition names an argument, any call to that procedure must supply the argument. In addition, the argument value must be the same data type in both locations. Notice that in the two calling procedures (cmdChangeMessage_Click and cmdChangeTitle_Click), the variable lngOriginalColor is declared as a Long Integer.

Another important point is that the *name* of the argument does not have to be the same in both locations. The ShowColor sub procedure will take whatever Long Integer value it is passed and refer to it as lngIncomingColor inside the procedure.

You may specify multiple arguments in both the sub procedure header and the call to the procedure. The number of arguments, their sequence, and their data types must match in both locations! You will see some examples of multiple arguments in the sections that follow.

Passing Arguments ByVal or ByRef

When you pass a value to a procedure you may pass it **ByVal** or **ByRef** (for by value or by reference). The ByVal sends a *copy* of the argument's value to the procedure so that the procedure cannot alter the original value. ByRef sends a reference indicating where the value is stored in memory, allowing the called procedure to actually change the argument's original value. You can specify how you want to pass the argument by using the `ByVal` or `ByRef` keyword before the argument. If you don't specify `ByVal` or `ByRef`, arguments are passed by reference.

```
Private Sub SelectColor(ByVal lngIncomingColor As Long)
```

Function Procedures versus Sub Procedures

When you insert a new procedure, recall that you can choose to create a sub procedure or a function procedure (refer to Figure 5.15). Let's consider the difference between these two types of procedures. A **sub procedure** is a procedure that performs actions. A **function procedure** may perform an action, but it also returns a value (the **return value**) to the point from which it was called.

Writing Function Procedures

In the past we have used predefined functions, such as the `FormatNumber` function and the `Val` function. The `FormatNumber` function returns the formatted characters; the `Val` function returns the numeric value of the named argument.

As a programmer, you may need to calculate a value that will be needed in several different procedures or programs. You can write your own function that will calculate a value and call the function from the locations where it is needed. As an example we will create a function procedure called `Commission`, which calculates and returns a salesperson's commission.

To create the new `Commission` function, follow the same steps as for creating a sub procedure. In the *Add Procedure* dialog box (refer to Figure 5.15), select the *Function* option button prior to selecting the OK command button.

When you insert a function procedure named `Commission`, your new Code window contains these statements:

```
Private Function Commission()

End Function
```

Notice that this procedure looks just like a sub procedure except that the word `Function` replaces the word `Sub` on both the first line and the last line.

Remember that functions also have arguments. You supply arguments to a function when you call the function by placing a value or values inside the parentheses. You can choose to pass the arguments `ByVal` or `ByRef`.

When you write a function, you declare the argument(s) that the function needs. You give each argument an identifier and a data type. The name that you give an argument in the function procedure header is the identifier that you will use inside the function to refer to the value of the argument.

Examples

```
Private Function Commission(ByVal curSalesAmount As Currency)
Private Function Payment(curRate As Currency, curTime As Currency, _
      curAmount As Currency)
```

In the function procedure the argument list you enter establishes the number of arguments, their type, and their sequence. When using multiple arguments, the sequence of the arguments is critical, just as when you use the predefined Visual Basic functions.

The main difference between coding a function procedure and coding a sub procedure is that in a function procedure you must set up the return value. This return value is placed in a variable that Visual Basic names with the same name as the function name. In the first of the preceding examples, the variable name is Commission. *Note:* Somewhere in the function, you *must* set the function name to a value.

You can also specify the data type of the return value by adding the As clause after the function name. Because the data type of the return value in this example is Currency, the function name has been changed to curCommission.

Writing a Commission Function

Code this function procedure to calculate a currency commission.

```
Private Function curCommission(ByVal curSalesAmount As Currency) As Currency
    'Calculate the sales commission

    If curSalesAmount < 1000 Then
        curCommission = 0
    ElseIf curSalesAmount <= 2000 Then
        curCommission = 0.15 * curSalesAmount
    Else
        curCommission = 0.2 * curSalesAmount
    End If
End Function
```

Calling the Commission Function

In another procedure in the project, you can call your function by using it in an expression.

```
Dim curSales as Currency
If IsNumeric(txtSales.Text) Then
    curSales = Val(txtSales.Text)
    lblCommission.Caption = curCommission(curSales)
End If
```

Notice in the preceding example that the argument named in the function call does not have the same name as the argument named in the function definition. When the function is called, a copy of curSales is passed to the function and is assigned to the named argument, in this case curSalesAmount. As the calculations are done (inside the function), for every reference to curSalesAmount, the value of curSales is actually used.

Writing a Function with Multiple Arguments

In creating a function with multiple arguments such as a Payment function, the list of arguments is enclosed within the parentheses. The following example indicates that three arguments are needed in the call: The first argument is the interest rate, the second is the time, and the third is the loan amount. All three argument values will have a data type of currency, and the return value will be currency. Look carefully at the following formula and notice how the identifiers in the parentheses are used.

```
Private Function curPayment(curRate As Currency, curTime As Currency, _
    curAmt As Currency) As Currency
    'Calculate the monthly payment on an amortized loan

    'Set the return value of the function
    curPayment = curAmt * (1 + curRate/12) ^ (curTime * 12)
End Function
```

Calling a Function with Multiple Arguments

To call this function from another procedure, use these statements:

```
curRate = Val(txtRate.Text)
curTime = Val(txtTime.Text)
curAmount = Val(txtAmount.Text)
lblPayment.Caption = curPayment(curRate, curTime, curAmount)
```

You can format the result, as well as pass the Val of the text boxes, by nesting functions:

```
lblPayment.Caption = FormatCurrency(curPayment(Val(txtRate.Text), _
    Val(txtTime.Text), Val(txtAmount.Text)))
```

Reusing Procedures

The function procedure in this example can be used for more than one situation. We use the curCalculateBonus function to calculate a gift certificate bonus amount for a shopper and also to calculate a salesperson's commission. The amount and rate values are passed to the function procedure from the appropriate event procedures.

Notice the general sub procedure used to clear the values on the interface.

```
'Project:              Chapter 5 reusable code example
'Programmer:           Theresa Berry
'Date:                 July 1999
'Folder:               CH05Shoppers
'Purpose:              This program uses menus, a reusable general
'                      sub procedure, and a function procedure.

Option Explicit
```

```
Private Sub mnuCalculateBonus_Click()
    'Calculate and display the amount of the
    'bonus earned by the shopper.

    Dim curPurchase           As Currency
    Dim curBonus              As Currency
    Const curBonusPercent     As Currency = 0.01

    curPurchase = Val(txtPurchaseAmount)
    If curPurchase > 0 Then
        curBonus = curCalculateBonus(curPurchase, curBonusPercent) 'Call _
            function procedure
        MsgBox txtName.Text & " has earned " & FormatCurrency(curBonus) & _
            " in gift certificates", vbInformation, "Congratulations"
        txtName.SetFocus
    Else
        MsgBox "You must input a value for the amount of purchase", _
            vbOKOnly, "Input Requested"
        With txtPurchaseAmount
            .Text = ""
            .SetFocus
        End With
    End If
End Sub
```

```
Private Sub mnuCalculateCommission_Click()
    'Calculate and display the salesperson's commission

    Dim curPurchase           As Currency
    Dim curCommission         As Currency
    Const curCommissionLimit  As Currency = 500
    Const curCommissionPercent  As Currency = 0.05

    curPurchase = Val(txtPurchaseAmount)
    If curPurchase >= curCommissionLimit Then
        curCommission = curCalculateBonus(curPurchase, curCommissionPercent) _
            'Call function procedure
        MsgBox "Salesman " & txtSalespersonID.Text & " earns " & _
            FormatCurrency(curCommission) & " in commission for this sale.", _
            vbInformation, "Congratulations"
        txtName.SetFocus
    Else
        MsgBox "No commission earned on this sale.", vbInformation, "Sorry"
    End If
End Sub
```

```
Private Sub mnuEditClear_Click()
    'Call the Clear procedure

    Clear                          'Call the sub procedure
End Sub
```

```
Private Function curCalculateBonus(curAmount As Currency, curRate As Currency) _
    As Currency
    'Calculate the amount of bonus earned based on the
    'sale amount and the percentage rate.

    curCalculateBonus = curAmount * curRate
End Function

Private Sub Clear()
    'Clear the text boxes on the form.

    txtName.Text = ""
    txtPurchaseAmount = ""
    txtSalespersonID = ""
    txtName.SetFocus
End Sub
```

Breaking Calculations into Smaller Units

A project with many calculation can be easier to understand and to write if you break the calculations into small units. In this example that calculates bowling statistics, separate function procedures calculate the average, handicap, and series total, and find the high game.

```
'Project:                   Chapter 5 Bowling Example
'Programmer:                A. Millspaugh
'Date:                      October 1999
'Folder:                    Ch05Bowling
'Description:               This project calculates bowling statistics using
'                           multiple function procedures

Option Explicit

Private Sub mnuFileCalc_Click()
    'Calculate individual and summary info

    Dim curAverage             As Currency
    Dim curHandicap            As Currency
    Dim intSeries              As Integer
    Dim strHighGame            As String
    Dim intGame1               As Integer
    Dim intGame2               As Integer
    Dim intGame3               As Integer
```

```vb
    If IsNumeric(txtScore1.Text) And
        IsNumeric(txtScore2.Text) And
        IsNumeric(txtScore3.Text) Then
            intGame1 = Val(txtScore1.Text)
            intGame2 = Val(txtScore2.Text)
            intGame3 = Val(txtScore3.Text)

            'Perform all calculations
            curAverage = curFindAverage(intGame1, intGame2, intGame3)
            intSeries = intFindSeries(intGame1, intGame2, intGame3)
            strHighGame = strFindHighGame(intGame1, intGame2, intGame3)
            curHandicap = curFindHandicap(curAverage)

            lblAverage.Caption = FormatNumber(curAverage, 1)
            lblHighGame.Caption = strHighGame
            lblSeries.Caption = intSeries
            lblHandicap.Caption = FormatNumber(curHandicap, 1)
    Else
            MsgBox "Please Enter three scores", vbOKOnly, "Missing Data"
    End If
End Sub
```

```vb
Public Function curFindAverage(intScore1 As Integer, _
    intScore2 As Integer, intScore3 As Integer) As Currency
    'Return the average of three games

    curFindAverage = (intScore1 + intScore2 + intScore3)/3
End Function
```

```vb
Private Function curFindHandicap(curAverage As Currency) As Currency
    'Calculate Handicap

    curFindHandicap = (200 - curAverage) * 0.8
End Function
```

```vb
Private Function intFindSeries(intGame1 As Integer, _
    intGame2 As Integer, intGame3 As Integer) As Integer
    'Calculate the series total

    intFindSeries = intGame1 + intGame2 + intGame3
End Function
```

```vb
Private Function strFindHighGame(intGame1 As Integer, _
    intGame2 As Integer, intGame3 As Integer) As String
    'Find the highest game in the series
```

```
If (intGame1 > intGame2) Then
    If (intGame1 > intGame3) Then
        strFindHighGame = "1"
    Else
        strFindHighGame = "3"
    End If
ElseIf (intGame2 > intGame3) Then
    strFindHighGame = "2"
Else
    strFindHighGame = "3"
End If
End Function
```

Feedback 5.1

You need to write a procedure to calculate and return the average of three integer values.

1. Should you write a sub procedure or a function procedure?
2. Write the first line of the procedure.
3. Write the calculation.
4. How is the calculated average passed back to the calling procedure?

Your Hands-On Programming Example

Modify the hands-on programming example from Chapter 4 by replacing some of the command buttons with menus. Use a function procedure to calculate the sales tax. You will need to move the constant for tax rate to the module level.

The project for R 'n R—for Reading 'n Refreshment calculates the amount due for individual orders and maintains accumulated totals for a summary. Have a check box for takeout items, which are taxable (8 percent); all other orders are nontaxable. Include option buttons for the five coffee selections—Cappuccino, Espresso, Latte, Iced Latte, and Iced Cappuccino. The prices for each will be assigned using these constants:

Cappuccino	2.00
Espresso	2.25
Latte	1.75
Iced (either)	2.50

Use a command button for Calculate Selection, which will calculate and display the amount due for each item. A button for Clear for Next Item will clear the selections and amount for the single item. Additional labels in a separate frame will maintain the summary information for the current order to include subtotal, tax, and total.

The *Next Order* menu will clear the bill for the current customer and add to the totals for the summary. The menu for *Summary* should display the total of all orders, the average sale amount per customer, and the number of customers in a message box.

The *Edit* menu contains options that duplicate the Calculate and Clear button. The Font and Color options change the contents of the subtotal, tax, and total labels.

The *About* selection on the *Help* menu will display a message box with information about the programmer.

<pre>
File   Edit   Help
   New Order   Calculate Selection   About
   Summary   Clear Item
   Exit   _____

                            Font
                            Color
</pre>

Planning the Project

Sketch a form (Figure 5.16), which your users sign as meeting their needs.

Figure 5.16

A sketch of the form for the hands-on programming example.

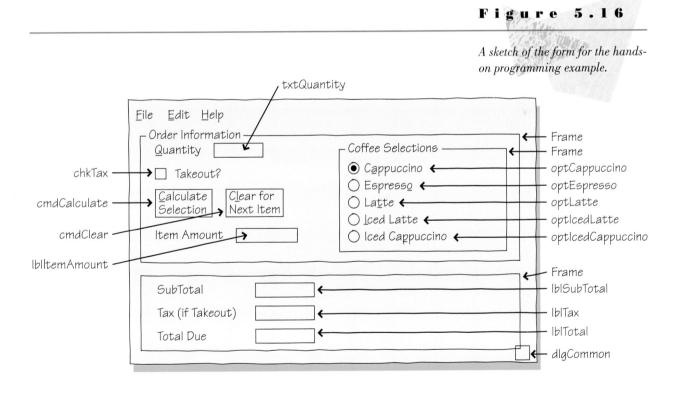

Plan the Objects and Properties

Plan the property settings for the form and each of the controls.

Object	Property	Setting
frmBilling	Name	frmBilling
	Caption	R 'n R for Reading 'n Refreshment
Frame1	Caption	Order Information
Frame2	Caption	Coffee Selections
Frame3	Caption	(blank)
optCappuccino	Name	optCappuccino
	Caption	C&appuccino
	Value	True
optEspresso	Name	optEspresso
	Caption	Espress&o
optLatte	Name	optLatte
	Caption	La&tte
optIcedLatte	Name	optIcedLatte
	Caption	&Iced Latte
optIcedCappuccino	Name	optIcedCappuccino
	Caption	Iced Ca&ppuccino
Label1	Caption	&Quantity
txtQuantity	Name	txtQuantity
	Text	(blank)
chkTax	Name	chkTax
	Caption	Takeout ?
Label2	Caption	Item Amount
Label3	Caption	SubTotal
Label4	Caption	Tax (if Takeout)
Label5	Caption	Total Due
lblItemAmount	Name	lblItemAmount
	Caption	(blank)
	BorderStyle	1 - FixedSingle
lblSubTotal	Name	lblSubTotal
	Caption	(blank)
	BorderStyle	1 - Fixed Single
lblTax	Name	lblTax
	Caption	(blank)
	BorderStyle	1 - Fixed Single

(continued)

Object	Property	Setting
lblTotal	Name	lblTotal
	Caption	(blank)
	BorderStyle	1 - Fixed Single
cmdCalculate	Name	cmdCalculate
	Caption	&Calculate Selection
	Default	True
cmdClear	Name	cmdClear
	Caption	C&lear for Next Item
	Cancel	True
mnuFile	Name	mnuFile
	Caption	&File
mnuFileNew	Name	mnuFileNew
	Caption	&New Order
mnuFileSummary	Name	mnuFileSummary
	Caption	&Summary
mnuFileExit	Name	mnuFileExit
	Caption	E&xit
mnuEdit	Name	mnuEdit
	Caption	&Edit
mnuEditCalc	Name	mnuEditCalc
	Caption	Calculate &Selection
mnuEditClear	Name	mnuEditClear
	Caption	C&lear Item
mnuSep1	Name	mnuSep1
	Caption	-
mnuEditFont	Name	mnuEditFont
	Caption	&Font
mnuEditColor	Name	mnuEditColor
	Caption	&Color
mnuHelp	Name	mnuHelp
	Caption	&Help
mnuHelpAbout	Name	mnuHelpAbout
	Caption	&About
dlgCommon	Name	dlgCommon

Plan the Event Procedures

You need to plan the actions for the command buttons and the actions of the menu commands.

Object	Procedure	Action
cmdCalculate	Click	Determine price per cup.
		Multiply price by quantity.
		Call tax procedure if needed.
		Add quantity to item total.
		Display the values.
cmdClear	Click	Clear the coffee selections.
		Clear the quantity and the item price.
		Disable the takeout check box.
		Set the focus to the quantity.
mnuFileNew	Click	Clear the previous order.
		Accumulate total and count.
		Set subtotal and total to 0.
mnuFileSummary	Click	Display the average.
		Display total sales.
		Display the number of customers.
mnuFileExit	Click	Terminate the project.
mnuEditCalc	Click	Call calculate command event.
mnuEditClear	Click	Call clear command event.
curFindTax	(call)	Calculate the sales tax.

Write the Project

Follow the sketch in Figure 5.16 to create the form. Figure 5.17 shows the completed form.

● Set the properties of each object according to your plan.

● Write the code. Working from the pseudocode, write each event procedure.

● When you complete the code, use a variety of data to thoroughly test the project.

The Project Coding Solution

```
'Project Name:        Billing
'Programmer:          A. Millspaugh
'Date:                July 1999
'Description:         This project calculates the
'                     amount due based on the customer selection
'                     and accumulates summary data for the day.
'                     The project incorporates menus and common
'                     dialog boxes.
'                     The common dialog box allows the user to change
'                     the color and font.
'Folder:              Ch0501
```

Figure 5.17

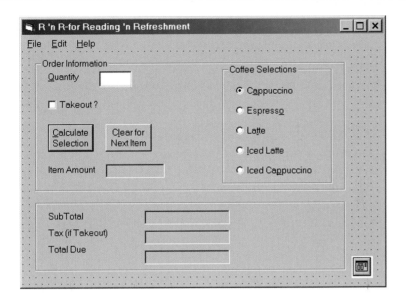

The form for the hands-on programming example.

```
Option Explicit

Dim mcurSubtotal               As Currency
Dim mcurTotal                  As Currency
Dim mcurGrandTotal             As Currency
Dim mintCustomerCount          As Integer
Const mcurTaxRate              As Currency = 0.08
```

```
Private Sub cmdCalculate_Click()
    'Calculate and display the current amounts, add to totals
    Dim curPrice               As Currency
    Dim intQuantity            As Integer
    Dim curTax                 As Currency
    Dim curItemAmount          As Currency
    Const curCappuccinoPrice   As Currency = 2
    Const curEspressoPrice     As Currency = 2.25
    Const curLattePrice        As Currency = 1.75
    Const curIcedPrice         As Currency = 2.5

    'Find the price
    If optCappuccino.Value = True Then
        curPrice = curCappuccinoPrice
    ElseIf optEspresso.Value = True Then
        curPrice = curEspressoPrice
    ElseIf optLatte.Value = True Then
        curPrice = curLattePrice
    ElseIf optIcedCappuccino.Value = True Or _
        optIcedLatte.Value = True Then
        curPrice = curIcedPrice
    Else
        MsgBox "Please Make Drink Selection", vbOKOnly, "Oops"
    End If
```

```vb
        'Add the price times quantity to price so far
        If IsNumeric(txtQuantity.Text) Then
            intQuantity = Val(txtQuantity.Text)
            curItemAmount = curPrice * intQuantity
            mcurSubtotal = mcurSubtotal + curItemAmount
            If chkTax.Value = Checked Then
                curTax = curFindTax(mcurSubtotal) 'Call a function procedure
            End If
            mcurTotal = mcurSubtotal + curTax
            lblItemAmount.Caption = FormatCurrency(curItemAmount)
            lblSubTotal.Caption = FormatCurrency(mcurSubtotal)
            lblTax.Caption = FormatNumber(curTax)
            lblTotal.Caption = FormatCurrency(mcurTotal)
        Else
            MsgBox "Quantity must contain a number", vbExclamation, "Missing Data"
            txtQuantity.SetFocus
        End If
End Sub


Private Sub cmdClear_Click()
    'Clear appropriate controls

    If mcurSubtotal <> 0 Then        'User should not be able to click if not yet
                                     'calculated
        optCappuccino.Value = True  'Make first button selected to begin
        optEspresso.Value = False
        optLatte.Value = False
        optIcedLatte.Value = False
        optIcedCappuccino.Value = False
        lblItemAmount.Caption = ""
        chkTax.Enabled = False       'Allow change for new order only
        With txtQuantity
            .Text = ""
            .SetFocus
        End With
    Else
        MsgBox "No New Order to Clear", vbExclamation, "Customer Order"
    End If
End Sub


Private Sub mnuEditCalc_Click()
    'Call the Calculate event

    cmdCalculate_Click
End Sub
```

```
Private Sub mnuEditClear_Click()
    'Call the Clear command event

    cmdClear_Click
End Sub
```

```
Private Sub mnuEditColor_Click()
    'Change the color of the total labels

    With dlgCommon
        .Flags = cdlCCRGBInit        'Set up initial color
        .Color = lblSubTotal.ForeColor
        .ShowColor
        lblSubTotal.ForeColor = .Color
        lblTax.ForeColor = .Color
        lblTotal.ForeColor = .Color
End Sub
```

```
Private Sub mnuEditFont_Click()
    'Change the font name for the subtotal labels

    With dlgCommon
        .Flags = cdlCFScreenFonts   'Set up Font dialog box fonts
        .ShowFont
        lblSubTotal.Font.Name = .FontName
        lblTax.Font.Name = .FontName
        lblTotal.Font.Name = .FontName
    End With
End Sub
```

```
Private Sub mnuFileExit_Click()
    'Terminate the project

    End
End Sub
```

```
Private Sub mnuFileNew_Click()
    'Clear the current order and add to totals

    cmdClear_Click
    lblSubTotal.Caption = ""
    lblTax.Caption = ""
    lblTotal.Caption = ""
```

```vb
    'Add to Totals
    If mcurSubtotal <> 0 Then        'Should not be able to add to counts if no
                                     'new order/customer. Prevents accidental
                                     'clicking.
        mcurGrandTotal = mcurGrandTotal + mcurTotal
        mcurSubtotal = 0
        mcurTotal = 0                'Reset for next customer
        mintCustomerCount = mintCustomerCount + 1
    End If

    'Clear appropriate display items and enable check box
    With chkTax
        .Enabled = True
        .Value = False
    End With
End Sub
```

```vb
Private Sub mnuFileSummary_Click()
    'Calculate the average and display the totals

    Dim curAverage                As Currency
    Dim strMessageString          As String
    Dim strFormattedAvg           As String

    If mintCustomerCount > 0 Then
        If mcurTotal <> 0 Then
            mnuFileNew_Click         'Make sure last order is counted
        End If
        curAverage = mcurGrandTotal / mintCustomerCount

        'Format the numbers
        strFormattedAvg = FormatCurrency(curAverage)
        'Concatenate the message string
        strMessageString = "Number Orders: " & mintCustomerCount & vbCr & _
            "Average Sale: " & strFormattedAvg
        MsgBox strMessageString, vbInformation, "Coffee Sales Summary"
    Else
        MsgBox "No data to summarize", vbExclamation, "Coffee Sales Summary"
    End If
End Sub
```

```vb
Private Sub mnuHelpAbout_Click()
    'Display a message box about the program

    MsgBox "R 'n R Billing" & vbCrLf & vbCrLf _
        & "Programmed by A Millspaugh", vbOKOnly, "About R 'n R Billing"
End Sub
```

```
Private Function curFindTax(curAmount As Currency) As Currency
    'Calculate the sales tax

    curFindTax = curAmount * mcurTaxRate
End Function
```

Programming Hints

Creating Executable Files

You can convert your project into an **executable file** that can be run from the Windows desktop. The resulting .exe file contains the information from all your project's files, including the form files and the modules. The .exe file will run much faster than the project runs in the VB environment.

After you create an .exe file, the original project files are still intact and can be used to make any modifications. Any time you make changes in the original project files, you must re-create the .exe file to incorporate the changes.

To create the .exe file, select the *Make . . .* command from the *File* menu. The *Make . . .* menu choice displays the name of the current project. Choose *Make Chap5Billing* from the *File* menu and the *Make Project* dialog box appears (Figure 5.18).

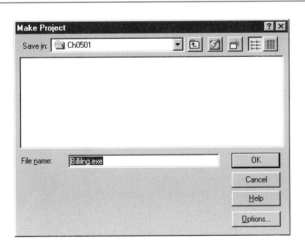

Use the Make Project dialog box to create an executable version of your project.

You will choose the location and name for your .exe file. You can also set properties for your project by clicking on the Options button. In the *Project Properties* dialog box (Figure 5.19), you can specify the version number, company name, and an icon for your file.

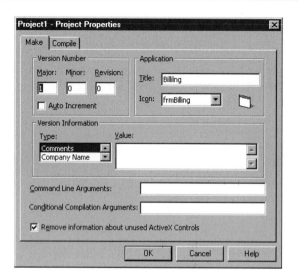

The Project Properties *dialog box allows you to specify version information, a company name, and an icon for your .exe file.*

S u m m a r y

1. The Visual Basic menu editor enables you to create menus, menu commands, and submenus, each with keyboard access keys.
2. The Caption and Name properties are required for each menu item.
3. In the menu editor, you can set and modify the order and level of menu items and the initial settings of the Enabled and Checked properties.
4. Each menu command has a Click event. The code to handle selection of a menu command belongs in the command's Click event procedure.
5. Common dialog boxes allow Visual Basic programs to display the predefined Windows dialog boxes for *Print, Open, Save, Fonts,* and *Colors.* These dialog boxes are part of the operating environment; therefore, it is an unnecessary duplication of effort to have each programmer re-create them.
6. The programmer can write reusable code in general procedures. These procedures may be sub procedures or sub functions and may be called from any other procedure in the form module.
7. Both sub procedures and sub functions can perform an action. However, sub functions return a value and sub procedures do not. The value returned by a sub function has a data type.
8. Arguments can be passed `ByRef` (the default) or `ByVal`. `ByRef` passes a reference to the actual data item; `ByVal` passes a copy of the data.
9. It is easy to convert a project to an .exe file that can be run from the Windows environment. Use the *Make Project* command on the *File* menu.

Key Terms

ByRef   *189*

ByVal   *189*

call (procedure call)   *188*

checked   *180*

common dialog   *181*

disabled   *180*

enabled   *180*

executable file   *205*

function procedure   *190*

general procedure   *187*

menu   *174*

return value   *190*

separator bar   *176*

sub procedure   *190*

submenu   *175*

Review Questions

1. Explain the difference between a menu and a submenu.
2. How can the user know if a menu command contains a submenu?
3. What is a separator bar and how is it created?
4. Explain the purpose of the Name and Caption properties of menu items.
5. What does the term *common dialog box* mean?
6. Name at least three types of common dialog boxes.
7. Why would you need procedures that are not attached to an event?
8. Code the necessary statements to produce a color dialog box and use it to change the background color of a form.
9. Explain the difference between a sub procedure and a function procedure.
10. What is a *return value*? How can it be used?
11. Explain the differences between ByRef and ByVal. When would each be used?
12. Give the steps required to convert a project into an .exe file.

Programming Exercises

5.1 Modify project 4.6 (Piecework Pay) to replace command buttons with menus and add a function procedure.

This project will input the number of pieces and calculate the pay for multiple employees. It also must display a summary of the total number of pieces, the total pay, and the average pay for all employees.

Menu: The menu bar must have these commands:

File	Edit	Help
Calc Pay	Clear	About
Summary	_____	
Exit	Font	
	Color	

Piecework workers are paid by the piece. Workers who produce a greater quantity of output may be paid at a higher rate.

Use text boxes to obtain the name and the number of pieces completed. The *Calc Pay* menu command calculates and displays the dollar amount earned. The *Summary* menu command displays the total number of pieces, the total pay, and the average pay per person in a message box. The *Clear* menu choice clears the name and the number of pieces for the current employee and resets the focus.

The *Color* and *Font* commands should change the color and font of the information displayed in the amount earned label.

Use a message box to display your name for the *About* option on the *Help* menu.

Use a function procedure to find the pay rate and return a value to the proper event procedure.

Pieces Completed	Price Paid per Piece for All Pieces
1 to 199	.50
200 to 399	.55
400 to 599	.60
600 or more	.65

5.2　Redo the checking account programming exercises from Chapter 4 (4.3, 4.4, and 4.5), using menus and sub procedures.
Menu:

```
File                    Edit                 Help
   Transaction             Clear                About
   Summary                 _____
   Exit                    Font
                           Color
```

Form: Use option buttons to indicate the type of transaction—deposit, check, or service charge. A text box will allow the user to enter the amount of the transaction. Display the balance in a label.

Include validation that displays a message box if the amount of the transaction is a negative number. If there is not enough money to cover a check, display a message box with the message "Insufficient Funds." Do not pay the check, but deduct a service charge of $10.

Use function procedures for deposits, checks, and service charges. The deposit function adds the deposit to the balance; the check function subtracts the transaction amount from the balance; the service charge function subtracts $10 from the balance.

The *Summary* menu command displays the total number of deposits and the dollar amount of deposits, the number of checks, and the dollar amount of the checks in a message box.

The *Clear* menu command clears the option buttons and the amount and resets the focus.

The *Color* and *Font* menu commands change the color and font of the information displayed in the balance label.

Use a message box to display your name as the programmer for the *About* option on the *Help* menu.

5.3 A salesperson earns a weekly base salary plus a commission when sales are at or above quota. Create a project that allows the user to input the weekly sales and the salesperson name, calculates the commission, and displays summary information.

Form: The form will have text boxes for the salesperson name and his or her weekly sales.

Menu:

```
File                Edit                Help
   Pay                 Clear               About
   Summary             _____
   Exit                Font
                       Color
```

Use constants to establish the base pay, the quota, and the commission rate.

The *Pay* menu command calculates and displays in labels the commission and the total pay for that person. However, if there is no commission, do not display the commission amount (do not display a zero-commission amount).

Use a function procedure to calculate the commission. The function must compare sales to the quota. When the sales are equal to or greater than the quota, calculate the commission by multiplying sales by the commission rate.

Each salesperson receives the base pay plus the commission (if one has been earned). Format the dollar amounts to two decimal places; do not display a dollar sign.

The *Summary* menu command displays a message box containing total sales, total commissions, and total pay for all salespersons. Display the numbers with two decimal places and dollar signs.

The *Clear* menu command clears the name, sales, and pay for the current employee and then resets the focus.

The *Color* and *Font* menu commands should change the color and font of the information displayed in the amount earned label.

Use a message box to display your name as programmer for the *About* option on the *Help* menu.

Test Data: Quota = 1000; Commission rate = .15; and Base pay = 250.

Name	Sales
Sandy Smug	1,000.00
Sam Sadness	999.99
Joe Whiz	2,000.00

Totals should be:

Sales	$3,999.99
Commissions	450.00
Pay	1,200.00

5.4   The local library has a summer reading program to encourage reading. The staff keeps a chart with readers' names and bonus points earned. Create a project using a menu and a function procedure that will determine the bonus points.
Menu:

File	Edit	Help
Points	Clear	About
Summary	_____	
Exit	Font	
	Color	

Form: Use text boxes to obtain the reader's name and the number of books read. Use a label to display the number of bonus points.

The *Points* menu command should call a function procedure to calculate the points using this schedule: the first three books are worth 10 points each. The next three books are worth 15 points each. All books over six are worth 20 points each.

The *Summary* menu command displays the average number of books read for all readers that session.

The *Clear* menu command clears the name, the number of books read, and the bonus points and then resets the focus.

The *Color* and *Font* menu commands change the color and font of the information displayed in the bonus points label.

Use a message box to display your name as programmer for the *About* option on the *Help* menu.

5.5   Modify project 2.2 (the flag viewer) to use a menu instead of option buttons, check boxes, and command buttons. Include check marks next to the name of the currently selected country and next to the selected display options.
Menu:

File	Country	Display
Print	United States	Title
Exit	Canada	Country Name
	Japan	Programmer
	Mexico	

CASE STUDIES

Modify the case study from Chapter 4, using menus and a function procedure. Refer to Chapter 4 for project specifications.

VB Mail Order

(Do not calculate shipping and handling on individual items—wait until the order is complete.)

Use a function procedure to calculate the shipping and handling based on the weight for an entire order.

Menu:

File	Edit	Help
Print Form	Next Item	About
Summary	Next Order	
Exit	————	
	Font	
	Color	

Modify the case study project from Chapter 4, using menus and a function procedure. Refer to Chapter 4 for project specifications.

VB Auto Center

Use a function procedure to calculate the sales tax.

Menu:

File	Edit	Help
Print Form	Calculate	About
Exit	Clear	
	————	
	Font	
	Color	

Video Bonanza

Modify the case study from Chapter 4 to use menus and a function procedure. Refer to Chapter 4 for project specifications.

Use a function procedure to calculate the rental fee based on the type of video.

The *Help* menu *About* option should display a message box with information about the program and the programmer. The *Color* option should change the background color of the form.

Menu:

```
File              Edit              Help
    Print Form        Next Item         About
    Summary           Order Complete
    Exit              _____
                      Font
                      Color
```

Optional extra: Set shortcut option for the menu commands: Ctrl+P for *Print Form* and Ctrl+X for *Exit.*

Very Very Boards

Modify your project from Chapter 4 to add a menu and a function procedure. Refer to Chapter 4 for the project specifications.

Use a function procedure to calculate the price of shirts; display the *About* box in a message box.

Allow the user to change the font size and font color of the labels that display the company slogan.

Include keyboard shortcuts for the menu commands.

Menu:

```
File          Sale                    Display          Help
    Summary       Add to Order            Font Size        About
    Print Form    Display Order Total     Font Color
    Exit          Begin New Order         _____
                                          Slogan
                                          Logo
```

The slogan and logo:

Make up a slogan for the company, such as "We're Number One" or "The Best in Boards." The logo should be a graphic that you can create with shape controls, an icon, any graphic you have available, or a graphic you create yourself with a draw or paint program. (Make sure to include the graphic on your project diskette.)

The *Slogan* and *Logo* menu choices must toggle and display a check mark when selected. For example, when the slogan is displayed, the *Slogan* menu command is checked. If the user selects the *Slogan* command again, hide the slogan and uncheck the menu command. The *Slogan* and *Logo* commands operate independently; that is, the user may select either, both, or neither item.

When the project begins, the slogan and logo must both be displayed and their menu commands appear checked.

6

Multiple Forms

At the completion of this chapter, you will be able to . . .

1. Create a project with multiple forms.

2. Use the Show and Hide methods to display and hide forms.

3. Create procedures that are accessible from multiple form modules.

4. Differentiate between variables that are global to a project and those visible only to a form.

5. Create an *About box* using a form.

6. Add a splash screen to your project.

7. Set the startup form or Sub Main to start project execution.

Multiple Forms

All the projects that you have created up to now have operated from a single form. It has probably occurred to you that the project could appear more professional if you could use different windows for different types of information. Consider the example in Chapter 5 in which summary information is displayed in a message box when the user presses the Summary button. You have very little control over the appearance of the message box. The summary information could be displayed in a much nicer format in a new window with identifying labels. Another window in Visual Basic is actually another form.

The first form a project displays is called the ***startup form***. You can add more forms to the project and display them as needed.

Creating New Forms

To add a new form to a project, select *Add Form* from the *Project* menu or click on the Form button on the toolbar (Figure 6.1). In the *Add Form* dialog box (Figure 6.2), you can select from a new form or an existing form. Notice in Figure 6.2 that VB provides several types of new forms that you can use; you will learn about some of these later in the chapter. For now, choose *Form* to add a regular new form.

F i g u r e   6 . 1

Add a new form to a project by clicking on the Add Form toolbar button.

F i g u r e   6 . 2

Select the type of new form you want in the Add Form dialog box.

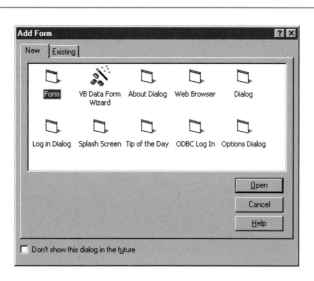

Steps for adding a new form to a project:

STEP 1: Select *Add Form* from the *Project* menu.
STEP 2: In the dialog box, select the *New* tab and indicate the type of form you want (Form, About, Splash).
STEP 3: Click on *Open*.

The new form will display on the screen and be added to the Project Explorer window (Figure 6.3).

Figure   6.3

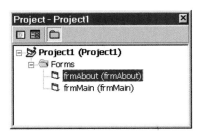

After adding a new form, the Project Explorer window shows the name of the new form.

If you want your newly created form to be the startup form (the one that appears when the project starts running), you will need to follow the steps for setting a startup form, which are found later in this chapter.

While in design time, you can switch between forms two ways. If you can see any part of the other form on the screen, just click on the form to make it active. You can also use the Project Explorer window. The Project Explorer window's View Form button and View Code button switch to the form or code of the module that is selected (highlighted). You can switch between forms by clicking on the form name in the Project Explorer window and clicking the View Form button, or by double-clicking on a form name.

Each form module is a separate file and a separate entity. The code that exists in one form module is not visible to any other form module. Note one exception: Any procedure declared with the `Public` keyword is callable from other modules in the project.

Adding and Removing Forms

The Project Explorer window shows the files that are included in a project. You can add new files and remove files from a project.

Adding Existing Form Files to a Project

Forms may be used in more than one project. You might want to use a form that you created for one project in a new project.

Each form is a separate module, which is saved as a separate file with an .frm extension. All information for the form resides in the file, which includes the code procedures and the visual interface as well as all property settings for the controls.

To add an existing form to a project, use the *Add Form* command on the *Project* menu and select the *Existing* tab (Figure 6.4). You will need to supply the name of the form and the folder where it can be found.

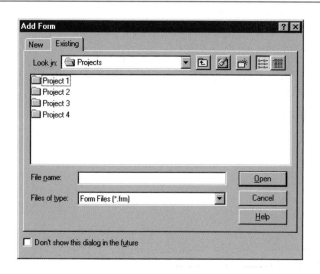

Select the Existing *tab to add an existing form to a project.*

Steps for adding an existing form to a project:

STEP 1: Select *Add Form* from the *Project* menu.
STEP 2: In the *Add Form* dialog box, select the *Existing* tab and locate the folder and file desired.
STEP 3: Click on *Open.*

Removing Forms from a Project

If you want to remove a file from a project, select its name in the Project Explorer window. You can then either choose *Remove File* from the *Project* menu or right-click on the filename to display the shortcut menu and choose *Remove Filename.*

The Hide and Show Methods

In code, you can display a form with the **Show method** and conceal a form with the **Hide method**. If both forms are the same size, the process of showing the second form will cover the first form on the screen. Use the Hide method when you want to make sure a form disappears.

The Show Method—General Form

```
FormName.Show [Style]
```

The FormName is the name of the form you wish to display. The optional *Style* determines whether the form will display modeless or modal. The values for

Style can be 0 (for modeless) or 1 (for modal); the default is 0. Better yet, use the VB intrinsic constants: vbModal and vbModeless.

When you display a form as **modal**, the user must respond to the form in some way, usually by clicking a command button. No other program code can execute until the modal form has been responded to and hidden or unloaded. However, if you display a **modeless** form, the user may switch to another form in the project without responding to the form. *Note:* Even with a modal form, the user can switch to another application within Windows.

The Show Method—Examples

```
frmSummary.Show 1              'Display the summary form, modal style
frmSummary.Show vbModal        'Display the summary form, modal style
frmSummary.Show vbModeless     'Display the summary form, modeless style
frmSummary.Show                'Display the summary form, modeless style
```

When you choose whether to display a form as modal or modeless, you must be aware of an important difference in the way VB executes the statements. As you already know, code statements within a procedure execute one after another, in sequence. When you have a modal Show method in code, VB executes the Show and pauses; it does not execute any further statements until the user responds to the modal form. Conversely, when VB encounters a modeless Show method, it displays the form and continues execution; if additional statements follow the Show, they will be executed immediately, without waiting for response from the user. In most cases you will want to display forms modally.

Recall the sample programs in Chapters 4 and 5, which display summary information in a message box. A nicer solution would be to display the summary data in a second form, called frmSummary. Replace the MsgBox statement in the cmdSummary_Click event procedure with this statement:

```
frmSummary.Show vbModal 'Display the summary form
```

The Form Load and Form Activate Events

The first time a form is displayed in a project, Visual Basic generates two events—a Form_Load and a Form_Activate. The Load event calls the form module into memory; the Activate event occurs after the Load event, just as control is passed to the form. Each subsequent time the form is shown, the Activate event occurs, but not the Load event. Therefore, if a form may be displayed multiple times, you may want to place initializing steps into the Form_Activate event procedure rather than into the Form_Load. Also, if you wish to set the focus in a particular place on the new form, place the SetFocus method in the Form_Activate procedure.

When you use a Show method, the size and location of the form depend on the Left, Top, Height, and Width properties of the form being displayed. You can calculate these properties when the form is shown by placing the calculations in the Form_Activate event. To make your form fill the screen, see the hints for working with maximized forms in the "Programming Hints" at the end of this chapter.

Tip

To write code for the Form_Activate event, display the code window and choose *Form* in the *Object* box and *Activate* in the *Procedure* box.

Hiding a Form

The Hide method is very similar to the Show method but is used to remove a form from the screen.

The Hide Method—General Form

```
FormName.Hide
```

The Hide Method—Example

```
frmSummary.Hide
```

The Load and Unload Statements

When you work with multiple forms, you may also want to use the **Load** and **Unload** statements. Although you can explicitly load a form, in most cases the Load isn't necessary. When you Show a form, the Load is done automatically. The only time you will code a Load statement is when you want to load a form, but not display it until later.

To remove a form from the screen, you can hide it or unload it. Hiding a form removes it from the screen, but the form still remains in memory and uses system resources. If you have many forms and you are sure you will not need a form again, it's best to unload it rather than to hide it.

The Load and Unload Statements—General Form

```
Load FormName
Unload FormName
```

The Load and Unload Statements—Examples

```
Load frmSummary
Unload frmSummary
```

The Me Keyword

You can refer to the current form by using the special keyword **Me**. Me acts like a variable and refers to the currently active form. You can use Me in place of the form name when coding form statements and methods.

Tip

You can quickly jump to another location in a project and then jump back to the same spot. Click on the name of a procedure or form where you want to jump and press Shift + F2. To jump back to the earlier spot, press Ctrl + Shift + F2.

The Me Keyword—Examples

```
Unload Me      'Unload the form that is currently executing code
Me.Hide        'Hide the form that is currently executing code
```

Referring to Objects on a Different Form

Each form is a separate module with its own variables, objects, properties, and code. When your project has only one form, you can refer to any object and its properties in any procedure. But when you use multiple forms, the code in one module cannot "see" the objects in another module without some help. One way to reference an object in another form module is to expand the reference to include the name of the form:

```
FormName.ObjectName.Property
```

Using this technique, you can set the properties of objects in a form before displaying it.

Example

```
frmSummary.lblTotalAmount.Caption = mcurTotal
frmSummary.Show vbModal
```

Consequently, you can use the same name for objects in two different forms. Although it may be confusing to have similarly named objects in multiple forms, it is perfectly acceptable. An example is having an OK button in two forms, both named cmdOK. The two buttons would be referred to as frmStartup.cmdOK and frmSummary.cmdOK.

Standard Code Modules

When using multiple forms in a project, it is important for you to consider each sub procedure or function procedure that you create. If the procedure will be used in only one form, then it should be included in the code for that form module. If, in fact, you will need to use the procedure in multiple forms, write the procedure in a **standard code module.** A *standard code module* is a Basic file with the extension **.bas**, which is added to the project. Standard code modules do not contain a form, only code.

Under "Project" drop-down

Create a new standard code module by selecting the *Add Module* command on the *Project* menu. Select *Module* on the *New* tab of the *Add Module* dialog box and click on *Open.* A new Code window titled *Module1* opens on the screen (Figure 6.5). Also note that Module1 is added to your Project Explorer window (Figure 6.6). Make sure that Module1 is highlighted in the Project Explorer window and choose *Save Module1* from the *File* menu to give the new file a name. It is a good idea to name this file the same as your project file unless you plan to use it for multiple projects. The file extension is .bas by default.

Figure 6.5

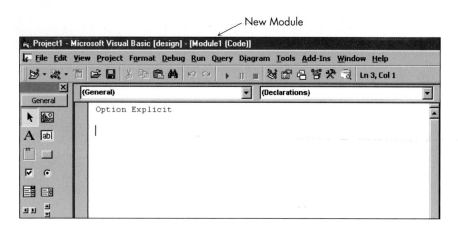

New Module

Figure 6.6

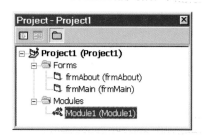

A standard code module has a General Declarations section and procedures, just like a form module. You can declare variables with the `Dim` statement in procedures or in the General Declarations section. Any `Dimmed` variables or constants in the General Declarations section of a standard code module are visible to all the procedures in that module, but not to the procedures in the form module(s).

From the *Add Module* menu option, you may also select an existing standard code module. This technique allows you to use a code module in more than one project.

Variables and Constants in Multiple-Form Projects

When a project has multiple modules, the scope of the variables and constants becomes a little more complicated. The variables and constants can be local to a procedure; module level, which are available to all procedures in the module; or **global**, which are available to all procedures in all modules in the project.

Global Variables and Constants

If you want variables and constants to be accessible to more than one form in the project, they must be global variables. To declare global variables, use the **Public** statement in place of the Dim statement.

The Public Statement—General Form

```
Public Identifier [As DataType]
Public Const Identifier [As DataType] = Value
```

The format of the Public statement is similar to the Dim and Const statements. If the data type is omitted for a variable, the type defaults to variant. For a constant, if you omit the data type, Visual Basic selects the type most appropriate for the value.

It is important to know the scope of a variable when programming. A module-level variable or constant has a prefix of "m", and a public variable or constant has a prefix of "g" (for global; "p" refers to private). Any variable or constant without a scope prefix is assumed to be local to a procedure.

The Public Statement—Examples

```
Public gcurGrandTotal As Currency
Public gPersonName 'Defaults to Variant data type
Public Const gsngTaxRate As Single = .0825
Public Const gstrCompany = "R 'n R -- for Reading and Refreshment" _
                          'Defaults to String data type
```

Note: Visual Basic also has a Private statement with the same syntax as the Public statement. Because all variables and constants are private by default, the Private statement is rarely used.

Static Variables

Another statement you can use to declare variables at the procedure level is the **Static** statement. Static variables retain their value for the life of the project, rather than being reinitialized for each call to the procedure. If you need to retain the value in a variable for multiple calls to a procedure, such as a running total, declare it as Static. (In the past we used module-level variables for this task. Using a static local variable is better than using a module-level variable because it is always best to keep the scope of a variable as narrow as possible.)

The Static Statement—General Form

```
Static Identifier [As DataType]
```

The format of the Static statement is the same as the format of the Dim statement. However, Static statements can appear only in procedures; Static statements never appear in the General Declarations section of a module.

The Static Statement—Examples

```
Static intPersonCount As Integer
Static curReportTotal As Currency
```

Static variables do not require a scope prefix, since all static variables are local.

Guidelines for Declaring Variables and Constants

When you declare variables and constants, select the location of the declaration carefully. These general guidelines will help you decide where to place declarations:

1. Place all local declarations (Dim, Const, Static) at the *top* of a procedure. Although Basic will accept declarations placed further down in the code, such placement is considered a poor practice. Your code will be easier to read, debug, modify, and maintain if you follow this guideline.
2. Use named constants for any value that doesn't change during program execution. It is far more clear to use named constants such as curMaximumRate and strCompanyName than to place the values into your code; and if in the future the values must be modified, having a constant name (at the top of your code) makes the task *much* easier.
3. Keep the scope of variables and constants as narrow as possible. Don't declare them all to be global or module level for convenience. There are books full of horror stories about strange program bugs popping up because the value of a variable was changed in an unknown location.
4. Consider making variables and constants local if possible.
5. If you need to keep the value of a variable for multiple executions of a procedure, but don't need the variable in any other procedure, make it Static.
6. If you need to use a variable both in a procedure and also in a second procedure called by the first procedure, declare the variable as local and pass it as an argument. (Refer to "Passing Variables to Procedures" in Chapter 5.)
7. If you need to use a variable in multiple procedures, such as to add to the variable in one procedure and to display it in another, use module-level variables. (Use a Dim statement in the General Declarations section of the module.)
8. If you need to use the value of a variable in multiple forms, you may still have two choices. Do you actually need to use the variable in the second form, or are you just displaying it in a control? Remember, you can assign

a variable to a property in another form by specifying FormName.Object.Property.

9. Finally, if you really need the value of a variable in more than one form, make it global. Declare the variable with the `Public` statement in the General Declarations section of a standard code module. *Note:* Visual Basic allows you to use the `Public` statement in the General Declarations section of *any* module, which means that you can declare global variables in any form module. Don't do it! Keep your `Public` declarations in a standard code module.

Feedback 6.1

For each of these situations, write the declaration statement and tell where it should appear. Assume the project will have multiple form modules and a standard code module. Be sure to give the proper prefixes to your identifiers.

1. The number of calories in a gram of fat (9), to use in the calculations of a procedure.
2. The name of the person with the highest score, which will be determined in one procedure and displayed in a label on a different form. (The value must be retained for multiple executions of the procedure.)
3. The name of the company ("Bab's Bowling Service"), which will appear in several forms.
4. A total dollar amount to be calculated in one procedure of a form, added to a grand total in a procedure of a second form, and formatted and displayed in a third form.
5. A count of the number of persons entered using a single form. The count will be used to help calculate an average in a second form.
6. The formatted version of a dollar total, which will be displayed in a label in the next statement.
7. For each of these identifiers, tell the scope and the data type.
   (a) mintLocations
   (b) gcurPayment
   (c) mcurPayment
   (d) curPayment
   (e) gstrTeamName
   (f) strTeamName
   (g) mstrTeamName

An About Box

One type of additional form in a project is an **About box**, such as the one you find in most Windows programs in *Help/About*. Usually, an About box gives the name and version of the project as well as information about the programmer or company. The About box may be displayed initially when the application begins or displayed when a specific event occurs (such as pressing a command button or selecting a menu command).

You can create your own About box by creating a new form and entering the information in labels. Of course, you may use any of the normal controls on this new form, but About boxes typically hold labels, an OK command button, and perhaps an image or shape controls for a logo. Figure 6.7 shows a typical About box.

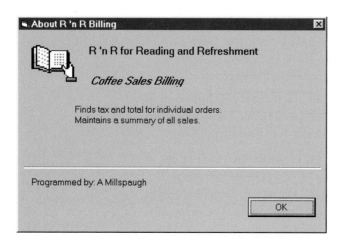

A typical About box containing labels, a line control, an image, and an OK command button.

You can also use VB's About Dialog template to create a new About box. Choose *Add Form* from the *Project* menu and on the *New* tab select *About Dialog* (Figure 6.8). A new form is added to your project with controls you can modify (Figure 6.9). You can change the captions and image by setting the properties as you would on any other form. Once you create the form in your project, it is yours and may be modified as you please.

*Select **About Dialog** from the New tab of the **Add Form** dialog box.*

About Dialog template file

| Form | VB Data Form Wizard | About Dialog | Web Browser | Dialog |

| Log in Dialog | Splash Screen | Tip of the Day | ODBC Log In | Options Dialog |

Open
Cancel
Help

☐ Don't show this dialog in the future

Figure 6.9

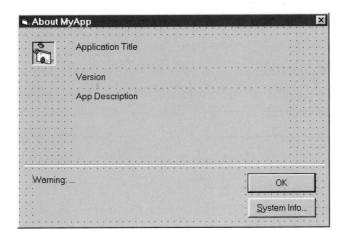

A Splash Screen

Perhaps you have noticed the logo or window that often appears while a program is loading, such as the one in Figure 6.10. This initial form is called a **splash screen**. Professional applications use splash screens to tell the user that the program is loading and starting. It can make a large application appear to load and run faster, since something appears on the screen while the rest of the application loads.

Figure 6.10

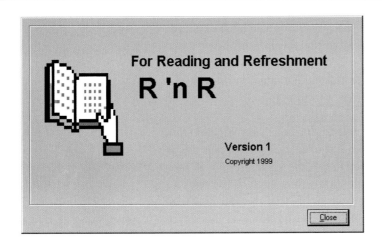

You can create your own splash screen or use the splash screen template included with VB (Figure 6.11). In the *Add Form* dialog box (refer to Figure 6.8), choose *Splash Screen* to add the new form; then modify the form to fit your needs. In the case of this splash screen, you will need to make major modifications to all the labels and to the code.

Figure 6 . 1 1

When you use this style of splash screen, your project does not display the main form as a startup form. Instead, when you run the project, execution begins with a sub procedure named Main, which is located in your .bas file.

Using Sub Main for Startup

A project may begin execution by displaying a startup form or by executing a procedure called Main, which you code in your standard code module. You use a Main sub procedure when you have tasks that should be done before the first form loads, such as when you want to display a splash screen while the main form loads.

When you begin execution with a Main sub procedure, you must explicitly load and/or show each form. In the following example, the splash screen is displayed as modeless so that the Load statement in the next statement will execute. In the Load statement the project's main form is loaded, but not shown. The last actions performed by the splash screen form is to unload the splash screen and show the main form.

You have some choices about when to unload the splash screen and show the main form. In a large application, in which it may take several seconds to load the main form, the logic is usually set up to exit the splash screen as soon as the main form finishes loading. In a small application, such as the ones we are writing in this text, the main form loads so quickly that the splash screen disappears before you can see it. We will place a Close button on the splash screen rather than have the form disappear automatically. You might also consider using a Timer control to close the form after an interval of time. See Chapter 13 or Visual Basic Help for information on the Timer control.

Coding the Standard Code Module

This code goes in the standard code module (.bas file):

Tip

To switch from one form to another in design time, use the Project Explorer window. Double-click on a form name to display the form. Or click on a form name and then click either the View Object or the View Code button.

```
Sub Main()
    'Display the splash screen while the main form loads

    frmSplash.Show vbModeless        'Display the splash form
    Load frmMain                     'Load the main form
End Sub
```

Coding the Splash Screen Event Procedure

The following code goes in the cmdClose_Click event procedure of the splash screen form. *Note:* If you started with the VB Splash Screen template, first remove all code that appeared automatically, add a cmdClose command button, and add this procedure:

```
Private Sub cmdClose_Click()
    'Unload splash screen and show the main form

    Unload Me                        'Unload the splash screen form
    frmMain.Show vbModal             'Show the main form
End Sub
```

Setting the Startup Form or Procedure

The startup form by default is the first form created in a project. However, you can select a different form to be the startup form, or you can specify that your Main sub procedure should begin when the project is run. In the *Project Properties* dialog box (Figure 6.12), you can choose one of the project's forms or *Sub Main*.

Figure 6.12

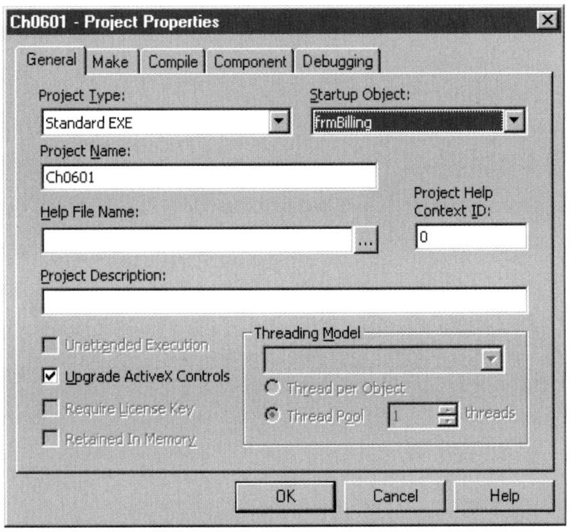

Set the startup form or procedure in the Project Properties *dialog box.*

To change the startup option:

STEP 1: Select *Project Properties* from the *Project* menu (or right-click on the project name in the Project Explorer window and choose *Project Properties*).

STEP 2: In the *Project Properties* dialog box, click on the *General* tab.

STEP 3: Drop down the list for *Startup Object* (Figure 6.13) and select the desired form or the *Sub Main* procedure.

STEP 4: Click OK.

F i g u r e   6 . 1 3

Drop down the Startup Object list to select a startup form or Sub Main.

Your Hands-On Programming Example

Modify the hands-on project from Chapter 5 to include multiple forms. This version of the project requires four forms: frmBilling, frmAbout, frmSplash, and frmSummary.

frmBilling: Add the frmBilling form from Chapter 5 to a new project. Do a *Save As*, create a new folder, and save the form into the new folder. This step creates a copy of the Chapter 5 form that you can modify for this project.

frmAbout: Replace the MsgBox About Box from Chapter 5 with a new form using the About Dialog template. Delete all of the code attached to the new form file. Delete the command button for system information from the form. (You may want to test this command on your own.)

frmSplash: Create a splash screen using the Splash Screen template. Customize the label captions and the image and delete all of the code attached to the new form file.

frmSummary: Replace the message box from the main form (frmBilling) with a separate form for the summary.

Startup Object: Create a standard code module with a Main sub procedure. Set the project properties Startup Object to Sub Main.

Reviewing the project requirements:

frmBilling: The user enters the number of items, selects the coffee type from option buttons, and selects the check box for taxable items. The price for each coffee is calculated according to these prices:

Cappuccino	2.00
Espresso	2.25
Latte	1.75
Iced (either)	2.50

The Calculate Selection command button calculates and displays the amount due for each item, adds the current item to the order, and calculates and displays the order information in labels. The Clear for Next Item button clears the selections and amount for the single item.

The *Next Order* menu command clears the bill for the current customer and add to the totals for the summary. The *Summary* menu command shows the summary form that displays the average sale amount per customer and the number of customers.

The *Edit* menu contains options that duplicate the Calculate and Clear buttons. The *Font* and *Color* options change the contents of the subtotal, tax, and total labels on the billing form.

The *About* selection on the *Help* menu displays the About form, which contains information about the program and the programmer.

File	Edit	Help
New Order	Calculate Selection	About
Summary	Clear Item	
Exit	_____	
	Font	
	Color	

Planning the Project

Sketch the four forms (Figure 6.14). Your user checks the sketches and signs off the design.

Figure 6.14

Sketches of the four forms for the hands-on programming example.

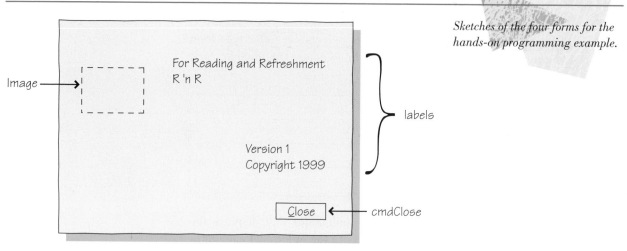

(a) *frmSplash*

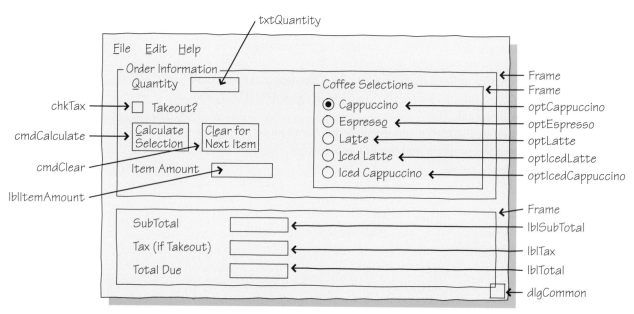

(b) *frmBilling*

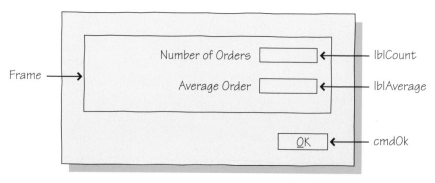

(c) *frmSummary*

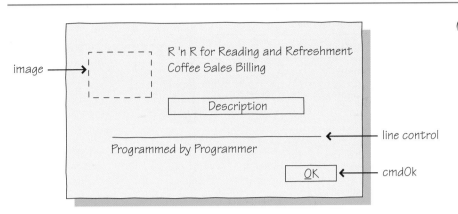

(d) frmAbout

The next step is to plan the property settings for the forms and the controls. *Note:* The frmBilling user interface is unchanged from Chapter 5.

frmBilling

Plan the Objects and Properties for frmBilling

Object	Property	Setting
frmBilling	Name	frmBilling
	Caption	R 'n R for Reading 'n Refreshment
	WindowState	Maximized
Frame1	Caption	Order Information
Frame2	Caption	Coffee Selections
Frame3	Caption	(blank)
optCappuccino	Name	optCappuccino
	Caption	C&appuccino
	Value	True
optEspresso	Name	optEspresso
	Caption	Espress&o
optLatte	Name	optLatte
	Caption	La&tte
optIcedLatte	Name	optIcedLatte
	Caption	&Iced Latte

continued

Object	Property	Setting
optIcedCappuccino	Name	optIcedCappuccino
	Caption	Iced Ca&ppuccino
Label1	Caption	&Quantity
txtQuantity	Name	txtQuantity
	Text	(blank)
chkTax	Name	chkTax
	Caption	Takeout ?
Label2	Caption	Item Amount
Label3	Caption	SubTotal
Label4	Caption	Tax (if Takeout)
Label5	Caption	Total Due
lblItemAmount	Name	lblItemAmount
	Caption	(blank)
	BorderStyle	1 - FixedSingle
lblSubTotal	Name	lblSubTotal
	Caption	(blank)
	BorderStyle	1 - Fixed Single
lblTax	Name	lblTax
	Caption	(blank)
	BorderStyle	1 - Fixed Single
lblTotal	Name	lblTotal
	Caption	(blank)
	BorderStyle	1 - Fixed Single
cmdCalculate	Name	cmdCalculate
	Caption	&Calculate Selection
	Default	True
cmdClear	Name	cmdClear
	Caption	C&lear for Next Item
	Cancel	True
mnuFileNew	Name	mnuFileNew
	Caption	&New Order
mnuFileSummary	Name	mnuFileSummary
	Caption	&Summary

(continued)

Object	Property	Setting
mnuFileExit	Name	mnuFileExit
	Caption	E&xit
mnuEditCalc	Name	mnuEditCalc
	Caption	Calculate Selection
mnuEditClear	Name	mnuEditClear
	Caption	C&lear Item
mnuEditFont	Name	mnuEditFont
	Caption	&Font
mnuEditColor	Name	mnuEditColor
	Caption	&Color
mnuHelpAbout	Name	mnuHelpAbout
	Caption	&About
dlgCommon	Name	dlgCommon

Plan the Event Procedures for frmBilling

Plan the actions for the event procedures for the menu commands and command buttons.

Object	Procedure	Action
cmdCalculate	Click	Determine price per cup. Multiply price by quantity. Call tax procedure if needed. Add quantity to item total. Display the values.
cmdClear	Click	Clear the coffee selections. Clear the quantity and the item price. Disable the takeout check box. Set the focus to the quantity.
mnuFileNew	Click	Clear the previous order. Accumulate total and count. Set subtotal and total to 0.
mnuFileSummary	Click	Display the average. Display the number of customers.
mnuFileExit	Click	Terminate the project.
mnuEditCalc	Click	Call calculate command event.
mnuEditClear	Click	Call clear command event.
curFindTax	(call)	Calculate the sales tax.

frmSplash

⌐ Plan the Objects and Properties for frmSplash

Object	Property	Setting
frmSplash	Name	frmSplash
	Caption	(blank)
	ControlBox	False (Already set by the form template)
	MaxButton	False (Already set by the form template)
	MinButton	False (Already set by the form template)
All labels	Caption	Program information (*Note:* Student information goes here.)
cmdClose	Name	cmdClose
	Caption	&Close

⌐ Plan the Event Procedures for frmSplash

Object	Procedure	Action
cmdClose	Click	Unload the splash form. Show the main form.

⌐ *frmAbout*

Plan the Objects and Properties for frmAbout

Object	Property	Setting
frmAbout	Name	frmAbout
	Caption	About R 'n R Billing
	MaxButton	False (Already set by the form template)
	MinButton	False (Already set by the form template)
All labels	Caption	Program and programmer information
cmdOK	Name	cmdOK
	Caption	&OK

⌐ Plan the Event Procedures for frmAbout

Object	Procedure	Action
cmdOK	Click	Hide the About form

frmSummary

Plan the Objects and Properties for frmSummary

Object	Property	Setting
frmSummary	Name	frmSummary
	Caption	Coffee Sales Summary
Frame1	Caption	(blank)
Label1	Name	Label1
	Caption	Number of Orders
Label2	Name	Label2
	Caption	Average Order
lblCount	Name	lblCount
	Caption	(blank)
	Alignment	Right Justify
lblAverage	Name	lblAverage
	Caption	(blank)
	Alignment	Right Justify
cmdOK	Name	cmdOK
	Caption	&OK

Plan the Event Procedures for frmSummary

Object	Procedure	Action
cmdOK	Click	Hide the Summary form

Form	Activate	If Count > 0 then
		    Calculate Average = Total / Count.
		Else
		    Average = 0.
		End If
		Format and display Count and Average.

Standard Code Module

Plan the Procedures for the Standard Code Module

Procedure	Action
Main	Show the Splash screen. Load frmBilling.

Write the Project

After completing the planning steps, create the forms following the sketches in
Figure 6.14. Figure 6.15 shows the completed forms.

*The four forms for the hands-on
programming example are
frmSplash, frmBilling,
frmSummary, and frmAbout.*

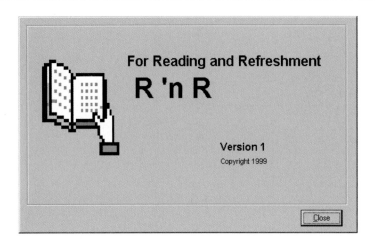

(a) frmSplash

(b) frmBilling

(continued)

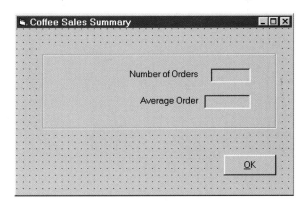

(c) frmSummary

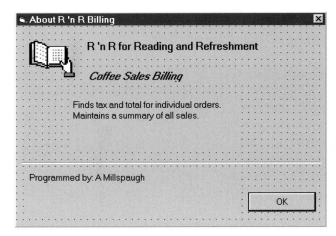

(d) frmAbout

frmBilling

STEP 1: Begin a new project.

STEP 2: Point to *Form1* in the Project Explorer window, right-click to display the shortcut menu, and select *Remove Form1*.

STEP 3: Select *Add Form* from the *Project* menu and click on the *Existing* tab.

STEP 4: Locate frmBilling in the Ch0501 folder (or wherever you placed the hands-on project from Chapter 5). Click on *Open*.

STEP 5: Click on *frmBilling* in the Project Explorer window and select *Save frmBilling.frm As* from the *File* menu. Open the *Save In* list and select the location you want for a new folder and then click on the *Create New Folder* button. Name your new folder *Ch0601*.

STEP 6: Double-click on your new folder so that it appears in the *Save In* box, check the filename, and click *Save*. Your Project Explorer window should resemble Figure 6.16.

STEP 7: Make the planned changes to the mnuFileSummary_Click and mnuHelpAbout_Click event procedures, as well as changes to global variables used for the summary.

Note: If you wish, you can continue adding forms to your project and return later to the steps that modify the forms and code.

Figure   6 . 1 6

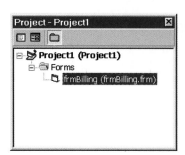

frmAbout

STEP 1: Select *Add Form* from the *Project* menu and click on the *New* tab.

STEP 2: Double-click on *About Dialog*.

STEP 3: Set the form's properties to match the plans detailed earlier.

STEP 4: Choose *Save frmAbout As* from the *File* menu, check the folder and filename, and save the new form.

STEP 5: Modify the label captions on the form to match your planning sketch.

STEP 6: Add the OK command button.

STEP 7: Switch to the code window and delete all code there except `Option Explicit`.

STEP 8: Write the code for frmAbout.

frmSplash

STEP 1: Select *Add Form* from the *Project* menu and click on the *New* tab.

STEP 2: Double-click on *Splash Screen*.

STEP 3: Set the form's properties to match the plans detailed earlier.

STEP 4: Choose *Save frmSplash As* from the *File* menu, check the folder and filename, and save the new form.

STEP 5: Modify the label captions on the form to match your planning sketch.

STEP 6: Add the Close command button.

STEP 7: Switch to the code window and delete all code there except `Option Explicit`.

STEP 8: Write the code for frmSplash.

frmSummary

STEP 1: Select *Add Form* from the *Project* menu and click on the *New* tab.

STEP 2: Double-click on *Form*.

STEP 3: Set the form's properties to match the plans detailed earlier.

STEP 4: Choose *Save Form1 As* from the *File* menu, check the folder, change the filename to *frmSummary*, and save the new form.

STEP 5: Create the controls on the form to match your planning sketch.

STEP 6: Set the properties for the controls.

STEP 7: Write the code for frmSummary.

Standard Code Module

STEP 1: Select *Add Module* from the *Project* menu and click on the *New* tab.

STEP 2: Double-click on *Module*.

STEP 3: Choose *Save Module1 As* from the *File* menu, check the folder, change the filename to *Ch0601*, and save the new code module. Your Project Explorer window should look like Figure 6.17.

STEP 4: Write the code for the standard code module, which includes declarations for the global variables and the Main sub procedure.

F i g u r e   6 . 1 7

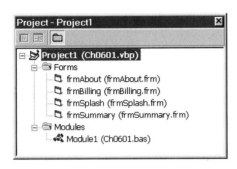

The completed project should show all four forms and the standard code module.

Set the Startup Object

STEP 1: Select *Project Properties* from the *Project* menu (or right-click on the project name in the Project Explorer window and choose *Project Properties*).

STEP 2: In the *Project Properties* dialog box, click on the *General* tab.

STEP 3: Drop down the list for *Startup Object* and select *Sub Main*. The Main sub procedure displays frmSplash and loads frmBilling.

STEP 4: Click on OK.

Write the Code

frmBilling

```
'Program Name:      Billing
'Programmer:        A. Millspaugh
'Date:              July 1999
'Description:       This project calculates the
'                   amount due based upon the customer selection
'                   and accumulates summary data for the day.
'                   The project incorporates menus, common dialog
'                   boxes, and multiple forms.
'Folder:            Ch0601

Option Explicit

Dim mcurSubtotal                   As Currency
Dim mcurTotal                      As Currency
Const mcurTaxRate                  As Currency = 0.08
```

```vb
Private Sub cmdCalculate_Click()
    'Calculate and display the current amounts, add to totals

    Dim mcurPrice                   As Currency
    Dim intQuantity                 As Integer
    Dim curTax                      As Currency
    Dim curItemAmount               As Currency
    Const curCappuccinoPrice        As Currency = 2
    Const curEspressoPrice          As Currency = 2.25
    Const curLattePrice             As Currency = 1.75
    Const curIcedPrice              As Currency = 2.5

    'Find the price
    If optCappuccino.Value = True Then
        mcurPrice = curCappuccinoPrice
    ElseIf optEspresso.Value = True Then
        mcurPrice = curEspressoPrice
    ElseIf optLatte.Value = True Then
        mcurPrice = curLattePrice
    ElseIf optIcedCappuccino.Value = True Or _
        optIcedLatte.Value = True Then
        mcurPrice = curIcedPrice
    Else
        MsgBox "Please Make Drink Selection", vbOKOnly, "Missing Data"
    End If

    'Add the price times quantity to running total
    If IsNumeric(txtQuantity.Text) Then
        intQuantity = Val(txtQuantity.Text)
        curItemAmount = mcurPrice * intQuantity
        mcurSubtotal = mcurSubtotal + curItemAmount
        If chkTax.Value = Checked Then
            curTax = curFindTax(mcurSubtotal) 'Call a function procedure
        End If
        mcurTotal = mcurSubtotal + curTax
        lblItemAmount.Caption = FormatCurrency(curItemAmount)
        lblSubTotal.Caption = FormatCurrency(mcurSubtotal)
        lblTax.Caption = FormatNumber(curTax)
        lblTotal.Caption = FormatCurrency(mcurTotal)
    Else
        MsgBox "Quantity must contain a number", vbExclamation, "Invalid Data"
        txtQuantity.SetFocus
    End If
End Sub
```

```
Private Sub cmdClear_Click()
    'Clear appropriate controls

    If mcurSubtotal<>0 Then           'Don't clear if not calculated
        optCappuccino.Value = True  'Make first button selected
        optEspresso.Value = False
        optLatte.Value = False
        optIcedLatte.Value = False
        optIcedCappuccino.Value = False
        lblItemAmount.Caption = ""
        chkTax.Enabled = False          'Allow change for new order only
        With txtQuantity
            .Text = ""
            .SetFocus
        End With
    Else
        MsgBox "No New Order to Clear", vbExclamation, "Customer Order"
    End If
End Sub
```

```
Private Sub mnuEditCalc_Click()
    'Call the Calculate event

    cmdCalculate_Click
End Sub
```

```
Private Sub mnuEditClear_Click()
    'Call the Clear command event

    cmdClear_Click
End Sub
```

```
Private Sub mnuEditColor_Click()
    'Change the color of the total labels

    With dlgCommon
        .Flags = cdlCCRGBInit           'Set up initial color
        .Color = lblSubTotal.ForeColor
        .ShowColor
        lblSubTotal.ForeColor = .Color
        lblTax.ForeColor = .Color
        lblTotal.ForeColor =.Color
    End With
End Sub
```

```
Private Sub mnuEditFont_Click()
    'Change the font name for the subtotal labels

    With dlgCommon
        .Flags = cdlCFScreenFonts      'Set up Font dialog box fonts
        .ShowFont
        lblSubTotal.Font.Name =.FontName
        lblTax.Font.Name =.FontName
        lblTotal.Font.Name =.FontName
    End With
End Sub
```

```
Private Sub mnuFileExit_Click()
    'Terminate the project

    End
End Sub
```

```
Private Sub mnuFileNew_Click()
    'Clear the current order and add to totals

    cmdClear_Click
    lblSubTotal.Caption = ""
    lblTax.Caption = ""
    lblTotal.Caption = ""

    'Add to Totals
    If mcurSubtotal <> 0 Then     'Prevent accidental clicking when no new order
        gcurGrandTotal = gcurGrandTotal + mcurTotal
        mcurSubtotal = 0              'Reset totals for next order
        mcurTotal = 0
        gintCustomerCount = gintCustomerCount + 1
    End If

    'Clear and enable tax check box
    With chkTax
        .Enabled = True
        .Value = False
    End With
End Sub
```

```
Private Sub mnuFileSummary_Click()
    'Load and display the summary information

    If mcurTotal <> 0 Then
        mnuFileNew_Click          'Make sure last order is counted
    End If
    frmSummary.Show vbModal
End Sub
```

```
Private Sub mnuHelpAbout_Click()
    'Display a message box about the program

    frmAbout.Show vbModal
End Sub
```

```
Public Function curFindTax(curAmount As Currency) As Currency
    'Calculate the sales tax

    curFindTax = curAmount * mcurTaxRate
End Function
```

frmAbout

```
'Module:         frmAbout
'Description:    Display information about the program and the
'                programmer.
'Folder:         Ch0601

Option Explicit
```

```
Private Sub cmdOK_Click()
    'Hide the form

    Me.Hide
End Sub
```

frmSplash

```
'Module:         frmSplash
'Description:    Splash screen to display while main form loads.
'Folder:         Ch0601

Option Explicit
```

```
Private Sub cmdClose_Click()
    'Unload the form and display the main form

    Unload Me                 'Close the Splash form
    frmBilling.Show vbModal    'Display the Billing form
End Sub
```

frmSummary

```
'Module:         frmSummary
'Description:    Display summary information on a separate form
'Folder:         Ch0601
```

```
Private Sub cmdOK_Click()
    'Return to the main form

    Unload Me
End Sub
```

```
Private Sub Form_Load()
    'Calculate the average and display the totals

    Dim curAverage              As Currency

    If gintCustomerCount > 0 Then
        curAverage = gcurGrandTotal / gintCustomerCount
    Else
        MsgBox "No sales have been recorded"
        curAverage = 0
    End If
    lblCount.Caption = gintCustomerCount
    lblAverage.Caption = FormatCurrency(curAverage)
End Sub
```

Standard Code Module

```
'Module:        Ch0601.BAS
'Programmer:    A. Millspaugh
'Date:          March 1999
'Description:   Code module to declare the global variables
'               and the Main procedure, which displays the
'               splash screen.
'Folder:        Ch0601

Public gcurGrandTotal          As Currency
Public gintCustomerCount       As Integer

Sub Main()
    'Display a splash screen while the main form is being loaded

    frmSplash.Show vbModeless   'Show the splash screen
    Load frmBilling             'Load the main form
End Sub
```

Programming Hints

Here are some useful tips for working with maximized forms.

Working with Maximized Forms

Until this point all of our forms have been smaller than the full screen. If you want your application's form to fill the entire screen, these techniques can help you in designing and running your project.

Design-Time Tips

Make your form run maximized by setting its WindowState property to *2-Maximized*. To work on the form in design time, click on the form's Maximize button, which will make the form larger. You can use the Form window's scroll bars to view the entire area of the form.

You can close the extra windows on the screen or undock them so that they float on top of your form. The borders of each window are resizable, and you can hide the toolbar. Figure 6.18 shows one possible screen setup for working on a maximized form.

The keyboard shortcut for the Code window is F7. Of course, you can always double-click on a control to display the Code window if you prefer.

Stopping Execution with a Maximized Form

To stop program execution, it is best to have a working Exit command button, but even if you don't, you can still stop your program. Click on your form's Close box, which exits the program, or click on the form's Restore button, which makes the form smaller so you have access to the Visual Basic toolbar buttons and menu bar.

Figure 6.18

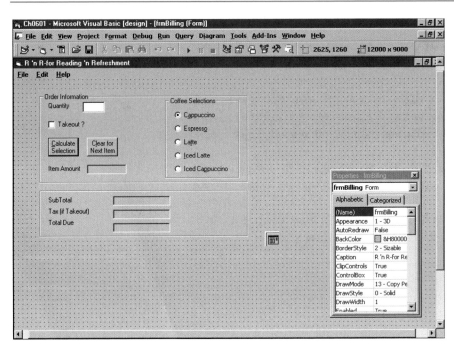

Modify the screen layout to make it easier to work on maximized forms. Here is one possible layout.

S u m m a r y

1. Projects may need more than one form—there is virtually no limit to the number of forms that can be used within a single project. Add forms by clicking the Form toolbar button or the *Add Form* command on the *Project* menu.

2. The first form displayed when a project runs is called the startup form.

3. Forms used for one project can be added to another project. Forms can also be removed from a project.

4. The `Show` and `Hide` methods are used to display or remove a form from the screen.

5. A form displayed as modal requires a response from the user; it must be closed or unloaded before any execution continues. When a form is displayed as modeless, the user can switch to another form without closing the form.

6. The `Load` statement loads a form but does not show it. The `Unload` statement hides a form, removes it from memory, and releases any system resources used by the form.

7. The `Me` keyword refers to the current active form. `Me` can be used to hide or unload the active form.

8. To refer to an object in a different form, use the form name, a period, and the object name.

9. A standard code module contains global declarations and procedures that may be used by multiple forms. To add a standard code module use the *Add Module* command on the *Project* menu; the file will have a .bas extension.

10. Global variables, which are visible to all forms within a project, are declared using the keyword `Public`. The `Public` statement can appear only in the General Declarations section of a module and *should* be placed in a standard code module.

11. Local variables may be declared with the keyword `Static`. Static variables retain their values for multiple calls to the procedure in which they are defined.

12. An About box, which typically contains information about the version of an application and the programmer and copyrights, may be created by adding a new form. VB has an About Dialog template form that you can use to create an About box.

13. A splash screen may be displayed while a program loads. VB provides a splash screen template that you can use to create a new splash screen form.

14. Program execution can start with a startup form or from a sub procedure called *Main*. Use a Sub Main to display a splash screen.

K e y   T e r m s

About box   *223*

.bas file extension   *219*

global   *220*

Hide method   *216*

Load statement   *218*

Me   *218*

modal   *217*

modeless   *217*

Public   *221*

Show method   *216*

splash screen   *225*

standard code module   *219*

startup form   *214*

Static   *221*

Unload statement   *218*

R e v i e w   Q u e s t i o n s

1. What does the phrase *standard code module* mean?
2. Discuss the difference between declaring a variable in the General Declarations section of a standard code module and declaring a variable in the General Declarations section of a form code module.
3. List some of the items generally found in an About box.
4. What is the purpose of a splash screen?
5. What is the term used for the first form to display in a project?
6. How can you choose a different form as the startup form after the project has been created?
7. Explain how to include an existing form in a new project.

P r o g r a m m i n g   E x e r c i s e s

6.1 Modify project 5.5 (the flag viewer) to include a splash screen and an About form.
Menus:

File	Country	Display	Help
Print	United States	Title	About
Exit	Canada	Country Name	
	Japan	Programmer	
	Mexico		

6.2 Create a project that will produce a summary of the amounts due for Pat's Auto Repair Shop. Display a splash screen first; then display the main form.

The main form menus:

File	Process	Help
Exit	Job Information	About

Job Information command:

The *Job Information* menu command will display the Job Information form.

Job Information form:

The Job Information form must have text boxes for the user to enter the job number, customer name, amount charged for parts, and the hours of labor. Include labels for Parts, Labor, SubTotal, Sales Tax, and Total.

Include command buttons for Calculate, Print, Clear, and OK.

The Calculate button finds the charges and displays them in labels. The tax rate and the hourly labor charge should be set up as named constants so that they can be easily modified if either changes. Current charges are $30 per hour for labor and 8 percent (.08) for the sales tax rate. Sales tax is charged only on parts, not on labor.

The Print button prints the current form.

The Clear button clears the text boxes and labels and resets the focus in the first text box.

The OK button hides the Job Information form and displays the main form.

6.3 Modify project 6.2 so that summary information is maintained for the total dollar amount for parts, labor, sales tax, and total for all customers.

Add a *Summary* command under the *Process* menu with a separator bar between the two menu commands. When the user selects the *Summary* command, display the summary information in a Summary form. The Summary form should have an OK button that hides the Summary form and returns the user to the main form.

6.4 A battle is raging over the comparative taste of Prune Punch and Apple Ade. Each taste tester rates the two drinks on a scale of 1 to 10 (10 being best). The proof of the superiority of one over the other will be the average score for the two drinks.

Display a splash screen and then the main form.

Main form menus:

```
File                Help
   New Tester          About
   Summary

   Exit
```

New Tester command:

The *New Tester* command displays a form that inputs the test results for each drink. The form contains an OK button and a Cancel button.

When the user clicks the OK button, add the score for each type of drink to the drinks' total, clear the text boxes, and reset the focus. Leave the form on the screen in case the next tester is ready to enter scores. If either score is blank when the OK button is pressed, display a message in a message box and reset the focus to the box for the missing data.

The Cancel button returns to the startup form without performing any calculation.

Summary command:

The *Summary* command displays a form that contains the current results of the taste test. It should display the winner, the total number of taste testers, and the average rating for each drink. The form contains an OK button that returns to the startup form. (The user will be able to display the summary at any time and as often as desired.)

About form:

The About form should display information about the program and the programmer. Include an OK button that returns the user to the main form.

6.5 Modify project 5.1 (piecework pay) to add a Splash form, an About form, and a Summary form. Add a slogan and a logo that the user can hide or display from menu choices.

Splash form:

The Splash form must appear only when the project begins execution. It should display the project name, programmer name, at least one graphic, and an OK button. When the user clicks the OK button, display the main form.

About form:

The About form should have the program name, version number, and programmer name, as well as a small image and an OK button. It must be displayed as modal.

Summary form:

The Summary form should display the summary information. Note that in Chapter 5 the summary information was displayed in a message box. You must remove the message box and display the summary information only on the Summary form.

Slogan and logo:

Make up a slogan for the company, such as "We're Number One" or "We Do Chicken Right." For the logo, you can create something with shape controls, use an icon, use any graphic you have available, or create one yourself with a draw or paint program.

The *Slogan* and *Logo* menu choices must toggle and display a check mark when selected. For example, when the slogan is displayed, the *Slogan* menu command is checked. If the user selects the *Slogan* command again, hide the slogan and uncheck the menu command. The *Slogan* and *Logo* commands operate independently; that is, the user may select either, both, or neither item.

When the project begins, the slogan and logo must both be displayed and their menu commands appear checked.

CASE STUDIES

Modify the VB Mail Order project from Chapter 5 to include a Splash screen, an About form, and a Summary form. Include

VB Mail Order

an image on both the Splash form and the About form.

VB Auto Center

Create a project that uses three forms. Add the form from the Chapter 5 case study and create a Splash screen and an About form.

Splash screen:
Display a Splash screen and then the Main form.

About form:
Include an image and identifying information about the program and programmer.

Main form:
The Main form should display "Valley Boulevard Auto Center—Meeting all your vehicle's needs" and appropriate image(s).

Main form menus:

File	Edit	Help
Input Sale	Color	About
Exit	Font	

The *Color* and *Font* commands should allow the user to change the large label on the form.

The *Input Sale* command should display the form from Chapter 5. You will need to modify the Chapter 5 form to hide itself rather than to terminate execution.

Video Bonanza

Modify the project from Chapter 5 to have three forms. Add a Splash screen and replace the *About* message box with an About form.

Include an image on both the Splash screen and the About form.

Very Very Boards

Modify your project from Chapter 5 to include a Splash form, an About form, and a summary form.

Make your project begin execution from a Sub Main procedure.

The Splash form:
The Splash form must appear only when the project begins execution. It should display the project name, programmer name, at least one graphic, and an OK button. The OK button should unload the splash form and show the main form.

The About form:
The About form should have the program name, version number, and programmer name, as well as a small image and an OK button. It must be displayed as modal and not be resizable by the user.

The Summary form:
Remove the *Summary* message box and display the summary in a separate form.

Lists, Loops, and Printing

At the completion of this chapter, you will be able to . . .

1. Create and use list boxes and combo boxes.

2. Enter items into list boxes at design time and during program execution.

3. Determine which item in a list is selected.

4. Use the ListCount property to determine the number of items in a list.

5. Display a selected item from a list.

6. Differentiate among the available types of combo boxes.

7. Use `Do/Loops` and `For/Next` statements to iterate through a loop.

8. Use the `MsgBox` function to determine the button pressed by the user.

9. Use the string functions `Left`, `Right`, and `Mid` to refer to part of a string and use the `Len` function to count the number of characters in a string.

10. Send information to the printer using the `Print` method.

11. Control the format of printing using commas, semicolons, the `Tab` function, and the `Spc` function.

Often you will want to offer the user a list of items from which to choose. You can use the Windows list box and combo box controls to display lists on a form. You may choose to add items to a list during design time, during run time, or perhaps using a combination of both. Several styles of list boxes are available; the style you use is determined by design and space considerations as well as by whether you will allow users to add items to the list.

List Boxes and Combo Boxes

Both **list box controls** and **combo box controls** allow you to have a list of items from which the user can make a selection. Figure 7.1 shows the toolbox tools for creating the controls; Figure 7.2 shows several types of list boxes and combo boxes, including simple list boxes, **simple combo boxes**, **dropdown combo boxes**, and **dropdown lists**. The list boxes on the left of the form in Figure 7.2 are all created with the list box tool; the boxes on the right of the form are created with the combo box tool. Notice the three distinct styles of combo boxes.

Combo box ⟶   ⟵ List box

Use the list box tool and the combo box tool to create list boxes and combo boxes on your forms.

List boxes and combo boxes have most of the same properties and operate in a similar fashion. One exception is that a combo box control has a Style property, which determines whether or not the list box also has a text box for user entry and whether or not the list will drop down (refer to Figure 7.2). Another exception is that combo boxes have a Text property that is available at design time; the Text property of list boxes is available only during program execution.

Both list boxes and combo boxes have a great feature. If the box is too small to display all the items in the list at one time, VB automatically adds a scroll bar. You do not have to be concerned with the location of the scroll box in the scroll bar; the scrolling is handled automatically.

Figure   7.2

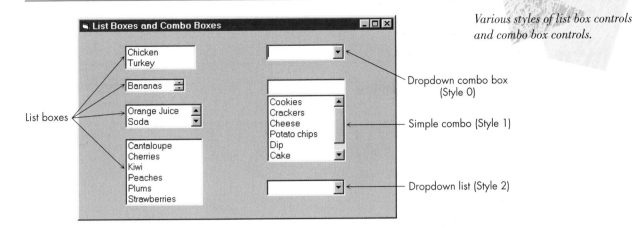

*Various styles of list box controls
and combo box controls.*

When you add a list box to a form, choose the style according to the space you have available and how you want the box to operate. Do you want the user to select from an existing list? If so, use a simple list box or a dropdown list (combo box style 2). Do you want the user to be able to type a new entry if necessary? In this case, use one of the two styles with an added text box: the dropdown combo box (style 0) or the simple combo box (style 1).

When you create a list box or combo box at design time, you determine the size of the control. For list boxes, Visual Basic displays the Name property in the control during design time, for combo boxes, the Text property displays. Don't spend any time trying to make a list box or dropdown list (combo box style 2) appear empty during design time; the box will appear empty at run time. Dropdown combo boxes and simple combos (styles 0 and 1) have a Text property, which you can set or remove at design time.

When you name list boxes and combo boxes, use the prefixes "lst" and "cbo".

Filling the List

You can use several methods to fill a list box and combo box. If you know the list contents at design time and the list never changes, you can define the list items in the Properties window. If you must add items to the list during program execution, you will use the `AddItem` method in an event procedure. In Chapter 10 you will learn to fill a list from a data file on disk. This method allows the list contents to vary from one run to the next.

Using the Properties Window

The List property holds the list of items for a list box or combo box. To define the List property at design time, select the control and scroll the Properties window to the List property (Figure 7.3). Click on the down arrow to drop down the empty list and type your first list item. Then press Ctrl + Enter to move to the next list item. Continue typing items and pressing Ctrl + Enter until you are finished (Figure 7.4). On the last list item, do not press Ctrl + Enter, or you will have an extra (blank) item on the list. Press Enter or click anywhere off the list to complete the operation.

Figure   7.3

Select the List property of a list box to enter the list items.

Figure   7.4

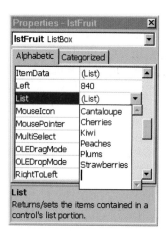

Type each list item and press Ctrl + Enter.

Using the AddItem Method

To add an item to a list box at run time, use the **AddItem method**. You may choose to add to a list the contents of the text box at the top of a combo box, a variable, a constant, or the property of another control.

The AddItem Method—General Form

```
Object.AddItem Value [, Index]
```

Value is the value to add to the list. If the value is a string literal, enclose it in quotation marks.

The optional *Index* specifies the position within the list to place the new item; the first element in the list has an Index of 0.

When you omit the Index, the new item generally goes at the end of the list. However, you can alter the placement by setting the control's **Sorted property** to True. Then the new item will be placed alphabetically in the list.

The AddItem Method—Examples

```
lstSchools.AddItem "Harvard"
lstSchools.AddItem "Stanford"
lstSchools.AddItem txtSchools.Text
cboMajors.AddItem cboMajors.Text
cboMajors.AddItem strMajor
```

When the user types a new value in the text box portion of a combo box, that item is not automatically added to the list. If you want to add the newly entered text to the list, use the `AddItem` method:

```
cboCoffee.AddItem cboCoffee.Text
```

Clearing the List

In addition to adding items during run time, you can also clear all items from a list. Use the **Clear method** to empty a combo box or list box.

The Clear Method—General Form

```
Object.Clear
```

The Clear Method—Examples

```
lstSchools.Clear
cboMajors.Clear
```

The ListIndex Property

When a project is running and the user selects (highlights) an item from the list, the index number of that item is stored in the **ListIndex property** of the list box. Recall that the ListIndex of the first item in the list is 0. If no list item is selected, the ListIndex property is set to negative 1.

You can use the ListIndex property to select an item in the list or deselect all items in code.

Example

```
lstCoffeeTypes.ListIndex = 3        'Select the fourth item in list
lstCoffeeTypes.ListIndex = -1       'Deselect all items in list
```

The ListCount Property

The application uses the **ListCount property** of a list box or combo box to store the number of items in the list. We will use the ListCount property later in this chapter to process each element in the list. ListCount is also handy when you need to display the count at some point in your project.

Remember, ListCount is always one more than the highest ListIndex, since ListIndex begins with 0. For example, if there are 20 items in a list, ListCount is 20 and the highest ListIndex is 19.

Example

```
intTotalItems = lstItem.ListCount
```

The List Property

If you need to display one item from a list, you can refer to one element of the **List property**. The List property of a list box or combo box holds the text of all list elements. You specify which element you want by including an index. This technique can be useful if you need to display a list item in another location. Later in this chapter we will use the List property to send the contents of the list box to the printer.

Using the List Property—General Form

```
Object.List(Index) [ = Value]
```

The index of the first list element is 0, so the highest index is ListCount − 1.

You can retrieve the value of a list element or set an element to a different value.

Using the List Property—Examples

```
lstSchools.List(5) = "University of California"
lblMyMajor.Caption = cboMajors.List(intIndex)
lblSelectedMajor.Caption = cboMajors.List(cboMajors.ListIndex)
```

To refer to the currently selected element of a list, you must combine the List property and the ListIndex property:

```
strSelectedFlavor = lstFlavor.List(lstFlavor.ListIndex)
```

You can also refer to the selected list element by using the Text property:

```
strSelectedMajor = cboMajor.Text
```

Removing an Item from a List

Earlier you learned how to clear all the elements from a list. However, you might want to remove individual elements from a list. To remove an element from the list, use the **RemoveItem method**.

The RemoveItem Method—General Form

```
Object.RemoveItem Index
```

The Index is required; it specifies which element to remove. The Index of the first list element is 0, and the Index of the last element is ListCount − 1.

The RemoveItem Method—Examples

```
lstNames.RemoveItem 0                      'Remove the first name from the list
cboSchools.RemoveItem intIndex             'Remove the element in position intIndex
cboCoffee.RemoveItem cboCoffee.ListIndex   'Remove the currently selected item
```

List Box and Combo Box Events

Later in the chapter we will perform actions in event procedures for events of list boxes and combo boxes. Some useful events are the Change, GotFocus, and LostFocus. *Note:* Although we haven't used these events up until this point, many other controls have these same events. For example, you can code event procedures for the Change event of text boxes.

The Change Event

As the user types text into the text box portion of a combo box (styles 0 and 1), the Change event occurs. Each keystroke generates another change event. This event will be used later to match the characters typed to the elements in the list. A list box does not have a Change event, because list boxes do not have associated text boxes.

The GotFocus Event

When a control receives the focus, a GotFocus event occurs. As the user tabs from control to control, a GotFocus event fires for each control. Later you will learn to make any existing text appear selected when the user tabs to a text box or the text portion of a combo box.

The LostFocus Event

You can also write code for the LostFocus event of a control. The LostFocus event fires as the control loses the focus. Often LostFocus event procedures are used for validating input data.

Feedback 7.1

Describe the purpose of each of the following methods or properties for a list box control.

1. ListCount
2. ListIndex
3. List
4. AddItem
5. Clear
6. RemoveItem
7. Sorted

Do/Loops

Until now, there has been no way to repeat the same steps in a procedure without calling them a second time. The computer is capable of repeating a group of instructions many times without calling the procedure for each new set of data. The process of repeating a series of instructions is called *looping*. The group of repeated instructions is called a **loop**. An **iteration** is a single execution of the statement(s) in the loop. In this section you will learn about the Do/Loop. Later in this chapter you will learn about another type of loop—a For/Next loop.

A **Do/Loop** terminates based on a condition that you specify. Execution of a Do/Loop continues *while* a condition is True or *until* a condition is True. You can choose to place the condition at the top or the bottom of the loop. Use a Do/Loop when the exact number of iterations is unknown.

Align the **Do** and **Loop statements** with each other and indent the lines of code to be repeated in between.

The Do and Loop Statements—General Form

```
Do {While | Until} Condition
    'statements in loop

Loop

or

Do
    'statements in loop

Loop {While | Until} Condition
```

The first form of the Do/Loop tests for completion at the top of the loop. With this type of loop, also called a **pretest**, the statements inside the loop may never be executed if the terminating condition is True the first time it is tested.

Example

```
intTotal = 0
Do Until intTotal = 0
    'statements in loop
Loop
```

Because intTotal is 0 the first time the condition is tested, the condition is True and the statements inside the loop will not execute. Control will pass to the statement following the Loop statement.

The second form of the Do/Loop tests for completion at the bottom of the loop, which means that the statements in the loop will *always* be executed at least once. This form of loop is sometimes called a **posttest**. Changing the example to a posttest, you can see the difference.

```
intTotal = 0
Do
    'statements in loop

Loop Until intTotal = 0
```

In this case the statements inside the loop will be executed at least once. Assuming the value for intTotal does not change inside the loop, the condition (intTotal = 0) will be True the first time it is tested and control will pass to the first statement following the Loop statement. Figure 7.5 shows flowcharts of pretest and posttest loops, using both While and Until.

Figure 7.5

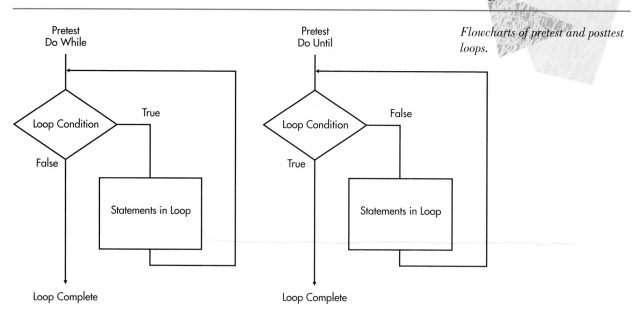

Flowcharts of pretest and posttest loops.

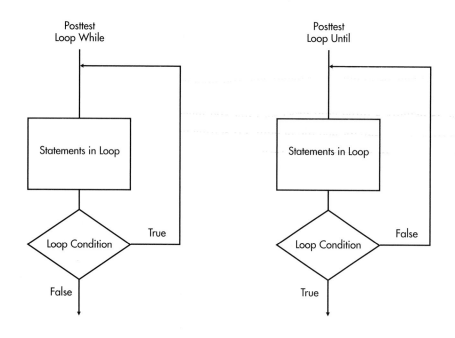

The Do and Loop Statements—Examples

```
Do Until intItemIndex = lstItems.ListCount - 1
    'Statements in loop

Loop

Do While curAmount >= 10 And curAmount <= 20
    'Statements in loop

Loop

Do
    'Statements in loop

Loop Until intTotal > 0
```

The Boolean Data Type Revisited

In Chapter 2 you learned about the Boolean data type, which holds only the values True or False. You will find Boolean variables very useful when setting and testing conditions for a loop. You can set a Boolean variable to True when a specific circumstance occurs and then write a loop condition to continue until the variable is True.

An example of using a Boolean variable is when you want to search through a list for a specific value. The item may be found or not found, and you want to quit looking when a match is found.

Using a Boolean variable is usually a three-step process. First you must dimension a variable and set its initial value (or use the default VB setting of False). Then, when a particular situation occurs, set the variable to True. A loop condition can then check for True.

```
Dim blnItemFound as Boolean
blnItemFound = False
Do Until blnItemFound     'Checks for True
    ...
```

A Boolean variable is always in one of two states—True or False. Many programmers refer to Boolean variables as *switches* or *flags*. Switches have two states: on or off; flags are considered either up or down.

Using a Do/Loop with a List Box

This small example combines a Boolean variable with a Do/Loop. Inside the loop each element of the list is compared to txtNewItem for a match. The loop will terminate when a match is found or when all elements have been tested. Follow through the logic to see what happens when there is a match, when there isn't a match, when the match occurs on the first list element, and when the match occurs on the last list element.

```
Private Sub cmdFind_Click()
    'Look for a match between the text box and list elements

    Dim blnItemFound As Boolean
    Dim intItemIndex As Integer

    blnItemFound = False
    intItemIndex = 0
    Do Until blnItemFound Or intItemIndex = lstItems.ListCount
        If txtNewItem.Text = lstItems.List(intItemIndex) Then
            blnItemFound = True
        End If
        intItemIndex = intItemIndex + 1
    Loop
    If blnItemFound Then
        MsgBox "Item is in the list", vbInformation, "Item match"
    Else
        MsgBox "Item is not in the list", vbInformation, "Item no match"
    End If
End Sub
```

Feedback 7.2

Explain the purpose of each line of the following code:

```
blnItemFound = False
intItemIndex = 0
Do Until blnItemFound Or intItemIndex = lstItems.ListCount
    If txtNewItem.Text = lstItems.List(intItemIndex) Then
        blnItemFound = True
    End If
    intItemIndex = intItemIndex + 1
Loop
```

For/Next Loops

When you want to repeat the statements in a loop a specific number of times, the **For/Next loop** is ideal. The For/Next loop uses the **For** and **Next statements** and a counter variable, called the *loop index*. The value of the loop index is tested to determine the number of times the statements inside the loop will execute.

```
Dim intLoopIndex as Integer
Dim intMaximum as Integer
intMaximum = lstSchools.ListCount - 1

For intLoopIndex = 0 To intMaximum
    'The statements inside of the loop are indented
    ' and referred to as the body of the loop
Next intLoopIndex
```

When the For statement is reached during program execution, several things occur. The loop index, intLoopIndex, is established as the loop counter and is initialized to 0. The final value for the loop index is set to the value of intMaximum, which was assigned the value of lstSchools.ListCount − 1 in the previous statement.

Execution is now "controlled by" the For statement. After the value of intLoopIndex is set, it is tested to see whether intLoopIndex is greater than intMaximum. If not, the statements in the body of the loop are executed. The Next statement causes the intLoopIndex to be incremented by 1. The control passes back to the For statement. Is the value of intLoopIndex greater than intMaximum? If not, the loop is again executed. When the test is made and the loop index is greater than the final value, control passes to the statement immediately following the Next.

A counter-controlled loop generally has three elements (see Figure 7.6 for a flowchart of loop logic).

1. Initialize the counter.
2. Increment the counter.
3. Test the counter to determine when it is time to terminate the loop.

Figure   7 . 6

A flowchart of the logic of a For/Next *loop.*

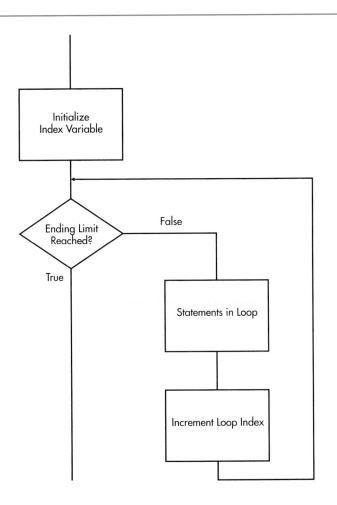

The For and Next Statements—General Form

```
For LoopIndex = InitialValue To TestValue [Step Increment]
    ::
    ::(Body of loop)
    ::
Next [LoopIndex]
```

LoopIndex must be a numeric variable; InitialValue and TestValue may be constants, variables, numeric property values, or numeric expressions. The optional word Step may be included, along with the value to be added to the loop index for each iteration of the loop. When the Step is omitted, the increment is assumed to be 1.

The For and Next Statements—Examples

```
For intIndex = 2 To 100 Step 2
For intCount = intStart To intEnding Step intIncrement
For intCounter = 0 To cboCoffeeType.ListCount - 1
For intNumber = (intNumberCorrect - 5) To intTotalPossible
For curRate = .05 To .25 Step .05
For intCountDown = 10 To 0 Step -1
```

Each For statement has a corresponding Next statement, which must follow the For. All statements between the For and Next are considered to be the body of the loop and will be executed the specified number of times.

The first For statement example will count from 2 to 100 by 2. The statements in the body of the loop will be executed 50 times—first with intIndex = 2, next with intIndex = 4, next with intIndex = 6, and so forth.

When the comparison is done, the program checks for *greater than* the test value—not equal to. When intIndex = 100 in the preceding example, the body of the loop will be executed one more time. Then, at the Next statement, intIndex will be incremented to 102, the test will be made, and control will pass to the statement following the Next. If you were to display the value of intIndex *after completion* of the loop, its value would be 102.

Negative Increment or Counting Backward

You may use a negative number for the Step increment to decrease the loop index rather than increase it. When the Step is negative, VB tests for *less than* the test value instead of greater than.

```
'Count Backwards
For intCount = 10 To 1 Step -1

Next intCount
```

Use a For/Next loop when you know the number of iterations needed for the loop. Use a Do/Loop when the loop should end based on a condition.

Conditions Satisfied before Entry

At times the final value will be reached before entry into the loop. In that case the statements in the body of the loop will not be executed at all.

```
'An unexecutable loop
intFinal = 5
For intIndex = 6 to intFinal
    'The execution will never reach here
Next intIndex
```

Altering the Values of the Loop Control Variables

Once a For loop has been entered, the values for InitialValue, TestValue, and Increment have already been set. Changing the value of these control variables within the loop will have no effect on the number of iterations of the loop. Many texts admonish against changing the values within the loop. However, Visual Basic just ignores you if you try.

```
'Bad Example—Changing the Control Variable
intFinal = 10
intIncrease = 2
For intIndex = 1 to intFinal Step intIncrease
    intFinal = 25
    intIncrease = 5
Next intIndex
```

If you tried this example and displayed the values of intIndex, you would find that the final value will remain 10 and the increment value will be 2.

The value that you *can* change within the loop is the LoopIndex. This practice is considered poor programming.

```
'Poor Programming
For intIndex = 1 To 10 Step 1
    intIndex = intIndex + 5
Next intIndex
```

Endless Loops

Changing the value of a LoopIndex variable is not only considered a poor practice but also may lead to an endless loop. Your code could get into a loop that is impossible to exit. Consider the following example; when will the loop end?

```
'More Poor Programming
For intIndex = 1 To 10 Step 1
    intIndex = 1
Next intIndex
```

Exiting For/Next Loops

In the previous example of an endless loop, you will have to break the program execution manually. You can click on your form's close box or use the Visual Basic menu bar or toolbar to stop the program. If you can't see the menu bar or toolbar, you can usually move or resize your application's form to bring it into view. If you prefer, press Ctrl + Break to enter break time; you may want to step program execution to see what is causing the problem.

Usually, For/Next loops should proceed to normal completion. However, on occasion you may need to terminate a loop before the loop index reaches its final value. Visual Basic provides an Exit For statement for this situation. Generally, the Exit For statement is part of an If statement.

The Exit For Statement—General Form

```
Exit For
```

The Exit For Statement—Example

```
For intLoopIndex = 1 to 10
    If txtInput.Text = "" Then    'Nothing was entered into the Input textbox
        MsgBox "You must enter something"
        Exit For
    End If
    ...    'Statements in loop
Next intLoopIndex
```

Feedback 7.3

1. Identify the statements that are correctly formed and those that have errors.
   For those with errors, state what is wrong and how to correct it.
   (a) ```
For curIndex = 3.5 To 6, Step .5
    Next curIndex
```
   (b) ```
For intIndex = intBegin To intEnd Step intIncrement
    Next intEnd
```
   (c) ```
For 4 = 1 To 10 Step 2
    Next For
```
   (d) ```
For intIndex = 100 To 0 Step -25
    Next intIndex
```
   (e) ```
For intIndex = 0 To -10 Step -1
    Next intIndex
```
   (f) ```
For intIndex = 10 To 1
    Next intIndex
```

2. How many times will the body of the loop be executed for each of these examples? What will be the value of the loop index *after* normal completion of the loop?

(a) `For intCounter = 2 To 11 Step 3` 4, 14
(b) `For intCounter = 10 To 1 Step -1` 10, 0
(c) `For curCounter = 3 To 6 Step .5` 7, 6.5
(d) `For intCounter = 5 To 1` not valid
(e) `For intCounter = 1 To 3` 3, 4

Using the MsgBox Function

You have been using the `MsgBox` statement to display messages since Chapter 4. In each case the box displayed only an OK button. You can also use the **MsgBox function** to display a dialog box with more than one button; the function returns a value to indicate which button was pressed.

Consider a message box that asks whether you really want to clear a combo box. You need to display Yes and No buttons and then be able to determine which button the user clicked. Figure 7.7 illustrates a message box with Yes and No buttons.

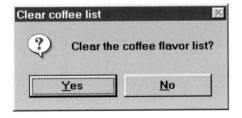

Display a message box with more than one button and check which button was clicked with the `MsgBox` *function.*

The MsgBox Function—General Form

```
MsgBox(Prompt [, Buttons] [, Title])
```

The MsgBox Function—Example

```
Dim intResponse As Integer
intResponse = MsgBox("Do you wish to continue?", vbYesNo + vbQuestion, "Title")
If intResponse = vbYes Then '...Continue processing

If MsgBox(stMsg, vbOKCancel) = vbOK Then
    ClearList
Else
    CancelOperation
End If
```

Function Return Values

The MsgBox function returns an integer value that can be tested in a condition using the value (numbers 1 through 7) or the associated intrinsic constant.

Return Values

Constant	Value	Button Pressed
vbOk	1	OK
vbCancel	2	Cancel
vbAbort	3	Abort
vbRetry	4	Retry
vbIgnore	5	Ignore
vbYes	6	Yes
vbNo	7	No

Specifying the Buttons and/or Icons to Display

You can specify which buttons to display by using numbers or the Visual Basic intrinsic constants. If you want to choose the buttons and an icon, use a plus sign to add the two values together.

Button and Icon Values

Buttons to Display	Value	Constant
OK	0	vbOKOnly
OK and Cancel	1	vbOKCancel
Abort, Retry, and Ignore	2	vbAbortRetryIgnore
Yes, No, and Cancel	3	vbYesNoCancel
Yes and No	4	vbYesNo
Retry and Cancel	5	vbRetryCancel

Icons to Display	Value	Constant
Critical Message	16	vbCritical
Warning Query	32	vbQuestion
Warning Message	48	vbExclamation
Information Message	64	vbInformation

To display Yes, No, and Cancel buttons along with a question mark icon, use one of these statements:

```
intResponse = MsgBox(strMsg, vbYesNoCancel + vbQuestion, "Good Question")
intResponse = MsgBox(strMsg, 3 + 32, "Good Question")
intResponse = MsgBox(strMsg, 35, "Good Question")
```

MsgBox Example

Earlier you learned to use the Clear method to clear the contents of a list box or combo box. In this example we will give the user a chance to confirm whether or not to really clear the list. (Refer to Figure 7.7 for the message box displayed by this procedure.)

```
Private Sub mnuEditClear_Click()
    'Clear the coffee list
    Dim intResponse As Integer

    intResponse = MsgBox("Clear the coffee flavor list?", _
        vbYesNo + vbQuestion, "Clear coffee list")
    If intResponse = vbYes Then
        cboCoffee.Clear
    End If
End Sub
```

Using String Functions

You can look at part of a string, rather than the entire string. Visual Basic provides the **Left**, **Right**, and **Mid functions** that return the specified section of a string.

The Left, Right, and Mid Functions—General Form

```
Left(StringExpression, NumberOfCharacters)
Right(StringExpression, NumberOfCharacters)
Mid(StringExpression, StartPosition, [NumberOfCharacters])
```

StringExpression in each of these statements may be a string variable, string literal, or text property. NumberOfCharacters and StartPosition are both numeric and may be variables, literals, or numeric expressions. In the Mid function, if you omit the NumberOfCharacters argument, the function returns all characters starting with StartPosition.

The Left, Right, and Mid Functions—Examples

```
Left(txtName.Text, 5)       'Returns first 5 characters
Right(strLongString, 1)     'Returns last 1 character
Mid("Mad Hatter", 5, 3)     'Returns 3 characters beginning with character 5
Mid(strProductID, 4)        'Returns all characters beginning with character 4
```

Examples Using Left, Right, and Mid Functions

```
Dim strExample As String
strExample = "It's a wonderful life"
lblMessage.Caption = Left(strExample, 1)       'Returns "I"
lblMessage.Caption = Left(strExample, 6)       'Returns "It's a"
lblMessage.Caption = Left(strExample, 21)      'Returns "It's a wonderful life"
lblMessage.Caption = Left(strExample, 50)      'Returns "It's a wonderful life"
lblMessage.Caption = Right(strExample, 1)      'Returns "e"
lblMessage.Caption = Right(strExample, 4)      'Returns "life"
lblMessage.Caption = Mid(strExample, 8, 9)     'Returns "wonderful"
lblMessage.Caption = Mid(strExample, 8)        'Returns "wonderful life"

If Left(txtDirection.Text, 1) = "N" Then
    lblDirection.Caption = "North"
End If
```

The Len Function

You can use the **Len function** to determine the length of a string expression. You may need to know how many characters the user has entered or how long a list element is.

The Len Function—General Form

```
Len(StringExpression)
```

The value returned by the Len function is an integer count of the number of characters in the string.

The Len Function—Examples

```
Len("Visual Basic")        'Returns 12
Len(txtEntry.Text)         'Returns the number of characters in the text box
Len(strSelection)          'Returns the number of characters in the string variable

If Len(txtName.Text) = 0 Then
    MsgBox "Enter a name", vbInformation, "Data Missing"
End If
```

You can combine the Len function with two new properties of text boxes and the text portion of a combo box—the SelStart and SelLength properties. The SelStart property sets or returns the position of the first selected character; the SelLength property sets or returns the number of selected characters. You can make the current contents of a text box or the Text property of a combo box appear selected when the user tabs into the control and it receives the focus.

```
Private Sub txtName_GotFocus()
    'Select the current entry

    With txtName
        .SelStart = 0              'Begin selection at start
        .SelLength = Len(.Text)    'Select the number of characters
    End With
End Sub
```

Selecting Entries in a List Box

When a list box has a very large number of entries, you can help users by selecting the matching entry as they type in a text box. This method is similar to the way the Help Topics list in Visual Basic works. For example, when you type *p*, the list quickly scrolls and displays words beginning with *p*. Then if you next type *r*, the list scrolls down to the words that begin with *pr* and the first such word is selected. If you type *i* next, the first word beginning with *pri* is selected. The following example implements this feature. See if you can tell what each statement does.

```
Private Sub txtCoffee_Change()
    'Locate first matching occurrence in the list

    Dim intIndex As Integer
    Dim blnFound As Boolean

    Do While Not blnFound And intIndex < lstCoffee.ListCount
        If UCase(Left(lstCoffee.List(intIndex), Len(txtCoffee.Text))) = _
            UCase(txtCoffee.Text) Then
            lstCoffee.ListIndex = intIndex
            blnFound = True
        End If
        intIndex = intIndex + 1
    Loop
End Sub
```

Sending Information to the Printer

So far, any printed output has been done with the PrintForm method. When you print using PrintForm, all output is produced as a graphic, which does not produce attractive text. In addition to printing forms, you will need to create reports or print small bits of information on the printer. You can use the **Print method** to print text on a form, on the Printer object, or in the Debug window.

Visual Basic was designed to run under Windows, which is a highly interactive environment. It is extremely easy to create forms for interactive programs, but not easy at all to print on the printer. Most professional programmers using Visual Basic use a separate utility program to format printer reports.

Several companies sell utilities that do a nice job of designing and printing reports. The VB Professional Edition and Enterprise Edition include a Data Report Designer for creating reports from database files.

Printing to the Printer

You can set up output for the printer using `Printer.Print` (Object.Method). Visual Basic establishes a Printer object in memory for your output. Each time you issue a `Printer.Print` method, your output is added to the Printer object. When your job terminates or it receives an `EndDoc` or `NewPage` method, VB actually sends the contents of the Printer object to the printer.

Formatting Lines

The format of a print line uses punctuation from earlier versions of Basic, the comma and semicolon, as well as a `Tab` function and a `Spc` function. When a line of output contains multiple items to be printed, the items will be separated by commas or semicolons. The list of items may contain literals, variables, or the contents of objects.

When you print on the printer, it is important to consider the font being used. Normally, printing is done with proportional fonts, which means that the amount of space for one character varies with the character. For example, a *w* takes more space than an *i*. You can use a fixed-pitch font, such as Courier, if you want every character to take the same amount of space.

Commas

The output page has preset tab settings with five columns per line. Each column is referred to as a **print zone**. Use a comma to advance the output to the next print zone.

The statement

```
Printer.Print , "R 'n R"
```

prints the "R 'n R" in the second print zone. You can use two commas to advance two print zones:

```
Printer.Print "Name", ,"Phone"
```

The string literal "Name" is printed in print zone 1, and "Phone" is placed in print zone 3. Note that the line prints as though print zone 2 had an empty string literal.

The only way to control the size of a print zone is to change the font size. The width of a print zone is 14 characters, based on the average size of a character for the font being used. Consequently, if you use many narrow characters, such as *i* and *t*, more than 14 characters will fit, but if you are printing many wide characters, such as *w* and *m*, fewer than 14 characters will print in a print zone. Therefore, you may find that some items you print exceed the width of the print zone.

Conceptually, print zones resemble tab stops in a word processor. Each comma means "Jump to the next tab stop." Sometimes you may print a string that extends further than you expected (past the beginning of the next print zone). Then the next comma jumps to the following print zone, perhaps causing your columns to align improperly. In the following example the label will be placed in print zone 4.

```
Printer.Print    "The average amount of sales for the current month is ", _
                 lblSales.Caption
```

When the number of print zones exceeds the number for a single line, the output automatically wraps to the next line on the printed page.

```
Printer.Print 1, 2, 3, 4, 5, 6
```

will output as

```
1                  2               3               4               5
6
```

Semicolons

If you need to separate items without advancing to the next print zone, use a semicolon between the two items. If you leave spaces between items, VB adds semicolons in the code for you. If the value of txtName.Text is "Mary", the line of code

```
Printer.Print "Name: "; txtName.Text
```

will output as

```
Name: Mary
```

Note that the number of spaces left inside the string literal will print out exactly as indicated. If you do not put spaces inside the quotes, you may well end up with one item printing right next to the previous one. The semicolon does not provide spacing on the output, only a means of listing items to print.

Trailing Commas and Semicolons

If the last character on a line of output is a comma or semicolon, the next `Print` method will continue on the same line without advancing the line.

```
Printer.Print "First this ",
Printer.Print "Then this"
```

will output as

```
First this     Then this
```

The print zone rule is still in effect because the first `Print` method ended with a trailing comma.

```
Printer.Print "First this ";
Printer.Print "Then this"
```

will output as

```
First this Then this
```

Printing Blank Lines

When you want to print a blank line on your printed report, use a `Print` method without any item to print:

```
Printer.Print      'Print a blank line
```

The Tab Function

Creating program output that is pleasing, properly spaced, and correctly aligned can be a difficult task. VB has functions to assist in the formatting process.

You can control the placement of variables and constants on a printed line by using the **Tab function**. In the `Tab` function you specify the column position where you want the output to appear. (*Note:* Basic uses the average character width to determine the column position.) The value of the column position argument must be numeric (fractional values will be rounded up), but it may be a constant, a variable, or a numeric expression (calculation).

The column position is absolute, meaning that the 1st position on the line is Tab(1) and the 20th position is Tab(20).

The Tab Function—General Form

```
Tab(Position)
```

The Tab Function—Examples

```
Printer.Print Tab(20); "R 'n R—for Reading 'n Refreshment"
Printer.Print Tab(10); "Name"; Tab(30); "Pay"
Printer.Print Tab(intColumn1); txtName.Text; Tab(intColumn2); curPay
```

If you try to tab to a column that precedes the previous output on the line, the Tab will advance to the specified column position on the next line. Do not use a comma following a `Tab` function; after tabbing to the specified position, it will still advance to the next print zone, destroying the effect of your `Tab` function.

The Spc Function

Another function that controls horizontal spacing on the line is the Spc (space) function. The **Spc function** differs from the `Tab` function in that you specify the number of spaces on the line that you want to advance *from the last item printed.*

The Spc Function—General Form

```
Spc(NumberOfCharacters)
```

The Spc Function—Examples

```
Printer.Print Tab(20); "Name"; Spc(5); "Phone"; Spc(5); "Address"
```

Notice that you can combine Tab and Spc on one print line.

Aligning String and Numeric Data

VB handles spacing for string and numeric data a little differently. String values print with no extra spacing between items. For example, the statement

```
Printer.Print "Sweet"; "Pea"
```

prints as

```
SweetPea
```

Numeric data prints with additional spacing. VB allows one space before each number for a sign. For negative values, a minus sign appears in the position; for positive values, the space remains blank. VB also adds a space following each numeric value. The statement

```
Printer.Print  1;  2;  3;  -1;  -2;  -3
```

outputs this line

```
 1  2  3 -1 -2 -3
```

If you combine string and numeric data, you must be aware of the difference in the spacing. This example combines string and numeric data using print zones.

```
Printer.Print "Item", "Quantity"
Printer.Print "Scissors", 10
Printer.Print "Rocks", -2
Printer.Print "Porcupines", 1
```

The output from these statements appears aligned like this:

```
Item         Quantity
Scissors         10
Rocks            -2
Porcupines        1
```

Tip

You can use the Printer object's CurrentX and CurrentY properties to position output on the page. See Help for more information.

Selecting the Font

Changing the font of printed output is similar to changing the font of a control. The Printer object has a Font property, which refers to the Font object. However, you cannot use the Properties window and *Font* dialog box to change the Font properties; you must change properties in code. When you change the font name, make sure you enter a font name supported by the target printer, spelled correctly. *Hint:* Display the *Font* dialog box for a control and make a note of the available font names. If you aren't sure which fonts your printer supports, stick with TrueType fonts (such as Arial and Times New Roman), which should work on any printer properly installed in Windows.

Examples

```
Printer.Font.Name = "Times New Roman"
Printer.Font.Size = 12
```

You need to change the font name and size only once, before the first item you print.

Terminating the Page or the Job

The `NewPage` method sends the current page to the printer and clears the printer object in memory so you can begin a new page. The `EndDoc` method sends the current page to the printer and terminates the printer job. *Note:* When your program terminates, Visual Basic automatically sends an `EndDoc`.

```
Printer.NewPage        'Send page and begin a new page
Printer.EndDoc         'Send page and terminate the print job
```

Use the `NewPage` or `EndDoc` methods after sending the information to the printer.

Example

```
Private Sub PrintReport()
    Printer.Print
    Printer.Print Tab(13); "Monthly Sales Summary"
    Printer.Print
    Printer.Print
    Printer.Print Tab(10); "Sales"; Tab(30); "Returns"
    Printer.Print Tab(10); "============================"
    Printer.Print
    Printer.Print Tab(10); FormatCurrency(mcurSalesTotal); _
                  Tab(30); FormatCurrency(mcurReturnsTotal)
    Printer.EndDoc    must have this to release spooled print
End Sub
```

Printing the Contents of a List Box

You can combine the techniques for printing, a loop, and the list box properties to send the contents of a list box to the printer. You know how many iterations to make, using the ListCount property. The List property allows you to print out the actual values from the list.

```
Private Sub mnuFilePrintAll_Click()
    'Print the contents of the coffee flavors
    'combo box on the printer

    Dim intIndex As Integer
    Dim intFinalValue As Integer
    intFinalValue = cboCoffee.ListCount - 1
    For intIndex = 0 To intFinalValue 'List index starts at 0
        Printer.Print cboCoffee.List(intIndex)
    Next intIndex
    Printer.EndDoc
End Sub
```

Printing the Selected Item from a List

When an item is selected in a list box or a combo box, the Text property holds the selected item. You can use the Text property to print the selected item.

```
Printer.Print Tab(10); "Coffee Flavor: "; cboCoffee.Text
Printer.Print              'Blank line
Printer.Print Tab(10); "Syrup Flavor: "; lstSyrup.Text
```

Aligning Decimal Columns

When the output to the printer includes numeric data, the alignment of the decimal points is important. One solution you may wish to use incorporates the Len function.

To right align numeric output:

STEP 1: Assign the formatted value to a string variable.
STEP 2: Determine the column position for the Tab at the position where you want the formatted value to *end*.
STEP 3: Tab the difference between the Tab position and the length of the formatted string variable.
STEP 4: Print the formatted value.

For example, if you want to right align a column for total pay on a printed report, you can use the following code:

```
Dim strFormattedNumber As String

strFormattedNumber = FormatCurrency(curTotalPay)
Printer.Print   Tab(10); strName ; Tab(50 - Len(strFormattedNumber)); _
              strFormattedNumber
```

The formatted curTotalPay will print right aligned at column 50.

Tip

While testing your program, use `Debug.Print` in place of `Printer.Print`. The output appears in the Immediate window.

Feedback 7.4

What will print for each of these code segments? Try to determine the results by hand; then enter them into the computer to verify your results.

1. ```
   Printer.Print "Half a loaf";
   Printer.Print "Is better than none"
   ```
2. ```
   Printer.Print "Half,","My Eye"
   ```
3. ```
   Printer.Print "Hawks";0,"Doves";0
   ```
4. ```
   Printer.Print 1,
   Printer.Print 2,
   Printer.Print 3,
   Printer.Print 4,
   Printer.Print 5,
   Printer.Print 6
   ```
5. ```
   Printer.Print 1, 2, 3, 4, 5, 6
   ```
6. ```
   Printer.Print Tab(10); 3; Tab(20); 5
   ```
7. ```
   Printer.Print Spc(10); 3; Spc(20); 5
   ```

Your Hands-On Programming Example

Create a project for R 'n R—for Reading 'n Refreshment that contains a drop-down combo box of the coffee flavors and a list box of the syrup flavors. Adjust the size of the boxes as needed when you test the project. The controls should have labels above them containing the words *Coffee* and *Syrup*. Enter the initial values for the syrup flavors and coffee flavors in the Properties window. The user will be able to add more coffee flavors to the list at run time.

Coffee Flavors	Syrup Flavors
Espresso Roast	Chocolate
Jamaica Blue Mountain	Irish Cream
Kona Blend	Hazelnut
Chocolate Almond	Orange
Vanilla Nut	

Include one menu item to print all the flavors on the printer and another to print only a selected item from each list. These two menu print commands belong on the *File* menu, along with the *Exit* command. Use a separator bar between the *Prints* and the *Exit*.

Include an *Edit* menu with commands to *Add coffee flavor*, *Remove coffee flavor*, *Clear coffee list*, and *Display coffee count*.

Add the About form from Chapter 6 into your project and add a *Help* menu with an *About* command.
   ```

After you have completed the project, try using different styles for the combo box and rerun the project. As an added challenge, modify the add coffee flavor routine so that duplicates are not allowed.

Planning the Project

Sketch a form (Figure 7.8), which your users sign off as meeting their needs.

F i g u r e   7 . 8

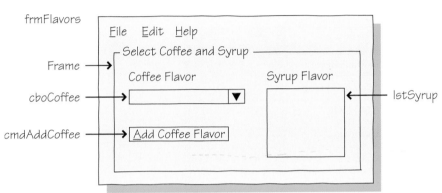

A sketch of the main form for the hands-on project.

Plan the Objects and Properties

Object	Property	Setting
frmFlavors	Name	frmFlavors
	Caption	R 'n R—for Reading 'n Refreshment
Frame1	Name	Frame1
	Caption	Select Coffee and Syrup
Label1	Caption	Coffee Flavor
Label2	Caption	Syrup Flavor
cboCoffee	Name	cboCoffee
	Style	0 - Dropdown combo
	Text	(blank)
	List	Chocolate Almond
		Espresso Roast
		Jamaica Blue Mtn.
		Kona Blend
		Vanilla Nut
	Sorted	True

(continued)

Object	Property	Setting
lstSyrup	Name	lstSyrup
	Sorted	True
	List	Chocolate
		Hazelnut
		Irish Creme
		Orange
cmdAddCoffee	Name	cmdAddCoffee
	Caption	&Add Coffee Flavor
mnuFile	Name	mnuFile
	Caption	&File
mnuFilePrintSelect	Name	mnuFilePrintSelect
	Caption	Print &Selected Flavors
mnuFilePrintAll	Name	mnuFilePrintAll
	Caption	Print &All Flavors
mnuSep	Name	mnuSep
	Caption	-
mnuFileExit	Name	mnuFileExit
	Caption	E&xit
mnuEdit	Name	mnuEdit
	Caption	&Edit
mnuEditAdd	Name	mnuEditAdd
	Caption	&Add coffee flavor
mnuEditRemove	Name	mnuEditRemove
	Caption	&Remove coffee flavor
mnuEditClear	Name	mnuEditClear
	Caption	&Clear coffee list
mnuEditCount	Name	mnuEditCount
	Caption	Count coffee &list
mnuHelp	Name	mnuHelp
	Caption	&Help
mnuHelpAbout	Name	mnuHelpAbout
	Caption	&About

Plan the Event Procedures

Main Form

Procedure	Actions

cmdAddCoffee	If text box in cboCoffee not empty then
	    Add contents of cboCoffee text box to list
	    Clear the text box in cboCoffee.
	Else
	    Display error message.
	End If
	Set the focus to cboCoffee.

mnuFilePrintSelect	If both coffee and syrup selected
	    Print only selected items.
	Else
	    Display error message.
	End If

mnuFilePrintAll	Print title and headings. Use a loop to send all flavor names to the printer.
mnuFileExit	Terminate the Project.
mnuEditAdd	Call cmdAddCoffee_Click.

mnuEditRemove	If coffee flavor selected then
	    Remove selected item.
	Else
	    Display error message.
	End If

mnuEditClear	Clear the coffee list.
mnuEditCount	Display list count in message box.
mnuHelpAbout	Display the About box.

About Form

Procedure	Action
cmdOK	Hide the About box.

Write the Project

- Follow the sketch in Figure 7.8 to create the form. Figure 7.9 shows the completed form.

- Set the properties of each object as you have planned.

- Write the code. Working from the pseudocode, write each event procedure.

- When you complete the code, use a variety of data to thoroughly test the project.

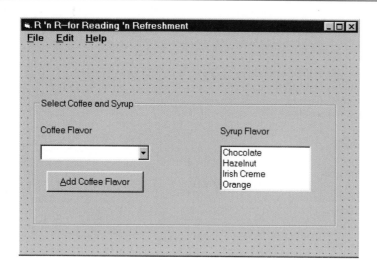

The form for the hands-on project.

The Project Coding Solution

Main Form

```
'Module:                  frmFlavors
'Programmer:              A. Millspaugh
'Date:                    July 1999
'Description:             Print the selected flavor of coffee and syrup
'                         or print a list of all of the coffee flavors.
'Folder:                  Ch0701

Option Explicit
```

```
Private Sub cmdAddCoffee_Click()
    'Add a new coffee flavor to the coffee list

    If cboCoffee.Text <> "" Then
        With cboCoffee
            .AddItem .Text
            .Text = ""
        End With
    Else
        MsgBox "Enter a coffee name to add", vbExclamation, "Missing data"
    End If
    cboCoffee.SetFocus
End Sub
```

```
Private Sub mnuEditAdd_Click()
    'Add a new coffee to list

    cmdAddCoffee_Click
End Sub
```

```vb
Private Sub mnuEditClear_Click()
    'Clear the coffee list

    Dim intResponse As Integer

    intResponse = MsgBox("Clear the coffee flavor list?", _
        vbYesNo + vbQuestion, "Clear coffee list")
    If intResponse = vbYes Then
        cboCoffee.Clear
    End If
End Sub
```

```vb
Private Sub mnuEditCount_Click()
    'Display a count of the coffee list

    MsgBox "The number of coffee types is " & cboCoffee.ListCount
End Sub
```

```vb
Private Sub mnuEditRemove_Click()
    'Remove the selected coffee from list

    If cboCoffee.ListIndex <> -1 Then
        cboCoffee.RemoveItem cboCoffee.ListIndex
    Else
        MsgBox "First select the coffee to remove", vbInformation, _
        "No selection made"
    End If
End Sub
```

```vb
Private Sub mnuHelpAbout_Click()
    'Display frmAbout

    frmAbout.Show
End Sub
```

```vb
Private Sub mnuFileExit_Click()
    'Terminate the project

    End
End Sub
```

```vb
Private Sub mnuFilePrintAll_Click()
    'Print the contents of the coffee flavors
    'combo box on the printer

    Dim intIndex        As Integer
    Dim intFinalValue   As Integer
```

```
        Printer.Print 'Blank line
        Printer.Print Tab(20); "Coffee Flavors"
        Printer.Print 'Blank line
        intFinalValue = cboCoffee.ListCount - 1
        'List index starts at 0
        For intIndex = 0 To intFinalValue
            Printer.Print Tab(20); cboCoffee.List(intIndex)
        Next intIndex
        Printer.EndDoc
End Sub


Private Sub mnuFilePrintSelect_Click()
    'Send the current selection of coffee flavor
    ' and syrup flavor to the printer

    If cboCoffee.ListIndex <> -1 And lstSyrup.ListIndex <> -1 Then
        Printer.Print 'Blank line
        Printer.Print Tab(15); "Coffee Selection"
        Printer.Print 'Blank line
        Printer.Print Tab(10); "Coffee Flavor: "; cboCoffee.Text
        Printer.Print 'Blank line
        Printer.Print Tab(10); "Syrup Flavor: "; lstSyrup.Text
        Printer.EndDoc
    Else
        MsgBox "Make a selection for coffee and syrup.", vbExclamation, _
            "Missing Data"
    End If
End Sub
```

About Form

```
'Module:            frmAbout
'Programmer:        A. Millspaugh
'Date:              July 1999
'Description:       Display information about the program
'                   and the programmer
'Folder:            Ch0701
Option Explicit


Private Sub cmdOK_Click()
    'Returns to the main form

    frmAbout.Hide
End Sub
```

S u m m a r y

1. List boxes and combo boxes hold lists of values. The three styles of combo boxes are simple combo boxes, dropdown combo boxes, and dropdown lists.
2. The size of a list box or combo box is determined at design time. If all of the items will not fit into the box, VB automatically adds scroll bars.
3. Initial values for the items in a list can be entered in the List property in the Properties window. At run time, items are added to lists using the `AddItem` method.
4. The `Clear` method may be used to remove the contents of a list box.
5. The ListIndex property can be used to select an item in the list or to determine which item is selected.
6. The ListCount property holds the number of elements in the list.
7. The List property holds all elements of the list. The individual elements can be referenced by using an index.
8. The `RemoveItem` method removes one element from a list.
9. Code can be written for several events of list boxes and combo boxes. Combo boxes have a Change event; both combo boxes and list boxes have GetFocus and LostFocus events.
10. A loop allows a statement or series of statements to be repeated. `Do/Loops` continue to execute the statements in the loop until a condition is met.
11. `Do/Loops` can have the condition test at the top or the bottom of the loop and can use a `While` or `Until` to test the conditon.
12. A `Do/Loop` can be used to locate a selected item in a combo box.
13. A loop index controls `For/Next` loops; the index is initialized to a starting value. After each iteration the loop index is incremented by the `Step` value, which defaults to 1. The loop is terminated when the loop index reaches the ending value.
14. The `Left`, `Right`, and `Mid` functions return a part of a string.
15. The `Len` function returns the number of characters in a string.
16. The `Printer.Print` statement sends lines of text to the printer, rather than printing the graphical form.
17. The `Print` method uses commas, semicolons, and the `Spc` function to control spacing. The `Tab` function can be used to align columns of information.
18. By default, the `Print` method uses proportional fonts, which allow a variable amount of space for a character, depending on the character width.

    With proportional fonts it is difficult to judge the number of characters in a print zone or the amount of space the text will require.
19. Aligning columns of numbers is difficult because print zones and the `Tab` function left align values. Numbers can be right aligned with the assistance of the `Len` function.

Key Terms

AddItem method   *254*
Clear method   *255*
combo box control   *252*
Do and Loop statements   *258*
Do/Loop   *258*
dropdown combo box   *252*
dropdown list   *252*
For and Next statements   *262*
For/Next loop   *262*
iteration   *258*
Left function   *269*
Len function   *270*
list box control   *252*
List property   *256*
ListCount property   *256*

ListIndex property   *255*
loop   *258*
loop index   *262*
Mid function   *269*
MsgBox function   *267*
posttest   *259*
pretest   *259*
Print method   *271*
print zone   *272*
RemoveItem method   *257*
Right function   *269*
simple combo box   *252*
Sorted property   *255*
Spc function   *274*
Tab function   *274*

Review Questions

1. What is a list box? a combo box?
2. Name and describe the three styles of combo boxes.
3. How can you make scroll bars appear on a list box or combo box?
4. Explain the purpose of the ListIndex property and the ListCount property.
5. When and how is information placed inside a list box or a combo box?
6. In what situation would a loop be used in a procedure?
7. Explain the difference between a pretest and a posttest in a Do/Loop.
8. Explain the differences between a Do/Loop and a For/Next loop.
9. What are the steps in processing a For/Next loop?
10. Discuss how and when the values of the loop index change throughout the processing of the loop.
11. What is the purpose of Printer.Print?
12. How do the Left, Right, and Len functions operate?
13. How do you control the horizontal spacing of printer output?

Programming Exercises

7.1 Create a project for obtaining student information.
Startup form controls are as follows:
- Text boxes for entering the name and units completed.
- Option buttons for Freshman, Sophomore, Junior, and Senior.
- Check box for Dean's List.
- Use a list box for the following majors: Accounting, Business, Computer Information Systems, and Marketing.

- A simple combo for name of high school—initially loaded with Franklin, Highland, West Highland, and Midtown. If the user types in a new school name, it should be added to the list.
- Print command button that will print the data from the form. Send the output to the printer, nicely formatted. (Do not use `PrintForm`.)
- An OK (for Enter) button that will clear the entries from the form and reset the focus. Set the button's Default property to True.

Menu: The *File* menu will have an option for *Print Schools* and *Exit*. The *Help* menu will have an option for the *About* box.

Note: Print your name at the top of the printer output for the schools.

7.2 R 'n R—for Reading 'n Refreshment needs a project that contains a form for entering book information.

Form Controls:

- Text boxes for author and title.
- Option buttons for type: fiction or nonfiction.
- Dropdown list for Subject that will include Best-Seller, Fantasy, Religion, Romance, Humor, Science Fiction, Business, Philosophy, Education, Self-Help, and Mystery.
- List box for Shelf Number containing RC-1111, RC-1112, RC-1113, and RC-1114.
- Print command button that will print the data from the form. (Do not use `PrintForm`.)
- An OK (for Enter) button that will clear the entries from the form and reset the focus. Set the Default property to True.

Menu: The *File* menu will have an option for *Print Subjects* and *Exit*. The *Help* menu will have an option for the *About* box.

Note: Print your name at the top of the printer output for the subjects.

7.3 Create a project to input chartering information about yachts and print a summary report showing the total revenue and average hours per charter.

Startup Form:

The startup form will contain a menu. The *File* menu will contain commands for *New Charter*, *Print Summary*, *Print Yacht Types*, and *Exit*. Place separator bars before *Print Summary* and after *Print Yacht Types*. The *Edit* menu should have commands for *Add Yacht Type*, *Remove Yacht Type*, and *Display Count of Yacht Types*. The *Help* menu will contain an *About* command.

New Charter Form:

- The new charter form will contain text boxes for responsible party and hours chartered.
- A dropdown combo box will contain the type of yacht: Ranger, Wavelength, Catalina, Coronado, Hobie, C & C, Hans Christian, and Excalibur. Any items that are added to the text box during processing must be added to the list.
- Another dropdown list will contain size: 22, 24, 30, 32, 36, 38, 45. (No new sizes can be entered at run time.)
- An OK command button will add to the totals, print a line on the summary report (do not end the page), and return to the startup form. The print line will contain the yacht type, size, responsible party, hours chartered, and total revenue for the hours chartered. The calculations will require price per hour—use the following chart:

Size	Hourly Rate
22	95.00
24	137.00
30	160.00
32	192.00
36	250.00
38	400.00
45	550.00

A Cancel command button will return to the startup form with no calculations.

Set the Default property of the OK button to True; set the Cancel property of the Cancel button to True.

Summary Report: The summary report will print the summary information and send the report to the printer. The summary information will include *Total Revenue* and *Average Hours Chartered*.

7.4 Create a project that contains a list box with the names of all U.S. states and territories. When the user types the first letters of the state into a text box, set the ListIndex property of the list box to display the appropriate name.

Alabama	Illinois	Nevada
Alaska	Indiana	New Hampshire
American Samoa	Iowa	New Jersey
Arizona	Kansas	New Mexico
Arkansas	Kentucky	New York
California	Louisiana	North Carolina
Colorado	Maine	North Dakota
Connecticut	Maryland	Ohio
Delaware	Massachusetts	Oklahoma
District of Columbia	Michigan	Oregon
Florida	Minnesota	Pennsylvania
Georgia	Mississippi	Puerto Rico
Guam	Missouri	Rhode Island
Hawaii	Montana	South Carolina
Idaho	Nebraska	South Dakota

(continued)

Tennessee	Vermont	West Virginia
Texas	Virgin Islands	Wisconsin
Trust Territories	Virginia	Wyoming
Utah	Washington	

7.5   Generate mailing labels with an account number for catalog subscriptions. The project will allow the user to enter Last Name, First Name, Street, City, State, ZIP Code, and Expiration Date for the subscription. A dropdown list box will contain the names of the catalogs: *Odds and Ends, Solutions, Camping Needs, ToolTime, Spiegel, The Outlet,* and *The Large Size.*

Use validation to make sure that entries appear in the Last Name, ZIP code, and Expiration Date fields.

The account number will consist of the first two characters of the last name, the first three digits of the ZIP code, and the expiration date. Display the account number in a label on the form when the user clicks on the *Display Account Number* button or menu option.

The menu or command buttons for the project should have options for *Print Label*, *Display Account Number*, *Exit*, and *Clear*.

The *Print label* menu command will print the label using the following format:

First Name Last Name Account Number

Street

City, State ZIP Code

7.6   Maintain a list of bagel types for Bradley's Bagels. Use a dropdown combo box to hold the bagel types and use command buttons or menu choices to *Add Bagel Type*, *Remove Bagel Type*, *Clear Bagel List*, *Print Bagel List*, *Display Bagel Type Count*, and *Exit.* Keep the list sorted in alphabetic order.

Do not allow a blank type to be added to the list. Display an error message if the user selects *Remove* without first selecting a bagel type.

Before clearing the list, display a message box to confirm the operation.

Here are some suggested bagel types. You can make up your own list.

Plain	Poppy seed
Egg	Sesame seed
Rye	Banana nut
Salt	Blueberry

C A S E   S T U D I E S

VB Mail Order

Modify your project from Chapter 6 to print invoices. The invoice will have customer information at the top, one detail line for each item ordered, and summary totals.

You will also add a dropdown combo box, which will hold the names of the catalogs: *Odds and Ends, Solutions, Camping Needs, ToolTime, Spiegel, The Outlet,* and *The Large Size.*

The user must be able to enter customer information to begin a new invoice. After entering customer information, the user can enter information about each item purchased. Do not allow the user to enter an item until after the customer information is entered. Also, do not allow the user to begin a new invoice until after the previous one is completed or canceled.

After entering the information for an item purchased, the user can choose to add the item to the invoice, clear the fields to enter another item, display the invoice summary, or cancel the order. If the user chooses to display the invoice summary, show the current invoice heading and summary information on an invoice summary form. The invoice summary form should have a *Print* button to print the summary information at the bottom of the current invoice.

You will have to modify the menus from the Chapter 6 project. Use menu choices that make it clear to the user what actions to take to enter and print an invoice. You may also choose to place command buttons on your forms.

When the user begins a new order, print the *Bill To* section and the invoice headings on the printer. Print one line for each item when it is added to the invoice; do not use the `EndDoc` method until after printing the summary information. Use `Printer.Print` statements for all printing—do not use `PrintForm`.

Add a *Print Catalog List* to your menu and remove the *Print* that uses a `PrintForm` from the menu.

Note: You may want to disable the *Print Catalog List* menu option while an invoice is in progress. Set mnuFilePrintCatalogList.Enabled = False when you begin an invoice and reset it to True after an invoice is complete.

Bill To: Customer Name
Customer Street Address
Customer City, State, ZIP

Catalog Name   Description   Quantity   Each Price

Total Price
Tax
Shipping and Handling
Total Due

Create a project for the car wash **VB Auto Center** located at VB Auto Center.

The form will contain three list box or combo box controls that do not permit the user to add items at run time. The first list will contain the names of the packages available for detailing a vehicle: Standard, Deluxe, Executive, or Luxury.

The contents of the other two lists will vary depending upon the package selected. Display one list for the interior work and one list for the exterior work. Store the descriptions of the items in string constants. The list for the interior and exterior must be cleared and new items added each time a selection is made from the package list.

Use a dropdown list to allow the user to select the fragrance. The choices are Hawaiian Mist, Baby Powder, Pine, Country Floral, Pina Colada, and Vanilla.

Include menu commands for *Print*, *Clear*, and *Exit*. The printout will contain the package name, the interior and exterior items being formed, and the fragrance selected. Use a `For/Next` loop when printing the interior and exterior lists.

	Item Description	S	D	E	L
Exterior	Hand Wash	√	√	√	√
	Hand Wax		√	√	√
	Check Engine Fluids			√	√
	Detail Engine Compartment				√
	Detail Under Carriage				√
Interior	Fragrance	√	√	√	√
	Shampoo Carpets		√	√	√
	Shampoo Upholstery				√
	Interior Protection Coat (dashboard and console)			√	
	Scotchgard™				√

Note: S—Standard; D—Deluxe; E—Executive; L—Luxury

Video Bonanza

Maintain a list of movie categories. Use a dropdown combo box to hold the movie types and use command buttons or menu choices to *Add a Category, Remove a Category, Clear all Categories, Print the Category List, Display the Movie Category Count,* and *Exit.* Keep the list sorted in alphabetic order.

Do not allow a blank type to be added to the list. Display an error message if the user selects *Remove* without first selecting a movie category. Before clearing the list, display a message box to confirm the operation.

The starting categories are

- Comedy
- Drama
- Action
- Sci-Fi
- Horror

Very Very Boards

Modify your project from Chapter 6 to include a dropdown combo box that holds the style of shirt, such as crew, turtle neck, or crop top. Add a *Style* menu with options to *Add Style, Remove Style, Clear Style List, Count Styles,* and *Print Style List.* Include keyboard shortcuts for the menu commands.

8

Arrays

At the completion of this chapter, you will be able to . . .

1. Set up and use a control array.

2. Code selection logic using a `Select Case` statement.

3. Establish an array of variables and refer to individual elements in the array with variable subscripts.

4. Use the `For Each/Next` to traverse the array.

5. Create user-defined data types for multiple fields of related data.

6. Accumulate totals using arrays.

7. Distinguish between direct access and indirect access of a table.

8. Combine the advantages of list box controls with arrays.

9. Coordinate lists and arrays using the ItemData property.

10. Store data in multidimensional arrays.

Control Arrays

When you plan to include a group of option buttons or check boxes on a form, it often makes sense to create a control array. A ***control array*** is a group of controls that all have the same name. All controls in an array must be the same class. An advantage of using a control array, rather than independent controls, is that the controls share one Click event. In the array's Click event, you can use a Case structure (discussed in the next section) to determine which button or box is selected.

For an example, assume that you are using a group of five option buttons to allow the user to choose a color. After creating the five buttons (Figure 8.1), begin setting the properties by setting the Name property. Name the first option button *optColor*. Then change the Name property of the second option button to *optColor* also (Figure 8.2); a message box (Figure 8.3) will ask whether you want to create a control array.

The five option buttons allow the user to choose the color

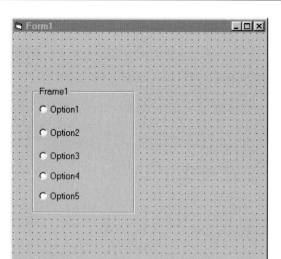

Set the name of the first button to optColor.

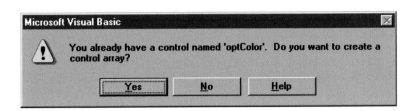

After you select Yes, the name in the top of the Properties window becomes *optColor(0)* for the first control and *optColor(1)* for the second. The number inside the parentheses is called an ***index*** and is used to refer to the specific control within the array. All subsequent controls given the same name will automatically have an index attached.

The option buttons in Figure 8.1 are named optColor(0), optColor(1), optColor(2), optColor(3), and optColor(4).

The Case Structure

In Chapter 4 you used the If statement for testing conditions and making decisions. Whenever you want to test a single variable or expression for multiple values, the Case structure provides a flexible and powerful solution. Any program decisions that you can code with a Case structure can also be coded with nested If statements, but usually the Case structure is simpler and clearer.

The Select Case Statement—General Form

```
Select Case expression
    Case constant list
        [statement(s)]
    [Case constant list
        [statement(s)]]

    .
    .
    .

    [Case Else]
        [statement(s)]
End Select
```

The expression in a Case structure is usually a variable or property you wish to test.

The constant list is the value that you want to match; it may be a numeric or string constant or variable, a range of values, a relational condition, or a combination of these.

There is no limit to the number of statements that can follow a Case statement.

The Select Case Statement—Example

```
Select Case intScore
    Case Is >= 100
        lblMessage1.Caption = "Excellent Score"
        lblMessage2.Caption = "Give yourself a pat on the back"
    Case 80 To 99
        lblMessage1.Caption = "Very Good"
        lblMessage2.Caption = "You should be proud"
    Case 60 To 79
        lblMessage1.Caption = "Satisfactory Score"
        lblMessage2.Caption = "You should have a nice warm feeling"
    Case Else
        lblMessage1.Caption = "Your score shows room for improvement"
        lblMessage2.Caption = ""
End Select
```

This example shows a combination of relational operators and constant ranges. Two points that were illustrated must be noted here:

When using a relational operator (e.g., `Is >= 100`) the word `Is` must be used.

To indicate a range of constants, use the word `To` (e.g., `80 To 99`).

The elements used for the constant list may have any of these forms:

```
constant [,constant...]              Case 2, 5, 9
constant To constant                 Case 25 To 50
Is relational-operator constant      Case Is < 10
```

When you want to test for a string value, you must include quotation marks around the literals.

Example

```
Select Case txtTeamName.Text
    Case "Tigers"
        (Code for Tigers)
    Case "Leopards"
        (Code for Leopards)
    Case "Cougars", "Panthers"
        (Code for Cougars and Panthers)
    Case Else
        (Code for any nonmatch)
End Select
```

Note that in the previous example, the capitalization must also match exactly. A better solution would be

```
Select Case UCase(txtTeamName.Text)
    Case "TIGERS"
        (Code for Tigers)
    Case "LEOPARDS"
        (Code for Leopards)
    Case "COUGARS", "PANTHERS"
        (Code for Cougars and Panthers)
    Case Else
        (Code for any nonmatch)
End Select
```

Although the `Case Else` clause is optional, generally you will want to include it in `Select Case` statements. The statements you code beneath `Case Else` execute only if none of the other `Case` conditions is matched. This clause provides checking for any invalid or unforeseen values of the expression being tested. If the `Case Else` clause is omitted and none of the `Case` conditions is True, the program continues execution at the statement following the `End Select`.

If more than one `Case` value is matched by the expression, only the statements in the first `Case` clause executes.

Testing Option Buttons with the Case Structure

The Case structure is ideal for testing which option button is selected. When the user selects one of the option buttons, their common Click event occurs. Notice in the following example that VB passes Index as an argument to the event procedure. Index holds the number of the selected button (0, 1, 2, 3, or 4). You can use the value of Index in a `Select Case` statement.

Note: The argument inside the parentheses, "Index as Integer," means that VB is passing a variable called *Index* with a data type of integer.

Example

```
Private Sub optColor_Click(Index As Integer)
    'Set the color to match the selected option button

    Select Case Index
        Case 0          'First button is selected
            lblMessage.ForeColor = vbBlue
        Case 1          'Second button is selected
            lblMessage.ForeColor = vbBlack
        Case 2          'Third button is selected
            lblMessage.ForeColor = vbRed
        Case 3          'Fourth button is selected
            lblMessage.ForeColor = vbWhite
        Case 4          'Fifth button is selected
            lblMessage.ForeColor = vbYellow
    End Select
End Sub
```

As you know, making changes occur for the Click event of an option button violates one of the standards for Windows programming. The color should actually be changed in the Click event for a command button. However, the option button's Index is not available in the command button's Click event. Therefore, the best practice is to set up a module-level variable to hold the selection. In the Click event for the option button, set the value of the module-level variable; in the Click event for the command button, check the value of the variable.

Example

```
'General Declarations
Option Explicit
Dim mlngSelectedColor As Long 'The color constants are long integers


Private Sub cmdDisplay_Click()
    'Change the color of the label

    lblMessage.ForeColor = mlngSelectedColor
End Sub


Private Sub optColor_Click(Index As Integer)
    'Save color selection

    Select Case Index
        Case 0                  'Blue button is selected
            mlngSelectedColor = vbBlue
        Case 1                  'Black button is selected
            mlngSelectedColor = vbBlack
        Case 2                  'Red button is selected
            mlngSelectedColor = vbRed
        Case 3          'White button is selected
            mlngSelectedColor = vbWhite
        Case 4              'Yellow button is selected
            mlngSelectedColor = vbYellow
    End Select
End Sub
```

Feedback 8.1

1. Convert the following If statement to a Select Case.

```
If intTemp <= 32 Then
    lblComment.Caption = "Freezing"
ElseIf intTemp > 80 Then
    lblComment.Caption = "Hot"
Else
    lblComment.Caption = "Moderate"
End If
```

2. Convert the following to a `Select Case` in the Click event procedure for optCoffee.

```
If optCoffee(0).Value = True Then
    curPrice = 2
ElseIf optCoffee(1).Value = True Then
    curPrice = 2.25
ElseIf optCoffee(2).Value = True Then
    curPrice = 1.75
ElseIf optCoffee(3).Value = True
    curPrice = 2.5
End If
```

[Handwritten annotation:]
```
Select Case intIndex
  Case (0)
     curCoffeePrice = 2
  Case 1
     curCoffeePrice = 2.25
  Case 2
     curCoffeePrice = 1.75
  Case 3
     curCoffeePrice = 2.5
End Select
```

3. Add a clause to the previous `Select Case` to display a message box if no option button is selected.

Single-Dimension Arrays

You have just seen how you can set up an array of controls in which several controls have the same name. Now you will find similar advantages to creating and using an array of variables.

A variable array can contain a list of values, similar to a list box or a combo box. In fact, Visual Basic actually stores the List property of a list box or a combo box in an array. You can think of an array as a list box without the box. Any time you need to keep a series of variables for later processing, such as reordering, calculating, or printing, you need to set up an array.

Consider an example that has a form for entering product information one product at a time. After the user has entered many products, you will need to calculate some statistics and perhaps use the information in different ways. Of course, each time the user enters the data for the next product, the previous contents of the text boxes are replaced. You could assign the previous values to variables, but they also would be replaced for each new product. Another approach might be to create multiple variables, such as strProduct1, strProduct2, strProduct3, and so on. This approach might be reasonable for a few entries, but what happens when you need to store 50 or 500 products?

When you need to store multiple values, use an array. An **array** is a series of individual variables, all referenced by the same name. Sometimes arrays are referred to as **tables** or **subscripted variables**. When you use a control array, the individual controls are referenced as optCoffee(0) or optCoffee(1). The same notation is used with variable arrays. Therefore, in an array for storing names, you may have strName(0), strName(1), strName(2), and so on.

Each individual variable is called an **element** of the array. The individual elements are treated the same as any other variable and may be used in any statement, such as an assignment or a `Printer.Print`. The **subscript** (which may also be called an *index*) inside the parentheses is the position of the element within the array. Figure 8.4 illustrates an array of 10 elements with subscripts from 0 to 9.

strName array

(0)	Janet Baker
(1)	George Lee
(2)	Sue Li
(3)	Samuel Hoosier
(4)	Sandra Weeks
(5)	William Macy
(6)	Andy Harrison
(7)	Ken Ford
(8)	Denny Franks
(9)	Shawn James

An array of string variables with 10 elements. Subscripts are 0 through 9.

Subscripts

The real advantage of using an array is not realized until you use variables for subscripts in place of the constants.

```
strName(intIndex) = ""
Printer.Print strName(intIndex)
```

Subscripts may be constants, variables, or numeric expressions. Although the subscripts must be integers, Visual Basic will round any noninteger subscript.

A question has probably occurred to you by now—how many elements are there in the strName array? The answer is that you must specify the number of elements in a Dim statement.

The Dim Statement for Arrays—General Form

```
Dim ArrayName([LowerSubscript To] UpperSubscript) [As Datatype]
```

The Dim Statement for Arrays—Examples

```
Dim strName(0 to 25)      As String
Dim curBalance(10)        As Currency
Dim gstrProduct(1 To 100) As String
Dim mintValue(-10 To 10)  As Integer
```

The Dim statement allocates storage for the specified number of elements and initializes each numeric variable to 0. In the case of string arrays, each element is set to an empty string (zero characters). It is not necessary to specify the lower subscript value. If no value is set for the lower subscript, then the lowest subscript is 0.

Arrays can be dimensioned with empty parentheses, such as

```
Public gstrCustomer() As String
```

An array dimensioned in this way is referred to as a *dynamic array* because the number of elements may change during program execution by using the `Redim` statement. All other arrays are fixed in size and referred to as *static arrays*. Each static array may be dimensioned only once in a project. Any attempt to change the size of a static array after its first use causes the following error message: *Array already dimensioned*. This text treats all arrays as static.

Note: The term "static array" should not be confused with static variables, which use the VB keyword `Static`. Static variables remain in memory for the lifetime of the module.

More on Subscripts

A subscript must reference a valid element of the array. If a list contains 10 names, it wouldn't make sense to ask: What is the 15th name on the list? or What is the 2½th name on the list? Visual Basic rounds fractional subscripts and gives the error message: *Subscript out of range* for invalid subscripts.

Feedback 8.2

```
Dim strName(20) As String
Const intValue As Integer = 10
```

After execution of the preceding statements, which of the following are valid subscripts?

1. strName(20)
2. strName(intValue)
3. strName(intValue * 2)
4. strName(intValue * 3) *Beyond range*
5. strName(0)
6. strName(intValue - 20) *Negative number*
7. strName(intValue / 3) *VB uses integer portion of decimal number*
8. strName(intValue / 5 - 2)

For Each/Next Statements

When you use an array, you need a way to reference each element in the array. `For/Next` loops, which you learned to use in Chapter 7, work well to traverse the elements in an array. Another handy loop construct is the `For Each` and `Next`. The significant advantage of using the **For Each/Next** is that you don't have to manipulate the subscripts of the array.

The For Each and Next Statements—General Form

```
For Each ElementName In ArrayName
    'statement(s) in loop
Next [ElementName]
```

Visual Basic automatically references each element of the array, assigns its value to ElementName, and makes one pass through the loop. If the array has 12 elements, for example, the loop will execute 12 times. The variable used for ElementName must be a variant data type.

In the following examples assume that the arrays strName and intTotal have already been dimensioned and that they hold data.

The For Each and Next Statements—Examples

```
Dim vntOneName As Variant
For Each vntOneName In strName
    Printer.Print vntOneName          'Print one element of the array
Next vntOneName

Dim vntTotal As Variant
For Each vntTotal In intTotal
    vntTotal = 0                      'Set one element of the array to zero
Next vntTotal
```

The For Each loop will execute if the array has at least one element. All the statements within the loop are executed for the first element. If the array has more elements, the loop continues to execute until all the elements are processed. When the loop finishes, execution of code continues with the line following the Next statement.

Note: You may use an Exit For statement within a loop to exit early, just as in a For/Next loop.

Initializing an Array Using For Each

Although all numeric variables are initially set to 0, it is sometimes necessary to reinitialize variables. To zero out an array, each individual element must be set to 0.

```
For Each vntTotal In intTotal
    vntTotal = 0 'Set value of each element to 0
Next vntTotal
```

User-Defined Data Types

You have been using the Visual Basic data types, such as integer, string, and currency, since Chapter 3. You can also define your own data types by combining multiple fields of data into a single unit. A **user-defined data type** can be used to combine several fields of related information. For example, an Employee data type may contain last name, first name, Social Security number, street, city, state, ZIP code, date of hire, and pay code. A Product data type might contain a description, product number, quantity, and price. The fields can be combined into a user-defined data type using the **Type** and **End Type** statements.

The Type Statement—General Form

```
Type NameOfNewDataType
    List of fields
End Type
```

The Type Statement—Examples

```
Type Employee
    strLastName                 As String
    strFirstName                As String
    strSocialSecurityNumber     As String
    strStreet                   As String
    strState                    As String
    strZipCode                  As String
    dtmHireDate                 As Date
    intPayCode                  As Integer
End Type

Type Product
    strDescription              As String
    strProductNumber            As String
    intQuantity                 As Integer
    curPrice                    As Currency
End Type

Private Type SalesDetail
    curSales(7)                 As Currency
End Type
```

Once you have created your own data type, you may use it to declare variables just as you use any other data type. The recommended prefix is "udt". It is also acceptable in a large project with multiple user-defined types to create an appropriate prefix starting with u such as upr for Product and usl for Sales.

```
Dim udtWidget                As Product
Dim udtInventory(1 To 100)   As Product
Dim udtHomeFurnishings       As SalesDetail
Dim udtHousewares            As SalesDetail
Dim udtOffice                As Employee
Dim udtWarehouse             As Employee
```

Type statements can appear only at the module level in the General Declarations section of a standard code module or a form module. When placed in a standard code module, they are Public by default. If Type statements are placed at the module level of a form, *they must be declared as* Private.

Example of a Type statement in a form module:

```
'General Declarations section
Option Explicit
Private Type Item
    intCount                 As Integer
    strDescription           As String
End Type
```

Accessing Information with User-Defined Data Types

Each field of data within a user-defined type is referred to as an *element* of the data type. To access the elements, use the dot notation similar to that used for objects: Specify Variable.Element.

```
udtWidget.strDescription
udtWidget.intQuantity
udtWidget.curPrice
udtInventory(intIndex).strDescription
udtInventory(intIndex).intQuantity
udtHomeFurnishings.curSales(intIndex)
udtOffice.strLastName
udtItem.intCount
```

Notice the use of indexes in the preceding examples. Each example was taken from the preceding Type and Dim statements. A variable that is not an array, such as udtWidget, does not need an index. However, for udtInventory, which was dimensioned as an array of 100, you must specify not only the udtInventory item but also the element within the data type. udtHomeFurnishings is a different situation: The variable was dimensioned as a single variable (not an array). Now look back at the Type statement for SalesDetail on the preceding page; there are eight elements in the data type. Therefore, you must use an index on the element within the data type.

Note: You could even declare an array of a data type that includes an array. This type of array requires an index on the variable name and another index on the element name.

Example

```
Dim udtClothing(3) as SalesDetail
```

The following line references one element:

```
udtClothing(intClothingIndex).curSales(intSalesIndex)
```

You specify the type name in the dimension, but you do not refer to the type name anywhere else in the program. This syntax is consistent with using the built-in data types such as currency and integer; we don't usually use the type names anywhere beyond the declaration.

Note: The `For Each` statement cannot be used with an array of user-defined Types. No problem; just use `For/Next` and keep track of the number of elements used.

Feedback 8.3

(Don't forget, subscripts start at 0 unless you declared them otherwise.)

1. Write a `Type` statement to hold student data containing last name, first name, student number, number of units completed, and GPA. The new data type should be called StudentInfo.
2. Declare an array of 100 students that will use the user-defined data type for student information.
3. Code the `Type` statement for a data type called Project containing project name, form name (up to 10), and the folder name.
4. Declare a variable called udtMyProject with a data type of Project.
5. Declare an array (with 100 elements) called udtOurProjects with a data type of Project.

Using Array Elements for Accumulators

Array elements are regular variables and perform in the same ways as all variables used so far. You may use the subscripted variables in any way you choose, such as for counters or total accumulators.

To demonstrate the use of array elements as total accumulators, eight totals will be accumulated. For this example, eight scout troops are selling raffle tickets. A separate total must be accumulated for each of the eight groups. Each time a sale is made, the number of tickets must be added to the correct total. The statement

```
Dim intTotal(1 To 8) As Integer
```

declares the eight accumulators.

Adding to the Correct Total

Assume that your user inputs a group number into txtGroup.Text and the number of tickets sold into txtSale.Text. The sales may be input in any order with multiple sales for each group. Your problem is to add each ticket count to the correct total (1 to 8).

You will use the group number as the subscript to add to the correct total. If the first sale of 10 tickets is for group 4, the 10 must be added to the group 4 total. (Figure 8.5 shows the form and the variables used for this example.)

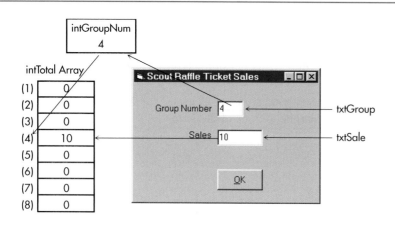

The group number entered in the txtGroup text box is used as a subscript to determine the correct intTotal array element to which to add.

```
intGroupNum = Val(txtGroup.Text)
intSale = Val(txtSale.Text)
intTotal(intGroupNum) = intTotal(intGroupNum) + intSale
```

Of course, there is always the danger that the user will enter an incorrect group number. Because it is undesirable for the user to get the error message *Subscript out of range*, the group number must be validated.

```
intGroupNum = Val(txtGroup.Text)
If intGroupNum >= 1 And intGroupNum <= 8 Then
    intSale = Val(txtSale.Text)
    intTotal(intGroupNum) = intTotal(intGroupNum) + intSale
Else
    MsgBox "Please Enter a Valid Group Number (1-8)", vbExclamation, "Data error"
End If
```

Using the group number as an index to the array is a technique called **direct reference**. The groups are assigned numbers from one to eight, which match the subscripts of the array.

Table Lookup

Things don't always work out so neatly as having sequential group numbers that can be used to access the table directly. Sometimes you will have to do a little work to find (look up) the correct value. Reconsider the eight scout troops and their ticket sales. Now the groups are not numbered 1 to 8, but 101, 103, 110, 115, 121, 123, 130, and 145. The group number and the number of tickets sold are still input, and the number of tickets must be added to the correct total. But now you must do one more step—determine to which array element to add the ticket sales, using a table **lookup.**

The first step in the project is to establish a user-defined type with the group numbers and totals and then dimension an array of the new type. Before any processing is done, load the group numbers into the table.

Place the following statements in the General Declarations section of a form module:

```
Private Type GroupInfo
    intNumber As Integer
    intTotal  As Integer
End Type
Dim mudtGroup(1 To 8) As GroupInfo
```

Then initialize the values of the array elements by placing these statements into the Form_Load procedure:

```
mudtGroup(1).intNumber = 101
mudtGroup(2).intNumber = 103
mudtGroup(3).intNumber = 110
```

etc.

During program execution the user still enters the group number and the number of tickets sold into text boxes.

The technique used to find the subscript is called a *table lookup*. In this example the object is to find the element number (1 to 8) of the group number and use that element number as a subscript to the total table. If the user enters the third group number (110), the sale is added to the third total. If the seventh group number (130) is entered, the sale is added to the seventh total, and so on. Hence, you need a way, given the group number in txtGroup.Text, to find the corresponding subscript of the mudtGroup array.

When Visual Basic executes the statement

```
mudtGroup(intGroupNum).intTotal = mudtGroup(intGroupNum).intTotal + intSale
```

the value of intGroupNum must be a number in the range 1 to 8. The task for the lookup operation is to find the number to place in intGroupNum, based on the value of txtGroup.Text. Figure 8.6 shows the variables used for the lookup. Figure 8.7 shows the flowchart of the lookup logic.

F i g u r e   8 . 6

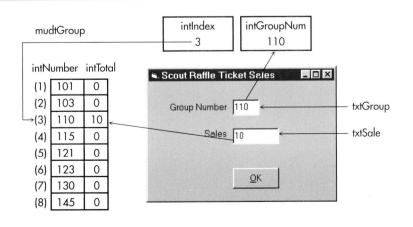

A lookup operation: The group number is looked up in the mudtGroup array; the correct subscript is found and used to add the sale to the correct intTotal.

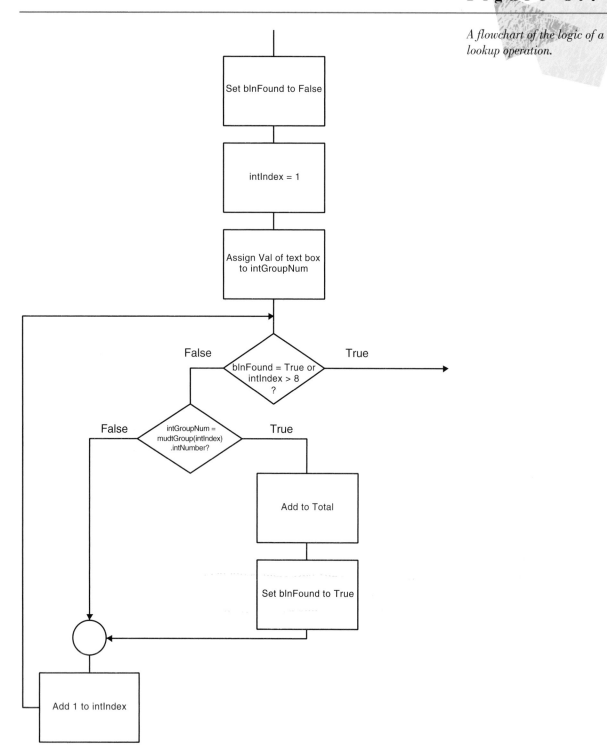

Coding a Table Lookup

For a table lookup, you will find that a Do/Loop works better than For Each. As you compare to each element in the array and eventually find a match, you need to know the subscript of the matching element.

```
Dim intGroupNum       As Integer
Dim intIndex          As Integer
Dim intSale           As Integer
Dim blnFound          As Boolean

blnFound = False
intIndex = 1
intGroupNum = Val(txtGroup.Text)
Do Until blnFound Or intIndex > 8
    If intGroupNum = mudtGroup(intIndex).intNumber Then
        intSale = Val(txtSale.Text)
        mudtGroup(intIndex).intTotal = mudtGroup(intIndex).intTotal + intSale
        blnFound = True
    End If
    intIndex = intIndex + 1
Loop
```

Once again, you should do some form of validation. If the user enters an invalid group number, you should display a message box. You can check the value of the Boolean variable blnFound after completion of the loop to determine whether the loop terminated because of a match or without a match.

```
If blnFound = False Then        'No match was found
    MsgBox "Invalid group number—Sale not added to a total", vbInformation, _
          "Data error"
End If
```

The table-lookup technique will work for any table, numeric or string. It isn't necessary to arrange the fields being searched in any particular sequence. The comparison is made to one item in the list, then the next, and the next—until a match is found. In fact, you can save processing time by arranging the table with the most-often-used entries at the top so that fewer comparisons must be made.

Using List Boxes with Arrays

In the previous example of a lookup, the user had to type some information into a text box, which was used to look up the information in an array. A more efficient and friendly solution might be to substitute a list box for the text box. You can store the eight group numbers in a list box and allow the user to select from the list.

The initial List property can contain the values 101, 103, 110, 115, 121, 123, 130, and 145.

You have probably already realized that you can use the ListIndex property to determine the array subscript. Remember that the ListIndex property holds the position or index of the selected item from the list. You could then use this index with one minor change to access the group total. Recall that the ListIndex property always begins with 0. If you plan to coordinate an array and a list, dimension the array with elements beginning with zero. For this example, we'll change the dimension in the General Declarations section to

```
Dim mudtGroup(0 to 7) As GroupInfo
```

In place of the lookup operation, we can use this code:

```
Dim intIndex              As Integer
Dim intSale               As Integer

If lstGroup.ListIndex <> -1 Then
    intSale = Val(txtSale.Text)
    intIndex = lstGroup.ListIndex
    mudtGroup(intIndex).intTotal = mudtGroup(intIndex).intTotal
Else
    MsgBox   "You must select a group number from the list", _
             vbInformation, "Data error"
End If
```

The ItemData Property

Visual Basic offers another handy property for list boxes and combo boxes that can be a big help when working with indexes. A problem can arise when you use the ListIndex of the items in the list as an array subscript. What happens if you sort the data in the list? The ListIndex of each list element could be different than it was previously, which means the position in the array would be incorrect. The **ItemData property** can associate a specific number with each item in the list. Each element of the List property can have a corresponding ItemData that does not change when the list is sorted.

You can set initial values for the ItemData property, just as you set initial values for the List property. If you add an item to the list during run time, you can also add a corresponding value to the ItemData property.

The ItemData Property—General Form

```
Object.ItemData(Index) [= number]
```

In this next example we'll use a combo box for a list of names and a corresponding array holding the phone numbers for each name in the list.

The array of phone numbers will have the same positions as the original list of names. When the data are first entered into the list, the ItemData property must also be assigned. The ListIndex and the ItemData properties match when first entered.

cboName.List	cboName.ItemData	cboName.ListIndex	strPhone()
Jones, Bill	0	0	111-1111
Lee, Brian	1	1	222-2222
Platt, Cece	2	2	333-3333
Adams, Keith	3	3	444-4444
Lopex, Ana	4	4	555-5555

Notice that after the sort the ItemData property stayed with the associated list item. The ListIndex still represents the position within the array.

cboName.List	cboName.ItemData	cboName.ListIndex
Adams, Keith	3	0
Jones, Bill	0	1
Lee, Brian	1	2
Lopex, Ana	4	3
Platt, Cece	2	4

You can use the ItemData property to access the proper array element.

```
Dim intIndex As Integer
intIndex = cboName.ItemData(cboName.ListIndex)    'Save position number of _
                                                   current selection

If intIndex <> -1 Then                            'If a selection is made
    lblPhone.Caption = strPhone(intIndex)         'Assign corresponding array _
                                                   element to label
Else
    MsgBox "Please select a name from the list", vbExclamation, "Data error"
End If
```

Using Nonsequential ItemData Values

The values that are placed in the ItemData property do not need to be in sequence. In our earlier scouting example, we could give names to the groups and have those names associated with the group numbers 101, 103, 110, 115, 121, 123, 130, and 145.

lstGroupName.List	lstGroupName.ItemData
Eagles	101
Bats	103
Wolves	110
Tigers	115
Bears	121
Mountain Lions	123
Panthers	130
Cobras	145

The value stored in the ItemData property is a long integer, but it may hold any numeric value you wish. Using ItemData is an easy way to assign such things as a product number to a description.

Adding Items with ItemData to a List

You learned in Chapter 7 to use the `AddItem` method to add a new item to a list box or combo box. If you want to store an ItemData property for the new list item, you must include an additional step. Assume that the user enters a new group name and number (using the previous scout group example), using txtGroupName and txtGroupNumber. You can use the `AddItem` method to add the group name. But then you must know the index of the new item in order to add the corresponding ItemData.

If your list is unsorted, the new item is always last—in the highest ListIndex position. (Remember that the highest ListIndex is one less than ListCount.) Therefore, these statements will add the group name and number to corresponding positions in the list:

```
lstGroupName.AddItem txtGroupName.Text
lstGroupName.ItemData(lstGroupName.ListCount - 1) = txtGroupNumber.Text
```

However, if your list is sorted, the `AddItem` method adds the new item alphabetically in the list. You can determine the index of the new item using the **NewIndex property**, which VB sets to the index of the new item.

```
lstGroupName.AddItem txtGroupName.Text
lstGroupName.ItemData(lstGroupName.NewIndex) = txtGroupNumber.Text
```

Note that you can use the second method (using the NewIndex property) for an unsorted list as well as a sorted list.

Multidimensional Arrays

You may need to use two subscripts to identify tabular data, where data are arranged in rows and columns.

Many applications of two-dimensional tables quickly come to mind—insurance rate tables, tax tables, addition and multiplication tables, postage rates, foods and their nutritive value, population by region, rainfall by state.

To define a two-dimensional array or *table*, the Dim statement specifies the number of rows and columns in the array. The **row** is horizontal and the **column** is vertical. The following table has three rows and four columns:

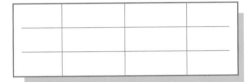

The Dim Statement for Two-Dimensional Arrays— General Form

```
Dim ArrayName([LowerLimit To] UpperLimit, [LowerLimit To] UpperLimit) As Datatype
```

The Dim Statement for Two-Dimensional Arrays— Examples

```
Dim strName(2, 3) As String
Dim strName(0 To 2, 0 To 3) As String
```

Either of these two statements establishes an array of 12 elements, with three rows and four columns. You must always use two subscripts when referring to individual elements of the table. Specify the row with the first subscript and the column with the second subscript.

(0,0)	(0,1)	(0,2)	(0,3)
(1,0)	(1,1)	(1,2)	(1,3)
(2,0)	(2,1)	(2,2)	(2,3)

The elements of the array may be used in the same ways as any other variable—in accumulators, counts, reference fields for lookup; in statements like assignment and printing; and as conditions. Some valid references to the table include

```
strName(1, 2) = "Value"
strName(intRowIndex, intColIndex) = "Value"
lblDisplay.Caption = strName(1, 2)
Printer.Print strName(intRowIndex, intColIndex)
```

Invalid references for the strName table would include any value greater than 2 for the first subscript or greater than 3 for the second subscript.

Initializing Two-Dimensional Arrays

Although numeric array elements are initially set to 0 and string elements are set to empty strings, many situations require that you initialize arrays to 0 or some other value. You can use nested `For/Next` loops or `For Each/Next` to set each array element to an initial value.

Nested For/Next Example

The assignment statement in the inner loop will be executed 12 times, once for each element of strName.

```
Dim intRow As Integer
Dim intCol As Integer

For intRow = 0 To 2
    For intColumn = 0 To 3
        strName(intRow, intColumn) = ""    'Initialize each element
    Next intColumn
Next intRow
```

For Each/Next Example

You can also perform the initialization with a `For Each` statement, which initializes all 12 elements.

```
Dim vntName As Variant
For Each vntName In strName
    vntName = ""                           'Initialize each element
Next vntName
```

Printing a Two-Dimensional Table

When you want to print the contents of a two-dimensional table, you can also use a `For Each/Next` loop.

```
Dim vntName As Variant
For Each vntName In strName
    Printer.Print vntName
Next vntName
```

If you wish to print an entire row in one line, use a `For/Next` loop and set up the print statements for multiple elements.

```
For intRowIndex = 0 To 2
    Printer.Print strName(intRowIndex, 0); Tab(15); strName(intRowIndex, 1); _
    Tab(30); strName(intRowIndex, 2); Tab(45); strName(intRowIndex, 3)
Next intRowIndex
```

Summing a Two-Dimensional Table

You can find the sum of a table in various ways. You may sum either the columns or the rows of the table; or, as in a cross-foot, you may sum the figures in both directions and double-check the totals.

To sum the array in both directions, each column needs one total field and each row needs one total field. Two one-dimensional arrays will work well for the totals. Figure 8.8 illustrates the variables used in this example.

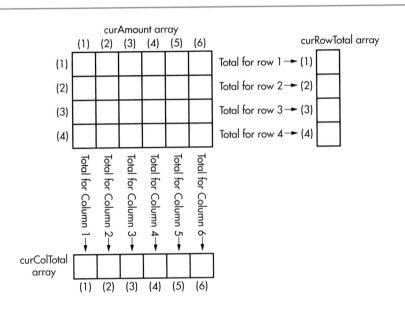

Two one-dimensional arrays hold totals for the two-dimensional array.

```
Dim curAmount(1 To 4, 1 To 6)  As Currency
Dim curRowTotal(1 To 4)        As Currency
Dim curColTotal(1 To 6)        As Currency
Dim intRowIndex                As Integer
Dim intColIndex                As Integer

For intRowIndex = 1 To 4
    For intColIndex = 1 To 6
        curRowTotal(intRowIndex) = curRowTotal(intRowIndex) _
            + curAmount(intRowIndex, intColIndex)
        curColTotal(intColIndex) = curColTotal(intColIndex) _
            + curAmount(intRowIndex, intColIndex)
    Next intColIndex
Next intRowIndex
```

Feedback 8.4

Write VB statements to do the following:

1. Dimension a table called curTemperature with five columns and three rows.
2. Set each element in the first row to 0.
3. Set each element in the second row to 75.
4. For each column of the table, add together the elements in rows 1 and 2, placing the sum in row 3.
5. Print the entire table.

Lookup Operation for Two-Dimensional Tables

When you look up items in a two-dimensional table, you can use the same techniques discussed with single-dimensional arrays—direct reference and table lookup. The limitations are the same.

1. To use a direct reference, row and column subscripts must be readily available. For example, you can tally the hours used for each of five machines (identified by machine numbers 1 to 5) and each of four departments (identified by department numbers 1 to 4).

```
intRowIndex = Val(txtMachine.Text)
intColIndex = Val(txtDepartment.Text)
curHours = Val(txtHours.Text)
curMachineTotal(intRowIndex, intColIndex) = curMachineTotal(intRowIndex, _
    intColIndex) + curHours
```

2. A table lookup is the most common lookup technique.

Many two-dimensional tables used for lookup require additional one-dimensional arrays or lists to aid in the lookup process. For an example, use a shipping rate table (Figure 8.9) to look up the rate to ship a package. The shipping rate depends on the weight of the package and the zone to which it is being shipped. You could design the project with the weight and zones in drop-down list boxes, or you could use a text box and let the user input the data.

Using List Boxes

In this example a list box holds the weight limits, and another list holds the zones. The values for the two lists are set with the List and ItemData properties at design time. The five-by-four rate table is two-dimensional, and the values are preloaded. The best way to preload values is to load the values from a data file, which is discussed in Chapter 10. The other alternative is to assign the values in the Form_Load procedure of the startup form.

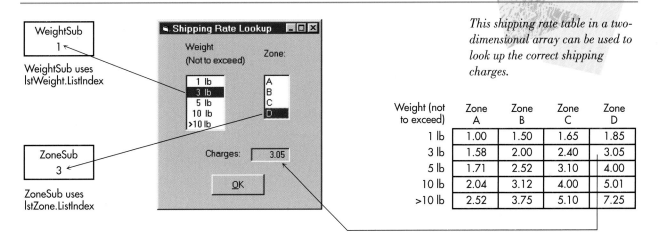

This shipping rate table in a two-dimensional array can be used to look up the correct shipping charges.

Weight (not to exceed)	Zone A	Zone B	Zone C	Zone D
1 lb	1.00	1.50	1.65	1.85
3 lb	1.58	2.00	2.40	3.05
5 lb	1.71	2.52	3.10	4.00
10 lb	2.04	3.12	4.00	5.01
>10 lb	2.52	3.75	5.10	7.25

```
Dim mcurRate(0 to 4, 0 to 3) As Currency 'Module-level array for lookup
Dim intWeightSub          As Integer
Dim intZoneSub            As Integer
intWeightSub = lstWeight.ListIndex
intZoneSub = lstZone.ListIndex

If intWeightSub <> -1 And intZoneSub <> -1 Then
    lblShipping.Caption = mcurRate(intWeightSub, intZoneSub)
Else
    MsgBox "Please select the weight and zone from the proper lists."
End If
```

Using Text Boxes

If you are using text boxes rather than list boxes for data entry, the input requires more validation. Both the weight and zone entries must be looked up before the correct rate can be determined. The valid zones and weight ranges will be stored in two separate one-dimensional arrays. The first step in the project is to establish and fill the two arrays. The five-by-four rate table is two-dimensional, and the values should be preloaded, as in the previous example.

```
Dim mcurRate(0 to 4, 0 to 3) As Currency 'Module-level array for lookup
Dim intWeight(0 To 4)       As Integer
Dim strZone(0 to 3)         As String
Dim intWeightSub            As Integer
Dim intZoneSub              As Integer
Dim intIndex                As Integer
Dim intWeightInput          As Integer
Dim blnWeightFound          As Boolean
Dim blnZoneFound            As Boolean
```

```
'Look up the weight to find the intWeightSub

intWeightInput = Val(txtWeight.Text)
blnWeightFound = False
intIndex = 0
Do Until blnWeightFound or intIndex > 4
    If intWeightInput <= intWeight(intIndex) Then
        intWeightSub = intIndex
        blnWeightFound = True
    End If
    intIndex = intIndex + 1
Loop
If Not blnWeightFound Then
    intWeightSub = 4
End If


'Look up the zone to find the intZoneSub
blnZoneFound = False
intIndex = 0
Do Until blnZoneFound or intIndex > 3
    If txtZone.Text = strZone(intIndex) Then
        intZoneSub = intIndex
        blnZoneFound = True
    End If
    intIndex = intIndex + 1
Loop


'Display the appropriate rate
If (intWeightSub >= 0 And intWeightSub <= 4) And _
    (intZoneSub >= 0 And intZoneSub <= 3) Then
    lblShipping.Caption = mcurRate(intWeightSub, intZoneSub)
Else
    MsgBox "Invalid zone or weight entered", vbExclamation, "Invalid data"
End If
```

Your Hands-On Programming Example

Create a project for R 'n R—for Reading 'n Refreshment that determines the price per pound for bulk coffee sales. The coffees are divided into categories: regular, decaf, and special blend. The prices are set by the ¼ pound, ½ pound, and full pound. Use a Find Price command button to search for the appropriate price based on the selections.

	Regular	Decaf	Blend
¼ pound	$2.60	$2.90	$ 3.25
½ pound	4.90	5.60	6.10
Full pound	8.75	9.75	11.25

Create a user-defined data type that contains the coffee type, amount, and price. Set up a variable called mudtTransaction that is an array of 20 elements of your data type. Each time the Find Price button is pressed, add the data to the array.

When the Exit button is pressed, print appropriate headings and the data from the mudtTransaction array.

Planning the Project

Sketch a form (Figure 8.10), which your users sign off as meeting their needs.

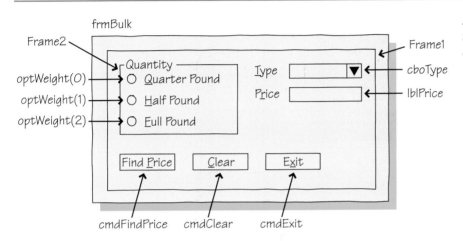

A planning sketch of the form for the hands-on programming example.

Plan the Objects and Properties

Object	Property	Setting
frmBulk	Name	frmBulk
	Caption	R 'n R—for Reading 'n Refreshment
Frame1	Caption	(blank)
Frame2	Caption	Quantity
Label1	Caption	&Type
Label2	Caption	&Price
lblPrice	Name	lblPrice
	Caption	(blank)
cboType	Name	cboType
	List	Regular
		Decaffeinated
		Special Blend

(continued)

Object	Property	Setting
	ItemData	0
		1
		2
	Sorted	True
	Style	2 - Dropdown list
optWeight(0)	Name	optWeight
	Caption	&Quarter pound
optWeight(1)	Name	optWeight
	Caption	&Half pound
optWeight(2)	Name	optWeight
	Caption	&Full pound
cmdFindPrice	Name	cmdFindPrice
	Caption	Find &Price
cmdClear	Name	cmdClear
	Caption	&Clear
cmdExit	Name	cmdExit
	Caption	E&xit

Plan the Event Procedures

You need to plan the actions for the event procedures and the Form_Load event.

Procedure	Actions
Form_Load	Create and load the price table.
cmdFindPrice	Look up the price in the table. Display the price in the label. Store type, quantity, and price in the array.
cmdClear	Erase the price. Set list box indexes to -1.
cmdExit	Print the Transaction array. Terminate the project.

Write the Project

- Follow the sketch in Figure 8.10 to create the form. Figure 8.11 shows the completed form.

- Set the properties of each object, according to your plan.

- Write the code. Working from the pseudocode, write each event procedure.

- When you complete the code, use a variety of data to thoroughly test the project.

Figure 8.11

The form for the hands-on programming example.

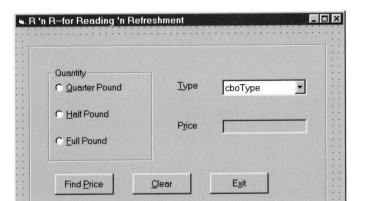

The Project Coding Solution

```
'Module:          frmBulk
'Programmer:      A. Millspaugh
'Date:            Oct 1999
'Description:     Look up the price for bulk coffee
'                 based on quantity and type.
'Folder:          Ch0801

Option Explicit
Dim mcurPrice(0 To 2, 0 To 2) As Currency

Private Type CoffeeSale
    strType           As String
    strQuantity       As String
    curPrice          As Currency
End Type
```

```
Dim mudtTransaction(20)         As CoffeeSale
Dim mintNumberTransactions      As Integer
Dim mlngWeight                  As Long
```

```
Private Sub cmdClear_Click()
    'Remove the selection from the lists and
    ' clear the price

    Dim intIndex As Integer

    cboType.ListIndex = -1 'Clear selection
    lblPrice.Caption = ""
    mlngWeight = 0
    For intIndex = 0 To 2
        optWeight(intIndex).Value = False
    Next intIndex
End Sub
```

```
Private Sub cmdExit_Click()
    'Print report and terminate the project

    Dim intIndex        As Integer
    Dim strPrintPrice   As String

    Printer.Print Tab(45); "Sales Report"
    Printer.Print ""
    Printer.Print Tab(15); "Type"; Tab(40); "Quantity"; Tab(60); "Price"
    Printer.Print ""
    For intIndex = 0 To mintNumberTransactions - 1
        strPrintPrice = FormatCurrency(mudtTransaction(intIndex).curPrice)
        Printer.Print Tab(10); mudtTransaction(intIndex).strType; _
            Tab(35); mudtTransaction(intIndex).strQuantity; _
            Tab(65 - Len(strPrintPrice)); strPrintPrice
    Next intIndex
    End
End Sub
```

```
Private Sub cmdFindPrice_Click()
    'Look up the price using the quantity and type

    Dim intRow      As Integer
    Dim intCol      As Integer
    Dim curPrice    As Currency

    intRow = mlngWeight
```

```
        If mintNumberTransactions <= 20 Then 'Allow only 20 transactions
            If cboType.ListIndex <> -1 Then
                intCol = cboType.ListIndex
                Select Case intRow
                    Case 0
                        mudtTransaction(mintNumberTransactions).strQuantity = _
                            "Quarter Pound"
                    Case 1
                        mudtTransaction(mintNumberTransactions).strQuantity = _
                            "Half Pound"
                    Case 2
                        mudtTransaction(mintNumberTransactions).strQuantity = _
                            "Full Pound"
                    Case Else
                        'Default to quarter pound
                        mudtTransaction(mintNumberTransactions).strQuantity = _
                            "Quarter Pound"
                End Select
                curPrice = mcurPrice(intRow, intCol)
                lblPrice.Caption = FormatCurrency(curPrice)
                mudtTransaction(mintNumberTransactions).strType = _
                    cboType.List(intCol)
                mudtTransaction(mintNumberTransactions).curPrice = curPrice
                mintNumberTransactions = mintNumberTransactions + 1
            Else
                MsgBox "Select a type and quantity", vbExclamation, "Entry Error"
            End If
        End If
End Sub
```

```
Private Sub Form_Load()
    'Load prices into the table

    mcurPrice(0, 0) = 2.6
    mcurPrice(0, 1) = 2.9
    mcurPrice(0, 2) = 3.25
    mcurPrice(1, 0) = 4.9
    mcurPrice(1, 1) = 5.6
    mcurPrice(1, 2) = 6.1
    mcurPrice(2, 0) = 8.75
    mcurPrice(2, 1) = 9.75
    mcurPrice(2, 2) = 11.25
End Sub
```

```
Private Sub optWeight_Click(Index As Integer)
    'Find the selected weight

    mlngWeight = Index
End Sub
```

Programming Hints

The Array Function

As you saw in the earlier programming example, initializing an array at run time is somewhat tedious (refer to the Form_Load procedure in the hands-on programming example). Visual Basic provides another method of initializing an array that uses a variant variable. You declare the variable to be an array and assign a list of values to it with the `Array` function.

The Array Function—General Form

```
Variable = Array(list of values)
```

The Array Function—Examples

```
vntNames = Array("Ann", "Mary", "Jorge", "Peter")
vntCodes = Array(45, 76, 53, 24)
```

The values within the array are accessed with the same subscript notation as a dimensioned array.

```
Dim vntMonth As Variant
vntMonth = Array("Jan", "Feb", "Mar", "Apr", "May", "Jun", "Jul", "Aug", _
          "Sep", "Oct", "Nov", "Dec")
```

After the previous declaration and assignment, the statement

```
Printer.Print vntMonth(4)
```

would print *May*. (As usual, the subscripts start at 0.)

S u m m a r y

1. A series of controls with the same name is called a control array. Each individual control is referenced using an index, which is its position number within the array.
2. The controls in a control array share one Click event procedure.
3. A `Select Case` statement may be used when an expression is being tested for many different values or ranges of values. The statement also can include a `Case Else` for the situation that none of the values specified was a match.

4. A series of variables with the same name is called an array. The individual values are referred to as elements, and each element is accessed by its subscript, which is a position number.

5. A special form of the For loop called For Each is available for working with arrays. The For Each eliminates the need for the programmer to manipulate the subscripts of the array.

6. In addition to the existing data types, programmers may use the Type statement to combine fields and create user-defined data types. Type statements must appear in the General Declarations section of a module.

7. Arrays can be used like any other variables; they can be used to accumulate a series of totals or to store values for a lookup procedure.

8. The information in arrays may be accessed directly by subscript, or a table lookup may be used to determine the correct table position.

9. List box and combo box controls have an ItemData property that can be used to assign a numeric value to each item in the list.

10. Arrays may be multidimensional. A two-dimensional table contains rows and columns and is processed similarly to a one-dimensional array. Accessing a multidimensional array frequently requires the use of nested loops.

Key Terms

array *299*
column *313*
control array *294*
direct reference *306*
element *299*
For Each and Next *301*
index *295*
ItemData property *310*

lookup *306*
NewIndex property *312*
row *313*
subscript *299*
subscripted variable *299*
table *299*
Type/End Type statements *325*
user-defined data type *303*

Review Questions

1. Define the following terms:
   (a) Array
   (b) Element
   (c) Subscript
   (d) Control array
   (e) Subscripted variable

2. Describe the logic of a table lookup.

3. Name some situations in which it is important to perform validation when working with subscripted variables.

4. Why would a list box control need both a ListIndex property and an ItemData property?

5. Compare a two-dimensional table to an array of a user-defined data type.

6. When initializing values in a two-dimensional table, what statements should be used?

P r o g r a m m i n g   E x e r c i s e s

8.1   (*Array of user-defined type*) Create a project to analyze an income survey. The statistics for each home include an identification code, the number of members in the household, and the yearly income. A menu will contain *File*, *Reports*, and *Help*. The *File* menu will contain *Enter Data* and *Exit*. As the data are entered, they should be assigned from the text boxes to the elements of a user-defined type.

The reports for the project will be sent to the printer and include the following:

(a) A three-column report displaying the input data.

(b) A listing of the identification number and income for each household that exceeds the average income.

(c) The percentage of households having incomes below the poverty level.

Test Data

Poverty Level: 8000 for a family of one or two, plus 2000 for each additional member.

ID Number	Annual Income	Number of Persons
2497	12500	2
3323	13000	5
4521	18210	4
6789	8000	2
5476	6000	1
4423	16400	3
6587	25000	4
3221	10500	4
5555	15000	2
0085	19700	3
3097	20000	8
4480	23400	5
0265	19700	2
8901	13000	3

Check Figures

Households exceeding average income:

You should have seven entries on the list.

Households below poverty level:

21.43%

8.2 (*Two-dimensional table*) Modify project 8.1 to assign the data to a multi-dimensional array rather than use an array of user-defined types.

8.3 Create a project to keep track of concert ticket sales by your club. Ticket prices are based on the section of the auditorium in which the seats are located. Your program should calculate the price for each sale, accumulate the total number of tickets sold in each section, display the ticket price schedule, and print a summary of all sales.

The form will contain a sorted list box of the sections for seating and use an ItemData property to store the ticket price subscript.

Section	Price
Orchestra	40.00
Mezzanine	27.50
General	15.00
Balcony	10.00

Special Consideration: Do not allow the user to receive a subscript-out-of-range error message.

8.4 (*Array of a user-defined type*) Create a project that will allow a user to look up state names and their two-letter abbreviations. The user will have the options to *Look up the Abbreviation* or to *Look up the State Name*. In the event that a match cannot be found for the input, print an appropriate error message.

Use an option button control array and a `Select Case` to determine which text box (state name or abbreviation) should have the focus and which should be disabled.

Data

AL	Alabama	DC	District of Columbia
AK	Alaska	FL	Florida
AS	American Samoa	GA	Georgia
AZ	Arizona	GU	Guam
AR	Arkansas	HI	Hawaii
CA	California	ID	Idaho
CO	Colorado	IL	Illinois
CT	Connecticut	IN	Indiana
DE	Delaware	IA	Iowa

continued

KS	Kansas	OH	Ohio
KY	Kentucky	OK	Oklahoma
LA	Louisiana	OR	Oregon
ME	Maine	PA	Pennsylvania
MD	Maryland	PR	Puerto Rico
MA	Massachusetts	RI	Rhode Island
MI	Michigan	SC	South Carolina
MN	Minnesota	SD	South Dakota
MS	Mississippi	TN	Tennessee
MO	Missouri	TX	Texas
MT	Montana	TT	Trust Territories
NE	Nebraska	UT	Utah
NV	Nevada	VT	Vermont
NH	New Hampshire	VA	Virginia
NJ	New Jersey	VI	Virgin Islands
NM	New Mexico	WA	Washington
NY	New York	WV	West Virginia
NC	North Carolina	WI	Wisconsin
ND	North Dakota	WY	Wyoming

8.5　(*Two-dimensional table*) Create a project that looks up the driving distance between two cities. Use two dropdown lists that contain the names of the cities. Label one list *Departure* and the other *Destination*. Use a command button to calculate distances.

Store the distances in a two-dimensional table.

	Boston	Chicago	Dallas	Las Vegas	Los Angeles	Miami	New Orleans	Toronto	Vancouver	Washington DC
Boston	0	1004	1753	2752	3017	1520	1507	609	3155	448
Chicago	1004	0	921	1780	2048	1397	919	515	2176	709
Dallas	1753	921	0	1230	1399	1343	517	1435	2234	1307
Las Vegas	2752	1780	1230	0	272	2570	1732	2251	1322	2420
Los Angeles	3017	2048	1399	272	0	2716	1858	2523	1278	2646
Miami	1520	1397	1343	2570	2716	0	860	1494	3447	1057
New Orleans	1507	919	517	1732	1858	860	0	1307	2734	1099
Toronto	609	515	1435	2251	2523	1494	1307	0	2820	571
Vancouver	3155	2176	2234	1322	1278	3447	2734	2820	0	2887
Washington DC	448	709	1307	2420	2646	1057	1099	571	2887	0

8.6   (*Two-dimensional table*) Create a project in which the user will complete a 10-question survey. Create a form containing labels with each of the questions and a group of option buttons for each question with the following responses: Always, Usually, Sometimes, Seldom, and Never.

Use a two-dimensional array to accumulate the number of each response for each question.

Have a menu or command option that will print an item analysis on the printer that shows the question number and the count for each response.

Sample of partial output:

Question	Always	Usually	Sometimes	Seldom	Never
1	5	2	10	4	6
2	2	2	10	2	1
3	17	0	10	0	0

CASE STUDIES

VB Mail Order

Create a project that will calculate shipping charges from a two-dimensional table of rates. The rate depends on the weight of the package and the zone to which it will be shipped. The Wt. column specifies the maximum weight for that rate. All weights over 10 pounds use the last row.

Wt.	Zone:	A	B	C	D
1		1.00	1.50	1.65	1.85
3		1.58	2.00	2.40	3.05
5		1.71	2.52	3.10	4.00
10		2.04	3.12	4.00	5.01
>10		2.52	3.75	5.10	7.25

VB Auto Center

VB Auto sells its own brand of spark plugs. To cross-reference to major brands, it keeps a table of equivalent part numbers. VB Auto wants to computerize the process of looking up part numbers in order to improve its customer service.

The user should be able to enter the part number and brand and look up the corresponding VB Auto part number. You may allow the user to select the brand (Brand A, Brand C, or Brand X) from a list or from option buttons.

You can choose from two approaches for the lookup table. Either store the part numbers in a two-dimensional table or in an array of user-defined types. In either case, use the part number and brand entered by the user; look up and display the VB Auto part number.

VB Auto	Brand A	Brand C	Brand X
PR214	MR43T	RBL8	14K22
PR223	R43	RJ6	14K24
PR224	R43N	RN4	14K30
PR246	R46N	RN8	14K32
PR247	R46TS	RBL17Y	14K33
PR248	R46TX	RBL12-6	14K35
PR324	S46	J11	14K38
PR326	SR46E	XEJ8	14K40
PR444	47L	H12	14K44

Create a project that displays the aisle number of a movie category in a label. The movie categories will be in a listbox in sorted order. Store the aisle numbers and categories in an array.

A *Search* command button should locate the correct location from the array and display it in a label. Make sure that the user has selected a category from the list and use the category's ItemData property from the listbox to find the appropriate aisle number.

Video Bonanza

Test Data	
Aisle1	Comedy
Aisle 2	Drama
Aisle 3	Action
Aisle 4	Sci-Fi
Aisle 5	Horror
Back Wall	New Releases

Modify your project from Chapter 7 **Very Very Boards** order, store the information in the array. When the user prints out the order, clear the array.

to keep track of each order in an array. You can then print out the entire order with detail lines for each type of shirt. You also will convert the option buttons to a control array and determine the shirt size in a shared-event procedure. Use a Case structure for selection.

Create an array of a user-defined type that holds the quantity, size, monogram (Boolean), pocket (Boolean), price, and extended price for each type of shirt ordered. As each shirt type is added to an

Add a menu option to print out the order, which will have the customer name and order number at the top and one line for each shirt type ordered. Use the following layout as a rough guide for your list. Make sure to align the numeric columns correctly. For the two Boolean fields (Monogram and Pocket), print Yes or No. Do not allow the user to print an invoice until the order is complete.

```
                    Very Very Boards Shirt Orders

                            By Your Name


Customer name:    xxxxxxxxxxxxxxxxxxxxx
Order Number:     xxxxx

     Quantity    Size    Monogram   Pocket    Price      Extended
                                              Each       Price

     ==================================================

       xxx       xxx       xxx       xxx       xxx       xxx,xxx


     Order Total:                                        xx,xxx
```

9

OOP—Creating Object-Oriented Programs

At the completion of this chapter, you will be able to . . .

1. Use object-oriented terminology correctly.

2. Differentiate between a class and an object.

3. Create a class that has properties and methods.

4. Use property procedures to set and retrieve private properties of a class.

5. Declare object variables and assign values to the variables using the Set statement.

6. Instantiate an object in a project using your class.

7. Understand the purpose of the Class_Initialize and Class_Terminate events.

8. Create a collection of objects.

9. Use the Object Browser to get information about available objects, properties, methods, events, and constants.

10. Store keys for a collection in a list box using the ItemData Property.

11. Add properties to a form.

Visual Basic and Object-Oriented Programming

You have been using objects since Chapter 1. As you know quite well by now, **objects** have properties and methods and generate events that you can respond to (or ignore) if you choose. Up until now the classes for all objects in your projects have been predefined; that is, you could choose to create a new object of the form class, a command button class, a text box class, or any other class of control in the VB toolbox. In this chapter you will learn to define your own new class and create objects based on the class.

Object-oriented programming (OOP) is currently the most accepted style of programming. Some computer languages, such as Java and SmallTalk, were designed to be object oriented (OO) from their inception. Other languages, such as Visual Basic 6.0, have been modified over the last few years to accommodate OOP.

Each version of Visual Basic brings it closer to what many consider a true object-oriented language. Although not all of the concepts of object-oriented programming are completely supported by Visual Basic, most are. Certainly VB is close enough to an OO language that you can write object-oriented programs.

Writing object-oriented programs is a mind set—a different way of looking at a problem. You must think in terms of using objects. As your projects become more complex, using objects becomes increasingly important.

Objects

Beyond the many built-in choices you have for objects to include in your projects, Visual Basic allows you to create your own new object types by creating a **class module.** Just like other object types, your **class** may have both properties and methods. Remember: Properties are characteristics, and methods are actions that can be performed by a class of object.

An object is a *thing* such as a command button. You create a command button object from the command button tool in the toolbox. In other words, *command button* is a class but *cmdExit* is an actual occurrence or **instance** of the class; the instance is the object. Just as you may have multiple command buttons in a project, you may have many objects of a new class type.

Defining your own class is like creating a new tool for the toolbox; the process does not create the object, only a definition of what that type of object looks like and how it behaves. You may then create as many instances of the class as you need. Your class may be a student, an employee, a product, or any other type of object that would be useful in a project.

Many people use a cookie analogy to describe the relationship of a class and an object. The cookie cutter is the class. You can't eat a cookie cutter, but you can use it to make cookies; the cookie is the object. When you make a cookie using a cookie cutter, you **instantiate** an object of the cookie class. You can use the same cookie cutter to make various kinds of cookies. Although all cookies will have the same shape, some may be chocolate, lemon, or vanilla; some may have frosting or colored sprinkles on top. The characteristics such as flavor and topping are the properties of the object. You could refer to the properties of your cookie object as

```
Cookie1.Flavor = "Lemon"
Cookie1.Topping = "Cream Frosting"
```

What about methods? Recall that a method is an action or behavior—something the object can do or have done to it, such as Move, Clear, or Print. Possible methods for our cookie object might be Eat, Bake, or Crumble. Using object terminology, you can refer to Object.Method:

```
Cookie1.Crumble
```

Sometimes the distinction between a method and an event is somewhat fuzzy. Generally, anything you tell the object to do is a method; if the object does an action and needs to inform you, that's an event. So if you tell the cookie to crumble, that is a method; if the cookie crumbles on its own and needs to inform you of the fact, that's an event.

Object-Oriented Terminology

The key features of an object-oriented language are **encapsulation, polymorphism,** and **inheritance.**

Encapsulation

Encapsulation refers to the combination of characteristics of an object along with its behaviors. You have one "package" that holds the definition of all properties, methods, and events. For example, when you create a command button, you can set or retrieve its properties, such as Caption or Width. You can execute its methods, such as SetFocus or Move, and you can write code for its events, such as Click or Double-click. But you cannot make up new properties or tell it to do anything that it doesn't already know how to do. It is a complete package; you can think of all of the parts of the package as being in a capsule.

Encapsulation is sometimes referred to as *data hiding*. Each object keeps its data (properties) and procedures (methods) hidden. Through use of the public and private keywords, an object can "expose" only those data elements and procedures that it wishes to allow the outside world to see.

Polymorphism

Polymorphism means "many shapes" and means that different classes of objects may have behaviors that are named the same but are implemented differently. Polymorphism allows you to request an action without knowing exactly what kind of object you are dealing with or how it will carry out its action. For example, you can specify Printer.Print, Form.Print, PictureBox.Print, and Debug.Print. Printer.Print sends its output to the printer object, Form.Print sends output to the form, PictureBox.Print sends output to a picture box control, and Debug.Print sends output to the VB Immediate window.

You can implement polymorphism in VB by using naming conventions. Always use standard names for your methods so that a programmer will recognize the action by its name. For example, don't use Clear for one class, BlankOut for another, and Empty for another.

Polymorphism also allows a single class to have more than one method with the same name. When the method is called, the argument type determines which version of the method to use. In VB 6.0 you can have similarly named methods in different classes, but not in the same class.

Inheritance

Inheritance is the ability to create a new class from an existing class. From the OOP purist point of view, VB 6.0 doesn't allow inheritance. For example, in theory you should be able to create a new class called MyCheckBox based on the check box class. It would have all of the properties, methods, and events of check boxes, but you would specify that the shape of the check box is your company logo. If checked, it appears red, and unchecked it is black—everything else remains unchanged. This VB 6.0 cannot do.

Note: Although VB 6.0 cannot do polymorphism and inheritance, don't give up. The public beta version of VB.NET (VB 7.0) at the time of this writing *does* implement these important OOP contructs. See Appendix D.

Reusability

The real purpose of inheritance is **reusability.** You need to be able to reuse or obtain the functionality from one class of object when you have another similar situation. VB *does* provide for reusability using interfaces and a concept known as *delegation.* Microsoft argues that reusability is the important concept, not inheritance, but it looks like true inheritance will be available in a future version of VB.

To share functionality using delegation, you place the code you want to share in a base class, also called a *superclass.* Then you create other classes, called *subclasses,* that can call the shared functions. This concept is very helpful if you have features that are similar in two classes. Rather than writing two classes that are almost identical, you can create a base class that contains the similar procedures.

An example of reusability could be the option button and check box classes, which contain very similar functionality and could share a "super" class. The subclass for each would call the shared procedure from the base class and would contain any procedures that are unique to the subclass.

Reusable Objects

A big advantage of object-oriented programming over traditional programming is the ability to reuse objects. When you create a new class by writing a class module, you can then use that class in multiple projects. Each object that you create from the class has its own set of properties. This process works just like the built-in VB controls you have been using all along. For example, you can create two image objects: imgOne and imgTwo. Each has its own Visible property and Picture property, which will probably be set differently for each.

As you begin using classes in your projects, you will find many situations in which classes are useful. You might want to create your own class to provide database access. You could include methods for adding and deleting data members. If you work frequently with sales, you might create a product class. The product class would likely have properties such as description, quantity, and cost. The methods would probably include finding the current value of the product.

By convention, class names are prefixed with C. For example, name the product class CProduct.

Classes

To design your own class, you need to analyze what characteristics and behaviors your object needs. The characteristics or properties are defined as variables, and the behaviors (methods) are sub procedures or function procedures.

Assigning Property Values

Inside your class module you define variables, which are the properties of the class. Theoretically you could declare all variables as Public so that all other project code could set and retrieve their values. However, this approach violates the rules of encapsulation that require each object to be in charge of its own data. Remember that encapsulation is also called data hiding. To accomplish encapsulation, you will declare all variables in a class module as Private. As a private variable, the value is available only to the procedures within the class module, the same way that module-level variables are available only to procedures within the form module.

When your program creates objects from your class, you will need to assign values to the properties. Because the properties are private variables, you will use special property procedures to pass the values *to* the class module and to return values *from* the class module.

The Property Procedures
The way that your class allows its properties to be set is through a **Property Let** procedure. And to retrieve the value of a property from a class, you must use a **Property Get** procedure. The Property Let and Property Get procedures serve as a gateway to assign and retrieve property values to the private members of the class module. You will find that the terms *let* and *get* make sense when you recall that a VB assignment statement is also called a *let statement*. Regular assignment statements can be written with the optional keyword Let:

```
Let intValue = 0 or
intValue = 0
```

When you define the Property Let and Property Get procedures, the name you use becomes the name of the property to the outside world. Create "friendly" procedure names that describe the property without using a prefix, such as LastName or EmployeeNumber.

The Property Get Procedure—Format
The Property Get returns the current value of a property.

```
[Public] Property Get ProcedureName([OptionalArgumentList]) [As DataType]
    [statements in procedure]
    ProcedureName = PropertyName
End Property
```

Property procedures are public by default, so you can omit the optional `Public` keyword. You can also define a property procedure to be private, which means that the property is available only inside the class module. We won't be using any private procedures in this text.

Property Get procedures are similar to function procedures in at least one respect: Somewhere inside the procedure, before the exit, you must assign a return value to the procedure name.

The Property Get Procedure—Example

```
Public Property Get LastName() As String
    LastName = mstrLastName
End Property
```

The Property Let Procedure—Format

The Property Let assigns a value to a property. Inside the Property Let procedure you can do validation to make sure the value is valid before assigning the incoming value to the property.

```
Public Property Let ProcedureName([OptionalArgumentList,] IncomingValue _
    [As DataType])
    [statements in procedure]
    PropertyName = IncomingValue
End Property
```

If you include any arguments in the argument list, the number of arguments, their data type, and order must exactly match the argument list in the Property Let procedure. If arguments are included, the incoming value must always follow the list.

The data type of the incoming value must match the type of the return value of the corresponding Property Get procedure.

The Property Let Procedure—Example

```
Property Let LastName(strLastName As String)
    mstrLastName = strLastName
End Property
```

Creating a New Class—Step-by-Step

In this step-by-step tutorial you will create a new class to hold product information.

Define a New Class Module

A class module is part of a Visual Basic project, so the first step is to create a new project.

The Project

STEP 1: Open a new project.

The Class

STEP 1: Select *Add Class Module* from the *Project* menu. The *Add Class Module* dialog box will appear (Figure 9.1).

Figure   9.1

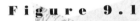

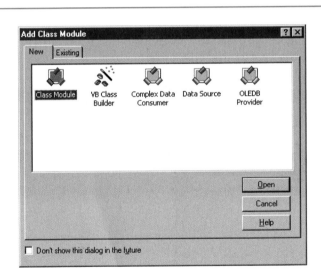

Add a new class to a project in the Add Class Module *dialog box.*

STEP 2: From the *New* tab choose *Class Module* and click on *Open*. You will see a code window similar to the code window for a standard code module.

STEP 3: Notice that the code window is labeled Class1. Change the class name to CProduct by changing the Name property in the Properties window (Figure 9.2).

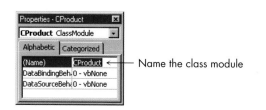

Change the module's Name property.

——— Name the class module

Define the Class Properties

STEP 1: In the General Declarations section of the code window, define the variables as Private. (If your code window doesn't have an `Option Explicit` statement, add one.) These module-level variables become the properties of your new class.

```
Private mcurPrice        As Currency
Private mintQuantity     As Integer
Private mstrDescription  As String
```

This class has three properties defined as private module-level variables: mcurPrice, mintQuantity, and mstrDescription (Figure 9.3). Because the properties and methods are declared as private, they can be accessed only by procedures within the class module. To allow access from outside the class module, you must add property procedures.

Tip

Use prefixes on the module-level variable to hold the property value; use a friendly name without a prefix for the property methods.

F i g u r e   9 . 3

Declare module-level variables for the class properties.

```
(General)                      (Declarations)

Option Explicit

Private mcurPrice        As Currency
Private mintQuantity     As Integer
Private mstrDescription  As String
```

Add Property Procedures

The Quantity Property

STEP 1: From the class module code window, select *Add Procedure* from the *Tools* menu.

STEP 2: Type Quantity for the Name and select the options for Property and Public (Figure 9.4). Click OK.

STEP 3: Look over the screen (Figure 9.5). Notice that you have both a Property Get Quantity and a Property Let Quantity() procedure. Note also that by default both procedures are declared as Variant return type.

Figure 9.4

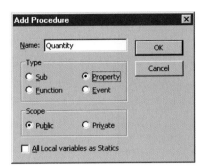

Create property procedures for the Quantity property in the Add Procedure dialog box.

Figure 9.5

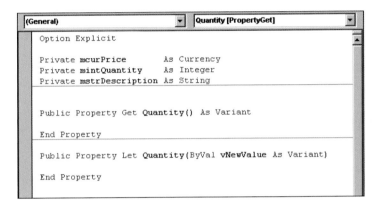

VB automatically creates the template for a Property Get and a Property Let procedure.

STEP 4: Change the return data type of the Property Get to Integer.

STEP 5: Write the code for the Property Get procedure.

```
Public Property Get Quantity() As Integer
    'Retrieve the current value

    Quantity = mintQuantity
End Property
```

STEP 6: Code the Property Let procedure, changing the incoming value and data type (Figure 9.6).

```
Public Property Let Quantity(ByVal intQuantity As Integer)
    'Assign the property value

    mintQuantity = intQuantity
End Property
```

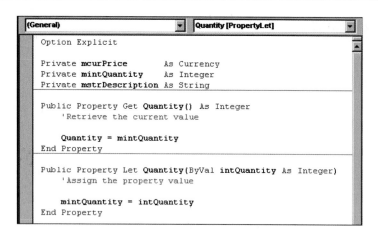

Code the Property Get and Property Let procedures.

The Price Property

STEP 1: Select *Add Procedure* from the *Tools* menu and add property procedures for Price.

STEP 2: Code the Property Get and Property Let procedures for the Price property.

```
Public Property Get Price() As Currency
    'Retrieve the current value

    Price = mcurPrice
End Property


Public Property Let Price(ByVal curPrice As Currency)
    'Assign the property value

    mcurPrice = curPrice
End Property
```

The Description Property

STEP 1: Select *Add Procedure* from the *Tools* menu and add a set of property procedures for Description.

STEP 2: Code the Property Get and Property Let procedures for the Description property.

```
Public Property Get Description() As String
    'Retrieve the current value

    Description = mstrDescription
End Property
```

```
Public Property Let Description(ByVal strDescription As String)
    'Assign the property value

    mstrDescription = strDescription
End Property
```

Code a Method

You can create methods by adding sub procedures and functions for the behaviors that the class needs. For this class you will add a function procedure to calculate the extended price, multiplying the price by the quantity.

STEP 1: From the class module code window, select *Add Procedure* from the *Tools* menu.
STEP 2: Name the new procedure ExtendedPrice and select the options for *Function* and *Public.*
STEP 3: Add Currency for the function's return data type and type the code.

```
Public Function ExtendedPrice() As Currency
    'Calculate the value of the product

    ExtendedPrice = mintQuantity * mcurPrice
End Function
```

Add General Remarks

STEP 1: Insert a new line before Option Explicit and add the general remarks.

```
'Class Name:       CProduct
'Programmer:       Your Name
'Date:             Today's Date
'Description:      Handle product information
```

Save the Class Module

STEP 1: Open the *File* menu and choose *Save CProduct As.* Note that VB assigns class modules the file extension .cls.
STEP 2: Select the path, creating a new folder called Ch09SBS for this new project. Save CProduct.cls in your new project folder.

Feedback 9.1

1. Write the property declarations for a class module for a student that will contain the properties: LastName, FirstName, StudentIDNumber, and GPA. Where will these statements appear?
2. Code the Property Let procedure to assign a value to the LastName property.
3. Code the Property Get procedure to retrieve the value of the GPA property.

Creating a New Object Using a Class

Creating a class module defines a new class; it does not create any objects. This process is similar to defining a new user-defined type; after you define the new data type, you must then dimension variables of the new type. To create an object using your new class, you must create an instance of the class using the **New keyword** and specify the class. This step is referred to as *instantiating* an object.

Dimensioning Objects Using the New Keyword— General Form

```
{Dim|Public|Private} VariableName As New ClassName
```

The New Keyword—Examples

```
Dim Emp                 As New CEmployee
Private mInventory      As New CInventory
Public NewForm          As New frmMain
```

The New keyword creates a new instance of an object class. The object class can be a class that you created or a standard Visual Basic object such as a form or a control.

Note: The New keyword sets up the memory location and references for the new object, but doesn't actually create it. The first time your project refers to a property or method of the new object, the object is created.

Define and Use a New Object

To continue the step-by-step tutorial for the CProduct class, you must define a form in your project. The form module creates an instance of the CProduct class. The user interface allows the user to enter the description, price, and quantity of a product. Your project then assigns the input values to the properties of the CProduct class. The `ExtendedPrice` method calculates the value of the product, which appears in a label on the form. Figure 9.7 shows the completed form.

Create the Form

STEP 1: Open the form module and create your interface with text boxes for the description, price, and quantity. Include a label for the value. Set appropriate properties for the form and the controls.

STEP 2: Create command buttons for Calculate and Exit. Set the Name and Caption properties of the buttons.

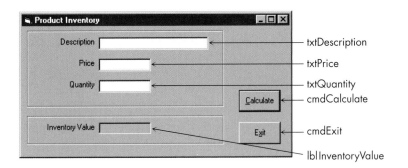

The completed form for the step-by-step tutorial.

Add Code

STEP 1: Type the comments and declare the new object.

```
'Project:         Calculate Product Inventory
'Programmer:      Your Name
'Date:            Today's Date
'Description:     Calculate product inventory amount using the CProduct _
                  class.
'                 Instantiate mProduct as a new object of the CProduct _
                  class.
'Folder:          Ch09SBS

Option Explicit
Private mProduct As New CProduct      'Instantiate the new object
```

STEP 2: Create a new sub procedure that will assign the values from the form's text boxes to the properties of the new object: Select *Add Procedure* from the *Tools* menu; name the new private sub procedure AssignProperties (Figure 9.8).

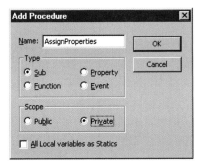

Create a new sub procedure for AssignProperties.

STEP 3: Write the code to assign the text box values to the corresponding properties (Figure 9.9).

```
Private Sub AssignProperties()
    'Assign properties from form

    mProduct.Description = txtDescription.Text
    mProduct.Price = Val(txtPrice.Text)
    mProduct.Quantity = Val(txtQuantity.Text)
End Sub
```

F i g u r e   9 . 9

```
Option Explicit
Private mProduct As New CProduct

Private Sub AssignProperties()
    'Assign properties from form

    mProduct.Description = txtDescription.Text
    mProduct.Price = Val(txtPrice.Text)
    mProduct.Quantity = val(txtQuantity.Text)|
End Sub
```

Assign the text box values to the class properties.

STEP 4: Code the command button event procedures. In the cmdCalculate event procedure, you will assign the text box values to the properties of the new object and use the curCalculateValue method of the mProduct object.

```
Private Sub cmdCalculate_Click()
    'Calculate the inventory value

    AssignProperties 'Assign all properties of form to object
    'Calculate value using the object's method
    lblInventoryValue.Caption = mProduct.ExtendedPrice
End Sub

Private Sub cmdExit_Click()
    'Terminate the project

    End
End Sub
```

Save the Form and the Project

STEP 1: Save the form as Product.frm.
STEP 2: Save the project as Product.vbp.
STEP 3: Close the code windows and Form Design window.

Run the Project

The next step is to watch the project run—hopefully without errors.

STEP 1: Click the Run button on the VB toolbar. Your form should appear.

STEP 2: Fill in test values for the description, price, and quantity. Click on Calculate. What did you get for the inventory value? Is it correct?

Watching the Project Run

If you got an error message or an incorrect answer, you will need to debug the project. The quickest and easiest way to debug is to single-step program execution. Single-stepping is an interesting exercise even if you *did* get the right answer.

If you have an error message, stop program execution. Press the F8 key to begin execution by single-stepping. Fill in the text boxes and click Calculate. Then repeatedly press F8 and watch each step; you will see execution transfer to the code for CProduct for each Property Let. If an error message halts program execution, point to the variable names and property names on the screen to see their current values.

When cmdCalculate_Click finishes, click on your project's task bar button to make the form reappear.

Feedback 9.2

1. What is the difference between an object and a class?
2. Is mProduct an object or class? What about CProduct?
3. What actions are performed by the following statement?

```
mProduct.Quantity = Val(txtQuantity.Text)
```

Choosing When to Create New Objects

There is more than one way to create a new object in VB. The method you choose can affect the scope of your object and the performance of your program.

You have already seen one method of creating a new object using the New keyword of the Dim statement:

```
Private mProduct As New CProduct
```

This statement creates a new variable that can hold a reference to an object. The first time your code refers to mProduct, the object is actually created.

Although in this example the object variable, mProduct, is a module-level variable, object variables may also be defined to be local or global. For example, if you need to create an object local to one procedure, you could use

```
Dim Product As New CProduct
```

For an object defined as local, each time the `Dim` is encountered VB recreates the object variable. And the first time the procedure references the variable, the object is actually created. When the procedure terminates and the object variable goes out of scope, the object is destroyed; that is, the system resources used by the object are released.

Using the Set Statement

Another way to create an object is to dimension the object variable without the `New` keyword and use the `Set` statement in a procedure when you are ready to create the object. This method gives you more control over when the object is actually created. Because this method can also improve program performance, it is the preferred way to create an object.

```
'General Declarations section of your form
Private mProduct As CProduct

'Inside a procedure—generally Form_Load
Set mProduct = New CProduct
```

The Set Statement—General Form

```
Set ObjectVariableName = {[New]ClassName | Nothing}
```

A `Set` statement is an assignment statement for object variables. The variable name must already be declared (with a `Dim`, `Public`, `Private`, or `Static` statement).

Setting an object variable to Nothing terminates the object reference and releases the system resources.

The Set Statement—Examples

```
Set mProduct = New CProduct
Set MyProduct = mProduct
Set mProduct = Nothing
```

When you create a new object, you have three choices for the statements. Note that all three methods use the `New` keyword either in the dimension or the `Set` statement.

Choice 1 (the preferred method)

```
Private mProduct As CProduct       'In the General Declarations section
Set mProduct = New CProduct        'In the procedure where you want to create _
                                    the object
```

The `Set` statement typically goes in the Form_Load procedure. The new object is created when the `Set` statement executes.

Choice 2 (the method used in the earlier step-by-step tutorial)

```
Private mProduct As New CProduct   'In the General Declarations section
```

This statement declares the new object; the object is actually created the first time mProduct is referenced in code. One disadvantage of this approach is that it is unclear exactly when the object is created; small changes to the project can alter the sequence and cause unexpected results.

Choice 3 (the least efficient method)

```
Private mProduct As Object          'Using a generic Object type
Set mProduct = New CProduct         'In the procedure where you want to create _
                                     the object
```

Declaring the object variable as a generic Object is legal. On occasion you may need to use this format if the actual object type cannot be determined until run time. The disadvantage of this format is that VB cannot resolve the references to the object during compile, but must wait until execution. This causes a condition called *late binding*.

Early Binding versus Late Binding

When you declare a new object, VB must locate the object definition to determine the available properties and methods. This process is called *resolving* the references. If the compiler can resolve the object references during compile, this is called **early binding** and is the most efficient method. Using either choice 1 or choice 2 in the preceding section causes early binding.

The third choice, with a variable declared as a generic object, is least efficient. This is an example of **late binding.** If you use late binding, your projects will run considerably slower.

The Initialize and Terminate Events

Each class module has two predefined events for which you can write code if you wish. The **Class_Initialize event** is triggered when an object is created, and the **Class_Terminate event** occurs when an object goes out of scope or is terminated with a `Set` *ObjectName* `=` `Nothing`. These event procedures are useful for doing any setup work or for making sure that the memory allocated for an object is released.

```
Public Sub Class_Initialize
    'Create the collection object

    Set mProducts = New Collection
End Sub

Public Sub Class_Terminate()
    'Remove the collection from memory

    Set mProducts = Nothing
End Sub
```

Terminating Projects

So far, all our projects terminate with an End statement. When VB encounters an End statement during execution, it stops execution right then and there. Often you actually need to do some housekeeping tasks before terminating the project. For example, you might want to ask the user whether to save any changed information (in Chapter 10 you will learn to save information in files on disk).

Before a project terminates, you need to release the system resources used for your objects and collections. If you just execute an End statement, the Class_Terminate events do not occur. Also, the Form_Unload events do not occur. Instead, you can end project execution by unloading all forms. This approach will terminate execution of the project and allow your cleanup events to occur.

Unless you are sure your project has no housekeeping tasks to perform, you should terminate all projects using the Unload statement. (Make sure to unload all forms that have been loaded.)
Examples:

```
Private Sub cmdExit_Click()
    'Terminate execution

    Unload frmMain
    Unload frmAbout
    End
End Sub
```

You can use a For Each to make sure to unload all loaded forms:

```
Private Sub cmdExit_Click()
    'Terminate execution

    Dim OneForm As Form
    For Each OneForm In Forms
        Unload OneForm
    Next
    End
End Sub
```

Note: The previous code uses the Forms collection, which is a predefined collection in each VB project. The next sections describe the use of collections in your projects.

Collections

When you program using objects, you usually need more than one of each object type. One CProduct object is not very useful—you are likely to need to define multiple products. You can accomplish this task by creating a collection of objects.

A **collection class** holds references for a series of objects created from the same class. Although in concept the collection *contains* the objects, actually the collection holds a reference to each of the objects, called *members* of the collection.

A collection can hold multiple objects, which is similar in concept to an array, which contains multiple variables. However, a collection can do more work for you. A collection object has an `Add` method, a `Remove` method, an `Item` method, and a Count property.

You can refer to the members of a collection in two different ways. Like an array, you can specify an index number, which is the object's position in the collection. This method is convenient only if the order of the members does not change. Alternatively, you can give each object a string key that uniquely identifies the object, and the collection object can store and retrieve the objects by their key. Sometimes objects already have a field that is unique and can be used as a key, such as a Social Security number, a customer number, or an account number. Or you can assign a sequential number to each object in order to have a unique key. When objects are removed from a collection, the indexes for the remaining objects change to reflect their new position, but the key fields never change.

Microsoft has adopted a consistent naming standard for collections: Always use the plural of an object for the name of the collection. Therefore, a collection of objects of the class CProduct would be called CProducts.

There are many collections built into VB. Each project has a Forms collection; each form has a Controls collection. You can refer to your project's forms as Forms(0), Forms(1), rather than their names. You can also refer to the controls on a form by their position in the collection, which is a handy way to set properties of all controls.

```
Dim AnyControl As Control
For Each AnyControl In frmDisplay.Controls
    AnyControl.Enabled = False
Next
```

Creating a Collection

A collection is another type of object. You create a collection by writing a new class module and declaring an object variable.

We will continue the CProduct tutorial by adding a CProducts collection.

Creating a Unique Key in the CProduct Class

Before we create a collection of CProduct objects, we need to modify the class to hold a unique key. Note that the key field for a collection must be string.

In this example you will assign the next sequential number to each object added to the collection. You will convert the sequential number to a string and assign the value to the new ProductCode property.

STEP 1: Open the CProduct class code window and add a module-level variable for the ProductCode property.

```
Private mstrProductCode As String
```

STEP 2: Add property procedures to allow access to the new ProductCode property.

```
Public Property Get ProductCode() As String
    'Retrieve the current value

    ProductCode = mstrProductCode
End Property

Public Property Let ProductCode(ByVal strProductCode As String)
    'Assign the property value

    mstrProductCode = strProductCode
End Property
```

Creating the CProducts Class

We're ready to create the collection class.

STEP 1: Drop down the list of object types from the Add Form button on the toolbar (Figure 9.10). Select *Class Module*; then select *Class Module* from the *New* tab of the *Add Class Module* dialog box.

F i g u r e   9 . 1 0

Add a new class module using the Add Form toolbar button.

STEP 2: In the Properties window change the Name property to CProducts.

STEP 3: Write the general remarks at the top of the module.

```
'Class Name:     CProducts
'Programmer:     Your Name
'Date:           Today's Date
'Description:    Maintain the collection of CProduct objects
```

STEP 4: Declare the new object variable in the General Declarations section. In this class we will use the preferred method of declaring an object variable without the New keyword. In the Class_Initialize procedure the Set statement will have the New keyword.

```
Option Explicit
Private mProducts As Collection
```

Tip

Before you can refer to properties or methods of a class, you must instantiate an object of the class.

STEP 5: Code the Class_Initialize event procedure.

```
Private Sub Class_Initialize()
    'Create the collection object

    Set mProducts = New Collection
End Sub
```

STEP 6: Code the Class_Terminate event procedure to release the object variable.

```
Private Sub Class_Terminate()
    'Release the collection reference

    Set mProducts = Nothing
End Sub
```

STEP 7: Write the private function that calculates the next product code. Use a static variable to keep the running count. Remember that a key field must be a string. You must use the Trim function, otherwise VB will add an extra space when converting from numeric to string.

```
Private Function NextProductCode() As String
    'Assign next ProductCode

    Static intProductCode As Integer

    intProductCode = intProductCode + 1
    'Convert number to string and trim any extra spaces
    NextProductCode = Trim(Str(intProductCode))
End Function
```

Adding Objects to a Collection

A collection object automatically has an Add method. If you declare the collection's object variable as public, code from any other module can use that Add method to add objects to the collection. However, to follow good OOP techniques, the collection should have control over each item added. Therefore, you should declare the object variable as private (we did) and write your own public Add method. This public Add method is called a *wrapper* method.

The Add method creates a new object from the passed arguments. It then executes the default (private) Add method of the collection, adding the newly created object.

STEP 1: Write the Add wrapper procedure.

```
Public Sub Add(ByVal strDescription As String, ByVal intQuantity As _
    Integer, ByVal curPrice As Currency)
    'Add a new member to the product collection
    Dim NewProduct As New CProduct    'Object variable to hold new object

    With NewProduct    'Set up the properties for the new object
        .ProductCode = NextProductCode    'Call the function to assign _
                                          the next key

        .Description = strDescription
        .Price = curPrice
        .Quantity = intQuantity

        mProducts.Add NewProduct, .ProductCode
    End With
End Sub
```

Removing a Member from a Collection

If you want to be able to remove objects from a collection, you must also write a public Remove wrapper method. The new Remove method executes the private Remove method.

Notice that the key is passed as an argument to the procedure. The key specifies which member object to remove. Recall that the key must be string. If you are using numeric indexes rather than keys, then you should pass a long (or variant) data type.

STEP 1: Write the Remove wrapper procedure.

```
Public Sub Remove(ByVal strKey As String)
    'Remove a member from the collection

    mProducts.Remove strKey
End Sub
```

Accessing a Member of a Collection

You also need to write a wrapper method to access an individual element of the collection. Again the string key is passed as an argument. This function returns the object referenced by the key.

STEP 1: Write the Item wrapper function.

```
Public Function Item(ByVal strKey As String) As CProduct
    'Return one member from the collection

    Set Item = mProducts.Item(strKey)
End Function
```

Returning the Count Property

Each collection has a Count property that holds the number of members in the collection. Because we declare the collection as private, we need a Property Get procedure to allow access to the count. *Note:* The Count property is read-only, so you don't need a Property Let procedure.

STEP 1: Write the Property Get procedure to return the count.

```
Public Property Get Count() As Long
    'Return the number of members in the collection

    Count = mProducts.Count
End Property
```

Setting a Default Property

Each of the controls you use on a form has a default property. Recall that you can refer to txtDescription.Text or txtDescription. The result is the same because Text is the default property of a text box control. You can also set a default property for your class. For a collection, normally the Item property is used as the default, since it is used the most, every time you access an object.

To set the default property, make sure you are displaying the code for your collection class and position the insertion point in the Item function. From the *Tools* menu, select *Procedure Attributes*. Click on the *Advanced* command button. Select *Item* from the *Name* dropdown list and then set the *Procedure ID* to *Default* (Figure 9.11).

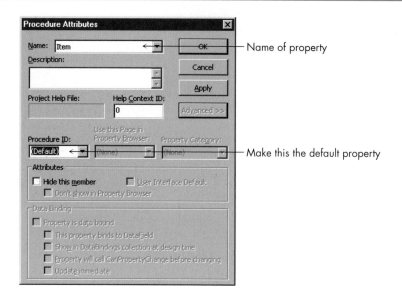

Make the Item property the default property of your class.

— Name of property

— Make this the default property

Using For Each/Next

When you want to access each object in a collection, you can use a For/Next statement. However, you must declare a loop index and use the Count property as the upper limit of the loop. For example:

```
'Display each product from the collection

Dim intIndex As Integer

For intIndex = 0 to mProducts.Count - 1
    picDisplay.Print mProducts(intIndex).Description
Next intIndex
```

Note: We are using a picture box control in this example for a "quick and dirty" display. A picture box allows you to use the Print method to quickly view output.

The For Each/Next statement is much handier than For/Next for stepping through a collection. Although the statement is not available for user-defined collections, with a small workaround we can make it available.

It takes a couple of steps to be able to use For Each. A collection has an enumerator that VB stores as a hidden property. You can "expose" the enumerator by referencing this hidden property (_NewEnum) in a function in the collection's code.

The NewEnum Function

STEP 1: In the CProducts collection class module, write the NewEnum function procedure.

```
Public Function NewEnum()
    'Allow for the For Each...Next enumeration

    Set NewEnum = mProducts.[_NewEnum]
End Function
```

Note: The square brackets around _NewEnum are required because the underscore is not a legal character for a property. A leading underscore in a property name indicates a hidden property.

STEP 2: Now for the really strange step: With the insertion point in the Function NewEnum statement, open the *Procedure Attributes* dialog box from the *Tools* menu, choose *Advanced*, and set the *Procedure ID* to −4 (negative four) and check the box for *Hide this member* (Figure 9.12).

F i g u r e   9 . 1 2

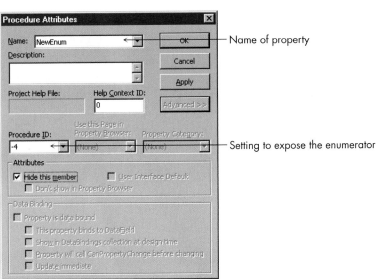

— Name of property

— Setting to expose the enumerator

To allow use of the For Each *statement, set the Procedure ID of the* NewEnum *function to* −4.

Once you have completed these two steps to expose the enumerator, you can step through the collection using For Each. Use this code in a form module to print out the descriptions of the objects in the collection.

```
'Display each product from the collection

Dim DisplayProduct As CProduct

For Each DisplayProduct In mProducts
    picDisplay.Print DisplayProduct.Description
Next
```

Note: As in the `For/Next` example above, we are using a picture box control for a "quick and dirty" display of items.

Using a Collection in a Form—Step-by-Step

Now it's time to put this code together and make it all run. We will modify the form from the chapter step-by-step tutorial to use a collection. We'll add command buttons to Add, Display, and Clear. Note that the new objects created in the cmdAdd_Click procedure are actually created by the collection; the objects you created earlier in the cmdCalculate_Click procedure are not affected.

Note: You must have completed all of the numbered steps so far in the chapter in order to complete this tutorial.

Modifying the User Interface

STEP 1: Open your form and add command buttons for Add, Display, and Clear. Add a picture box control. Figure 9.13 shows the completed form.

F i g u r e   9 . 1 3

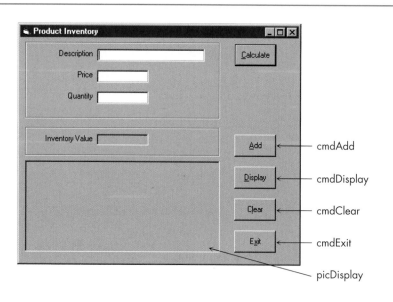

The form for the step-by-step example with an added picture box control.

STEP 2: Change the Name and Caption properties of the command buttons; name the picture box control picDisplay.

Assuming that you have completed all of the numbered steps in the chapter, your CProducts collection class module has procedures for Add, Remove, Item, and Count, and has exposed the enumerator so that you can use the `For Each` statement on the collection. This would be a good time to check your CProducts code to make sure all procedures are present.

Declaring the Collection Object

You must declare a new object of the collection class in the form's General Declarations section.

STEP 1: Switch to the code window and add the declaration statement.

```
Private mProduct As New CProduct      'This line should already appear
Private mProducts As New CProducts    'Add this line to declare the _
                                       collection
```

Coding the Add Procedure

Your cmdAdd_Click procedure takes the contents of the text boxes on the form and uses the Add method of the mProducts collection. Recall that the Add method generates the next sequential ProductID, creates a new object, and adds the object to the collection.

STEP 1: Code the cmdAdd_Click procedure in your form module.

```
Private Sub cmdAdd_Click()
    'Add product to collection

    If txtDescription.Text <> "" Then
        mProducts.Add txtDescription.Text, _
        Val(txtQuantity.Text), Val(txtPrice.Text)
    End If
    cmdClear_Click 'Clear out the form controls
End Sub
```

Coding the Display Procedure

The cmdDisplay_Click procedure uses the For Each statement to step through the collection. For an easy way to print quickly, we will use the Print method of a picture box control. The techniques you know for printing to the printer object work the same here—you can use commas and semicolons for spacing, as well as the Tab and Spc functions.

STEP 1: Code the cmdDisplay_Click procedure in your form module.

```
Private Sub cmdDisplay_Click()
    'Display each product from the collection

    Dim DisplayProduct As CProduct

    For Each DisplayProduct In mProducts
        picDisplay.Print DisplayProduct.Description
    Next
End Sub
```

Coding the Clear Procedure

In the cmdClear_Click procedure, clear out the form's text boxes, label, and the picture box. Notice the Cls (clear screen) method used to clear the contents of the picture box.

STEP 1: Code the cmdClear_Click procedure in your form module.

```
Private Sub cmdClear_Click()
    'Clear form controls

    txtDescription.Text = ""
    txtPrice.Text = ""
    txtQuantity.Text = ""
    lblInventoryValue.Caption = ""
    picDisplay.Cls
    txtDescription.SetFocus
End Sub
```

Running the Project

It's time to run the project. Test each button on your form. A good way to see what's happening in the project is to single-step program execution by repeatedly pressing F8.

Using the Object Browser

The Object Browser is an important tool for working with objects in VB. The Object Browser can show you the names of objects, properties, methods, events, and constants for VB objects; your own objects; and objects available from other applications.

Select *View / Object Browser*, click on the Object Browser toolbar button (Figure 9.14), or press F2 to display the Object Browser (Figure 9.15). In the *Project/Library* dropdown list, you can choose to display the objects in your own project or in one of the VB libraries. You can type search text in the Search Text box to display matching text in the selected library or project.

F i g u r e   9 . 1 4

Click on the Object Browser toolbar button.

Figure 9.15

The Object Browser window. Notice the icons to indicate the member type.

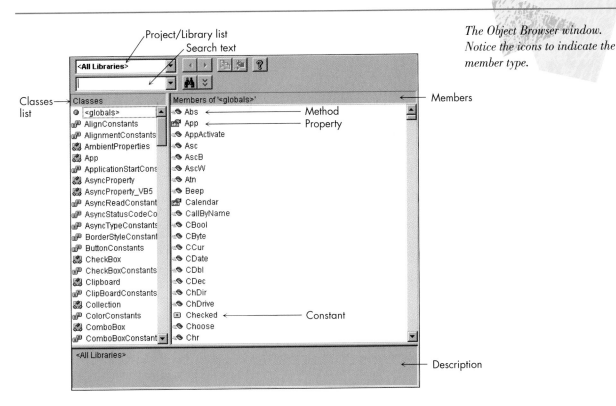

The Object Browser uses several icons to represent items. Notice in Figure 9.15 the icons that represent properties, methods, and constants. At the bottom of the window you can see a description of any item you select.

Note: You can find more information about the Object Browser in Appendix C. The MSDN Library has extensive information on using the Object Browser.

Examining VB Objects

The Object Browser is the quickest and most reliable way to look up the available properties, methods, events, or constants of a Visual Basic object. You will find the lists to be more complete than those found in Help.

Try this: Select VB in the *Project/Library* list and click on *ComboBox* in the *Classes* list (Figure 9.16). Then examine the list that shows members of the ComboBox class; you will see the names of properties, methods, and events. Try clicking on a member name in the list; the description of that item shows up in the bottom pane of the window. And if you want more information on any member, click to select it and press F1 for its Help topic.

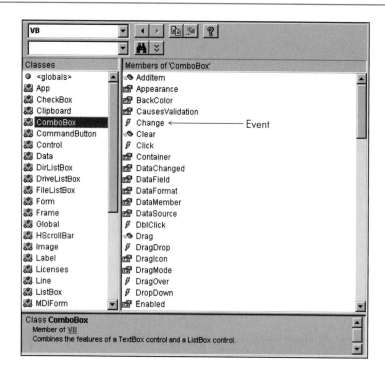

Display the properties, methods, and events for a VB combo box control.

Examining Your Own Classes

You can see your own classes listed in the Object Browser. Make sure that the chapter step-by-step sample project is open and then open the Object Browser. Select *Project1* from the *Project/Library* list and see the project's classes listed in the Classes list. Try clicking on each class name and viewing the list of properties and methods (Figure 9.17).

You can use the Object Browser to jump to the definition of any property or method by double-clicking on its name in the Members list. This technique is also a great way to jump to any of the procedures in your forms. Select your form name in the Classes list and then double-click on the name of the procedure you want to view.

Using a List Box to Store the Keys

When you want to reference a member of a collection, you need to know the key. However, keeping track of keys is inconvenient. Who wants to remember keys?

A slick visual solution to the key problem is to display the name or identifying information in a list box. The list box can have its Sorted property set to True, which makes it easy for the user to find the desired member. Each list entry's corresponding ItemData property can hold the key. When the user selects an item from the list, you can use the number stored in ItemData to retrieve the correct member of the collection. Figure 9.18 illustrates the use of a list box for selecting an object from a collection.

Figure 9.17

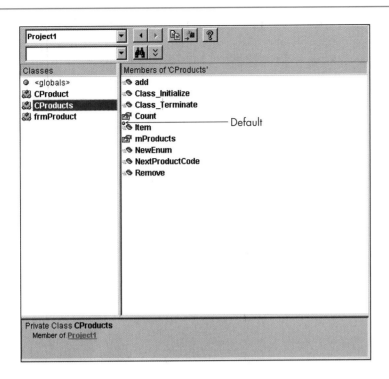

View the properties and methods for your own classes.

Figure 9.18

List box List property	ItemData property
Brooks, Barbara	5
Chen, Diana	3
Dunning, Daniel	1
Khan, Brad	6
Lester, Les	2
Nguyen, Ahn	4
Potter, Pete	8
Stevens, Roger	7

User selects this name from list.

Program displays the member with a key of 6.

The list box holds employee names in the List property and corresponding keys in the ItemData property.

The following code segment concatenates a first and last name, adds to the list box, and then assigns the key to the ItemData property. Recall that a collection's key is string and the ItemData property must be a long integer (data type Long).

```
'Add to the list box and set ItemData to object's key
strName = txtLastName.Text & ", " & txtFirstName.Text
With lstEmployee
    .AddItem strName
    lngKey = Val(strKey)
    .ItemData(.NewIndex) = lngKey
End With
```

When concatenating fixed-length strings, the entire string length, including the spaces, is used. You can use the `Trim` function to avoid including the extra spaces.

Using the List Box to Display an Object

When your user selects a name from the list box, you can use the corresponding ItemData, converted to string, to reference the correct member of the collection.

When converting the numeric ItemData to string, make sure to trim off the extra space inserted by VB.

```
If lstEmployee.ListIndex <> -1 Then
    With lstEmployee
        strKey = Trim(Str(.ItemData(.ListIndex)))
    End With
    With mEmployees(strKey)
        txtLastName.Text = .LastName
        txtFirstName.Text = .FirstName
        txtStreet.Text = .Street
        txtCity.Text = .City
        txtState.Text = .State
        txtZip.Text = .ZipCode
        txtPhone.Text = .Phone
        txtEmail.Text = .Email
    End With
Else
    MsgBox "Please Select Item from list"
End If
```

Using the List Box to Remove an Object

You can use nearly the same procedure to remove an object. When your user selects a name from the list box, use the name's ItemData to remove the correct object. Use the `Trim` function to remove the extra space when converting from numeric to string. You must also remove the name from the list box to keep the list synchronized with the collection.

```
If lstEmployee.ListIndex <> -1 Then
    With lstEmployee
        strKey = Trim(Str(.ItemData(.ListIndex)))
    End With
    'Remove from Collection
    mEmployees.Remove strKey
    'Remove from list box
    lstEmployee.RemoveItem lstEmployee.ListIndex
Else
    MsgBox "Please Select Item from list"
End If
```

Avoiding Global Variables

If you want your project's objects, including the forms, to be encapsulated, avoid global variables. Although global variables may occasionally be unavoidable, most times they are unnecessary. If a class must know about and use a global variable, then it isn't really encapsulated. You can create properties for objects and set the properties from any other module when you need to pass a value.

Adding Properties to Forms

You know how to set and retrieve properties for the objects you create. But what about when you need to pass a value from one form to another? Not a problem. Each form is actually a class; you can define new properties for a form and set those properties from other objects. You define a property for a form just as you do for a property in a class module: Declare a private module-level variable and write Property Get and Property Let procedures.

```
'General Declarations section of frmEmployee
Private mstrKey          As String 'Key property of form
Private mstrAction       As String 'Action property of form

Public Property Let Key(ByVal strKey As String)
    'Assign the Key property

    mstrKey = strKey
End Property

Public Property Let Action(ByVal strAction As String)
    'Assign the Action property

    mstrAction = strAction
End Property
```

Once these procedures are in place, another form may set the form's properties.

```
With frmEmployee
    .Key = Trim(Str(lstEmployee.ItemData(lstEmployee.ListIndex)))
    .Action = "D"
    .Show vbModal
End With
```

Your Hands-On Programming Example

Create a project with two forms: a main form and an employee data form for employees for R 'n R.

The main form has a list box displaying employee names and command buttons for Add, Delete, Display, and Exit. When the user clicks on one of the command buttons, the data form displays, set for the correct action.

The data form displays the employee data in text boxes and provides OK and Cancel buttons for changes to the data.

The project uses the list box on the main form for navigation. The user selects an employee by clicking on the employee name; the program then displays the complete information for that employee from the correct object from the collection.

Add option

Display the data form with the text boxes empty. When the user clicks the OK button, save the employee data in the collection.

Delete option

Display the data form with the information for the selected employee displayed. The user can then choose OK to delete the object from the collection or cancel the operation.

Display option

Display the data form with the data for the selected employee displayed in the text boxes.

Planning the Project

Sketch a main form (Figure 9.19) and a data form (Figure 9.20), which your users sign off as meeting their needs.

F i g u r e   9 . 1 9

The planning sketch of the main form for the hands-on programming example.

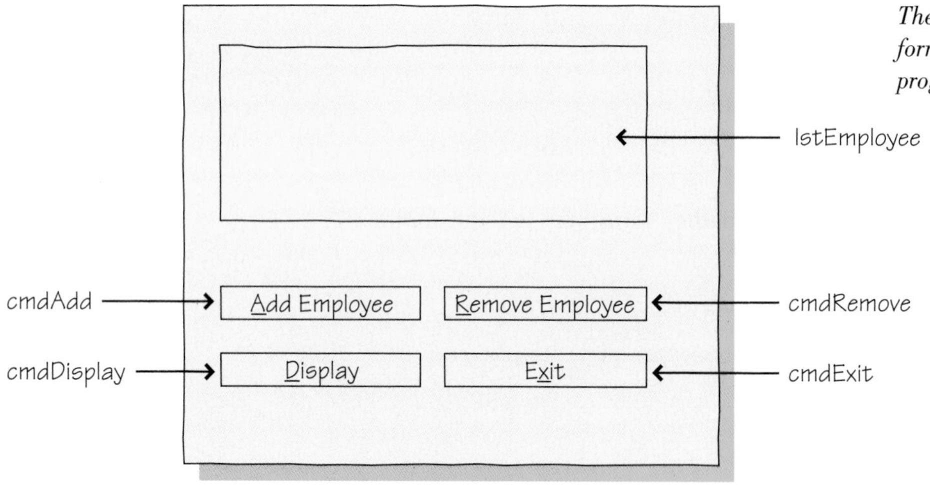

Figure 9.20

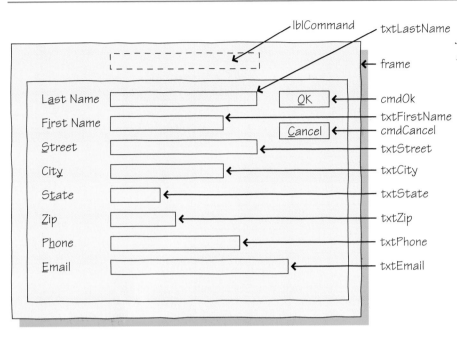

The planning sketch of the data form for the hands-on programming example.

Plan the Objects and Properties: Main Form

Object	Property	Setting
lstEmployee	Name	lstEmployee
	Sorted	True
cmdAdd	Name	cmdAdd
	Caption	&Add Employee
	Default	True
cmdRemove	Name	cmdRemove
	Caption	&Remove Employee
cmdDisplay	Name	cmdDisplay
	Caption	&Display
cmdExit	Name	cmdExit
	Caption	E&xit

Plan the Objects and Properties: Employee Data Form

Object	Property	Setting
lblCommand	Name	lblCommand
	Caption	(blank)
Label1	Name	Label1
	Caption	L&ast Name
txtLastName	Name	txtLastName
	Caption	(blank)
Label2	Name	Label2
	Caption	F&irst Name
txtFirstName	Name	txtFirstName
	Caption	(blank)
Label3	Name	Label3
	Caption	&Street
txtStreet	Name	txtStreet
	Caption	(blank)
Label4	Name	Label4
	Caption	Cit&y
txtCity	Name	txtCity
	Caption	(blank)
Label5	Name	Label5
	Caption	S&tate
txtState	Name	txtState
	Caption	(blank)
Label6	Name	Label6
	Caption	&Zip
txtZip	Name	txtZip
	Caption	(blank)
Label7	Name	Label7
	Caption	P&hone
txtPhone	Name	txtPhone
	Caption	(blank)

(continued)

Object	Property	Setting
Label8	Name	Label8
	Caption	&Email
txtEmail	Name	txtEmail
	Caption	(blank)
cmdOK	Name	cmdOK
	Caption	&OK
cmdExit	Name	cmdExit
	Caption	E&xit

Plan New Properties: Data Form

Action property	String, Write-only	Used to pass the form action from main form.
Key	String, Write-only	Used to pass the selected key from the main form.

Plan the Procedures: Main Form

Procedure	Actions
cmdAdd_Click	Set action to "A". Show frmEmployee.

cmdRemove_Click	If a name is selected in list Then
	    Set key for selected employee.
	    Set action to "R".
	    Show frmEmployee.
	Else
	  Display error message.
	End If

cmdDisplay_Click	If a name is selected in list Then
	    Set key for selected employee.
	    Set action to "D".
	    Show frmEmployee.
	Else
	  Display error message.
	End If

cmdExit_Click	Unload both forms

Plan the Procedures: Data Form

Procedure	Actions
cmdCancel_Click	Hide this form

cmdOK_Click	Select Case for action
	    Case "A" (Add)
	        Concatenate last and first name.
	        Add name to list box.
	        Calculate next employee key.
	        Set list box ItemData to new employee's key.
	        Create new employee object and add to collection.
	    Case "R" (Remove)
	        Remove selected employee from list box.
	        Remove selected employee member from collection.
	End Select
	Hide frmEmployee.

Form_Activate	Select Case for action
	Case "A" (Add)
	        Set label caption for add.
	        Clear text boxes.
	        SetFocus to first text box.
	Case "R" (Remove)
	        Set label caption for remove.
	        Display data for selected employee.
	Case "D" (Display)
	        Set label caption for display.
	        Display data for selected employee.
	End Select

Form_Load	Create the new collection object.
Form_Unload	Release collection object references.
DisplayData	Display all employee data from the selected object in text boxes.
ClearTextBoxes	Clear all text boxes on form.

Plan the Employee Object Class

Actions
Declare private module-level variables for all properties.
Write Property Get and Property Let procedures for all public properties: LastName, FirstName, Street, City, State, ZipCode, Phone, Email, EmployeeCode

Plan the Employees Collection Class

Procedure	Actions
Class_Initialize	Create new collection object.
Class_Terminate	Remove the collection object from memory.
Add	Declare new employee object. Set all object properties to corresponding argument value. Add new object to collection.
Remove	Remove selected employee object from collection.
Item	Return selected employee object from collection.
Count	Get count of number of objects in collection.
NextEmployeeCode	Add 1 to previous employee code. Return next employee code.
NewEnum	Set collection to allow `For Each` statement. *Note:* Make sure to set the procedure's ID to −4 in the *Procedure Attributes* dialog box.

Write the Project

● Follow the sketches in Figures 9.19 and 9.20 to create the forms. Figures 9.21 and 9.22 show the completed forms.

● Set the properties of each of the objects according to your plan.

● Write the code. Working from the pseudocode, write each procedure.

● When you complete the code, use a variety of data to thoroughly test the project.

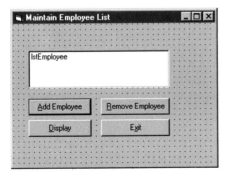

The completed main form for the hands-on programming example.

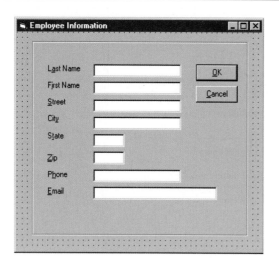

The completed data form for the hands-on programming example.

The Project Coding Solution

Employee Class

```
'Class:          CEmployee
'Programmer:     A. Millspaugh
'Date:           Oct 1999
'Description:    Declare properties and methods
'                for the Employee class
'Folder:         Ch0903
Option Explicit
```

```
Private mstrLastName        As String
Private mstrFirstName       As String
Private mstrStreet          As String
Private mstrCity            As String
Private mstrState           As String
Private mstrZipCode         As String
Private mstrPhone           As String
Private mstrEmail           As String
Private mstrEmployeeCode    As String
```

```
Public Property Get LastName() As String
    'Retrieve the current value

    LastName = mstrLastName
End Property
```

```
Public Property Let LastName(ByVal strLastName As String)
    'Assign the property value

    mstrLastName = strLastName
End Property
```

```
Public Property Get FirstName() As String
    'Retrieve the current value

    FirstName = mstrFirstName
End Property
```

```
Public Property Let FirstName(ByVal strFirstName As String)
    'Assign the property value

    mstrFirstName = strFirstName
End Property
```

```
Public Property Get Street() As String
    'Retrieve the current value

    Street = mstrStreet
End Property
```

```
Public Property Let Street(ByVal strStreet As String)
    'Assign the property value

    mstrStreet = strStreet
End Property
```

```
Public Property Get City() As String
    'Retrieve the current value

    City = mstrCity
End Property
```

```
Public Property Let City(ByVal strCity As String)
    'Assign the property value

    mstrCity = strCity
End Property
```

```
Public Property Get State() As String
    'Retrieve the current value

    State = mstrState
End Property
```

```
Public Property Let State(ByVal strState As String)
    'Assign the property value

    mstrState = strState
End Property
```

```
Public Property Get ZipCode() As String
    'Retrieve the current value

    ZipCode = mstrZipCode
End Property
```

```
Public Property Let ZipCode(ByVal strZipCode As String)
    'Assign the property value

    mstrZipCode = strZipCode
End Property
```

```
Public Property Get Phone() As String
    'Retrieve the current value

    Phone = mstrPhone
End Property
```

```
Public Property Let Phone(ByVal strPhone As String)
    'Assign the property value

    mstrPhone = strPhone
End Property
```

```
Public Property Get Email() As String
    'Retrieve the current value

    Email = mstrEmail
End Property
```

```
Public Property Let Email(ByVal strEmail As String)
    'Assign the property value

    mstrEmail = strEmail
End Property
```

```
Public Property Get EmployeeCode() As String
    'Retrieve the current value

    EmployeeCode = mstrEmployeeCode
End Property
```

```
Public Property Let EmployeeCode(ByVal strEmployeeCode As String)
    'Assign the property value

    mstrEmployeeCode = strEmployeeCode
End Property
```

Employees Collection

```
'Class:          CEmployees Collection
'Programmer:     A. Millspaugh
'Date:           Oct 1999
'Description:    Create a collection of Employees
'Folder:         Ch0903

Option Explicit
Private mEmployees As Collection
```

```
Public Sub Add(ByVal strLastName As String, _
        ByVal strFirstName As String, _
        ByVal strStreet As String, _
        ByVal strCity As String, _
        ByVal strState As String, _
        ByVal strZipCode As String, _
        ByVal strPhone As String, _
        ByVal strEmail As String, _
        ByVal strEmployeeCode As String)
    'Add a member to the collection

    Dim NewEmployee As New CEmployee

    With NewEmployee
        .EmployeeCode = strEmployeeCode
        .LastName = strLastName
        .FirstName = strFirstName
        .Street = strStreet
        .City = strCity
        .State = strState
        .ZipCode = strZipCode
        .Phone = strPhone
        .Email = strEmail

        mEmployees.Add NewEmployee, .EmployeeCode
    End With
End Sub
```

```vb
Public Sub Remove(ByVal strKey As String)
    'Remove a member from the collection

    mEmployees.Remove strKey
End Sub
```

```vb
Public Function Item(ByVal strKey As String) As CEmployee
    'Select a member from the collection

    Set Item = mEmployees.Item(strKey)
End Function
```

```vb
Public Sub Class_Initialize()
    'Create the collection object

    Set mEmployees = New Collection
End Sub
```

```vb
Public Sub Class_Terminate()
    'Remove the collection from memory

    Set mEmployees = Nothing
End Sub
```

```vb
Public Function NextEmployeeCode() As String
    'Find next available code
    Static intEmployeeCode

    intEmployeeCode = intEmployeeCode + 1
    NextEmployeeCode = Trim(Str(intEmployeeCode))
End Function
```

```vb
Public Property Get Count() As Long
    'Find the number of members in the collection

    Count = mEmployees.Count
End Property
```

frmMain

```vb
'Project:        New Employee Collection
'Form:           frmMain
'Programmer:     A. Millspaugh
'Date:           Oct. 1999
'Description:    Maintain a list of Employees
'Folder:         Ch0903
Option Explicit
```

```vb
Private Sub cmdAdd_Click()
    'Display the Employee Data form with action set to Add

    With frmEmployee
        .Action = "A"
        .Show vbModal
    End With
End Sub
```

```vb
Private Sub cmdDisplay_Click()
    'Display the Employee Data form with selected Employee

    If lstEmployee.ListIndex <> -1 Then
        With frmEmployee
            .Key = Trim(Str(lstEmployee.ItemData(lstEmployee.ListIndex)))
            .Action = "D"
            .Show vbModal
        End With
    Else
        MsgBox "Please select name from list"
    End If
End Sub
```

```vb
Private Sub cmdExit_Click()
    'Terminate the project

    Unload frmEmployee
    Unload Me
    End
End Sub
```

```vb
Private Sub cmdRemove_Click()
    'Display the Employee Data form with selected Employee for delete

    If lstEmployee.ListIndex <> -1 Then
        With frmEmployee
            .Key = Trim(Str(lstEmployee.ItemData(lstEmployee.ListIndex)))
            .Action = "R"
            .Show vbModal
        End With
    Else
        MsgBox "Please select name from list"
    End If
End Sub
```

frmEmployee

```
'Project:              New Employee Collection
'Form:                 frmEmployee
'Programmer:           A. Millspaugh
'Date:                 Oct 1999
'Description:          Obtain and display data for an employee
'Folder:               Ch0903
Option Explicit
Private mEmployees     As CEmployees
Private mstrKey        As String      'Holds form's Key property
Private mstrAction     As String      'Holds form's Action property
```

```
Private Sub cmdCancel_Click()
    'Return to main form with no action

    frmEmployee.Hide
End Sub
```

```
Private Sub cmdOK_Click()
    'Choose action depending upon the action setting
    Dim strName As String
    Dim strKey As String

    Select Case mstrAction
    Case "A"            'Add an employee object
        'Add to listbox and set ItemData to new object's key
        strName = txtLastName.Text & ", " & txtFirstName.Text
        With frmMain.lstEmployee
            .AddItem strName
            strKey = mEmployees.NextEmployeeCode
            .ItemData(.NewIndex) = Val(strKey)
        End With
        'Add employee object to collection, setting the key
        mEmployees.Add txtLastName.Text, txtFirstName.Text, _
            txtStreet.Text, txtCity.Text, txtState.Text, _
            txtZip.Text, txtPhone.Text, txtEmail.Text, strKey
    Case "R" 'Remove an employee object
        'Remove from list box
        With frmMain.lstEmployee
            .RemoveItem .ListIndex
        End With
        'Remove from Collection
        mEmployees.Remove mstrKey
    End Select

    'Return to main form
    frmEmployee.Hide
End Sub
```

```
Private Sub Form_Activate()
    'Set up the form for the selected action

    Select Case mstrAction
        Case "A"
            lblCommand.Caption = "Add New Employee Info"
            ClearTextBoxes
            txtLastName.SetFocus
        Case "R"
            lblCommand.Caption = "Remove this record?"
            DisplayData
        Case "D"
            lblCommand.Caption = "Employee Display"
            DisplayData
    End Select
End Sub
```

```
Private Sub Form_Load()
    'Create the employee collection object

    Set mEmployees = New CEmployees
End Sub
```

```
Private Sub Form_Unload(Cancel As Integer)
    'Remove the employee collection object from memory

    Set mEmployees = Nothing
End Sub
```

```
Private Sub DisplayData()
    'Transfer from the collection to text fields

    With mEmployees.Item(mstrKey)
        txtLastName.Text = .LastName
        txtFirstName.Text = .FirstName
        txtStreet.Text = .Street
        txtCity.Text = .City
        txtState.Text = .State
        txtZip.Text = .ZipCode
        txtPhone.Text = .Phone
        txtEmail.Text = .Email
    End With
End Sub
```

```
Private Sub ClearTextBoxes()
    'Clear all of the text boxes

    txtLastName.Text = ""
    txtFirstName.Text = ""
    txtStreet.Text = ""
    txtCity.Text = ""
    txtState.Text = ""
    txtZip.Text = ""
    txtPhone.Text = ""
    txtEmail.Text = ""
End Sub
```

```
Public Property Let Key(ByVal strKey As String)
    'Assign the Key property

    mstrKey = strKey
End Property
```

```
Public Property Let Action(ByVal strAction As String)
    'Assign the Action property

    mstrAction = strAction
End Property
```

Programming Hints

Multitier Applications

A common use of classes is to create applications in multiple "tiers" or layers. Each of the functions of a **multitier application** can be coded in a separate component and the components may be stored and run on different machines.

One of the most popular approaches is a three-tier application. The tiers in this model are User Services, Business Services, and Data Services (Figure 9.23). You also hear the term "*n*-tier" application, which is an expansion of the three-tier model. The middle tier, which contains all of the business logic, may be written in multiple classes that can be stored and run from multiple locations.

F i g u r e   9 . 2 3

The three-tier design model.

User Services	Business Services	Data Services
User Interface Forms, controls, menus	**Business Objects** Validation Calculations Business logic Business rules	**Data Retrieval** Data storage

In a multitier application, the goal is to create components that can be combined and replaced. If one part of an application needs to change, such as a redesign of the user interface or a new database format, the other components do not need to be replaced. A developer can simply "plug in" a new user interface and continue using the rest of the components of the application.

The User Services tier refers to the user interface, which in VB is the form. Consider that in the future the user interface could be redesigned or even converted to a Web page.

The Business Services tier is a class or classes that handle the data. This layer can include validation to enforce business rules as well as the calculations.

The Data Services tier includes retrieving and storing the data in a database. Occasionally an organization will decide to change database vendors or need to retrieve data from several different sources. The Data Services tier retrieves the data and passes the results to the Business Services tier, or takes data from the Business Services tier and writes them in the appropriate location. Database handling is covered in Chapters 11 and 12.

S u m m a r y

1. Objects have properties and methods, and can generate events.
2. You can create a new class module that can then be used to create new objects. The new object is called an *instance* of the class.
3. In object-oriented terminology, *encapsulation* refers to the combination of the characteristics and behaviors of an item into a single class definition. *Polymorphism* allows different classes of objects to have similar methods that behave differently for that particular object. *Inheritance* provides a means to derive a new object class based on an existing class. VB does not allow true inheritance but allows for reusability in another manner, using interfaces and delegation.
4. One of the advantages of object-oriented programming is that objects that you create for one project may be reused in another project.
5. Properties inside a class should be private so that data values are accessible only by procedures within the class.
6. The way to make the properties of a class available to code outside the class is to use Property Get and Property Let procedures.
7. The methods of a class are public sub procedures and functions.
8. To instantiate an object of a class, you must use the New keyword either on the declaration statement or the Set statement. The location of the New keyword determines when the object is created.
9. Declaring an object variable as a specific object type allows early binding; dimensioning a variable as a generic Object type causes late binding, which is much less efficient.
10. The Class_Initialize event occurs when an object is created; the Class_Terminate event is triggered when an object is destroyed.
11. You should unload each project's forms rather than use the End statement to terminate a project. This approach allows the forms' Unload events to occur along with Class_Terminate events.

12. A collection holds a series of objects. You can create a new collection class and declare a new instance of the class. Members of a class can be referenced by a unique string key or by a numeric index.

13. Each collection class automatically has methods for `Add`, `Remove`, and `Item`, and a Count property. These methods should be made private, and new public wrapper methods should be written to give the class control over its methods.

14. You can set a default property of a class, as well as enable the enumerator to allow using the `For Each` statement.

15. The Object Browser displays all properties, methods, and events for your new classes as well as all VB objects and objects from other available applications.

16. A sorted list box can be used to store entries from a collection using the ItemData property to store the key field for easy access to the complete data.

17. A multitier application divides a program into components that can be combined and replaced. The three tiers are User Services, Business Services, and Data Services.

Key Terms

class *334*
class module *334*
Class_Initialize event *349*
Class_Terminate event *349*
collection class *351*
early binding *349*
encapsulation *335*
inheritance *335*
instance *334*
instantiate *334*

instantiating *344*
late binding *349*
multitier application *380*
New keyword *344*
object *334*
polymorphism *335*
Property Get *337*
Property Let *337*
reusability *336*

Review Questions

1. What is an object? a property? a method?
2. What is the purpose of a class module?
3. Why should properties of a class be declared as private?
4. What are property procedures and what is their purpose?
5. Explain how to create a new object.
6. What steps are needed to assign property values to an object?
7. What actions trigger the Initialize event and the Terminate event of an object?
8. How can you write methods for a new class?
9. What is a collection? Name one collection that is automatically built into VB.

10. What properties and methods are provided by the Collection object?
11. What are the advantages of a multitier application over a traditional application? Name the three tiers of a three-tier application.

P r o g r a m m i n g   E x e r c i s e s

9.1 Create a project that contains a collection of sandwich objects. Each sandwich member should have properties for name, bread, meat, cheese, and condiments.

Use two forms, one with a list for names of the sandwiches, and options to add, remove, display, or exit. A second form should contain the detail information.

9.2 Create a project for a collection of pets. Each member will contain pet name, animal type, breed, and color. The form should contain text boxes to enter the information for the pets and command buttons for add, display, clear, and exit. The display command button must display the information about each pet. You may display the information in a message box or a picture box control.

Use only one form for this project.

9.3 Modify project 7.1 (student information) to store the information for a student in a collection of student objects. The existing form will serve as a data form (with some modification). Add a main form that gives options to add a new student, remove a student, and display the information for the selected student. Maintain a list of students in a list box on the main form.

This project requires you to save the student's major and high school name, both selected from list boxes. The easy way to save the selected item from a list box is to use its Text property. Example:

```
mStudent.Major = lstHighSchool.Text
```

Hint: To change the startup form, change the Startup Object in the project properties.

9.4 Modify project 7.2 (R 'n R book information). Each book entered should be a member of a books collection. The existing form will serve as a data form. *Hint:* You must change the project's Startup Object.

Add a main form with a list box showing all books entered. The form should have options to add a new book, remove a book, or display the information about the selected book.

See exercise 9.3 for help in saving the subject and shelf number, which are stored in list boxes.

9.5. Modify project 7.5 (mailing labels) to keep the customer information in a collection of customer objects. Use the account number for the collection key and display the list of customers in a list box.

The user should be able to select one customer and print a mailing label or choose to print labels for all customers.

Allow the user to add a new customer, remove a customer, or display the information for a selected customer.

Note: When you use the account number for the collection key, you will not use the ItemData property of the list. Instead, store the account numbers in the List property of the list box.

See exercise 9.3 for help in saving the name of the catalog, which is stored in a list box.

. . . .

C A S E   S T U D I E S

VB Mail Order

Create a project that uses a collection of objects to hold customer information. Allow the user to add a customer, remove a customer, and display the information for a selected customer. Use the Customer ID for the key. Display a count of the number of customers on the form.

The class should have the following properties, with appropriate property procedures for accessing the property values.

Properties
Customer ID
LastName
FirstName
Address
City
State
ZipCode

Create a project that stores vehicle information in a collection of objects. Allow the user to add a vehicle, remove a vehicle, display the information for a selected vehicle, or display a count of the number of vehicles. Assign sequential numbers for the VehicleID and use it as a key.

Set up your project with two forms, similar to the chapter hands-on project. On the main form, use a list box to hold the InventoryID, ModelName, and Year,

VB Auto Center

concatenated together. For example, the entry for an '89 Chevrolet Suburban with an ID of 10 would be

```
10 Suburban 1989
```

The class should have the following properties, with the appropriate property procedures for accessing the property values.

Properties
InventoryID
Manufacturer
ModelName
Year
VehicleID
CostValue

Create a project that stores video information in a collection of objects. Allow the user to add a video, remove a video, display the information for a selected video, or display a count of the number of videos. Use the movie number as the key.

Video Bonanza

The properties for each object will be Movie Number, Title, Studio ID, Category, and Length (in minutes). Include the appropriate property procedures for accessing the property values.

Very Very Boards

The management of Very Very Boards wants a computer application to store and display product information.

Create a project that stores product information in a collection of objects. Allow the user to add a product, remove a product, or display the values for a product.

Assign sequential numbers for the ProductID field and use that as the key.

Set up your project with two forms, similar to the chapter hands-on example. On the main form, use a list box to hold the ProductID and product description, concatenated together. For example, the list box item for a snowboard with a ProductID of 5 would be

```
5 Snowboard
```

The class should have the properties listed in the table.

The Unit property will hold string values, such as "pair," "dozen," or "each."

Properties
ProductID
Description
Manufacturer
Unit
Cost
Last order date
Last order quantity

Hint: To update the values of an object, set the properties of the object to the new values. You also must update the object's description in the list box on the main form.

10

Data Files

At the completion of this chapter, you will be able to . . .

1. Create data files.

2. Read and write records to disk.

3. Determine the appropriate locations for data file–related code.

4. Understand the significance of Open and Close statements.

5. Differentiate between sequential and random files.

6. Trap user errors and handle errors to avoid run-time errors.

7. Incorporate fixed-length strings into user-defined data types.

8. Read and write objects in a random file.

9. Perform add, delete, and edit operations on random files.

10. Allow the user to input data using the InputBox function.

Data Files

In all of your projects so far, the user has entered information through text boxes. Although this input method is satisfactory for many applications, some situations require large quantities of data or information to be processed week after week.

Many computer applications require data to be saved from one run to the next. Some examples are personal tasks, such as budgeting, mailing lists, and sports-team records, and business applications, such as inventory records, customer files, and master files. This chapter deals with methods to store and access **data files** on disk.

Data Files and Project Files

In computer terminology anything that you store on a diskette or hard disk is given its own unique name and called a **file**. Each of your Visual Basic projects requires multiple files—for the forms, standard code modules, and project information. However, the files you will create now are different; they contain actual data, such as names and addresses, inventory amounts, and account balances.

Data File Terminology

The entire collection of data is called a file. The file is made up of **records**— one record for each entity in the file. Each record can be broken down further into **fields** (also called *data elements*). For example, in an employee file, the fields for one employee are one record. In a name and address file, the fields for one person are a record.

In the name and address file, each person has a last name field, a first name field, address fields, and a phone number field. Each field in a record pertains to the same person. Figure 10.1 illustrates a name and address file.

F i g u r e   1 0 . 1

The rows in this data file represent records; the columns represent fields.

Last Name	First Name	Street	City	State	Zip	Phone	Email
Maxwell	Harry	795 W. J Street	Ontario	CA	91764	909-555-1234	
Helm	Jennifer	201 Cortez Way	Pomona	CA	91766	818-555-2222	JHelm@ms.org
Colton	Craig	1632 Granada Place	Pomona	CA	91766	909-555-3333	

A record

A field

The data stored in files is nearly always entered in an organized manner. Records may be stored in account number order, alphabetically by name, by date, or by the sequence in which they are received. One field in the record is the organizing factor for the file (such as account number, name, or date). This field, which is used to determine the order of the file, is called the **record key**, or **key field.**

A key field may be either a string or numeric field. In an employee file, if the records are in order by an employee number, then the employee number is the key field. If the order is based on employee name, then the name is the key field, although key fields are normally unique data items.

File Organizations

The manner in which data are organized, stored, and retrieved is called the *file organization.* Two common file organizations are *sequential* and *random*. In this chapter you will learn to read and write both sequential and random files.

Opening and Closing Data Files

Three steps are necessary to process data files:

1. *Open* the file. Before any data may be placed on the disk or read from the disk, the file must be opened. Generally, you will open the file in the Form_Load procedure.
2. *Read* or *write* the data records. You will read or write in a save procedure associated with the data entry form.
3. *Close* the file. You must always close a file when you are finished with it.

The Open Statement—General Form

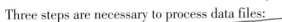

Drive\Path\ Filename.ext

```
Open "FileName" For {Input | Output | Append | Random} As #FileNumber [Len = RecLength]
```

The **Open statement** elements shown in the braces are the **file mode**, indicating the way that you will access the file. The braces indicate that you must make a choice, but that the entry is required. The first three choices are used for sequential files. The FileNumber may be from 1 to 511. The record length can be up to 32,767 characters.

The Open Statement—Examples

```
Open "A:\DataFile.Dat" For Output As #1
Open "C:\VB6\Ch0701\Names.txt" For Input As #2
```

The first example opens a file called *DataFile.Dat* as an output file, calling it file #1. The second example opens a file in the C: drive called *Names.txt* as an input file, calling it file #2.

File Mode	Description
Output	Data are output from the project and written on the disk. New data is written at the beginning of the file, overwriting any existing data.
Input	Data are input into the project from the disk. This mode reads data previously stored on the disk.
Append	Data are output from the project and written on the disk. The new data are added to the end of the file.
Random	Data can be input or output, and records may be accessed in any order.

Remember that a data file must always be opened prior to being used. When a data file is opened, the following actions are taken:

1. The directory is checked for the named file. If the file does not exist, a directory entry is created for this file, with the exception of Input mode, which will cause an error message if the file does not exist.
2. For sequential files a **buffer** is established in memory. A buffer is simply an area of main storage. As the program instructs VB to write data on the disk, the data are actually placed in the buffer. When the buffer is filled, the data are physically written to the disk. The size of the buffer for a random file is the number specified in the Len = clause of the Open statement.
3. A **file pointer** is created and set to the beginning of the file for all modes except Append, in which it is set to the end of the file. The pointer is always updated to indicate the current location in the file.
4. The file is given a **file number** for future reference. Each file used in a project must be assigned a unique number; however, the numbers need not begin with 1. After a file is closed, the number may be reused for a different file.

The Close Statement—General Form

```
Close [#filenumber...]
```

The Close Statement—Examples

```
Close #1
Close #1, #2
Close
```

The **Close statement** terminates processing of a disk file. When used without a file number, all open files are closed. The Close statement performs many housekeeping tasks:

1. Physically writes the last partially filled buffer on the disk (sequential files only). The `Write` statement places data in the buffer, and the data are written to the disk when the buffer is filled. Generally, the buffer will contain data when the project terminates. Those data must be written to the disk.
2. Writes an end-of-file mark (**EOF**) at the end of the file.
3. Releases the buffer.
4. Releases the file number.

Note: Executing an `End` statement automatically closes all open files, but you should not rely on this technique. A good rule is to always explicitly `Close` every file that has been opened in the project.

The FreeFile Function

When you open a file, you must assign a file number to each file. For a small project with one or two data files, most programmers assign #1 and #2. But in a larger project, selecting a file number can be a problem. If your code will be part of a larger project with code from other programmers and other libraries, you must make sure to avoid any conflicting file numbers. To solve this problem, you can allow the system to assign the next available file number. Use the `FreeFile` function to assign the next available file number to your file, and you will never have conflicts.

```
Dim intFileNumber As Integer
intFileNumber = FreeFile 'Get next available file number
Open "File.dat" For Output As #intFileNumber
```

Viewing the Data in a File

When you wish to look at the data in your file, use the Notepad or Wordpad application available in Windows Accessories (or any other text editor). Sequential files appear as text with comma-separated fields. When viewing random data files, you may notice some strange characters in your file; these represent numeric fields. Numeric data types such as integer, single, and currency are stored in 2 or 4 bytes that can be reread by a project but look cryptic when displayed by a text editor. When you finish viewing your data file, make sure to exit without saving; your text editor may insert special control characters that will corrupt your file.

Sequential File Organization

Sequential files contain data elements that are stored one after another in sequence. When you read the data from the disk, it must be read in the same sequence in which it was written. To read any particular element of data, all preceding elements must first be read.

As data elements are written on disk, string fields are enclosed in quotation marks and the fields are separated by commas. Records are generally terminated by a carriage return character.

A sequential name and address file on the disk might look like this:

"Maxwell", "Harry", "795 W. J. Street", "Ontario", "CA", "91764"<CR>
"Helm", "Jennifer", "201 Cortez Way", "Pomona", "CA", "91766"<CR>
"Colton", "Craig", "1632 Granada Place", "Pomona", "CA", "91766"<EOF>

Writing Data to a Sequential Disk File

Use the **Write # statement** to place data into a sequential data file. Before the Write # statement can be executed, the file must be opened in either Output mode or Append mode. Remember that for Append mode, the file pointer is placed at the end of the file. If there are no records, the beginning of the file *is* the end of the file. In Output mode, the pointer is placed at the beginning of the file. Use Output mode to create a new file or write over old data.

The list of fields to write may be string expressions, numeric expressions, or both and may be separated by commas or semicolons.

The Write Statement—General Form

```
Write #FileNumber, ListOfFields
```

The Write Statement—Examples

```
Write #1, txtAccount.Text, txtDescription.Text, txtPrice.Text
Write #2, strAccount
Write #intFileNum, mintCount; mintQuantity; mcurTotal
```

The Write # statement outputs data fields to the disk. As the elements are written on disk, commas are written between elements, string data are enclosed in quotation marks, and a carriage return and a line feed are inserted after the last element.

Creating a Sequential Data File

Sequential files are most commonly used to store small quantities of data that will rarely change. A common use of the sequential file is to store the information from a list box from one run to the next. In Chapter 7 your project added, removed, and cleared items from a list. These changes were not saved, so on the next execution of the project, the list reverted to its original contents stored in the List property of the control. The following save procedure writes the contents of a list box to a sequential file:

```
Private Sub mnuFileSave_Click()
    'Save the list box contents to a sequential file
    Dim intIndex        As Integer
    Dim intMaximum      As Integer

    Open "Coffee.Dat" For Output As #1
    intMaximum = cboCoffee.ListCount - 1
    For intIndex = 0 To intMaximum
        Write #1, cboCoffee.List(intIndex)
    Next intIndex
    Close #1
End Sub
```

After execution of this procedure, the Coffee.Dat file on disk will hold the elements from the list box. VB automatically writes a carriage return at the end of each `Write #` statement and an EOF mark at the end of the file.

Disk File Contents

"Chocolate Almond"<CR>"Espresso Roast"<CR>
   "Jamaica Blue Mtn."<CR>"Kona Blend"<CR> "Vanilla Nut"<EOF>

Reading the Data in a Sequential File

When you want to read a sequential file from the disk, you must open it for input. A successful `Open` sets the file pointer to the beginning of the file. After you have opened the file in Input mode, you can read the records using the **Input # statement**. One word of warning: Recall that if you open a file for input and it does not exist, a run-time error occurs and the program terminates. Later in this chapter you will learn to check for errors and avoid the error message.

The Input # Statement—General Form

```
Input #FileNumber, ListOfFields
```

The Input # Statement—Examples

```
Input #1, lblName.Caption, lblStreet.Caption, lblCity.Caption, lblZipCode.Caption
Input #2, strAccount
Input #intFileNum, intSavedCount, intSavedQuantity, curSavedTotal
```

The FileNumber named on the `Input #` statement must be the number of a previously opened data file. The fields named should be separated by commas. It doesn't matter what variable names were used when the data were written to the disk. When the data elements are read from the disk, they may be called by the same variable names or by completely different ones.

If you plan to load a list box from the data stored in a sequential file, the Open in the Form_Load must be followed by a loop that adds the data to the list. The loop will terminate when the EOF marker is read.

Finding the End of a Data File

When reading data from the disk, you must know when to stop. Recall that closing the file creates an EOF mark. You can read until the EOF mark has been reached. (Attempting to read past the EOF mark causes a run-time error.)

The EOF(N) Function—General Form

```
EOF(FileNumber)
```

The **EOF(n) function** returns True when the EOF mark is read on the last good record. You can test for EOF using an If statement, but a better solution is to use a loop that continues until the condition is True. This example uses a Do/Loop:

```
Do Until EOF(1)                          'Continue processing until EOF is True
    Input #1, strCoffeeFlavor            'Read a record from the data file
        cboCoffee.AddItem strCoffeeFlavor    'Assign the variables to the list boxes
Loop
```

Locating a File

When you code the Open statement for a file, you can include the entire path, including the drive letter. However, this approach can cause problems if you move the file to a new location. If you ever work on the hard drive and then transfer the project to diskette, you will generate "File not found" errors.

The best approach is to keep the data file in the same folder as your project. You will be able to move the entire folder to a new location and still find the file if you use this helpful technique. The predefined VB object called *App* holds properties for your application. You can use App.Path to refer to the path from which the current application is running:

```
Dim strFilePath   As String
strFilePath = App.Path & "\FileName.Ext"
Open strFilePath for Input As #1
```

You can also code the path directly in the `Open`, skipping the variable for the filename:

```
Open App.Path & "\FileName.Ext" for Input As #1
```

Note: The App.Path method will fail if your project is running in the root directory. Your project must be stored in a folder.

Feedback 10.1

1. Write the Visual Basic statements to
   (a) Open a sequential file called Vendor.dat for Output.
   (b) Write the items in the lstVendor list box to the Vendor.dat file.
   (c) Close the Vendor.dat file.
   (d) Open the Vendor.dat file so it can be used to read the records.
   (e) Read the records from the disk file into a list box.
2. What function is used to find the end of the file?
3. What is the purpose of App.Path and where would it be used?

Trapping Program Errors

You have already learned to use `If` statements to test field values and shield the user from nasty run-time errors. When you start coding for data files, you will find that some problems cannot be avoided, but must be anticipated. One such case is opening a data file for input when the file does not exist. It may be that the user has not inserted the proper disk containing the file or has selected an incorrect option.

When a run-time error occurs, Visual Basic generates an error number and checks it against a table of error codes. You can intercept the error number and take action without terminating the project. The statements used in this **error-trapping** process are the **On Error statement** and the Err object.

For you to trap errors, you must do the following:

1. Turn on the error-handling feature using the `On Error` statement.
2. Create error-handling code routines, which are set off from your other code with line labels.
3. Determine how and where the program is to continue after the error is taken care of.

The On Error Statement

You must place an `On Error` statement at the beginning of any procedure where errors might occur, such as before opening a sequential file for input. The following procedure has minimal error trapping. The individual statements and options will be explained in the sections that follow.

```
Private Sub Form_Load()
    'Open the file

    On Error Go To HandleErrors                'Turn on error trapping
    Open "A:\Datafile.txt" For Input As #1

Form_Load_Exit:
    Exit Sub

HandleErrors:                                  'Error-handling routine
    'Code here to determine cause of error and display message
    Resume
End Sub
```

You may not want to add error-handling statements until you have tested and debugged your project (assuming the possibility that your projects don't always run perfectly the first time you test them). You want your error-handling code to trap user errors, not any programming errors. You may want to include the error-handling statements but remark them out while debugging. An alternative is to set the environment to disable error handlers while you complete your normal debugging. Choose *Options* on the *Tools* menu. On the *General* tab select *Break on All Errors* and then click OK.

Although there are three forms of the On Error statement, you will want to use form 1 and form 3 in most of your work. Form 1 turns on error trapping, and form 3 turns it off. Anytime error trapping is turned off, the project is subject to terminating with an *Error* dialog box.

The On Error Statement—General Form 1

```
On Error Go To LineLabel
```

The On Error Go To specifies the label of the line where your error-handling code begins. A **line label** is a name (following identifier naming conventions) on a line by itself and followed by a colon. The error-handling code must be in the same procedure as the On Error statement.

The On Error Statement—General Form 2

```
On Error Resume Next
```

Using the Resume Next option of error handling causes execution to skip the line that generated the error and continue execution with the following line of code.

The On Error Statement—General Form 3

```
On Error Go To 0
```

The Go To 0 option of the On Error turns off error handling. Any error that occurs after this statement executes will cause a run-time error.

The Err Object

The **Err object** holds information about an error that has occurred. You can check the properties of the Err object to determine the error number and a description of the error. The name of the object or application that caused the error is stored in the **Source property**. The **Number property** contains the error number (ranging from 0 to 65,535), which is described in the **Description property**.

You don't need to define or include the Err object. It has global scope and is automatically a part of your project, similar to the Printer object.

If you transfer execution of your project to another procedure or execute a Resume statement, the properties of the Err object are cleared. If you will need these values for further processing, make sure to assign them to variables before performing any action that causes them to clear.

The Err.Number Property

The following table includes a partial list of errors. The complete list of errors may be found in VB Help under the heading *Trappable Errors*.

Err.Number	Err.Description
7	Out of memory
9	Subscript out of range
11	Division by zero
13	Type mismatch
52	Bad file name or number
53	File not found
54	Bad file mode
58	File already exists
61	Disk full
67	Too many files
68	Device unavailable
70	Permission denied
71	Disk not ready
75	Path/file access error
76	Path not found
482	Printer error

Raising Error Conditions

You can use the `Raise` method to set the error code, effectively "turning on" an error, or making it occur. This step may be necessary when an error that occurs is not among those that you anticipated and coded for; you may want to turn on the error so that the system handles the error and displays a dialog box for the user.

```
Err.Raise Number:=71
Err.Raise Err
```

The full `Raise` method allows several arguments—only the error number is required.

The Raise Method—General Form

```
Object.Raise Number:=NumericValue
Err.Raise Err        'Raise the previous unhandled error
```

The numeric value that you assign may be a constant, a named constant, or a variable.

The Raise Method—Examples

```
Err.Raise Number:=76
Err.Raise Number:=intPathNotFound
```

Coding Error-Handling Routines

The code that you use to handle errors begins with a line label. Assuming that you have used the statement:

```
On Error Go To HandleErrors
```

your error-handling code begins with the line label:

```
HandleErrors:
```

A line label follows the rules for naming identifiers and is followed by a colon. It must appear on a line by itself and will begin in column 1. If you attempt to insert spaces or a tab before the line label, the editor deletes them.

```
HandleErrors:
    'Check to make sure the user put a disk in the drive
    Dim strMsg                  As String
    Dim intResponse             As Integer
    Const intErrorNoDisk        As Integer = 71
    strMsg = "Make sure there is a disk in the drive"

    If Err.Number = intErrorNoDisk Then         'Check for Err 71
        intResponse = MsgBox(strMsg, vbOKCancel)    'Returns button pressed
        If intResponse = vbOK Then              'OK button pressed
            Resume                              'Try again
        Else
            mnuFileExit_Click                   'Exit the project
        End If
    Else                                        'Any other error
        Err.Raise Err                           'Cancel with error message
    End If
```

The preceding example includes a routine that continues execution if the error is solved and also handles the situation for any unsolved errors.

Using Select Case to Check for Errors

You will find the Select Case statement very handy when you have a series of errors to check.

```
Select Case Err.Number
    Case 53                     'File not found
        'Code to handle File not found error
    Case 71                     'Disk not ready
        'Code to handle Disk not ready error
    Case 76                     'Path not found
        'Code to handle Path not found error
    Case Else                   'All other errors
        Err.Raise Err           'Make the error reappear
End Select
Resume
```

The Resume Statement

When you have resolved the problem causing an error, your program should continue execution if possible. This is accomplished with the **Resume statement**. You can choose to continue with the statement that caused the error, with the statement following the one causing the error, or at a specified location in the code.

The Resume Statement—General Form 1

```
Resume
```

If you use the `Resume` statement in the procedure that originally generated the error, execution of the project continues with the line of code that caused the error to occur. If the error-handling routine calls a different procedure that contains a `Resume`, execution continues with the statement that called the second procedure.

The Resume Statement—General Form 2

```
Resume Next
```

Using the `Next` option of `Resume` continues execution with the statement immediately following the line that caused the error (assuming that the `Resume Next` appears in the same procedure as the line of code causing the error). Similar to form 1, if you call another procedure from the error-handling routine, `Resume Next` continues execution at the line following the call.

The Resume Statement—General Form 3

```
Resume LineLabel
```

Execution continues at the line label, which *must be in the same procedure* as the `Resume`.

Handling Errors

Your error-handling routine should do *something* to handle each error:

- If you identify the error type and the user can correct the problem (such as insert the correct diskette in the drive), use `Resume`, which will reexecute the statement that caused the error. If another error occurs, it will return to the error handler.

- If you identify the error type and execution can proceed without the error-causing statement, use `Resume Next`.

- If you prefer to check in-line for a particular type of error (following the `Open`, for example), use `Resume Next`.

- If the error number is unexpected or unidentified, raise the error again so that Visual Basic will handle it. The system error message will display for the user.

- If you want to exit the current procedure and continue project execution, use `Resume LineLabel`. Make sure to code a line label before your

Tip

Make sure that you cannot reach a `Resume` statement without an error occurring. This condition causes an error that generates the message *Resume without an Error*.

`Exit Sub` statement. For an example, see the following section describing the `Exit Sub` statement.

- If you want to end your project execution without displaying the system error message, call your exit procedure code (e.g., mnuFileExit_Click or cmdExit_Click).

- If you want to turn off error trapping, use `On Error Go To 0`. (Any further error will cause a run-time error and display the system error message to the user.)

The Exit Function and Exit Sub Statements

The statements in your procedure execute sequentially. To include an error-handling routine that will not execute accidentally (when no error occurs), you must exit the procedure before the line label. Precede the error-handling line label with an **Exit Sub** or **Exit Function statement** (depending on whether the code is in a sub procedure or a function procedure). The `Exit Sub` or `Exit Function` causes execution to exit the procedure immediately.

You can simplify your error-handling code if you adopt the following pattern for any procedure with error trapping:

1. Include an `On Error` statement at the top of any procedure that might require error handling.
2. Code a line label just before the `Exit Sub` statement. Name the line label the same as the procedure name, plus an underscore and Exit. Example: mnuFileSave_Click_Exit.
3. After the `Exit Sub` statement, code your error-handling routine.

```
Private Sub Form_Load()
    'Template for procedure that includes error handling

    On Error Go To HandleErrors                 'Turn on error trapping
    Open "A:\Filename.txt" For Input As #1

Form_Load_Exit:
    Exit Sub

HandleErrors:                                   'Error-handling routine
    'Code here to determine cause of error and display message

    Select Case Err.Number
        Case n
            'Code to handle error
        Case n
            'Code to handle error
        Case Else
            'Code to handle any other errors
    End Select
    Resume
End Sub
```

Here is an error-handling sub procedure to handle any errors that occur when opening a sequential file for input.

```vb
Private Sub Form_Load()
    'Load the Coffee list
    Dim strCoffee As String

    On Error GoTo HandleErrors
    Open "Coffee.Dat" For Input As #1
    Do Until EOF(1)
        Input #1, strCoffee
        cboCoffee.AddItem strCoffee
    Loop
    Close #1

Form_Load_Exit:
    Exit Sub

HandleErrors:
    Dim intResponse As Integer

    Select Case Err.Number
        Case 53, 76                     'File or path not found
            intResponse = MsgBox("Create a new file?", _
                vbYesNo + vbQuestion, "File not Found")
            If intResponse = vbYes Then
                Resume Form_Load_Exit
            Else
                mnuFileExit_Click
            End If
        Case 71                         'Disk not ready
            intResponse = MsgBox("Disk not ready. Retry?", _
                vbRetryCancel + vbQuestion, "Disk Error")
            If intResponse = vbRetry Then
                Resume                  'Try again
            Else
                mnuFileExit_Click       'Exit project
            End If
        Case Else                       'All other errors should cancel execution
            Err.Raise Err
    End Select
    Resume
End Sub
```

Feedback 10.2

What is the purpose of the following statements?

1. `On Error Go To 0`
2. `On Error Go To WhatToDo`
3. `Err.Raise Number:=53`
4. `Resume`
5. `Resume Next`

Saving Changes to a File

If your project allows users to make changes to data during program execution, it's a good idea to ask them if they want to save the changes before the program ends. This is like working in a word processing program or the VB editor. If you close the file after making changes, you receive a message asking if you want to save the file. But if you haven't made any changes since the last save, no message appears.

To keep track of data changes during execution, you will need a module-level Boolean variable. Because the standard practice in programming is to refer to the data as "dirty" if changes have been made, we will call the variable *mblnIsDirty*. In each procedure that allows changes (Add, Remove, Edit), you must set mblnIsDirty to True. After saving the file, set the variable to False.

Just before the project ends, you must check the value of mblnIsDirty; if True, ask the user if he or she wants to save; if False, you can just exit without a message.

The Form_QueryUnload Procedure

Recall the discussion in Chapter 9 about ending your project. To allow your project to perform housekeeping tasks, you should unload the forms before executing an End statement. This approach allows each form's Unload event and each class's Terminate event to occur.

If you want to do something before the project ends, such as ask the user to save the file, the best location is the form's **QueryUnload event** procedure. This procedure executes before the Unload when the user clicks on your Exit button or menu command, clicks on the window's Close button, or even exits Windows. (However, if your Exit button or menu command procedure has an End statement, the QueryUnload event will not occur.)

```
Private Sub Form_QueryUnload(Cancel As Integer, UnloadMode As Integer)
    'Ask user to save the file
    Dim intResponse As Integer

    If mblnIsDirty = True Then
        intResponse = MsgBox("Coffee list has changed. Save the list?",_
            vbYesNo + vbQuestion, "Coffee List Changed")
        If intResponse = vbYes Then
            mnuFileSave_Click
        End If
    End If
End Sub
```

Notice the Cancel argument on the QueryUnload procedure header. If you determine inside this event that the Unload shouldn't be allowed to complete, set Cancel = True. When the procedure finishes, the Unload cancels.

Sequential File Programming Example

This programming example is based on the hands-on example at the end of Chapter 7, which contains a dropdown combo box with the flavors of coffee (Figure 10.2). The user can add new flavors to the list, remove items from the list, or clear the list. However, in Chapter 7 those changes were not saved from one program run to the next. If you wish to allow the user to update the list of flavors, the data should be stored in a data file. For each program run, the list will be loaded from the data file during the Form_Load procedure of the startup form. If the flavors file does not yet exist, the program skips over loading the combo box to allow the user to add coffee flavors and create the file.

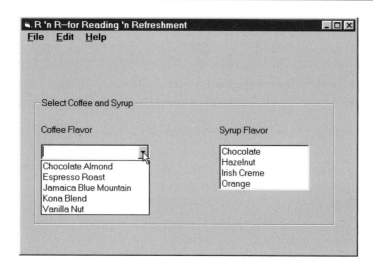

The dropdown combo box from Chapter 7. Users can add new flavors, delete flavors, and clear the list.

The user can choose to save the coffee list into a disk file by selecting a menu choice. Also, when the *Exit* menu choice is selected, if any changes have been made to the list, the project prompts the user to save the file. A Boolean variable is used to determine if any changes have been made since the file was last saved.

Notice that this example is only a partial program, showing the changes made to the hands-on program example from Chapter 7. Only a few procedures are changed.

```
'Module:              frmFlavors
'Programmer:          Bradley/Millspaugh
'Date:                Oct 1999. Updated 6/2001.
'Description:         Allow the user to add coffee flavors, remove
'                     flavors, clear the list, display a count, and
'                     save the list from one run to the next.
'Folder:              Ch1001


Option Explicit
Dim mblnIsDirty As Boolean
```

```
Private Sub cmdAddCoffee_Click()
    'Add a new coffee flavor to the coffee list

    With cboCoffee
        If .Text <> "" Then
            .AddItem .Text
            .Text = ""
            mblnIsDirty = True
        Else
            MsgBox "Enter a coffee name to add.", vbExclamation, "Missing data"
        End If
    .SetFocus
    End With
End Sub
```

```
Private Sub Form_Load()
    'Load the Coffee list
    Dim strCoffee   As String
    Dim strFilePath As String

    On Error GoTo HandleErrors
    strFilePath = App.Path & "\Coffee.Dat"
    Open strFilePath For Input As #1
    Do Until EOF(1)
        Input #1, strCoffee
        cboCoffee.AddItem strCoffee
    Loop
    Close #1

Form_Load_Exit:
    Exit Sub
```

```
HandleErrors:
    Dim intResponse As Integer

    Select Case Err.Number
        Case 53, 76                     'File or path not found
            intResponse = MsgBox("Create a new file?", _
                vbYesNo + vbQuestion, "File not Found")
            If intResponse = vbYes Then
                Resume Form_Load_Exit 'Exit the procedure
            Else
                mnuFileExit_Click       'Exit the project
            End If
        Case 71                         'Disk not ready
            intResponse = MsgBox("Disk not ready. Retry?", _
                vbRetryCancel + vbQuestion, "Disk Error")
            If intResponse = vbRetry Then
                Resume                   'Try again
            Else
                mnuFileExit_Click       'Exit project
            End If
        Case Else                       'All other errors should cancel execution
            Err.Raise Err
    End Select
End Sub
```

```
Private Sub Form_QueryUnload(Cancel As Integer, UnloadMode As Integer)
    'Ask user to save the file
    Dim intResponse As Integer

    If mblnIsDirty = True Then
        intResponse = MsgBox("Coffee list has changed. Save the list?", _
            vbYesNo + vbQuestion, "Coffee List Changed")
        If intResponse = vbYes Then
            mnuFileSave_Click
        End If
    End If
End Sub
```

```
Private Sub mnuEditAdd_Click()
    'Add a new coffee to list

    cboAddCoffee_Click
End Sub
```

```vb
Private Sub mnuEditClear_Click()
    'Clear the coffee list
    Dim intResponse    As Integer

    intResponse = MsgBox("Clear the coffee flavor list?", _
        vbYesNo + vbQuestion, "Clear Coffee List")
    If intResponse = vbYes Then
        cboCoffee.Clear
        mblnIsDirty = True
    End If
End Sub
```

```vb
Private Sub mnuEditCount_Click()
    'Display a count of the coffee list
    Dim strMsg        As String

    strMsg = "The number of coffee types is " & cboCoffee.ListCount
    MsgBox strMsg, vbInformation, "Coffee List Count"
End Sub
```

```vb
Private Sub mnuEditRemove_Click()
    'Remove the selected coffee from list
    Dim strMsg        As String

    With cboCoffee
        If .ListIndex <> -1 Then
            .RemoveItem .ListIndex
            mblnIsDirty = True
        Else
            strMsg = "First select the coffee to remove."
            MsgBox strMsg, vbInformation, "No Coffee Selection Made"
        End If
    End With
End Sub
```

```vb
Private Sub mnuFileSave_Click()
    'Save the list box contents to a sequential file
    Dim intIndex     As Integer
    Dim intMaximum   As Integer
    Dim strFilePath As String

    strFilePath = App.Path & "\Coffee.Dat"
    Open strFilePath For Output As #1
    intMaximum = cboCoffee.ListCount - 1
    For intIndex = 0 To intMaximum
        Write #1, cboCoffee.List(intIndex)
    Next intIndex
    Close #1
    mblnIsDirty = False
End Sub
```

```
Private Sub mnuFileExit_Click()
    'Terminate the project

    Unload Me
    End
End Sub
```

The preceding procedures demonstrate loading a combo box from a sequential file. Notice that the error handling in the Form_Load procedure traps for any error on the Open. If there is no error, the combo box is loaded with a Do/Loop.

If error number 53 or 76 occurs (File not found or Path not found), a message box asks the user whether or not to create the file. An answer of No terminates the program, but a Yes continues execution without attempting the read.

The user can enter new flavors during program execution, remove flavors, or clear the list. If any changes are made to the list, the Boolean variable mblnIsDirty is set to True. When the project exits, if mblnIsDirty is True, the user is prompted to save the list. Placing the user prompt in the QueryUnload procedure guarantees that it will execute even when the user exits the program using the window's close button or closes Windows.

Random Data Files

The primary difference between sequential files and random files is that you may read and write the data in any order in a **random file**. With sequential files you must always start at the beginning of the file and proceed in order through the file. Random files offer greater speed as well as the capability for random access.

You can visualize random files as a table in which each entry may be referenced by its relative position. Each entry in a file is one record, which is referred to by its record number. Any record in the file may be read or written without accessing the preceding records. Figure 10.3 illustrates the table concept of random files.

F i g u r e   1 0 . 3

	Last Name Field	First Name Field	Phone Number Field
(1)			
(2)			
(3)			
(4)			
(5)			
(6)			
(7)			
(8)			
....			

Layout of a random file. Each record consists of a Last Name field, a First Name field, and a Phone Number field.

All records in a random file are exactly the same size. The fields within the record are fixed in length and position. That is, if the name takes the first 30 bytes (characters) in one record, every record will allocate the first 30 bytes for the name. This scheme is a departure from sequential files with their variable-length fields and records. Before reading or writing a random file, the record structure or layout must be defined. The `Type/End Type` statements set up record structures. The only modification you will need is to use fixed-length strings.

Fixed-Length Strings

String variables may be variable length or fixed length. Until this point, all strings have been variable length. But for random files you need to specify fixed-length strings. You can define a specific number of characters for elements of user-defined data types and dimension fixed-length single variables and arrays.

If the value you store in a field is less than its specified length, the extra positions are filled with spaces. If you assign a value that is longer than the fixed length, the extra characters are truncated (chopped off) when the value is stored in the fixed-length string.

To specify the string length, add an asterisk (*) followed by the size of the string declaration.

```
Dim strName            As String * 30

Type FullName
    strLastName        As String * 20
    strFirstName       As String * 20
End Type
```

Defining a Record for a Random File

To define a record for a random file, first set up its structure with a `Type` statement. Then dimension a record variable of the data type.

Note: You can code `Type` statements in a standard code module or the General Declarations section of a form module or a class module. In a form module or a class module, you must specify `Private`.

```
Private Type MemberStructure
    strLastName        As String * 20
    strFirstName       As String * 20
    strPhone           As String * 12
End Type
Dim mudtMemberRecord   As MemberStructure
```

Opening a Random File

The `Open` statement for a random file is the same as for sequential files, using a file mode of Random. This mode allows you to input and output to the same file without closing and reopening it.

```
Open "B:\Data\Names.txt" For Random As #1 Len = 52
Open "A:Members.dat" For Random As #2 Len = Len(mudtMemberRecord)
```

For a random file, the Len (length) entry refers to the length of a single record. In the second example the second Len is actually the Length function that returns the size in bytes of the item enclosed in parentheses. The item in parentheses is the name used for the record variable you declared.

Determining Whether a File Exists

When you open a random file, the file can have both input and output. Therefore, if the file doesn't exist when the Open executes, no error is generated. Instead, VB sets up an empty file so you can start adding records.

Sometimes you want the user to know that no file was found; maybe he or she didn't specify the correct file or load the right disk. You can check for the existence of a file using the **Dir function.** The Dir function returns the path of the named file; if the file doesn't exist, Dir returns an empty string.

```
If Dir(mstrFilePath) <> "" Then        'The file exists
    'Code to open and read file
Else
    'Code to inform user and confirm file creation
End If
```

Reading and Writing a Random File

The input/output statements that you use for a random file differ from those used for sequential files. When accessing a random file, the data are handled a record at a time. The statements used are Get and Put, which include the record position in the file and the name of the variable defined as the record.

You can Get and Put records in a random file in any order you choose. That is, you may first write record #5, then #1, then #20, or any other order. When record #5 is written in the file, VB skips enough space for four records and writes in the fifth physical location. Record positions 1 to 4 are skipped until records are written in those locations. See the diagram in Figure 10.4.

F i g u r e   1 0 . 4

Writing record # 5. The record is written into the fifth location in the file.

	Last Name Field	First Name Field	Phone Number Field
(1)			
(2)			
(3)			
(4)			
(5)				← Write record #5
(6)			
(7)			
(8)			
....			

The record numbers start at record 1. This rule will probably feel strange to you, since you are used to arrays and lists beginning with an index of 0. If you attempt to Get or Put a record number of 0, you receive a *Bad Record Number* error.

The Get Statement—General Form

```
Get [#]FileNumber, [RecordNumber], RecordName
```

The Get Statement—Examples

```
Get #2, intRecNumber, mudtMemberRecord
Get #1, intRecordNumber, mudtInventoryRecord(intRecordNumber)
Get #2, intCustomerNumber, gudtCustomerRecord(intIndex)
Get #3, 4, udtAccountRecord
Get #1, , mudtMemberRecord
```

The **Get statement** reads data from a random disk file and places the data into the record-name variable. This variable should be one declared with a user-defined data type. If the variable is an array, the appropriate subscript number must be included.

When you omit the record number, the *next* record (after the last Get or Put that was processed) is read from the file. Either a variable or a constant may be used for the record number. Generally, you will want to use a variable to allow selection of any record in the file.

The Put Statement—General Form

```
Put [#]FileNumber, [RecordNumber], RecordName
```

The Put Statement—Examples

```
Put #2, intRecNumber, mudtMemberRecord
Put #1, intRecordNumber, mudtInventoryRecord(intRecordNumber)
Put #2, intCustomerNumber, gudtCustomerRecord(intIndex)
Put #3, 4, udtAccountRecord
Put #1, , mudtMemberRecord
```

The **Put statement** takes the contents of the specified record and writes it on the disk. The record number determines the relative location within the file for the record. If the record number is omitted, the record will be placed in the *next* location from the last Get or Put. Note that the next location is likely not the end of the file. Be careful not to write over other data by accident. If you wish to add a record to the end of the file, add 1 to the current number of records and Put the record at that position.

Tip

If you omit the record number in a Get or Put, make sure to include the extra comma, as shown in the last example for each.

Accessing Fields in a Random Record

The Get and Put statements always read or write an entire record. To access the individual fields within the record, you must reference the elements by the record name, a period, and the element name that is defined with the Type statement.

```
Get #1, intRecordNumber, mudtMemberRecord
lstName.AddItem mudtMemberRecord.strLastName
```

Finding the End of a Random File

To find the end of a random file, use the **LOF function** (length of file) rather than the EOF function. The LOF function returns the size of the file in bytes. Although EOF can sometimes be used, problems can occur if records are written randomly and any gaps exist in the file.

The LOF Function—General Form

```
LOF(FileNumber)
```

The FileNumber entry is the file number from a currently open file.

To determine the highest record number in the file, divide the return value of the LOF function by the size of one record (the name dimensioned using the user-defined data type).

The LOF Function—Example

```
intNumberRecords = LOF(1) / Len(mudtMemberRecord)
```

You can use the LOF function to find out how many records are in the file prior to using a For/Next loop that might load the data into a table or list.

```
'Read a random file and store member names into a list box
Dim intNumberRecords As Integer
Dim intIndex As Integer 'Index for the loop

intNumberRecords = LOF(1) / Len(mudtMemberRecord)
For intIndex = 1 To intNumberRecords
    Get #1, intIndex, mudtMemberRecord
    lstNames.AddItem mudtMemberRecord.strLastName
Next intIndex
```

When you are adding to the end of the file, you can use a calculation to find the next record number.

```
intRecordNumber = LOF(1) / Len(mudtMemberRecord) + 1
Put #1, intRecordNumber, mudtMemberRecord
```

The Seek Function

At times you may need to determine the position of the file pointer within the file. The **Seek function** returns the current location of the pointer. For a sequential file, the current byte number is returned. For a random file, Seek returns the position (record number) of the *next* record in the file.

The Seek Function—General Form

```
Seek(FileNumber)
```

FileNumber is the file number of a currently open file.

The Seek Function—Example

```
intNextRecord = Seek(1)
```

Using a List Box to Store a Key Field

When you Get or Put a record in a random file, you need to know the record number. You can use the method introduced in Chapter 9 to use a list box. Display the name or identifying information in a sorted list box, which makes it easy for the user to find the desired record. Each name's corresponding ItemData property can hold the record number. When the user selects a record from the list, you can use the number stored in ItemData to retrieve the correct record. Figure 10.5 illustrates using a list box for record selection.

Figure 10.5

List box List property	ItemData property
Brooks, Barbara	5
Chen, Diana	3
Dunning, Daniel	1
Khan, Brad	6
Lester, Les	2
Nguyen, Ahn	4
Potter, Pete	8
Stevens, Roger	7

User selects this name from list.

The list box holds employee names in the List property and corresponding record numbers in the ItemData property.

Program displays record 6 from file.

The following code segment concatenates a first and last name, adds to the list box, and then assigns the record number to the ItemData property.

```
Private Sub AddToList(intRecordNum As Integer)
    'Add an employee to the list and to ItemData
    Dim strName     As String

    strName = Trim(txtLastName.Text) & ", " & txtFirstName.Text
    With cboEmployee
        .AddItem strName
        .ItemData(.NewIndex) = intRecordNum
    End With
End Sub
```

When concatenating fixed-length strings, the entire string length, including the spaces, is used. You can use a `Trim` function to avoid including the extra spaces.

Trimming Extra Blanks from Strings

The **`Trim`, `LTrim`, and `RTrim` functions** remove extra blank characters in a string. When you have fixed-length strings, such as the fields in a random file, the strings are likely padded with extra spaces. The `LTrim` function removes extra spaces at the left end of the string, `RTrim` removes extra spaces on the right, and `Trim` removes extra spaces from both the left and right ends.

The Trim, LTrim, and RTrim Functions—General Form

```
Trim(StringExpression)
LTrim(StringExpression)
RTrim(StringExpression)
```

The `Trim`, `LTrim`, and `RTrim` functions return a string with the extra spaces removed.

The Trim, LTrim, and RTrim Functions—Examples

```
Trim(" Harry Rabbit ")     'Returns "Harry Rabbit"
LTrim(" Harry Rabbit ")    'Returns "Harry Rabbit "
RTrim(" Harry Rabbit ")    'Returns " Harry Rabbit"
```

Retrieving a Record from the File

You can easily retrieve any record from the random file. After the user chooses a name from the list box, use the ItemData property as the record number.

```
Private Sub cboEmployee_Click()
    'Read the record for the selected employee
    Dim intRecordNum    As Integer
    Dim strMsg          As String

    If cboEmployee.ListIndex <> -1 Then     'Employee selected
        intRecordNum = cboEmployee.ItemData(cboEmployee.ListIndex)
        Get #1, intRecordNum, mudtEmployee
        DisplayData                              'Display the record fields
    Else
        strMsg = "Select an employee name to display."
        MsgBox strMsg, vbInformation, "Employee File"
    End If
End Sub
```

Displaying the Selected Record

After you read a record, you can display the individual fields from the record in controls.

```
Private Sub DisplayData()
    'Display the data for the selected employee

    With mudtEmployee
        txtLastName.Text = .strLastName
        txtFirstName = .strFirstName
        txtStreet = .strStreet
        txtCity = .strCity
        txtState = .strState
        txtZip.Text = .strZipCode
        txtPhone.Text = .strPhone
        txtEmail.Text = .strEmail
    End With
End Sub
```

Updating a Random File

A file update generally consists of routines to add records, edit (modify) records, and delete records. The procedures for these options might be selected from command buttons or menu commands.

In the example random file update, the user can display the information for an employee, edit the information, remove an employee record, or add a record for a new employee. The form for the update contains text boxes for each field of the record along with the appropriate labels. (Figure 10.6 shows the form for the random file update in the chapter hands-on programming example.)

F i g u r e   1 0 . 6

The form for the hands-on programming example.

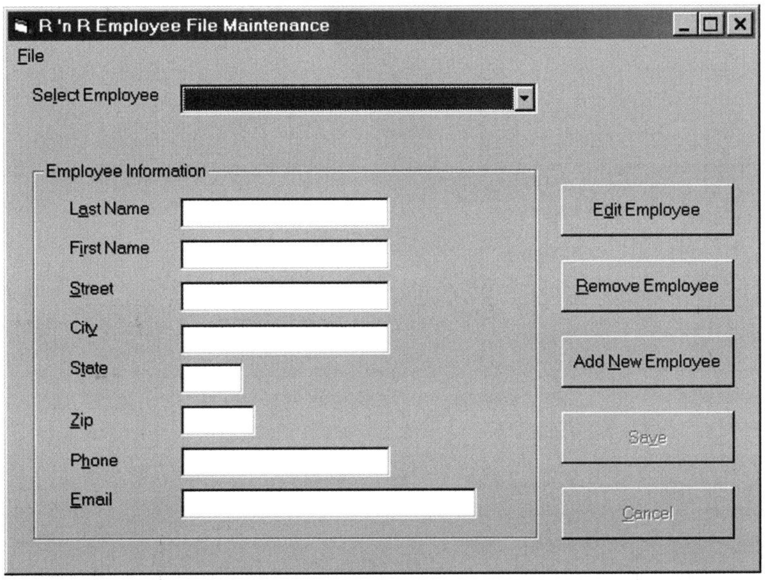

The Update Program

In the update program, the user can select a name from the list (Figure 10.7). The program reads the corresponding record from the file and displays the data in the text boxes. Notice in Figure 10.8 that the current action is *Display*. In Display mode, the text boxes are locked so that the user cannot modify any data.

Figure 10.7

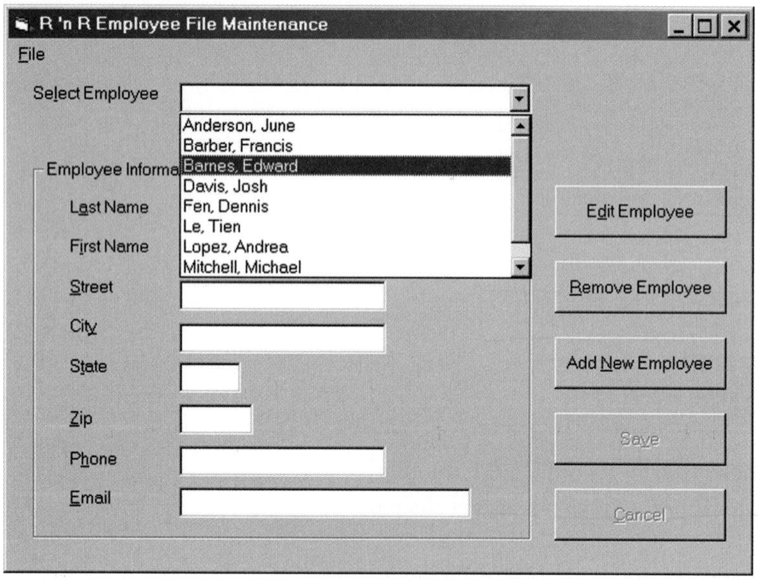

The user can drop down the list and select a name. The program uses the list element's ItemData property for the record number and reads the corresponding record from the disk.

Figure 10.8

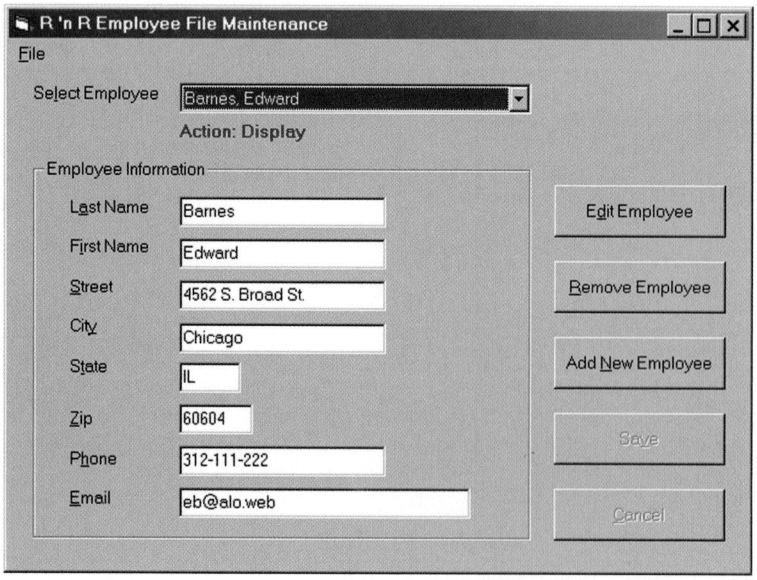

The current record showing in Display mode. The text boxes are locked.

To edit or remove a record, the user must first display it. With the correct record showing, clicking on the *Edit* button changes the action to *Edit* and unlocks the text boxes. To keep the user from making mistakes, you also disable the update buttons, enable the *Save* and *Cancel* buttons, and disable the combo box holding the names. Once an edit begins, the only actions the user can take are to save or cancel (Figure 10.9).

In Edit mode the text boxes are unlocked. The user can only save or cancel the changes.

Locking the Contents of Controls

A good technique for keeping the user out of trouble is to lock text boxes when you don't want to allow any changes. Although you can set the Enabled property of a text box to False, the contents display as grayed. A better approach is to set its Locked property to True. If you lock text boxes, make sure to unlock them again when you *do* want to allow changes.

```
txtLastName.Locked = True
txtFirstName.Locked = True
txtStreet.Locked = True
```

Adding Records

When the user wants to add a record, you must clear all the text boxes, and unlock the text boxes. To keep the user out of trouble, disable the update button and enable only the *Save* and *Cancel* buttons. After the user enters the fields of data for the new record and clicks the *Save* button, you will write the new record at the end of the file, add the new employee's name to the list box, and store the record number in the ItemData property.

```
'Add a record
intRecordNum = LOF(1) / Len(mudtEmployee) + 1 Find next record number
SetupRecord                          'Send text box fields to record variables
WriteRecord intRecordNum             'Write the new record in the file
With cboEmployee                     'Add name to list and record number to ItemData
    strName = Trim(mudtEmployee.strLastName) & ", " & mudtEmployee.strFirstName
    .AddItem strName
    .ItemData(.NewIndex) = intRecordNum
End With
```

An alternative approach would be to search through the records in the file to find the location of a deleted record. You could add a new record in the location of the deleted record. For this example we will add all new records at the end of the file.

Deleting a Record

You can delete a record from a random file in several ways. A common method is to mark a record in some way to indicate that the record is deleted, rather than to actually remove it. If you were to actually remove a record, you would also have to move forward all of the remaining records. That procedure would take time and also change the record numbers. (Often the record number is used as a form of identification.)

One technique is to write some special character in a field of the record to indicate that the record has been deleted. A drawback of this method is that the data in the record cannot be recovered later if you want to add undelete routines.

A more popular method is to add a special field to the record description. The field, commonly called a *delete flag* or *delete code*, holds one of two values, such as *Y* and *N*; or *A* for *active* and *D* for *deleted*; or True/False values. We will use this approach.

In the following data type, the field strDeleteCode indicates whether a record is deleted. A *D* in strDeleteCode means that the record is deleted. When a record is added, *A* (for active) is placed in the field.

```
Private Type udtEmployee
    strLastName            As String * 15
    strFirstName           As String * 10
    strStreet              As String * 20
    strCity                As String * 15
    strState               As String * 2
    strZipCode             As String * 11
    strPhone               As String * 11
    strEmail               As String * 20
    strEmployeeCode        As String * 4
    strDeleteCode          As String * 1 'D = deleted; A = active
End Type
Private mudtEmployee       As udtEmployee
```

To mark a record as deleted, store a *D* in the strDeleteCode field.

```
mudtEmployee.strDeleteCode = "D"
```

When you add records to the dropdown list, add only those with the *A*.

```
If mudtEmployee.strDeleteCode = "A" Then 'Active record
    AddToList (intRecordNum)
End If
```

Keep the List Box Up-to-Date

Whenever you delete a record from the file, you must update the list box. Use the RemoveItem method to delete the reference to the deleted record from the list. The next code segment demonstrates the steps for deletion.

```
mudEmployee.strDeleteCode = "D"
With cboEmployee
    intRecordNum = .ItemData(.ListIndex)
    WriteRecord intRecordNum       'Write delete code in file
    .RemoveItem .ListIndex         'Remove from list
End With
ClearTextBoxes
```

Confirm the Deletion

You may want to verify that the record is really to be deleted. If you do so, make sure to offer the user a chance to cancel the delete.

Editing Records

You can allow the user to make changes to a record.

When the user clicks the *Save* button, you must save the changed record. And because the user can change the employee's first or last name, you must update the list box after the update.

```
'Save updated record and update the list
Dim intRecordNum    As Integer
Dim strName         As String

intRecordNum = cboEmployee.ItemData(cboEmployee.ListIndex)
With cboEmployee             'Remove name from list
    .RemoveItem .ListIndex
End With
SetupRecord                 'Send text box fields to record variables
WriteRecord intRecordNum    'Write updated record in the file
With cboEmployee            'Add name to list and record number to ItemData
    strName = Trim(mudtEmployee.strLastName) & ", " & mudtEmployee.strFirstName
    .AddItem strName
    .ItemData(.NewIndex) = intRecordNum
End With
```

The Read and Write Procedures

Good programming technique calls for a single procedure for reading a file and one for writing to the data file. Write one procedure to write a record and call that procedure from any location that needs to write. Then code a single procedure to read a record and call it as needed. This procedure writes the current record in the file, the record number is passed in as an argument.

```
Private Sub WriteRecord(intRecordNum As Integer)
    'Write the current record in the file

    Put #1, intRecordNum, mudtEmployee
End Sub
```

The Read procedure is similar, but it must determine which record to read by checking the selection in the list. Notice that the ItemData property is used to get the record number, intRecordNum.

```
Private Sub ReadRecord()
    'Read the record for the selected employee
    Dim intRecordNum    As Integer
    Dim strMsg          As String

    If cboEmployee.ListIndex <> -1 Then     'Employee selected
        intRecordNum = cboEmployee.ItemData(cboEmployee.ListIndex)
        Get #1, intRecordNum, mudtEmployee
    Else
        strMsg = "Select an employee name to display."
        MsgBox strMsg, vbInformation, "Employee File"
    End If
End Sub
```

Feedback 10.3

1. Write the Type statement called *Inventory*, which contains 30 characters for a description, 5 characters for a part number, a price (currency), and a quantity (integer).
2. Declare a variable called *udtInventoryRecord* that will use the Inventory data type.
3. Write the statement to open a random file using the disk file Inventory.dat on the C: drive.
4. Write the statement(s) to find the number of records in the Inventory.dat file.
5. Write the statement to write one record to the Inventory.dat file using a record number called *intRecordNumber*.
6. What value is returned by the Seek function if the current record is record # 5?
7. Write the statement to read one record from the Inventory.dat file.

Your Hands-On Programming Example

The hands-on project for this chapter maintains employee information for R 'n R using a random file. Create a project with a single form that has text boxes for entering and displaying employee information. Place a sorted dropdown list of employee names at the top of the form. The user can select a name from the list and the entire record for that employee will display. Refer to Figure 10.5 for an illustration of the list box.

Include buttons for *Edit Employee, Remove Employee, Add New Employee, Save,* and *Cancel.* The *Save* and *Cancel* buttons should be disabled except during an Edit or Add operation.

Display a label at the top of the form to show the current action: Display, Edit, Add, or Remove. Also, change the label to indicate that a record was saved or an operation was cancelled.

Include a *File / Exit* menu item to exit the project.

Display Employee option   When the user selects a name from the dropdown list (the list's Click event), display the employee's information in the text boxes and indicate Action: Display. The text boxes should be locked and the *Save* and *Cancel* buttons disabled.

Edit Employee option   In the *Edit Employee* option, make sure that the user has selected the record. Then unlock the text boxes, enable the *Save* and *Cancel* buttons, and disable the update buttons (*Edit Employee, Remove Employee,* and *Add New Employee*). The only choices the user should have are to save the changes or cancel the operation. If the user clicks *Cancel,* restore the text box fields to their previous contents.

Remove Employee option   The user must first select a record before removing it. If a record is selected, display a message box confirming the removal. Give the user the option of not completing the remove operation.

Add New Employee option   When the user clicks on the *Add* button, set up the screen for entry of a new record. Clear the text boxes and clear any selection in the dropdown list. Unlock the text boxes, enable the *Save* and *Cancel* buttons, and disable the update buttons. The user should only be able to save the new record or cancel the operation.

Save and Cancel options   The *Save* and *Cancel* buttons are enabled only during an *Edit* or an *Add* operation. When the user clicks *Save,* save the current record. For *Cancel,* do not save the record. In either case, set the Action label to indicate what happened and reset the form controls to their default state: text boxes locked, update buttons enabled, *Save* and *Cancel* buttons disabled.

Planning the Project

Sketch the form (Figure 10.10), which your users sign off as meeting their needs.

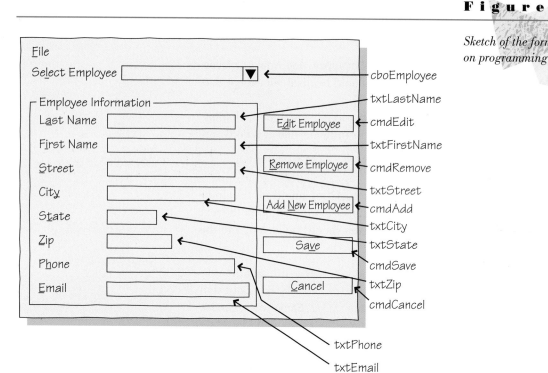

Sketch of the form for the hands-on programming example.

Plan the Objects and Properties

Object	Property	Setting
cboEmployee	Sorted	True
	Style	2 – Dropdown List
cmdEdit	Caption	E&dit Employee
cmdRemove	Caption	&Remove Employee
cmdAdd	Caption	Add &New Employee
cmdSave	Caption	Sa&ve
	Enabled	False
cmdCancel	Caption	&Cancel
	Enabled	False
	Cancel	True

(continued)

Object	Property	Setting
lblAction	Caption	(blank)
	Forecolor	Blue
Frame1	Caption	Employee Information
Label1	Caption	L&ast Name
txtLastName	Text	(blank)
Label2	Caption	F&irst Name
txtFirstName	Text	(blank)
Label3	Caption	&Street
txtStreet	Text	(blank)
Label4	Caption	Cit&y
txtCity	Text	(blank)
Label5	Caption	S&tate
txtState	Text	(blank)
Label6	Caption	&Zip
txtZip	Text	(blank)
Label7	Caption	P&hone
txtPhone	Text	(blank)
Label8	Caption	&Email
txtEmail	Text	(blank)
mnuFile	Caption	&File
mnuFileExit	Caption	E&xit

Plan the Event Procedures

Procedure	Actions

cboEmployee_Click	If not an Add
	    Read a Record.
	      Display a Record.
	End If

cmdAdd_Click	Set lblAction to Add. Deselect any entry in cboEmployee. Unlock text boxes. Clear text boxes. Disable update buttons.

cmdEdit_Click	If record selected
	    Set lblAction to Edit.
	    Disable cboEmployee.
	    Disable update buttons.
	    Unlock text boxes.
	Else
	    Display error message box.
	End If

cmdRemove_Click	If record selected
	    Set lblAction to Remove.
	    Display confirmation message box (Yes or No).
	    If Yes
	        Set record delete code to D.
	        Write changed record in file.
	        Remove employee name from cboEmployee.
	        Clear text boxes.
	        Set lblAction to Record Deleted.
	    Else
	        Set lblAction to Record Not Deleted.
	    End If
	Else
	    Display error message box.
	End If

cmdSave_Click	If a name is present
	    Save the record.
	    Set lblAction to Record Saved.
	    Enable cboEmployee.
	    Enable update buttons.
	    Lock text boxes.
	Else
	    Display error message box.
	    Set the focus in txtLastName.
	End If

(continued)

Procedure	Actions

cmdCancel_Click	If current action is Edit
	    Redisplay the selected record.
	Else (Action = Add)
	    Clear text boxes.
	End If
	Enable update buttons.
	Lock text boxes.
	Enable cboEmployee.
	Set lblAction to Operation Cancelled.

Form_Load	Read file into list.
mnuFileExit	Close the file. Unload the form. End.
AddToList (intRecordNum)	Set up name by concatenating last and first names. Add name to cboEmployee. Add record number to ItemData for new list item.
ClearTextBoxes	Clear all text boxes.
DisableButtons	Disable Edit, Add, and Remove buttons. Enable Save and Cancel buttons.
DisplayData	Set each text box to corresponding record field. Set lblAction to Display. Lock the text boxes. Enable update buttons.
EnableButtons	Enable Edit, Add, and Remove buttons. Disable Save and Cancel buttons.
LockTheControls	Lock all text boxes.

ReadFileIntoList	Open the file.
	If the file is not empty
	    Loop through all records
	        Get next record.
	        If active record
	            AddToList, passing record number.
	        End If
	    End loop
	Else
	    Display message asking whether to create new file.
	    If No
	        mnuFileExit_Click.
	    End If
	End If

ReadRecord	If record selected
	    Get record number from ItemData.
	    Read the selected record.
	Else
	    Display an error message box.
	End If

(continued)

Procedure	Actions

SaveRecord	If current action is Edit
	    Get the record number from ItemData.
	    Remove the name from the list (in case user changed
	      name).
	Else
	    Calculate the next record number.
	End If
	Set up the record.
	Write the record, passing the record number.
	Concatenate and add the name to the list.
	Add the record number to ItemData.
	Enable the update buttons.
	Lock the controls.
	Set lblAction to Record Saved.
	Enable cboEmployee.

SetUpRecord	Trim each text box field and assign to corresponding record field.
UnlockTheControls	Unlock each text box.
WriteRecord(intRecordNum)	Write the current record in the file.

Write the Project

- Follow the sketch in Figure 10.10 to create the form. Figure 10.11 shows the completed form.

- Set the properties of each object according to your plan.

- Write the code. Working from the pseudocode, write each event procedure.

- When you complete the code, use a variety of data to thoroughly test the project. Add records, clicking both *Save* and *Cancel*. Edit records, testing both *Save* and *Cancel*. And remove records, testing both the Yes and No options. Run the project multiple times to make sure the changes are saved and that the list loads correctly after adds and deletes.

Figure 1 0 . 1 1

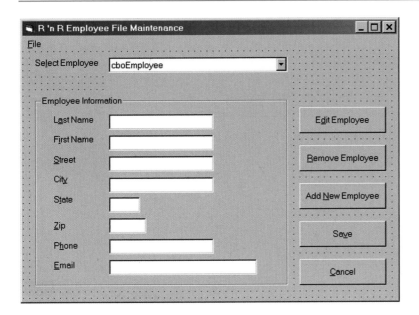

The form for the hands-on programming example.

The Project Coding Solution

```
'Project:         Chapter 10 Employee Random File Maintenance
'Form:            frmMain
'Programmer:      Bradley/Millspaugh
'Date:            6/2001
'Description:     Display and update a random file for employee information.
'Folder:          Ch1002
Option Explicit

Private Type udtEmployee
    strLastName        As String * 15
    strFirstName       As String * 10
    strStreet          As String * 20
    strCity            As String * 15
    strState           As String * 2
    strZipCode         As String * 11
    strPhone           As String * 11
    strEmail           As String * 20
    strEmployeeCode    As String * 4
    strDeleteCode      As String * 1    'D = deleted; A = active
End Type


Dim mudtEmployee       As udtEmployee
```

```vb
Private Sub cboEmployee_Click()
    'Display data for selected employee

    If lblAction.Caption <> "Action: Add" Then
        ReadRecord
        DisplayData
    End If
End Sub
```

```vb
Private Sub cmdAdd_Click()
    'Add a new record

    lblAction.Caption = "Action: Add"
    With cboEmployee
        .ListIndex = -1      'Deselect current entry
        .Enabled = False
    End With
    UnlockTheControls
    ClearTextBoxes
    DisableButtons
End Sub
```

```vb
Private Sub cmdCancel_Click()
    'Cancel an Edit or Add operation

    If lblAction.Caption = "Action: Edit" Then
        DisplayData      'Redisplay the selected record
    Else                 'Action: Add
        ClearTextBoxes
    End If
    'Return controls to standard positions
    EnableButtons
    LockTheControls
    cboEmployee.Enabled = True
    lblAction.Caption = "Action: Operation Cancelled"
End Sub
```

```vb
Private Sub cmdEdit_Click()
    'Edit the current employee information
    Dim strMsg       As String

    If cboEmployee.ListIndex <> -1 Then    'Record selected
        lblAction.Caption = "Action: Edit"
        cboEmployee.Enabled = False
        DisableButtons
        UnlockTheControls
    Else
        strMsg = "Select record to edit."
        MsgBox strMsg, vbInformation, "Employee List"
    End If
End Sub
```

```
Private Sub cmdRemove_Click()
    'Remove the selected record
    Dim strMsg          As String
    Dim intResponse     As Integer
    Dim intRecordNum    As Integer

    If cboEmployee.ListIndex <> -1 Then     'Record selected
        lblAction.Caption = "Action: Remove Record"
        strMsg = "Delete this record?"
        intResponse = MsgBox(strMsg, vbYesNo + vbQuestion, "Employee List")
        If intResponse = vbYes Then
            mudtEmployee.strDeleteCode = "D"
            With cboEmployee
                intRecordNum = .ItemData(.ListIndex)
                WriteRecord intRecordNum     'Write delete code in file
                .RemoveItem .ListIndex       'Remove from list
            End With
            ClearTextBoxes
            lblAction.Caption = "Action: Record Deleted"
        Else
            lblAction.Caption = "Action: Record Not Deleted"
        End If
    Else
        strMsg = "Select record to delete."
        MsgBox strMsg, vbInformation, "Employee List"
    End If
End Sub
```

```
Private Sub cmdSave_Click()
    'Save the contents of the controls in file
    'After an Edit or Add
    Dim strMsg      As String

    If txtLastName.Text <> "" And txtFirstName.Text <> "" Then
        SaveRecord
        lblAction.Caption = "Action: Record Saved"
        cboEmployee.Enabled = True
        EnableButtons
        LockTheControls
    Else
        strMsg = "Name is a required entry."
        MsgBox strMsg, vbInformation, "Employee List"
        txtLastName.SetFocus
    End If
End Sub
```

```
Private Sub Form_Load()
    'Initialize file and controls

    ReadFileIntoList
End Sub
```

```vb
Private Sub mnuFileExit_Click)()
    'Terminate the project

    Close #1
    Unload Me
    End
End Sub
```

```vb
Private Sub AddToList(intRecordNum As Integer)
    'Add an employee to the list and to ItemData
    Dim strName     As String

    strName = Trim(mudtEmployee.strLastName) & ", " & mudtEmployee.strFirstName
    With cboEmployee
        .AddItem strName
        .ItemData(.NewIndex) = intRecordNum
    End With
End Sub
```

```vb
Private Sub ClearTextBoxes()
    'Clear all text boxes

    txtLastName.Text = ""
    txtFirstName.Text = ""
    txtStreet.Text = ""
    txtCity.Text = ""
    txtState.Text = ""
    txtZip.Text = ""
    txtZip.Text = ""
    txtPhone.Text = ""
    txtEmail.Text = ""
End Sub
```

```vb
Private Sub DisableButtons()
    'Disable standard buttons in Edit or Add mode

    cmdEdit.Enabled = False
    cmdAdd.Enabled = False
    cmdRemove.Enabled = False
    'Enable only Save and Cancel buttons
    cmdSave.Enabled = True
    cmdCancel.Enabled = True
End Sub
```

```
Private Sub DisplayData()
    'Display the data for the selected employee

    With mudtEmployee
        txtLastName.Text = .strLastName
        txtFirstName.Text = .strFirstName
        txtStreet.Text = .strStreet
        txtCity.Text = .strCity
        txtState.Text = .strState
        txtZip.Text = .strZipCode
        txtPhone.Text = .strPhone
        txtEmail.Text = .strEmail
    End With
    lblAction.Caption = "Action: Display"
    LockTheControls
    EnableButtons
End Sub
```

```
Private Sub EnableButtons()
    'Enable standard buttons after an Edit or Add

    cmdEdit.Enabled = True
    cmdAdd.Enabled = True
    cmdRemove.Enabled = True
    'Disable Save and Cancel buttons
    cmdSave.Enabled = False
    cmdCancel.Enabled = False
End Sub
```

```
Private Sub LockTheControls()
    'Do not allow changes

    txtLastName.Locked = True
    txtFirstName.Locked = True
    txtStreet.Locked = True
    txtCity.Locked = True
    txtState.Locked = True
    txtZip.Locked = True
    txtPhone.Locked = True
    txtEmail.Locked = True
End Sub
```

```
Private Sub ReadFileIntoList()
    'Read the file and store in the sorted combo box
    'Store the relative record number into ItemData

    Dim intRecordNum    As Integer
    Dim intResponse     As Integer
    Dim strMsg          As String

    On Error GoTo HandleErrors
    Open App.Path & "\Employee.dat" For Random As #1 Len = Len(mudtEmployee)
    If LOF(1) / Len(mudtEmployee > 0 Then      'If file not empty
        For intRecordNum = 1 To LOF(1) / Len(mudtEmployee)
            Get #1, intRecordNum, mudtEmployee
            If mudtEmployee.strDeleteCode = "A" Then 'Active record
                AddToList (intRecordNum)
            End If
        Next intRecordNum
    Else
        strMsg = "File does not exist. Create new file?"
        intResponse = MsgBox(strMsg, vbQuestion + vbYesNo, "Employee File")
        If intResponse = vbNo Then
            mnuFileExit_Click
        End If
    End If

ReadFile_Exit:
    Exit Sub

HandleErrors:
    If Err.Number = 71 Then
        strMsg = "No disk. Retry?"
        intResponse = MsgBox(strMsg, vbRetryCancel + vbQuestion, _
          "Employee File")
        If intResponse = vbRetry Then
            Resume                          'Try again
        Else
            mnuFileExit_Click               'Exit project
        End If
    Else
        On Error GoTo 0                     'Turn off error handling
    End If
End Sub
```

```
Private Sub ReadRecord()
    'Read the record for the selected employee
    Dim intRecordNum    As Integer
    Dim strMsg          As String

    If cboEmployee.ListIndex <> -1 Then     'Employee selected
        intRecordNum = cboEmployee.ItemData(cboEmployee.ListIndex)
        Get #1, intRecordNum, mudtEmployee
    Else
        strMsg = "Select an employee name to display."
        MsgBox strMsg, vbInformation, "Employee File"
    End If
End Sub
```

```
Private Sub SaveRecord()
    'Save the current record for an Edit or Add

    Dim intRecordNum    As Integer
    Dim strName         As String

    If lblAction.Caption = "Action: Edit" Then
        intRecordNum = cboEmployee.ItemData(cboEmployee.ListIndex)
        With cboEmployee    'Remove name from list
            .RemoveItem .ListIndex
        End With
    Else                        'Action: Add
        intRecordNum = LOF(1) / Len(mudtEmployee) + 1 'Find next record number
    End If
    SetupRecord
    WriteRecord intRecordNum
    With cboEmployee    'Add name to list
        strName = Trim(mudtEmployee.strLastName) & ", " & _
            mudtEmployee.strFirstName
        .AddItem strName
        .ItemData(.NewIndex) = intRecordNum
    End With
    EnableButtons
    LockTheControls
    lblAction.Caption = "Action: Record Saved"
    cboEmployee.Enabled = True
End Sub
```

```
Private Sub SetupRecord()
    'Set up record from screen controls

    With mudtEmployee
        .strListName = Trim(txtLastName.Text)
        .strFirstName = Trim(txtFirstName.Text)
        .strStreet = Trim(txtStreet.Text)
        .strCity = Trim(txtCity.Text)
        .strState = Trim(txtState.Text)
        .strZipCode = Trim(txtZip.Text)
        .strPhone = Trim(txtPhone.Text)
        .strEmail = Trim(txtEmail.Text)
        .strDeleteCode = "A"
    End With
End Sub
```

```
Private Sub UnlockTheControls()
    'Allow changes to text boxes

    txtLastName.Locked = False
    txtFirstName.Locked = False
    txtStreet.Locked = False
    txtCity.Locked = False
    txtState.Locked = False
    txtZip.Locked = False
    txtPhone.Locked = False
    txtEmail.Locked = False
End Sub
```

```
Private Sub WriteRecord(intRecordNum As Integer)
    'Write the current record in the file
    'Used for Edit, Add, and Delete

    Put #1, intRecordNum, mudtEmployee
End Sub
```

Programming Hints

The InputBox Function

When you need to request input from the user, you can always use a text box, either on the current form or on a new form. Visual Basic also provides a quick and easy way to pop up a new form that holds a text box, using the `InputBox` function.

The `InputBox` function is similar to `MsgBox`. In the input box you can display a message, called the *prompt*, and allow the user to type input into the text box (Figure 10.12).

Figure 10.12

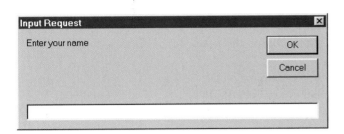

The InputBox *function produces a dialog box with a prompt and a text box for entering program input.*

The InputBox Function—General Form

```
VariableName = InputBox("Prompt" [, "Title"] [, Default] [, XPos] [, YPos])
```

The prompt must be enclosed in quotation marks and may include NewLine characters (vbCrLf) if you want the prompt to appear on multiple lines. The Title displays in the title bar of the dialog box; if the Title is missing, the project name appears in the title bar. Any value you place in *Default* appears in the text box when it is displayed; otherwise, the text box is empty. (If *Default* is a string, it must be enclosed in quotation marks.) *XPos* and *YPos*, if present, define the measurement in twips for the left edge and top edge of the box.

The InputBox Function—Examples

```
strName = InputBox("Enter your name.")
intQuantity = Val(InputBox("How many do you want?", "Order Quantity"))
```

Using the InputBox to Randomly Retrieve a Record

You will find the input box to be a great tool when you need to retrieve a record from a random file. Many applications use the record number as a method of identification, such as customer number or product number. If you request this number, you can read the correct record in the random file directly.

```
Dim intRecordNumber As Integer
intRecordNumber = Val(InputBox("Enter Customer Number"))
If intRecordNumber >= 0 And intRecordNumber <= LOF(1) / Len(mudtCustomer) Then
    Get #1, intRecordNumber, mudtCustomer
Else
    MsgBox "Invalid Customer Number"
End If
```

S u m m a r y

1. A data file is made up of records, which can be further broken down into fields or data elements. The field used for organizing the file is the key field.

2. An Open statement is needed to access data files. The Open allows modes for Input, Output, Append, and Random. A FileNumber is associated with a file at the time the file is opened.

3. A Close statement should be used prior to the termination of a program that uses data files.

4. The FreeFile function can be used to find the next available file number.

5. Sequential files use the Write # and Input # statements for writing and reading records. Each field to be written or read is listed in the statement.

6. The records in a sequential file must be accessed in order, and the file is either input or output, not both. With a random file the records may be accessed in any order and may be read or written without closing the file.

7. The EOF function returns True when the end of a file is reached.

8. Specifying App.Path for the path of a data file allows the project to find the file when its folder is moved.

9. The On Error statement allows the programmer to test for known error situations and to handle errors without the application aborting. An example of the type of error that can be found through error trapping is the failure of the user to place a disk in the disk drive.

10. The Err object holds the error number and description of the current error.

11. The Resume statement continues execution after an error condition.

12. Confirm a save of "dirty" data in the form's QueryUnload event procedure.

13. Random file access uses fixed-length records and requires the string fields to be a specified length. Use the Type statement to define the record structure for a random file.

14. The Get and Put statements read and write records in a random file. The amount of data transferred is always a complete record.

15. A file update program allows the user to make changes to the data file, such as adding a record, changing the contents of a record, and deleting a record.

16. The LOF function returns the length of a random file in bytes. You can use the result to calculate the number of records in the file and the record number of the next-available record.

17. You can use a list box to allow the user to select a record from a random file. The ItemData property of the list box is set to the record number so that random reads can retrieve the correct record.

18. The Trim, LTrim, and RTrim functions remove extra spaces from strings.

19. To allow deletion of records in a random file, usually a deletion code is included in the record. Records are not actually deleted but are coded as a deleted record.

20. The input box is similar to a message box; it allows the user to enter information that can be returned to the project.

Key Terms

buffer   *390*
Close statement   *390*
data element   *388*
data file   *388*
Description property   *397*
Dir function   *410*
EOF   *391*
EOF(n) function   *394*
Err object   *397*
error trapping   *395*
Exit Function statement   *401*
Exit Sub statement   *401*
field   *388*
file   *388*
file mode   *389*
file number   *390*
file pointer   *390*
Get statement   *411*
Input # statement   *393*

key field   *389*
line label   *396*
LOF function   *412*
LTrim function   *414*
Number property   *397*
On Error statement   *395*
Open statement   *389*
Put statement   *411*
QueryUnload procedure   *403*
random file   *408*
record   *388*
record key   *389*
Resume statement   *399*
RTrim function   *410*
Seek function   *412*
sequential files   *391*
Source property   *397*
Trim function   *414*
Write # statement   *392*

Review Questions

1. What is the difference between a Visual Basic project file and a data file?
2. Explain what occurs when an Open statement is executed.
3. List and explain the file modes for data files.
4. What is the significance of a file number?
5. Explain the differences between the Output and Append modes.
6. What is the format for the statements to read and write sequential files?
7. What function can be used to determine an available file number?
8. When would an On Error statement be used?
9. Explain the function and use of the Err object.
10. What are the differences between a random file and a sequential file?
11. What does *updating a data file* mean?
12. Give examples for using the InputBox function.

Programming Exercises

10.1 (*Sequential file*) Rewrite project 8.4 using a sequential file to store the state names and abbreviations. You need two projects. The first will allow the typist to enter the state name and the abbreviation in text boxes and store them in a sequential file. The second project will perform the functions specified in project 8.4.

10.2 Create a *sequential file* for employee information and call it *Employee.dat*. Each record will contain fields for first name, last name, Social Security number, and hourly pay rate.

Write a project to process payroll. The application will load the employee data into an array of user-defined types from the sequential file with an extra field for the pay. The form will contain labels for the information from the array and display one record at a time.

A command button called *FindPay* will use a `For Next` loop to process the array. First you will display an input box for the number of hours worked, calculate the pay, and add to the totals. Then you will display the labels for the next employee. (Place the pay into the extra field in the array.)

The Exit button will print a report on the printer and terminate the project. (Print the array.)

Processing: Hours over 40 receive time-and-a-half pay. Accumulate the total number of hours worked, the total number of hours of overtime, and the total amount of pay.

Sample Report

	Ace Industries			
Employee Name	Hours Worked	Hours Overtime	Pay Rate	Amount Earned
Janice Jones	40	0	5.25	210.00
Chris O'Connel	35	0	5.35	187.25
Karen Fisk	45	5	6.00	285.00
Tom Winn	42	2	5.75	247.25
Totals	162	7		929.50

10.3 (*Sequential file*) Modify project 7.6 to store the list box for Bradley's Bagels in a sequential file. Load the list during the Form Load and then close the file. Be sure to use error checking in case the file does not exist.

In the exit procedure prompt the user to save the bagel list back to the disk.

10.4 (*Random file*) Create a project that stores and updates personal information for a little electronic "black book." The fields in the file should include name, phone number, pager, cell phone, voice mail, and email.

Allow the user to add a new record, remove a record, edit a record, save a new or changed record, or cancel an operation.

10.5 Create a random file project that stores and updates student information. Use a dropdown list box to display the student names and store record numbers in the ItemData property, similar to the chapter hands-on example project.

The fields include

Name

Major—Use a dropdown combo box to list available majors.

Class level—Use option buttons for Freshman, Sophomore, Junior, and Senior.
Dean's list—Use a check box.

Hint: Although check boxes, option buttons, and list boxes do not have a Locked property, you can place all these controls inside a frame and set the frame's Enabled property to True or False.

C A S E   S T U D I E S

VB Mail Order

Sequential file and random file ~~Only Sequential~~

Modify the projects created in Chapters 6 and 7. You will use a sequential file to store catalog names and a random file to store customer information.

The list of catalog names must be stored in a sequential file and loaded into a dropdown combo box during the initial processing. Any catalogs that are added during execution of the program must be written to the disk. (You can use catalogs.dat from your CD or allow the user to create it using the combo box and the Add button.)

You must create the customer random file and provide routines to add, remove, display, and edit the records. Fields include name, street, city, state, and Zip.

VB Auto Center

Create a project that maintains a random file for vehicle inventory.

The fields are inventory ID, manufacturer, model name, year, vehicle ID number, and cost value.

Refer to the hands-on project in this chapter for ideas for the form, menu, and command buttons.

Video Bonanza

Sequential File

Modify your project from Chapter 7 to display the category list in a sequential file.

Create a menu option to save the category list. In addition, before exiting, query the user to save the category list. Optionally you can query the user only when changes have been made to the list (set up a Boolean variable to keep track of any changes).

Each time the project runs, the category list must be loaded from the disk file so that the list appears as it was in the previous run.

Make sure that the category list data file is stored in the diskette folder with your project and that the

project will run from a computer other than the one on which it was written.

Random File

Create an application to store video information in a random file. Allow the user to add a video, remove a video, and display or edit the information for a selected video.

The fields are Movie Number (a 5-character string), Title (25 characters), Studio ID (5 character), Category (15 characters), and Length (Integer).

Assignment 1; Sequential File

Modify your project from Chapter 8 to store the style list in a sequential file. Each time the project runs, the style list must be loaded from the disk file so that the list appears as it was in the previous run.

Create a menu option to save the style list. In addition, before exiting, query the user to save the style list. Optionally, you can query the user only when changes have been made to the list (set up a Boolean variable to keep track of any changes).

Make sure that the style list data file is stored in the diskette folder with your project and that the project will run from a computer other than the one on which it was written.

Assignment 2; Sequential File

Modify your Chapter 9 project to display the manufacturer names in a dropdown combo box. Allow the user

Very Very Boards

to add and remove manufacturer names on the list.

Create a menu option to save the manufacturer list. In addition, before exiting, query the user to save the manufacturer list. Optionally, you can query the user only when changes have been made to the list (set up a Boolean variable to keep track of any changes).

Each time the project runs, the manufacturer list must be loaded from the disk file so that the list appears as it was in the previous run.

Make sure that the manufacturer list data file is stored in the diskette folder with your project and that the project will run from a computer other than the one on which it was written.

Assignment 3; Random File

Modify your project from Chapter 9 (or the sequential file project above) to store the product information in a random file.

11

Accessing Database Files

At the completion of this chapter, you will be able to . . .

1. Use database terminology correctly.

2. Differentiate between the data control and data-bound controls.

3. Create a project to view an existing database table.

4. Set up a lookup table for a database field.

5. Change records, add new records, and delete records in a database table.

6. Write code to help prevent user errors.

Visual Basic and Database Files

You can use Visual Basic to write projects that view and update database files. You can use the data control in the Learning Edition to create database applications with very little coding. However, if you want to use the more advanced features, including creating new databases and modifying the structure of existing database tables, you will need the Professional Edition or Enterprise Edition of Visual Basic. The applications in this text can be done with the Standard Edition or the Learning Edition.

Database Formats Supported by Visual Basic

Visual Basic directly supports database files in several formats. The native format is Microsoft Access, using the Jet database engine. However, by setting just one property, VB can access files created with dBASE III, dBASE IV, dBASE 5.0, Excel, FoxPro, Lotus, Paradox, or text files. With the Professional Edition and Open DataBase Connectivity (ODBC), you can use many other database formats, such as SQL Server, Oracle, and DB2.

Database Terminology

To use database files, you must understand the standard terminology of relational databases. Although there are various definitions of standard database terms, we will stick with those used by Access.

An Access **file** (with an .mdb extension) can hold multiple **tables.** Each table can be viewed as a spreadsheet—with **rows** and **columns.** Each row in a table represents the data for one item, person, or transaction and is called a *record.* Each column in a table is used to store a different element of data, such as an account number, a name, address, or numeric amount. The elements represented in columns are called *fields.* You can think of the table in Figure 11.1 as consisting of rows and columns or of records and fields.

Most tables use a **key field** (or combination of fields) to identify each record. The key field is often a number, such as employee number, account number, identification number, or Social Security number; or it may be a text field, such as last name, or a combination, such as last name and first name.

Any time a database table is open, one record is considered the **current record.** As you move from one record to the next, the current record changes.

ISBN	Title	Author	Publisher
0-15-500139-6	Business Programming in C	Millspaugh, A. C.	The Dryden Press
0-446-51652-X	Bridges of Madison County	Waller, Robert James	Warner Books
0-451-16095-9	The Stand	King, Stephen	Signet
0-517-59905-8	How to Talk to Anyone, Anytime, Anywhere	King, Larry	Crown
0-534-26076-4	A Quick Guide to the Internet	Bradley, Julia Case	Integrated Media Group
0-670-85332-1	How to Be Hap-Hap-Happy Like Me	Markoe, Merrill	Viking
0-671-66398-4	Seven Habits of Highly Effective People	Covey, Stephen R.	Fireside
0-697-12897-0	QuickBasic and QBasic Using Modular Structure	Bradley, Julia Case	B & E Tech
0-697-21361-7	Desktop Publishing Using PageMaker 5.0	Bradley, Julia Case	B & E Tech
0-8007-1213-7	Secrets of Closing the Sale	Ziglar, Zig	Revell
1-55615-484-4	Code Complete	McConnell, Steve	Microsoft Press

A database table consists of rows (records) and columns (fields).

Record or row

Field or column

Creating Database Files for Use by Visual Basic

Although you cannot create a new database file with the VB Standard Edition or Working Model, you have other options. You can use Access to create the database, or you can use the Visual Data Manager add-in application that comes with Visual Basic.

You can run the VB Visual Data Manager by selecting *Visual Data Manager* from the *Add-Ins* menu (Figure 11.2). The VisData application window opens (Figure 11.3); you can create a new file or open and modify an existing database file. The application is quite straightforward; you can use Help if you need instructions.

Figure 11.2

Select Visual Data Manager *from the* Add-Ins *menu to run the VB Visual Data Manager.*

Figure 11.3

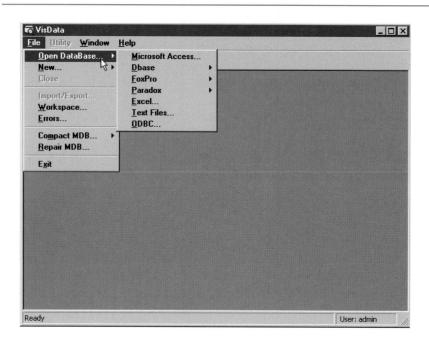

Create a new database or modify an existing one using the Visual Data Manager window.

Using the ADO Data Control

You will find programming with a data control quite easy and powerful. VB has several controls for accessing data, including the intrinsic data control that automatically appears in the toolbox and the more powerful ActiveX Data Object Data Control (ADODC). You can add the ADODC to your toolbox: select *Components* from the *Project* menu and choose *Microsoft ADO Data Control 6.0* (Figure 11.4).

Figure 11.4

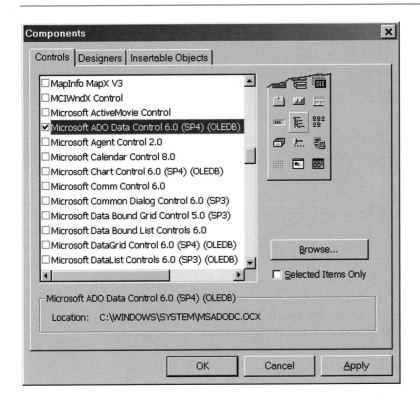

ADO is Microsoft's newer database access technology. The goal of ADO is to allow programmers to use a standard set of objects to access any type of data from any application on any type of computer.

The exercises in this chapter all refer to the ADO data control rather than the older data control. When you read the words "data control," assume that the term is used generically for the ADODC. Figure 11.5 shows the toolbox tool for creating an ADO data control and Figure 11.6 shows an ADO data control on a form.

Figure 11.5

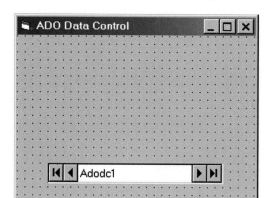

The Data Control and Data-Bound Controls

Using a data control is a two-step process. First you place a data control on a form and set the properties to link it to a database file and table. Then you create the controls, such as labels and text boxes, to display the actual data. Each control is bound to a particular field in the table. In this example the label is called a ***data-bound control*** and automatically displays the contents of the bound field when the project runs. Figure 11.7 shows a form with a data control and two data-bound labels.

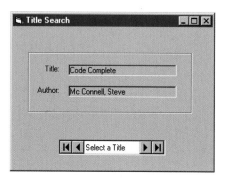

Microsoft also uses the term *data aware* for controls that can be bound to a database table. You might say that labels are data aware; therefore, you can use a label to create a data-bound control. The standard data-aware controls are labels, text boxes, check boxes, list boxes, combo boxes, images, picture boxes, data-bound list boxes, data-bound combo boxes, and data-bound grids.

A data control generally links one form with one table. If you want to have data-bound controls on a second form, you must place a data control on that form. You may place more than one data control on a single form when you wish to reference more than one table.

Properties of the Data Control

After you place a data control on a form, you must set its properties (Figure 11.8). By default, the Name and Caption are set to Adodc1. Change the Name property using "ado" as its three-character prefix. The Caption appears inside the control (refer to Figure 11.7).

F i g u r e   1 1 . 8

Set the properties for a data control in the Properties window.

Required properties   In order to access data, the minimum you must do is:

● Specify a **ConnectionString property,** which declares the database path, file name, and an optional UserID and password.

● Specify the **RecordSource** and **CommandType properties,** which select the data you want from within the database file. The RecordSource may be a table name, a stored procedure name, or an SQL statement. The CommandType property specifies which type of RecordSource you are using.

The ConnectionString Property   Click the ConnectionString property's builder button to display the *Property Pages* dialog box (Figure 11.9). Then click on the *Build* button to display the *Data Link Properties* dialog box (Figure 11.10).

Create the ConnectionString property by using the **Property Pages** *dialog box.*

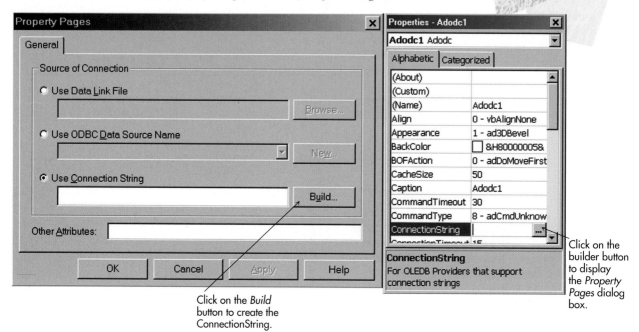

Click on the *Build* button to create the ConnectionString.

Click on the builder button to display the *Property Pages* dialog box.

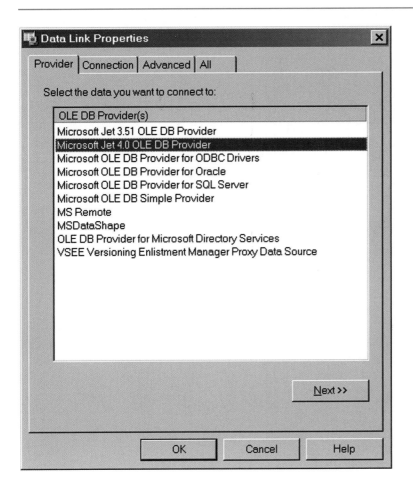

Select the OLE DB provider on the Provider tab of the Data Link Properties dialog box.

First, set the *OLE DB Provider* on the *Provider* tab. For Access files, select *Microsoft Jet 4.0 OLE DB Provider.* Then click the *Connection* tab (Figure 11.11). You can enter or browse for the file name and then click on the *Test Connection* button, which verifies the access to the file.

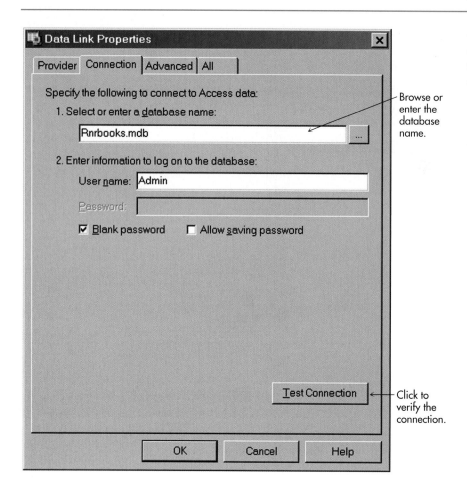

Specify the database name and location on the **Connection** *tab of the* **Data Link Properties** *dialog box.*

The RecordSource and CommandType properties   The RecordSource and CommandType properties specify the data within the file to select. Click on RecordSource's builder button to display the *Property Pages* dialog box (Figure 11.12). The default setting for RecordSource is adCmdUnknown but you will change that to adCmdTable to select a specific table from the database.

Figure   11.12

Display the **Property Pages** *dialog box for the RecordSource and CommandType properties.*

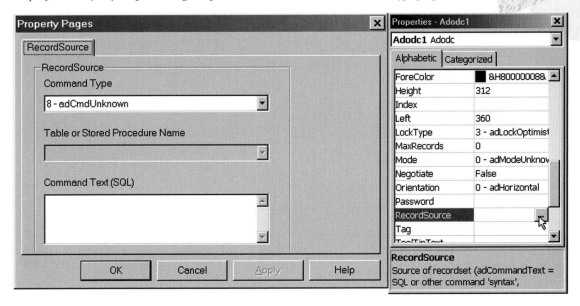

After you set the RecordSource to 2 - adCmdTable, a *Table or Stored Procedure Name* list appears, filled with the names of the tables from the database selected in the connection string. Drop down the list to select the table name (Figure 11.13).

Figure   11.13

After you set the CommandType property to 2 - adCmdTable, a list appears with the names of the tables defined in the file.

Properties of Data-Bound Controls

Place the controls that you want to display in the database fields on the form and then change their properties. Use labels for any fields you don't want the user to change; use text boxes if the field content is user updateable. Use check boxes for fields with a True/False or Yes/No value; the check box will display a check mark for True or Yes and remain blank for False or No.

After setting the Name and Text or Caption properties of your text boxes or labels, set the two properties that bind the control to a particular field in a table.

First set the **DataSource property** of the text box or label to point to the data control. Click on the down arrow in the Settings box to drop down the list of data controls on the form (Figure 11.14). Once you have selected the data control, VB knows the name of the file and table. Next you specify the particular field to bind to the control.

Select the name of the data control for the data-bound control's DataSource property.

Properties - txtTitle	
txtTitle TextBox	

Alphabetic | Categorized

(Name)	txtTitle
Alignment	0 - Left Justify
Appearance	1 - 3D
BackColor	&H80000005&
BorderStyle	1 - Fixed Single
CausesValidation	True
DataField	Title
DataFormat	
DataMember	
DataSource	adoBooks
DragIcon	adoBooks
DragMode	0 - Manual
Enabled	True

DataSource
Sets a value that specifies the Data control through which the current control is bound

Set the **DataField property** by clicking on the down arrow in the Settings box. The list of fields in the selected table will appear (Figure 11.15). After choosing the field name for one of your data-bound controls, set the DataSource and DataField properties for the rest of your controls.

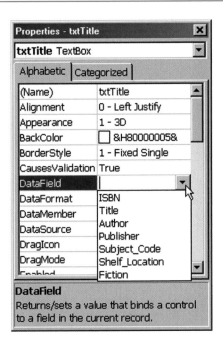

Set the DataField property to the name of the field to bind to the control.

That's all there is to it. After you bind the table and fields to the controls on your form, you are ready to run the application. With no code at all, the fields will fill with data when your project begins. You can use the navigation buttons on the data control to move from one record to the next.

Viewing a Database File—Step-by-Step

In this step-by-step tutorial, you will create a simple project to display the data from the Books table for R 'n R—for Reading 'n Refreshment. The only code required is for the Exit procedure.

Design and Create the Form

Figure 11.16 shows the user interface for this project.

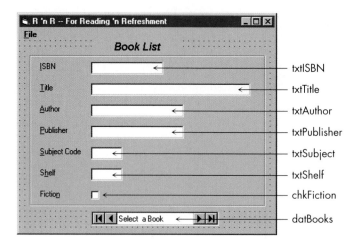

The user interface for the database step-by-step tutorial.

The Project

STEP 1: Begin a new project and add the ADODC control to the toolbox by selecting *Project/Components.* Check the box for *Microsoft ADO Data Control 6.0* (Figure 11.17).

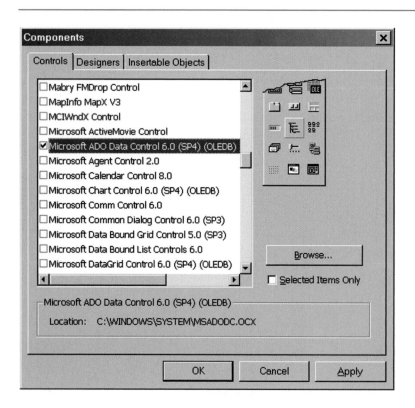

Add the ADO Data Control 6.0 to your toolbox.

STEP 2: Save your project in a new folder.

STEP 3: Place a copy of RnRBooks.mdb in your project folder. (The file is on the text CD in the StudentData folder.)

The Form

STEP 1: Create a new form large enough to hold the controls (see Figure 11.16).

The Controls

STEP 1: Click on the ADO data control tool and draw a data control along the bottom of the form.

STEP 2: Create a large frame to hold the labels and text boxes; then delete the frame's Caption property.

STEP 3: Create labels that describe the data and the form title (Book List).

STEP 4: Create the controls to hold the data. Use text boxes for ISBN, Title, Author, Publisher, Subject Code, and Shelf; use a check box for Fiction.

The Menu

STEP 1: Open the Menu Editor window and create a *File* menu with an *Exit* command. Name the menu mnuFile and the command mnuFileExit.

Set the Properties for the Data Control

STEP 1: Select the ADO data control and display the Properties window.

STEP 2: Change the Name property to adoBooks.

STEP 3: Change the Caption property to Select a Book.

STEP 4: Select the ConnectionString property and click on the builder button. The *Property Pages* dialog box appears (Figure 11.18).

F i g u r e   1 1 . 1 8

Create the ConnectionString property by using the Property Pages dialog box.

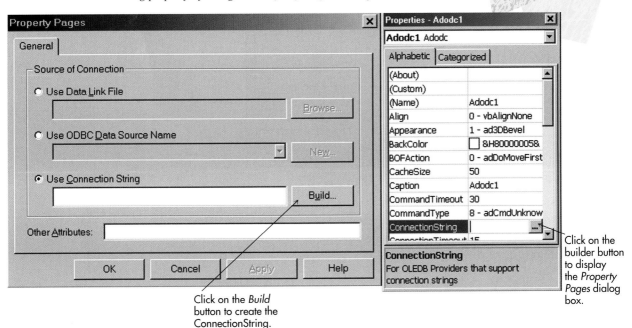

STEP 5: Click on the *Build* button to display the *Data Link Properties* dialog box.

STEP 6: On the *Provider* tab, select *Microsoft Jet 4.0 OLE DB Provider.* Click Next (or select the *Connection* tab).

STEP 7: On the *Connection* tab, under *Select or Enter a Database Name,* click on the builder button. Browse to select the RnRBooks.mdb file that you placed in your folder (Figure 11.19). Click on *Text Connection.* You should have good news. Click OK on the message box, OK again on the Data Link Properties window, and OK again on the *Property Pages* dialog box.

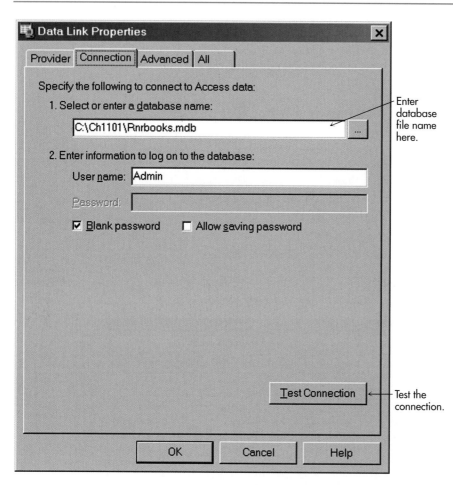

Browse to find your database file or type its name directly in the box.

STEP 8: Click on the RecordSource property's builder button to display the *RecordSource* tab of the *Property Pages* dialog box. Change the command type to *2 - adCmdTable.* Then select *Books* from the dropdown list of tables (Figure 11.20).

Figure 11.20

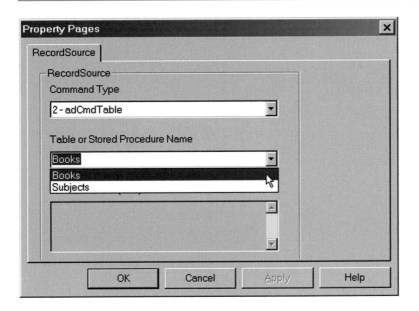

Set the Properties for the Data-Bound Controls

STEP 1: Select the text box to hold the ISBN number; switch to the Properties window.

STEP 2: Set the following properties:

Name	txtISBN
Caption	(blank)

STEP 3: Click on the Settings down arrow for the DataSource property and select adoBooks (the name of the data control).

STEP 4: Click on the Settings down arrow for the DataField property; the list of fields in the Books table appears. Click on ISBN.

STEP 5: Set the properties for the rest of the data-bound controls.

Object	Property	Setting
txtTitle	Name	txtTitle
	Text	(blank)
	DataSource	adoBooks
	DataField	Title
txtAuthor	Name	txtAuthor
	Text	(blank)
	DataSource	adoBooks
	DataField	Author
		(continued)

Object	Property	Setting
txtPublisher	Name	txtPublisher
	Text	(blank)
	DataSource	adoBooks
	DataField	Publisher
txtSubject	Name	txtSubject
	Text	(blank)
	DataSource	adoBooks
	DataField	Subject_Code
txtShelf	Name	txtShelf
	Text	(blank)
	DataSource	adoBooks
	DataField	Shelf_Location
chkFiction	Name	chkFiction
	Caption	(blank)
	DataSource	adoBooks
	DataField	Fiction

Write the Code

The coding for this project will surprise you. All you need are a few remarks and an Exit procedure.

STEP 1: Select the *Exit* command from the *File* menu to open the mnuFileExit_Click procedure.

STEP 2: Type the following code:

```
'Exit the project

End
```

STEP 3: Switch to the General Declarations section and type the remarks:

```
'Program Name:      R 'n R Book List Database
'Programmer:        Your Name
'Date:              Today's date
'Purpose:           Display book information in the
'                   R 'n R Book database
'Folder:            Ch1101
```

STEP 4: Save your form and project. You will use them again later in this chapter.

Run the Project

STEP 1: Start the project running. You should see your form on the screen filled
with the data for the first record. (Maybe a "Wow" is in order?)

STEP 2: Try the navigation buttons on the data control: Click on the arrows for
Move Next, Move Previous, Move First, and Move Last (Figure 11.21).

F i g u r e   1 1 . 2 1

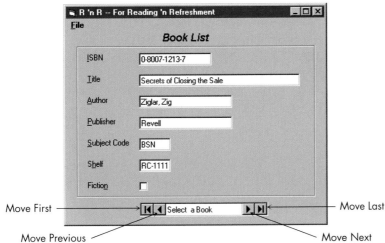

*Click on the navigation buttons to
display different records.*

Feedback 11.1

Use this information to fill in the answers to the following questions:

Database name:	Classes.mdb
Table name:	Teachers
Field name:	Name
Data control name:	adoClasses
Text box name:	txtTeacher

You want to display the Name field in txtTeacher. How should these properties be set?

1. adoClasses.CommandType
2. adoClasses.RecordSource
3. txtTeacher.DataSource
4. txtTeacher.DataField
5. txtTeacher.Text

Navigating the Database in Code

The navigation buttons on the data control can be used to move from record to record, or you can make the data control invisible and provide the navigation in code. You can use the **Recordset object** to manipulate the database.

The Recordset Object

When you set the RecordSource property of a data control to the name of a table or query, you are defining a new object called a *Recordset*. The Recordset object has its own set of properties and methods, which you can use to move from record to record, check for the beginning or end of the file, and search for records to match a condition (covered in Chapter 12).

When you refer to the Recordset object, you must first name the data control:

```
DataControl.Recordset.Property
DataControl.Recordset.Method
```

Using the MoveNext, MovePrevious, MoveFirst, and MoveLast Methods

The MoveNext, MovePrevious, MoveFirst, and MoveLast methods provide the same functions as the data control buttons. Each method is applied to the Recordset object created by the data control.

```
adoBooks.Recordset.MoveNext        'Move to the next record
adoBooks.Recordset.MoveLast        'Move to the last record
adoBooks.Recordset.MovePrevious    'Move to the previous record
adoBooks.Recordset.MoveFirst       'Move to the first record
```

Checking for BOF and EOF

Two handy properties of the Recordset object are **BOF** (beginning of file) and **EOF** (end of file). The BOF property is automatically set to True when the record pointer is before the first record in the Recordset. This condition happens when the first record is current and the user chooses MovePrevious. The BOF property is also True if the Recordset is empty (contains no records).

The EOF property is similar to BOF; it is True when the record pointer moves beyond the last record in the Recordset and when the Recordset is empty.

When you are doing your own navigation in code, you need to check for BOF and EOF so that run-time errors do not occur. If the user clicks MoveNext when on the last record, what do you want to do? Have the program cancel with a run-time error? display a message? wrap around to the first record? keep the record pointer on the last record? (The last approach matches the action of the navigation buttons on the data control.)

In the examples that follow, we will use the wraparound method. If the user clicks on the MoveNext button from the end of the table, the first record becomes the active record.

```
Private Sub cmdNext_Click()
    'Move to the next record

    adoBooks.Recordset.MoveNext
    If adoBooks.Recordset.EOF Then
        adoBooks.Recordset.MoveFirst
    End If
End Sub
```

Just as with any other object reference in Visual Basic, you can use the `With/End With` statements to refer to the Recordset object. This style of coding not only simplifies the VB code but also makes a project run a little faster.

```
Private Sub cmdNext_Click()
    'Move to the next record

    With adoBooks.Recordset
        .MoveNext
        If .EOF Then
            .MoveFirst
        End If
    End With
End Sub
```

Using List Boxes and Combo Boxes as Data-Bound Controls

Beginning with release 4.0 of Visual Basic, list boxes and combo boxes are data aware. You can see the value of using data-bound lists when you have a list of acceptable values for a field. The user can select an item from the list when updating records or adding new ones.

Setting Up a Lookup Table for a Field

To set up a lookup table of acceptable values for a field, use a combo box. You can bind the combo box to a field in the database *and* specify initial values for the List property. Figure 11.22 shows a combo box as a data-bound control, displaying the Subject field from the database. When the user selects a subject from the dropdown combo box, the bound field's contents are updated to the new value.

Figure   11.22

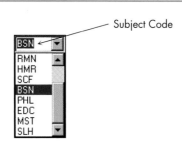

Subject Code

The List property of the combo box shows the acceptable choices for the field. Select an entry from the list to change the contents of the field.

Adding a Lookup Table and Navigation—Step-by-Step

For this step-by-step example, we add navigation buttons and two lookup combo boxes to the previous programming example.

Modify the User Interface

STEP 1: Open the previous program example.
STEP 2: Resize the form and add four command buttons for navigation. (See Figure 11.23.)

Figure   11.23

Add the four command buttons to use for navigation.

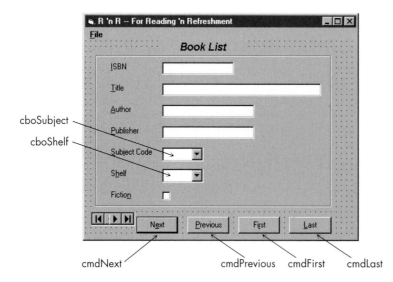

STEP 3: Delete the text box for Subject Code and add a combo box in its place.
STEP 4: Delete the text box for Shelf and add a combo box in its place.

Change the Properties

STEP 1: Set the properties of the four command buttons.

Object	Property	Setting
cmdNext	Name	cmdNext
	Caption	&Next
	Default	True
cmdPrevious	Name	cmdPrevious
	Caption	&Previous
cmdFirst	Name	cmdFirst
	Caption	Fi&rst
cmdLast	Name	cmdLast
	Caption	&Last

STEP 2: Change the Visible property of the data control to False.

STEP 3: Change the Locked property of txtISBN to True. This setting prevents the user from changing the ISBN, which is the key field for the table.

STEP 4: Set the properties of the two combo boxes as described in the following table:

Object	Property	Setting
cboSubject	Name	cboSubject
	Text	(blank)
	DataSource	adoBooks
	DataField	Subject_Code
	List	BSS (Ctrl + Enter after each)
		FNT
		RLG
		RMN
		HMR
		SCF
		BSN
		PHL
		EDC
		MST
		SLH

(continued)

Object	Property	Setting
cboShelf	Name	cboShelf
	Text	(blank)
	DataSource	adoBooks
	DataField	Shelf_Location
	List	RC-1111 (Ctrl + Enter after each)
		RC-1112
		RC-1113
		RC-1114

Reset the Tab Order for the Controls

STEP 1: Click on the ISBN label on the form, switch to the Properties window, and change the TabIndex to 0; then click on the text box for the ISBN (txtISBN) and change its TabIndex to 1.

STEP 2: Click on the second label (Title), and the TabIndex property for the label should appear in the Properties window. Change it to 2. Then change the TabIndex property for txtTitle to 3.

STEP 3: Change the TabIndex property of the Author label to 4; change the TabIndex of txtAuthor to 5.

STEP 4: Set the TabIndex property of the Publisher label to 6 and the TabIndex of txtPublisher to 7.

STEP 5: Change the Subject label's TabIndex to 8 and the combo box for subject (cboSubject) to 9.

STEP 6: Set the TabIndex properties for the rest of the controls.

cboShelf	10
chkFiction	11
cmdNext	12
cmdPrevious	13
cmdFirst	14
cmdLast	15

Write the Code

STEP 1: Change the remarks in the General Declarations section to reflect the changes.

STEP 2: Add coding for each command button. See the following listing for help.

Caution: Make sure that the datafile, RnRbooks.mdb, does not have its ReadOnly property set to True.

```
'Program Name:     R 'n R Book List Database
'Programmer:       Bradley/Millspaugh
'Date:             Jan 2002
'Purpose:          Display and update book information in the
'                  R 'n R Book database, using buttons for
'                  navigation and combo boxes for field lookup
'Folder:           Ch1102
```

```
Private Sub cmdFirst_Click()
    'Move to first record

    adoBooks.Recordset.MoveFirst
End Sub
```

```
Private Sub cmdLast_Click()
    'Move to last record

    adoBooks.Recordset.MoveLast
End Sub
```

```
Private Sub cmdNext_Click()
    'Move to next record

    With adoBooks.Recordset
        .MoveNext
        If .EOF Then
            .MoveFirst
        End If
    End With
End Sub
```

```
Private Sub cmdPrevious_Click()
    'Move to previous record

    With adoBooks.Recordset
        .MovePrevious
        If .BOF Then
            .MoveLast
        End If
    End With
End Sub
```

```
Private Sub mnuFileExit_Click()
    'Exit the project

    End
End Sub
```

Testing the Navigation and Lookup Tables

Save the project; then test it. Try each of your navigation buttons. Make sure that you can move forward and backward and that the project properly handles moving before the first record and after the last.

As you move from record to record, notice the contents of the two lookup combo boxes. Try selecting a new subject for a record; then move to the next record. Move back to the changed record, and you will see that the change has been made. *Caution:* All changes you make to the data records are permanently saved when you move to another record or exit the database. You do not have an option to abandon changes; all changes are recorded in the file.

Updating a Database File

As you saw in the previous example, a project that displays data from a database allows updates automatically. If you don't want the user to change the data, you can keep the user from making changes to the data by displaying fields in labels rather than in text boxes or setting the Locked property of the text boxes to True.

The Recordset object has an **Update method,** which you can use to save any changes in the data. Most of the time, updating is automatic, since Visual Basic automatically executes the Update method any time the user clicks one of the navigation buttons or one of the Move methods executes.

Adding Records

When you want to add new records to a database, you have a couple of choices. If you are using the data control's navigation buttons (rather than your own code for navigation), you can allow Visual Basic to do the adds automatically. Set the data control's EOFAction property to 2 - adDoAddNew. When the user moves to the end of the table and clicks the arrow for Next Record, an *Add* operation begins. The data in all bound controls are cleared so that new data can be entered. Then, when the user clicks one of the arrow buttons, the Update method is automatically executed and the new record is written in the file.

You need a different approach when you use code to accomplish record navigation. Assume that you have a command button or menu choice to add a new record. In the Click event for the command button, use the Recordset's **AddNew method:**

```
adoBooks.Recordset.AddNew
```

When this statement executes, all bound controls are cleared so that the user can enter the data for the new record. After the data fields are entered, the new record must be saved in the file. You can explicitly save it with an Update method; or, if the user moves to another record, the Update method is automatically executed.

```
adoBooks.Recordset.Update
```

You may want to use two buttons for adding a new record—an Add button and a Save button. For the Add button, use an `AddNew` method; for the Save button, use the `Update` method.

When adding new records, some conditions can cause errors to occur. For example, if the key field is blank on a new record, a run-time error halts program execution. See "Preventing Errors" later in this chapter for some solutions.

In the sample project for this chapter, the Locked property for txtISBN should be set to False. If you are going to allow adds, the user must be able to enter a new key field. (You might consider setting the Locked property to False during an Add operation and True the rest of the time.)

Deleting Records

The **Delete method** deletes the current record. The user should display the record to delete and click a Delete command button or menu choice. When a record is deleted, the current record is no longer valid. Therefore, a `Delete` method must be followed by a `MoveNext` (or any other `Move`) method.

```
With adoBooks.Recordset
    .Delete
    .MoveNext
End With
```

But what if the record being deleted is the last record in the table? Remember that if the navigation buttons are used to navigate, moving beyond EOF just resets the current record to the last record. No problem. However, if you are using event procedures for navigation, you must take care of this situation. If a `MoveNext` causes an EOF condition, then the program should do a `MovePrevious`.

```
Private Sub cmdDelete_Click()
    'Delete the current record

    With adoBooks.Recordset
        .Delete                'Delete the current record
        .MoveNext              'Move to the following record
        If .EOF Then           'If last record deleted
            .MovePrevious
        End If
    End With
End Sub
```

Did you find another problem with this code? Stop and look at the preceding delete routine a moment. What will happen if the user deletes the *only* record in the Recordset?

Did you spot the problem? If the user deletes the last and only record in the Recordset, you must check for both EOF and BOF.

```
Private Sub cmdDelete_Click()
    'Delete the current record

    With adoBooks.Recordset
        .Delete                  'Delete the current record
        .MoveNext                'Move to the following record
        If .EOF Then             'If last record deleted
            .MovePrevious
            If .BOF Then         'If BOF and EOF true, no records remain
                MsgBox "The recordset is empty.", vbInformation, "No records"
                'Take any other desired action for empty recordset
            End If
        End If
    End With
End Sub
```

Preventing Errors

Allowing your users to get run-time errors is considered very poor programming style. Catching errors before they can cancel a program is called ***error trapping.*** In Chapter 10 you learned to use the On Error statement for error trapping with data files; in Chapter 12 you will learn to use error trapping and validation with the ADO data control.

In the meantime you can do some simple things, such as disabling command buttons, to prevent user errors. You can keep a user from causing many errors by disabling navigation buttons during an Add or a Delete operation.

Protecting an Add Operation

When the user clicks on the Add button, the cmdAdd_Click event will occur:

```
Private Sub cmdAdd_Click()
    'Add a new record

    adoBooks.Recordset.AddNew 'Clear out fields for new record
End Sub
```

Once the Add operation starts, you want the user to fill in the text boxes for the new record and click on *Save*. However, if the user clicks on one of the navigation buttons first, any data already entered in the text boxes is saved automatically. How can the user be forced to click on *Save*? How can she or he be allowed to cancel the operation?

Limiting User Actions

The best way to avoid errors is to avoid any extra options that can cause trouble. Once the Add begins, the user should have two choices only: *Save* or *Cancel*. The navigation buttons and the *Delete* button should be disabled. Figure 11.24 illustrates a data form used for updating; Figure 11.25 shows the same form during an Add operation with only two buttons available.

Figure 11.24

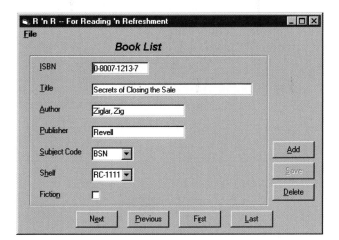

The update form as it appears before the user clicks on Add.

Figure 11.25

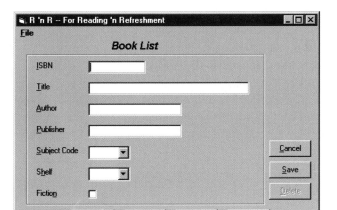

The update form as it appears during the Add operation. The Caption on the Add button changes to Cancel.

In the following example, when the user clicks on the Add button, several actions occur:

1. An AddNew method clears the bound controls to await entry of new data.
2. The focus is set in the first text box.
3. The navigation buttons and the *Delete* button are disabled.
4. The *Save* button is enabled.
5. The caption of the *Add* button changes to *Cancel*, which gives the user only two choices: *Save* or *Cancel*.

Sharing the Functions of a Command Button

Sometimes the best technique is to have one command button perform different actions, depending on the situation. Notice in Figures 11.24 and 11.25 that the

A good programming practice is to disable buttons when they shouldn't be used. It is not good practice to make buttons invisible and make them suddenly appear.

Save button becomes the *Cancel* button during an Add operation. Of course, this isn't the only solution: You could create a separate Cancel button and disable it.

To make a command button perform more than one action, you must change its Caption when appropriate. Then in the button's Click event, check the Caption before responding to the event.

```
Private Sub cmdAdd_Click()
    'Add a new record or cancel an add

    If cmdAdd.Caption = "&Add" Then
        'Code to handle Add
        cmdAdd.Caption = "&Cancel"    'Change the button's Caption
    Else                             'A Cancel action is selected
        'Code to handle Cancel
        cmdAdd.Caption = "&Add"       'Reset the button's Caption
    End If
End Sub
```

Coding the New Add Procedure

The new cmdAdd_Click event performs two distinct operations: Add or Cancel. A new statement, the **CancelUpdate method**, also appears in the Cancel operation. CancelUpdate does what it sounds like—it cancels the Add and returns to the record that was active before the Add started.

```
Private Sub cmdAdd_Click()
    'Add a new record

    If cmdAdd.Caption = "&Add" Then
        adoBooks.Recordset.AddNew       'Clear out fields for new record
        txtISBN.SetFocus
        DisableButtons                  'Disable navigation
        cmdSave.Enabled = True          'Enable the Save button
        cmdAdd.Caption = "&Cancel"      'Allow a Cancel option
    Else                                'A Cancel action is selected
        adoBooks.Recordset.CancelUpdate 'Cancel the Add
        EnableButtons                   'Enable navigation
        cmdSave.Enabled = False         'Disable the Save button
        cmdAdd.Caption = "&Add"         'Reset the Add button
    End If
End Sub
```

Procedures to Disable and Enable Buttons

These two new general procedures simplify the disable/enable operations.

```
Private Sub DisableButtons()
    'Disable navigation buttons

    cmdNext.Enabled = False
    cmdPrevious.Enabled = False
    cmdFirst.Enabled = False
    cmdLast.Enabled = False
    cmdDelete.Enabled = False
End Sub

Private Sub EnableButtons()
    'Enable navigation buttons

    cmdNext.Enabled = True
    cmdPrevious.Enabled = True
    cmdFirst.Enabled = True
    cmdLast.Enabled = True
    cmdDelete.Enabled = True
End Sub
```

The Save Procedure

When the user clicks on Save, you must first save the new record by executing the Update method. Then reset the controls to their "normal" state.

```
Private Sub cmdSave_Click()
    'Save the current record

    adoBooks.Recordset.Update
    EnableButtons
    cmdSave.Enabled = False
    cmdAdd.Caption = "&Add"
End Sub
```

Your Hands-On Programming Example

This example displays and maintains a database table to keep track of books for R 'n R—for Reading 'n Refreshment. This project puts together all the examples shown in this chapter. If you have completed the second example, you can just add the buttons and coding for Add, Cancel, Save, and Delete and change the Locked property for txtISBN.

Planning the Project

Sketch the modified form (Figure 11.26). Your user checks it over and approves the design.

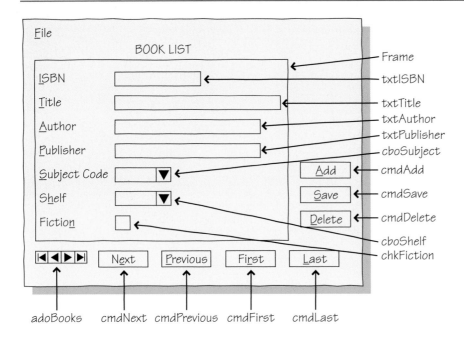

The planning sketch of the data entry form for the hands-on programming example.

Plan the Objects and Properties

Object	Property	Setting
frmBookData	Name	frmBookData
	Caption	R 'n R—for Reading 'n Refreshment
adoBooks	Name	adoBooks
	ConnectionString	(Select MS Jet OLE DB 4.0 and data file path)
	CommandType	2 - adCmdTable
	RecordSource	Books
	Visible	False
Frame1	Caption	(blank)
Label1	Caption	&ISBN
Label2	Caption	&Title
Label3	Caption	&Author
Label4	Caption	&Subject Code
Label5	Caption	S&helf
Label6	Caption	Fictio&n

(continued)

Object	Property	Setting
txtISBN	Name	txtISBN
	Text	(blank)
	DataSource	adoBooks
	DataField	ISBN
	Locked	False
txtTitle	Name	txtTitle
	Text	(blank)
	DataSource	adoBooks
	DataField	Title
txtAuthor	Name	txtAuthor
	Text	(blank)
	DataSource	adoBooks
	DataField	Author
txtPublisher	Name	txtPublisher
	Text	(blank)
	DataSource	adoBooks
	DataField	Publisher
cboSubject	Name	cboSubject
	Text	(blank)
	DataSource	adoBooks
	DataField	Subject_Code
	List	BSS
		FNT
		RLG
		RMN
		HMR
		SCF
		BSN
		PHL
		EDC
		MST
		SLH
cboShelf	Name	cboShelf
	Text	(blank)
	DataSource	adoBooks
	DataField	Shelf_Location

(continued)

Object	Property	Setting
	List	RC-1111
		RC-1112
		RC-1113
		RC-1114
chkFiction	Name	chkFiction
	Caption	(blank)
	DataSource	adoBooks
	DataField	Fiction
cmdAdd	Name	cmdAdd
	Caption	&Add
cmdSave	Name	cmdSave
	Caption	&Save
	Enabled	False
cmdDelete	Name	cmdDelete
	Caption	&Delete
cmdNext	Name	cmdNext
	Caption	N&ext
	Default	True
cmdPrevious	Name	cmdPrevious
	Caption	&Previous
cmdFirst	Name	cmdFirst
	Caption	Fi&rst
cmdLast	Name	cmdLast
	Caption	&Last
mnuFile	Name	mnuFile
	Caption	&File
mnuFileExit	Name	mnuFileExit
	Caption	E&xit

Plan the Code Procedures

Plan the actions for the event procedures and the general procedures.

Procedure	Actions
mnuFileExit_Click	Terminate the project.

cmdAdd_Click	If button caption = "Add" Then
	    AddNew record.
	    Set the focus in txtISBN.
	    Disable buttons.
	    Enable the Save button.
	    Set Add button caption to "Cancel".
	Else
	    CancelAdd method.
	    Enable buttons.
	    Disable the Save button.
	    Set button caption to "Add".
	End If

cmdDelete_Click	Delete record.
	Move to next record.
	If EOF Then
	    Move to the previous record.
	    If BOF Then (no records in recordset)
	        Display message.
	        Disable buttons.
	    End If
	End If

cmdSave_Click	Update record. Enable buttons. Disable the Save button. Set cmdAdd caption to "Add".

cmdNext_Click	Move to next record.
	If EOF Then
	    Move to first record.
	End If

cmdPrevious_Click	Move to previous record
	If BOF Then
	    Move to last record.
	End If

cmdFirst_Click	Move to first record.
cmdLast_Click	Move to last record.

Write the Project

- Follow the sketch in Figure 11.26 to create the form. Figure 11.27 shows the completed form. If you have done the preceding step-by-step examples in this chapter, you can just modify the previous project.

- Set the properties of each of the objects as you have planned.

● Write the code. Working from the pseudocode, write each procedure.

● Thoroughly test the project. Make sure to try every option, including canceling an Add and deleting the last record in a table.

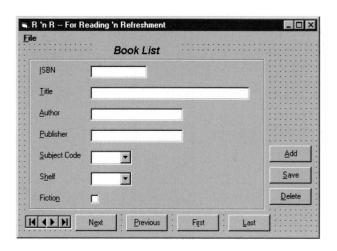

The data entry form for the hands-on programming example.

The Project Coding Solution

```
'Program Name:      R 'n R Book List Database
'Programmer:        Bradley/Millspaugh
'Date:              Jan 2002
'Purpose:           Display and update book information in the
'                   R 'n R Book database, using buttons for
'                   navigation and combo boxes for field lookup
'Folder:            Ch1103
```

```
Private Sub cmdAdd_Click()
    'Add a new record

    If cmdAdd.Caption = "&Add" Then
        adoBooks.Recordset.AddNew        'Clear out fields for new record
        txtISBN.SetFocus
        DisableButtons                   'Disable navigation
        cmdSave.Enabled = True           'Enable the Save button
        cmdAdd.Caption = "&Cancel"       'Allow a Cancel option
    Else
        adoBooks.Recordset.CancelUpdate  'Cancel the Add
        EnableButtons                    'Enable navigation
        cmdSave.Enabled = False          'Disable the Save button
        cmdAdd.Caption = "&Add"          'Reset the Add button
    End If
End Sub
```

```vb
Private Sub cmdDelete_Click()
    'Delete the current record

    With adoBooks.Recordset
        .Delete                    'Delete the current record
        .MoveNext                  'Move to the following record
        If .EOF Then               'If last record deleted
            .MovePrevious
            If .BOF Then           'If BOF and EOF true, no records remain
                MsgBox "The recordset is empty.", vbInformation, "No records"
                DisableButtons
            End If
        End If
    End With
End Sub
```

```vb
Private Sub cmdFirst_Click()
    'Move to first record

    adoBooks.Recordset.MoveFirst
End Sub
```

```vb
Private Sub cmdLast_Click()
    'Move to last record

    adoBooks.Recordset.MoveLast
End Sub
```

```vb
Private Sub cmdNext_Click()
    'Move to next record

    With adoBooks.Recordset
        .MoveNext
        If .EOF Then
            .MoveFirst
        End If
    End With
End Sub
```

```vb
Private Sub cmdPrevious_Click()
    'Move to previous record

    With adoBooks.Recordset
        .MovePrevious
        If .BOF Then
            .MoveLast
        End If
    End With
End Sub
```

```
Private Sub cmdSave_Click()
    'Save the current record

    adoBooks.Recordset.Update
    EnableButtons
    cmdSave.Enabled = False
    cmdAdd.Caption = "&Add"
End Sub
```

```
Private Sub mnuFileExit_Click()
    'Exit the project

    End
End Sub
```

```
Private Sub DisableButtons()
    'Disable navigation buttons

    cmdNext.Enabled = False
    cmdPrevious.Enabled = False
    cmdFirst.Enabled = False
    cmdLast.Enabled = False
    cmdDelete.Enabled = False
End Sub
```

```
Private Sub EnableButtons()
    'Enable navigation buttons

    cmdNext.Enabled = True
    cmdPrevious.Enabled = True
    cmdFirst.Enabled = True
    cmdLast.Enabled = True
    cmdDelete.Enabled = True
End Sub
```

Programming Hints

1. If you have trouble with your project running correctly, try single-stepping through the execution. Place a breakpoint at the top of a suspect procedure and begin execution. When the program halts at the breakpoint, press F8 (the shortcut for Step) repeatedly and watch the execution. While the project is in break time, you can highlight any expression in code and wait a second; the current value of the expression will display.
2. You can look up all properties, events, and methods for the data control in the Object Browser (Figure 11.28). Select *Object Browser* from the *View* menu, drop down the *Project/Library* list, and choose *MSAdodcLib*; then select *Adodc.*

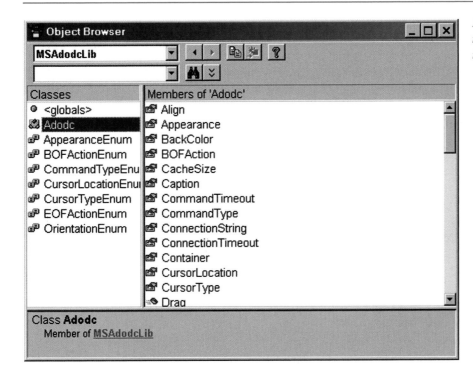

Look up the properties and methods for the ADO data control in the Object Browser.

S u m m a r y

1. Microsoft Access is Visual Basic's native format for database files.
2. In database terminology a *file* consists of *tables*, which consist of *rows* or *records*, which consist of *columns* or *fields*. Each record is identified by its *key* field. One record is always the *current* record.
3. A data control placed on a form links to a database file and a particular table within that file. Data-bound controls link to a data control for the table name and to a particular field within the table.
4. Data-aware controls (those that can become data bound) are labels, text boxes, check boxes, list boxes, combo boxes, images, picture boxes, data-bound list boxes, and data-bound grids.
5. Set the ConnectionString, CommandType, and RecordSource properties of a data control to link it to a database table.
6. Set the DataSource and DataField properties of data-aware controls to bind them to a field in a database table.
7. The Recordset object defined by the data control has its own properties and methods. Use the MoveNext, MovePrevious, MoveFirst, and MoveLast methods to navigate the database. The BOF and EOF properties indicate the beginning or end of file.
8. A combo box can be used as a data-bound control, and its List property can hold the possible choices for the field.

9. Any data that the user changes on the screen is automatically written into the file unless the file or the bound controls are locked.

10. The `AddNew` method clears the fields on the screen to allow the user to add a new record. After the Add, an `Update` method is needed; however, an `Update` occurs automatically when the user moves to another record.

11. The `Delete` method removes a record from the table. A `Move` must be executed after a `Delete`, because the current record is no longer valid.

12. To protect the user from making errors, you can disable and enable buttons. During an Add operation, the user should have only the options to Save or to Cancel. A `CancelUpdate` method cancels an Add operation.

K e y   T e r m s

`AddNew` method   *466*

`BOF`   *460*

`CancelUpdate` method   *470*

column   *442*

CommandType property   *447*

ConnectionString property   *447*

current record   *442*

data-bound control   *446*

DataField property   *452*

DataSource property   *452*

`Delete` method   *467*

`EOF`   *460*

error trapping   *468*

field   *442*

file   *442*

key field   *442*

record   *442*

Recordset object   *460*

RecordSource property   *447*

row   *442*

table   *442*

`Update` method   *466*

R e v i e w   Q u e s t i o n s

1. Assume you have a database containing the names and phone numbers of your friends. Describe how the terms *file, table, row, column, record, field,* and *key* apply to your database.

2. Explain the difference between a data control and a data-bound control.

3. Which controls can be data bound?

4. Explain how the BOF and EOF properties are set and how they might be used in a project.

5. Which properties must be set to bind a combo box to a field in a database and display a dropdown list of the choices for that field?

6. What steps are needed to add a new record to a database?

7. What steps are needed to delete a record from a database?

8. What steps are needed to change the data in a database record?

9. How can you check for the user deleting the only record in a Recordset?

Programming Exercises

11.1 The Rnrbooks.mdb database file holds two tables: the Books table used in this chapter and the Subjects table. The Subjects table has only two fields: the Subject Code (the key) and the Subject Name. Write a project that will display the Subjects table. Include command buttons for record navigation and make the data control invisible. Lock the text boxes so the user cannot change the data.

11.2 Write a project to maintain the Subjects table described in project 11.1. Use the (visible) data control for record navigation. Include command buttons for Add, Delete, and Save. Use a menu item for Exit.

11.3 Write a project to maintain the Subjects table described in project 11.1. Use menu choices rather than command buttons for the following program functions:

Menus

File	Record	Help
Exit	Next	About
	Previous	
	First	
	Last	
	Add New	
	Delete Current	

Give each menu command a keyboard shortcut (in the menu editor) if you wish, to make selecting a command quicker.

Include two command buttons on the form—a Save button and a Cancel button, which are both disabled most of the time. When the user chooses Add New, make the Save and Cancel buttons enabled. If the user clicks on Save, update the record; a click on Cancel cancels the Add operation. After either a Save or Cancel, make both buttons disabled again.

Make the Save button the default button. Set the Cancel property to True on the Cancel button.

Disable the menu options for navigation, Add, and Delete when an Add is in progress.

11.4 Write a project to display the Publishers table from the Biblio.mdb database that comes on the Visual Basic CD. (Biblio.mdb is not installed automatically on your computer, but it is on the CD.) Include command buttons for record navigation and hide the data control. Do not allow the user to change the data.

Hint: Copy the Biblio.mdb file to the directory where your project will be stored before setting the properties for the data control.

Note: The Biblio.mdb database included with VB4 was 288 KB, small enough to easily fit on a diskette. The version included with VB5 and VB6 is 3.5 MB—too large for a diskette. The older version is included on your student diskette. The two versions of the file have the same structure; the size difference is due to the large number of records added to the newer version.

Fields in the Publishers Table

PubID (Publisher Identification—key field)

Name

Company Name

Address

City

State

ZIP

Telephone

Fax

11.5 Write a project to maintain the Publishers table described in project 11.4. Allow Adds and Deletes to the database. On an Add, disable the navigation and Delete buttons so that the only options are Save or Cancel.

    Hint: Copy the Biblio.mdb file to the directory where your project will be stored before setting the properties for the data control. See the note in Exercise 11.4 about the file size.

CASE STUDIES

VB Mail Order Assignment 1—Display Only

VB Mail Order

Create a project to display the VB Mail Order Customer table from the Vbmail.mdb database on your student diskette. Do not allow the user to change the data.

Make the data control invisible; instead, include command buttons for Next, Previous, First, and Last.

VB Mail Order Assignment 2—Display and Update

Create a project to display and maintain the customer table. See project 11.3 for a list of the menu choices.

Allow adds and deletions to the database through menu selections. During an Add, allow the user to Save or to Cancel only.

Fields
Customer ID
LastName
FirstName
Address
City
State
ZipCode

VB Auto Center Assignment 1—Display Only

VB Auto Center

Create a project to display the VB Auto Center Vehicle table from the Vbauto.mdb database on your student diskette. Do not allow the user to change the data.

Make the data control invisible; instead, include command buttons for Next, Previous, First, and Last.

VB Auto Center Assignment 2—Display and Update

Create a project to display and maintain the Auto Center Vehicle table. See project 11.3 for a list of the menu choices.

Allow adds and deletions to the database through menu selections. During an Add, allow the user to Save or to Cancel only.

Fields
InventoryID
Manufacturer
ModelName
Year
VehicleID
CostValue

Video Bonanza

Video Bonanza Assignment 1—Display Only

Create a project to display the information from the Studio table in the VBVideo.mdb database. Do not allow the user to change the data.

The Studio table contains these fields:

Fields	Data Type
Studio ID	Text, 3 characters
Studio Name	Text, 30 characters
Contact Person	Text 25 characters
Phone	Text, 20 characters

Make the data control invisible and include command buttons for Next, Previous, First, and Last.

Video Bonanza Assignment 2—Display and Update

Create a project to display and maintain the Video Bonanza Studio table. Use either command buttons or menu options for the following program functions:

Next
Previous
First
Last
Add a Product
Delete a Product

The user will be able to make changes to the data, add records, or remove records. When an Add is in progress, allow the user to Save or Cancel only.

Hint: You can prevent some user errors by setting the MaxLength property of text boxes so that the user cannot enter too many characters in a field.

Very Very Boards

Very Very Boards Assignment 1— Display Only

Create a project to display the Product table from the VeryBoards.mdb database file on your student diskette. The Product table contains these fields:

Fields	Data Type
ProductID	Text, 4 characters
Description	Text, 20 characters
MfgID	Text, 3 characters
Unit	Text, 10 characters
Cost	Currency, 2 decimal places
LastOrderDate	Date/time
LastOrderQuantity	Integer

Do not allow the user to change the data. Make the data control invisible.

You can use command buttons or menu choices for record navigation. Provide options for Next, Previous, First, and Last.

Very Very Boards Assignment 2—Display and Update

Create a project to display and maintain the Very Very Boards Product table. Use either command buttons or menu options for the following program functions:

Next
Previous
First
Last
Add a Product
Delete a Product

The user will be able to make changes to the data, add records, or remove records. When as Add is in progress, allow the user to Save or Cancel only.

Hint: You can prevent some user errors by setting the MaxLength property of text boxes so that the user cannot enter too many characters in a field.

12

Data Handling— Grids, Validation, Selection, and Sorting

At the completion of this chapter, you will be able to . . .

1. Write a database application using the DataGrid control.

2. Improve database validation techniques with error trapping.

3. Find records that meet a specific criterion using both the `Find` and the `Filter` methods.

4. Reorder table type recordsets using the `Sort` method.

5. Set up a parent and child relationship using a Data Environment.

Displaying Data in Grids

In Chapter 11 you learned to display database tables in bound controls, such as labels, text boxes, check boxes, and list boxes. Another good way to display data is in **grids**, which present tables in rows and columns similar to a spreadsheet.

Visual Basic comes with several grid controls. In addition, many companies sell powerful grid controls that you can include in your project. In the following example, you will create a simple application using Microsoft's DataGrid control.

Note: This example cannot be completed with the VB 6 Working Model software.

A Grid Control—Step-by-Step

This step-by-step tutorial shows you how to create an application that displays the Books table for R 'n R. Although the application is quite simple, it allows the user to add, change, and delete data records. You also learn how to display the record number and record count. Figure 12.1 shows the completed form.

F i g u r e   1 2 . 1

The completed form using the grid control.

Create the Form and Controls

STEP 1: Begin a new project and widen the form. You may want to close the Project Explorer and Form Layout windows and float the Properties window to allow room to work on the wide form (Figure 12.2).

STEP 2: Save the project in a new folder called Ch1201. Call the project file Grid.vbp and the form file Grid.frm. Place a copy of the RnRBooks.mdb file in the folder.

STEP 3: Select *Project/Components* to display the *Components* dialog box (or right-click on the toolbox and choose *Components*). Locate and select these two components:

Microsoft ADO Data Control 6.0

and

Figure   12.2

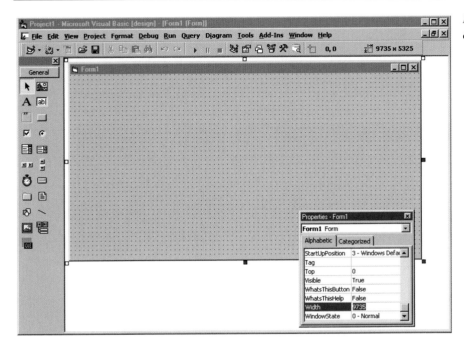

Modify the screen layout to work on a wide form.

Microsoft DataGrid Control 6.0.

After selecting the two components, close the dialog box. You should see the two new tools in the toolbox (Figure 12.3).

Figure   12.3

a. *b.*

The toolbox tools for this project: (a) the ADO data control and (b) the DataGrid control.

STEP 4: Add an ADO data control along the bottom of the form. Set the following properties:

Property	Setting
Name	adoBooks
ConnectionString	*Provider* tab: Microsoft Jet 4.0 OLE DB Provider *Connection* tab: Database name: RnRBooks.mdb
CommandType	2 - adCmdTable
RecordSource	Books

STEP 5: Click on the DataGrid tool and draw a large grid on the form (Figure 12.4). Then, using the Properties window, change the control's Name property to *dbgBooks* and its DataSource property to *adoBooks*.

F i g u r e　　1 2 . 4

Draw a large grid control on your form.

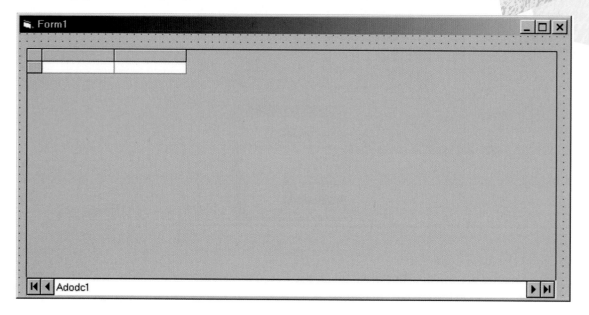

STEP 6: Create the menu bar. It should have a *File* menu with only an *Exit* command.

STEP 7: Create the large label at the top of the form with the form's title: *Book List*. Change the font and size to something you like.

Set the Properties of the Form

STEP 1: Set the form's Name property to *frmBookGrid* and its Caption property to *R 'n R--For Reading and Refreshment*.

Set the Properties of the Grid

STEP 1: Point to the grid control and right-click to display the shortcut menu. Select *Retrieve Fields* and click Yes to *"Replace existing grid layout with new field definitions?"* Then watch as the grid changes to display all the fields from the Books table. One column is set up for each field, with the field name at the top of the column as a caption.

We are going to set more properties to improve the display of the table, but at this point the application will work. We'll make a quick test before setting the rest of the properties.

STEP 2: Start the project running. You should see the grid fill with data. Scroll to the right and view all the fields. You can also scroll down to see more records.

Next we will resize the columns, change captions for some columns, fix the display format of the Yes/No field (Fiction), and make the long titles and names wrap to a second line.

STEP 3: Stop program execution, point to the grid control, and right-click to display the shortcut menu. Select *Properties* (Figure 12.5), and the custom *Property Pages* dialog box appears (Figure 12.6). Although you can change the properties in the regular Properties window, the process is much easier from this custom dialog box.

Figure 12.5

Right-click on the grid control to display the shortcut menu; select *Properties.*

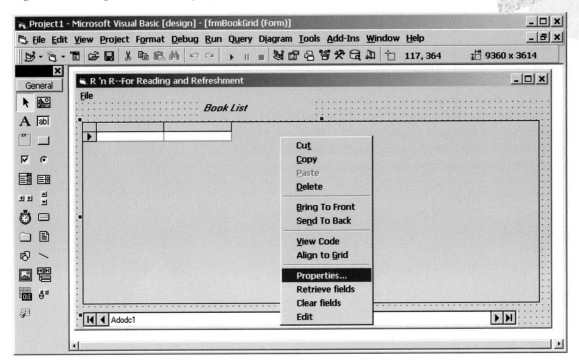

Modify the properties of the grid control using the custom Property Pages *dialog box.*

STEP 4: On the *General* tab select *AllowAddNew* and *AllowDelete*. Change the *Row Height* entry to *400* (approximately double the default entry). Allow the rest of the entries to remain at their default values.

STEP 5: Change to the *Columns* tab and make these changes:

Column4 (Subject_Code)
    Caption: *Subject*
Column5 (Shelf_Location)
    Caption: *Shelf*

STEP 6: Change to the *Format* tab and make this change:

Column6 (Fiction)
    FormatType: *Boolean*

STEP 7: Click *Apply* to apply the changes without closing the *Property Pages* dialog box.

STEP 8: Change to the *Layout* tab and make the following changes. You may want to click *Apply* after each change.

Column0 (ISBN)
    Locked: Checked
    Width: *1200* (measurements in twips)
Column1 (Title)
    WrapText: Checked
    Width: *2000*
Column2 (Author)
    WrapText: Checked
    Width: *2000*
Column3 (Publisher)
    WrapText: Checked
    Width: *2000*

Column4 (Subject_Code)
> *Width:*   *700*

Column5 (Shelf_Location)
> *Width:*   *700*

STEP 9: Click OK to close the custom *Property Pages* dialog box.

STEP 10: Resize the form and data control as you wish.

Write the Exit Procedure

STEP 1: Code the mnuFileExit_Click procedure with an `Unload Me` and an `End` statement.

> You could run the project now and have a functioning database grid. However, we are going to add one more feature to the project and make the record number appear in the data control.

Displaying the Record Number and Record Count

Often it is useful to display the record number and record count when viewing database records. You can use the **RecordCount** and **AbsolutePosition properties** of the data control's recordset to display both, for example: *Record 10 of 45.*

The RecordCount and AbsolutePosition Properties

The RecordCount property holds the number of records in a recordset; the AbsolutePosition holds the position of the current record in the recordset.

Example

```
intCurrentRecord = adoBooks.Recordset.AbsolutePosition
```

If the recordset is at BOF or EOF, the AbsolutePosition property has a value of 0.

Note: You cannot use the AbsolutePosition property as a record number, because the position number changes as records are added and deleted.

To display the record number and the count in the caption of the data control, create a sub procedure and use this code:

```
Private Sub SetRecordNumber()
    'Display the record number
    Dim intRecordCount      As Integer
    Dim intCurrentRecord    As Integer

    With adoBooks.Recordset
        intRecordCount = .RecordCount
        intCurrentRecord = .AbsolutePosition
        If .EOF Then
            adoBooks.Caption = "EOF"
        Else
            adoBooks.Caption = "Record " & intCurrentRecord & _
                " of " & intRecordCount
        End If
    End With
End Sub
```

Tip

Quickly switch back and forth between the Code window and the Form window using keyboard shortcuts. F7 takes you to the Code window; Shift+F7 switches to the Form window.

In the procedure to begin an Add (cmdAdd_Click), include this statement:

```
txtISBN.Locked = False
```

Because the only two actions that the user can take after beginning an Add are Save and Cancel, you should include the following statement in both routines:

```
txtISBN.Locked = True
```

Validating Data in the Validate Event

When you want to make sure that a required field has an entry or that a field has valid data, the **Validate event** is a good location to check. If the field is not valid, you can display an error message and cancel the operation.

New to VB 6, most controls now have a new property and a new event that greatly aid in validating the entries in controls. The **CausesValidation property** can be set to True or False, which indicates whether validation will be performed on the control about to lose the focus. The Validate event occurs for the control just before it loses the focus.

For example, assume you have txtISBN and txtTitle. The user is expected to enter a value in txtISBN and tab to txtTitle. If you have the CausesValidation property of txtTitle set to True, then the Validate event of txtISBN will occur. Of course, the user may do something else, such as click in a different field, on a command button, or exit the program. You must set the CausesValidation property to True for all controls that the user might select if you want validation to occur. Fortunately, the default setting for CausesValidation is True.

The Validate Event—General Form

```
Private Sub ControlName_Validate(Cancel As Boolean)
```

The Validate Event—Example

```
Private Sub txtISBN_Validate(Cancel As Boolean)
```

In the Validate event procedure, you can perform any error checking and display a message for the user. If the data doesn't pass the error checking, set Cancel to True. When the sub procedure completes, the focus will remain in the control you are checking.

```
Private Sub txtISBN_Validate (Cancel As Boolean)
    'Validate the ISBN for an Add
    Dim strMessage As String

    If Len(txtISBN.Text) > 13 Then          'All ISBNs must be <= 13 characters
        strMessage = "Invalid ISBN"
        MsgBox strMessage, vbExclamation, "Data Entry Error"
        With txtISBN
            .SelStart = 0                   'Select the current entry
            .SelLength = Len(.Text)
        End With
        Cancel = True                       'Keep the focus
    End If
End Sub
```

Make sure to allow your user a way out. If *all* the controls on the form have CausesValidation set to True, *any* action puts the focus back in the text box. For example, if you have a Cancel button to cancel the operation, set its CausesValidation property to False.

Trap Errors with On Error

Error trapping with `On Error` is very important when working with database files. You need to include the `On Error` in every procedure that accesses the database, such as the Add, Delete, Update, and all Moves. In each case trap for any errors you think are likely. For many routines you can just code an `On Error Resume Next`, which ignores the error and continues execution.

```
Private Sub cmdFirst_Click()
    'Move to first record

    On Error Resume Next
    adoBooks.Recordset.MoveFirst
End Sub
```

Handling Error Conditions That Cancel an Operation

If an error occurs that will cancel an operation, such as a Delete or Add operation, the user should be notified. You can display a message and continue with program execution.

```
Private Sub cmdDelete_Click()
    'Delete the current record

    On Error GoTo HandleDeleteError
    With adoBooks.Recordset
        .Delete                    'Delete the current record
        .MoveNext                  'Move to the following record
        If .EOF Then               'If last record deleted
            .MovePrevious
            If .BOF Then           'If BOF and EOF true, no records remain
                MsgBox "The recordset is empty.", vbInformation, "No records"
                DisableButtons
            End If
        End If
    End With

cmdDelete_Click_Exit:
    Exit Sub

HandleDeleteError:
    Dim strMessage As String
    strMessage = "Cannot complete operation." & vbCrLf & vbCrLf _
                & Err.Description
    MsgBox strMessage, vbExclamation, "Database Error"
    On Error GoTo 0                       'Turn off error trapping
End Sub
```

Handling Errors after an Add Operation

When the user clicks *Save* after an Add operation, several errors are possible.
A duplicate key will cause an error, as will a missing key field.

You must decide what action you want to take when the user has entered a
complete new record and the ISBN duplicates one already in the file. Do you
want to clear the data? Do you want to display a message and abort the operation? In this example we will allow the user to change the ISBN and continue
with the Add if desired. To make this happen, you must save the contents of the
screen controls, execute an AddNew method, and replace the contents of the
controls. We will place this code in a separate sub procedure.

```
Private Sub cmdSave_Click()
    'Save the current record

    On Error GoTo HandleSaveErrors
    adoBooks.Recordset.Update
    txtISBN.Locked = True             'Reset all
    EnableButtons
    cmdSave.Enabled = False
    cmdAdd.Caption = "&Add"
```

```
cmdSave_Click_Exit:
    Exit Sub

HandleSaveErrors:
    Dim strMessage As String

    strMessage = "Record could not be saved." & vbCrLf _
                        & Err.Description 'Display system error message
    MsgBox strMessage, vbExclamation, "Database Error"
    SetUpAddRecord      'Allow user to change ISBN and complete Add
    Resume cmdSave_Click_Exit
End Sub
```

```
Private Sub SetUpAddRecord()
    'Set up a new Add to allow the user another try
    Dim strISBN As String, strTitle As String, strAuthor As String
    Dim strPublisher As String, strSubject As String
    Dim strLocation As String, vntFiction As Variant

    On Error Resume Next

    'Save the contents of the form controls
    strISBN = txtISBN.Text
    strTitle = txtTitle.Text
    strAuthor = txtAuthor.Text
    strPublisher = txtPublisher.Text
    strSubject = cboSubject.Text
    strLocation = cboLocation.Text
    vntFiction = chkFiction.Value

    'Start a new Add
    adoBooks.Recordset.AddNew

    'Place saved data back in form controls
    With txtISBN
        .Text = strISBN
        .SelStart = 0
        .SelLength = Len(.Text)
        .SetFocus
    End With
    txtTitle.Text = strTitle
    txtAuthor.Text = strAuthor
    txtPublisher.Text = strPublisher
    cboSubject.Text = strSubject
    cboLocation.Text = strLocation
    chkFiction.Value = vntFiction
End Sub
```

Feedback 12.1

1. Write the statement(s) to display the record number in a label.
2. Write the statement(s) to instruct VB to ignore any error and just keep processing.
3. What statement(s) would appear in a text box Validate event procedure to prevent the user from exiting the control?
4. Write the statement(s) to check for an empty string in txtName (a data-bound control) in the txtName_Validate event procedure. If no data exists, display a message box.
5. Explain what will display for this statement:

```
MsgBox "Error " & Err.Description
```

Programming Example Showing Validation Techniques

This example starts with the hands-on programming example from Chapter 11 and adds numerous validation routines that combine many of the techniques discussed in the previous sections. Figure 12.7 shows the form for this project.

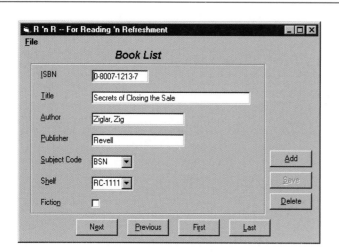

The form for the database validation example.

```
'Program Name:      R 'n R Book List Database
'Programmer:        Bradley/Millspaugh
'Date:              Jan 2002
'Purpose:           Display and update book information in the
'                   R 'n R Book database. Handles program errors
'                   and validates the ISBN.
'Folder:            Ch1202

Option Explicit
```

```
Private Sub cmdAdd_Click()
    'Add a new record

    On Error GoTo HandleAddErrors
    If cmdAdd.Caption = "&Add" Then
        adoBooks.Recordset.AddNew          'Clear out fields for new record
        txtISBN.Locked = False
        txtISBN.SetFocus
        DisableButtons                     'Disable navigation
        cmdSave.Enabled = True             'Enable the Save button
        cmdAdd.Caption = "&Cancel"         'Allow a Cancel option
    Else
        adoBooks.Recordset.CancelUpdate    'Cancel the Add
        txtISBN.Locked = True
        EnableButtons                      'Enable navigation
        cmdSave.Enabled = False            'Disable the Save button
        cmdAdd.Caption = "&Add"            'Reset the Add button
    End If

cmdAdd_Click_Exit:
    Exit Sub

HandleAddErrors:
    Dim strMessage As String
    strMessage = "Cannot complete operation." & vbCrLf & vbCrLf _
                & Err.Description
    MsgBox strMessage, vbExclamation, "Database Error"
    On Error GoTo 0                        'Turn off error trapping
End Sub
```

```
Private Sub cmdDelete_Click()
    'Delete the current record

    On Error GoTo HandleDeleteError
    With adoBooks.Recordset
        .Delete                           'Delete the current record
        .MoveNext                         'Move to the following record
        If .EOF Then                      'If last record deleted
            .MovePrevious
            If .BOF Then                  'If BOF and EOF true, no records remain
                MsgBox "The recordset is empty.", vbInformation, "No records"
                DisableButtons
            End If
        End If
    End With

cmdDelete_Click_Exit:
    Exit Sub
```

```
HandleDeleteError:
    Dim strMessage As String
    strMessage = "Cannot complete operation." & vbCrLf & vbCrLf _
                & Err.Description
    MsgBox strMessage, vbExclamation, "Database Error"
    On Error GoTo 0                     'Turn off error trapping
End Sub
```

```
Private Sub cmdFirst_Click()
    'Move to first record

    On Error Resume Next
    adoBooks.Recordset.MoveFirst
End Sub
```

```
Private Sub cmdLast_Click()
    'Move to last record

    On Error Resume Next
    adoBooks.Recordset.MoveLast
End Sub
```

```
Private Sub cmdNext_Click()
    'Move to next record

    On Error Resume Next
    With adoBooks.Recordset
        .MoveNext
        If .EOF Then
            .MoveFirst
        End If
    End With
End Sub
```

```
Private Sub cmdPrevious_Click()
    'Move to previous record

    On Error Resume Next
    With adoBooks.Recordset
        .MovePrevious
        If .BOF Then
            .MoveLast
        End If
    End With
End Sub
```

```vb
Private Sub cmdSave_Click()
    'Save the current record

    On Error GoTo HandleSaveErrors
    adoBooks.Recordset.Update
    txtISBN.Locked = True           'Reset all
    EnableButtons
    cmdSave.Enabled = False
    cmdAdd.Caption = "&Add"

cmdSave_Click_Exit:
    Exit Sub

HandleSaveErrors:
    Dim strMessage As String

    strMessage = "Record could not be saved." vbCrLf _
                        & Err.Description 'Display system error message
    MsgBox strMessage, vbExclamation, "Database Error"
    SetUpAddRecord         'Allow user to change ISBN and complete Add
    Resume cmdSave_Click_Exit
End Sub
```

```vb
Private Sub mnuFileExit_Click()
    'Exit the project

    Unload Me
    End
End Sub
```

```vb
Private Sub DisableButtons()
    'Disable navigation buttons

    cmdNext.Enabled = False
    cmdPrevious.Enabled = False
    cmdFirst.Enabled = False
    cmdLast.Enabled = False
    cmdDelete.Enabled = False
End Sub
```

```vb
Private Sub EnableButtons()
    'Enable navigation buttons

    cmdNext.Enabled = True
    cmdPrevious.Enabled = True
    cmdFirst.Enabled = True
    cmdLast.Enabled = True
    cmdDelete.Enabled = True
End Sub
```

```
Private Sub SetUpAddRecord()
    'Set up a new Add to allow the user another try
    Dim strISBN As String, strTitle As String, strAuthor As String
    Dim strPublisher As String, strSubject As String
    Dim strLocation As String, vntFiction As Variant

    On Error Resume Next

    'Save the contents of the form controls
    strISBN = txtISBN.Text
    strTitle = txtTitle.Text
    strAuthor = txtAuthor.Text
    strPublisher = txtPublisher.Text
    strSubject = cboSubject.Text
    strLocation = cboLocation.Text
    vntFiction = chkFiction.Value

    'Start a new Add
    adoBooks.Recordset.AddNew

    'Place saved data back in form controls
    With txtISBN
        .Text = strISBN
        .SelStart = 0
        .SelLength = Len(.Text)
        .SetFocus
    End With
    txtTitle.Text = strTitle
    txtAuthor.Text = strAuthor
    txtPublisher.Text = strPublisher
    cboSubject.Text = strSubject
    cboLocation.Text = strLocation
    chkFiction.Value = vntFiction
End Sub
```

```
Private Sub txtISBN_Validate(Cancel As Boolean)
    'Validate the ISBN for an Add
    '  Note: The control is locked unless an Add is in progress.
    Dim strMessage As String

    If Len(txtISBN.Text) > 13 _
        Or Len(txtISBN.Text) = 0 Then 'All ISBNs must be <= 13 characters
        strMessage = "Invalid ISBN"
        MsgBox strMessage, vbExclamation, "Data Entry Error"
        With txtISBN
            .SelStart = 0                    'Select the current entry
            .SelLength = Len(.Text)
        End With
        Cancel = True                        'Keep the focus
    End If
End Sub
```

Searching for Records

You can search for specific records using the **Find method** or the Filter property of a recordset. The **Find** method locates a single record and the Filter property creates a subset of the records that match your criteria.

The Find Method

You can search for a particular value in any field. For example, you can request a certain name, account number, phone number, book title, author—any field stored in the database and bound to one of your controls. Use the **Find** method to locate the first record that matches the criteria

The Find Method—General Form

```
adoDatControl.Recordset.Find Criteria [, [RowsToSkip] , [SearchDirection]]
```

The criteria specify the field name from the database and the contents for which you are searching.

The RowsToSkip argument allows you to specify the number of rows from the current position to begin the find. SearchDirection allows you to search either forward or backward; use one of the two ADO constants: adSearchForward or adSearchBackward. Since a forward search is the default, the only time you need to specify the direction is when you want to search backward through the recordset.

The Find Method—Examples

```
adoBooks.Recordset.Find "ISBN = '123-456-789-X'"
adoMembers.Recordset.Find "FirstName = 'Dennis'"
adoMembers.Recordset.Find "FirstName = '" & txtName.Text & "'"
adoMembers.Recordset.Find "Amount > 100"
adoMembers.Recordset.Find "Amount > " & txtAmount.Text
```

For a string search criterion, the string must be enclosed in single quotes, as in the first two examples. In the third example, the confusing mix of quotes produces the correct search string. If txtName.Text holds the name "Theresa", then the search string is `FirstName = 'Theresa'`.

When searching in a numeric field, do not enclose the numeric value in single quotes. The fourth example above includes a numeric constant, and the fifth example searches for the value entered in a text box. Assuming that the text box holds the number "123", the search string will be `Amount > 123`.

If you are searching a field that has any spaces in its name, the field name must be enclosed in square brackets:

```
adoEmployees.Recordset.Find "[Pay Rate] > 30000"
```

The `Find` operation always begins with the current record and moves through the file. If you want to locate the first record in the recordset, it's a good idea to use a `MoveFirst` method before performing the Find.

```
With adoBooks.Recordset
    .MoveFirst
    .Find "Author Like '" & strName & "*'"
End With
```

For the comparison operator, you can use =, >, <, <=, >=, <>, `Like`, `Between`, and `In`. To use the `Like` operator, use an asterisk as a wildcard character to match any character(s) in that position. *Note:* Some databases use a percent sign, rather than an asterisk, for a wildcard.

Examples

```
"PayRate <= 50000"
"LastName Like 'Br*'"                     'Find a last name beginning with "Br"
"Amount Between 50 And 100"
"LastName Not Like 'A*'"                   'A last name not beginning with "A"
"LastName In('Adams', 'Baker', 'Charles')" 'A matching last name
```

No Record Found

If no record is found on a `Find`, the Recordset is at EOF (BOF for a forward search). Always test for end-of-file after a `Find` method.

```
With adoBooks.Recordset
    .MoveFirst
    .Find "Author Like '" & strName & "*'"
    If .EOF Then
        MsgBox "No matching records found", , "Find Author"
    End If
End With
```

If a match is found, the record becomes current and is displayed in the data-bound controls. If no match is found, the current record number is unpredictable. A good way to take care of a no-match situation is to use a bookmark.

Bookmarks

You can set a bookmark on any record in a recordset and use the bookmark later to return to that record. Set a variable equal to the recordset's **BookMark property** to save it for future reference. Any time you set the BookMark property to the variable name, the bookmarked record becomes the current record. *Note:* Use variant datatype for a variable to hold a bookmark.

```
Private Sub mnuFindAuthor_Click()
    'Locate first record by selected author
    Dim strName     As String
    Dim vntBookmark As Variant

    strName = InputBox("Enter Last Name (or partial name)", "Find Author")
    With adoBooks.Recordset
        vntBookmark = .Bookmark
        .MoveFirst
        .Find "Author Like '" & strName & "*'"
        If .EOF Then
            MsgBox "No matching records found", , "Find Author"
            .Bookmark = vntBookmark
        End If
    End With
End Sub
```

The Filter Property

The **Filter property** allows you to create a new temporary recordset by selecting records that match a specified criterion. For example, you might select all records for the same last name. ADO creates a temporary recordset for display purposes; no changes are made to the underlying table.

The Filter Property—General Form

```
Object.Recordset.Filter = FilterString
```

Use the same criteria rules for the filter as you used with the Find method.

The Filter Property—Examples

```
adoBooks.Recordset.Filter = "Author = 'Bradley'"
adoBooks.Recordset.Filter = "Author = '" & txtAuthor.Text & "'"
adoBooks.Recordset.Filter = "Author = 'Bradley' AND Title = 'Programming*'"
adoBooks.Recordset.Filter = strSearch
```

You can use multiple criteria by combining the comparisons with AND or OR. Although you can combine multiple ANDs and ORs, there is no precedence for the AND/OR operators. Use parentheses to specify the order of evaluation.

If you want to display all records after you have set the Filter property, you must set the Filter property to empty quotes "" or use the ADO constant adFilterNone.

```
adoBooks.Recordset.Filter = ""
```

or

```
adoBooks.Recordset.Filter = adFilterNone
```

Sorting a Recordset

You can sort a recordset by any field using the recordset's **Sort property.** Assign the property a field name or multiple field names, separated by commas.

The Sort Property—General Form

```
Object.Recordset.Sort = "FieldName[, MoreFields]"
```

The Sort Property—Examples

```
adoBooks.Recordset.Sort = "Author"
adoBooks.Recordset.Sort = "Author, Title"
```

To allow your users to select a sort field, you can create menu options or create a list box with choices. In the following example for R 'n R, the user can choose to sort by Author, ISBN, or Subject (Figure 12.8).

F i g u r e   1 2 . 8

The Sort By menu offers choices to display the Books table in three orders. Change the recordset's Sort property to change the order. Set the menu item's Checked property to match the sort order.

```
Private Sub mnuSortAuthor_Click()
    'Sort by Author

    adoBooks.Recordset.Sort = "Author"
    mnuSortAuthor.Checked = True
    mnuSortISBN.Checked = False
    mnuSortSubject.Checked = False
End Sub

Private Sub mnuSortISBN_Click()
    'Sort by ISBN

    adoBooks.Recordset.Sort = "ISBN"
    mnuSortISBN.Checked = True
    mnuSortAuthor.Checked = False
    mnuSortSubject.Checked = False
End Sub

Private Sub mnuSortSubject_Click()
    'Sort by Subject

    adoBooks.Recordset.Sort = "Subject_Code"
    mnuSortSubject.Checked = True
    mnuSortISBN.Checked = False
    mnuSortAuthor.Checked = False
End Sub
```

Feedback 12.2

1. Write the statement(s) to find the first record in adoProducts where the Quantity field is less than 20.
2. Write the statement(s) to create a subset of records in adoProducts with a Quantity field of less than 20.
3. Write the statement(s) to sort adoAcmePayroll by
   (a) Rate
   (b) Employee Name
4. Write the statement(s) to select records from adoAcmePayroll. Create the set of records that contains a YTD salary of more than 45000. The name of the field is YTD.

Working with Database Fields

In the section that follows, we will be referencing individual fields from a recordset by name, reading the contents of fields, and loading field values into a list box.

Referring to Database Fields

At times you may want to refer to a single field in the current recordset. Use either of these formats to refer to a field:

```
adoDatControl.Recordset!FieldName
```

or

```
adoDatControl.Recordset("FieldName")
```

If the field name in the table is more than one word, you must enclose the name in quotes or square brackets:

```
adoBiblio.Recordset![Year Published]
```

or

```
adoBiblio.Recordset("Year Published")
```

Loading Database Fields into a List Box

In the earlier examples for `Find` and `Filter`, the user entered the search value into an input box or a text box. A better approach might be to offer a list of possible values.

To fill a list with values from a recordset, use a `Do/Loop`. You can place the loop in the Form_Load procedure.

```
Private Sub Form_Load()
    'Fill the Subject Code list

    With adoSubjects.Recordset
        Do Until .EOF
            If !Subjectcode <> "" Then
                cboSubjects.AddItem !Subjectcode
            End If
            .MoveNext
        Loop
        .Close
    End With
End Sub
```

An Example with Find, Filter, and Sort

This example puts together the `Find`, `Filter`, and `Sort`. For the Filter option, a list box appears with the subject codes from the Subjects table. The user can select the subject on which to filter and a temporary recordset is created with only those records. The form has two data controls: one for the Books table and another for the Subject table, used to fill the Subject list. Figure 12.9 shows the form.

The Find, Filter, *and* Sort *example program. The Subject list appears only when the user chooses to select by subject.*

```
'Project:        R 'n R Book List Selection
'Programmer:     Bradley/Millspaugh
'Date:           Jan 2002
'Purpose:        Display book information in the R 'n R Book database.
'                Allow user to select criteria to create a subset of records,
'                to sort by specific fields, or to find a record.
'Folder:         Ch1203

Option Explicit
```

```
Private Sub adoBooks_MoveComplete(ByVal adReason As ADODB.EventReasonEnum, _
        ByVal pError As ADODB.Error, adStatus As ADODB.EventStatusEnum, _
        ByVal pRecordset As ADODB.Recordset)
    'Display the record number

    With adoBooks.Recordset
        If .EOF Then
            adoBooks.Caption = "End of File"
        Else
            adoBooks.Caption = "Record " & .AbsolutePosition & " of " _
                            & .RecordCount
        End If
    End With
End Sub
```

```
Private Sub cboSubjects_Click()
    'Update the text boxes to match criteria

    With cboSubjects
        adoBooks.Recordset.Filter = "Subject_Code Like  '" & _
                .List(.ListIndex) & "*'"
    End With
End Sub
```

```
Private Sub Form_Load()
    'Fill the Subject Code List

    With adoSubjects.Recordset
        Do Until .EOF
            If !Subjectcode <> "" Then
                cboSubjects.AddItem !Subjectcode
            End If
            .MoveNext
        Loop
        .Close
    End With
End Sub
```

```
Private Sub mnuFileExit_Click()
    'Exit the project

    Unload Me
    End
End Sub
```

```
Private Sub mnuFindAuthor_Click()
    'Locate first record by selected author

    Dim strName     As String
    Dim vntBookmark As Variant

    On Error GoTo HandleError
    strName = InputBox("Enter Last Name (or partial name)", "Find Author")
    With adoBooks.Recordset
        vntBookmark = .Bookmark
        .MoveFirst
        .Find "Author Like '" & strName & "*'"
        If .EOF Then
            MsgBox "No matching records found", , "Find Author"
            .Bookmark = vntBookmark
        End If
    End With
```

```
mnuFindAuthor_Click_Exit:
    Exit Sub

HandleError:
    MsgBox "Unable to carry out requested operation", vbInformation, _
        "Find Author"
End Sub
```
___

```
Private Sub mnuFindISBN_Click()
    'Locate record by ISBN
    Dim strISBN     As String
    Dim vntBookmark  As Variant

    On Error GoTo HandleError
    strISBN = InputBox("Enter ISBN (Partial OK)", "Find ISBN")
    With adoBooks.Recordset
        vntBookmark = .Bookmark
        .MoveFirst
        .Find "ISBN Like '" & strISBN & "*'"
        If .EOF Then
            MsgBox "No matching records found", , "Find ISBN"
            .Bookmark = vntBookmark
        End If
    End With

mnuFindISBN_Click_Exit:
    Exit Sub

HandleError:
    MsgBox "Unable to carry out requested operation", vbInformation, _
        "Find ISBN"
End Sub
```
___

```
Private Sub mnuSelectAll_Click()
    'Display all records in table

    adoBooks.Recordset.Filter = adFilterNone
    fraSubject.Visible = False
    mnuSelectAll.Checked = True
    mnuSelectSubject.Checked = False
End Sub
```
___

```
Private Sub mnuSelectSubject_Click()
    'Display Selection list

    fraSubject.Visible = True
    mnuSelectSubject.Checked = True
    mnuSelectAll.Checked = False
End Sub
```

```
Private Sub mnuSortAuthor_Click()
    'Sort by Author

    adoBooks.Recordset.Sort = "Author"
    mnuSortAuthor.Checked = True
    mnuSortISBN.Checked = False
    mnuSortSubject.Checked = False
End Sub
```

```
Private Sub mnuSortISBN_Click()
    'Sort by ISBN

    adoBooks.Recordset.Sort = "ISBN"
    mnuSortISBN.Checked = True
    mnuSortAuthor.Checked = False
    mnuSortSubject.Checked = False
End Sub
```

```
Private Sub mnuSortSubject_Click()
    'Sort by Subject

    adoBooks.Recordset.Sort = "Subject_Code"
    mnuSortSubject.Checked = True
    mnuSortISBN.Checked = False
    mnuSortAuthor.Checked = False
End Sub
```

The Data Environment Designer

Warning: The Data Environment Designer is not available in the Working Model version of VB. The procedures in the remainder of this chapter cannot be done with the Working Model.

The **Data Environment Designer** is a visual interface that allows you to set up all of the database connections and recordsets for a project in one location. Then all forms and modules can refer to those recordsets. Using the Data Environment Designer (Figure 12.10), you can specify a hierarchy among the data in the project. You also can drag and drop fields to your forms, which automatically creates bound controls.

Figure 12.10

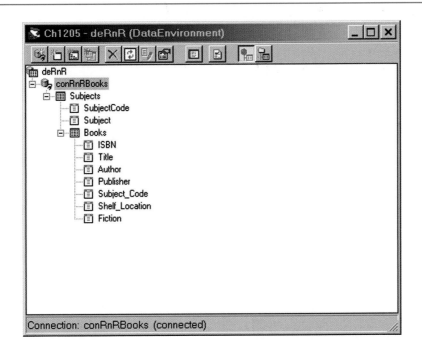

A Data Environment Designer
can manage all Connections and
Commands in a project.

If you choose to use a Data Environment instead of an ADO data control, you no longer have the visible navigation buttons available. You will have to code the navigation as you did in the hands-on program for Chapter 11 and Ch1202 in this chapter.

Using the Data Environment Designer, you set up and refer to a series of objects. A **DataEnvironment** is an object that consists of **Connections.** Each Connection can hold one or more **Command** objects.

Connection and Command Objects

Connection: Specifies the physical database file, how it will be accessed, and with what permissions. Also called a **DEConnection.**

Command: Source of the data within the file. May be a table name, a stored procedure name, or an SQL statement. A Command corresponds to the RecordSource property of an ADO data control. The Command also can specify actions to perform on the data, such as grouping and updating. Also called a **DECommand.**

Adding a Data Environment Designer

You can add a Data Environment Designer to a VB project by selecting *Project/Add Data Environment* (or *Project/Add ActiveX Designers/Data Environment* in some configurations). If *Add Data Environment* doesn't appear on the *Project* menu, select *Project/Components,* switch to the *Designers* tab, select *Data*

Environment, and close the *Components* dialog box. Then you can select *Project/ Add Data Environment.*

When the Data Environment (DE) window appears (Figure 12.11), you will see an icon for the Data Environment and an icon for one Connection. (Each Data Environment must have at least one Connection.) In the DE window, you can rename each of the objects, add Connections and Commands, and set the properties for each of the objects.

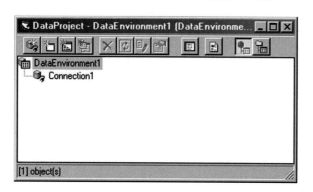

A new Data Environment Designer window displays icons for the Data Environment and the first Connection.

It's a good idea to rename the Data Environment before adding any Connections or Commands. Click on the DE icon and change the name in the Properties window; the recommended prefix for a Data Environment is "de"; for example, *deRnR* or *deCompanyDatabase.*

Creating Connections

You will want to rename the Connection. You can select the Connection and rename it in the Properties window, or right-click on the Connection and choose *Rename* from the shortcut menu. Name each Connection with a prefix of "con"; for example *conBooks* or *conAuthors.*

You can set many properties of the Connection object. Right-click on the icon and choose *Properties.* You will see the *Data Link Properties* dialog box; you used this same dialog box to set up a ConnectionString for the ADO data control. You can set the provider and the database name, as well as test the connection.

Adding Commands

Although the term *command* can be somewhat confusing, for now just think of a Command as a table name or a query that returns a set of data, similar to the RecordSource property of an ADO data control. A Command creates a Recordset object with the data it returns. You will be able to use the recordset in code, just as you used the ADO data control's recordset.

To add a Command, right-click on the icon for a Connection and select *Add Command* from the shortcut menu. Change the name of the Command in the Properties window or the *Rename* command of the shortcut menu. Most pro-grammers do not use a prefix for a Command, but rather choose a name that describes the data in the recordset, such as Books, Subjects, Employees, or Products.

The Data Environment Designer works well to separate the database operations from your coding.

Creating a Data Environment—Step-by-Step

The following step-by-step tutorial creates a form with bound controls using a Data Environment. Note that the Working Model version of VB does not include the Data Environment Designer.

Begin a Project

STEP 1: Create a new folder and add the RnRBooks.mdb data file to the folder.

STEP 2: Open a new standard project in VB.

STEP 3: Save the project into the new folder. Call the form BookGrid.frm and the project Ch1205.vbp.

Add a Data Environment

STEP 1: Open the *Project* menu and select *Add Data Environment.* If you don't see it, look under *Project/Add ActiveX Designers/Data Environment.* A Data Environment window will open.

Note: If *Add Data Environment* is not listed in the *Project,* menu, open the *Components* dialog box, select the *Designers* tab, click on *Data Environment.*

STEP 2: Click on the icon for DataEnviroment1 and change its Name property to *deRnR.*

Set Up the Connection

STEP 1: Click on Connection1 and change its Name property to *conRnRBooks.*

STEP 2: Right-click on conRnRBooks and select *Properties;* the *Data Link Properties* dialog box appears.

STEP 3: On the *Provider* tab, select *Microsoft Jet 4.0 OLE DB Provider* and click *Next.*

STEP 4: On the *Connection* tab, for the database name, browse to find and select RnRBooks.mdb. Click the *Test Connection* button to verify that your connection is set up correctly. Then click OK to close the dialog box.

Note: If you accidentally close the Data Environment window, reopen it by double-clicking on deRnR in the Project Explorer.

Add a Command

STEP 1: In the deRnR Data Environment window, right-click on conRnRBooks and select *Add Command* from the shortcut menu.

STEP 2: Name the command *Books.*

STEP 3: For the CommandType property select adCmdTable. Click OK on the message about Command Text.

STEP 4: Set the CommandText property to *Books* (the name of the table in the database). Click on the plus sign for Books to see a listing of the fields in the table (Figure 12.12).

Figure   12.12

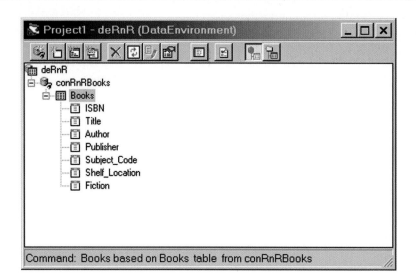

Expand the Command to view the field names for the Books table.

Create Bound Controls

STEP 1: You may want to resize and move the Data Environment window so that you can view both the form and the fields in the window. Widen the form to allow room for a grid.

STEP 2: Drag and drop the Books command to the form. You now have labels and data-bound text boxes.

While the controls are still selected, adjust their placement (Figure 12.13).

Figure   12.13

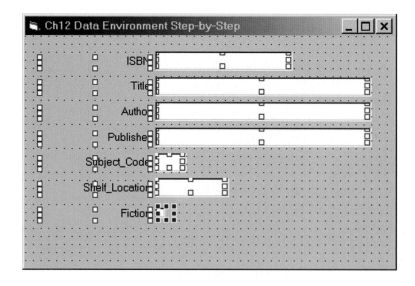

Drag the Command to the form to create bound controls and identifying labels. Adjust the placement of the controls while they are selected.

Run the Project

STEP 1: Run the project. You should see the fields filled with the first record in the recordset.

Note that there are no navigation buttons. To navigate the record-set, you will have to add the MoveNext coding, as you did in the Chapter 11 hands-on exercise.

STEP 2: Stop execution. You can use the Properties window to view the proper-ties set for data-bound controls. Notice that the Datesource is set to the Data Environment (deRnR) and the DataMember is set to the Command (Books). Also notice the names of the automatically created bound controls.

Navigating Recordsets for Data Environment Objects

A Command object creates a Recordset object, to which you can refer in code. The recordset is automatically named with the name of the Command plus a pre-fix of "rs". For example, in the previous step-by-step tutorial, you created a Data Environment object called deRnR with a Connection object conRnRBooks, which contains a Command object called Books. The recordset is automatically created as "rsBooks". You reference the recordset in code as

```
DataEnvironmentName.RecordsetName.Property
```

or

```
DataEnvironmentName.RecordsetName.Method
```

Because the Data Environment does not provide an automatic navigation tool, you need to code command buttons to perform the navigation functions. You can use the same navigation methods as with the ADO data control's recordset: MoveFirst, MoveLast, MoveNext, and MovePrevious.

The MoveNext method would appear as

```
deRnR.rsBooks.MoveNext
```

Add a Next Button to the Step-by-Step Example

STEP 1: Reopen the project, if necessary.

STEP 2: Add a command button to the form. Change the button's Name prop-erty to cmdNext, the Caption to &Next, and the Default property to True.

STEP 3: In the cmdNext_Click event procedure, write this code:

```
Private Sub cmdNext_Click()
    'Move to next record

    With deRnR.rsBooks
        .MoveNext
        If .EOF Then
            .MoveFirst
        End If
    End With
End Sub
```

STEP 4: Test the project again.
STEP 5: Close the project, saving the Data Environment.

One-to-Many Relationships

You can set options in the Data Environment Designer to create hierarchies of data, joining data from more than one table. This is especially useful for one-to-many relationships, which join a primary (parent) table with a secondary (child) table.

The hierarchy can display orders for a specific customer, classes for a student, or any information with a relationship between the data in one table and another. Figure 12.14 shows a hierarchical recordset for the RnR database. The Subject table has one entry for each subject code; the Books table may have many records with any one subject code. The subject code joins the two tables; Subjects is the primary table; Books is the secondary (child) table.

F i g u r e   1 2 . 1 4

Two Commands form a hierarchical recordset. The Subjects Command is the parent and the Books Command is the child.

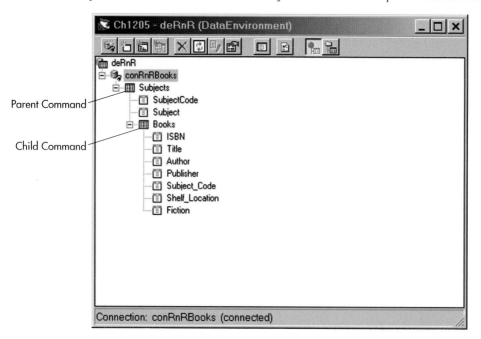

VB 6 includes a special control for displaying the data in a relation hierarchy called the Microsoft Hierarchical FlexGrid control (MSHFlexGrid). In the following sections you will create a hierarchical recordset and display it in an MSHFlexGrid control.

An MSHFlexGrid is also similar to the DataGrid control but is more secure because the user is not allowed to change the data. However, resourceful programmers can allow users to update the data in an MSHFlexGrid by adding a text box on top of the cell to edit.

To use the control, you need to select *Microsoft Hierarchical FlexGrid Control 6.0 (OLE DB)* from the *Components* dialog box; the suggested naming prefix is "flex".

Relation Hierarchies

Creating a **relation hierarchy** is similar to joining two related tables of data. Using the Data Environment Designer, you create a parent Command object and a child Command object. For the example that follows, we will use the Subjects and Books tables of the R 'n R database, relating the tables using the subject code. The Subjects table is the parent (primary) table and Books is the child (secondary) table.

You can use either of two methods for creating the parent–child relationship. In both methods you need a Command object for each table. In the first method you create both Commands at the same level and convert one into a child, in the second method you first create the parent, then add the child directly beneath the parent. The following step-by-step tutorial uses the first method.

Creating a Relation Hierarchy—Step-by-Step

Create the Project

STEP 1: Create a folder for the project and add the RnRBooks.mdb database to the folder.

STEP 2: Open a new VB project and save the project into the new folder. Call the form BooksHierarchy.frm and the project Ch1205.vbp.

Add a Data Environment

STEP 1: Select *Project/Add Data Environment.*

STEP 2: In the Data Environment Designer, click on the icon for DataEnvironment1 and change its Name property in the Properties window to *deRnR.*

Set Up the Connection

STEP 1: Select the Connection and rename it to conRnRBooks.

STEP 2: Right-click on the Connection and select *Properties.*

STEP 3: On the *Provider* tab, select *Microsoft Jet 4.0 OLE DB Provider* and click *Next.*

STEP 4: On the *Connection* tab, type *RnR.mdb.*

You also can browse for the filename, which stores the path with the filename. If you want the project to be portable, omit the path and the current folder will be used.

Build the Relation Hierarchy

STEP 1: Add a Command object and name it *Books*. Set the CommandType property to *adCmdTable* and the CommandText property to *Books* (the Books table).

STEP 2: Add a second Command object named *Subjects*. The CommandType should be *adCmdTable* and the CommandText *Subjects* (the Subjects table). See Figure 12.15.

Figure 12.15

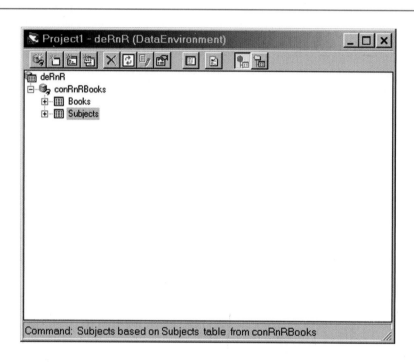

Add two Command objects to the conRnRBooks Connection.

STEP 3: Right-click on the Books Command object and select *Properties* from the shortcut menu.

STEP 4: On the *Relation* tab, check the box for *Relate to a Parent Command Object*.

STEP 5: Select *Subjects* for the *Parent Command*.
At this point VB tries to guess which fields form the relationship.

STEP 6: For *Relation Definition*, make *Subject Code* relate to *Subject_Code*, if necessary.

STEP 7: Click *Add* and the relation will appear in the text box (Figure 12.16).

Figure   12.16

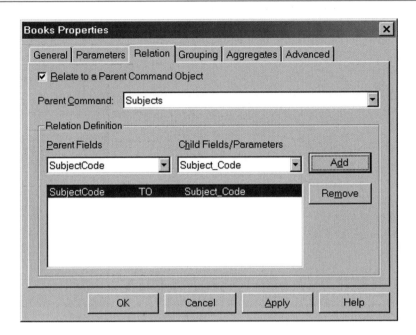

Click **Add** *to make the relationship appear in the text box.*

STEP 8: Click on OK. Note the indentation and relationship in the Data Environment. (Refer to Figure 12.14, Page 518.)

STEP 9: Save your project.

Add the Grid

STEP 1: Widen the form, change the form Name to *frmHierarchy*, and the Caption to *R 'n R Books by Subject*.

STEP 2: Drag the Subjects command to your form. While the controls are still selected, adjust the placement (Figure 12.17).

STEP 3: Notice the controls, their names, and their DataSource and DataMember properties.

Figure   12.17

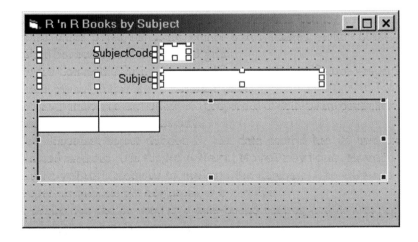

Drag the Books Command to the form to create the data-bound controls.

Modify the Project

STEP 1: Run the project. The first subject appears at the top and all books that match that subject (Art) appear in the MSHFlexGrid.

STEP 2: Stop the execution so we can add navigation to the form. Resize the form and grid if you want more data to show.

STEP 3: Add a command button, name it cmdNext, set the Caption to &Next, and the Default property to True.

STEP 4: Add the coding:

```
Private Sub cmdNext_Click()
    'Move to the next subject

    With deRnR.rsSubjects
        .MoveNext
        If .EOF Then
            .MoveFirst
        End If
    End With
End Sub
```

STEP 5: Run the project. Step through the subjects to see the books for each subject (Figure 12.18).

STEP 6: Stop execution and save the project.

Step through the subjects. Each subject appears in the text boxes at the top and the books that match that subject appear in the grid.

Your Hands-On Programming Example

In this project for R 'n R, you will create a project that allows the user to display books by subject using a Data Environment, a hierarchical recordset, and an MSHFlexGird control. This is essentially a more finished version of the chapter step-by-step tutorial.

Note that the Working Model version of VB does not support the Data Environment and cannot be used for this exercise.

Planning the Project

Sketch the form. Your users check over the design and you are ready to proceed. Figure 12.19 shows the completed form.

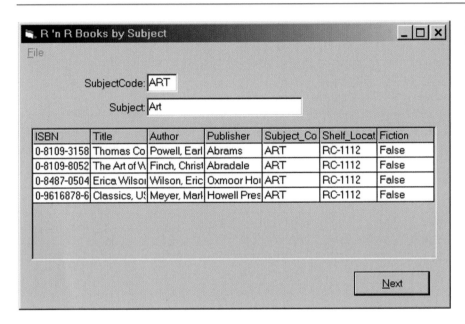

The completed form for the hands-on example.

Plan the Objects and Properties

Object	Property	Setting
frmBooks	Name	frmBooks
cmdNext	Caption	&Next
	Default	True
mnuFile	Caption	&File
mnuFileExit	Caption	E&xit

Plan the Event Procedures

Object	Procedure	Actions
cmdNext	Click	Move to the next record If end of recordset Move to the first record
mnuFileExit	Click	Unload the form. End.

Write the Project

- If you have completed the chapter hands-on tutorial, you are nearly done.

- Set the properties of each of the objects according to the plan.

- Write the code. Working from the pseudocode, write each event procedure.

- Thoroughly test the project.

The Project Coding Solution

```
'Program Name:        R 'n R Book List Database
'Programmer:          Bradley/Millspaugh
'Date:                Jan 2002
'Purpose:             Display related information (books within a subject area)
'                     in the R 'n R Book database.
'Folder:              Ch1205

Option Explicit


Private Sub cmdNext_Click()
    'Move to the next subject

    With deRnR.rsSubjects
        .MoveNext
        If .EOF Then
            .MoveFirst
        End If
    End With
End Sub


Private Sub mnuFileExit_Click()
    'Terminate the project

    Unload Me
    End
End Sub
```

Summary

1. The DataGrid control can be used to display and/or update database recordsets. The grid displays records in rows and columns, resembling a spreadsheet.
2. The data control's RecordCount property holds the number of records in a recordset; the AbsolutePosition property holds the record number of the current record.

3. The data control's MoveComplete event occurs each time a new record becomes current. Use the event procedure to perform any checking on the individual record.

4. Use the Validate event of controls to check for input errors.

5. Most procedures that perform database access need error trapping with an On Error statement.

6. When the user clicks Save after an Add operation, you must trap for a duplicate or missing key field.

7. The Find method may be used to search for any value in any field of a recordset. The EOF property is set to True if a match is not found.

8. Use the recordset's Bookmark property to store or set the current record number.

9. Set the Filter property to create a subset of records that match a criterion.

10. Display a recordset in a different order by setting the Sort property to a field name.

11. The Data Environment Designer can be used to set up all Connections and Commands for database access.

12. A Data Environment (DE) provides a Connection that can be used by all forms in the project. The DE may include multiple tables and queries.

13. A DE can easily set up a one-to-many relationship in a relational database. The "one" side is the parent Command and the "many" side is the child Command.

14. The MSHFlexGrid is designed to display hierarchical recordsets.

Key Terms

AbsolutePosition property *491*

BookMark property *505*

CausesValidation property *494*

Command *513*

Connection *513*

Data Environment *513*

Data Environment Designer *512*

DECommand *513*

DEConnection *513*

Filter property *505*

Find method *503*

grid *486*

MoveComplete event *492*

RecordCount property *491*

recordset *499*

relation hierarchy *519*

Sort property *506*

Validate event *494*

Review Questions

1. When would it be a good idea to use a grid control?

2. When does a control's Validate event occur? How is the Cancel argument used?

3. Explain the differences between the Find and Filter properties of a recordset.

4. How can you reorder a recordset?

5. What is the purpose of the Data Environment? How is it used?

P r o g r a m m i n g   E x e r c i s e s

12.1 *Grid:* Write a project that will display the Publishers table in a grid. Use the Biblio.mdb sample database that comes with Visual Basic. (Biblio.mdb is not installed automatically on your computer but it is on the CD.) Make sure that the grid cells are large enough to display all the data, and display the record number and record count in the caption of the data control.

   Hint: Copy the Biblio.mdb file to the directory where your project will be stored before setting the properties for the data control.

   Note: The Biblio.mdb database included with VB4 was 288 KB, small enough to easily fit on a diskette. The version included with VB5 and VB6 is 3.5 MB—too large for a diskette. The older version is included on your Student Diskette. The two versions of the file have the same structure; the size difference is due to the large number of records added to the newer version.

12.2 *Validation and error trapping:* Modify project 11.2 or 11.3, which maintains the Subjects table in the R 'n R database. Validation required: Do not allow the user to change the Subject Code (the primary key) except during an Add. Make sure that no error can cause a run-time error. Do not allow a duplicate key field or deletion of the last record to cancel the project.

   If you are modifying project 11.2, add a Cancel button to allow the user to back out of an Add operation.

12.3 *Validation, error trapping, and selection:* Modify project 11.5, which maintains the Publishers table in the Biblio.mdb sample database. Include validation: Do not allow any run-time errors; the primary key field (PubID) can be changed only during an Add. Do not allow a duplicate key field or deletion of the last record to cancel the project.

   Include menu choices or command buttons to search for a name or a company name using a Find or Filter.

   Note: See the note in Exercise 12.1 about the size of the file.

12.4 *Reorder:* Write a project that will display a recordset in order by one of three fields. Use the Titles table in the Biblio.mdb sample database, which comes with Visual Basic. Allow the user to select Title Order, ISBN Order, or Publisher's ID Order.

   Display the following fields from the Titles table:

Title	(indexed)
Year Published	
ISBN	(PrimaryKey)
PubID	(indexed)

   Note: See the note in Exercise 12.1 about the size of the file.

12.5 *Data Environment and hierarchical recordset:* This project displays fields from the Titles table and the Publishers table in the Biblio.mdb database. The layout of the Publishers table (shown in project 11.4) has a primary key of PubID; the Titles table (described in project 12.4) includes a PubID field, which can be used to relate the two tables.

Create a Data Environment with the Titles table as a child of the Publishers table. Drag the grid to the form and add navigation buttons. *Hint:* After dragging the parent Command to the form, remove extra fields.

Optional: Display the data in labels rather than a grid. Use the appropriate Data Environment Command for the DataMember property of the labels.

Note: See the note in Exercise 12.1 about the size of the file.

C A S E S T U D I E S

VB Mail Order

Grid

Display the Product table of VBMail.mdb in a grid. Include the record number and record count either in the caption of the data control or in a label. Make sure the grid cells are large enough to display all the data.

Validation, Error Trapping, and Selection

Modify the VB Mail Order database project from Chapter 11. The new menu will add choices to search for a customer by last name or by customer ID. A *Sort* menu will allow the user to display the information in order by LastName or CustomerID.

Do not allow the user to change the CustomerID field (the primary key) except during an Add operation. Make sure that no error can cause a run-time error.

Include a Cancel button to allow the user to back out of an Add operation.

Data Environment, Hierarchical Recordset

In this project for VB Mail Order, you will create an application that allows the user to select products by catalog name from VBMail.mdb. A grid displays the product information.

Tables

Product
ProductNumber (indexed) (compound primary key)
Catalog Number (indexed) (compound primary key)
Description
Price
Weight

Catalog
Number (primary key)
Name (indexed)
Phone

Grid

Display the Vehicle table of VBAuto.mdb in a grid. Include the record number and record count either in the caption of the data control or in a label. Make sure the grid cells are large enough to display all the data.

Validation, Error Trapping, and Selection

Modify the VB Auto database project from Chapter 11. The new menu will add choices to search for a vehicle by inventory ID or by manufacturer. An *Organize* menu will allow the user to display the information in order by Manufacturer or InventoryID.

Do not allow the user to change the InventoryID field (the primary key) except during an Add. Make sure that no error can cause a run-time error.

Include a Cancel button to allow the user to back out of an Add operation.

Data Environment, Hierarchical Recordset

In this project for VB Auto Center, you will create a program that allows the user to view records by vehicle

VB Auto Center

and customer. Make the Vehicle table the parent Command and the Customer table the child. Display in an MSHFlexGrid.

Tables

Vehicle

Inventory ID (indexed) (primary key)

Manufacturer

Model

Year

Cost Value

VehicleID

Customer

Number (primary key)

Name (indexed)

InventoryIDNumber

Video Bonanza

Grid

Display the Video table of VBVideo.mdb in a grid. Include the record number and record count either in the caption of the data control or in a label. Make sure the grid cells are large enough to display all the data.

Validation, Error Trapping, Selection, and Sort

Modify the Video Bonanza database project from Chapter 11. New options:

* Find a studio by Studio Name or by Studio ID

* Display in order by Studio Name or Studio ID

The new menu will add choices to search for a studio by Studio Name or by Studio ID. An *Organize* menu will allow the user to display the information in order by Studio Name or Studio ID.

Do not allow the user to change the Studio ID field (the primary key) except during an Add operation. Make sure that no error can cause a run-time error.

Include a *Cancel* button to allow the user to back out of an Add operation.

Data Environment, Hierarchical Recordset

In this project for Video Bonanza, you will create an application that displays videos by studio. Use a Data Environment to create a hierarchical recordset. Display the studio information at the top and the video information in an MSHFlexGrid.

Tables

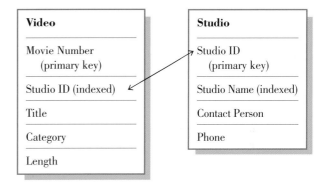

Very Very Boards

Grid

Display the Product table of VeryBoards.mdb in a grid. Include the record number and record count in the caption of the data control. Make sure the grid cells are large enough to display all the data.

Validation, Error Trapping, Sort, Selection

Modify the Very Very Boards database project from Chapter 11. New options:

- Find a product by ProductID or by MfgID.

- Display in order by ProductID.

- Display in order by MfgID.

Do not allow the user to change the ProductID field (the primary key) except during an Add. The Product Description field must not be empty. Make sure that no error can cause a run-time error.

Include a *Cancel* button to allow the user to back out of an Add operation.

Hierarchical Grid

In this project for Very Very Boards, you will create a project that displays the products by Manufacturer. Use a Data Environment to create a hierarchical recordset. Display the manufacturer information at the top and the product information in a MSHFlexGrid.

Tables

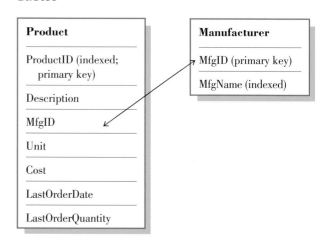

Product	Manufacturer
ProductID (indexed; primary key)	MfgID (primary key)
Description	MfgName (indexed)
MfgID	
Unit	
Cost	
LastOrderDate	
LastOrderQuantity	

13

Drag-and-Drop

At the completion of this chapter, you will be able to . . .

1. Explain the difference between the source and target in a drag-and-drop operation.

2. Code a program that incorporates drag-and-drop.

One of the handy visual tools of Windows is the drag-and-drop operation. In this chapter you will learn how to incorporate drag-and-drop into your programs.

Drag-and-Drop Terminology

Before you are ready to code a drag-and-drop operation, you need to know some terminology. Also, you need to understand the properties that must be set and the difference between a DragOver event and a DragDrop event.

The Source and the Target

In a drag-and-drop operation, an object is moved from one location to another. The object being moved (dragged) is called the **source**; the location to which it is moved is called the **target**. Figure 13.1 shows a form with a source image and a target image. In the example, imgPaper is the source and imgTrash is the target.

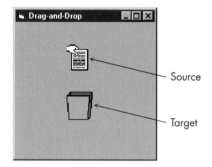

The Source object is dragged to the Target

Source Object Properties

To make a source object movable, set its **DragMode property** to 1 - Automatic. You will also want to set the **DragIcon property** to display an icon; otherwise, when you drag the object, you see only an outline.

DragOver and DragDrop Events

As an object is dragged across a form, events are occurring. The events are for the target objects, not the source. For example, as you drag an image across a form, the form's **DragOver event** occurs. If you drag the image across a control, such as a command button, the command button's DragOver event occurs. As long as you keep the mouse button down and keep moving, DragOver events occur for the form and every control over which you move. When you release the mouse button with the image over a control, the control's **DragDrop event** occurs; of course, if you release the mouse button over the form, the *form's* DragDrop event occurs.

Therefore, for any drag-and-drop operation, multiple DragOver events may occur. Only one DragDrop event occurs—when the operation is complete. All the events occur to the target objects, not to the source object.

Note: You can also code for events that occur for the source object, such as the Click event and the MouseDown, MouseUp, and MouseMove events. This brief introduction focuses on the events for the target objects.

A Step-by-Step Example

In this example you will develop a small application that allows the user to drag the airplane icon into the hangar (use your imagination for the hangar). Notice that Figure 13.2 contains two airplane icons—the source (imgPlane) and another inside the target (imgPlaneParked). The second image has its Visible property set to False, so it won't be seen until the plane is inside the hangar.

F i g u r e   1 3 . 2

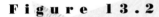

The form for the airplane step-by-step example.

This example uses a picturebox control. For further information about pictureboxes, see Chapter 14.

Create the User Interface

STEP 1: Begin a new project and place the picturebox and the two image controls (for the two airplanes) on the form. Make sure to create the second airplane image *inside* the picturebox, which is its container. (If you try to drag the image on top of the picturebox, it will disappear behind the control because of the way the graphic controls are layered on the form. You can either draw the image inside the picturebox or cut-and-paste it inside; dragging does not place the image inside the picturebox.)

STEP 2: Create the label under the picturebox (the one captioned Hangar).

Set the Properties

STEP 1: Set the properties for the form.

Property	Value
Name	frmPlane
Caption	Fly the Plane to the Hangar

STEP 2: Set the properties for the first airplane image.

Note: The graphic image files are not stored on your computer automatically. You must perform a custom setup when you install VB on your computer. The location of the files can vary, depending on your configuration and whether you installed Visual Studio or only Visual Basic. After you locate the files on your system, adjust the path specifications for all image files.

Property	Value
Name	imgPlane
Stretch	True
Picture	Graphics\Icons\Industry\Plane.ico
DragIcon	Graphics\Icons\Industry\Plane.ico
DragMode	1 - Automatic

STEP 3: Set the properties for the second airplane image.

Property	Value
Name	imgPlaneParked
Stretch	True
Picture	Graphics\Icons\Industry\Plane.ico
Visible	False

STEP 4: Set the Name property of the picturebox to picHangar.
STEP 5: Set the Caption property of the label to Hangar.

Write the Code

STEP 1: Try a test run of the program before you write any code. Click the Run button and try dragging the plane image.

You should see an icon as you drag, but the original image still appears (Figure 13.3). The next step will be to make the source image invisible as you begin to drag the image over the form.

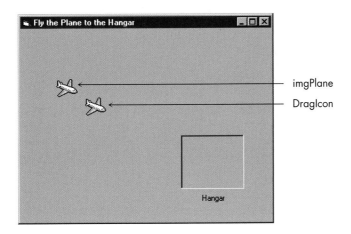

The icon moves as you drag it, but the original image is still visible.

STEP 2: Stop program execution.

Code the Drag Operation

STEP 3: In the Code window, click on *Form* for the object and *DragOver* for the procedure.

STEP 4: Code the following remark and line of code in the Form_DragOver event.

```
'Make the plane invisible

imgPlane.Visible = False
```

STEP 5: Run the program again. When you begin dragging the plane image, the original should disappear so that it looks like you are actually dragging the image (Figure 13.4). Try dropping it anywhere. (Disappears, doesn't it?) Now it's time to take care of the drop operation.

Stop program execution.

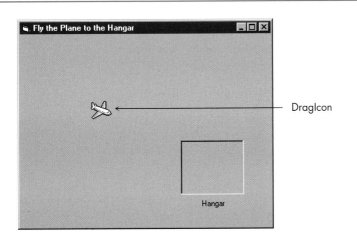

For a proper drag, the original image should disappear.

Code the Drop Operation

A DragDrop event may occur for the intended target (the picturebox), but perhaps the user misses (how?) or has a change of heart. If a DragDrop event occurs for the form or for any control other than the intended target, the drop is in error and the original image must become visible again.

STEP 6: Code the DragDrop event for the picturebox (picHangar).

```
Private Sub picHangar_DragDrop(Source As Control, X As Single, _
         Y As Single)
   'Good Drop

      imgPlaneParked.Visible = True
End Sub
```

STEP 7: Code the DragDrop event for the form.

```
Private Sub Form_DragDrop(Source As Control, X As Single, Y As Single)
   'Bad Drop

      imgPlane.Visible=True
End Sub
```

STEP 8: Code a DragDrop event for the label control. If the user drops the plane on the label, it's another bad drop.

```
Private Sub Label1_DragDrop(Source As Control, X As Single, Y As Single)
   'Bad Drop

      imgPlane.Visible = True
End Sub
```

Run the Project

STEP 1: Start the project running. Try dragging and dropping the plane on the hangar (Figure 13.5). Then stop the project; restart and try dropping on the form. Stop, restart, and try dropping on the label. For each bad drop, the plane should reappear in its original location.

If you have problems, check the event procedure names. You must code the DragDrop event for the picturebox, the form, and the label.

Wouldn't it be helpful to have command buttons to exit the project and to reset the image to its original location?

Figure 13.5

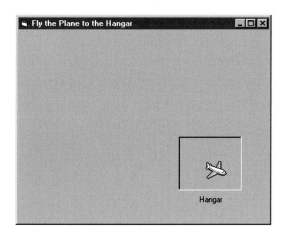

A good drag-and-drop with the airplane in the hangar.

Add Command Buttons

STEP 1: Add two command buttons to the form (Figure 13.6) and set their properties.

Object	Property	Value
cmdReset	Name	cmdReset
	Caption	&Reset
cmdExit	Name	cmdExit
	Caption	E&xit

Figure 13.6

Add Reset and Exit command buttons to the form.

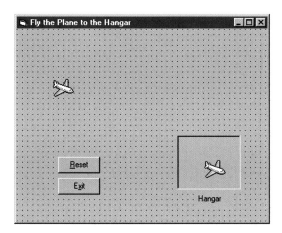

STEP 2: Code the cmdReset_Click event.

```
Private Sub cmdReset_Click()
    'Reset to original condition

    imgPlaneParked.Visible = False
    imgPlane.Visible = True
End Sub
```

STEP 3: Code the cmdExit_Click event.

```
Private Sub cmdExit_Click()
    'Exit the project

    Unload me
    End
End Sub
```

You *could* test the project to see what happens when you drop the plane on a command button now, but the plane would disappear from the screen (from radar?). A better practice is to code the DragDrop event for the two command buttons first.

STEP 4: Copy and paste the statements from the Form_DragDrop event procedure into the cmdReset_DragDrop event procedure.

```
Private Sub cmdReset_DragDrop(Source As Control, X As Single, Y As Single)
    'Bad Drop

    imgPlane.Visible = True
End Sub
```

STEP 5: Paste another copy into the DragDrop event for the cmdExit button.

```
Private Sub cmdExit_DragDrop(Source As Control, X As Single, Y As Single)
    'Bad Drop

    imgPlane.Visible = True
End Sub
```

Run the Completed Project

STEP 1: Try each option. Drag the plane and drop it anywhere on the form. Drag it to its hangar and try the Reset button. Then test your Exit button.

Dragging and Dropping Multiple Objects

In the previous example only one object was enabled for drag-and-drop. Recall that the source object becomes invisible in the form's DragOver event procedure. What if the form has more than one possible source object (as in Figure 13.7)? Which object should become invisible? Fortunately, there's an easy answer. Notice the first line of the DragOver event procedure:

```
Private Sub cmdExit_DragOver(Source As Control, X As Single, Y As Single)
```

Figure 13.7

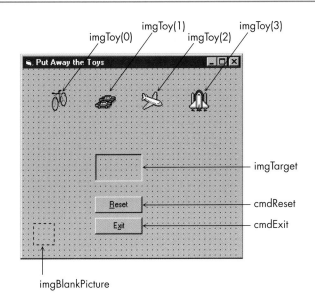

imgToy(0) imgToy(1) imgToy(2) imgToy(3)

imgTarget

cmdReset

cmdExit

imgBlankPicture

All four toy icons on this form can be dragged to the target (a toybox).

The Source argument holds the name of the control that caused the DragOver event to occur. You can use the name *Source* to reference the source control in code.

```
Source.Visible = False
```

Passing the Source Argument

There may be times when you want to call another procedure from a DragOver or a DragDrop event procedure. Recall from the previous example that if a source object is dropped on any control other than the target, it is considered a "bad drop." In a bad drop, the source control must be made visible again. Rather than place identical code in the DragDrop event for all other controls on the form, consider writing one BadDrop sub procedure and calling it wherever necessary. The Source argument that is passed to the DragDrop event procedure can be passed along to the BadDrop sub procedure.

```
Private Sub cmdExit_DragDrop(Source As Control, X As Single, Y As Single)
    'Bad drop

    BadDrop Source 'Call the BadDrop procedure and pass along Source
End Sub
```

```
Private Sub cmdReset_DragDrop(Source As Control, X As Single, Y As Single)
    'Bad drop

    BadDrop Source 'Call the BadDrop procedure and pass along Source
End Sub
```

```
Private Sub BadDrop(Source)
    'Make source control visible

    Source.Visible = True
End Sub
```

Note: In this example the BadDrop sub procedure has only one line of code, so it could be argued that it is efficient to place that line in each DragDrop event. In many situations, such as the chapter hands-on programming example, there are several things to do for a bad drop. In that case it is best to create a separate general sub procedure.

Changing the Icon of the Target Image

In the airplane step-by-step example, a successful drag-and-drop operation caused a second image to become visible. Another approach is to change the icon of the target image. Continuing with the toybox example (Figure 13.7), when a successful drop is made, the icon of the target changes. Notice in the following code how the Picture property of the target is changed to match the Picture property of the source.

```
Private Sub imgTarget_DragDrop(Source As Control, X As Single, Y As Single)
    'Got a hit

    imgTarget.Picture = Source.Picture
End Sub
```

Setting the DragIcon Property of Source Controls

In most cases you want the DragIcon of a source control to be the same as its Picture property. You can set both properties to the same filename in the Properties window, as you did in the earlier step-by-step example. But a better approach is to set only the Picture property at design time. Then in the Form_Load event, set the control's DragIcon property to its Picture property. That way the file is loaded from disk only once.

```
imgPlane.DragIcon = imgPlane.Picture
```

If you have multiple images that can be dragged, consider making them a control array. In the toybox example, the four images are named imgToy(0), imgToy(1), imgToy(2), and imgToy(3). A loop in the Form_Load event procedure will set the DragIcon property for all images. (Note that the number of lines of code remains the same for 15 or 20 or 4 toy images.)

```
Private Sub Form_Load()
    'Set up DragIcon properties
    Dim intCounter As Integer

    For intCounter = 0 To 3
        imgToy(intCounter).DragIcon = imgToy(intCounter).Picture
    Next intCounter
End Sub
```

Blanking Out an Image

If you want to remove an icon from an image, you have two choices. You can either use the LoadPicture function with a blank filename or set the image's Picture property to another (blank) image. The second approach is the more efficient but requires you to place an extra image, with no Picture property, on the form.

Method 1
```
imgTarget.Picture = LoadPicture("")
```

Method 2
```
imgTarget.Picture = imgBlank.Picture
```

Feedback 13.1

1. Name two properties of the source object that should be changed for drag-and-drop operations.
2. To which object does the DragDrop event belong?
3. To which object does the Source argument of the DragOver event refer?

The Toybox Program

Here are the program specifications for the toybox example shown in Figure 13.7. Try entering and running it.

Object	Property	Setting
frmToys	Name	frmToys
	Caption	Put Away the Toys
imgToy(0)	Name	imgToy(0)
	DragMode	1 - Automatic
	Picture	Graphics\Icons\Industry\Bicycle.ico
imgToy(1)	Name	imgToy(1)
	DragMode	1 - Automatic
	Picture	Graphics\Icons\Industry\Cars.ico
imgToy(2)	Name	imgToy(2)
	DragMode	1 - Automatic
	Picture	Graphics\Icons\Industry\Plane.ico
imgToy(3)	Name	imgToy(3)
	DragMode	1 - Automatic
	Picture	Graphics\Icons\Industry\Rocket.ico
imgTarget	Name	imgTarget
	BorderStyle	1 - Fixed Single
	Stretch	True
imgBlank	Name	imgBlank
cmdReset	Name	cmdReset
	Caption	&Reset
cmdExit	Name	cmdExit
	Caption	E&xit

The Procedures

Object	Procedure	Actions
frmToys	Load	Set DragIcon to Picture property for all four images.
	DragOver	Set source control invisible.
	DragDrop	Call BadDrop procedure.

(continued)

Object	Procedure	Actions
imgTarget	DragDrop	Set Picture property to picture of source.
cmdExit	Click	Exit the project.
	DragDrop	Call BadDrop procedure.
cmdReset	Click	Set Visible = True for all four images. Set Picture property of target to blank.
	DragDrop	Call BadDrop procedure.
General	BadDrop	Set Visible = True for source image.

The Project Coding Solution

```
'Program:              Toybox Drag-and-Drop Example
'Programmer:           J.C. Bradley
'Date:                 September 1999
'Purpose:              Drag-and-drop multiple objects.
'Folder:               Ch1302

Option Explicit


Private Sub cmdExit_Click()
    'Exit the project

    Unload me
    End
End Sub


Private Sub cmdExit_DragDrop(Source As Control, X As Single, Y As Single)
    'Bad drop

    BadDrop Source
End Sub


Private Sub cmdReset_Click()
    'Replace images
    Dim intCounter As Integer

    For intCounter = 0 To 3
        imgToy(intCounter).Visible = True
    Next intCounter
    imgTarget.Picture = imgBlank.Picture
End Sub
```

```
Private Sub cmdReset_DragDrop(Source As Control, X As Single, Y As Single)
    'Bad drop

    BadDrop Source
End Sub
```

```
Private Sub Form_DragDrop(Source As Control, X As Single, Y As Single)
    'Bad drop

    BadDrop Source
End Sub
```

```
Private Sub Form_DragOver(Source As Control, X As Single, _
        Y As Single, State As Integer)
    'Make the source control invisible

    Source.Visible = False
End Sub
```

```
Private Sub Form_Load()
    'Set up DragIcon properties
    Dim intCounter As Integer

    For intCounter = 0 To 3
        imgToy(intCounter).DragIcon = imgToy(intCounter).Picture
    Next intCounter
End Sub
```

```
Private Sub BadDrop(Source)
    'Make source control visible

    Source.Visible = True
End Sub
```

```
Private Sub imgTarget_DragDrop(Source As Control, X As Single, Y As Single)
    'Got a hit

    imgTarget.Picture = Source.Picture
End Sub
```

Your Hands-On Programming Example

This drag-and-drop example combines many of the techniques from the chapter. In addition, you must change target icons more than once. Figure 13.8 shows a sketch of the form; Figures 13.9, 13.10, and 13.11 show the form during run time.

Figure 13.8

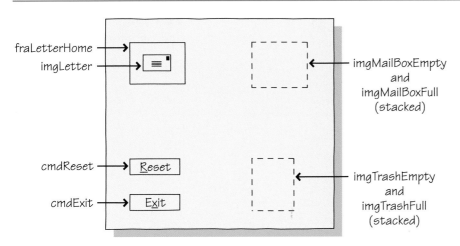

The planning sketch for the hands-on programming example.

Figure 13.9

The form as it appears when the project begins execution.

Figure 13.10

When the letter is placed in the mailbox, the flag goes up.

When the letter is dropped on the mailbox, the icon changes to a mailbox with the flag up and a letter inside. The letter can be dragged from the mailbox and dropped in the trash can or back in its original frame. When the letter is dropped in the trash can, the icon changes to a trash can with visible trash inside. The letter can also be dragged out of the trash can and dropped either on the mailbox or on the letter's original frame.

Because you want to drag a letter from the mailbox or the trash can, the DragIcon property of each must be set to the same icon as the letter image. (You want to drag a picture of a letter, not a picture of a trash can.)

The two icons for the mailbox are stored in two image controls—one visible and one invisible. Manipulating the two images gets a little tricky but remember what you learned about multiple controls: You can select multiple controls by dragging a selection box around them or Ctrl-click on them, or you can set similar properties on multiple selected controls in the Properties window (such as their Top, Left, and Width properties). You can also select one control and choose *Send to Back* or *Bring to Front* on the *Edit* menu.

The two image controls for the trash cans are developed in the same way as the mailboxes.

Planning the Project

Sketch the form, which is shown in Figure 13.8.

Plan the Objects and Properties

Object	Property	Setting
frmMail	Name	frmMail
	Caption	Mail the Letter
fraLetterHome	Name	fraLetterHome
	Caption	(blank)
imgLetter	Name	imgLetter
	DragMode	1 - Automatic
	Stretch	True
	Picture	Graphics\Icons\Mail\Mail02a.ico
imgMailBoxEmpty	Name	imgMailBoxEmpty
	Stretch	True
	Picture	Graphics\Icons\Mail\Mail16a.ico
imgMailBoxFull	Name	imgMailBoxFull
	Stretch	True
	Picture	Graphics\Icons\Mail\Mail16b.ico
	DragMode	1 - Automatic
	Visible	False
imgTrashEmpty	Name	imgTrashEmpty
	Stretch	True
	Picture	Graphics\Icons\Computer\Trash04b.ico
imgTrashFull	Name	imgTrashFull
	Stretch	True
	Picture	Graphics\Icons\Computer\Trash04a.ico
	DragMode	1 - Automatic
	Visible	False
cmdReset	Name	cmdReset
	Caption	&Reset
cmdExit	Name	cmdExit
	Caption	E&xit

Plan the Event Procedures

Plan the actions for the event procedures.

Object	Procedure	Actions
frmMail	Load	Set DragIcon of imgLetter, imgMailboxFull, and imgTrashFull to imgLetter.Picture.

	DragOver	Case imgLetter
		   Set Visible = False for imgLetter.
		Case imgTrashFull
		   Set Visible = False for imgTrashFull.
		   Set Visible = True for imgTrashEmpty.
		Case imgMailBoxFull
		   Set Visible = False for imgMailBoxFull.
		   Set Visible = True for imgMailBoxEmpty.

	DragDrop	Call BadDrop procedure.
imgMailBoxEmpty	DragDrop	Set Visible = False for imgMailBoxEmpty. Set Visible = True for imgMailBoxFull.
imgTrashEmpty	DragDrop	Set Visible = False for imgTrashEmpty. Set Visible = True for imgTrashFull.
fraLetterHome	DragDrop	Set Visible = True for imgLetter.
cmdExit	Click	Unload the form. Exit the project.
	DragDrop	Call BadDrop procedure.

cmdReset	Click	Set Visible = True for imgLetter,
		   imgMailBoxEmpty, and imgTrashEmpty.
		Set Visible = False for imgMailBoxFull
		   and imgTrashFull

	DragDrop	Call BadDrop procedure.

General sub procedure	BadDrop	Case imgLetter
		   Set Visible = True for imgLetter.
		Case imgTrashFull
		   Set Visible = True for imgTrashFull.
		   Set Visible = False for imgTrashEmpty.
		Case imgMailBoxFull
		   Set Visible = True for imgMailBoxFull.
		   Set Visible = False for imgTrashEmpty.

Write the Project

Follow the sketch in Figure 13.8 to create the form. Figures 13.9, 13.10, and 13.11 show the completed form at different stages of run time.

Set the properties of each object according to your plan.

The next step is to write the code. Working from the pseudocode, write each event procedure.

When you complete the code, thoroughly test the project by dragging the letter to each target and resetting from each position.

The Project Coding Solution

```
'Program:                Drag-and-Drop Hands-On Example
'Programmer:             J.C. Bradley
'Date:                   September 1999
'Purpose:                Mail or trash a letter using drag-and-drop.
'Folder:                 Ch1303

Option Explicit


Private Sub cmdExit_Click()
    'Exit the project

    Unload me
    End
End Sub


Private Sub cmdExit_DragDrop(Source As Control, X As Single, Y As Single)
    'Bad drop

    BadDrop Source
End Sub


Private Sub cmdReset_Click()
    'Initialize setup

    imgLetter.Visible = True
    imgMailBoxEmpty.Visible = True
    imgMailboxFull.Visible = False
    imgTrashEmpty.Visible = True
    imgTrashFull.Visible = False
End Sub


Private Sub cmdReset_DragDrop(Source As Control, X As Single, Y As Single)
    'Bad drop

    BadDrop Source
End Sub


Private Sub Form_DragDrop(Source As Control, X As Single, Y As Single)
    'Bad drop

    BadDrop Source
End Sub
```

```vb
Private Sub Form_DragOver(Source As Control, X As Single, _
         Y As Single, State As Integer)
    'Check source of DragOver and determine action

    Select Case Source
        Case imgLetter
            imgLetter.Visible = False
        Case imgTrashFull
            imgTrashFull.Visible = False
            imgTrashEmpty.Visible = True
        Case imgMailboxFull
            imgMailboxFull.Visible = False
            imgMailBoxEmpty.Visible = True
    End Select
End Sub
```

```vb
Private Sub Form_Load()
    'Set DragIcon to Letter

    imgLetter.DragIcon = imgLetter.Picture
    imgMailboxFull.DragIcon = imgLetter.Picture
    imgTrashFull.DragIcon = imgLetter.Picture
End Sub
```

```vb
Private Sub fraLetterHome_DragDrop(Source As Control, X As Single, _
         Y As Single)
    'Good drop

    imgLetter.Visible = True
End Sub
```

```vb
Private Sub imgMailBoxEmpty_DragDrop(Source As Control, X As Single, _
         Y As Single)
    'Good drop

    imgMailBoxEmpty.Visible = False
    imgMailboxFull.Visible = True
End Sub
```

```vb
Private Sub imgTrashEmpty_DragDrop(Source As Control, X As Single, _
         Y As Single)
    'Good drop

    imgTrashEmpty.Visible = False
    imgTrashFull.Visible = True
End Sub
```

```
Private Sub BadDrop(Source As Control)
    'Reset source after a bad drop

    Select Case Source
        Case imgLetter
            imgLetter.Visible = True
        Case imgTrashFull
            imgTrashFull.Visible = True
            imgTrashEmpty.Visible = False
        Case imgMailboxFull
            imgMailboxFull.Visible = True
            imgMailBoxEmpty.Visible = False
    End Select
End Sub
```

Programming Hints

Manual Drag-and-Drop

Sometimes you don't want to set the DragMode property of controls to True, because then normal mouse clicks and keystrokes are not recognized for that control. You can use the **Drag method** to drag-and-drop in code. For example, you can begin a Drag operation in the MouseDown event for a control (a text box in this example).

```
Private Sub txtEntry_MouseDown(Button As Integer, Shift As Integer, _
            X As Single, Y As Single)
    txtEntry.Drag
End Sub
```

This action begins a drag operation that behaves just like the automatic dragging in the chapter examples.

S u m m a r y

1. In a drag-and-drop operation, the control being dragged is the source, and the destination is the target.
2. Set the source control's DragMode property and DragIcon property.
3. The DragOver event and DragDrop event belong to the target control. DragOver occurs as the source control is moving over the target; DragDrop occurs when the mouse button is released over the target.
4. The system passes the name of the source control to the DragOver and DragDrop event procedures.

K e y   T e r m s

Drag method   *551*   DragOver event   *532*

DragDrop event   *532*   source   *532*

DragIcon property   *532*   target   *532*

DragMode property   *532*

R e v i e w   Q u e s t i o n s

1. Explain the differences between the source and target in a drag-and-drop operation.
2. Which properties must be set for the source control in order to do drag-and-drop?
3. An image of a car is dragged across the form and dropped on an image of a garage. Describe the events that occur (and the objects to which they belong) as the operation takes place.
4. In a form's DragOver event, it is necessary to make the source control invisible. How can you determine which control is the source control?

P r o g r a m m i n g   E x e r c i s e s

13.1 Write a drag-and-drop program to play a game of darts. Use the icon files Graphics\Icons\Misc\Bullseye.ico and Graphics\Icons\Point10.ico. Place an invisible dart in the center of the target and make it visible when the target is hit. Also, keep track of the number of hits and display a running count.

The Reset button should reset the dart to its starting location.

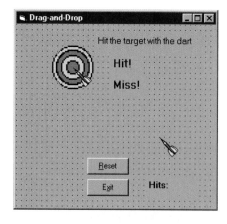

13.2 Create a project for a card-suit guessing game. The user will drag the images to the boxes along the lower edge of the form. When the correct image is placed in a box, make the image remain there. When all four images are in the correct location, display a message box congratulating the user. The Reset button should replace the suit images at the top of the form and clear out the lower boxes. (*Hint:* For the boxes, use image controls with a border.) Consider using control arrays.

The four images are in the Graphics\Icons\Misc folder and are called Misc34.ico, Misc35.ico, Misc36.ico, and Misc37.ico.

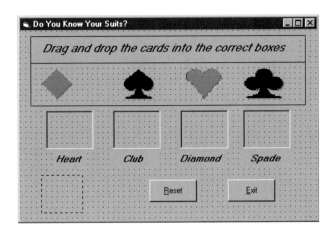

13.3 Create a project that keeps track of the food for the company picnic. The user will enter each person's name into the text box and then drag it to the correct list. Use drag-and-drop to move the names to the lists. (*Hint:* Use AddItem in the DragDrop event procedure.)

Do not allow a blank name to be added to a list; keep the three lists in alphabetic order; clear out the text box and set the focus after adding a name to one of the lists.

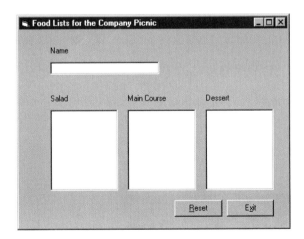

13.4 Modify project 13.3 to include a menu bar. Include a *Print* command with a submenu to select the item (salads, main courses, or desserts). Allow the user to print any of the lists, one at a time.

13.5 Create your own drag-and-drop application using graphic files available to you (or create your own using a draw or paint program). You can use files with the extensions .ico, .wmf, .bmp, .dib, .gif, .jpg, .emf, and .cur.

CASE STUDIES

VB Mail Order

Create a form that allows the user to select express delivery or freight through the use of drag-and-drop. Include a label that will display the words *Express Delivery—overnight* or *Freight—10 working days* after the user drops the appropriate icon in the mailbox.

For this project the empty mailbox (Mail16a.ico) is the empty target. The source will be Mail05b.ico for freight and Mail03.ico for express. When the selected type of delivery reaches the target, change the empty mailbox to have the flag up (Mail16b.ico).

VB Auto Center

Create a game project using drag-and-drop for the VB Auto Center. The form will contain the following images:

Graphics\Icons\Traffic\Trffc16.ico in the upper-left corner.
Graphics\Icons\Misc\Face01.ico in the upper-right corner (visible to begin).

Arranged horizontally across the center of the screen:

Graphics\Icons\Industry\Wrench.ico
Graphics\Icons\Industry\Gaspump.ico
Graphics\Icons\Elements\Water.ico

At the bottom of the screen:

Graphics\Icons\Misc\House.ico at the lower-left corner.
Graphics\Icons\Misc\Face03.ico at the lower-right corner (invisible to begin).

The car may be dragged to the icons only in the proper order before it goes home. The correct order: wrench for service, gas pump, and then water for the car wash. When the drops have been made in the proper order and the vehicle gets home, the top face becomes invisible and the lower face becomes visible.

Video Bonanza

Design an interface that contains a text box for movie titles and two list boxes, one labeled DVD and the other Videotapes. The user should be able to type a title and then drag it and drop it in either list box.

Include a *File* menu with options for *Print, Clear,* and *Exit.* The *Print* option should contain a submenu allowing the user to print a list of DVD titles or a list of videotape titles.

Very Very Boards

Very Very Boards keeps a weather forecast poster on the wall. Create a project using drag-and-drop that will display an icon for the forecast for each day of the week.

Use frames for each day of the week, and another frame that holds the icon from which to choose. Allow the user to drag an icon to each day of the week to show the weather forecast. Since each icon may be used more than once, do not hide the icon being dragged (the source).

Provide menu commands to reset the forecast, print the form, and exit.

You can find the weather icon files in Microsoft Visual Studio \ Common \ Graphics \ Icons. The file-names are Cloud.ico, Litening.ico, Rain.ico, Snow.ico, and Sun.ico.

14

Graphics

At the completion of this chapter, you will be able to . . .

1. Understand the measurements in the graphics coordinate system.

2. Display and change colors using the RGB and QBColor functions.

3. Create graphics using graphics methods.

4. Understand the graphics-layering principles.

5. Load and change pictures at run time.

6. Create simple animation.

7. Use the timer control.

8. Use scroll bars to move and resize an image.

In past chapters you learned how to incorporate graphics using the shape, image, and line controls. In this chapter you will learn how to enhance the use of the controls and to use the graphics methods. New controls include the picturebox, the timer, and scroll bar controls.

The Graphics Environment

The measurement system you use in a project is known as the *scale*. You can set the scale to twips, points, pixels, inches, or centimeters, or you can create your own scale.

The default scale is twips. A **twip** is ½₀ of a point. Because a **point** is a printer's measurement of ½₂ of an inch, a twip is ½₁₄₄₀ of an inch; in other words, an inch has 1,440 twips.

The term **pixel** is an abbreviation of *picture element*, a dot that makes up a picture. You are probably most familiar with pixels in the determination of the resolution of a monitor. A display of 1,280 by 1,024 is a reference to the number of pixels horizontally and vertically.

You can change the scale with the ScaleMode property. The examples in this chapter are based on twips.

The Coordinate System

Graphics are measured from a starting point of 0,0 for the *x* and *y* coordinates beginning in the upper-left corner. The *x* is the horizontal position, and *y* is the vertical measurement. The starting point depends on where the graphic is being placed. If the graphic is going directly on a form, the 0,0 coordinates are the upper-left corner of the form. You can also place graphics in containers, such as pictureboxes. In this case the picturebox has its own 0,0 **coordinate system** to be used as the starting point for measuring the location of items within the control (Figure 14.1).

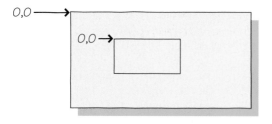

The coordinates for graphics begin with 0,0 in the upper-left corner of a form or container.

You can change the starting point of the coordinate system, the scale, or both. You control these with the ScaleLeft, ScaleTop, ScaleWidth, and ScaleHeight properties. For more information on changing these properties refer to the Help files in Visual Basic.

Picturebox Controls

The **picturebox control** is very similar to the image control, but a picturebox does not contain a Stretch property. However, it does have many other properties for graphics including those relating to the scale. Pictureboxes use more system resources than images use. For that reason, the recommended practice is to use an image control unless you need the added capabilities of a picturebox.

Figure 14.2 shows the toolbox tool for creating a picturebox, and Figure 14.3 shows a picturebox on a form. The three-character prefix for a picturebox name is "pic". Use the chart on the inside back cover of the text to compare the properties that apply to the image and to the picturebox.

The picturebox tool from the toolbox.

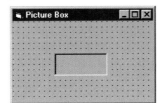

A picturebox control on a form.

Colors

You can specify colors for your graphics in a number of ways. The graphic controls have properties for ForeColor, BackColor, and FillColor. The VB graphics methods use the RGB color functions or the intrinsic color constants (such as vbRed and vbBlue).

The RGB Function

The **RGB function** specifies the quantities of red, green, and blue for the largest variety of colors. The value for each color ranges from 0 to 255, with 0 being the least intense. The color arguments are in the same order as their letters in the function name—red, green, and then blue. You can use the function to assign a color to a property or specify the color in a graphics method. Table 14.1 shows the RGB values for a few colors.

Color	Red Value	Green Value	Blue Value
Black	0	0	0
Blue	0	0	255
Green	0	255	0
Cyan	0	255	255
Red	255	0	0
Magenta	255	0	255
Yellow	255	255	0
White	255	255	255

The RGB values for some standard colors.

The RGB Function—General Form

```
RGB(RedValue, GreenValue, BlueValue)
```

The RGB Function—Examples

```
lblWarning.BackColor = RGB(255, 0, 0)          'Red
txtName.Forecolor = RGB(255, 0, 255)           'Blue and red make magenta
Line (0, 0) - (1000, 1000), RGB(100, 100, 100) 'A gray line
```

The Visual Basic Intrinsic Color Constants

You can use the VB color constants introduced in Chapter 2 to specify colors for properties and for drawing graphics using the graphics methods. The color constants are

vbBlack
vbBlue
vbGreen
vbCyan
vbRed
vbMagenta
vbYellow
vbWhite

The QBColor Function

For compatibility with older versions of Basic, VB allows you to use color numbers that range from 0 to 15. To use these color numbers you must use the **QBColor function**, which converts the color numbers to their RGB equivalent.

Example

```
frmMyForm.BackColor = QBColor(1) 'Blue
```

Table 14.2 shows the 16 color numbers that you can use with the QBColor function.

T a b l e   1 4 . 2

The QBColor *numbers, included in VB for compatibility with older versions of Basic.*

Number	Color
0	Black
1	Blue
2	Green
3	Cyan
4	Red
5	Magenta
6	Yellow
7	White
8	Gray
9	Light Blue
10	Light Green
11	Light Cyan
12	Light Red
13	Light Magenta
14	Light Yellow
15	Bright White

The Graphics Methods

You can use the graphics methods to draw in a Form object, a Picturebox object, or the Printer object. The object you choose becomes the **container** for your graphics. If you omit the name of the object, it defaults to the form.

Using the graphics methods, such as Cls, Pset, Line, and Circle to draw graphics differs from using the graphics controls. Controls, such as shapes, lines, and images, appear on the form as it loads. If the form is resized or covered by another window and redisplayed, the graphics controls reappear. But the graphics you draw with code display when the code is executed. They do not redraw automatically. Therefore, if you want your graphics to redisplay each time the form is redisplayed, place the statements in the Paint event for the form or picturebox. You may also place graphics methods in a user event such as a command button's Click event.

The Cls Method

The **Cls method** clears the specified object. You could use Cls to clear an existing picture and change the background color of the form or picturebox. Remember that if the object is omitted on any of the graphics methods, the default is the form.

The CLS Method—General Form

```
[Object].Cls
```

The CLS Method—Examples

```
Cls                         'Clear the background of the form
picLogo.Cls                 'Clear a picture box
```

The PSet Method

The **PSet method** places a single point on the object in the location specified by the x and y coordinates. You may also specify the color for the point.

The PSet Method—General Form

```
[Object].PSet (x, y)[, Color]
```

The PSet Method—Examples

```
picLogo.PSet (100, 100)
PSet (1000, 1000), vbCyan
```

When the color is omitted, the ForeColor property setting of the object is used. The x and y coordinates may also be variables.

The **Rnd function** returns "random" numbers between 0 and the upper limit specified. Try the following code from the Ch1401 programming example, which demonstrates the use of the Rnd function. Figure 14.4 shows the screen generated by this code.

```
'Program:        PSet
'Programmer:     A. Millspaugh
'Date:           December 1999
'Description:    Place colored dots randomly on the
'                form.
'Folder:         Ch1401

Option Explicit

Private Sub cmdExit_Click()
    'Terminate the Project

    Unload Me
    End
End Sub

Private Sub Form_Paint()
    'Place random dots in random colors on form

    Dim intIndex As Integer
    Dim intColor As Integer
    Dim X, Y

    For intIndex = 1 To 1000
        X = Rnd * ScaleWidth
        Y = Rnd * ScaleHeight
        intColor = Rnd * 15
        PSet (X, Y), QBColor(intColor)
    Next intIndex
End Sub
```

The **DrawWidth property** determines the size of the point. Change the DrawWidth of the form in the Ch1401 PSet program to 5. Next try changing the form WindowState to Maximized and experiment with the ScaleHeight and ScaleWidth properties.

You can try this again, placing the dots within an object using Object.Width and Object.Height to control the upper limit.

If you wish to erase a point, place a new point on top of the old one using the BackColor property as the color.

The Line Method

Because a line is used to connect two points, the **Line method** needs two sets of coordinates specified for the line. If the first coordinate is not specified, the line is drawn from the last graphics point created on the screen.

The Line Method—General Form

```
[Object].Line [(x1, y1)]-(x2, y2)[, [Color][, B [ F ] ] ]
```

The Line Method—Examples

```
Printer.Line (5, 0)-(5,1000)
picLogo.Line - (500,100), QBColor(2)
picLogo.Line - (500,300), vbBlue
Line (intXStart, intYStart)-(intXEnd, intYEnd), intLineColor
```

This program draws an *X* in a picturebox called picX. (See Figure 14.5.)

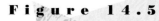

F i g u r e   1 4 . 5

The screen for project Ch1402.

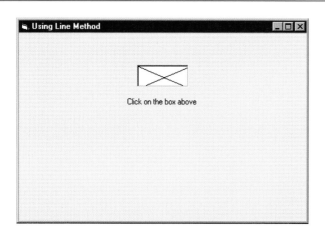

```
'Program:              Line
'Programmer:           A. Millspaugh
'Date:                 December 1999
'Description:          Draw lines in a picture box.
'Folder:               Ch1402

Option Explicit

Private Sub picX_Click()
    'Create an X in the picture box

    picX.Line (0, 0)-(picX.Width, picX.Height)
    picX.Line (0, picX.Height)-(picX.Width, 0)
End Sub
```

Rectangles

You can also use the Line method to create boxes by adding the *B* parameter. The *B* stands for *box*. You can fill a box without specifying a color; the box will use the FillColor property. However, make sure to include the commas to indicate that the color argument is missing.

```
Line ( 0, 0)-(500, 500), ,B
```

The box may be filled with a solid color or a pattern, depending on the setting of the FillStyle property.

FillStyle	Name	Pattern
0	Solid	Uses the FillColor to fill the box.
1	Transparent (default)	No fill regardless of the FillColor setting.
2	Horizontal lines	
3	Vertical lines	
4	Upward diagonal lines	
5	Downward diagonal lines	
6	Crosshatch	
7	Diagonal crosshatch	

The *F* option listed in the general form of the Line method may be used to *fill* the box, instead of using the FillStyle and the FillColor properties. You cannot use the *F* option without the *B*.

The Circle Method

You can draw rounded shapes using the **Circle method**. These shapes include circles, ovals, arcs, and pie-shaped wedges. To draw a circle, specify

Tip

Use the Line method with the Printer object to add interest to your output.

the coordinates of the center and the radius of the circle. You may also specify the color or let it default to the ForeColor.

```
picFace.Circle (160,100), 60
```

You can choose whether or not the circle is filled by setting the FillStyle property.

```
FillStyle = 0
Circle (1000, 1000), 500      'A filled circle
FillStyle = 1
Circle (2000, 1000), 500      'Outline of a circle
```

The full form of the `Circle` method includes an argument for start angle and end angle that will determine arcs and wedges. The aspect ratio argument is used to make ellipses (ovals).

The Circle Method—General Form

```
[Object].Circle (x, y), Radius [, Color [, StartAngle, EndAngle [, AspectRatio] ] ]
```

Arcs of a Circle

To draw parts of a circle, you can specify the beginning and ending points of the arc. The endpoints for the arc are determined by a measurement in radians, counterclockwise from 0 to 2 PI. The angle reference is illustrated below:

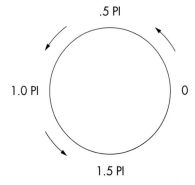

The statements

```
Const PI = 3.14159
Circle (500, 500), 500, , 0, PI
```

draw the top half of a circle, beginning at the right side (angle 0) and proceeding over the top to the left side (angle PI).

The following program uses circles and arcs to draw a happy face. Place the code in the form's Paint event. (See Figure 14.6.)

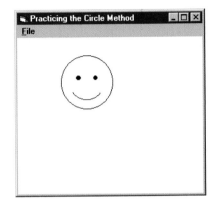

The screen for project Ch1403.

```
'Program:          Circle
'Programmer:       A. Millspaugh
'Date:             December 1999
'Description:       Draw a happy face.
'Folder:           Ch1403


Option Explicit


Private Sub Form_Paint()
    'Draw a happy face on the form
    Const PI = 3.14159

    FillStyle = 1
    Circle (1600, 1000), 600             'Outline of the face
    Circle (1600, 1000), 400, , PI * 1.2, PI * 1.8 'Smile
    FillStyle = 0
    Circle (1400, 900), 50, vbBlue       'Left eye
    Circle (1800, 900), 50, vbBlue       'Right eye
End Sub


Private Sub mnuFileExit_Click()
    'Terminate the project

    Unload Me
    End
End Sub
```

Segments of a Pie

You can draw an arc with its endpoints connected to the center of the circle, creating a slice of pie. If you specify an endpoint as a negative number, a radius is drawn from the endpoint to the center point. *Note:* The minus sign preceding the endpoint specifies the radius; not a negative angle.

```
Circle (50, 100), 30, , -PI / 2, -PI
```

will produce

Ellipses

By setting the AspectRatio parameter of the `Circle` method, you can draw ellipses and elliptical arcs. The aspect ratio refers to the comparative length of a radius drawn vertically to a radius drawn horizontally. When this parameter is omitted, the aspect ratio is assumed to be one and the figure drawn is a circle. When the aspect ratio is less than one, the elliptical figure will be wider than it is tall. When the aspect ratio is greater than one, the ellipse will display taller than it is wide. (Notice the commas in the statements that indicate omitted parameters.)

```
Circle (1000,1000), 1000, , , , .5       'Wide ellipse
Circle (3000,1000), 1000, , , , 1.5      'Tall ellipse
```

Give the preceding lines of code a try.

The Step Keyword

Each graphics method discussed here can also use the **Step method**, which changes the coordinates from an absolute position to a relative position. Coordinates are normally measured from the starting point of the object (**absolute position**) on which they are drawn. By adding the `Step`, coordinates begin from the last point that was drawn, hence the starting point is a **relative position**.

A variation of the `PSet` method is the `PSet Step` statement that indicates that the *x* and *y* coordinates specified are relative to the last point drawn. The statement

```
PSet Step (100, 100)
```

draws a point 100 twips to the right and 100 twips down from the last point specified in a graphics method. If there are no previous graphics methods, the offset is from the 0, 0 coordinate.

With the `Line` method you can give the second set of coordinates as an offset from the first.

```
Line -Step(1000, 1000)
```

Try the following lines of code:

```
PSet Step(100, 100)
Line -Step(1000, 1000)
Line -Step(2000, 0)
```

Feedback 14.1

1. Write the statement to draw a vertical line down the center of a form that has the following settings: ScaleWidth 6720, ScaleHeight 4230.
2. Write the statements to draw a Pacman.

Layering

When displaying information on an object, different types of items are placed on different layers. The complete set of layers produces the output that we can see. (See Figure 14.7.)

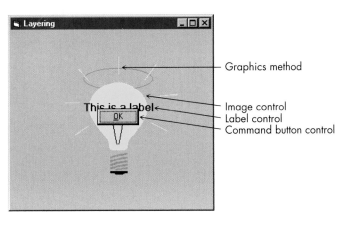

Most controls appear on the top layer, graphics controls appear on the middle layer, and graphics created with graphics methods appear on the bottom layer.

Layer	Contents
Front	Command buttons, check boxes, and other nongraphic controls.
Middle	Labels; graphics controls.
Back	Shapes created with graphics methods.

The items in the back layer are covered by items in the middle layer, which are then covered by controls in the front layer. Usually this arrangement is what you want, allowing your graphics to form a background for the controls. However, these default layers may behave differently depending on the settings of the AutoRedraw and ClipControls properties, which contain Boolean values, and on whether the graphics methods are located in the Paint event or elsewhere.

If you set the container's **AutoRedraw property** to True, you will get **persistent graphics**, which save an image in memory so that it can be redisplayed. Although Windows takes care of windows and controls when objects are moved or resized, it is up to you to control the redraw for graphics. Although it sounds easy to just set AutoRedraw to True, there is a trade-off in performance because the process requires a large amount of memory. The default setting of AutoRedraw is False for forms and True for pictureboxes. It is to your advantage to place graphic images in pictureboxes rather than on forms because less memory is required.

One technique is to leave AutoRedraw set to False and call the Paint event procedure when needed.

The **clipping region** determines which portions of the screen will be painted. A form, frame, or picturebox has a **ClipControls property**. Setting ClipControls to False can also speed up the repainting process but may cause items to be mixed in the layering.

Use these guidelines for redrawing graphics:

1. When AutoRedraw is set to False, place graphics methods in the Paint event of the form or container.
2. Setting AutoRedraw to True always provides normal layering but will slow the performance because too much memory is required. (Setting ClipControls to False may speed up the form display.)

You can also adjust the stacking order of items within a layer using the **ZOrder method**. This method can be used for forms or controls. Refer to Help for more information on the `ZOrder` method.

More Properties for Your Graphics Controls

You have used icons for the Picture property of an image control. Pictures in the form of bitmaps, icons, or metafiles may be added to a project during design time or at run time. You can create your own pictures in a Paint or Draw program and then copy and paste them using the Clipboard. Pictures may be placed in an image control, a picturebox control, or a form.

Controlling Pictures at Design Time

All three controls that can contain a picture have a Picture property. If you set the Picture property of a form, the graphic displays behind the controls. An advantage of using the image control rather than the picturebox control is that an image has a Stretch property that can be used to adjust the size of the picture when set to True.

Another way to insert a picture in a control is by using the Clipboard. First copy a picture from clip art or one that you created into the Clipboard. Then switch to Visual Basic and the *Paste* command on the *Edit* menu will be available to transfer the picture from the Clipboard onto the control.

To remove a picture, double-click the setting in the Picture property and press the Delete key.

Controlling Pictures at Run Time

You may also want to add or change a picture at run time. You can do so by having images or pictures that have their original Visible property set to False or by using the **LoadPicture function**.

If you store a picture in an invisible control, you can change the Visible setting to True; or you may decide to copy it to another control.

```
picLogo.Visible = True
imgLogo.Picture = picLogo.Picture
```

You can use the LoadPicture function to retrieve a file during run time. The problem with this method is that the path must be known. When you are running an application on multiple systems, the path names may vary.

```
picLogo.Picture = LoadPicture("C:\VB\LOGO.BMP")
```

To remove a picture from the display, either hide it or use the LoadPicture function with empty quotes.

```
imgLogo.Visible = False
picLogo.Picture = LoadPicture("")
```

Moving a Picture

You can move picture controls by changing the values of the Left and Top properties. Another choice is the **Move method**. Since line controls do not have Top and Left properties, you must use the Move method to move them. The Move method produces a smoother appearing move than changing the Top and Left properties of controls.

The Move Method—General Form

```
[Object].Move Left [, Top[, Width[, Height]]]
```

Only the new setting for the Left property is required, but the Top, Width, and Height may also be changed. If no object is specified, the move applies to the current form.

The Move Method—Examples

```
Move 100                          'Changes the Left property of the current form
imgLogo.Move 100, 200
imgLogo.Move imgLogo.Left + 50    'Moves relative to current position
```

Notice that a move can be relative to the current location by performing calculations in the Move method.

Simple Animation

You can create animation by toggling between two pictures, moving a picture, or rotating through a series of pictures. You can also create graphics with the various graphics methods.

Many of the icons in the icon library have similar sizes but opposite states such as a closed file cabinet and an open file cabinet; a mail box with the flag up and with the flag down; a closed envelope and an open envelope; or a traffic light in red, yellow, or green. In Chapter 2 you used the two light bulbs: LightOn and LightOff.

This sample program demonstrates switching between two phone icons (a phone and a phone being held). The two icons are Phone12.ico and Phone13.ico in the Graphics\Icons\Comm folder. Two images, imgWithHand and imgNoHand, are set to invisible (Visible = False) and then assigned to imgPhone at run time. (See Figure 14.8.)

F i g u r e   1 4 . 8

The screen for project Ch1404.

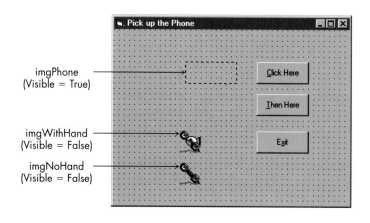

```
'Program:      Phones
'Programmer:   A. Millspaugh
'Date:         December 1999
'Description:  Change a picture of a phone to
'              show someone holding it.
'Folder:       Ch1404

Option Explicit
```

```
Private Sub cmdChange_Click()
    'Change the phones

    imgPhone.Picture = imgWithHand.Picture
End Sub
```

```
Private Sub cmdExit_Click()
    'Terminate the project

    Unload Me
    End
End Sub
```

```
Private Sub cmdStart_Click()
    'Display the phone

    imgPhone.Picture = imgNoHand.Picture
End Sub
```

The Timer Control

You can cause events to occur at a set interval using the **timer control** and its Timer event. Place the control anywhere on the form; it is invisible at run time. The tool for the timer control is represented by the little stopwatch in the toolbox (Figure 14.9). The three-character prefix for naming a timer is "tmr".

Figure 14.9

The tool for the timer control.

When you have a timer control on a form, it "fires" each time an interval elapses. You can place any desired code in the Timer event procedure; the code executes each time the event occurs. You choose the interval for the timer by setting its **Interval property**, which can have a value of 0 to 65,535. This value specifies the number of milliseconds between the calls to the Timer event. One second is equivalent to 1,000 milliseconds. Therefore, for a 3-second delay, set the timer's Interval property to 3,000. You can set the value at run time or at design time.

You can keep the Timer event from occurring by setting its **Enabled property** to False. The default value is True.

Your Hands-On Programming Example

In this project you will use a timer control to create simple animation. Place an airplane icon in an image control, move it across the screen, and also make it appear larger as it goes.

First, sketch a plan of the form (Figure 14.10).

A planning sketch for the hands-on programming example.

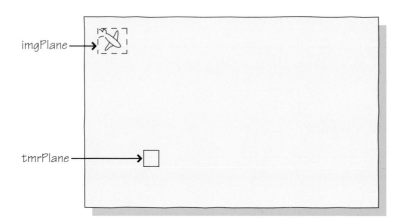

Plan the Objects and Properties

Object	Property	Setting
frmPlane	Name	frmPlane
	Caption	Fly the Plane
tmrPlane	Name	tmrPlane
	Interval	50
imgPlane	Name	imgPlane
	Icon	Graphics\Icons\Industry\Plane.ico

Plan the Event Procedures

Plan the actions for the event procedure.

Procedure	Actions
tmrPlane_Timer	Move the plane.
	Adjust the size.

Write the Project

● Follow the sketch in Figure 14.10 to create the form. Figure 14.11 shows the completed form.

● Set the properties of each object according to your plan.

● Write the code. Working from the pseudocode, write each event procedure.

● Thoroughly test the project.

The form for the hands-on programming example.

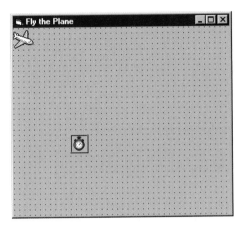

The Programming Coding Solution

```
'Program:        Plane
'Programmer:     A. Millspaugh
'Date:           December 1999
'Description:    Move a plane with the timer.
'Folder:         Ch1405


Option Explicit


Private Sub tmrPlane_Timer()
    'Fly the Plane

    imgPlane.Move imgPlane.Left + 10, _
                  imgPlane.Top + 10, _
                  imgPlane.Width + 2, _
                  imgPlane.Height + 2
End Sub
```

More Graphics Techniques

Custom Coordinate Systems

You can specify a custom scale for your graphics by changing the coordinate system. Perhaps you would like the upper-left corner to start at 0,0 and the lower-right corner to be 100,100. Then all your coordinates for graphics will be between 0 and 100. This change can be accomplished with the Scale method.

The Scale Method—General Form

```
[Object].Scale (x1 , y1) - (x2, y2)
```

The Scale Method—Example

```
picLogo.Scale (0, 0) - (100, 100)
```

The handy result of this statement is that you could then use ratios. The midpoint would be (50, 50).

The Scale method performs the same function as individually altering the settings in ScaleLeft, ScaleTop, ScaleWidth, and ScaleHeight.

PaintPicture Method

Another graphics method that you have available is the **PaintPicture method**, which can be used to place a graphic file on a form, on the printer object, or in a picturebox.

This method is faster than moving picture controls around and can be used to copy graphics, such as when tiling a picture on the screen. You can flip the graphic horizontally by making the destination width a negative number.

The PaintPicture Method—General Form

```
[Object].PaintPicture Picture, x1, y1[, DestinationWidth, _
    DestinationHeight]
```

The PaintPicture Method—Example

```
PaintPicture picLogo.Picture, 100, 100
```

The following program creates a tiled image on the form (Figure 14.12).

Figure 14.12

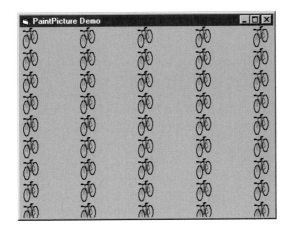

The form for example Ch1406.

```
'Program:           Tile
'Programmer:        A. Millspaugh
'Date:              December 1999
'Description:       Create a tiled background on a form.
'Folder:            Ch1406

Option Explicit


Private Sub Form_Paint()
    'Tile the background of the form
    Dim intIndex1 As Integer
    Dim intIndex2 As Integer

    For intIndex1 = 0 To 10
        For intIndex2 = 0 To 10
            frmTile.PaintPicture picTile.picture, _
                intIndex2 * picTile.Width, _
                intIndex1 * picTile.Height
        Next intIndex2
    Next intIndex1
End Sub
```

The Scroll Bar Controls

You can add **horizontal scroll bars** and **vertical scroll bars** to your form
(Figure 14.13). These **scroll bar controls** are similar to the scroll bars in
Windows that can be used to scroll through a document or window. Often scroll
bars are used to control sound level, color, size, and other values that can be
changed in small amounts or large increments.

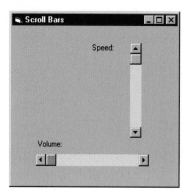

Properties for scroll bars are somewhat different from the controls we have worked with previously. Because the scroll bars represent a range of values, they have the following properties: **Min** for the minimum value, **Max** for the maximum value, **SmallChange** for the distance to move when the user clicks on the scroll arrows, and **LargeChange** for the distance to move when the user clicks on the gray area of the scroll bar (Figure 14.14).

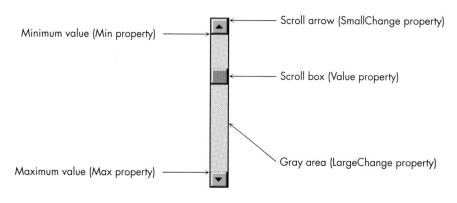

The Value property indicates the current position of the scroll box and its corresponding value within the scroll bar. When the user clicks the up arrow of a vertical scroll bar, the Value property decreases by the amount of SmallChange (if the Min value has not been reached). Clicking the down arrow causes the Value property to increase by the amount of SmallChange.

When naming scroll bars, use a prefix of "hsb" for horizontal scroll bars and "vsb" for vertical scroll bars. Figure 14.15 shows the horizontal scroll bar tool and vertical scroll bar tool from the toolbox.

Horizontal scroll bar ————— Vertical scroll bar

Scroll Bar Events

The events that occur for scroll bars differ from the ones used for other controls. Although a user might click on the scroll bar, there is no Click event; rather there are two events: a Change event and a Scroll event.

When the user clicks on a scroll arrow or the gray area of the scroll bar, a **Change event** occurs. If the user drags the scroll box instead, a **Scroll event** occurs. In fact, multiple scroll events occur, as long as the user continues to drag the scroll box. As soon as the user releases the mouse button, the Scroll events cease and a Change event occurs. When you write code for a scroll bar, usually you will want to code both a Change event procedure and a Scroll event procedure.

A Fun Programming Example

You can try the scroll bars and the shape controls with this little exercise. Open a new project and create a rectangle on the form using a shape control. Make a note of the shape's Location properties—Left, Top, Width, and Height. Then create an image inside the rectangle with its Picture property set to an icon of a car.

A horizontal scroll bar will make the image move sideways in the rectangle, and the vertical scroll bar will make it move up and down. Make sure that you set the Max and Min properties of the scroll bar to reflect the screen location of the rectangle. The SmallChange and LargeChange also need to be set.

Design and Create the Form

Figure 14.16 shows the form for this scroll bar example.

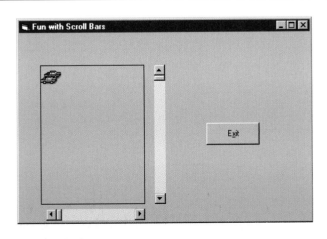

Set the Properties

Control	Property	Setting
Form1	Caption	Fun with Scroll Bars
	Name	frmScroll
shpRectangle	Name	shpRectangle
	Shape	0 - Rectangle
	Height	3135
	Left	480
	Top	720
	Width	2415
imgCar	Name	imgCar
	Picture	Graphics\Icons\Industry\Cars.ico
	Height	480
	Width	480
hsbMoveCar	Name	hsbMoveCar
	Min	480
	Max	1935 (rectangle width - image width)
	LargeChange	50
	SmallChange	10
vsbMoveCar	Name	vsbMoveCar
	Min	720 (top of rectangle)
	Max	3135 (rectangle height)
	LargeChange	50
	SmallChange	10
cmdExit	Name	cmdExit
	Caption	E&xit

Write the Code

Procedure	Actions
cmdExit_Click	Terminate the project.
vsbMoveCar_Change	Assign the scroll bar Value to the Top property of the image.
vsbMoveCar_Scroll	Assign the scroll bar Value to the Top property of the image.
hsbMoveCar_Change	Assign the scroll bar Value to the Left property of the image.
hsbMoveCar_Scroll	Assign the scroll bar Value to the Left property of the image.

The Project Coding Solution

```
'Program:              Scroll
'Programmer:           A. Millspaugh
'Date:                 December 1999
'Description:          Use scroll bars to move an image
'                      horizontally and vertically within the
'                      limits of a rectangle.
'Folder:               Ch1407

Option Explicit
```

```
Private Sub cmdExit_Click()
    'Terminate the project

    Unload Me
    End
End Sub
```

```
Private Sub hsbMoveCar_Change()
    'Controls the side-to-side movement
    'Used for arrow clicks

    imgCar.Left = hsbMoveCar.Value
End Sub
```

```
Private Sub hsbMoveCar_Scroll()
    'Controls the side-to-side movement
    'Used for scroll box movement

    imgCar.Left = hsbMoveCar.Value
End Sub
```

```
Private Sub vsbMoveCar_Change()
    'Positions the up-and-down movement
    'Used when arrow is clicked

    imgCar.Top = vsbMoveCar.Value
End Sub
```

```
Private Sub vsbMoveCar_Scroll()
    'Positions the up-and-down movement
    'Used when the scroll box is moved

    imgCar.Top = vsbMoveCar.Value
End Sub
```

S u m m a r y

1. Graphics may be measured in twips, points, pixels, inches, or centimeters. The measurement is known as the scale.
2. The coordinate system normally begins with 0,0 at the upper-left corner of the container object.
3. Colors are available using the RGB function, the intrinsic color constants, and the QBColor function.
4. The graphics methods include PSet, Line, and Circle. You can use the Line method to create a rectangular shape. The Circle method may be used for ellipses, arcs, and wedges.
5. Graphics and controls are created in three layers that produce a single display. The AutoRedraw and ClipControls properties affect the order of the layering.
6. Pictures can be loaded, moved, and resized at run time.
7. Animation effects can be created by using similar pictures and by controlling the location and visibility of controls.
8. The timer control can enable a Timer event that occurs at specified intervals.
9. Scroll bar controls are available for both horizontal and vertical control. Properties include Min, Max, SmallChange, and LargeChange. Scroll and Change events are used to control the action.

K e y   T e r m s

absolute position   *566*
AutoRedraw property   *568*
Change event   *577*
Circle method   *563*
ClipControls property   *568*
clipping region   *568*
Cls method   *560*
container   *559*
coordinate system   *556*
DrawWidth property   *562*
Enabled property   *571*
horizontal scroll bars   *575*
Interval property   *571*
LargeChange property   *576*
Line method   *562*
LoadPicture function   *569*
Max property   *576*
Min property   *576*
Move method   *569*

PaintPicture method   *574*
persistent graphics   *568*
picturebox control   *557*
pixel   *556*
point   *556*
PSet method   *560*
QBColor function   *558*
relative position   *566*
RGB function   *557*
Rnd function   *560*
scale   *556*
scroll bar control   *575*
Scroll event   *577*
SmallChange property   *576*
Step method   *566*
timer control   *571*
twip   *556*
vertical scroll bars   *575*
ZOrder method   *568*

R e v i e w   Q u e s t i o n s

1. How big is a twip?
2. To which controls do the graphics methods apply?
3. What happens when no object is specified for a graphics method such as PSet or Cls?
4. Name three methods available for graphics.
5. How is a pie-shaped wedge created?
6. What is the advantage to setting the AutoRedraw to True? to False?
7. Which function loads a picture at run time?
8. How is a picture removed at run time?
9. What steps are necessary to change an image that contains a turned-off light bulb to a turned-on light bulb?
10. What is the purpose of the timer control?

P r o g r a m m i n g   E x e r c i s e s

14.1 Create a project that contains a picturebox and two buttons labeled *Smile* and *Frown*. The Smile button will display a happy face in the picturebox; Frown will display a sad face. Use graphics methods to draw the two faces.

14.2 Use graphics methods to create the background of a form. Draw a picture of a house, including a front door, a window, and a chimney.

14.3 Use an image control with a .bmp file from Windows. Set the Stretch property to True. Use a scroll bar to change the size of the image.

14.4 Use graphics from a clip art collection to create a project that has a command button for each month of the year. Have an appropriate image display in a picturebox for each month.

14.5 Use the bicycle icon from Visual Basic and a timer control to move the bicycle around the screen. Add a Start button and a Stop button. The Stop button will return the bicycle to its original position. (The bicycle icon is stored as Graphics\Icons\Industry\Bicycle.ico.)

CASE STUDIES

VB Mail Order

Create a logo for VB Mail Order using graphics methods. Place the logo in the startup form for the project from Chapter 6. Add appropriate images and graphics to enhance each form. The graphics may come from .bmp files, clip art, or your own creation from a draw or paint program.

VB Auto Center

Have the startup screen initially fill with random dots in random colors. Use graphics methods to draw an Auto Center advertisement that will appear on the screen. Make various appropriate images (icons) appear in different locations, remain momentarily, and then disappear.

Video Bonanza

Use the timer control and the random number generator to create a promotional game for Video Bonanza customers. Create three image controls that will display an image selected from five possible choices. When the user clicks on the *Start* command button a randomly selected image will display in each of the image controls and continue to change for a few seconds (like a "slot machine") until the user presses the *Stop* command button. If all three images are the same, the customer receives a free video rental.

Display a message that says "Congratulations" or "Better Luck Next Visit."

Very Very Boards

Modify your Very Very Boards project from Chapter 6, 7, or 8 to add a moving graphic to the Splash form. Use the graphic Skateboard.wmf or other graphic of your choice. Include a timer control to move the graphic across the form. When the graphic reaches the edge of the form, reset so that the graphic will appear at the opposite edge and begin the trip again.

Hint: Depending on the direction of movement, you can check for the edge of the form by checking the Left or Top property of the image, which is zero when the graphic is at the edge of the form. To determine the right or bottom edge of the form, you will need to use the Width or Height of the form and the Width or Height of the image.

15

Advanced Topics in Visual Basic

At the completion of this chapter, you will be able to . . .

1. Use ActiveX controls to extend the functionality of your projects.

2. Create a link from a Visual Basic project to a Web site.

3. Include procedures from dynamic link libraries (DLLs) in your projects.

4. Realize the potential for programming using the Windows API.

5. Use an OLE container control for linking or embedding objects.

6. Recognize the relationship between Visual Basic and VBA.

7. Understand the difference between MDI and SDI.

8. Create a report using Report Designer.

In addition to the large variety of controls, statements, and functions that are a part of the language, as a Visual Basic programmer you can turn to many other sources for your application needs. Controls have been referred to as *objects*. Objects go far beyond the controls that are a part of Visual Basic. Think of objects as programming components. You can incorporate those available from word processors, spreadsheets, graphics programs, and the multitude of software available.

Programs that run under Windows have access to other applications' objects through ActiveX controls, the object linking and embedding (OLE) container control, and dynamic link libraries (DLLs). This chapter introduces these topics as well as some components designed specifically for use with Visual Basic.

To have more control of the forms (windows) within a project, you may wish to use a multiple document interface (MDI), which allows you to set up a single parent form that controls its child forms.

ActiveX

The term ***ActiveX*** originally referred to controls that could be used with the Internet. Since then the term has been expanded to refer to executable files, controls (COM, or Component Object Model, objects), and DLLs that are used by multiple applications. These controls were called ***OLE*** controls for a period of time, but the term OLE currently refers only to the process of object linking and embedding. The terminology has been changing rapidly and likely will change somewhat in the next few years as the use of the Internet expands.

Using ActiveX Controls

You have used many controls built into Visual Basic, plus some others, such as the grid and the common dialog box, that had to be added to the Visual Basic environment. In general, Microsoft refers to any controls as *ActiveX controls*. These controls may be part of Visual Basic, created by other companies, or created by you. The controls that are part of Visual Basic are called *intrinsic controls*; those that must be added later are called *components*. Many ActiveX controls are available in the Professional and Enterprise Editions of Visual Basic, as well as from other software developers.

A large selection of ActiveX controls are available to solve many problems. You can purchase controls to display various types of gauges and indicators, display data in grids, send and receive faxes, display video, scan bar codes, display calendars and appointments, and perform many other functions. Many ActiveX controls are available as shareware, and a few are freeware. Many can be downloaded from various Web sites.

The files for ActiveX controls have extensions of .ocx or .vbx. (Any controls developed for Visual Basic 4.0 or later should be .ocx files.)

When you select the *Components* command from the *Project* menu, you see a list of the controls available on your system (Figure 15.1). As you select a component name from the list, a line at the bottom of the dialog box shows the name and location of the selected control file. In most cases the file extension will be .ocx.

Tip

To include objects that are available from other applications, use the *References* dialog box, which you can select from the *Project* menu.

Figure 15.1

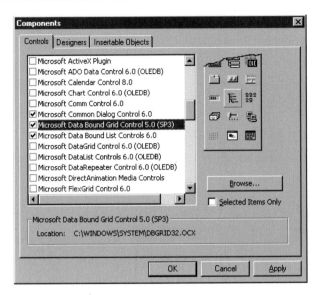

Available ActiveX controls appear in the Components dialog box.

The Tabbed Dialog Control

One of the handy extra controls that comes with Visual Basic is the Microsoft Tabbed Dialog Control 6.0. The tabbed dialog is a convenient way for placing a large amount of related material in one dialog box. You can find many examples of tabbed dialogs in Visual Basic, such as the *Components* dialog box (Figure 15.1) that has three tabs: *Controls*, *Designers*, and *Insertable Objects*. Figure 15.2 shows a dialog box with a **Tabbed Dialog control**.

Figure 15.2

The tabs in this form were created with the Tabbed Dialog control.

To add a Tabbed Dialog control to your project, you must first add the control to your toolbox. Select *Microsoft Tabbed Dialog Control 6.0* from the *Components* dialog box (Figure 15.3). Figure 15.4 shows the Tabbed Dialog tool in the toolbox and a control on a form.

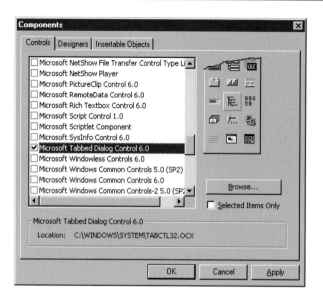

*Select the Tabbed Dialog control from the **Components** dialog box.*

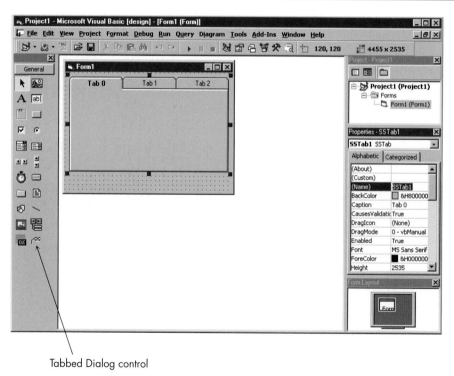

Tabbed Dialog control

The tool for the Tabbed Dialog control as it appear in the toolbox and a control on a form.

The Tabbed Dialog control has many properties and methods that you can set or check at run time or at design time. The default name of the tab is SSTab1. Use the prefix "tab" when naming your control.

The easiest way to initially set up the control is to use the custom *Property Pages* dialog box (Figure 15.5). To display this dialog box, either click on the builder button for *Custom* in the control's Properties window (Figure 15.6) or right-click the control and select *Properties* from the shortcut menu (Figure 15.7). In this dialog box you can specify the number of tabs, tabs per row, and the tab caption of each tab. *Note:* The first tab is tab 0, the next is tab 1, and so forth.

Figure 15.5

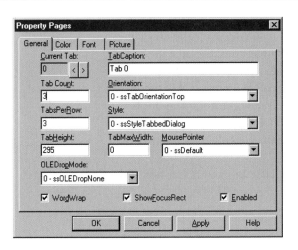

Set the properties for the Tabbed Dialog control in its custom Property Pages dialog box.

Figure 15.6

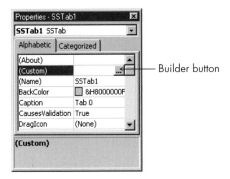

One way to display the Property Pages dialog box is to click on the builder button for the Custom entry in the Property window.

Figure 15.7

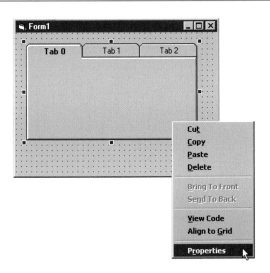

You can display the Property Pages dialog box by right-clicking on the control to display the shortcut menu and selecting Properties.

You can also set up the Tabbed Dialog control using the Properties window. To set the tab captions, click on each tab to select it and then change the caption in the Properties window.

Placing Controls on the Tab Sheets of a Tabbed Control

When you place controls such as text boxes and labels on top of a Tabbed Dialog control, usually you want the controls to appear on only the one tab page. Select the desired control's toolbox tool and manually draw the new control on top of the Tabbed Dialog control (do not double-click to place the control). If you double-click on a control in the toolbox, you are actually placing the control on the form and the control will appear on every tab. (This process is similar to the way you place controls inside frame controls; the Tabbed Dialog control is a container for the controls that "belong to" it.) If you *do* want a control to appear on all tabs, such as an Exit button, then place the control by double-clicking.

The Tabbed Dialog control for R 'n R has a *Coffee* tab with a list box and another tab containing a combo box. See Figures 15.8 and 15.9.

F i g u r e   1 5 . 8

The form for R 'n R has a Tabbed Dialog control with two tabs.

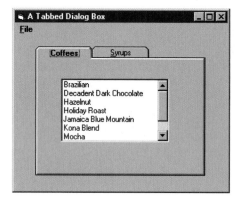

F i g u r e   1 5 . 9

The tabs on the form for R 'n R hold different lists.

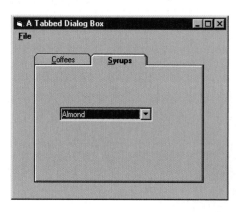

Browsing the Web from a Visual Basic Project

Another ActiveX control available on the *Components* dialog box is the **Web Browser control**. To add this control to your toolbox, place a check on the Microsoft Internet Controls (Figure 15.10) in the *Components* selection of the *Project* menu. You can now link your Visual Basic application to the Internet.

Figure 15.10

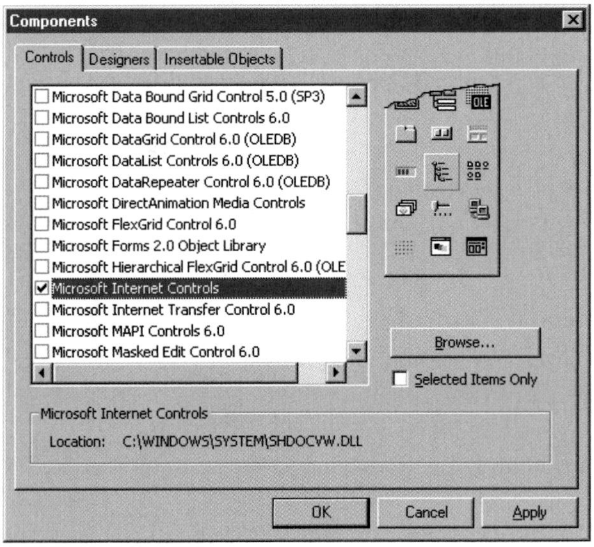

Add a Web Browser control to a project by selecting **Microsoft Internet Controls** *in the* **Components** *dialog box.*

When you add this control to your project, a new window is created (Figure 15.11). Web pages will appear in this window on your form. The default name is WebBrowser1. When naming your control use the prefix "web".

Figure 15.11

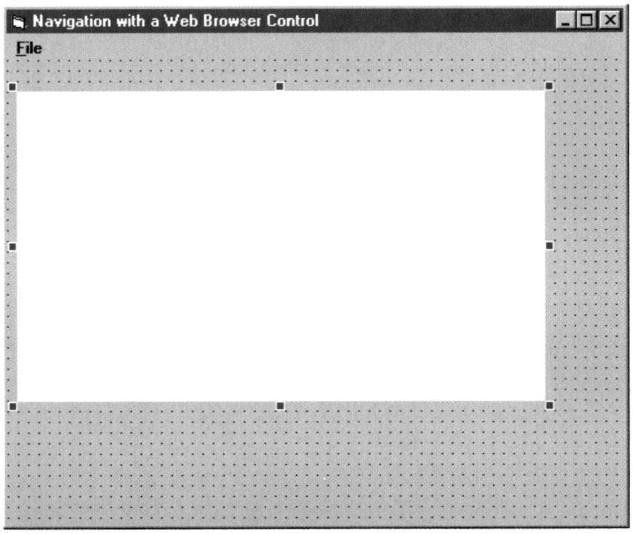

A Web Browser control on a form. Web pages will appear in the window created by the control.

One of the methods of the control is `Navigate`, which allows you to specify a Web site URL. Place the link as a string following the call to the method. The following code will bring up the Microsoft home page if there is a current connection to the Internet:

```
webBrowser.Navigate "Microsoft.com"
```

The computer system must be connected through an Internet provider for this control to work. If no browser is open, the project attempts to open Internet Explorer. The program will work using Netscape Navigator; open the browser before executing your Visual Basic project.

Creating Your Own ActiveX Controls

In VB it is easy to create your own controls. In the *New Project* dialog box, you can choose to begin a new project for an ActiveX control, an ActiveX EXE, or an ActiveX DLL.

An ActiveX Control Project Using the Calendar Control

We will create a new ActiveX control that contains a Microsoft calendar control, a text box, and a command button. The user will enter a date in the text box and click the command button, and the corresponding date will appear on the calendar. Figure 15.12 shows the custom control; the following steps explain how to create it.

F i g u r e   1 5 . 1 2

This form and controls make up a new custom control created with VB.

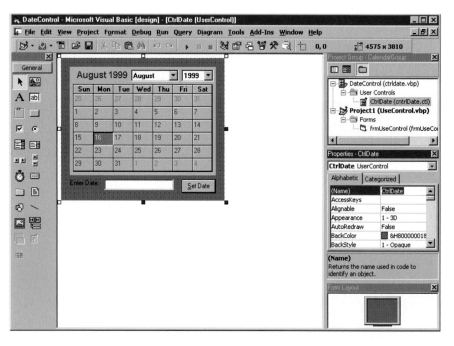

STEP 1: Open a new project selecting the ActiveX control option (Figure 15.13).

Figure 15.13

Select New Project from the File menu and select ActiveX Control to create a new control.

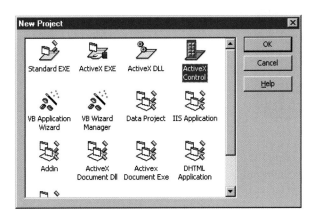

STEP 2: Use the *Components* dialog box to add *Microsoft Calendar Control 8.0* to your project and form (Figure 15.14).

Figure 15.14

Select Microsoft Calendar Control in the Components dialog box to add the control to your toolbox.

STEP 3: Design the interface and the code as you would for any other project (Figure 15.15).

STEP 4: Enter the code for the new control. (You can see the code in the next section.)

Set up the form and controls for the new custom control.

STEP 5: Select *Make .ocx* from the *File* menu to compile the code. Name your new control calDate.ocx; the control is automatically placed in the *Components* dialog box.

STEP 6: Close the window for the control project before adding your new control to a regular VB project.

The Code for the ActiveX Control

The following program code converts the contents of the text box to a date data type. Date functions extract the year, month, and day from the date data type. Setting the properties of the calendar control (calDate) makes the date appear in the calendar.

```
'Project:          Calendar Activex
'Programmer:       A. Millspaugh
'Date:             Oct 1999
'Description:      Create an ActiveX control
'                  that displays the date entered
'                  in a text box.
'Folder:           Ch1503

Private Sub cmdDate_Click()
    'Use the date in the text box
    'to set the calendar
    Dim dtmDate As Date
```

```
    If IsDate(txtDate.Text) Then
        dtmDate = txtDate.Text            'Convert the text box to a date data _
                                          type
        calDate.Year = Year(dtmDate)      'Find the year and assign to the _
                                          calendar year
        calDate.Month = Month(dtmDate)    'Find the month and assign to the _
                                          calendar month
        calDate.Day = Day(dtmDate)        'Find the day and assign to the _
                                          calendar day
        calDate.Refresh                   'Display the Calendar again
    Else
        MsgBox "Not a valid date", vbOKOnly, "Date Check"
    End If
End Sub
```

Using Your New ActiveX Control

The steps for using the new control in a project are the same as for using any other control. If your new control does not appear in the toolbox, open the *Components* dialog box; you will find its name there. Select the new control name, and the control will appear in your toolbox. Then add your new control to a form and test the control.

New to VB6, you can also run your ActiveX control on a Web page. After creating the new control, you can click VB's Start button; your Web browser will open with your new control on a page. You can test your new control on the page.

Dynamic Link Libraries

Libraries store commonly used procedures. As a project executes, it can call procedures from libraries. This technique is especially useful for procedures used by multiple projects; only one copy of the library is kept in memory, and its procedures can be called by more than one project. Windows uses **dynamic link libraries (DLLs)** to store collections of procedures. The DLL file is then linked to your project when it runs. *Note:* Look at the list of library selections in the Visual Basic *References* dialog box from the *Project* menu. The line near the bottom of the dialog box shows the path including the .DLL extension (Figure 15.16). Use the Windows Explorer to look in the Windows and Windows\System folders; you will see many library files with the .DLL extension.

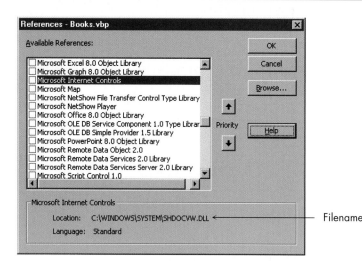

Select a DLL file from the **References** *dialog box. The DLL filenames appear at the lower edge of the form.*

Windows applications routinely use DLLs. A project can call a function from the library and pass arguments if needed. The function is maintained separately from the programs that call it. Therefore, changes are made to the internal workings of a function in a dynamic link library without having to recode all the projects that call the function.

One extremely useful feature of Visual Basic is that a project can call and use library procedures used by the Windows system. Consequently, functions available in Windows but not available in Visual Basic can still be used. The DLLs that Windows applications use for tasks such as moving and resizing windows are referred to as the Windows application programming interface (**API**). Visual Basic uses many API DLLs to create the Visual Basic environment.

Most of the Windows DLL code is written in the C language and requires some use of C syntax. Don't worry if you don't know C. You don't have to write any C statements; you only have to pass arguments to the library procedures.

Two steps are required for using a DLL. Any time you call a procedure that is in a library, you must include a **Declare statement**. `Declare` statements tell Visual Basic the name of the procedure and the library where it can be found, along with the arguments the procedure needs. Once you have included the `Declare`, you can call the procedure as you would call one of your own. You can call both sub procedures and function procedures from DLLs; the `Declare` statement specifies the type of procedure. (Recall that a function returns a value.)

The Declare Statement

`Declare` statements appear at the module level. You can include them in the General Declarations section of a form module or in a standard code module. Calls to the library procedures may appear in any module in the scope of the `Declare`.

The Declare Statement—General Form

```
Declare Sub Name Lib LibName$ [Alias AliasName$] _
    ([ArgumentList])
Declare Function Name Lib LibName$ [Alias AliasName$] _
    ([ArgumentList]) [As Datatype]
```

The Name parameter refers to the name of the procedure. If the name of the procedure is the same as a reserved word in Visual Basic or one of your existing procedures, you must use an alias to give the procedure a new name within your project. The word *Lib* precedes the name of the DLL library file. The argument list specifies the arguments expected by the procedure.

In the first of the following examples, the function procedure is called `sndPlaySound` from the MMSystem library.

The Declare Statement—Examples

```
Declare Function sndPlaySound Lib "winmm" Alias "sndPlaySoundA" _
    (ByVal lpszSoundName As String, ByVal uFlags As Long) As Long

Declare Function GetWindowsDirectory Lib "kernel32" Alias "GetWindowsDirectoryA" _
    (ByVal lpBuffer As String, ByVal nSize As Long) As Long
```

The arguments may have a datatype specified and can be passed `ByVal` or `ByRef`.

To place `Declares` in a form module, use the `Private` keyword.

Passing Arguments ByVal and ByRef

Remember that arguments may be passed to a called procedure by value or by reference. When passed `ByVal`, only a copy of the original value is passed; the called procedure cannot alter the original value. When items are passed `ByRef`, the memory address of the original value is passed to the procedure, allowing the procedure to change the original value. You will pass `ByVal` or `ByRef` based on the requirements of the specific DLL. If no specification is made, the default is `ByRef`.

When you are calling Windows API procedures, always declare a string argument `ByVal`. Visual Basic and C do not store strings in the same way. A Visual Basic string holds the length of the string at the beginning; strings in C are variable in length and terminated by a NULL character. C does not actually have a string data type, but treats strings as an array of characters.

String arguments and array arguments are treated differently than other (nonarray) arguments. You should declare them as passing `ByVal`, but what is actually passed is the address of the first element of the array.

Calling a DLL Procedure

You can call a DLL procedure from within any procedure in the scope of the `Declare` statement. The call will look the same as calls to procedures that you have written. The passed arguments may be either variables or constants.

The following procedure uses the `sndPlaySound` function to play a sound wave file (.wav extension). This shareware wave file sounds like the Laurel and Hardy "Look at the fine mess you've gotten us into now" routine. Although this example plays the sound when a command button is clicked, you might consider playing it in a validation routine when the user makes a mistake.

```
Private Sub cmdSound_Click()
    'Play a sound file
    Dim lngTalk     As Long
    Dim strWaveFile As String
    Const lngSync = 1

    strWaveFile = App.Path & "\l&h.wav"
    lngTalk = sndPlaySound(ByVal CStr(strWaveFile), lngSync)
End Sub
```

The first parameter converts the path and filename string to a "C string" by using the `CStr` function. The second argument being passed is a long constant. Compare these arguments with the `Declare` used for this DLL procedure. (*Note:* The path indicated must be valid for your system. This shareware file is included on your CD.)

```
Declare Function sndPlaySound Lib "winmm" Alias "sndPlaySoundA" _
    (ByVal lpszSoundName As String, ByVal uFlags As Long) As Long
```

The `sndPlaySound` function is very useful for including sounds in a multimedia type of program. You might consider scanning in your own pictures, recording a voice description, and playing back the sound file when the appropriate selection is made from a menu or command button.

Finding the Reference Information for DLLs

You are not expected to learn the names and arguments for DLL procedures. You will find small code samples in magazines, in articles that present tips, or in question-and-answer features. If you ask a "How do I do . . . " question online, the answer you receive may contain a few lines of code that include a `Declare` and a call to the procedure.

Visual Basic comes with a reference database for the procedures in the Windows API. You can use the API Viewer VB Add-In to look up the names of library files, procedures, constants, and the format of the `Declare` for each call. To use the Add-In, it must be selected when you install VB on your system. Then select *Add-Ins/Add-In Manager* and select *VB API Viewer* from the dialog box to add the API Viewer to the *Add-Ins* menu. Open the viewer and open its text file, Win32api.txt. The path for the text file varies, depending on how VB was installed, but should be located in the Tools\Winapi folder. After you locate the desired `Declare` and `Const` statements, you can copy and paste them into your project.

Accessing System Information with a DLL

Your project may need to know the specific hardware or software on the computer system running the program. Windows maintains this information, and you can access it with a DLL. The following program will determine the Windows folder and system folder.

Figure 15.17 shows the form for this program example.

Figure 15.17

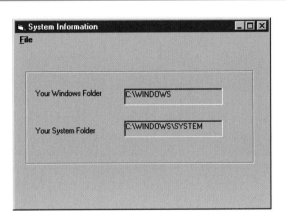

The form for the system information example program using a Windows API DLL.

```
'Project:              Ch1504.bas - Standard code module
'Programmer:           A. Millspaugh
'Date:                 December 1999
'Description:          Declares the DLL procedures to find the
'                      Windows and System folders.
'Folder:               Ch1504

    'Declare the DLL procedures
    Declare Function GetWindowsDirectory _
        Lib "kernel32" Alias "GetWindowsDirectoryA" _
        (ByVal lpBuffer As String, ByVal nSize As Long) _
        As Long
    Declare Function GetSystemDirectory Lib _
        "kernel32" Alias "GetSystemDirectoryA" _
        (ByVal lpBuffer As String, ByVal nSize As Long) _
        As Long
```

```
'Project:              Ch1504 frmSysInfo
'Programmer:           A. Millspaugh
'Date:                 December 1999
'Description:          Uses DLL procedures to find the Windows
'                      and System folders.
'Folder:               Ch1504

Option Explicit
```

```
Private Sub Form_Load()
    'Call the DLL procedures and assign return
    ' values to labels
    Dim strWinPath As String
    Dim vntTemp

    'Create a string of 145 null characters
    strWinPath = String(145, Chr(0))
    'Fill the string with the path name
    vntTemp = GetWindowsDirectory(strWinPath, 145)
    'Take the left characters up to the null
    lblWindowsDir.Caption = Left(strWinPath, InStr(strWinPath, Chr(0)) - 1)
    strWinPath = String(145, Chr(0))
    vntTemp = GetSystemDirectory(strWinPath, 145)
    lblSystemDir.Caption = Left(strWinPath, InStr(strWinPath, Chr(0)) - 1)
End Sub
```

```
Private Sub mnuFileExit_Click()
    'Terminate the project

    Unload Me
    End
End Sub
```

Placing Tabs for Columns in a List Box

Visual Basic list boxes and combo boxes do not have tab settings. At times you may want to fill a list with two or more columns. This example uses a Windows DLL to set tab stops in a list box. The project opens the Publishers table from the Visual Basic Biblio.mdb database and fills a list box with the data in three columns (Figure 15.18).

Figure 15.18

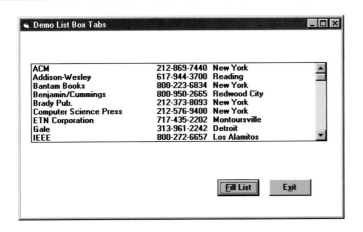

The columns in the list box created by using a Windows DLL to set tab stops.

```
'Project:              Demo Tabs
'Date:                 Oct 1999
'Programmer:           J.C. Bradley
'Description:          Use a DLL to place tab stops in a list box.
'Folder:               Ch1505
Option Explicit

Private Declare Function SendMessage Lib "user32" Alias "SendMessageA" _
    (ByVal hwnd As Long, ByVal wMsg As Long, ByVal wParam As Long, _
    lParam As Any) As Long
Const LB_SETTABSTOPS = &H192
```

```
Private Sub cmdExit_Click()
    'Exit the project

    Unload Me
    End
End Sub
```

```
Private Sub cmdFill_Click()
    'Fill the list box

    SetTabs lstData            'Call procedure, passing name of list box
    With datBiblio.Recordset
        Do Until .EOF          'Chr$(9) is a Tab character
            lstData.AddItem !Name & Chr$(9) & !Telephone & Chr$(9) _
                & !City
            .MoveNext
        Loop
    End With
End Sub
```

```
Private Sub SetTabs(Lst As ListBox)
    'Set the tab stops in a listbox

    ReDim lngTabs(0 To 1) As Long      'Two tab stops needed
    Dim lngRtn As Long                 'DLL function returns a Long variable
    lngTabs(0) = 110                   'Twips measurement for 1st tab stop
    lngTabs(1) = 160                   'Twips measurement for 2nd tab stop
    lngRtn = SendMessage(Lst.hwnd, LB_SETTABSTOPS, 2, lngTabs(0)) 'Set the stops
End Sub
```

Object Linking and Embedding

OLE enables you to link or embed objects from other applications into your project, either at run time or at design time. You can access objects from other types of applications without writing the code. Think how much time it would take to program a spreadsheet application. Why should you spend that time when excellent spreadsheets are available? OLE is the means by which each programmer can avoid "reinventing the wheel." The types of objects available to use in a project depend on the applications that are installed on your computer system or network.

Object Linking

Linking causes your program to access an object that is actually maintained by the application that creates it. A reference to the linked object is kept in your code, but the actual object is kept in the other application. Consequently, any application that has linking ability can access the linked object and change it. When your application runs, you can access the current state of the object.

An example of a linked object could be a spreadsheet showing the current status and costs for a project. The spreadsheet object could be included in a Visual Basic project, included in a word processing document, or displayed from the spreadsheet application. The data in the linked spreadsheet can also be updated from each application. Because each application is using the same object, any changes made to the spreadsheet would be available to all applications linked to it.

Object Embedding

Embedding places a copy of the object into your project. Hence your copy of the object is maintainable only from within your project and cannot be accessed by other projects. Another result of embedding is that the Visual Basic project file becomes significantly larger because of the embedded code.

Consider a project that includes a spreadsheet object created in Excel. You can choose to create a new spreadsheet file or to include an existing spreadsheet. The steps to accomplish the two tasks are similar. First, create a new control on a form using the OLE tool from the toolbox (Figure 15.19); the *Insert*

Object dialog box (Figure 15.20) appears automatically. Notice the option buttons for *Create New* or *Create from File*. Try clicking on the buttons and viewing the changes to the dialog box (Figure 15.21). If you want to create a new item within your project, you must make a selection from the *Object Type* list box.

Figure   15.19

Use the OLE tool from the toolbox to link or embed an OLE object in a project.

Figure   15.20

The Insert Object dialog box with its initial settings for creating a new object.

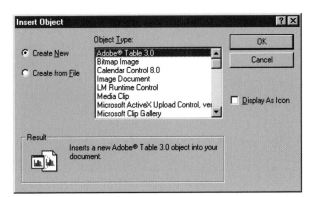

Figure   15.21

The Insert Object dialog box as it appears for Create from File.

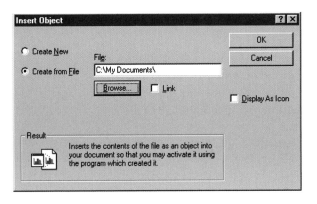

The following example places an existing spreadsheet for R 'n R on a form as an embedded object. Figure 15.22 shows the form for this example. The steps are as follows:

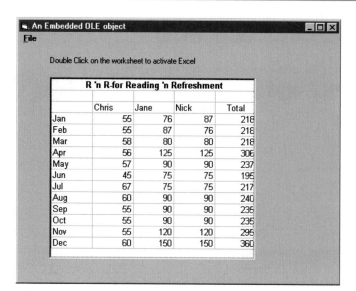

The form for the OLE example project showing an embedded Excel spreadsheet object.

STEP 1: Create a control on your form using the OLE tool from the toolbox; the *Insert Object* dialog box will display (refer to Figure 15.20).

STEP 2: Select the option button for *Create from File*.

STEP 3: Type the filename Rnr.xls in the File text box (or use the Browse button to locate the file in the Ch1506 folder).

STEP 4: Make sure that the Link check box is not selected so that the object will be embedded.

The project Ch1506 displays the interface shown in Figure 15.22 when the program is running.

Creating OLE Objects at Run Time

You can embed and link objects while a project is executing by using the properties and methods of the OLE control. You can create a link to an existing object by setting the control's SourceDoc property and using the `Create Link` method. If you are linking to a datafile and want a specific range of the file, you can set the control's SourceItem property.

To embed an object, set the SourceDoc property and use the `Create Embed` method.

You can also allow the user to select the type of object to be linked or embedded as the project is running. Use the `InsertObjDlg` or the `PasteSpecialDlg` method. These methods display the *Object* dialog box or the *Paste Special* dialog box, respectively.

Visual Basic for Applications

Each Microsoft Office application, such as Excel, Word, PowerPoint, and Access, includes **Visual Basic for Applications (VBA)** for writing procedures. Most of the Visual Basic features that you have learned carry over to programming in VBA. Take a look at the Code window (Figure 15.23), the Visual Basic toolbar (Figure 15.24), and the Controls Toolbox toolbar (Figure 15.25) in Excel 97. You will find many items that look familiar.

F i g u r e   1 5 . 2 3

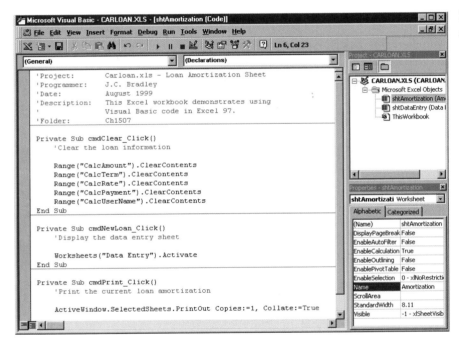

The Visual Basic Code window in Excel 97.

F i g u r e   1 5 . 2 4

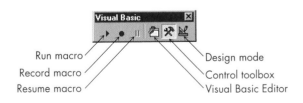

The Excel 97 Visual Basic toolbar.

Figure   1 5 . 2 5

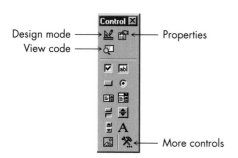

Recording an Excel Macro

If Excel 97 is installed on your computer, you may be interested in trying the activities in this section. Start by recording an Excel macro: Select *Tools/Macros/Record New Macro*, and a dialog box will ask for the name of your macro. Give it the name *Demo;* a little Stop button appears in a toolbar. Then try typing something into your worksheet, such as your name and the date. Then click the Stop button.

Display the Visual Basic toolbar (*View/Toolbars*) and click on the Visual Basic Editor button (Figure 15.26). Then double-click on Module1 in the Project Explorer window. Your procedure (recorded macro) should appear in the Code window (Figure 15.27).

Figure   1 5 . 2 6

	A	B	C	D	E	F
1	This is a demo					
2	Today is	7/20/99				
3				Visual Basic		
4						
5						
6				Visual Basic Editor		
7						

Investigate the environment—the windows, the menus, and the toolbars. This environment is the same Visual Basic environment you are accustomed to. Now look at the code. The Visual Basic notation for remarks includes the name *Demo* that you called your macro. Notice the procedure begins with Sub and ends with End Sub. The statements inside the procedure reflect the steps you took while the macro was recording.

The structure of VBA is the same as the structure for Visual Basic. However, a spreadsheet has different objects, properties, events, and methods than those you are familiar with.

Figure 15.27

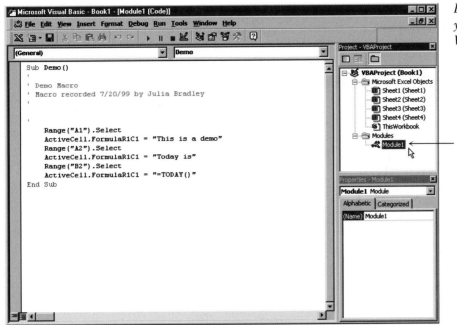

Double-click on Module1, and your new macro appears in the Visual Basic Code window.

Select Module 1

You can add objects with which you are familiar. Return to the Worksheet window by clicking on its Taskbar button. Then display the Control Toolbox toolbar (*View/Toolbars*). Create a command button. The tools are the same, but you must click the tool and then draw it; the double-click method does not work in VBA.

After you create a new button, change to the design mode of Excel by clicking on the Design mode button on the Visual Basic toolbar. You can toggle between design mode and regular mode with the Design mode button. When you are in design mode, you can display the Properties window, change properties of controls, and write code.

A Sample Excel Visual Basic Application

Your student disk has a file called Carloan.xls for calculating loan payments and printing loan amortizations. It contains two sheets: a worksheet that resembles a dialog box for data entry (Figure 15.28*a*) and a second worksheet for the loan amortization (Figure 15.28*b*). The data entry worksheet has three command buttons: Calculate Payment, Display Amortization, and Clear. The loan amortization worksheet has buttons for Print, Clear, and New Loan. You can load the workbook file, run the application, and examine the Visual Basic procedures.

a.

This Excel spreadsheet demonstrates using Visual Basic for Applications in Excel. This demo workbook has two worksheets: (a) the Data Entry sheet and (b) the Amortization sheet.

b.

Note: Because there are no validation routines, you must enter all fields.
The form is designed to print out the first three years of the loan.

The Code for the Data Entry Worksheet

```
'Project:              Carloan.xls - Data Entry Sheet
'Programmer:           J.C. Bradley
'Date:                 August 1999
'Description:          This Excel workbook file demonstrates using
'                      Visual Basic in Excel 97.
'Folder:               Ch1507


Option Explicit


Private Sub cmdCalculateLoan_Click()
    'Calculate the payment

    Range("CalculatedPayment").Value = _
        "=-PMT(YearlyRate/1200, TermInYears*12, Principal)"
End Sub


Private Sub cmdClear_Click()
    'Clear the sheet

    Range("UserName").ClearContents
    Range("Principal").ClearContents
    Range("YearlyRate").ClearContents
    Range("TermInYears").ClearContents
    Range("CalculatedPayment").ClearContents
    Range("UserName").Select
End Sub


Private Sub cmdDisplay_Click()
    'Display Amortization worksheet

    cmdCalculateLoan_Click
    With Worksheets("Amortization")
        .Range("CalcAmount") = Range("Principal")
        .Range("CalcRate").Value = Range("YearlyRate") / 100
        .Range("CalcTerm").Value = Range("TermInYears")
        .Range("Payment").Value = Range("CalculatedPayment")
        .Range("CalcUserName").Value = Range("UserName")
        .Activate
    End With
End Sub


Private Sub Worksheet_Activate()
    'Set up the worksheet

    Range("UserName").Select
End Sub
```

The Code for the Loan Amortization Worksheet

```
'Project:             Carloan.xls - Loan Amortization Sheet
'Programmer:          J.C. Bradley
'Date:                August 1999
'Description:         This Excel workbook demonstrates Visual Basic code.
'Folder:              Ch1507

Option Explicit
```

```
Private Sub cmdClear_Click()
    'Clear the loan information

    Range("CalcAmount").ClearContents
    Range("CalcTerm").ClearContents
    Range("CalcRate").ClearContents
    Range("CalcPayment").ClearContents
    Range("CalcUserName").ClearContents
End Sub
```

```
Private Sub cmdNewLoan_Click()
    'Display the data entry sheet

    Worksheets("Data Entry").Activate
End Sub
```

```
Private Sub cmdPrint_Click()
    'Print the current loan amortization

    ActiveWindow.SelectedSheets.PrintOut Copies:=1, Collate:=True
End Sub
```

Help with Visual Basic in Excel

Another area that can help you learn more about VBA is Excel's *Help* menu. Under *Help/Contents* and *Index/Contents* select the topic *Microsoft Excel Visual Basic Reference* and expand the topics list. The Visual Basic section of *Help* gives a new index of topics that relate specifically to VB.

In addition to the Help screens, you can also try some demo programs that come with Excel.

Multiple Document Interface (MDI)

Each of your projects so far has been a single document interface **(SDI)**. VB also allows you to create a multiple document interface **(MDI)** project. For an example of MDI, consider an application such as Microsoft Word. Word has a **parent form** (the main window) and **child** forms (each document window). You can open multiple child windows, maximize, minimize, restore, or close each child window, which always stays within the boundaries of the parent window. And when you close the parent window, all child windows close automatically.

Your VB projects can use MDI or SDI. With SDI each form acts independently of the others; an MDI has a parent form that controls the other forms, referred to as *child forms.* In an MDI project, when you unload the main form, all child forms are also unloaded. Another advantage is that the child forms display within the boundaries of the parent, giving more control to the user resizing forms.

Creating an MDI Project

In any one VB project you can have only one MDI form, which is the parent. You can make any other forms into child forms by setting the MDIChild property to True. Note that in an MDI project, you *should* make all nonparent forms into child forms. Any forms not set as child forms will operate independently and not be confined to the parent window.

To add an MDI (parent) form to a project, choose *Project / Add MDI Form.* Notice in the Project Explorer window that the symbols for the MDI parent form and child forms differ from the symbols for SDI forms (Figure 15.29).

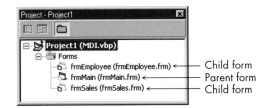

The icons indicate an MDI form and child forms.

Adding Menus to an MDI Project

If you add menus to an MDI project, you need to consider carefully the location to specify the menus. If an MDI (parent) form has a menu, its menu will display only if no child form with a menu is displaying. If any child form that has a menu is displaying, its menu replaces the parent's menu. You can see this concept in action by opening Word or Excel and watching the menus. If no document (child) is open, you see one menu; if a document *is* open, you see a different menu on the main window.

Creating a Window Menu

You can make your MDI project behave like other Windows applications by adding a Window menu. The Window menu typically has options to cascade and tile the child windows. Also, a list of open child windows displays with the active window checked. The user can switch to another window by selecting it from the menu.

Arranging the Child Windows

Give your user the option of arranging the open child windows within the parent window using the **Arrange method.**

The Arrange Method—General Form

```
formname.Arrange vbConstant
```

The constant can be vbCascade, vbTileHorizontal, or vbTileVertical.

The Arrange Method—Examples

```
frmMain.Arrange vbCascade
frmMain.Arrange vbTileHorizontal
```

Displaying the List of Open Windows

It's easy to display the list of open windows. When you define the menus, select the WindowList option for the Window menu (Figure 15.30); the list will display and function correctly.

F i g u r e   1 5 . 3 0

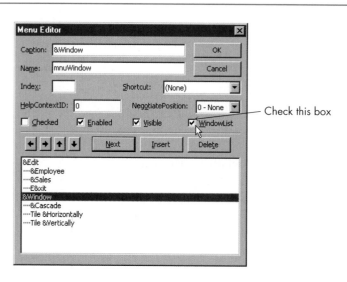

Select the WindowList option to make a list of open windows appear on the selected menu.

— Check this box

MDI Example

Here is an example of an MDI project. The menu is defined in the MDI parent form.

```
'Project:            MDI Project Example--Main Form
'Programmer:         A. Millspaugh
'Date:               Oct 1999
'Description:        A demonstration using an MDI form with two child
'                    forms. Menu offers cascade, tile, and Window
'                    list options.
'Folder:             Ch1508

Option Explicit


Private Sub mnuEditEmployee_Click()
    'Show employee form

    frmEmployee.Show
End Sub


Private Sub mnuEditSales_Click()
    'Show Sales Form

    frmSales.Show
End Sub


Private Sub mnuFileExit_Click()
    'Exit the project

    Unload Me
    End
End Sub


Private Sub mnuWindowCascade_Click()
    'Cascade Open Forms

    frmMain.Arrange vbCascade
End Sub


Private Sub mnuWindowTileHorizontally_Click()
    'Tile Open forms horizontally

    frmMain.Arrange vbTileHorizontal
End Sub


Private Sub mnuWindowTileVertically_Click()
    'Tile open forms vertically

    frmMain.Arrange vbTileVertical
End Sub
```

Defining Shortcut Menus

When running Windows applications, do you use **shortcut menus** (also called pop-up menus, context menus, and right-mouse menus)? You can use the Menu Editor and a new event to add shortcut menus to your projects. A right-click can display different menus, depending on the location of the pointer at run time.

Defining the Menu

You can choose to display one of your existing menus when the user right-clicks, or you can create a separate menu specifically as a shortcut menu. To create a menu as a shortcut menu, make the top-level menu name invisible (Visible property unchecked). See Figure 15.31. Create the menu items, following the standard naming conventions. Your menu must have at least one command beneath the menu name.

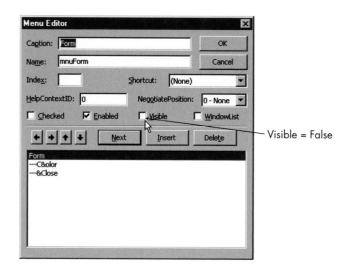

To create a shortcut menu, make the top level menu name invisible.

Menu	Control Name
Form	mnuForm
....C&olor	mnuFormColor
....&Close	mnuFormClose

Coding for the Menu

You can make a shortcut menu pop up for a form or any control on the form. Write code in the MouseUp or MouseDown event for the selected form or control. (Microsoft recommends using the MouseUp event.) For example, the code for a form's MouseUp event appears as follows:

```
Private Sub Form_MouseUp(Button As Integer, Shift As Integer, X As Single, _
     Y As Single)
```

The Button argument holds an integer that indicates which button was pressed: 1 = left button; 2 = right button. You can use the numeric constant in your code or use the intrinsic constant vbKeyRButton for the right button.

The statement that causes the menu to appear is the `PopupMenu` statement. Follow the command with the name of the menu (the top-level menu name).

```
Private Sub Form_MouseUp(Button As Integer, Shift As Integer, X As Single, _
     Y As Single)
   'Display a menu when the right mouse button is pressed

   If Button = vbKeyRButton Then      'Constant value = 2
      PopupMenu mnuForm
   End If
End Sub
```

> **Tip**
>
> Find the VB intrinsic constants using the Object Browser. The mouse and key constants are listed in KeyCodeConstants.

The Report Designer

When you need to create a printed report based on a database, you can use the **Report Designer**, which is new to VB 6.0. You first set up a data source using the **Data Environment**, also new to VB 6.0, then lay out the design of the report using Report Designer. Both the Data Environment and report become modules in your project. After you create the report, you can display it on the screen using the report's `Show` method, or send the report to the printer with the `PrintReport` method.

When you design a report, you are creating a template for a report. Each time you display or print the report, VB uses current data values from the data source that you specify.

You can add a data source and report(s) to an existing project or create a new project for the report. In this step-by-step tutorial, we will create a new project that displays a report on the screen or sends it to the printer. Figure 15.32 shows the completed report.

Figure   15.32

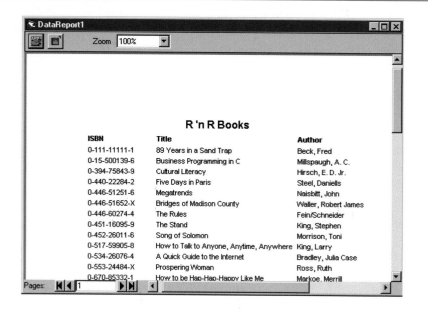

Note: The Working Model Edition of VB 6.0 does not include the Data Environment or the Report Designer, so this exercise cannot be done.

Begin the Project

STEP 1: Open a new standard project.

STEP 2: Save the project in a new folder called Ch15Report. Name the form file Reports.frm and the project file Reports.vbp.

STEP 3: Use the Windows Explorer to move a copy of RnRBooks.mdb into the new folder. (You can find RnRBooks.mdb on the Student Data CD in the Chap 11 & 12 Data Files folder.)

Set Up the Data Source

Each report must be based on a data source, which can be any one of many relational database formats, or even nonrelational data.

STEP 1: Open the *Project* menu and select *Add Data Environment*. A Data Environment window will open (Figure 15.33).

    Note: If *Add Data Environment* is not listed in the *Project* menu, open the *Components* dialog box, select the *Designers* tab, and click on *Data Environment*. If your system has more than four designers selected, you may find *Add Data Environment* under *More ActiveX Designers*.

You can display the *Components* dialog box by right-clicking on the toolbox.

Figure 15.33

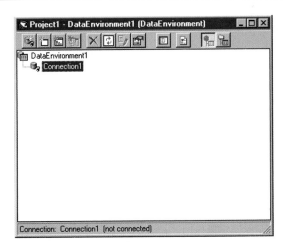

The Data Environment window.

STEP 2: Click on *DataEnvironment1*, and change its Name property to deBooks (Figure 15.34).

Figure 15.34

Change the Name property of the data environment in the Properties window.

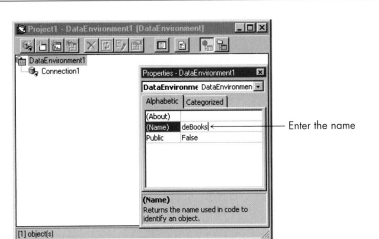

STEP 3: Click on *Connection1* and change its Name property to conBooks.

STEP 4: Right-click on conBooks and select Properties; the *Data Link Properties* dialog box appears (Figure 15.35).

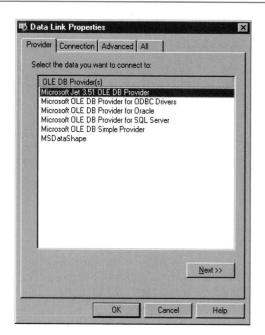

Set properties for the connection in the Data Link Properties dialog box.

STEP 5: On the *Provider* tab, select *Microsoft Jet 4.0 OLE DB Provider* and click *Next*.

STEP 6: On the *Connection* tab, click on the builder button (ellipsis button) for database name, navigate to your new folder (Ch15Report), and select RnRBooks.mdb. Click the *Test Connection* button to make sure that your connection is set up correctly, then click OK to close the dialog box.

STEP 7: In the deBooks Data Environment window, right-click on conBooks and select *Add Command* from the shortcut menu.

STEP 8: Right-click on *Command1* and select *Properties* from the shortcut menu.

STEP 9: On the *General* tab, enter Books for *Command Name*. The Connection should be set to conBooks.

STEP 10: For *Source of Data*, drop down the list for *Database Object* and select *Table*.

STEP 11: For *Object Name*, drop down the list and choose *Books*. Click OK to close the dialog box. You have now set the data source to the Books table of the RnRBooks.mdb database. Click on the plus sign for Books to see a listing of the fields in the table (Figure 15.36).

Figure 15.36

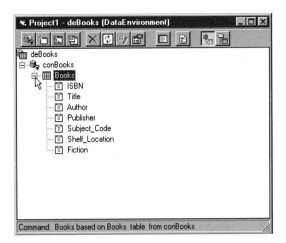

Design the Report

You will want to keep the Data Environment window open during most of the report design. At times you may close the window to better view the report design. You can open the window again by clicking on the deBooks icon in the Project Explorer window.

Begin the Report

STEP 1: Open the *Project* menu and select *Add Data Report*. The Data Report window opens. Resize the window to see more of the report.

Notice the bands or sections on the report layout. You can add bound controls, labels, images, and other controls to each of the sections of the report.

When you are working on a report object, the toolbox changes to display the tools for a report. Take a minute to look over the available controls.

Set the Report's Properties

STEP 1: In the Properties window, change the Name property of the report to rptBooks (Figure 15.37).

Figure 15.37

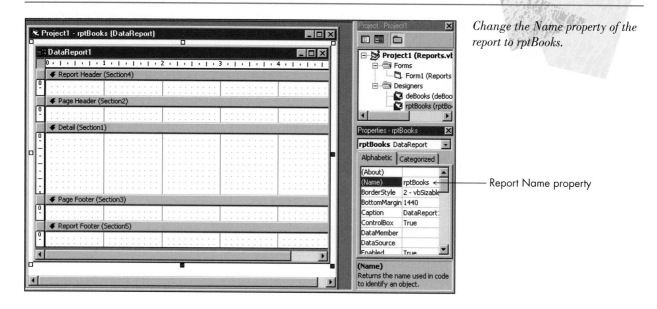

Change the Name property of the report to rptBooks.

STEP 2: Drop down the list for the DataSource property and select deBooks.

STEP 3: Set the DataMember property to Books.

Close the Report Header Section

STEP 1: Point to the dividing line at the top of the Page Header section. When your pointer changes to the two-headed arrow, drag upwards to close the Report Header section. Anything you place in the Report Header section appears at the top of the first page of a report.

Place a Title in the Page Header Section

STEP 1: Select the RptLabel tool in the toolbox and draw a label in the Page Header section. Change the label's Caption property to "R 'n R Books" (Figure 15.38).

STEP 2: Modify the label's properties to set the Font to 12-point bold and the alignment to centered.

While the label is still selected, you may want to resize the control and/or move it into a better position.

STEP 3: Drag the bottom edge of the section down to allow room for the column headings.

Figure   15.38

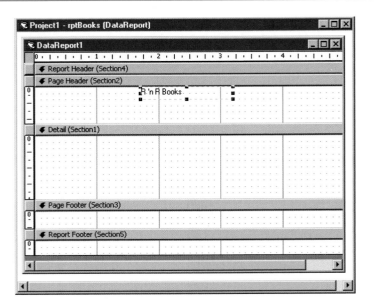

Change the Caption of the report title label to R 'n R Books.

Place Bound Controls in the Detail Section

STEP 1: Arrange your screen so that you can see the report layout and the Data Environment window. You may want to close the toolbox, the Project Explorer window, and the Properties window.

STEP 2: Click on ISBN in the Data Environment window and drag a control onto the Detail section of the report layout. Drop the icon at approximately the 1-inch mark at the top of the section (Figure 15.39).

Figure   15.39

Drag the icon for the ISBN field onto the Detail section.

The designer creates a text box as a bound control and a label to indicate the field name. You can move the two controls independently, change their properties, or delete them to match your planning design.

STEP 3: Drag the Title and Author fields to the Detail section. You will move the fields and labels to match the report design next.

Move the Detail Fields and Column Headings into Position

STEP 1: Referring to Figure 15.40, move and resize the labels and text boxes. The labels should appear in the Page Header section, which appears once at the top of each page. The text boxes should appear in the Detail section, because that section repeats once for every record in the data source.

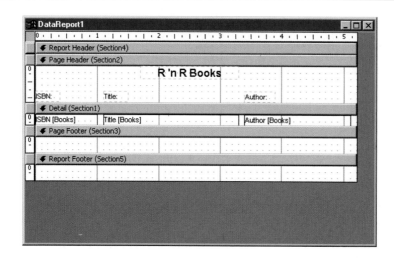

Move and resize the controls.

STEP 2: Resize the Page Header section and the Detail section to remove any extra space. Any extra space in the Detail section is repeated for every row, giving the report wide spacing between lines.

STEP 3: Select the three column heading labels and change their font to bold.

STEP 4: Remove the colons from the Captions of the labels.

STEP 5: Drag the dividers upward to close the Page Footer and Report Footer sections.

Save the Report Design

STEP 1: Select *Save rptBooks As* from the *File* menu and save the report file. It will be named rptBooks.dsr. Your screen should resemble Figure 15.41.

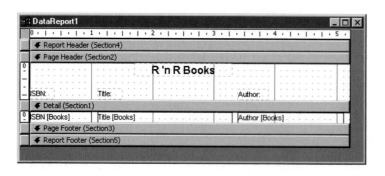

The final layout of the report design.

Print the Report from a Form

Set up the Form Properties

STEP 1: Set up your screen for working on a form: Click on the toolbox *General* tab to display form controls; display the form and the Properties window.

STEP 2: Change the form's Name property to frmReport and its Caption to R 'n R Book Report.

STEP 3: Open the menu editor and create a menu with these commands:

Caption	Name
&File	mnuFile
&Report	mnuFileReport
&Display	mnuFileReportDisplay
&Print	mnuFileReportPrint
E&xit	mnuFileExit

Write the Code

STEP 1: In the mnuFileReportDisplay_Click procedure, code these lines:

```
Private Sub mnuFileReportDisplay_Click()
    'Display the report on the screen

    rptBooks.Show
End Sub
```

STEP 2: In the mnuFileReportPrint_Click procedure, code these lines:

```
Private Sub mnuFileReportPrint_Click()
    'Print the report on the printer

    rptBooks.PrintReport
End Sub
```

STEP 3: Code the mnuFileExit_Click procedure:

```
Private Sub mnuFileExit_Click()
    'End the project

    Unload rptBooks
    Unload frmReport
    End
End Sub
```

Test the Code and Report Layout

STEP 1: Save your project and run it.

STEP 2: Test the *File / Report / Display* command. Your report should display on the screen. You may need to return to the Report Designer to modify the layout of the report.

S u m m a r y

1. ActiveX refers to controls and procedures that can be used by different applications. You can access objects other than the ones in the toolbox by selecting options from the *Components* or *References* dialog boxes from the commands on the *Project* menu.
2. Visual Basic enables you to create new controls and to make the .ocx files that are registered in the *Components* dialog box.
3. Dynamic link libraries are procedures in library files, outside of Visual Basic, that can be linked and called when a project is running.
4. DLLs used by Windows are referred to as the Windows application programming interface (API).
5. DLL procedures may pass arguments by value (pass a copy of the value) or by reference (pass the address of the value).
6. Objects created by other applications can be linked to a Visual Basic project using the OLE container control. The object can appear on a Visual Basic form and be manipulated by the user of the Visual Basic project. Linked objects are actually maintained by the application that created them.
7. OLE embedded objects are similar to linked objects except that the files relating to the objects are stored with the Visual Basic project, which greatly increases the size of the project.
8. Visual Basic for Applications is the standard language used for generating procedures (macros) in other Microsoft application packages, such as Word, Excel, and Access.
9. A VB project can use an MDI form as a parent form and specify other forms as child forms.
10. You can specify a shortcut menu to pop up when the user right-clicks over the form or a control.
11. The VB Report Designer can be used to design reports for a database that can be printed from a VB project.
12. The Report Designer requires that a data source first be created.

K e y   T e r m s

ActiveX *584*
API *594*
Arrange method *610*
child *608*
Data Environment *613*
Declare statement *594*
dynamic link libraries (DLL) *593*
embedding *600*
linking *600*
MDI *608*

OLE *584*
parent form *608*
Report Designer *613*
SDI *608*
shortcut menu *612*
Tabbed Dialog control *585*
Visual Basic for Applications (VBA) *603*
Web Browser control *589*

R e v i e w   Q u e s t i o n s

1. What is an ActiveX control? Give an example.
2. What is a DLL?
3. What does *API* mean?
4. What are the purposes of a `Declare` statement?
5. Explain the difference between `ByVal` and `ByRef`. When is each used?
6. Explain the difference between linking and embedding an object into a Visual Basic project.
7. What determines the list of objects that can be used with OLE in a particular system?
8. What does *MDI* mean?
9. What are the advantages of having parent and child forms?
10. How can a child form be created? a parent form?

P r o g r a m m i n g   E x e r c i s e s

15.1 Add an OLE control to a form and select *Create New File*. Look over the list of OLE objects available on your system. Try linking and embedding an object and compare the file size of your projects.

15.2 Examine the .wav files in your Windows directories. Write a project that prompts the user to guess a number. Have the project generate a random number from 1 to 100. Allow the user to enter a number. Display a message that indicates whether the response is too high or too low. If the user gives the correct answer, use the Tada.wav file to play a sound.

15.3 If you have access to a multimedia system with a microphone, record a short message to a .wav file. Write a project that plays back the sound file—a description of an item being displayed, for example.

15.4 Convert one of your previous projects with multiple forms to an MDI project. Make the main form the MDI form and all other forms child forms.

15.5 Start with one of your previous projects and add shortcut menus to the form and any controls that could benefit from the menu.

CASE STUDIES

VB Mail Order

Create an ActiveX control to perform the actions of VB Mail from Chapter 1. The class should display the name and telephone number for the contact person of the selected department.

Include command buttons for the customer relations, marketing, order processing, and shipping departments. When the user clicks on the button for a department, display the name and telephone number for the contact person in two labels. Also include identifying labels with Captions *Department Contact* and *Telephone Number*.

Test your control in a form that includes buttons to print the form and to exit.

Test Data

Department	Department Contact	Telephone Number
Customer Relations	Tricia Mills	500-1111
Marketing	Michelle Rigner	500-2222
Order Processing	Kenna DeVoss	500-3333
Shipping	Eric Andrews	500-4444

VB Auto Center

Create a new ActiveX control that includes a list box and a label. Selecting the department name from the list box should display the appropriate special in a label. Create a form module that incorporates the new control.

Test Data

List Box	Special to Display in Label
Auto Sales	Family wagon, immaculate condition $12,995
Service Center	Lube, oil, filter $25.99
Detail Shop	Complete detail $79.95 for most cars
Employment Opportunities	Sales position: Contact Mr. Mann 551-2134 x475

Video Bonanza

Modify your project for Chapter 14 to include sound. You may use an existing sound file (.wav) or create one of your own using a microphone on a multimedia computer system.

Very Very Boards

Modify one of your Very Very Boards projects from Chapter 11 or 12 to add a report using the Microsoft Report Designer. (*Note:* The Report Designer is not available in the Working Model edition of VB.)

Base the report on the Product table in VeryBoards.mdb. Include the ProductID, Description, MfgID, and Unit fields.

Include a report title, column headings, and detail lines for your report. Add your name to the page header section of the report.

A

Answers to Feedback Questions

Feedback 2.1

Property	Setting
Name	imgBig
Stretch	True
Appearance	1 - 3D
BorderStyle	1 - Fixed Single
Visible	True

Feedback 2.2

1. `txtCompany.Text = ""`
   `txtCompany.SetFocus`
2. `lblCustomer.Caption = ""`
   `txtOrder.SetFocus`
3. (a) Check box is checked.
   (b) Option button is not selected.
   (c) Image is not visible.
   (d) The appearance is set to three-dimensional; border style is fixed.
   (e) Assigns the value in txtCity.Text to lblCity.Caption.

Feedback 3.1

1. Does not indicate the data type with a prefix.
2. Cannot contain special characters such as #.
3. No blank spaces are allowed within an identifier.
4. The periods separate items such as object and property and should not be used in a variable identifier.
5. Cannot contain special characters such as $.
6. *Sub* is a reserved word in Visual Basic.
7. Valid name. Is it meaningful? That would depend upon the situation.
8. *Caption* is a property name and, as such, is a reserved word.
9. Follows the naming rules but not the conventions. A prefix should be used to indicate the data type.
10. A prefix should be used to specify the data type.
11. Valid.
12. Valid.

Feedback 3.2

Note: Answers may vary; make sure the prefix indicates the data type.

1. (a) sngHoursWorked
   (b) strEmployeeName
   (c) strDepartmentNumber
2. (a) intQuantity
   (b) strDescription
   (c) strPartNumber
   (d) curCost
   (e) curSellingPrice

Feedback 3.3

Note: Answers may vary; make sure the prefix indicates the data type.

1. `Dim mcurTotal As Currency`, declared at module level.
2. `Const mcurSalesTaxRate As Currency = .07`, declared at module level.
3. `Dim mintParticipantCount As Integer`, declared at module level.

Feedback 3.4

1. 18
2. 1
3. 6
4. 5
5. 22
6. 4 to the power of 5; then multiply by 2 (2048).
7. 22
8. 38

Feedback 3.5

1. `lblAveragePay.Caption = FormatCurrency(mcurAveragePay)`
   $123.46
2. `lblPercentCorrect.Caption = FormatPercent(sngCorrect)`
   76.00%
3. `lblTotal.Caption = FormatNumber(mcurTotalCollected)`

Feedback 4.1

1. True
2. True
3. True
4. False
5. False
6. True
7. True
8. False
9. True
10. True

Feedback 4.2

1. The frogs option button on; the toads off.
2. It's the toads and the polliwogs.
3. It's true.
4.
```
If txtApples.Text > txtOranges.Text Then
    lblMost.Caption = "Apples"
Else
    lblMost.Caption = "Oranges"
End If
```
5.
```
If curBalance > 0 Then
    chkFunds.Value = Checked
    curBalance = 0
    intCounter = intCounter + 1
Else
    chkFunds.Value = Unchecked
End If
```

Feedback 5.1

1. Function procedure; a value is returned.
2.
```
Private Function intCalculateAverage (intValue1 As Integer, _
    intValue2 As Integer, intValue3 As Integer) As Integer
```
3. `intCalculateAverage = (intValue1 + intValue2 + intValue3) / 3`
4. The answer is assigned to a field with the name of the function.

Feedback 6.1

1. `Const mintFatCalories As Integer = 9  'module level`
2. `Public gstrNameHighest As String       'standard code module`
3. `Const gstrCompanyName As String = "Babs Bowling Service"`
   `    'standard code module`
4. `Public gcurTotalAmount As Currency       'standard code module`
5. `Public gintPersonCount As Integer        'standard code module`
6. `Dim curTotal As Currency                 'local to procedure`
7. (a) Module-level integer.
   (b) Standard code module currency.
   (c) Module-level currency.
   (d) Local currency.
   (e) Standard code module string.
   (f) Local string.
   (g) Module-level string.

Feedback 7.1

1. Tracks the physical number of elements in the list.
2. Stores the position of the currently selected item; has a value of 21 if nothing is selected.
3. String value of an item in the list.
4. Adds an item during run time.
5. Removes all items from the list.
6. Removes the selected or specified item from the list.
7. Displays the list in alphabetic order.

Feedback 7.2

```
blnItemFound = False                'Set initial value of found flag to False
intItemIndex = 0                    'Initialize counter for index
'Loop until the item is found or the end of list is reached
Do Until blnItemFound Or intItemIndex = lstItems.ListCount
    'Test if the text box entry matches item in list
    If txtNewItem.Text = lstItems.List(intItemIndex) Then
        blnItemFound = True         'Set the found flag to True
    End If
    intItemIndex = intItemIndex + 1  'Increment counter for index
Loop
```

Feedback 7.3

1. (a) There should not be a comma after the ending value.
   (b) The Next statement must contain the control variable that follows the For, intIndex in this case.
   (c) The item following the word For must be a variable and must be the same as the one on the Next statement.
   (d) Valid.
   (e) Valid.
   (f) Will never execute; should have a negative Step argument.

2. (a) Will execute four times with an ending value in intCounter of 14.
   (b) Will execute 10 times with an ending value in intCounter of 0.
   (c) Will execute seven times with an ending value of 6.5.
   (d) Will not execute.
   (e) Will execute three times; intCounter will have an ending value of 4.

Feedback 7.4

1. Half a loaf is better than none

2. Half,   My Eye

3. Hawks0   Doves0

4.	1	2	3	4	5	6
5.	1	2	3	4	5	6
6.		3	5			
7.		3		5		

Feedback 8.1

```
1. Select Case intTemp
      Case Is > 80
         lblComment.Caption = "It's Hot"
      Case Is > 32
         lblComment.Caption = "It's Moderate"
      Case Else
         lblComment.Caption = "It's Freezing"
   End Select
```

2. 'General Declarations
```
Dim mcurCoffeePrice As Currency

Private Sub optCoffee_Click(Index As Integer)
    'Find the price
    Select Case intIndex
        Case 0
            curCoffeePrice = 2
        Case 1
            curCoffeePrice = 2.25
        Case 2
            curCoffeePrice = 1.75
        Case 3
            curCoffeePrice = 2.5
    End Select
End Sub
```
3. Use a Case Else:
```
Case Else
    MsgBox "You must select an option from the Coffee Selections"
```

Feedback 8.2

1. Valid.
2. Valid.
3. Valid.
4. Invalid, beyond the range.
5. Valid.
6. Invalid, negative number.
7. Yields a decimal number, but Basic will use the integer portion.
8. Valid.

Feedback 8.3

1.
```
Type StudentInfo
    strLastName         As String
    strFirstName        As String
    strStudentNumber    As String
    curUnits            As Currency
    curGPA              As Currency
End Type
```
2. `Dim udtStudents(99) As StudentInfo`

3. Type Project
```
     strName              As String
     strForm(9)           As String
     strSubdirectory      As String
   End Type
```
4. Dim udtMyProject As Project
5. Dim udtOurProjects(99) As Project

Feedback 8.4

1. Dim curTemperature(1 to 3, 1 to 5) As Currency
2. For intColumn = 1 To 5
```
       curTemperature(1, intColumn) = 0
   Next intColumn
```
3. For intColumn = 1 To 5
```
       curTemperature(2, intColumn) = 75
   Next intColumn
```
4. For intColumn = 1 To 5
```
       curTemperature(3, intColumn) = curTemperature(1, _
           intColumn) + curTemperature(2, intColumn)
   Next intColumn
```
5. For Each vTemp in curTemperature
```
       Printer.Print vTemp
   Next vTemp
```

Feedback 9.1

1. The following code will be placed at the module level of the class module.
```
   Private mstrLastName           As String
   Private mstrFirstName          As String
   Private mstrStudentIDNumber    As String
   Private mcurGPA                As Currency
```
2. Public Property Let LastName(ByVal strLastName As String)
```
       'Assign the property Value

       mstrLastName = strLastName
   End Property
```
3. Public Property Get GPA() As Currency
```
       'Retrieve the current Value

       GPA = mcurGPA
   End Property
```

Feedback 9.2

1. A class defines an item type (like the cookie cutter defines the shape), whereas the object is an actual instance of the class (as the cookie made from the cookie cutter).
2. mProduct follows the naming conventions for an object, whereas CProduct would be the class.
3. The quantity property of the mProduct object is assigned the value contained in the text box.

Feedback 10.1

1. (a) `Open "Vendor.Dat" For Output As #1`
   (b) `For intIndex = 0 to lstVendor.ListCount - 1`
   `        Write #1, lstVendor.List(intIndex)`
   `    Next intIndex`
   (c) `Close #1`
   (d) `Open "Vendor.Dat" For Input As #1`
   (e) `Do Until EOF(1)`
   `        Input #1, strVendor`
   `        lstVendor.AddItem strVendor`
   `    Loop`
2. `EOF()`
3. The Path property of the App object returns the folder path for the current application.

Feedback 10.2

1. Turns off error trapping.
2. Branches execution to the line labeled `WhatToDo` when an error occurs.
3. Sets the error code to 53 and triggers the error condition so that the system will handle it.
4. Continues execution with the statement that caused the error.
5. Continues execution with the statement following the one that caused the error.

Feedback 10.3

1. ```
Type Inventory
    strDescription   As String * 30
    strPartNumber   As String * 5
    curPrice   As Currency
    intQuantity   As Integer
End Type
```
2. `Dim udtInventoryRecord As Inventory`
3. ```
Open "C:\Inventory.dat" For Random As #1 Len = _
    Len(udtInventoryRecord)
```
4. `intNumberRecords = LOF(1) / Len(udtInventoryRecord)`
5. `Put #1, intRecordNumber, udtInventoryRecord`
6. 6, the position number of the next record.
7. `Get #1, intRecordNumber, udtInventoryRecord`

Feedback 11.1

adoClasses.CommandType	adCmdTable
adoClasses.RecordSource	Teachers
txtTeacher.DataSource	adoClasses
txtTeacher.DataField	Name
txtTeacher.Text	Not important—will display name from table

Feedback 12.1

1. ```
intRecordNumber = adoControl.Recordset.AbsolutePosition
If adoControl.Recordset.EOF then
    lblRecordNumber.Caption = "EOF"
Else
    lblRecordNumber.Caption = intRecordNumber
End If
```
2. `On Error Resume Next`
3. `Cancel = True`
4. ```
If txtName.Text = "" Then
    MsgBox "Name required", vbExclamation, "Data Missing"
End If
```

5. A message box will appear with the error description.

Feedback 12.2

1. adoProducts.Recordset.Find "Quantity < 20"
2. adoProducts.Recordset.Filter = "Quantity < 20"
3. (a) adoAcmePayroll.Recordset.Sort = "Rate"
   (b) adoAcmePayroll.Recordset.Sort = "[Employee Name]"
4. adoAcmePayroll.Recordset.Filter = "YTD > 45000"

Feedback 13.1

1. The DragMode property and the DragIcon property.
2. The target.
3. The name *Source* can be used to refer to the source control (the control being dragged over the target).

Feedback 14.1

1. Line (3360, 0) – (3360, 4230)
2. Const PI = 3.14159
   Circle (1600, 1000), 600, , -PI * 0.2, -PI * 1.8

B

Functions for Working with Dates, Financial Calculations, Mathematics, and String Operations

Visual Basic includes a wealth of functions that you can use in your projects. The preceding chapters cover only a few of the available functions. Some of the string functions are covered in Chapter 7. Other functions that are covered include `MsgBox`, `Val`, `UCase`/`LCase`, and `Format`.

This appendix introduces some additional functions for handling dates, for performing financial calculations and mathematical operations, for converting between data types, and for performing string operations.

Date Functions

Visual Basic has several functions specifically for dealing with dates. The date functions can retrieve the system date, break down a date into component parts, test whether the contents of a field are compatible with the date data type, and convert other data types to a date.

Accessing the System Date

You can retrieve the system date from your computer with the `Date` function, which returns the current date, or the `Now` function, which returns both the date and the time. These functions can be very handy in "time stamping" data or for inclusion in a report heading.

The Date and Now Functions—General Form

```
Now

Date
```

The Date and Now Functions—Examples

```
lblDate.Caption = Date      'Assign the system date to a label

Printer.Print Now
```

Date Variables

The date data type may hold values of many forms that represent a date. Examples could be May 22, 1998 or 5/22/98 or 5-22-1998. When a value is assigned to a date variable, it must be enclosed in # signs.

```
Dim datMyDate as Date
datMyDate = #3-1-97#
```

You can use the `FormatDateTime` function to format dates and times.

Converting Values to a Date Format

In order to store values in a date data type, you may need to convert the value of the data to a date type. You can accomplish this task with the CDate (convert to date) function.

The CDate Function—General Form

```
CDate(Variable or Property)
```

The CDate Function—Example

```
datMyDate = CDate(txtDate.Text)
```

When you want to compare two date fields from different sources, you can use the CDate function to assure that you are comparing compatible formats. This condition may occur when comparing a date from a database or file with the contents of a text box or date variable.

The DatePart Function

Another handy date function is the DatePart function, which can tell you whether a date is a weekday, what day of the week, what month, and so on. The part of the date that you extract is determined by a part type (interval) according to the following chart:

Part Type/Interval	Part of Date
yyyy	Year
q	Quarter
m	Month
y	Day of year
d	Day
w	Weekday
ww	Week
h	Hour
n	Minute
s	Second

The DatePart Function—General Form

```
DatePart("PartType", Date)
```

The DatePart Function—Example

```
MsgBox "The Month is " & DatePart("m", datMyDate)
```

Notice in the example that the *m* for the part type is enclosed in quotes.

Finding the Difference between Dates

You can use the `DateDiff` function to calculate with dates. The `DateDiff` function uses the same intervals as the `DatePart` function shown earlier. The `DateDiff` function uses two dates as arguments.

The DateDiff Function—General Form

```
DateDiff("Interval", Date1,Date2)
```

DateDiff Function—Example

```
MsgBox "It has been " & DateDiff("m", datMyDate, Now) & " months"
```

You could use this function to calculate the number of days prior to an event or how many days a payment is overdue.

Summary of Date Functions

Function	Purpose
CDate	Converts text data to date data type.
Date	Retrieves system date.
DateDiff	Finds the difference between two dates.
DatePart	Allows part of date to be accessed.
IsDate	Tests whether data can be converted to date data type.
MonthName	Returns the name of the month as a string.
Now	Retrieves system date and time.

Financial Functions

Visual Basic provides functions for many types of financial and accounting calculations, such as payment amount, depreciation, future value, and present value. When you use these functions, you eliminate the need to know and code the actual formulas yourself. Each financial function returns a value that you can assign to a variable, or to a property of a control.

Category	Purpose	Function
Depreciation	Double-declining balance.	DDB
	Straight line.	SLN
	Sum-of-the-years digits.	SYD
Payments	Payment.	Pmt
	Interest payment.	IPmt
	Principal payment.	PPmt
Return	Internal rate of return.	IRR
	Rate of return when payments and receipts are at different rates.	MIRR
Rate	Interest rate.	Rate
Future value	Future value of an annuity.	FV
Present value	Present value.	PV
	Present value when values are not constant.	NPV
Number of periods	Number of payments.	NPer

You must supply each function with the necessary values, called the *arguments*. You specify the name of the function, followed by parentheses that enclose the arguments.

The Visual Basic editor helps you type the arguments of functions. When you type the parentheses, the arguments will be specified in order. The one to be entered next is in bold. The order of the arguments is important because the function uses the values in the actual formula based on their position in the argument list. For example, the following Pmt function has three arguments: the interest rate, number of periods, and amount of loan. If you supply the values in a different order, the Pmt function will calculate with the wrong numbers.

The PMT Function

You can use the Pmt function to find the amount of each payment on a loan if the interest rate, the number of periods, and the amount borrowed are known.

The Pmt Function—General Form

```
Pmt(interest rate per period, number of periods, amount of loan)
```

The interest rate must be specified as a decimal and adjusted to the interest rate per period. For example, if the loan is made with an annual rate of 10 percent and monthly payments, the interest rate must be converted to the monthly rate. Convert the annual rate to the monthly rate by dividing by the number of months in a year (.10/12).

The number of periods for the loan is the total number of payments. If you want to know the monthly payment for a 5-year loan, you must convert the number of years to the number of months. Multiply the number of years by 12 months per year (12 * 5).

The Pmt Function—Example

```
curMonthlyRate = Val(txtRate.Text) * 12
curMonths = Val(txtYears.Text)/12
curAmount = Val(txtAmount.Text)
lblMonthlyPayment.Caption = Pmt(curMonthlyRate, curMonths, curAmount)
```

Notice in the example that the fields used in the payment function are from text boxes that the user can enter, and the answer is displayed in a label. It would also be wise to use the Format function on the result.

The Rate Function

You can use the Rate function to determine the interest rate per period when the number of periods, the payment per period, and the original amount of the loan are known.

The Rate Function—General Form

```
Rate(number of periods, payment per period, loan amount)
```

The Rate Function—Example

```
curMonths = Val(txtYears.Text) * 12
curPayment = Val(txtPayment.Text)
curAmount = Val(txtAmount.Text)
msngPeriodicRate = Rate(curMonths, curPayment, curAmount)
msngAnnualRate = msngPeriodicRate * 12
```

Functions to Calculate Depreciation

If you need to calculate the depreciation of an asset in a business, Visual Basic provides three functions: the double-declining-balance method, the straight-line method, and the sum-of-the-years-digits method.

The DDB function calculates the depreciation for a specific period within the life of the asset, using the double-declining-balance method formula. Once again, you do not need to know the formula but only in what order to enter the arguments. Incidentally, the *salvage value* is the value of the item when it is worn out.

The DDB (Double-Declining Balance) Function—General Form

```
DDB(original cost, salvage value, life of the asset, period)
```

The DDB Function—Example

```
curCost = Val(txtCost.Text)
curSalvage = Val(txtSalvage.Text)
curYears = Val(txtYears.Text)
curPeriod = Val(txtPeriod.Text)
lblDepreciation.Caption = DDB(curCost, curSalvage, curYears, curPeriod)
```

The other financial functions work in a similar manner. You can use the *Help* menu to find the argument list, an explanation, and an example.

Numeric Functions

Visual Basic includes functions for many mathematical operations.

Function	Returns
Abs(x)	The absolute value of x. $\|x\| = x$ if $x \geq 0$ $\|x\| = -x$ if $x \leq 0$
Atn(x)	The angle in radians whose tangent is x.
Cint(x)	The even integer closest to x (rounded).
Cos(x)	The cosine of x where x is in radians.
Exp(x)	The value of e raised to the power of x.
Fix(x)	The integer portion of x (truncated).
Int(x)	The largest integer $\leq x$.
Log(x)	The natural logarithm of x, where $x \geq 0$.
Rnd	A random number in the range 0–1 (exclusive).
Round(x[,DecimalPlaces])	The rounded value of x, rounded to the specified number of decimal positions. *Note:* Values round to the nearest even number.
Sgn(x)	The sign of x. -1 if $x < 0$ 0 if $x = 0$ 1 if $x > 0$
Sin(x)	The sine of x where x is in radians.
Sqr(x)	The square root of x where x must be ≥ 0.
Tan(x)	The tangent of x where x is in radians.

Functions for Working with Strings

Visual Basic provides many string functions for working with text. Although several of the functions are covered in this text, many more are available.

Function	Returns
Asc(*StringExpression*)	The number corresponding to the ASCII or ANSI code for the first character of String.
Chr(*NumericCode*)	A string character that corresponds to the ASCII or ANSI code in the range 0–255. Reverse of the Asc function.
Instr([*StartingPosition,*] StringExpression, SubString)	A numeric value that is the position within the string where the substring begins; returns 0 if the substring is not found.
InstrRev(*StringExpression, SubString [, StartingPosition[, CompareSetting]]*)	A numeric value that is the position within the string where the substring begins, starting from the end of the string; returns 0 if the substring is not found.
LCase(*StringExpression*)	The string converted to lowercase.
Left(*StringExpression, NumberOfCharacters*)	The leftmost characters of the string for the indicated number of characters.
Len(*StringExpression*)	A numeric count of the number of characters in the string.
Mid(*StringExpression, StartingPosition [, NumberOfCharacters]*)	A substring taken from the string, beginning at StartingPosition for the specified length.
Replace(*StringExpression, FindString, ReplacementString[, StartingPosition[, Count[, CompareSetting]]]*)	A string that has the FindString replaced with the ReplacementString the specified number of times.
Right(*StringExpression, NumberOfCharacters*)	The rightmost characters of the string for the indicated number of characters.
Space(*NumberOfCharacters*)	A string of blank spaces for the specified number of characters.
Str(*NumericExpression*)	The string value of the numeric expression; used to convert numeric values to strings. Reverse of the Val function.
String(*NumberOfCharacters, StringExpression*)	A string of the named character(s) for a length of the specified number of characters.
StrReverse(StringExpression)	A string with the characters reversed.
UCase(*StringExpression*)	The string converted to uppercase.
Val(*StringExpression*)	The numeric value of the string expression; used to convert strings to numeric values. Reverse of the Str function.

Functions for Converting between Data Types

Each of the following functions converts an expression to the named data type.

Function	Return Value
CBool(*Expression*)	Boolean
CDate(*Expression*)	Date
CDbl(*Expression*)	Double
CInt(*Expression*)	Integer
CLng(*Expression*)	Long
CSng(*Expression*)	Single
CStr(*Expression*)	String
CVar(*Expression*)	Variant

C

Tips and Shortcuts for Mastering the VB Environment

Set Up the Screen for Editing Convenience

As you work with the VB environment, you will find many ways to save time. Here are some tips and shortcuts that you can use to become more proficient in using the environment to design, code, and run your projects.

Close Extra Windows

Arrange your screen for best advantage. While you are entering and editing code in the Code window, you don't need the toolbox, the Project Explorer window, the Properties window, or the Form Layout window. Click each window's close button; you can quickly and easily open each window again when you need it.

Display Windows Quickly

An easy way to display windows is to use the VB standard toolbar.

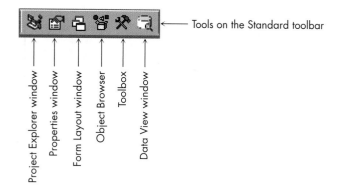

Tools on the Standard toolbar

Project Explorer window
Properties window
Form Layout window
Object Browser
Toolbox
Data View window

Display Windows Using Keyboard Shortcuts

Project Explorer window	Ctrl + R
Properties window	F4

Jump between the Form Window and Code Window

Form window	Shift + F7
Code window	F7
Jump back and forth	Ctrl + Tab

Dock and Float Windows for Your Convenience

All the toolbars and windows in the VB environment can be docked or floating. Windows toolbars can always be docked or floating; you can set the VB windows to be dockable or not on the *Docking* tab of the *Options* dialog box.

Moving Toolbars

To drag a toolbar, point to a gray area of the toolbar (not on a button), press the mouse button, and drag to a new location. If you drop the toolbar somewhere in the middle of the screen, it will display as an independent window; the toolbar is *floating*. A docked toolbar is attached along one of the edges of the screen. You can dock a toolbar at the top; under the menu bar (the default); or along the bottom, the left, or the right edges of the screen.

Docking the VB Windows

Docking the VB Project Explorer, Properties, and Form Layout windows can be a challenge. Each can be docked independently along any edge of the screen. The windows can also be docked together, which is the default and the way the windows appear in most figures in this text. To dock the three windows along the right edge of the screen, first dock the Project Explorer window. Then drag the Properties window to the lower edge of the Project Explorer window and drop. Sometimes you need more than one try to dock a window correctly. You can watch the window's outline change shape to indicate its floating or docking position. Then drag the Form Layout window to the bottom of the Properties window and drop it. Again, you may need more than one try to dock the window in the right location.

After you dock the three windows, you can resize them by dragging on their borders.

Display the Edit Toolbar

You can save yourself time by displaying and using the Edit toolbar while you are editing code. Choose *View/Toolbars* to select the Edit toolbar. Or you can right-click on any toolbar to pop up a list of the available toolbars and turn any toolbar on or off.

Here is the recommended screen setup to use while entering and editing code in the Code window:

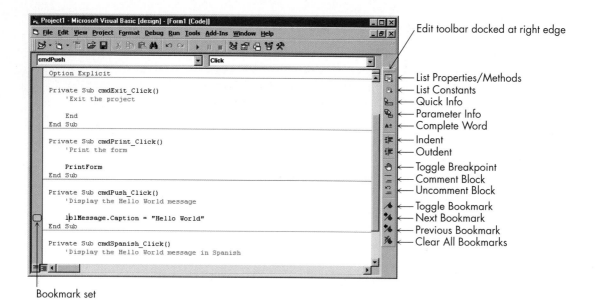

Edit toolbar docked at right edge

← List Properties/Methods
← List Constants
← Quick Info
← Parameter Info
← Complete Word
← Indent
← Outdent
← Toggle Breakpoint
← Comment Block
← Uncomment Block
← Toggle Bookmark
← Next Bookmark
← Previous Bookmark
← Clear All Bookmarks

Bookmark set

Comment Block: Use this command when you want to convert some code to comments, especially while you are testing and debugging projects. You can remove some lines from execution to test the effect, without actually removing them. Select the lines and click the Comment Block button; each line will have an apostrophe appended at the left end.

Uncomment Block: This command undoes the Comment Block command. Select some comment lines and click the Undo Uncomment Block button; the apostrophes at the beginning of the lines will be deleted.

Toggle Bookmark: This button sets and clears individual bookmarks. Bookmarks are useful when you are jumping around in the Code window. Set a bookmark on any line by clicking in the line and clicking the Toggle Bookmark button; you will see a mark in the margin area to the left of the marked line. You may want to set bookmarks in several procedures where you are editing or testing code.

Next Bookmark and *Previous Bookmark:* Use these buttons to quickly jump to the previous or next bookmark in the code.

Clear All Bookmarks: You can clear individual bookmarks with the Toggle Bookmark button or clear all bookmarks using this button.

Indent and *Outdent:* You can use these buttons to indent or outdent single lines or blocks of code. The buttons work the same way as the Tab and Shift + Tab keys.

The buttons for List Properties/Methods, List Constants, Quick Info, and Parameter Info can be helpful. By default, these options are turned on, and the lists automatically appear as you are typing code. You might prefer to keep the automatic features turned off and click the buttons when you actually want the lists to appear.

Try clicking the Complete Word button as you are typing the name of an object or a variable. If you have typed enough for the editor to identify the word, it will automatically fill in the rest. You can also press Ctrl + Spacebar for this function.

Set Options for Your Convenience

The VB environment is customizable, and you may find that you prefer changing some of the options. Choose *Tools/Options* to display the *Options* dialog box. *Note:* If you are working in a shared lab, check with the instructor or lab technician before changing any options.

Editor Tab: For optimum editing you will want to make sure that *Drag-and-Drop Text Editing, Default to Full Module View,* and *Procedure Separator* are selected.

General Tab: In the *Form Grid Settings* frame, you can set up the way you want the grid to appear as you work on forms. You can turn the grid off or on, or modify the spacing of the grid dots.

Use Shortcuts When Editing Code

While you are editing code, save yourself time by using keyboard shortcuts.

Task	Shortcut
Delete the current line (insertion point anywhere in line).	Ctrl + Y
Delete from insertion point left to beginning of word.	Ctrl + Backspace
Delete from insertion point right to end of word.	Ctrl + Delete
Complete the word.	Ctrl + Spacebar
Jump to a procedure (insertion point on procedure name). Use this shortcut while working on the general sub procedures and functions that you write. For example, when writing a call to a function, you want to check the coding in the function. Point to the procedure name in the *Call* and press Shift + F2. After you finish looking at the function, press Ctrl + Shift + F2 to return to the original position (the *Call*).	Shift + F2
Jump back to original position after a jump.	Ctrl + Shift + F2
Jump to the top of the current module.	Ctrl + Home
Jump to the bottom of the current module.	Ctrl + End
Indent a block of code.	Highlight lines and use the Edit toolbar button or Tab key.
Outdent (Unindent) a block of code.	Highlight lines and use the Edit toolbar button or Shift + Tab.

Split the Edit Window

You can view more than one procedure at a time by splitting the Code window. Point to the Split bar at the top of the vertical scroll bar and drag the bar down to the desired location. To remove the split, you can either drag the split bar back to the top or double-click the split bar.

Use Drag-and-Drop Editing

You can use drag-and-drop to move or copy text to another location in the Code window, to the Code window for another project, to the Immediate window, or to the Watch window.

To move code, select the text, point to the selection, and drag it to a new location. You can copy text (rather than move it) by holding down the Ctrl key as you drag.

Use Shortcuts in the Form Window

You can save time while creating the user interface in the Form window by using shortcuts.

Create Multiple Controls of the Same Type

When you want to create several controls of the same class, you must select the toolbox tool each time you draw a new control. That is, unless you use this method: When you select the toolbox tool for the first control, hold down the Ctrl key as you click. After you create your first new control, the tool will stay selected so that you can create as many more controls of that class as you wish.

When you are finished, press Esc to deselect the tool or click on another toolbox tool.

Display the Form Editor Toolbar

You can display the Form Editor toolbar to save yourself time when working with multiple controls. Turn toolbars on and off from the *View/Toolbars* menu command or by right-clicking any toolbar.

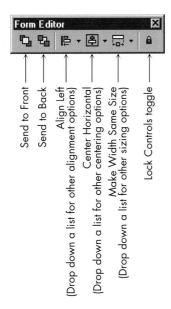

Nudge Controls into Place

Sometimes it is difficult to place controls exactly where you want them. Of course, you can use the alignment options on the *Format* menu or the Form Editor toolbar. You can also nudge controls in any direction by holding down the Ctrl key and pressing one of the arrow keys. *Nudging* moves a control one grid dot in the desired direction. If the grid is turned off, the control(s) moves by one pixel.

For example: Ctrl + right arrow moves a selected control one grid dot to the right.

Use Shortcuts to Execute a Project

You can use keyboard shortcuts to start and stop project execution.

Task	Shortcut
Run the current project (from Design time).	F5
Continue execution (from Break time).	F5
Restart execution from the beginning (from Break time).	Shift + F5
Stop execution.	Ctrl + Break
Begin execution, single-stepping through code.	F8

Use the Object Browser

The VB Object Browser can be a valuable source of information. You can use the Object Browser to examine objects, properties, methods, and events for VB objects; objects from other applications; and ActiveX controls. You can view a list of the objects, properties, procedures, and variable declarations in your project and jump to a section of your code.

Finding Lists of Constants

You can find listings of the VB constants using the Object Browser. The constants are grouped by function. Select *<All Libraries>* in the *Project/Library* box and then scroll the Classes list and click on the desired group; the constants will appear in the Members list. Or you can type something in the Search Text box and click the Search button.

This example shows the VB color constants:

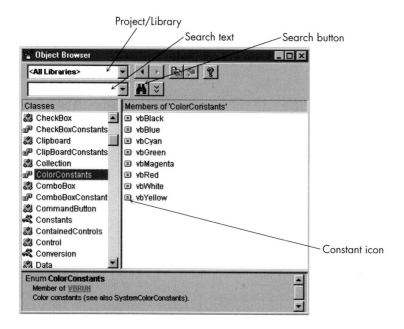

Learning about Objects

The Object Browser can show you all properties, methods, and events for an object. You can choose any of the VB objects; objects from other applications, such as Excel or Project; or an ActiveX control. Before you can display information about an object, it must be selected in the References list (*References* dialog box from the *Project* menu). *Note:* You can display the *References* dialog box directly from the Object Browser if you right-click to display the shortcut menu.

This example shows the listing for a vertical scroll bar control in the VB library.

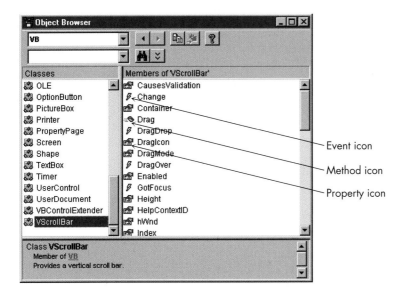

Jumping in Your Code

As soon as you develop a project with several modules, jumping to different sections of your code becomes more difficult. You can use the Object Browser for reference to recall the name you have given to any procedure, variable, or constant or to quickly jump to any position in your code.

Select your project name in the *Project/Library* box, and the Classes list will show the modules in your project. The Members list displays all objects, properties, and coded procedures (the methods). To jump to any procedure listing, double-click on the desired name.

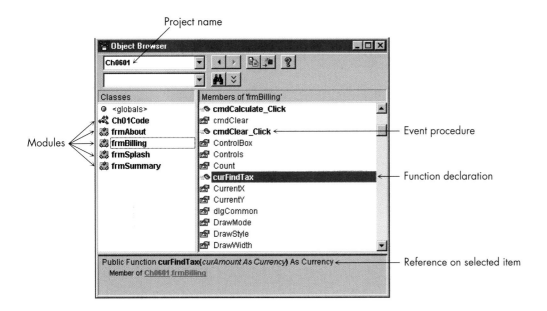

D

A Preview of Microsoft's VB.NET

The new version of Visual Basic, scheduled for release in late 2001, is called VB.NET. You also will see it referred to as Visual Basic 7, since it's the version that follows Visual Basic 6. This appendix is based on the public beta 1 version plus further information released by Microsoft during development.

A Major Revision

VB.NET is a major revision of Visual Basic, designed to fit into Microsoft's Internet development vision. VB.NET is one part of Visual Studio.NET Framework, which includes Visual C++, VB, and the new language C# (pronounced C-*sharp*).

The primary goals for VB.NET are interoperability with other languages, increased object-oriented programming capabilities, and easier development of Web-based applications. In order to achieve these goals, major changes were needed, both in the language syntax and in the way that data are stored and referenced.

Don't expect all VB developers to immediately switch to VB.NET. The consensus of VB programmers is that VB.NET is an entirely new language but that it will be somewhat familiar to anyone who already knows VB. Developers on the VB.NET newsgroup (news.microsoft.com:microsoft.public.dotnet.languages.vb) have expressed these conflicting points of view:

- Great new language. We plan to do all development in VB.NET.

- The changes in VB.NET will break our existing code base. We may do some future development in VB.NET but will not modify any existing applications.

- The new features are not worth the tremendous cost. We will stick with VB 6.

Interoperability

Using VB.NET you can create instances of classes written in other .NET languages, call methods from classes without knowing the original language, and pass variables and objects to and from components written in various languages. To make this happen, Microsoft had to make data types and calling protocol consistent for all .NET languages.

Common Language Runtime

Each of the languages in the .NET Framework compiles to a common machine language called Microsoft Intermediate Language (MSIL). The MSIL code is called *Managed Code* and runs in the Common Language Runtime (CLR).

Object-Oriented Programming

One of the biggest criticisms of VB 6 is that it isn't purely object oriented. Although you can create classes, interfaces, objects, properties, methods, and events, VB (6 and earlier) is missing a few important constructs to make it match up to other OOP languages. The primary missing feature is inheritance, which is the ability to create a new class based on an existing class, inheriting all the properties and methods of the base (or super) class. VB.NET finally has inheritance, the cost is that VB programmers must learn a new way of programming and a new set of keywords.

Common Features

The Visual Studio.NET languages, VB, C#, and C++, share several features:

- The new integrated development environment (IDE), which resembles the VB 6 IDE.

- The forms engine for creating Windows forms, called WindowsForms. Creating WindowsForms is very much like creating VB 6 forms.

- The forms engine for creating Web forms, called WebForms. The components that you place on WebForms are the components commonly available for HTML pages. The server converts your WebForm definition into standard HTML.

The IDE

You can use the New Visual Studio.NET integrated development environment to create VB solutions, as well as C# and C++ solutions. Figure D.1 shows the VS IDE (beta 2) with its Start Page displayed. Recent projects appear on the list, or you can choose to create a new project.

F i g u r e   D . 1

The shared Visual Studio.NET IDE Start Page.

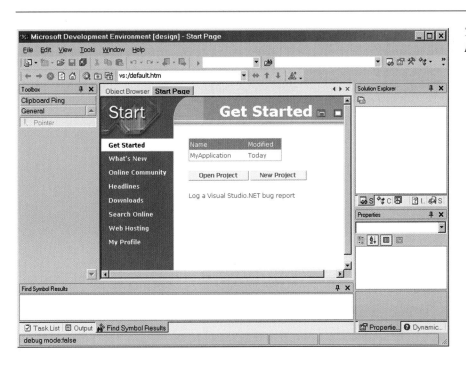

In the New Project dialog (Figure D.2) you can select *Windows Application* to create a project using WindowsForms. This is a form-based application familiar to VB programmers. Selecting *Web Application* begins a project based on WebForms.

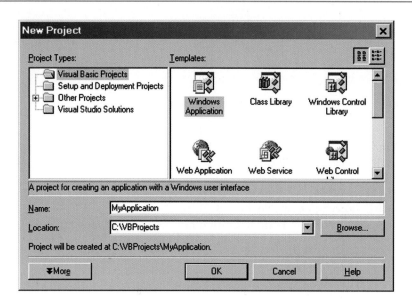

Begin a new VB.NET project using WindowsForms.

Figure D.3 shows the Form Designer and Figure D.4 shows the code for the current form. Notice the tabs at the top of the window that you can use to switch back and forth between form design and form coding. If you have several forms and code modules in the project, each will have its own tab.

The VS.NET Form Designer.

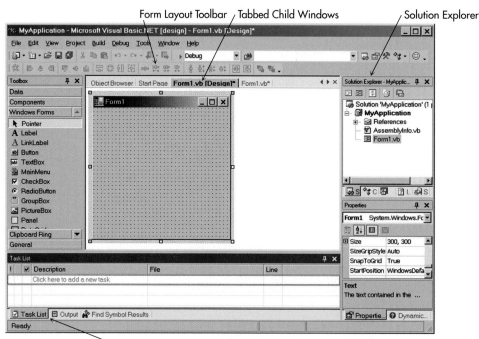

The VS.NET Code window. Collapse and expand sections of code using the plus and minus signs along the left edge of the window.

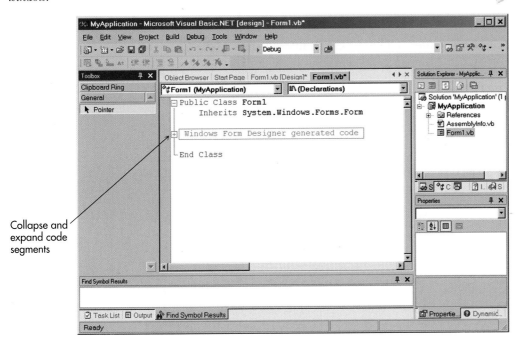

Collapse and
expand code
segments

Looking at the code in Figure D.4, you can see a couple of the big changes in VB.NET. You can use the plus and minus signs along the left edge to expand and hide sections of code. This can be a big help in a large project.

The code showing in the window was generated by the Form Designer. In fact, there's lots more code that is currently collapsed. Click a plus sign to expand the code if you want to see it.

In VB 6, the code to create the form and controls was hidden from the programmer. In VB.NET, that's no longer true. All of the code necessary to create a form is generated by the Form Designer. You should not change the generated code, because the next time you compile the project, the Form Designer will regenerate the code. If you want to make changes, you should switch back to design mode and make your changes there; the Form Designer will then generate the correct code to reflect the current design.

Changes to Visual Basic

The following sections introduce you to the major changes to the language. For a much more complete list along with discussions and examples, see the http://msdn.microsoft.com/net/Website.

Data Types

Big changes were made to the VB data types. Gone are the Variant and Currency types, and the integer types, Integer and Long, have changed.

- The default or universal data type is now Object. A variable of Object type can hold any type of data. Variant is no longer supported.

- In place of the Currency type, VB now has a Decimal type. Decimal variables hold decimal fractions with more digits to the left and to the right of the decimal point than the old Currency type.

- VB.NET does not support user-defined types (UDT). Instead you can use the new `Structure/End Structure` statements.

- Fixed-length strings are no longer allowed in the new VB.
  Unsupported code:
  ```
  Dim strName As String * 20
  ```

Size	New VB.NET Data Type	VB.NET Class	Visual Basic 6 (and earlier) Data Type
16 bits	Short	Int16	Integer
32 bits	Integer	Int32	Long
64 bits	Long	Int64	(not available)
(varies)	Object	Object	Variant
96 bits	Decimal	Decimal	Currency (64 bits)

Type Conversions

VB.NET is now a strongly typed language, which means that you must pay much closer attention to the type of data you are using. VB can perform an implicit conversion only if you are converting from a "narrow" data type into a "wider" data type. For example, you can convert an Integer type into a Long type like this:

```
lngNumber = intNumber
```

But to convert to a narrower type, where significant digits might be lost, you must explicitly convert from one type to another using conversion functions. To convert from a Long type into an Integer, use this statement:

```
intNumber = CInt(lngNumber)
```

When you convert user input from a text box, you must convert to the correct data type rather than use the `Val` function.

```
intCount = CInt(txtCount.Text)     'Convert text to Integer
decNumber = CDec(txtNumber.Text)   'Convert text to Decimal
```

Option Strict

You can set the new Option Strict option to Off to tell the compiler to ignore data type conversion problems. VB.NET will then operate pretty much like VB 6. This process is not recommended.

Place this statement at the tope of the module for each form or code module that you want type-checking turned off. Option Strict is On by default.

```
Option Strict Off
```

Declarations

VB.NET has a couple of new handy shortcuts. You can declare multiple variables on one line, naming the data type only once. And you can give a variable an initial value when you declare it.

Declaration	Creates
`Dim intCount, intIndex As Integer`	Two integer variables.
`Dim intMax As Integer = 100`	An integer variable with an initial value.

Arrays

There are some changes in the way that you declare arrays. Gone is the `Option Base` statement and the `To` option. All arrays begin with element zero. For example, these statements, which were considered preferred practices in VB 6, are no longer allowed:

VB 6 syntax:

```
    Dim strNames (1 To 10) As String
```
or
```
    Option Base 1
    Dim strNames (10) As String
```

When you declare an array in VB.NET, the number in parentheses is the upper bound of the array. So the statement

```
    Dim strNames (10)
```

declares an array of 11 elements—numbered 0 through 10.

The function of the `ReDim` statement is also changed. In VB 6 you could declare a dynamic array with `ReDim`. In VB.NET, all arrays are dynamic. Use `Dim` to declare an array; use the `ReDim` statement to change the number of elements in an array.

You also can assign initial values to an array when you declare it:

```
    Dim intCode(4) As Integer = (0, 2, 4, 5, 7)
    Dim strDept(3) As String = ("Art", "Business", "Math", "English")
```

New Keywords for Declaring Functions

The OOP extensions in VB.NET necessitate some new keywords for declaring functions and sub procedures. The new keywords, in addition to `Public` and `Private`, are

- Overloads—Procedure has the same name as another procedure in this class but with a different set of arguments.

- Overrides—Procedure has the same name as a procedure in the base class. This procedure will be called rather than the similarly named procedure in the base class.

- Overrideable—Any class that inherits from this class may have a similarly named procedure that overrides this procedure.

- MustOverride—Any class that inherits from this class *must* have a similarly named procedure that overrides this procedure.

- Protected—This procedure is available only to this class and any classes that inherit from this class. Protected is similar to Private in its interaction with objects, but has the added advantage of allowing inheritance.

- Friend—This procedure is available from all classes in the current project, but is unavailable from classes outside this project.

- Protected Friend—This procedure is available to classes that inherit from this class and to classes in the current project.

Example:

```
Overrides Function SetName (strName) As String

End Function
```

Passing Arguments

The default for arguments in VB.NET is ByVal; in VB 6 the default was ByRef. Passing arguments by reference (ByRef) is dangerous, since the called procedure can change the value of the argument in the calling procedure. If that's what you really want to do, specify by reference (ByRef).

Method Calls

In VB 6 you can choose whether or not to use parentheses when calling a method. In fact, if you use the Call keyword, you *must* use parentheses, and if you omit the Call keyword, you *cannot* use parentheses.

VB 6:

```
Call CalculateResult (intOne, intTwo)
```
or
```
CalculateResult intOne, intTwo
```

In VB.NET, you must always use the parentheses; the keyword Call is optional.

VB.NET:

```
Call CalculateResult (intOne, intTwo)
```
or
```
CalculateResult (intOne, intTwo)
```

Scope

VB.NET introduces an additional level of scope: block-level scope. If you declare a variable within a block, the variable is visible only within that block. A block is defined as a set of statements terminated by an `End`, `Loop`, or `Next` statement.

Example:

```
If intTotal > intMax Then
   Dim intCount As Integer
   intCount = intCount + 1
   lblOverMax.Caption = "Number over max: " & Str(intCount)
End If
```

Note that the lifetime of a block-level variable is the same as the lifetime of the entire procedure. Although the value of the variable is not available outside of the block, the variable holds its value as long as the procedure is running. If you re-enter the block while the procedure is executing, the block-level variable still has its previous value.

Namespaces

As you look over the documentation for VB.NET, you see many references to namespaces. Namespaces are used for organizing classes, interfaces, and methods into hierarchies and providing a way to refer to them.

A namespace is the hierarchy of names that you use to refer to a class, interface, or method. For example, to use the drawing methods, you must refer to System.Drawing.Graphics. The namespace is System.Drawing.Graphics for the methods `DrawLine` and `DrawEllipse`.

Namespaces prevent naming conflicts. In any one namespace, there can be only one class with any one name. However, a class name can appear in more than one namespace and not cause conflict. For example, the VS.NET Framework has a Button class in the System.Windows.Forms namespace and another Button class in the System.Web.UI.WebControl namespace. The reference to each of the Button classes includes the namespace:

System.Windows.Forms.Button
System.Web.UI.WebControl.Button

You can think of namespaces a little like libraries. You might want to reference all classes in the System library. However, in VB.NET, the classes that make up the System library do not have to be stored in one physical location. VB.NET can find and make available all classes declared with the System namespace, regardless of their location.

You also can declare your own namespaces for your projects, as a way of identifying all classes that belong to the application. The `NameSpace` statement goes at the top of the class definition.

```
NameSpace MyApplicationName
```

Imports

To use classes in the various namespaces, you need to explicitly import the namespaces into your code. The Form Designer generates the `Imports` statements necessary to create the form and controls (refer to Figure D.4). You can add `Imports` statements for namespaces that you want to use.

Syntax

New Assignment Operators

Anyone who knows C++ or Java will be pleased to see the addition of new assignment operators to VB. You can use either the new operators or the old syntax.

VB 6:

```
sngTotal = sngTotal + sngAmount     'Add sngAmount to sngTotal
intCount = intCount + 1             'Add 1 to intCount
```

VB.NET:

```
sngTotal += sngAmount               'Add sngAmount to sngTotal
intCount += 1                       'Add 1 to intCount
```

Operator	Operation
+=	Add the expression on the right side of the equal sign to the variable named on the left
−=	Subtract the expression on the right side of the equal sign from the variable named on the left.
*=	Multiply the variable by the expression on the right side of the equal sign and assign the result to the variable.
/=	Divide the variable by the expression on the right side of the equal sign and assign the result to the variable.
\=	Divide the variable by the expression on the right side of the equal sign and assign the integer result to the variable.
^=	Raise the variable to the exponent named on the right side of the equal sign and assign the result to the variable.
&=	Concatenate the string expression on the right side of the equal sign to the string variable on the left.

No Default Properties

VB.NET no longer has a default property for objects. In VB 6 you could omit the property name for the default property, but in VB.NET you must always specify the property name.

VB 6:

```
txtName.Text = "Bill"
```

or

```
txtName = "Bill"
```

VB.NET:

```
txtName.Text = "Bill"
```

In the new version of VB, assigning something to an object name does an object assign. For example, the statement:

```
objName = txtName
```

assigns the entire object txtName to objName, so that you could then refer to the properties of objName. Note that in previous versions of VB you needed a Set statement to perform an object assign; in VB.NET the Set statement is no longer supported.

Constants

The "vb" has been dropped from the names of the intrinsic constants. Instead you must specify the class in which the constant is declared. For example, the colors vbRed and vbBlue are now Color.Red and Color.Blue (plus many more choices, such as Fushia, HotPink, and ForestGreen).

The control characters change from vbCrLf, vbCr, and vbTab to ControlChars.CrLf, ControlChars.Cr, and ControlChars.Tab.

The message box constants are now MessageBox.OkOnly, Message Box.OKCancel, MessageBox.IconExclamation, MessageBox.IconInformation, and many more that are defined in the MessageBox class.

To see all of the constants for each of these classes, type the name of the class and the dot into the editor; the list will pop up with all of the choices.

Graphics

Gone are the PSet, Line, Circle, and Scale statements. You can draw by executing methods of the Graphics class. For example, use the Graphics.DrawLine and Graphics.DrawEllipse methods to draw lines and circles or ellipses.

Math Functions

The built-in math functions disappear in VB.NET. Instead you can use methods of the Math class: Math.Sqrt, Math.Sign, Math.Round, and Math.Atan.

Keywords Removed

A few keywords are no longer supported as part of the VB language. Most of these keywords are holdovers from early versions of Basic. The removed keywords include Let, On...GoSub, On...GoTo, Set, Wend, Type, LSet, and RSet.

The On Error GoTo statement is still supported for error trapping, but VB.NET introduces Try and Catch, which is a much better way to trap program errors. See the section on "Error Handling."

Debug.Print Replaced

The `Debug.Print` method is replaced by different methods of the Debug object: `Debug.Write`, `Debug.WriteIf`, `Debug.WriteLine`, and `Debug.WriteLineIf`.

Form_PrintForm Removed

VB.NET drops support of the `Form.PrintForm` method.

MsgBox Function Replaced

The standard `MsgBox` function is no longer supported. Instead you will use the `Show` method of the MessageBox class along with constants defined in the MessageBox class, such as the button and icons to display.

VB 6:

```
intAnswer = MsgBox ("My Message to You", vbYesNo + vbExclamation, _
                    "Dialog Title Bar")
if intAnswer = vbYes Then
  'Take some action
End If
```

VB.NET:

```
intAnswer = MessageBox.Show("My Message to You", "Dialog Title Bar", _
                    MessageBox.OKCancel + MessageBox.IconExclamation)
If intAnswer = DialogResult.OK Then
  'Take some action
End If
```

Toolbox Control Changes

Some of the standard toolbox controls are changed in VB.NET.

VB.NET Control	VB 6 Control
Button	CommandButton
TextBox	Text
GroupBox	Frame
RadioButton	OptionButton
FontDialog	CommonDialog
OpenFileDialog	
SaveFileDialog	
PrintDialog	
ColorDialog	
PrintPreviewDialog	
None (removed)	Shape
None (removed)	Line

Property Changes

You may be surprised to see some property changes for familiar controls. For example, the Form and the Label no longer have a Caption property; instead they both have Text properties.

Menu Changes

You create menus with two new controls: MainMenu and ContextMenu. You cannot popup a MainMenu as a context menu.

Error Handling

You will like the new structured error trapping, especially if you are familiar with C, C++, or Java. VB.NET now includes the `Try...Catch...Finally` block, so you can drop the unstructured `On Error GoTo` statement.

Enclose any program code that might cause an error in a `Try` block. If an error occurs, called an *exception,* control transfers to the `Catch` block. The optional `Finally` block executes last, whether or not an exception occurred.

```
Try
   [statements to execute that could cause an error]
Catch [Variable As ExceptionType]
   [statements to execute to handle the exception]
Finally
   [statements to execute whether or not an exception occurred]
End Try
```

Any time you write statements that could cause errors, such as division by zero, file processing, or database access, enclose the statements in a `Try...Catch` block. If no exception occurs, the `Catch` block is skipped and processing continues with the first statement following the `End Try` statement.

```
Try
   intCount = CInt(txtCount.Text)
   intAverage = intTotal \ intCount
   lblAverage.Text = "Average: " & intAverage
Catch
   MessageBox.Show("Cannot divide by zero.", "MyApp Error Message")
End Try
```

You can use the new `Throw` keyword to generate an exception, similar to the VB 6 `Err.Raise` statement. You also can exit a `Try` block using the optional `Exit Try` statement.

Property Procedures

The syntax for writing property procedures changes in VB.NET. Rather than write separate Property Get and Property Let procedures, you write a single Property block. The block has sections for `Get` and `Set` (there is no `Let`. Let is replaced by `Set`).

```
'In the Declarations section
Private strMyProperty As String

'Property procedure
Public Property MyProperty As String
   Get
        MyProperty = strMyProperty
   End Get

   Set    'The intrinsic variable Value is the argument passed in
        strMyProperty = Value
   End Set
End Property
```

You can omit either the Get or Set. For example, to create a read-only property, write only a Get. To create a write-only property, code only the Set.

ADO.NET

A new version of ADO accompanies Visual Studio.NET, called ADO.NET. This enhanced version of ADO provides many new features, including increased support for Extensible Markup Language (XML) and better interoperation with many database formats.

ADO.NET replaces the recordset with the data set. A data set has many of the same features as a recordset but can be passed across the Internet as an XML document.

Disappearing Features

Two features that were new to VB 6 disappear in VB.NET: the Data Environment and the Data Report features. Microsoft has returned to Crystal Reports for database report writing.

Glossary

About box A dialog box that contains information about a program.

absolute position Measurement from the starting point of a graphic object.

access key Key to press to activate a control rather than using the mouse. Also called a *keyboard shortcut*.

ActiveX A custom control, program, or DLL that can be added to a project.

ADO ActiveX Data Objects. The object model used for database access; intended to allow access any type of data from any application on any type of computer.

ANSI code The code used to represent characters in a string. (American National Standards Institute)

API Application program interface; a collection of DLLs used for Windows programming.

argument A value being passed to or from a procedure.

array A series of items, such as a control array or a variable array.

assignment statement Assigns a value to a variable or property of an object.

.bas file File used to store standard code modules.

BOF Beginning of file, used for the Recordset object of the data control.

Boolean A data type that evaluates to True or False.

break time Temporary break in execution of a program used for debugging.

breakpoint Indicated point in project code where execution should break; used for debugging.

buffer Temporary storage area used for reading and writing data files. On a write, data are placed in the buffer until it is filled and then written to disk.

ByRef Specifies that an argument passed to a procedure should be passed as the address of the data so that both calling and called procedures have access to the same memory location. Default type of argument used in DLLs.

ByVal Specifies that an argument passed to a procedure should be passed as a copy of the data. The calling and called procedures do not have access to each other's variables.

cell Intersection of a row and a column; used for the grid control.

check box A control used to indicate a value that may be True or False. In any group of check boxes, any number may be selected.

checked Selected. A menu command preceded by a check mark or a check box containing an X.

class A prototype or blueprint for an object indicating the properties and methods.

class module Code used to define a new class of object.

clipping region Graphics area that defines the area to be redrawn.

code Programming statements in the Basic language.

Code window The Visual Basic window in which code is displayed and written.

collection class An object type that holds references to a group of objects.

color constant Predefined constants for specifying colors, such as vbRed and vbBlue.

column A vertical section of a grid control.

combo box control A control that is a combination of a list box and a text box.

command button A control used to activate a procedure.

common dialog boxes A set of Windows dialog boxes available to Visual Basic programmers for

Open, *Save*, *Fonts*, *Print*, and *Color*.

compile error A syntax error (usually spelling or punctuation) found by the compiler before execution begins; causes Visual Basic to enter break time.

compound condition Multiple conditions combined with the use of the logical operators, And or Or.

concatenation Joining string (text) fields. The ampersand (&) is used to concatenate text.

condition An expression that will evaluate True or False. May be a comparison of two values (variables, properties, constants) using relational operators.

constant A value that cannot be changed during program execution.

context-sensitive Help Use of the F1 function key to directly access the Help topic related to the selected code or element.

control An object used on a graphical interface, such as an option button, text box, command button, or label.

control array A group of controls sharing the same name and event procedures.

coordinate system A measurement system used for creating graphics.

current record The position of the pointer in a database table or data file.

custom controls Additional controls that may be added to the toolbox for inclusion in a project. Also called *ActiveX* controls.

data element Unit within a user-defined data type or a data record. Also called a *field*.

Data Environment A VB module that sets up access to the data used by a project. Used instead of a data control.

data file Disk file that holds values for data records.

data tip A small label that displays the current value of a variable, property, or expression. Available only at break time by placing the pointer over the desired value.

data type Specifies the type of value to be stored in a variable or constant. May be used to indicate the return type for a function. Examples of data types are integer, currency, and string.

debug window A window that appears when a project is executing. It contains information about the status of the project and can be used to display or change program values.

debugging Finding and eliminating computer program errors.

declaration Nonexecutable code that sets up variables and constants, declares data types, and allocates memory. Can be used to set up arrays and specify the data type returned by a function. Example declaration statements are Dim, Const, Static, Public, and Private.

design time The status of the Visual Basic environment while a project is being developed, as opposed to run time or break time.

direct reference Accessing an element of an array by a subscript

when the value of the subscript is known.

DLL Dynamic link library; a file with an extension of .dll, used to hold procedures.

dropdown combo box A combo box control with a down-pointing arrow that allows the user to pull down the list. Allows efficient use of space on a form.

dropdown list A list box with a down-pointing arrow allowing the user to pull down the list. Allows efficient use of space on a form.

early binding References to objects that can be resolved by the compiler before a program is run. Preferable to late binding.

element Single item within a table, array, list, or grid.

embed An OLE action causing an object from a different application to be contained within a VB application. An embedded object cannot be modified from other applications.

empty string A string with a length of zero characters.

enabled A command button or menu command that is available to the user; indicated by a black Caption rather than a gray Caption.

encapsulation The combination of an object's properties, methods, and events, which operate independently.

EOF End of file; a condition that evaluates True when reading sequential files or accessing a database using a Recordset object.

Err object A special pre-defined Visual Basic object that stores the error number and its description when a run-time error occurs.

error trapping Coding to control the action when an error occurs.

event An action that may be taken by the user, such as a click, drag, key press, or scroll. Events can also be triggered by an internal action, such as repainting the form or validating a database action.

event-driven programming Applications designed to respond to actions taken by the user.

event procedure A procedure written to respond to an action taken by the user.

field A group of related characters used to represent one characteristic or attribute of an entity in a data file or database.

file mode Specification for the manner that data can be accessed from a disk file, including Input, Output, Append, Random, and Binary.

file number Buffer number used to read and write records in a data file.

file pointer Used to keep track of the current position when reading or writing a data file.

flag A variable, usually of Boolean type, used to indicate status, such as True or False, On or Off, Found or NotFound. Also called a *switch*.

focus The currently selected control, indicated by an I-beam, selected text, highlighted Caption, or a dotted border. The control

with the focus is ready to receive user input.

form An object that acts as a container for the controls in a graphical interface.

form file A file with an .frm extension; contains the code and control information for a single form.

form module The code related to a single form.

Form window The window in which the form is displayed at design time; can be displayed by pressing the Show Form button in the Project window.

format A specification for the way information will be displayed, including dollar signs, percent signs, and number of decimal positions.

format string A string of characters used to specify a custom-designed format.

frame A control used as a container to group other controls.

function A procedure that returns a value when it is called.

general declarations section The portion of a code module used to declare variables that will be available throughout that module.

global The scope of a variable, constant, or procedure that makes it available in all modules of a project.

graphical user interface (GUI) Program application containing icons, buttons, and menu bars.

grid control A control that has rows and columns and displays data in cells.

handle A small square on a selected control at design time; used to resize a control.

identifier A programmer-supplied name for a variable, constant, procedure, or control.

image A control that can contain a picture; has a stretch property to adjust the size of the contained graphic.

index A variable or a property that stores the position number of the elements in a series; used for list box controls, control arrays, variable arrays, and database records.

inheritance The ability to reuse classes by basing a new class on an existing class. Visual Basic 6 does not implement true inheritance.

instance An object created from a class.

instant watch A debugging feature that allows you to quickly see the current value of a variable or expression.

instantiate The process of creating a new object from a class.

intrinsic constants Constants supplied with VB, such as vbBlue.

intrinsic controls Basic controls provided in the toolbox.

iteration A single pass through the body of a loop.

key field The field (or fields) on which a data file is organized; used to search for a record.

label A control that displays text as a Caption; cannot be altered by the user.

late binding References in a program that cannot be resolved until run time. Slower and less efficient than early binding.

line-continuation character A space and underscore; used in program code to indicate that a Basic statement continues on the next line.

link An OLE relationship that places an object in your project but allows other applications to access and modify the object. A linked OLE object is not stored inside your project and is maintained by the creating application.

list box control A control that holds a list of values; the user cannot add new values at run time.

literal A string expression enclosed in quotation marks.

local The scope of a variable or constant that limits its visibility to the current procedure.

logic error An error in a project that does not halt execution but causes erroneous results in the output.

logical operator The operators And, Or, and Not; used to construct compound conditions and to reverse the truth of a condition.

lookup An operation that searches a table or an array to find a value when the subscript is not directly known.

loop A control structure providing for the repetition of statements.

loop index A counter variable used in a For/Next loop.

MDI Multiple document interface. Using a parent form and child forms for an application.

menu A list of choices; the available commands displayed in a menu bar.

message box A dialog box displaying a message to the user. The MsgBox function returns a value indicating the user's response.

method The actions (procedures) associated with objects.

modal A form that requires the user to respond before transferring to any other form in the project.

modeless A form that does not prevent the user from accessing any other form before responding.

module A collection of procedures; may be a form module, a standard code module, or a class module. Each file in a project is a separate module.

navigation Stepping through the records of a database file: next record, previous record, first record, or last record.

nested A statement completely contained within another statement, such as a loop within a loop or a decision within a decision.

object An occurrence of a class type that has properties and methods. A specific instance of a control type or form.

object-oriented programming (OOP) An approach to programming that uses objects and their properties. Each type of object behaves in a certain way. Applications are built by combining objects and coding the actions to be taken when events occur. Visual Basic has many (but not all) of the characteristics of an object-oriented language.

OLE Object linking and embedding; a process used to share objects among applications.

option button A control used to indicate a value that may be True or False (selected or not selected). In any group of option buttons, only one button may be selected.

order of precedence Hierarchy of mathematical operations; the order in which operations are performed.

persistent graphics Graphics that are saved in memory and can be redisplayed.

picturebox A control used as a container; may hold graphics, pictures, text, or other controls.

pixel Picture element; a single dot on the screen; a unit of measurement for displaying graphics.

point A printer's measure used to define the size of a font; 1/72 of an inch.

polymorphism The ability to have more than one method with the same name, which behave differently depending on the object and/or arguments.

posttest A loop that has its test condition after the body of the loop; the statements within the loop will always be executed at least once.

pretest A loop that has its test condition at the top; the statements inside the loop may never be executed.

print zone Preset column width used with the Printer object.

private Specifies the scope in a declaration. A procedure declared as private can be called only from another procedure in that module. A private variable is available only in the module in which it is declared.

procedure   A unit of code; may be a sub procedure, a function procedure, or a property procedure.

Professional Edition   A version of Visual Basic that includes more controls than the Standard Edition and allows more robust database programming.

project file   A file with a .vbp extension; used to store the information displayed in the Project window.

Project window   A window that displays a list of the forms and standard code modules used for a project.

Properties window   A window that shows the properties for each object in a form.

property   Characteristic or attribute of an object; value may be set at design time or run time depending on the specific property.

public   Specifies scope as global. A procedure declared as public can be called from other modules; a public variable is available in other modules in the project.

random file   A data file that may be read or written in any order; has fixed-length records.

record   A group of related fields; relates to data files and database tables.

recordset   The current group of records associated with a data control, or Data Environment.

relational operator Comparison operators, including $<$, $>$, and $=$.

relative position   In graphics, the position in relation to the last point drawn.

remark   A Basic statement used for documentation; not interpreted by the compiler; also called a *comment*.

row   A horizontal section of a grid control.

run time   While a project is executing.

run-time error   An error that occurs as a program executes; causes execution to break.

scope   The extent of visibility of a variable or constant. The scope may be global, module level, or local.

SDI   Single document interface. An application with independent forms with no parent/child relationship; as opposed to MDI.

search argument   The value to be matched in a lookup operation.

separator bar   A horizontal line used to separate groups of menu commands.

shortcut menu   The menu that pops up when the right mouse button is clicked. Also called popup menus, context menus, or right mouse menus.

simple combo box   A control that combines a text box and a list box, with no dropdown capability.

single step   A debugging feature that executes the project code one line at a time and displays each line.

source   The object being dragged in a drag-and-drop operation.

SQL   Structured Query Language; an industry-standard database language available in Visual Basic.

standard code module   A file with a .bas extension used to declare global variables and constants; can contain procedures that will be called from multiple forms.

startup form   The first form to appear when a project begins execution; a project must have a startup form or a Sub Main procedure.

statement   A line of Visual Basic code.

static   A setting for local variables that retains the value for multiple calls to the procedure.

string literal   A constant enclosed in quotation marks.

sub procedure   A procedure that takes actions but does not return a value.

subscript   The position of an element within an array.

subscripted variable   An element of an array.

switch   See *flag*.

tabbed dialog   A control that adds tabs that resemble folder tabs. Used to increase the usable portion of a window and to organize functions.

table   A two-dimensional array.

table recordset   A recordset defined using a single table in a database file.

text box   A control for data entry; its value can be entered and changed by the user. Also called an *edit box*.

third-party control   A custom control produced by a company other than Microsoft.

timer control   A control that can be made to fire an event at a specified interval; can be used to perform actions repeatedly.

toolbar   The group of buttons beneath the menu bar; used as shortcuts for menu commands.

toolbox   A window that holds buttons used to create controls on a form.

ToolTip   A small label that appears when the mouse pointer pauses over a control.

twip   A unit of measure for the display screen; $\frac{1}{20}$ of a point or $\frac{1}{1,440}$ of an inch.

user-defined data type Grouping of data elements to create a new data type that can be used in declaration statements.

user interface   The display and commands seen by a user; how the user interacts with an application. In Windows, the graphical display of an application containing controls and menus.

validation   Verification of the values entered by the user. Validation may include checking for a range of values, checking for specific values, or verifying the data type.

variable   A memory location referred to by a name. The value of a variable can change during execution of an application.

Visual Basic environment The Visual Basic elements used for program development at design time; includes the menu bar, toolbar, toolbox, Form window, Property window, Project window, and Menu editor.

Visual Basic for Applications (VBA)   A version of Visual Basic that is included in many Microsoft application programs, such as Excel and PowerPoint.

watch   A debugging tool that allows the programmer to view the value of a variable or expression as the project executes.

Web browser   A control that has methods to navigate the Internet.

`ZOrder` **method**   Changes the stacking order of graphical elements.

Index

A

About box. *See also* Form
in general, 223–225
Access file, 442
Access key, defining, 62–63
Accumulator, array element for, 305–306
ActiveX controls. *See also* ActiveX Data Object Data Control; Controls
browsing Web from VB project, 589-590
creating, 590–593
in general, 584
components, 584
intrinsic controls, 584
Tabbed Dialog control, 585–588
using, 584
Web Browser control, 589
ActiveX Data Object Data Control (ADODC)
CommandType property, 450–451
ConnectionString property, 448–449
data-bound controls, 446–447
in general, 444–445
properties, 447
RecordSource property, 450–451
Add operation
error with, 496–497
protecting
coding new Add procedure, 470
limiting user actions, 468–469
procedures to disable and enable buttons, 470–471
Save procedure, 471

sharing command button functions, 469-470
AddItem method, 254–255
AddNew method, 466
ADODC. *See* ActiveX Data Object Data Control
Alignment property, 53
Animation. *See also* Graphics
in general, 570–571
ANSI code, 132
API. *See* Application programming interface
Appearance property, 56
Application. *See also* Visual Basic for Applications
multitier application, 380–381
Application programming interface (API), 594
Argument
defined, 99
multiple, calling, 192
passing ByVal or ByRef, 189-190, 595
passing source argument, 539-540
Arithmetic operations. *See also* Calculations
in general, 100
order of operations, 101
using calculations in code, 102
Array. *See also* Control arrays; Multidimensional arrays; Single-dimension arrays
defined, 299
initializing, with For Each, 302
with list box
adding items with ItemData, 312

Array—*Cont.*
in general, 309-310
ItemData property, 310–311
nonsequential ItemData values, 311–312
subscript of, 299, 300–301
two-dimensional, 313
Array element, 299
for accumulator, 305–306
Array function, 324
Assignment statement, 22, 23
AutoRedraw property, 568
Average. *See also* Calculations
calculating, 112

B

.bas extension, 5, 219
BASIC, 3
Beginning of file (BOF), checking for, 460–461
Binding, objects, 349
.bmp extension, 54
BookMark property, 505
Boolean data type, 261. *See also* Data types
Border. *See also* Graphics
setting control, 56
Break, inserting breakpoint, 156
Break button, pausing execution with, 156
Break time, 8
Buffer, 390
Button. *See also* specific buttons
enabling and disabling, 470–471
ByRef, passing arguments, 189-190, 595
ByVal, passing arguments, 189-190, 595

C

C, 3
C++, 3
Calculation programming, example, 106–111
Calculations. *See also* Arithmetic
operations; Constants; Variables

breaking into smaller units, 194–196
in code, 102
counting and accumulating sums, in general, 111
discussed, 99
Calendar control, for ActiveX control, 590
Call, event procedures, 147–149
Call statement, 148
Cancel button, 63
Cancel property, Command button, 63
Caption property
for Label, 17–20
Menus, 175
Case structure
in general, 295–297
testing option buttons with, 297–298
Change event, 257, 577
Check box
control, 53–54
with If statement, in general, 140–141
multiple, testing value of, 142–143
testing value of, 141–142
value property, 66–67
Circle method, 563–566
ellipses, 566
Class. *See also* Class module; Collection
assigning property values, 337–338
control arrays, 294
creating, 339-343
creating new object with, 344–347
examining, 362
instance, 334
object, 18
subclass, 336
superclass, 336
Class module
defining, 339
initialize and terminate events, 349-350
object, 334
Class_Initialize event, 349
Class_Terminate event, 349

Clear method, 255
ClipControls property, 568
Close statement, 390
Cls method, 560
COBOL, 3
Code. *See also* Code statements;
          Controls; Standard code
          module
    compiling, 39
    printing, 37
    pseudocode and, 4
Code module, standard code
          module, 219-220
Code statements
    assignment statement, 22, 23
    End statement, 22, 23
    remark statement, 22–23
Code window, 24
Collating sequence, ANSI code, 132
Collection. *See also* Class; Object
    creating, 351
        accessing member, 355
        adding objects to, 353–354
        CProducts class, 352–353
        For Each/Next, 356–358
        removing member from, 354
        returning count property, 355
        setting default property, 355
        unique key creation, 352
    in general, 351
    key storage in list box, 362–364
    using in form, 358–360
Collection class, 351
Color, 62. *See also* Graphics
    color dialog box, 184–185
    QBColor function, 558–559
    RGB function, 557–558
    text, 68
    VB color constants, 558
Color constants, 68. *See also*
          Constants
Color dialog box, 184–185
Column. *See also* Table
    aligning decimal columns, 277
    array, 313
    placing in list box, 598–600
    table, 442
COM. See Component Object Model
Combo box. *See also* Combo box
          event; List box

AddItem method, 254–255
    as data-bound control, 461–462
    dropdown, 252
    filling the list, 253–255
    simple, 252
Combo box controls, 252. *See also*
          Controls
Combo box event
    Change event, 257
    in general, 257
    GotFocus event, 257–258
    LostFocus event, 258
Comma
    printing, 272–273
    trailing, 273–274
Command, adding to Data
          Environment Designer,
          514–515
Command button, 14
    Cancel property, 63
    Caption properties, 20–21
    Default property, 63
    sharing functions, 469-470
Command object, 513
CommandType property, 447,
          450–451
Comments, 22
Compile errors. *See also* Error
          trapping
    finding and fixing, 39-40
Component Object Model
          (COM), 584
Components, controls, 584
Concatenation, text, 69
Conditions
    comparing text property of text
          box, 135
    comparing upper/lower-case
          characters, 136
    compound conditions
        combining And and Or, 137
        in general, 136–137
    in general, 130–131
        relational operator, 130
    implied condition, 135
    numeric variables and constants,
          compared, 131–132
    strings, 132–134
    testing for True or False, 135
Connection, creating, 514

Connection object, 513
ConnectionString property, 447,
    448–449
Const statement, 92–93
Constants
    adding values to, 93
    color constants, 68
    data types, 89-90
        variant, 89
    declaring, guidelines, 222–223
    in general, 88–89
        declaration statement, 89
    global, 221
    intrinsic, 92, 93–94
    in multiple-form project, 220
    named, 92
    naming conventions, 90–91
    naming rules, 90
    numeric, 131–132
    string constants, 93
Container, graphics, 559
Control arrays. *See also* Array;
        Single-dimension arrays
    in general, 294–295
Controls, 2. *See also* ActiveX
        controls
    border and style, 56
    check boxes, 53–54
    coding
        changing multiple properties,
            68–69
        Check Box value property,
            66–67
        clearing text boxes and
            labels, 66
        concatenating text, 69
        continuing long program lines,
            69-70
        font properties, 67–68
        Option button value property,
            66–67
        resetting focus, 66
        text color, 68
    custom, 5
    default property, 70–71
    frames, 53
    in general, 52
    images, 54–56
    index, 295
    intrinsic, 584

line control, 57
locking, 417
menu commands, 174
multiple
    aligning, 59-61
    deselecting group, 58
    in general, 57–58
    moving group, 58–59
    setting properties, 59
as objects, 3, 584
option button, 54
placing on form, 14–17
shape control, 56–57
tab order, 63–64
text boxes, 53
Coordinate system, graphics, 556
Counting and accumulating sums.
        See also Calculations
    calculating an average, 112
    counting, 111
    in general, 111
    summing numbers, 111
    summing a two-dimensional table,
        315–316
.cur extension, 54
Currency, 90
    FormatCurrency function, 103

D

Data control. *See* ActiveX Data
        Object Data Control
Data element, 388
Data Environment Designer. *See also*
        Report Designer
    adding, 513–514
    adding commands, 514–515
    creating, 515–517
    creating connections, 514
    in general, 512–513, 613
    one-to-many relationships,
        518–519
    Recordset navigation, 517–518
    relation hierarchies, 519
        creating, 519-522
Data file. *See also* Random data file;
        Sequential file
    end-of-file (EOF) mark, 391, 394
    file mode, 389

Data file—*Cont.*
  finding end of, 394
  FreeFile function, 391
  in general, 388
  locating, 394–395
  opening and closing, 389-391
  organization, 389
    random, 389
    sequential, 389
  project file and, 388
  terminology, 388–389
  viewing, 391
Data formatting. *See* Formatting data
Data hiding, 335
Data types. *See also* Constants;
      Variables
  Boolean, 261
  in general, 89-90
    variant data type, 89
  user-defined
    accessing information with,
      304–305
    in general, 303–304
Data-bound controls
  data control and, 446–447
  list box and combo box as,
      461–462
  properties, 452–453
Database. *See also* Database field;
      Database file
  navigating
    checking for BOF and EOF, 460
    MoveFirst method, 460
    MoveLast method, 460
    MoveNext method, 460
    MovePrevious method, 460
    Recordset object, 460
Database field. *See also* Field
  example, with Find, Filter, Sort,
      508–513
  in general, 507
  loading in list box, 508
  referring to, 508
Database file
  creating, for use by Visual
      Basic, 443
  formats supported by Visual
      Basic, 442
  in general, 442
  terminology, 442

updating
  adding records, 466–467
  deleting records, 467–468
  in general, 466
  viewing, 453–459
DataEnvironment, connections, 513
DataField property, 452
DataSource property, 452
Date, FormatDateTime function, 105
DB2, 442
dBASE 5.0, 442
dBASE III, 442
dBASE IV, 442
Debugging, 41. *See also* Error
      trapping
  checking values of
        expressions, 158
  forcing a break, 156–157
  in general, 156
  Immediate window, 157
  pausing execution with Break
      button, 156
  stepping through code, 158–159
    Step Into command, 159
    Step Over command, 159
  stopping execution with
      Maximized form, 245
  tutorial, 159-165
Declare statement, 594–595
DECommand, 513
DEConnection, 513
Default button, 63
Default property, Command
      button, 63
Delegation, 336
Delete method, 467
Description property, 397
Design
  command buttons, 63
  form location, 64–65
  keyboard access keys, 62–63
  maximized form, 245
  Tab Order for controls, 63–64
  ToolTip, 65
  user interface, 61–62
Design time, 8
Dialog box
  common dialog control, 181
  in general, 181–183
  information from

Dialog box—*Cont.*
    color dialog box, 184–185
    font dialog box, 185–186
  setting current values, 186–187
  using, 183
.dib extension, 54
Dim statement, 94. *See also*
      Variables
  arrays, 300
  entering, 95
  two-dimensional array, 313
Dir function, 410
Direct reference, arrays, 306
DLL. *See* Dynamic link libraries
Do statement, 259, 261
Documentation, printing, 35–36
Do/Loop
  Boolean data type, 261
  in general, 258–261
  with list box, 261–262
Drag method, 551
Drag-and-drop
  example, 533–538
  manual, 551
  multiple objects
    blanking out an image, 541
    changing icon of target
       image, 540
    in general, 539
    passing source argument,
       539-540
    setting DragIcon property of
       source controls,
       540–541
  terminology
    DragOver/DragDrop events,
       532–533
    source, 532
    source object properties, 532
    target, 532
  Toybox program, 542–544
DragDrop event, 532–533
DragIcon property, 532
  source controls, 540–541
DragMode property, 532
DragOver event, 532–533
DrawWidth property, 562
Dynamic link libraries (DLLs). *See*
    also Object linking and
    embedding

  accessing system information with,
    597–598
  calling DLL procedure, 596
  Declare statement, 594–595
  in general, 584, 593–594
  passing arguments ByVal and
    ByRef, 595
  placing Tabs for columns in list
    box, 598–600
  reference information for,
    596–597

E

Element, array, 299
Ellipse, 566
Embedding. *See also* Object linking
    and embedding
  in OLE, 600–602
.emf extension, 54
Encapsulation, OOP, 335
End statement, 22, 23, 350
End Type statement, 303
End With statement, 69
End-of-file (EOF), 391, 394
  checking for, 460–461
Endless loop, 265
EOF. *See* End-of-file mark
Err object. *See also* Error
  coding error-handling routines,
    398–399
  Err.Number property, 397
  in general, 397
    Description property, 397
    Number property, 397
    Source property, 397
  raising error conditions, 398
  Resume statement, 399-400
Error. *See also* Error trapping
  compile errors, 39-40
  debugging, 41
  handling, 400–401
  logic errors, 40–41
  naming rules and conventions,
    objects, 41–42
  run-time errors, 40
Error trapping. *See also* Debugging;
    Validation
  Add operation protection

Error trapping—*Cont.*
    coding new Add procedure, 470
    limiting user actions, 468–469
    procedures to disable and
            enable buttons, 470–471
    Save procedure, 471
    sharing command button
            functions, 469-470
    Exit Function statement, 401–403
    Exit Sub statement, 401–403
    in general, 395, 468
    On Error statement, 395–397
    using, 495–503
    saving changes to file,
            Form_QueryUnload event,
            403–404
    sequential file programming
            example, 404–408
    validation and
        in general, 493
        locking text boxes, 493–494
        Validate event, 494–495
Event, Visual Basic event, 22
Event procedures, 22. *See also*
        General procedures
    calling, 147–149
    coding, 24–26
    naming, 22
    subprocedures, 22
Event-driven programming, 2, 3
Excel, 442, 600
    Help with, 608
    macro recording, 604–605
Executable file, creating, 205
.exe extension, 205
Exit button, coding, 25–26
Exit For statement, 266
Exit Function statement, 401–403
Expression, checking value of, 158

F

Field. *See also* Database field;
        Key field
    accessing in random record,
            411–412
    files, 388
    lookup table for, 461–462
    table, 442

File. *See also* Data file
    beginning of file, 460–461
    defined, 388
    end-of-file, 391, 394, 460–461
File mode, data file, 389
File number, 390
File pointer, 390
    Seek function, 412–414
Filter property, 505–506, 508–513
Find method
    record search, 503–504
        BookMarks, 505
        Filter property, 505–506
        no record found, 504
Find property, 508–513
Flags, 261
Focus
    controls, 63
    resetting, 66
Folder, creating, 28
Font, 62
    font dialog box, 185–186
    selecting, 276
Font properties, controls, 67–68
For Each statement, 302
For Each/Next, collections, 356–358
For statement, 262, 264
For/Next loop
    altering values of loop control
            variables, 265
    conditions satisfied before entry,
            265
    endless loop, 265
    exiting, 266
    in general, 262–263
    negative increment, 264
For/Next statement, in general,
        301–302
ForeColor property, 68
Form, 2. *See also* Multiple-form
        project
    about box, 223–225
    adding form file to project,
            215–216
    adding properties to, 365
    adding and removing, 215
    Caption properties, 21
    collection use in, 358–360
    creating, 214–215
    displaying

Form, 2—*Cont.*
  modal, 217
  modeless, 217
  Hide method, 216–218
  hiding, 218
  Load and Unload statements, 218
  location on screen, 64–65
  location and size, 8
  maximized, 244–245
  Me keyword, 218–219
  multiple, 214
  objects and, 3
  objects on different form, 219
  removing from project, 216
  Show method, 216–218
  startup form, 214
    coding, 227–228
  as text, 38–39
Form Activate event, 217–218
Form file, 5
  adding to project, 215–216
  saving, 28–29
Form image, printing, 36
Form Layout window, 7
Form Load event, 217–218
Form module, 5
Form window, 6
FormatCurrency function, 103
FormatDateTime function, 105
FormatNumber function, 104
FormatPercent function, 104–105
Formatting data, in general,
    102–106
Form_QueryUnload event,
    403–404
FORTRAN, 3
FoxPro, 442
Frames, control, 53
FreeFile function, 391
.frm extension, 5
Function. *See also* Function
    procedure; *specific functions*
  calling, with multiple
      arguments, 192
  defined, 99
  with multiple arguments, 192
  reusing procedures, 192–194
  shared functions, 336
Function procedure. *See also*
    General procedures

breaking calculations into smaller
    units, 194–196
in general, 190–191

G

General procedures. *See also* Event
    procedures; Function
    procedure
  function procedures vs. sub
      procedures, 190
  in general, 187
  new sub procedure creation,
    187–188
  passing arguments ByVal or
    ByRef, 189-190
  passing variables to procedures,
    188–189
Get statement, 411
.gif extension, 54
GotFocus event, 257–258
Graphical user interface (GUI), 2
Graphics. *See also* Animation; Color;
    Graphics methods
  AutoRedraw property, 568
  border, 56
  clipping region, 568
  controlling pictures
    at design time, 568–569
    moving pictures, 569-570
    at run time, 569
  coordinate system, 556
  in general, 556
    pixel, 556
    point, 556
    scale, 556
    twip, 556
  layering, 567–568
  persistent, 568
  picturebox controls, 557
  techniques
    custom coordinate system, 574
    PaintPicture method, 574–575
Graphics files, 54
Graphics methods
  Circle method, 563–566
  Cls method, 560
  DrawWidth property, 562
  in general, 559-560

Graphics methods—*Cont.*
  Line method, 562–563
    rectangles, 563
  PSet method, 560–562
  Step keyword, 566–567
Grid, in general, 486
Grid control, 486–493
GUI. *See* Graphical user interface

H

Handles, label, 15
Help
  context-sensitive, 44
  in general, 8, 42–43
  MSDN viewer, 43
  with VB in Excel, 608
Hide method, forms, 216–218

I

.ico extension, 54
Identifier. *See also* Constants;
    Variables
  defined, 89
  naming rules, 90
  sample, 91
  scope in, 98
If statement. *See also* Nested if
    statement
  conditions and, 130–131
  flowcharting, 130
  in general, 128–129
  with Option button and Check
    box, in general, 140–141
If . . . Then . . . Else statement, 129
Image, controls, 54–56
Immediate window, 157
Index
  arrays, 299
    direct reference, 306
  controls, 295
Inheritance, OOP, 336
Input # statement, 393
InputBox function, 434–435
Instance, class, 334
Instantiate, object, 334, 344
Integer, 90
IsNumeric function, 145

ItemData property
  adding items with, 312
  in general, 310–311
  nonsequential ItemData values,
    311–312

J

Java, 334
.jpg extension, 54

K

Key. *See also* Collection
  access key, 62–63
  storing in list box, 362–364
Key field. *See also* Field
  file, 389
  storing in list box
    displaying selected record, 415
    in general, 413–414
    retrieving record from file, 414
    trimming extra blanks from
      strings, 414
  table, 442
Keyboard access keys, defining,
    62–63
Keywords, defined, 90

L

Label, 14
  appearance property, 56
  Caption properties for, 17–20
  clearing, 66
  handles, 15
  line label, 396
  properties, 64
Layering. *See also* Graphics
  graphics, 567–568
LCase, 136
Left function, 269
  example, 270
Len function, 270–271
Line, printing blank line, 274
Line control, using, 57
Line method, 562–563
  rectangles, 563

Line-continuation character, 70
Linking. *See also* Object linking and
     embedding in OLE, 600
List. *See also* List box
  clearing, 255
  dropdown, 252
  printing items from, 277
  removing item from, 257
List box. *See also* List box controls;
     List box event
  AddItem method, 254–255
  with arrays
    adding items with ItemData, 312
    in general, 309-310
    ItemData property, 310–311
    nonsequential ItemData values,
      311–312
  as data-bound control, 461–462
  displaying object with, 364
  with Do/Loop, 261–262
  filling the list, 253–255
  loading database field in, 508
  menus, 176
  placing Tabs in, 598–600
  printing contents, 276–277
  removing object with, 364
  selecting entries in, 271
  to store key field
    displaying selected record, 415
    in general, 413–414
    retrieving a record from file, 414
    trimming extra blanks from
      strings, 414
  to store keys, 362–364
  with two-dimensional table,
    316–317
List box controls, 252. *See also*
    Controls
List box event
  Change event, 257
  in general, 257
  GotFocus event, 257–258
  LostFocus event, 258
List property, 256–257
ListCount property, 256
ListIndex property, 255–256
Literal, 23
Load and Unload statements, 218
LoadPicture function, 569
LOF function, 412

Logic errors, 40–41
Logical operator, conditions, 136
Lookup table. *See also* Table
  adding, 462–466
  coding, 309
  for field, 461–462
  in general, 306–308
Loop
  defined, 258
  pretest, 259
Loop index, 262
Loop statement, 259, 261
Looping, 258
LostFocus event, 258
Lotus, 442
LTrim function, 414

M

.mak extension, 5
MDI. *See* Multiple document
    interface
Me keyword, forms, 218–219
Member, collection, 351, 354, 355
Menu. *See also* Menu command
  Caption property, 175
  coding, 179
  creating, 176–178, 609-611
  defining, 174
  in general, 174
  list box, 176
  modifying, 179-181
  Name box, 175
  naming standards, 175
  separator bars, 176
  shortcut menu
    coding for, 613
    defining, 612
  standards, 181
  subMenu, 175
  toggling check mark, 181
Menu command
  disabled, 180
  enabled, 180
Message, size and alignment
    modification, 30–32
Message box
  displaying message in
    in general, 143

Message box—*Cont.*
  displaying message in—*Cont.*
    selecting MsgBox icon, 144
    displaying message string,
      144–145
Message string, 143. *See also* String
  displaying, 144–145
Methods, objects, 3, 3–4
Microsoft Developer Network
    (MSDN)
  library, 8, 42
  viewer, 43
Microsoft Office, 61
Mid function, 269
  example, 270
Module. *See* Class module
Move method, 569-570
MoveFirst method, 460
MoveLast method, 460
MoveNext method, 460
MovePrevious method, 460
MSDN. *See* Microsoft Developer
    Network
MsgBox function
  example, 269
  function return values, 268
  in general, 267
  specifying buttons or icons,
    268–269
MsgBox statement, 143
Multidimensional arrays. *See also*
    Array
  For Each/Next example, 314
  in general, 313–314
  nested For/Next example, 314
  two-dimensional array,
    initializing, 314
  two-dimensional table
    lookup operations, 316–318
    printing, 314–315
    summing, 315–316
Multiline property, 53
Multiple document interface
    (MDI)
  in general, 584, 608–609
  project creation, 609
    menus, 609
    Windows menu, 609-611
Multiple-form project. *See also*
    Form

variables and constants in, in
    general, 220
Multitier application, 380–381

N

Name
  Menu, 175
  variables and constants, 90–91
Name box, Menu, 175
Name keyword, 90
Navigation button, adding, 462–466
Nested if statement. *See also* If
    statement
  in general, 137–140
New keyword, 344
NewEnum function, collections,
    357–358
NewIndex property, 312
Next statement, 262, 264, 302
Null string, 66. *See also* String
Number. *See also* Arithmetic
    operations; Calculations
  FormatNumber function, 104
  summing numbers, 111
Number property, 397
Numeric values, checking for,
    145–146

O

Object. *See also* Collection; Object
    browser
  adding to collection, 353–354
  class, 18
  class module, 334
  controls as, 3, 584
  creating
    choosing when to create,
      347–349
    with class, 344–347
    early vs. late binding, 349
    set statement, 348–349
  displaying in list box, 364
  examining in browser, 361
  in general, 3, 334–335
  instantiating, 334, 344
  naming rules and conventions,
    41–42

Object—*Cont.*
  removing in list box, 364
  reusable, 336–337
Object browser
  examining classes, 362
  examining VB objects, 361
  in general, 360–361
Object linking and embedding
      (OLE). *See also* Dynamic link
      libraries
  creating OLE object at run
      time, 602
  embedding, 600–602
  in general, 584, 600
  linking, 600
Object-oriented programming
      (OOP), 3
  in general, 334
  reusable objects, 336–337
  terminology
    encapsulation, 335
    inheritance, 336
    polymorphism, 335–336
    reusability, 336
.ocx extension, 5, 584
OLE. *See* Object linking and
      embedding
On Error statement. *See also*
      Error trapping
  in general, 395–397
  using, 495–503
OOP. *See* Object-oriented
      programming
Open statement, 389
Option button
  checking value, 142
  control, 54
  with If statement, in general,
      140–141
  testing with case structure,
      297–298
  value property, 66–67
Oracle, 442
Order of operations, arithmetic
      operations, 101
Order of precedence, arithmetic
      operations, 101
Output, multiple lines, 145

P

PaintPicture method, 574–575
Paradox, 442
Pascal, 3
Percent, FormatPercent function,
      104
Picture property, 54
Picturebox controls, graphics, 557
Pixel, 556
PL/I, 3
Planning, Visual Basic project,
      4–5
Point, 556
Polymorphism, OOP, 335–336
Print keyword, 90
Print method, 271
Print zone, 272
Printing
  aligning decimal columns, 277
  blank lines, 274
  font selection, 276
  formatting lines, 272
    commas, 272–273
    semicolons, 273
  in general, 271–272
  list box contents, 276–277
  list items, 277
  sample printout, 36–39
  Spc function, 274–275
  string and numeric data
      alignment, 275
  Tab function, 274
  terminating page or job, 276
Procedural languages, 3
Programming, event-driven
      programming, 2
Programming languages, procedural
      languages, 3
Project Explorer window, 6
  Project file, 5
  data file and, 388
  saving, 29
project. *See* Visual Basic project
Properties window, 7
  using, 253–254
Property
  adding to forms, 365

Property—*Cont.*
    controls, 52
    objects, 3
Property Get procedure, 337
Property Let procedure, 337
Property values, assigning to class,
        337–338
Pseudocode, 4. *See also* Code
Public statement, 221
Push Me button, coding, 24–25
Put statement, 411

Q

Query_Unload event, 403

R

Raise method, 398
Random data file. *See also* Data file
    accessing fields in, 411–412
    finding end of, 412
    fixed-length strings, 409
    in general, 408–409
    InputBox function, 434–435
        to retrieve record, 435
    opening, 409-410
    reading and writing, 410–411
    record definition for, 409
    Seek function, 412–413
    updating
        adding records, 417–418
        deleting records, 418–419
        editing records, 419
        in general, 415–417
        locking contents of controls, 417
        Read and Write procedure, 420
Read procedure, 420
Record. *See also* Recordset
    adding
        to database file, 466–467
        to random file, 417–418
    current record, 442
    defining for random file, 409
    deleting
        from database file, 467–468
        from random file, 418–419

displaying, 415
    editing, 419
    files, 388–389
    retrieving
        from file, 414
        randomly, 435
    searching, Find method,
        503–506
Record key, file, 389
Recordset
    navigating, 517–518
    sorting, 506–507
Recordset object, 460
RecordSource property, 447,
        450–451
Rectangles, 563
Relation hierarchy
    creating, 519-522
    in general, 519
Relational operator, conditions, 130
Relationships, one-to-many,
        518–519
Remark statement, discussed,
        22–23
RemoveItem method, 257
Report Designer. *See also* Data
        Environment Designer
    discussed, 613–621
Resume statement, error, 399-400
Reusability, OOP, 336
RGB function, color, 557–558
Right function, 269
    example, 270
Rnd function, 560
Row. *See also* Array; Table
    array, 313
    table, 442
RTrim function, 414
Run time, 8
Run-time errors, 40. *See also* Error
        trapping

S

Save procedure, 471
Saving, project, 28–29
Scale method, 574

Scope. *See also* Variables
　variables, 96–99
Scroll bar. *See also* Scroll bar
　　　controls; Scroll bar events
　horizontal, 575
　programming example, 577–579
　vertical, 575
Scroll bar controls
　in general, 575–576
　　LargeChange, 576
　　Max, 576
　　Min, 576
　　SmallChange, 576
Scroll bar events
　Change event, 577
　in general, 577
　Scroll event, 577
Scroll event, 577
SDI. *See* Single document interface
SDK. *See* Software development kit
Seek function, file pointer, 412–413
Select Case statement, 295–296
Semicolon
　printing, 273
　trailing, 273–274
Separator bars, Menu, 176
Sequential file. *See also* Data file
　creating, 392–393
　error trapping, 404–408
　in general, 391–392
　reading data in, 393–394
　writing data to, 392
Set statement, 348–349
SetFocus method, 66
Shape control, using, 56–57
Show Method, 183
　forms, 216–218
Single document interface
　　　(SDI), 608
Single-dimension arrays. *See also*
　　　Array; Control arrays
　in general, 299-300
SmallTalk, 334
Software development kit (SDK), 43
Sort property, 506, 508–513
Sorted property, 255
Source, passing source argument,
　　　539-540
Source property, 397
Spc function, 274–275

Splash screen
　coding, 227
　discussed, 225–226
Spreadsheet, 442, 600. *See also*
　　　Table
SQL Server, 442
Standard code module, 5. *See also*
　　　Code
　coding, 226–227
Static statement, 221–222
Step Into command, 159
Step keyword, 566–567
Step Over command, 159
Stretch property, 56
String, 90, 93. *See also* String
　　　function; Text
　comparing, 132–134
　empty string, 66
　fixed-length strings, 409
　message string, 143, 144–145
　null string, 66
　trimming extra blanks from, 414
String function
　in general, 269
　Left, Right, Mid function, 269-270
　Len function, 270–271
　selecting entries in List box, 271
String literal, defined, 93
Style, setting control, 56
Sub procedure, 190. *See also*
　　　General procedures
　creating, 187–188
　using sub main for startup, 226
SubMenu, 175. *See also* Menu
Subprogram, 22
Subroutine, 22
Subscript
　array, 299, 300–301
　finding, 307
Switches, 261

T

Tab, for columns, placing in list box,
　　　598–600
Tab function, 274
Tab Order, controls, 63–64
Tab stop, 273
Tabbed Dialog control, 585–588

TabIndex property, 63
Table. *See also* Column; Lookup table
  array and, 299
  defining, 313
  multiple, 442
  two-dimensional
    list boxes, 316–317
    lookup operations, 316
    printing, 314–315
    summing, 315–316
TabStop property, 63
Text. *See also* String; Text box
  color, 68
  concatenating, 69
Text box
  clearing, 66
  control, 53
  locking text boxes, 493–494
  text property comparison, 135
  with two-dimensional table,
    317–318
Text file, 442
Text property, 53
  comparing, 135
Time, FormatDateTime
    function, 105
Timer control
  in general, 571
    Enabled property, 571
    Interval property, 571
Toolbar, 7
Toolbox, 7
ToolTip, creating, 65
ToolTipText property, 65
Toybox program, 542–544
Trim function, 414
True or false, testing for, 135
Twip, 15, 556
  defined, 61
Type statement, 303

U

UCase, 136
Unicode, 132
Update method, 466
User interface, 4
  defining, 13–17
  designing, 61–62

V

Val function
  discussed, 99-100
    examples, 100
Validate event, data validation,
    494–495
Validation, 145. *See also* Error
    trapping
  error trapping and
    in general, 493
    locking text boxes, 493–494
    Validate event, 494–495
  input validation, 145
  multiple validations, 147
  numeric values, 145–146
  programming example, 498–502
  range of values, 146
  required field, 146–147
Value. *See also* Property values
    adding to constants, 93
Value keyword, 90
Value property, 53
  Check box, 66–67
  Option button, 66–67
Variables
  Boolean, 261
  data types, 89-90
    variant, 89
  declaring, 94–96
    coding module-level variables,
      98
    guidelines, 222–223
    including scope in identifiers,
      98
    local declarations, 96–97
    module-level declarations,
      97–98
  in general, 88–89
    declaration statement, 89
  global, 96, 220, 221
    avoiding, 364–365
  lifetime of, 96
  local, 96
    declaring, 96–97
  module-level, 96
    coding, 98
    declaring, 97–98
  in multiple-form project, 220
  naming conventions, 90–91

Variables—*Cont.*
  naming rules, 90
  numeric, 131–132
  passing to procedures, 188–189
  scope, 96–99
  static, 221–222
  subscripted, 299
  visibility, 96
VBA. *See* Visual Basic for
    Applications
.vbx extension, 5, 584
Visibility, variables, 96
Visible property, 56
Visual Basic
  versions, 4
    Enterprise Edition, 4
    Learning Edition, 4
    Professional Edition, 4
    Working Model, 4
Visual Basic for Applications
    (VBA). *See also* Application
  Excel macro recording, 604–605
  in general, 603
  sample application, 605–608
Visual Basic environment
  break time, 8
  design time, 8
  Form Layout window, 7
  form location and size, 8
  Form window, 6
  in general, 6
  Help
    in general, 8, 42–43
    MSDN viewer, 43
  Main Visual Basic window, 7
  Project Explorer window, 6
  Properties window, 7
  run time, 8
  toolbar, 7
  toolbox, 7
Visual Basic program, Hands-On
    Programming Example,
    71–77, 112–118, 149-155,
    196–205, 228–244, 278–284,
    318–323, 365–380, 421–434,
    471–478, 522–524, 544–551,
    572–573

Visual Basic project
  browsing Web from, 589-590
  code statements, 22–23
  code writing, 22
  documentation, printing, 35–36
  event procedures, 24–26
  modifying, message size and
    alignment, 30–32
  opening, 30
  running, 26–27
  sample printout, 36–39
  saving, 28–29
  terminating, 350–351
  writing process, 4–5
    form file, 5
    form module, 5
    in general, 8
    project file, 5
    set properties, 17–21
    standard code module, 5
    user interface, 13–17
    Visual Basic workspace, 9–12
Visual C++, 43
Visual FoxPro, 43
Visual InterDev, 43
Visual J++, 43
Visual SourceSafe, 43
Visual Studio, 43

W

Windows, 2, 584
  controls, 2
  forms, 2
  main Visual Basic window, 7
With statement, 69
.wmf extension, 54
Word
  child form, 608
  parent form, 608
Write procedure, 420
Write statement, 392

Z

ZOrder method, 568